MαRKETING

PRINCIPLES

&

PERSPECTIVES

THE IRWIN SERIES IN MARKETING

Gilbert A. Churchill, Jr., Consulting Editor

University of Wisconsin, Madison

Alreck & Settle
The Survey Research Handbook,   2/e

Arens & Bovee
Contemporary Advertising,   5/e

Bearden, Ingram & LaForge
Marketing: Principles & Perspectives,   1/e

Belch & Belch
Introduction to Advertising and Promotion: An Integrated Marketing Communications Approach,   3/e

Berkowitz, Kerin, Hartley & Rudelius
Marketing,   4/e

Bernhardt & Kinnear
Cases in Marketing Management,   6/e

Bonoma & Kosnik
Marketing Management: Text & Cases,   1/e

Boyd, Walker & Larréché
Marketing Management: A Strategic Approach,   2/e

Burstiner
Basic Retailing,   2/e

Cadotte
The Market Place: A Strategic Marketing Simulation,   1/e

Cateora
International Marketing,   8/e

Churchill, Ford & Walker
Sales Force Management,   4/e

Cole & Mishler
Consumer and Business Credit Management,   10/e

Cravens
Strategic Marketing,   4/e

Cravens & Lamb
Strategic Marketing Management Cases,   4/e

Crawford
New Products Management,   4/e

Dillon, Madden & Firtle
Essentials of Marketing Research,   1/e

Dillon, Madden & Firtle
Marketing Research in a Marketing Environment,   3/e

Engel, Warshaw & Kinnear
Promotional Strategy,   8/e

Faria, Nulsen & Roussos
Compete,   4/e

Futrell
ABC's of Selling,   4/e

Hawkins, Best & Coney
Consumer Behavior,   6/e

Lambert & Stock
Strategic Logistics Management,   3/e

Lehmann & Winer
Analysis for Marketing Planning,   3/e

Lehmann & Winer
Product Management,   1/e

Levy & Weitz
Retailing Management,   2/e

Mason, Mayer & Ezell
Retailing,   5/e

Mason, Mayer & Wilkinson
Modern Retailing,   6/e

Mason & Perreault
The Marketing Game! 2/e

McCarthy & Perreault
Basic Marketing: A Global-Managerial Approach,   11/e

McCarthy & Perreault
Essentials of Marketing: A Global-Managerial Approach,   6/e

Meloan & Graham
International and Global Marketing: Concepts and Cases,   1/e

Patton
Sales Force: A Sales Management Simulation Game,   1/e

Peter & Donnelly
A Preface to Marketing Management,   6/e

Peter & Donnelly
Marketing Management: Knowledge and Skills,   4/e

Peter & Olson
Consumer Behavior and Marketing Strategy,   3/e

Peter & Olson
Understanding Consumer Behavior,   1/e

Quelch
Cases in Product Management,   1/e

Quelch, Dolan & Kosnik
Marketing Management: Text & Cases,   1/e

Quelch & Farris
Cases in Advertising and Promotion Management,   4/e

Quelch, Kashani & Vandermerwe
European Cases in Marketing Management,   1/e

Rangan
Industrial Marketing Strategy: Cases & Readings,   1/e

Rangan
Readings in Industrial Marketing Strategy,   1/e

Smith & Quelch
Ethics in Marketing,   1/e

Stanton, Buskirk & Spiro
Management of a Sales Force,   9/e

Thompson & Stappenbeck
The Marketing Strategy Game,   1/e

Walker, Boyd & Larréché
Marketing Strategy: Planning and Implementation,   1/e

Weitz, Castleberry & Tanner
Selling: Building Partnerships,   2/e

MαRKETING

PRINCIPLES & PERSPECTIVES

WILLIAM O. BEARDEN
University of South Carolina

THOMAS N. INGRAM
The University of Memphis

RAYMOND W. LAFORGE
University of Louisville

IRWIN

Chicago • Bogotá • Boston • Buenos Aires • Caracas
London • Madrid • Mexico City • Sydney • Toronto

About the cover

When tomorrow comes, the messages sent to students today will help them survive in the complex and turbulent marketplace of tomorrow. To be successful, students need an accurate overall picture of contemporary marketing. Seeing into the future of marketing is represented on the cover by a shaft of light streaming through the dense forest. Bearden, Ingram, and LaForge deliver this vision to help students develop the understanding and skills necessary for future marketing success. It is held together by the ten vantage points of marketing called the Ten Key Marketing Perspectives.

The Ten Key Marketing Perspectives are interwoven throughout the book. They are the framework that applies the basic concepts of marketing defined in real-world situations. The handwritten script, used as an underlying texture behind the overall picture, represents the Ten Key Marketing Perspectives. This emphasizes the importance of the ten perspectives as the basic structure that holds the many complex pieces of marketing together. The handwriting is a reminder of the essential role people play in the marketing around the world.

Other images and objects, rendered in a collage fashion, focus on marketing's interaction within its internal and external environments. A laser disc emphasizes technology and reminds marketers of its importance when establishing a competitive edge. A globe represents the vast number of global markets and the need to search for marketing opportunities around the world. The initials Q/V symbolize quality & value and direct marketers toward generating customer satisfaction. Ecology is pictured as clouds and suggests that marketers consider the environmental consequences when making marketing decisions. Together, these images form a fragile, yet crucial, connection within the marketing environment of the future.

Sponsoring editor: Nina McGuffin
Managing development editor: Eleanore Snow
Marketing manager: Jim Lewis
Project editor: Ethel Shiell
Production manager: Ann Cassady
Designer: Mercedes Santos
Cover photographer: Tom Collicott
Art studio: Boston Graphics, Inc.
Art coordinator: Mark Malloy/Kim Meriwether
Photo research coordinator: Charlene Breeden
Photo researcher: Michael J. Hruby
Compositor: William C. Brown Communications, Inc.
Typeface: 10/12 Sabon
Printer: Von Hoffmann Press, Inc.

Library of Congress Cataloging-in-Publication Data

Bearden, William O.
    Marketing: principles & perspectives/William O.
Bearden, Thomas N. Ingram, Raymond W. LaForge.
        p.   cm.—(Irwin series in marketing)
        Includes index.
        ISBN 0–256–11319–X
        1. Marketing—United States. I. Ingram, Thomas
N. II. LaForge, Raymond W. III. Title. IV. Series
HF5415.1.B4155 1995
658.8—dc20   94–31421

Printed in the United States of America
1 2 3 4 5 6 7 8 9 0 VH 1 0 9 8 7 6 5 4

To Patti, Anna, Wallace, and my parents

Bill Bearden

To Jacque and my parents

Tom Ingram

To Susan, Alexandra, Kelly, and my parents

Buddy LaForge

Meet the Authors . . .

A note from the publisher:

We knew going into this project that Bill Bearden, Tom Ingram, and Buddy LaForge were eminent researchers and scholars and highly acclaimed teachers; and we were tremendously pleased when this illustrious team agreed to publish an introductory marketing textbook with IRWIN.

What we didn't know, but soon found out, was that they are also extremely hardworking, dedicated, and patient authors, sensitive and open to reviewer and Publisher suggestions for improving and polishing the various manuscript drafts. Their passionate commitment to facilitating student learning with the most current material and to making marketing *fun* for their students is unsurpassed. Through it all they kept a sense of humor, needling each other (and IRWIN) whenever the opportunity arose—which happened often over the course of the project. As Publisher, however, IRWIN gets the last word. And so we present Achievement Awards to Bill, for meeting all deadlines and submitting the longest chapters; to Tom, for taking the most minivacations; and to Buddy, for not failing to miss every single deadline.

WILLIAM O. BEARDEN (Ph.D., University of South Carolina)
University of South Carolina

Bill Bearden is Distinguished Foundation Fellow and Professor of Marketing at the University of South Carolina. He has focused his teaching and research interests in consumer behavior and marketing research. In addition, Bill teaches principles of marketing and marketing management.

His teaching awards include Outstanding MBA Teacher, the College of Business Administration Alfred G. Smith Excellence in Teaching Award, and the University of South Carolina AMOCO Award for Excellence in Undergraduate Teaching.

He is currently a member of the Editorial Review Boards for the *Journal of Consumer Research*, the *Journal of Marketing Research*, the *Journal of the Academy of Marketing Science*, the *Journal of Retailing*, the *Journal of Business Research*, and the *Marketing Education Review*. His professional experience includes past president of the Southern Marketing Association, past vice president of the American Marketing Association, Education Division, and member of the American Marketing Association Board of Directors. He is currently Co-Director of the USC Lilly Endowment Teaching Fellows Program.

Bill lives in Columbia, South Carolina, with his wife Patti, while his two daughters, Anna and Wallace, attend the University of Tennessee and Clemson University. Bill and his entire family are active in tennis and enjoy frequent trips to the SC coast.

THOMAS N. INGRAM (Ph.D., Georgia State)
The University of Memphis

Tom Ingram is holder of the Sales and Marketing Executives of Memphis Chair of Excellence at The University of Memphis, where he teaches principles of marketing, sales management, and professional selling courses. Previously, he was on the faculty at the University of Kentucky, where he received the university's highest recognition for teaching, the National Alumni Association's Great Teacher Award. Prior to his academic career, Tom worked in sales, product management, and sales management with Exxon Company, USA, and Mobil Corporation.

In 1990, Tom was named educator of the year by Sales and Marketing Executives International (SMEI), an organization of 9,600 members. He is Chair of the SMEI Accreditation Institute, which oversees professional certification programs in marketing management, professional selling, and sales management. In 1994, he was recognized by national honorary Mu Kappa Tau for his contributions to the sales/sales management discipline.

Tom has published extensively in professional journals, including the *Journal of Marketing,* the *Journal of Marketing Research,* the *Journal of the Academy of Marketing Science,* and the *Journal of Personal Selling and Sales Management.* He is past editor of the latter journal, and is coauthor of *Sales Management: Analysis and Decision Making,* 2nd ed.

Currently, Tom is vice president of development for the Academy of Marketing Science, and has just completed a term as vice president of research and publications for the Southern Marketing Association. He and his wife Jacque enjoy life in Memphis, home of some of the world's best music and barbecue.

RAYMOND W. (BUDDY) LAFORGE (DBA, University of Tennessee)
University of Louisville

Buddy LaForge is the Brown-Forman Professor of Marketing at the University of Louisville. He is the founding editor of the *Marketing Education Review* and served as senior vice president of teaching and information dissemination for the American Marketing Association Academic Council.

Buddy teaches principles of marketing, sales management, and professional selling courses, and is coauthor of *Sales Management: Analysis and Decision Making,* 2nd ed. His research in the sales management and marketing strategy/entrepreneurship areas has been published in various journals, including the *Journal of Marketing* and the *Journal of Marketing Research.* He received the 1993 Best Paper Award from the *Journal of Personal Selling and Sales Management.*

Buddy lives in Louisville, Kentucky, with his wife Susan and daughters Alexandra and Kelly. He enjoys golf, tennis, and breeding/racing thoroughbred horses.

Preface

∎∎∎∎∎

*T*he marketing world is changing rapidly. Global economic conditions, political situations, and competitive landscapes are in constant flux. Marketing approaches that worked yesterday may not work tomorrow. Increasingly, marketing success requires doing things differently.

Our students will face a marketing environment different than the one discussed in our classes today. Learning what was done in the past will not prepare them sufficiently for what they need to do tomorrow. We must prepare our students to operate in the complex and dynamic marketing environment of the future.

Preparing students for marketing in the future

Our major objective in writing this text is to help students develop the understanding and skills necessary for marketing success in the future. Yes, students must still learn basic marketing terms and concepts. But more important, they need to develop the capacity to think and act like marketers in a difficult and uncertain environment. This requires the ability to assess complex and changing marketing situations, to determine the best marketing strategies for these situations, and to execute the strategies effectively and efficiently.

Everything in our text and in the accompanying teaching resources is intended to help students develop the understanding and skills to become successful marketers. The text is designed to facilitate student learning from individual reading and study. The teaching resources provide useful tools for instructors to go beyond what is covered in the text. Together, the text and teaching resources represent an integrated package for preparing students for marketing in the future.

This package differs from currently available products in many important ways. The critical differences stand out in the integration of ten key marketing perspectives throughout the text, the presentation of comments from an Executive Roundtable of practicing marketers, the implementation of an integrated marketing communications (IMC) approach, and an intense emphasis on student learning.

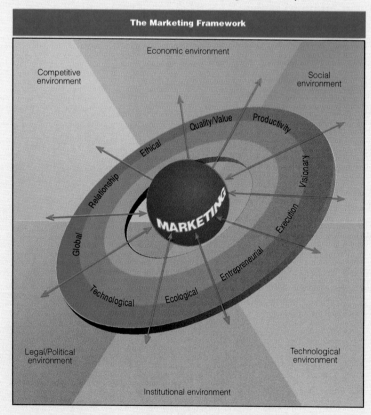

The Marketing Framework

Economic environment

Competitive environment

Social environment

Quality/Value

Productivity

Ethical

Visionary

Relationship

MARKETING

Execution

Global

Entrepreneurial

Technological

Ecological

Legal/Political environment

Technological environment

Institutional environment

x

Ten Key Marketing Perspectives

We studied emerging trends in business and identified ten key marketing perspectives to help marketers identify and respond to opportunities in the marketing environment. These perspectives provide unifying themes for the text. The perspectives are introduced in the contemporary marketing framework in Chapter 1, discussed in detail in Chapter 2, and covered in the remaining chapters in various ways.

The text concludes with an illustrated essay, **Epilog: Key Perspectives Revisited,** where the perspectives are examined in relation to the marketing efforts of The Timberland Company. The Epilog ties everything together by synthesizing and summarizing the major points presented in the text.

A brief overview of each perspective and examples of the integration illustrate the value of the perspectives:

A global perspective

This perspective helps marketers cultivate a global view of the marketplace that includes searching for marketing opportunities around the world, competing against international competitors, and working with multicultural suppliers, employees, channel partners, and customers. The global perspective is integrated throughout the text by discussion, real-world company examples, photos, and ads. Examples of detailed coverage of the global perspective include the global marketing environment (Chapter 3), international marketing strategies (Chapter 4), and international considerations in marketing research (Chapter 7).

P
R
E
F
A
C
E

Coca-Cola for example, uses a largely standardized marketing strategy, where the brand name, concentrate formula, positioning, and advertising are virtually the same worldwide, but the artificial sweetener and packaging differ across countries.[24] TGI Friday's restaurants are successsful in the Far East using the same concept as in the United States. The mix of American memorabilia and chatty, high-fiving waiters produces high sales per store. In fact, the TGI Friday's in Seoul generates double the sales volume of an average restaurant in the United States.[25]

Nissan, in contrast, uses a more customized marketing strategy by tailoring cars to local needs and tastes. One success has been the Nissan Micra, designed specifically to negotiate the narrow streets in England.[26] Similarly, Campbell Soup gets higher sales by adapting its products to local tastes. For example, sales accelerated when it introduced a cream of chile poblano soup to the Mexican market.[27]

Exhibit 2.3 | **Transaction marketing versus relationship marketing**

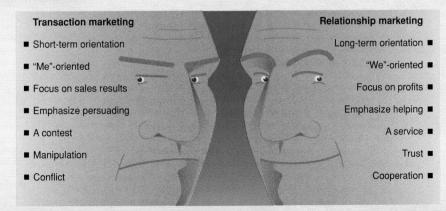

Transaction marketing	Relationship marketing
■ Short-term orientation	Long-term orientation ■
■ "Me"-oriented	"We"-oriented ■
■ Focus on sales results	Focus on profits ■
■ Emphasize persuading	Emphasize helping ■
■ A contest	A service ■
■ Manipulation	Trust ■
■ Conflict	Cooperation ■

A relationship perspective

This perspective orients marketers toward long-term mutually beneficial relationships that include customer relationships, organizational partnerships, and teamwork within a company. Examples of specific attention to the relationship perspective include teamwork in the new-product development process (Chapter 10), channel relationships (Chapter 14), and a relationship approach to personal selling and sales management (Chapter 20).

An ethical perspective

The ethical perspective helps marketers incorporate moral and social responsibility issues into marketing decisions and activities. Many chapters conclude with a discussion of ethics and social responsibility—for example, ethical issues in marketing research (Chapter 7), FTC guidelines against deceptive pricing (Chapter 13), and ethical and legal issues in advertising (Chapter 18).

Exhibit 20.11	Unethical sales behaviors

Research indicates sales behaviors that are unethical in the eyes of customers:

- Exaggerates the features & benefits of his/her products/ services.
- Lies about availability to make a sale.
- Lies about the competition to make a sale.
- Sells products/services people don't need.
- Is interested only in own interests, not the clients'.
- Gives answers when doesn't really know the answers.
- Lies about competitors.
- Falsifies product testimonials.

- Passes the blame for something he/ she did onto someone else.
- Poses as a market researcher when conducting telephone sales.
- Misrepresents guarantees/warranties.
- Makes oral promises that are not legally binding,
- Does not offer information about an upcoming sale that will include merchandise the customer is planning to buy.
- Accepts favors from customers so the seller will feel obliged to bend the rules/ policies of the seller's company.
- Sells dangerous or hazardous products.

Consumers have general expectations about market prices and a range of acceptable prices, as this ad suggests.

A quality/value perspective

This perspective directs marketers toward generating customer satisfaction by providing the quality desired at the best prices. It emphasizes continuous quality improvement as a way to increase the value customers receive. Examples of specific quality/value coverage include: product quality (Chapter 9), prototype development for new products (Chapter 10), and customer price evaluations (Chapter 12).

A productivity perspective

The productivity perspective focuses attention toward improving the productivity of marketing resources. Sometimes, this requires doing the same things better. At other times, this perspective leads marketers to do things differently. Examples of an emphasis on the productivity perspective include: corporate objectives and resource allocation (Chapter 4), new-product development process (Chapter 10), and budget development for integrated marketing communications planning (Chapter 17).

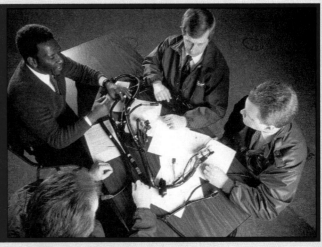

To increase productivity, Ford Motor Company outsources the electrical distribution systems for its 1995 Taurus and Sable models from United Technologies.

A technological perspective

The technological perspective orients marketers toward looking for ways to use the latest technological advances to improve marketing practice and as a source for new products. The use of new technologies in marketing is discussed throughout the text. Each chapter also includes a sidebar entitled **The Technological Edge** that presents a specific example of the technological perspective. Examples of these sidebars include "CATS Provide Single-Source Data" (Chapter 7), "Driving on the Information Highway" (Chapter 10), and "Charles Schwab and Discount Brokerage Marketing" (Chapter 12).

W. W. Grainger, a nationwide distributor of equipment, components, and supplies to commercial, industrial, contractor, and institutional markets, provides and example of the *technological perspective* with its use of an electronic catalog to reach more than 4,000 customers.

An ecological perspective

This perspective helps marketers consider the environmental consequences of marketing decisions and capitalize on environmental marketing opportunities. Examples of particular coverage include environmentalism (Chapter 3), packaging (Chapter 9), and environmental concerns in logistics (Chapter 16).

Fordwerke emphasizes an *ecological perspective* with an appeal to the environmental concerns of German consumers. The headline reads "I was a car," because the child's toy was made from recycled auto parts.

PREFACE

xiii

Sony illustrates an *entrepreneurial perspective* in the unique approach used to introduce its new MiniDisc.

An entrepreneurial perspective

The entrepreneurial perspective encourages marketers to emphasize creativity, innovation, and risk-taking in their marketing efforts. This perspective, discussed throughout the text, is important to both smaller, growth-oriented firms and to the largest corporations. Each chapter features a sidebar entitled **The Entrepreneurial Spirit** to highlight specific situations. Examples include: "America's Greatest 18 Holes" (Chapter 10), "Pricing to Cover Exporting Costs" (Chapter 13), and "sMall Shops Test Big Ideas" (Chapter 15).

DHL suggests the importance of an *execution perspective* in a global marketplace.

An execution perspective

This perspective emphasizes the effective implementation of sound marketing strategies. Determining what to do is one thing; doing it is another. The execution perspective focuses on *doing* it. Examples of specific coverage of the execution perspective include executing strategic plans (Chapter 4), implementing channel strategy (Chapter 14), and the sales process (Chapter 20).

A visionary perspective

The visionary perspective focuses on developing a broad, long-term view of what a company is trying to accomplish. This vision provides direction for all marketing efforts. Examples of specific attention to the visionary perspective include: megatrends (Chapter 3), corporate vision (Chapter 4), and new-product objectives (Chapter 10). ■

Exhibit 4.5   **Corporate vision components**

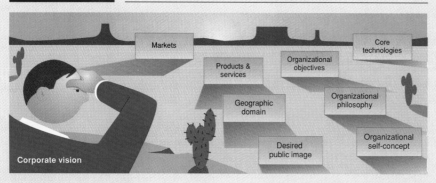

Executive Roundtable

What better way to prepare students for the future than by having active marketers tell them how their companies view things and what they are doing now to be successful in the future? We researched the viability of this issue and based on our findings assembled a group of practicing marketers into an Executive Roundtable to do just that. The Roundtable members represent a broad spectrum of marketing positions at many different types of organizations operating in a variety of industries. We introduce the Executive Roundtable members at the end of the Preface.

Each Roundtable member prepared specific comments for our text. We asked them to discuss how their organization views the changing marketing world and to describe what they were doing to be successful now and in the future. We also gave them a copy of the ten key marketing perspectives and encouraged them to indicate how—or whether—specific perspectives were important to their situation.

The diversity of the Executive Roundtable is evident from some of the titles and companies:

- Partner, Arthur Andersen

- International marketing manager, Diebold

- Vice president, branch manager, Smith Barney

- Manager of small and medium business marketing, Apple Computer

- Assistant vice president for quality planning, NationsBank

- Vice president, product development, Gibson Greetings

- Vice president of sales, Ruddell & Associates

- President, Stuckey's Family Favorites

- Regional sales manager, Pomeroy Computer Products

- Traffic manager, Sharp Manufacturing

An example illustrates the value of the Executive Roundtable:

EXECUTIVE ROUNDTABLE COMMENT | **Mark Oshnock, partner at Arthur Andersen, suggests how important marketing is in a major public accounting firm:**

Marketing became a formal function in public accounting beginning in the early 1980s. Today, most offices of any size in international, national, regional, and local firms emphasize marketing activities to support their practice. Only a few employees at Arthur Andersen have *marketing* in their titles, but an in-depth understanding of marketing is vitally important to everyone in our firm. The successful professional employs a targeted marketing plan to satisfy the needs of current clients and to generate new clients.

(Chapter 1)

Students respond favorably when we inject realism into our classes. This is especially noticeable when we have marketers visit our classes as guest speakers. The three Executive Roundtable comments in each chapter incorporate this realism into the text. Think of it as having guest lecturers from the business world in each chapter. Our reviewers say the Roundtable's specific comments will stimulate student interest and provide realistic commentary on what marketers in different situations are doing now and plan to do in the future. ■

Integrated Marketing Communications

*T*he marketing communications element of the marketing mix is one area where many firms are making tremendous changes. Traditionally, marketers viewed advertising and personal selling as the major communication tools. Other forms of marketing communications, including sales promotion, were relegated to minor, supporting roles. This is the way marketing communications is still presented in most existing texts.

Our research indicates the reality is that firms of all sizes are integrating a variety of communication tools into comprehensive programs designed to achieve specific objectives. The current term for this approach is **integrated marketing communications (IMC)**. Total expenditures for sales promotion today are higher than those for advertising, for example; and direct marketing communications is growing faster than any other communications approach.

Tools such as coupons, cross-promotions, contests, premiums, point-of-purchase displays, interactive computer services and kiosks, and even fax machines are emerging as major elements in an IMC program. Personal selling and sales management are also changing from a manipulative, transaction-oriented focus to an emphasis on trust-building and long-term relationships.

The SpokesMannequin comes to life through video or laser disc technology to answer questions, gather information, and accept cash or credit cards.

We agree with leading practitioners that the emerging trend toward IMC programs must be emphasized in a principles of marketing text. We therefore introduce the IMC approach in Chapter 17, and in succeeding chapters discuss the importance and usage of the communication tools in contemporary marketing practice, paying special attention to the tools likely to be of critical importance in the future. This means our coverage of marketing communications differs considerably from and is more comprehensive than available texts, but also reflects more clearly the current trends in marketing practice.

| Exhibit 20.3 | The sales process: A relationship approach |

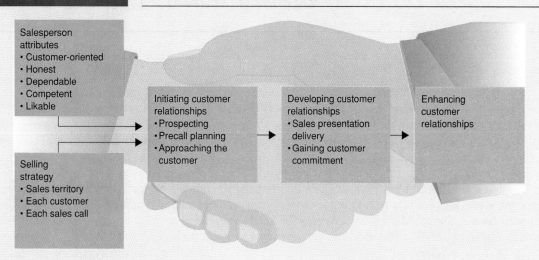

Salesperson attributes
• Customer-oriented
• Honest
• Dependable
• Competent
• Likable

Selling strategy
• Sales territory
• Each customer
• Each sales call

Initiating customer relationships
• Prospecting
• Precall planning
• Approaching the customer

Developing customer relationships
• Sales presentation delivery
• Gaining customer commitment

Enhancing customer relationships

If we are to prepare students for tomorrow's marketing world, we must present these accurate pictures of current marketing and future trends. Our emphasis on IMC, full-chapter coverage of sales promotion (19) and direct marketing (21), and timely presentation of personal selling and sales management (20) ensures that our students are exposed to the latest in marketing thought and practice. ■

P R E F A C E

Direct mail can be as simple as a one-piece flyer or a multipiece mailer. Landmark Products, distributor of products to the food-service industry, won the 1993 Echo Gold Mailbox award for the most innovative use of direct mail.

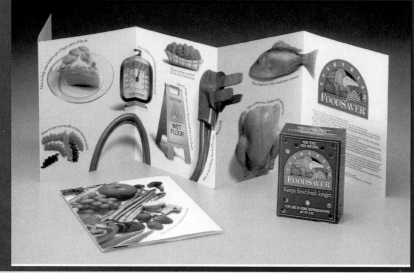

An Emphasis on Student Learning

We see important trends emerging in marketing education. For one thing, teaching is receiving more emphasis at most colleges and universities—but not teaching as traditionally viewed and practiced. It really does not matter *what* we teach, if students do not learn. And student learning is viewed differently, too. Learning is not just the recall of facts by passive students, but the understanding of concepts and the ability to apply them appropriately. Such learning requires the active participation of students.

The complete package for **MARKETING: PRINCIPLES & PERSPECTIVES** is oriented toward student learning; and the text and teaching resources are designed to complement each other toward that end. In keeping with our philosophy that students should be able to understand the text material largely from their own reading and study, we wrote in a lively, interesting, informal manner to capture their attention and interest. We discussed major concepts clearly and simply in a way that students can understand. Our reviewers tell us we succeeded in this effort. Encouraged by our reviewing panels, we did not include everything we know about a major topic, but only what we believe students at this level need to know. We simplified the discussion of concepts and then reinforced them with interesting examples and exciting visuals, and incorporated a number of learning tools to facilitate the learning process (*see pp. xxv–xxviii*).

The teaching resources—*Teaching Resource Guide, Manual of Tests,* Color Print Acetates and Electronic Acetates, Video Library, Laser Disc, *Media Resource Guide*—go beyond text coverage so that instructors can easily add value to the learning process. We provide more detail and additional examples on some concepts; and we present additional concepts not included in the text for instructors to introduce in class sessions.

But the major purpose of the teaching resources is to offer instructors innovative ideas for teaching concepts. We suggest different approaches to actively involve students in learning both during and outside of class sessions. We offer a number of options so that instructors can select the approaches that best fit their needs and can add variety to the classes in a given term. This focus on **active learning** is integrated throughout the teaching resources—such as the **Ideas for Student Learning** offered for each chapter in the *Teaching Resource Guide.*

Research indicates our intensified attention to student learning is necessary to prepare students for marketing in the future. Actively involving students in the learning process makes class sessions and courses more interesting and helps students develop the understanding and skills they need for success. Students must begin to take responsibility for their learning now, because they surely will be involved in lifelong learning throughout their careers. ■

Student Learning Tools

We carefully designed the chapter formats so that each element has a specific purpose in the student learning process.

Student Learning Guides

Every chapter begins with several learning guides to help students focus attention on major concepts in reading and studying the chapter.

Opening Vignettes

Chapter-opening vignettes generate student involvement by presenting interesting marketing examples that illustrate important concepts covered in the chapter. Company situations featured in the vignettes include:

- Domino's Pizza: Pizza delivery and freebies
- Blockbuster Entertainment: Exploding into new markets
- Levi Strauss: A "stitched niche" strategy
- Snapple: Grapples with premium price and premium value
- MCI Communications: Commodities or brands?
- ALICO: Ensuring successful selling from Japan to Pakistan
- Direct marketing communications: Circling the Pacific Rim

Immediately following the vignette, brief follow-up comments tying it to the major chapter concepts make a logical transition into the body of the chapter.

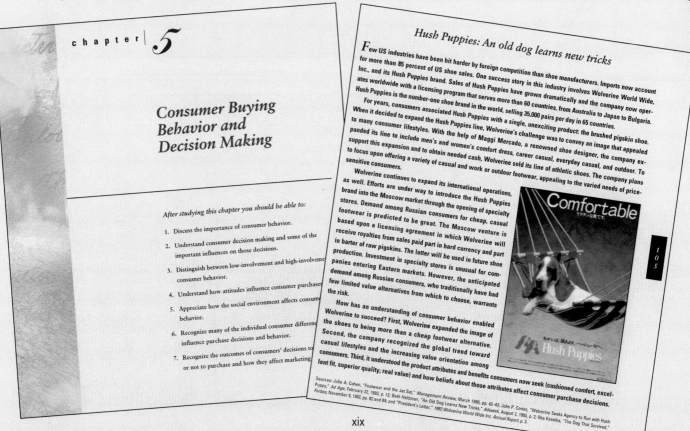

chapter | *5*

Consumer Buying Behavior and Decision Making

After studying this chapter you should be able to:

1. Discuss the importance of consumer behavior.

2. Understand consumer decision making and some of the important influences on those decisions.

3. Distinguish between low-involvement and high-involvement consumer behavior.

4. Understand how attitudes influence consumer purchases.

5. Appreciate how the social environment affects consumer behavior.

6. Recognize many of the individual consumer differences that influence purchase decisions and behavior.

7. Recognize the outcomes of consumers' decisions to purchase or not to purchase and how they affect marketing.

Hush Puppies: An old dog learns new tricks

Few US industries have been hit harder by foreign competition than shoe manufacturers. Imports now account for more than 85 percent of US shoe sales. One success story in this industry involves Wolverine World Wide, Inc., and its Hush Puppies brand. Sales of Hush Puppies have grown dramatically and the company now operates worldwide with a licensing program that serves more than 60 countries, from Australia to Japan to Bulgaria. Hush Puppies is the number-one shoe brand in the world, selling 35,000 pairs per day in 65 countries.

For years, consumers associated Hush Puppies with a single, unexciting product: the brushed pigskin shoe. When it decided to expand the Hush Puppies line, Wolverine's challenge was to convey an image that appealed to many consumer lifestyles. With the help of Maggi Mercado, a renowned shoe designer, the company expanded its line to include men's and women's comfort dress, career casual, everyday casual, and outdoor. To support this expansion and to obtain needed cash, Wolverine sold its line of athletic shoes. The company plans to focus upon offering a variety of casual and work or outdoor footwear, appealing to the varied needs of price-sensitive consumers.

Wolverine continues to expand its international operations, as well. Efforts are under way to introduce the Hush Puppies brand into the Moscow market through the opening of specialty stores. Demand among Russian consumers for cheap, casual footwear is predicted to be great. The Moscow venture is based upon a licensing agreement in which Wolverine will receive royalties from sales paid part in hard currency and part in barter of raw pigskins. The latter will be used in future shoe production. Investment in specialty stores is unusual for companies entering Eastern markets. However, the anticipated demand among Russian consumers, who traditionally have had few limited value alternatives from which to choose, warrants the risk.

How has an understanding of consumer behavior enabled Wolverine to succeed? First, Wolverine expanded the image of the shoes to being more than a cheap footwear alternative. Second, the company recognized the global trend toward casual lifestyles and the increasing value orientation among consumers. Third, it understood the product attributes and benefits consumers now seek (cushioned comfort, excellent fit, superior quality, real value) and how beliefs about those attributes affect consumer purchase decisions.

Sources: Julie A. Cohen, "Footwear and the Jet Set," *Management Review*, March 1990, pp. 42–43; Beth Heitzman, "An Old Dog Learns New Tricks," *Adweek*, August 2, 1993, p. 12; John P. Cortez, "Wolverine Seeks Agency to Run with Hush Puppy," *Ad Age*, February 22, 1993, p. 12; Rita Koselka, "The Dog That Survived," *Forbes*, November 9, 1992, pp. 82 and 84; and "President's Letter," *1992 Wolverine World Wide Inc. Annual Report*, p. 3.

Comfortable

Hush Puppies

105

Executive Roundtable Comments

Each chapter contains three comments from members of the **Executive Roundtable.** The comments were prepared specifically for our text. The Roundtable members focus on the most interesting changes in their industries and at their companies and reinforce the importance of the ten key marketing perspectives. (*See example on p. xv.*)

Sidebars

Each chapter presents one **The Technological Edge** and one **The Entrepreneurial Spirit** sidebar that offer expanded examples of the technological and entrepreneurial perspectives in various marketing situations. The sidebars are referenced in the text so that students can read them at the relevant time.

Personal touch pays off

*I*n the 1980s, Brenda French's French Rags label sold about $10 million (wholesale price) in upscale apparel through leading department stores such as Neiman Marcus, Bonwit Teller, and Bloomingdales. Yet, Ms. French was not happy with her chosen marketing channel.

A lack of personal selling attention in the large stores, along with dissatisfaction with how much of the profit went to the retailer, led to a withdrawal from the department store channel. French set up a direct salesforce of 45 women in high-income locales such as Grosse Pointe, Michigan, Kenilworth, Illinois, and Pasadena, California. These women show the French Rags line in their homes four times a year, mostly to friends and social contacts. They are paid a 15 percent commission.

Brenda French sells half as much now as she did through department stores, but makes more money with the new channel. French Rags now earns about $750,000 per year in net profit, compared to $200,000 per year in the past.

Source: Damon Darlin, "Rags to Riches," *Forbes,* March 28, 1994, p. 108.

Driving on the information highway

*T*echnological advancements, such as the capacity to translate all audio and video communications into digital information and new methods for storing, compressing, and sending this information into homes, are producing an information highway that links video, telephones, and computers. Major telephone companies and cable operators are working together to make the information highway a reality.

Once established, the information highway is likely to give birth to a tremendous number of new products. The possibilities include interactive cable systems with 500 or more channels that deliver programs on demand. Viewers will be able to select what they want to watch from a computer menu on their TV screens. Also, specific ads targeted to individual homes may allow customers to take shopping trips over TV. For example, an individual could take a 15-minute trip around an auto showroom without leaving the couch. Or finally, videophones will transmit onto a TV screen the images of the people talking to each other.

Sources: Philip Elmer-Dewitt, "Take a Trip into the Future on the Electronic Superhighway," *Time,* April 12, 1993, pp. 50–58; and John Naisbitt, *Global Paradox* (New York: William Morrow and Company, Inc., 1994), pp. 53–102.

Exhibits and Photos

The visual aspects of each chapter were designed to increase student learning. We use colorful and appealing art work to make complex relationships and data tables more understandable. Photos and ads with descriptive captions also illustrate important points. Every spread in the text includes some type of visual enhancement beyond the basic chapter discussion. This helps to maintain student interest and facilitate learning.

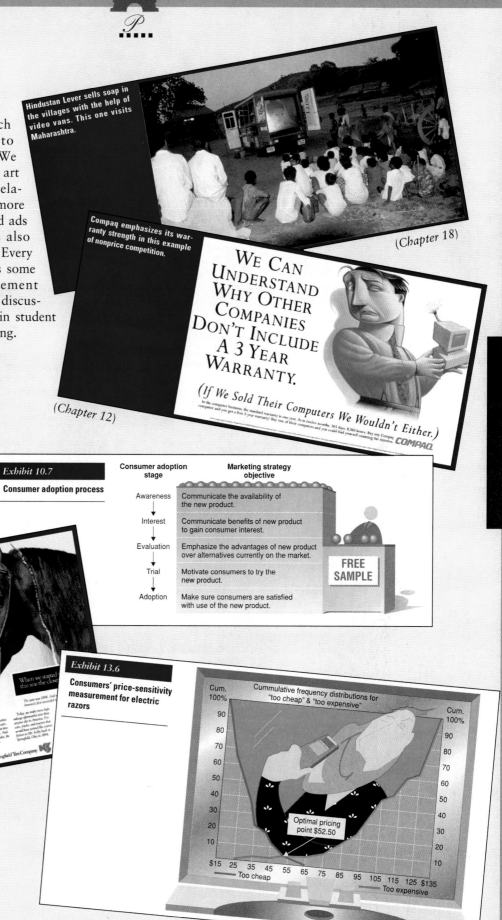

Hindustan Lever sells soap in the villages with the help of video vans. This one visits Maharashtra.

(Chapter 18)

Compaq emphasizes its warranty strength in this example of nonprice competition.

WE CAN UNDERSTAND WHY OTHER COMPANIES DON'T INCLUDE A 3 YEAR WARRANTY.

(If We Sold Their Computers We Wouldn't Either.)

(Chapter 12)

When the automobile was introduced, it was truly a new-to-the-world product.

The Kelly-Springfield Tire Company

(Chapter 10)

Exhibit 10.7

Consumer adoption process

Consumer adoption stage	Marketing strategy objective
Awareness	Communicate the availability of the new product.
Interest	Communicate benefits of new product to gain consumer interest.
Evaluation	Emphasize the advantages of new product over alternatives currently on the market.
Trial	Motivate consumers to try the new product.
Adoption	Make sure consumers are satisfied with use of the new product.

FREE SAMPLE

Exhibit 13.6

Consumers' price-sensitivity measurement for electric razors

Cummulative frequency distributions for "too cheap" & "too expensive"

Optimal pricing point $52.50

Too cheap — Too expensive

Chapter Summaries

The summary at the end of each chapter is keyed to the **Learning Guides** presented at the beginning of it. This further reinforces what students should learn from each chapter.

Key Terms & Concepts

The most important **terms and concepts** are bolded when first introduced in a chapter, and followed directly by their definitions. Less important but significant terms and concepts are presented in *italics*. Each bolded term is listed at the end of the chapter with the page number where it is defined. This pedagogical device helps students identify and learn the most important terms and guides them to the correct page for further study.

Summary

1. *Discuss the importance of consumer behavior.* Marketers must understand consumer behavior to develop successful strategies and identify target market segments. Furthermore, awareness of emerging trends in the consumer marketplace is essential for quick recognition of and response to problems and opportunities with sound marketing strategies.

2. *Understand consumer decision making and some of the important influences on those decisions.* Consumer behavior describes the mental and physical activities that people engage in when they select, purchase, use, and dispose of products and services purchased to satisfy needs and desires. The traditional view of consumer decision making is sequential: recognition of problem, search for information (either internal or external), evaluation of alternatives, purchase, and postpurchase evaluation.

3. *Distinguish between low-involvement and high-involvement consumer behavior.* Involvement represents the level of importance or interest generated by a duct's attributes and the relative evaluation of those attributes.

5. *Appreciate how the social environment affects consumer behavior.* Social influences on behavior must be understood prior to the development of sound marketing strategies. Social class and family influences affect consumer behavior and can be used to identify market segments.

   The culture in which consumers are raised is also critical in determining the values that matter to them; culture may be used to identify segments with unique needs (subcultures). A great deal of learning also comes from observing and interacting with others (informational interpersonal influence). Some behavior occurs with the expectations of others in mind (utilitarian influences) and some with how they will react to our own behavior (value-expressiveness). The latter two are normative social influences. Consumers are also influenced by the situations in which behavior occurs or is expected to occur.

6. *Recognize many of the individual consumer differ-*

Key terms & concepts

consumer behavior *106*	values *112*	opinion leaders *117*
involvement *110*	ethnic patterns *113*	market mavens *118*
high-involvement decisions *110*	social classes *114*	psychographics *119*
low-involvement decisions *110*	childhood consumer	consumer learning *122*
routinized response behavior *110*	socialization *114*	negative disconfirmation *122*
extensive problem solving *111*	family life cycle *115*	positive disconfirmation *122*
limited problem solving *111*	reference groups *117*	voice responses *123*
consumer attitudes *111*	informational influence *117*	private responses *123*
culture *112*	utilitarian influence *117*	third-party responses *123*
socialization *112*	value-expressive influence *117*	cognitive dissonance *123*

Review & Discussion Questions

Each chapter contains 10 review and discussion questions, two of which refer to the sidebars in the chapter. Answers to several questions in each chapter require critical thinking that goes beyond strict recall of what is covered in the chapter. The *Teaching Resource Guide* presents different ways the critical thinking questions might be used to actively involve students in class discussion.

Application Exercises

Every chapter includes three application exercises. These exercises provide varied and interesting ways for students to apply what they are reading and what is being covered in class sessions. Some of the exercises are intended to be homework assignments; others can be performed completely during a class period. The *Teaching Resource Guide* presents different ways the application exercises might be used to improve student learning.

Review & discussion questions

1. How does a firm's corporate vision affect its marketing operations?

2. How does marketing differ for a new, single-product venture and a large, multiproduct corporation?

3. What are the basic options for a corporate growth strategy?

4. Look at **The Technological Edge: Prodigy Goes after Everybody.** How might Prodigy grow through related diversification?

5. How do business marketing strategies and product marketing strategies differ?

6. What are the keys to effective execution of strategic plans?

7. Refer to **The Entrepreneurial Spirit: America Online Targets a Few.** How might America Online grow through related diversification?

8. How does an understanding of the marketing environment, as discussed in Chapter 3, help in the development of strategic plans?

9. Why do firms change their business composition?

10. How do corporate objectives affect marketing operations?

Application exercises

1. Read an annual report for any company. Using only the information in the report, describe the firm's corporate, business, and marketing strategies.

2. Pick a recent issue of *Business Week*, *Fortune*, or any other business publication. Review it to identify examples of corporate growth strategies used by different firms.

3. Interview a marketing executive at a local firm. Ask the executive what types of strategic plans the firm develops and what is included in each strategic plan. Also, inquire about the firm's strategic planning process.

Cases

All chapters conclude with two cases representing well-known companies and current situations. Examples include:

- Fidelity Investments: People, technology, and service
- Nike: Sneakers go European
- Polaroid: Captivating customers with the Captiva
- PepsiCo: Fiasco in the Philippines
- Clearly Canadian: Clearly successful
- Burger King: Now serving dinner
- Saturn: Taking a STEP to equip its salesforce
- Sega versus Nintendo: A game of pricing technology
- QVC Network: TV home shopping takes off
- Coldwater Creek: Cataloging customers

Three or four questions guide students in analyzing the case. At least one of these is a critical thinking question that requires students to make and support judgments based on the case situation. Ideas for involving students in the cases are presented in the *Teaching Resource Guide.*

Case 3.1   *Nike: Sneakers go European*

Philip Knight is the billionaire founder of Nike, Inc. While continuing to focus on sneakers, the company has expanded into outdoor footwear and apparel and even into sports licensing. Growth has slowed somewhat, but 1993 results indicate a sales increase of 15 percent and a profit increase of 11 percent.

The sneaker business in Europe is experiencing fast growth. Marketing efforts have expanded that market to $4.5 billion annually, twice the 1985 level. And Nike is getting a larger share of this growing market. Sales in Spain, Britain, and Italy, for example, are increasing nicely.

A few years ago, many Europeans looked at sneakers with disdain, wearing them only in gyms and on tennis courts. When government official Josef Fisher wore sneakers to his German office 15 years ago, he was featured on the evening news! The sneaker situation has changed dramatically since then. Chanel models now stroll down fashion runways in Paris wearing canvas high-top sneakers. A standard outfit for Austrian Prince Karl von Hapsburg is a coat, tie, black denim pants, and sneakers.

These changes are due to several factors. One is that the US image, especially as it relates to sports, has become much more popular in Europe. US professional basketball, especially, is surging in popularity in Europe. Nike has built on and fueled this interest by featuring National Basketball Association stars in advertising. The company has also sent Michael Jordan and Charles Barkley to Europe to participate in basketball clinics and to sign autographs.

Nike has also improved the quality and design of its sneakers. The company introduces about 800 different styles a year, so almost everyone can find some type that is acceptable. Nike spends around $100 million a year on advertising in Europe to promote both the quality image and the variety of designs available.

Nike expects to generate much of its future growth from Europe. Although there are about 130 million more people in Europe than in the US, European sneaker sales are only a third of current US sales, indicating the potential for substantial growth. Nike plans to take advantage of this opportunity, but will face fierce competition from Reebok, Adidas, and other firms. Europe's lingering recession has limited sales growth as well, as many Europeans perceive sneaker prices to be high. In addition, Nike must adapt to cultural nuances in sneaker distribution and purchasing behavior.

Questions:

1. What trends in the marketing environment have produced the increases in the size of the sneaker market in Europe?

2. What has Nike done to take advantage of the opportunities offered by these marketing environment trends?

3. What types of cultural nuances in sneaker distribution and purchasing behavior might Nike face?

4. What is your assessment of Nike's marketing strategy in Europe?

Sources: Joseph Pereira, "Nike and Reebok Sell Sneakers to Europe," *The Wall Street Journal*, July 22, 1993, pp. A1, A8; Fleming Meeks, "Be Ferocious," *Forbes*, August 2, 1993, pp. 40–41; and Dori Jones Young, Michael O'Neal, Charles Hoots, and Robert Neff, "Can Nike Just Do It?" *Business Week*, April 18, 1994, pp. 86–90.

Glossary of Marketing Terms

The comprehensive glossary provided at the end of the text includes definitions of all bolded and italicized terms used in the text and the page number where the term is first presented and defined. These alphabetized definitions make it easy for students to review important terms and definitions during study sessions. ■

Glossary of Marketing Terms

ability the consumer's knowledge about the product category sufficient to understand the advertised message, *p. 446*

acceptable price range the range of prices buyers are willing to pay for a product; prices above the range may be judged unfair, while prices below the range may generate concerns about quality, *p. 320*

accessibility the degree to which a firm can reach intended target segments efficiently with its products and communications, *p. 184*

adaptive selling a salesperson's adjustment of his or her

Teaching Resources

*T*he teaching resources accompanying **MARKETING: PRINCIPLES & PERSPECTIVES** were carefully selected based on feedback from teachers of marketing principles. In addition, all of the authors were closely involved in the design of each element of the teaching resources. Our goal was to make it as easy as possible for instructors to add value to the student learning process. We meticulously reviewed all supplements during the preparation process for accuracy and to ensure their integration with the text. The *Teaching Resource Guide* and *Manual of Tests* were also reviewed by a panel of professors to ensure accuracy and maximum usefulness. Both of these supplements are available in printed form and on computer disc.

Teaching Resource Guide and *Electronic Teaching Resource Guide*

The *Teaching Resource Guide* was prepared by Scott Inks (The University of Memphis). We worked closely with Scott to develop a comprehensive, useable, and useful *Resource Guide.*

Teaching Map

Each chapter of the *Teaching Resource Guide* begins with a teaching map that visually illustrates the important teaching resources in the chapter.

Student Learning Guides, Chapter Outlines, and Key Terms & Concepts

These items from the text provide a quick overview of what students should be learning and what is covered in each chapter.

Ideas for Student Learning

We believe this section of the *Teaching Resource Guide* is extremely important, and we spent a tremendous amount of time in its preparation. As the role of teaching changes from transferring information to facilitating student learning, teaching becomes much more than determining *what* material to cover. The emphasis moves to: **What can we do to get students motivated and actively involved in learning?**

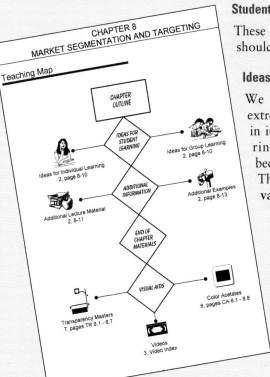

Ideas for Student Learning

Individual learning

IL 8.1
Purpose: To give students practical experience in positioning and, to help students improve their chances of getting a job after graduation.

Procedure: Very simply, students are to develop a strategy for positioning themselves in the minds of prospective employers. Students are to write a 3 - 5 page paper describing their strategy and the basis for its development. First, students will have to determine the job market segment in which they are interested in working. Second, the students will have to make a determination as to what qualifications are associated with successful candidates for positions in that market segment. Third, the student should describe any steps to be taken prior to graduation that will help provide him/her with the necessary qualifications. Finally, the student should provide an outline as to how he or she will achieve the desired positioning in the minds of prospective employers (e.g. cover letters, portfolios, etc.).

IL 8.2
Purpose: To give students insight into how marketers use television programs to gain access to specific target markets.

Procedure: Students are to watch a network television channel for 1 hour, between each of the following times:

Ideas for Student Learning presents many suggestions for the instructor to use during class sessions, for outside homework assignments, or both. Because instructors face different teaching situations—class size, course objectives, teaching styles—we present a variety of ideas for maximum flexibility, including **discussion starters, active learning exercises,** and different **discussion formats.** Some suggestions are borrowed from marketing training programs where it is imperative to actively involve trainees in their learning. All **Ideas for Student Learning** are presented in a format conducive to easy use in a principles of marketing class.

Additional Examples and Additional Lecture Materials

Although the text is extremely current, there is always a delay between when a book is written and when it is used. During this time, company situations change and relevant examples emerge. We also believe that everything a student should learn about a topic should not be included in the text. The **Additional Examples** and **Additional Lecture Materials** can be introduced into class sessions as desired: the instructor can update some examples, present new ones, expand on text coverage, and introduce new concepts by referring to these sections. This shortens preparation time but adds considerable value to the course and specific class sessions.

Additional Lecture Materials

LM 5.1
Concept: Attitude Theory - A Compensatory Attitude Model

Summary: Theory and research in psychology over the last 30 to 40 years have provided a conceptualization of consumer brand attitudes in the model:

$$Aact_{jk} = \sum_{i=1}^{n} b_{ijk}\, e_{ik}$$

Where:
Σ = summation of beliefs x evaluations
n = number of salient product attributes
$Aact_{jk}$ = consumer k's attitude toward the purchase of brand j
b_{ijk} = belief held by consumer k that brand j possesses attribute i
e_{ik} = evaluation (goodness - badness) of attribute i held by consumer k

The model is simpler than it may appear. Basically, it proposes that attitudes toward purchase of a brand or product are based upon a combination of both the consumer's beliefs about a brand's attributes and the relative importance of those attributes (e.g., price, style). Note that this model focuses on attitudes toward an action, the purchase of a particular brand, not general attitudes about the brand. No doubt, your immediate attitude toward a Mercedes Benz differs from your attitude toward the purchase of one.

Additional Examples

AE 8.1
Concept: Segmentation

Citation: Stewart L. Allyson (19

Before presenting this
segment the market for

Summary: This article examines h
unlike most other prod
market to market. "Lik
home video, home shop
geographic markets, bu
localized." The market
localized market. Markets develop segments based on genre, retail channels used, format purchased (and degree of CD penetration). For example, 76% of all Dutch music is sold on CDs, while on 23% is sold this way in Greece.

AE 8.2
Concept: Targeting

Citation: Siegle, Candice (1994), "Sewing It Up," *World Trade,* (May) 122-124

Summary: While most foreign companies have ignored Mexico's working class, Singer has identified it as having a high profit potential. Singer has targeted Mexico's working class for its lower end sewing machines and has taken steps to enhance its market penetration. For example, each of the 140 Singer shops employs its own credit investigator. This makes it possible to sell machines to individuals who have never established credit. In a country where cash payment is the cultural norm, the number of consumers without established credit is substantial. Because it has targeted Mexico's working class, Singer's sales of white-line and sewing machines has increased %500 since 1988.

End-of-Chapter Materials

This section provides suggested answers to the text's **Review & Discussion Questions, Application Exercises,** and **Cases.** It also presents ideas for using these materials in different ways to actively involve students.

Transparency Masters (TRs)

More than 200 **Transparency Masters (TRs)** are provided, all different than the **Color Print Acetates** and **Electronic Acetates.** One TR for each chapter is a collage of relevant article titles that instructors can show before class begins to focus students on the material to be covered. Some **TRs** come in two parts to generate class discussion: **Part A** contains issues or questions with room for the instructor to write student responses directly on the **TM; Part B,** suitable for a lecture format, contains selected answers to the questions or issues in **Part A.**

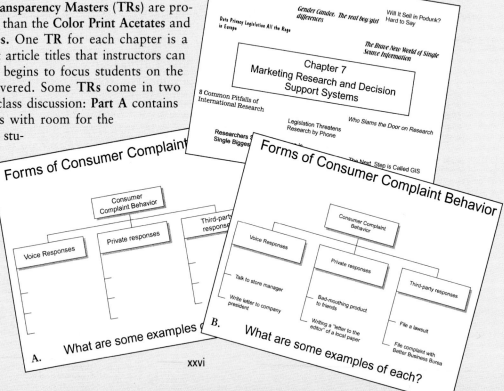

Manual of Tests

The *Manual of Tests* was prepared by Ron Weir (East Tennessee State University). We worked with Ron in planning the *Manual of Tests* and reviewed all questions. The *Manual of Tests,* comprising over 3,500 test items, includes multiple choice, short answer, fill-in-the-blank, and critical thinking questions. The three types of questions—basic recall, comprehension, and application—are graded for level of difficulty, page-referenced to the text, and a **rationale** is given for each correct answer.

Color Print Acetates

The package, prepared by Robert Gwinner (Arizona State), contains approximately 200 original, full-color acetates of **compelling ads** and **striking graphics** that illustrate key marketing concepts. None of the images in the **Color Print Acetates** package comes directly from the text. Detailed **Teaching Notes** accompany each **Color Print Acetate**, relating it to the text concept. Many **Teaching Notes** also include provocative questions to stimulate class discussion and promote active learning. The **Color Print Acetates** are also available in **35mm slides.**

A12-1 Daffy's: Discounting from the suggested list price

A12-1 DAFFY'S: DISCOUNTING FROM THE SUGGESTED LIST PRICE

In a number of product areas such as name brand clothing, discounting from suggested list prices is quite common. The advertisement in this transparency is presented by Daffy's, a discount clothier that discounts men's, women's, and children's fashion and designer clothing by 40-75%. From the ad, it may be observed that Daffy's cleverly offers "clothes that will make you, not break you."

Question: How significant are list prices in today's marketplace? As demonstrated in this example, list prices are always subject to reductions. These may occur in the form of discounts, allowances, or rebates. As a practical matter, consumers seldom pay list prices if they are smart shoppers. Even in the traditional full-service department store, list prices are vulnerable to reductions when merchandise is on the shelf for an unsatisfactory period of time. That merchandise would be put on sale and discounted well below the original price that was marked on the merchandise. Sales are commonplace today, and most consumers look for and expect to see their favorite products and brands offered at less than list price.

Electronic Acetates

In addition to the printed **Color Print Acetates,** we also offer 100 **graphic acetates** on disk, compatible with *Powerpoint*. More than a third of these images are unique from the hardcopy printed **Color Print Acetates.** The **Electronic Acetates** also come with **Teaching Notes.**

Video Library

This current, dynamic **Video Library** includes 21 videos, one for each chapter. The segments, which run from 6 to 15 minutes, visually demonstrate the marketing concepts from the text and are tied closely to specific chapter coverage. The **videos** offer a variety of classroom uses: as video cases, to present important marketing concepts and approaches, to emphasize the ten key marketing perspectives, or to introduce **Executive Roundtable** members.

Laser Disc

The **Laser Disc** includes the **Video Library, Color Print Acetates, Electronic Acetates,** and additional concepts from the text. This new medium for classroom presentation gives the instructor instant access to any of the visual supplements that accompany **MARKETING: PRINCIPLES & PERSPECTIVES.** The **Laser Disc** can be accessed through bar code or manual remote control.

Media Resource Guide

This manual describes each video segment and offers suggestions for using the **Video Library** and **Laser Disc** to facilitate classroom interaction. The suggestions go beyond just showing the complete video and then answering specific questions—**outlines, exercises,** and **additional discussion questions** are also included. **Teaching Notes** for the **Electronic Acetates** also appear in the *Media Resource Guide.*

Irwin Link™

A computer bulletin board service —**Irwin Link**™—is available to every adopter of **MARKETING: PRINCIPLES & PERSPECTIVES.** With a modem and communications software, instructors can dial IrwinLink and leave messages for editors, authors, or other adopters. And they can download new cases, readings, test questions, and teaching tips. A full list of Irwin's other offerings is also available.

Student Resources

The complete **MARKETING: PRINCIPLES & PERSPECTIVES** package offers several additional resources for student learning, all prepared by or under the guidance of the Authors. The resources are described in detail in **A NOTE TO THE STUDENT** (*p. xxx*) and briefly listed here.

• *Student Learning Workbook,* prepared by Nick Sarantakes (Austin Community College), provides review material, self-test **Learning Exercises** (with answers), and a visual **Study Poster** for each chapter.

• *Marketing Careers, Marketing in Other Careers, and Marketing Your Career* provides information on careers in marketing, the importance of marketing in careers outside of marketing, and experiential exercises to help students in career planning and job search.

• *Marketing Planning Software* is a windows-based program that takes students step-by-step through the marketing planning process. Students can import documents from other software programs such as *Excel* and *Powerpoint* to create a professional and complete marketing plan.

• *Student Software* takes students through 10 decision-making exercises that give hands-on experience in key areas of marketing such as marketing research, pricing, communications, and sales. This windows-based software has a virtual-reality-like design and integrates the ten key perspectives in each exercise. ■

In Conclusion

*L*ooking back over the three years we spent developing **MARKETING: PRINCIPLES & PERSPECTIVES,** we realized how the entire project came to fruition through our application of the ten key marketing perspectives. First we developed a vision—we envisioned a marketing principles package that would make an important contribution to marketing education throughout the 90s and into the 21st century. Achieving our vision required an **entrepreneurial** effort to research and capture the exciting changes in marketing thought and practice, and to present them in innovative ways that would help instructors teach and students learn.

We took a **global perspective** from the beginning by examining marketing around the world, integrating global issues into the text, and having our work reviewed by professors from different countries. The entire process was driven by a **relationship perspective.** Our objective was not just to write a book to be sold, but to produce a complete package that instructors and students will find of value in the teaching and learning process for years to come. We also established partnerships with several individuals and organizations to assemble the package materials. And we emphasized teamwork by working together as authors and with our teammates at Irwin.

We emphasized **quality/value** and **productivity** throughout the project. Before anything was written, we researched and studied the needs of instructors for principles of marketing courses. We designed everything in the package to meet these needs and had our work evaluated by instructors on a continuing basis. The result is a package that offers the quality desired by marketing instructors as defined by them. We tried to add value in every aspect of the text and supplements. And everything has been evaluated from a productivity perspective so that we can offer the highest quality and the best value.

A **technological perspective** helped us to be more productive in developing the package and providing materials in different technological formats. Information and communication technologies facilitated the entire development and production process. The text exhibits were generated by state-of-the-art computer design; and the text itself was typeset and the artwork incorporated into it electronically and then printed on high-tech color presses. Offering many materials in various electronic formats gives instructors several teaching alternatives and is ecologically responsible by reducing the use of paper for many of these items.

All of our careful planning would be wasted, however, if the plans were not **executed** effectively. We constantly focused on doing things right. Everything in the package was reviewed and reviewed, and revised and revised. And revised again. Positive feedback from many reviewers indicates that we indeed executed our plans successfully. We incorporated an **ethical perspective** into the development and production processes. Effective partnerships with our teammates required the trust that can only be established through ethical behavior. Our integrated marketing communications also highlight only the parts of our package that have clear and demonstrable differences from existing products.

As we put the finishing touches on this project, we are truly proud of what has been accomplished. We feel good about it. The ten key marketing perspectives helped us in this process. We think they will also be valuable to you in your teaching and to your students in their learning.

We are now ready for the ultimate test—the response of the marketplace. Please let us know what you think about all aspects of **MARKETING: PRINCIPLES & PERSPECTIVES.** We are especially interested in any ideas you might have for improving any part of the text or teaching resources. Your comments are important and appreciated. ■

Bill Bearden
Tom Ingram
Buddy LaForge

Note to the Student

......

Congratulations! You are about to begin studying the exciting field of marketing. This could not happen at a better time. Today, marketing is increasingly important in all types of organizations and situations. Businesses, hospitals, museums, nonprofit organizations, and even government agencies emphasize marketing and offer marketing positions. They also realize the importance of focusing everyone in the organization toward satisfying the needs of their customers. That's a *marketing philosophy.* So, even if you are not in an official marketing job, you are likely to be involved in marketing in one way or another. Finally, you are continually marketing yourself and your ideas in your everyday life, and will be even more so as you enter the job market. Effective marketing can help you get the jobs you want and advance through your career.

MARKETING: PRINCIPLES & PERSPECTIVES is written to and for you—the student. We present the most important marketing concepts in a way that you can understand and apply. Many text examples, photos, and exhibits reinforce the concepts and show how real organizations and people use marketing concepts effectively. Our objective is to help you learn and understand the basics of marketing so that you can think and act like a marketer in any type of career situation.

"The little box for head and tummy aches." Campaign for Alka-Seltzer in Belgium.

Norwegian Cruise Lines ad for trips to the Caribbean.

"If I were you, I'd order steak." Campaign for a steak restaurant in Amsterdam.

(Chapter 18)

To achieve this objective, however, you have to become actively involved in the learning process. Use all of the available resources—the text, *Student Learning Workbook,* your instructor, your classmates, practicing marketers—to learn as much as possible about marketing. The more you learn, the better prepared you will be to operate successfully in the complex and turbulent world of the 90s and the 21st century.

We recommend that you review the **Learning Guides** at the beginning of each chapter to identify what you should learn from the chapter. Then, read and study the chapter carefully and pay special attention to the bolded and italicized terms—these are the terms and concepts you need to understand. After studying the chapter, try to answer the **Review & Discussion Questions.** Some answers come directly from the text, but others require you to think more critically about what has been read. Do

---

Exhibit 10.9 **Marketing research support for new products**

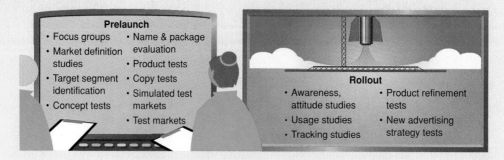

Prelaunch
- Focus groups
- Market definition studies
- Target segment identification
- Concept tests
- Name & package evaluation
- Product tests
- Copy tests
- Simulated test markets
- Test markets

Rollout
- Awareness, attitude studies
- Usage studies
- Tracking studies
- Product refinement tests
- New advertising strategy tests

the **Application Exercises.** Many of them have you contact a firm to talk with someone in a marketing position or with the public relations department to obtain an annual report. Don't feel intimidated. Most people will be glad to help! They will be delighted to talk about their marketing operations or to send an annual report.

The *Student Learning Workbook* is a valuable learning tool. It outlines and summarizes each chapter and presents definitions of the key terms. Then it offers various **Learning Exercises.** Working the exercises increases your learning and understanding of marketing, and you can check answers to identify areas where further study is needed. When you think you have learned the material, take the **Marketing Master Quiz** to evaluate your progress. The *Workbook* also includes a **Marketing Journal** where you can log examples of marketing encountered in your daily activities. Once you start looking for them, you'll be surprised at the abundance of marketing examples you'll see in the environment around you. Finally, the *Student Learning Workbook* provides a **Questions to Ask in Class** section where you can jot down issues or questions you want to ask about in class or marketing experiences or examples to share with your classmates.

Are you interested in a career in marketing? We prepared *Marketing Careers, Marketing in Other Careers,* and *Marketing in Your Career* to help you with this important decision. *Careers* contains information about different types of positions in the field of marketing. Comments from successful marketers who are specialists in various fields offer insight into the positions they hold. *Careers* also shows how marketing skills are needed in business careers outside of the field of marketing itself and gives hints for conducting a job search, writing a resumé and preparing for a job interview. The self-tests and exercises will help you identify areas of interest. Overall, *Marketing Careers, Marketing in Other Careers,* and *Marketing in Your Career* should expand your marketing horizons with the possibility of more career possibilities and then help you narrow your choices to the most viable options.

We wish you the best in the study of marketing. *Everyone* is involved in marketing in some way—so, the real question is whether you are an effective or ineffective marketer. You can learn the basics needed to be an effective marketer by applying yourself in this course. Read the text, answer the questions, perform the application exercises, use the *Student Learning Workbook,* go to class, participate in class discussions, ask questions, interact with your classmates, talk with people in marketing positions, and look for the marketing examples that are all around you. Do these things and you will learn about marketing. Learning about marketing will help you in your future career, no matter what it may be. We invite you to call or write us if you have questions about anything in the text itself or about marketing in general. We believe marketing is the most exciting and interesting of topics; and we hope we have conveyed this excitement to you. Best wishes, and happy marketing!

Bill Bearden
Tom Ingram
Buddy LaForge

Executive Roundtable

The Executive Roundtable members hold diverse positions in a variety of industries. The brief bios below list their current and previous career positions and educational backgrounds. All Roundtable members also hold leadership positions in professional, civic, and charitable organizations too numerous to list here.

Richard L. Bohy Vice president/professional services, Sioux Valley Hospital, Sioux Falls, SD (South Dakota's largest hospital). Responsibilities include the marketing program and the surgical, laboratory, cardiovascular, radiology, and ambulatory services. West Central Regional Director for Sales and Marketing Executives International (SMEI). B.A., English and education, Nebraska Weslyan University; M.A., educational psychology, University of Nebraska.

Claudia J. Bowers Executive vice president, owner and partner in TRC Industries, Inc., Stow, OH, which makes polymers. In 1990–92 TRC Industries was named one of the top 100 fastest-growing companies in Northeast Ohio by the Weatherhead School of Business at Case Western Reserve University; and in 1991 chosen Ohio's small business of the year by the US Small Business Administration. Elected SMEI president July 1994. Certified sales executive (CSE). Magna cum laude, social work, University of Akron.

Sheila K. Burroughs Quality consultant with NationsBank in Charlotte, NC. Previous positions at NationsBank include branch development analyst and marketing research analyst. Received specialized training in facilitating, motivating, and customer/supplier relationship skills. B.S., honors, business administration, University of South Carolina.

Paul C. Casey Vice president/ branch manager, Smith Barney, Inc., Louisville, KY. Previous positions include commercial banking, Montgomery, AL; office manager, E. F. Hutton, Pensacola, FL; sales manager, Shearson Lehman Brothers, Atlanta. Graduated Troy State University, Montgomery, AL.

Dorothy Brazil Clark Director, business development/ volume food services for Protein Technologies International, St. Louis. Previous positions at PTI include manager/market research and marketing manager/school food service segment. Was sales representative and assistant manager/ market research with Norden Laboratories, subsidiary of SmithKline-Beecham; and division food specialist for Interstate United Corporation Management Company. B.A., University of Iowa; M.B.A., University of Missouri.

Anthony Donnan General manager/European government affairs for Avon Products Inc., Rontigax, France. Joined Avon in Montreal in 1968 as purchasing manager, then division sales manager; moved to Europe where responsible for merchandising in 8 European countries; national sales manager in France for 5 years and in Germany for 3 years. General manager for Avon in Saudi Arabia 1984–87; in Indonesia 1987–91; in France, 1991–93. Also chair of FEDSA, the European Association of Direct Marketing. Born and educated in Australia; attended Sydney University.

Gerald W. Evans Vice President/field sales, L'eggs Products, Inc., Winston-Salem, NC. Previously L'eggs marketing director, including advertising development and promotional spending; product manager for SHEER EN-ERGY and ACTIVE SUPPORT brands concurrently, including research and advertising functions; product manager/ new product development; assistant product manager for SHEER ENERGY brand; and marketing assistant for SHEER ENERGY brand. B.S., marketing, and M.B.A., University of South Carolina.

Robert C. Heimbrock Regional sales manager, Pomeroy Computer Resources, Erlanger, KY, which designs, provides, and manages information technology for business, specializing in providing professional computer services. Previously sales representative for ComputerLand of Cincinnati. Undergraduate and masters degrees, marketing, University of Kentucky.

Don C. Johnson Traffic manager for Sharp Manufacturing Co. of America, Memphis, TN, a leading electronics manufacturer. Involved in all phases of logistics, including import/export operations in domestic and international markets. Previously held logistics management positions with Schering-Plough and Kroger. Undergraduate degree, transportation and traffic management, University of Alabama; masters degree, operations management, University of Arkansas.

Thomas W. Kapella Vice president/product development for Gibson Greetings, Inc., Cincinnati. Responsible for product marketing, creative, editorial, licensing, and communications. Previous positions include commodity buyer and sales promotion manager for a Los Angeles investment firm; positions at small, privately held Dallas greeting card company that merged with American greetings; vice president/ marketing for American Greetings. B.S., Oklahoma State University.

John V. O. Kennard Executive director of spirits marketing, Brown-Forman Beverages Worldwide, Louisville, KY. Supervises the market research department and is member of the firm's management committee. Previously held marketing positions for General Foods, White Plains, NY; senior brand manager for R. J. Reynolds, Winston-Salem, NC; then group product manager for its Del Monte division, San Francisco. B.A., English literature, and M.B.A., business administration, University of Virginia.

Richard Kitaeff District manager, business communications services business unit, AT&T, Basking Ridge, NJ. Responsible for all marketing research conducted on 800-services and related applications. Earlier AT&T positions include conducting research studies using internal databases and other research-related assignments, and in the marketing and regulatory areas. Formerly went through the management development program and worked as business manager for New York Telephone. B.A., sociology/anthropology, New York University.

Robert W. Kyle International marketing manager, Diebold, Inc., Canton, OH. Responsible for the marketing and support of major security systems in Diebold's two international divisions. Did installation/repair work and sold major key telephone systems and switchboards for Bell Canada. Was sales manager in marketing electronic stock quotation equipment across Canada; Canadian sales manager for Mosler (Safe Co.); then US international sales manager, director of international marketing and managing director for Mosler in Europe. Degree in marketing from Sir George Williams University, Montreal.

David Moore Vice president/ sales with Ruddell and Associates, Inc., a gift and greeting card manufacturer's representative firm in San Francisco. Formerly worked with gift industry firms of Hallmark Cards, American Greetings, Leadworks, and Roserich Designs. National director of field sales at Carlton Cards division of American Greetings, managing 200 salespeople, district and regional managers, and sales specialists and in-house customer service, sales training, and telemarketing departments. B.S., industrial management, Bowling Green State University.

Stephen Eugene Martin Director of marketing and economic development, Westplains Energy, a division of UtiliCorp United, Pueblo, CO. Previously marketing manager for South Carolina Electric & Gas Company (SCE&G); president of M.M.R. & Associates (company he helped co-found while in graduate school); vice president/director of marketing for American Health Services Corporation. B.A., journalism (advertising management major); M.S., business administration (marketing management major), University of South Carolina.

William D. Neal Founder and principal in SDR, Inc., Atlanta, GA, which specializes in processing and statistical analysis of marketing research information. Currently employs more than 100 people in the Atlanta and Chicago offices. Works with marketing research departments and marketing research companies to apply data processing and statistical procedures to marketing problems. Lectures and teaches seminars on market segmentation, multivariate analysis, and applied statistical analysis of marketing research data. B.S., commerce and engineering, Drexel University; M.S., industrial management (specialization in operations research), Georgia Tech.

Shaun Singleton Masters Director of merchandising for Signal Artwear division of Signal Apparel, Chattanooga, TN. Markets licensed products to major retail customers. Previously held merchandising and marketing positions with Duck Head Apparel Company. Experienced in advertising, event marketing, point-of-purchase, in-store promotions, and in sales, purchasing, and product development. Bachelor's, merchandising and marketing, University of Georgia.

Donald C. North President and CEO, Stuckey's Family Favorites, Inc., Bethesda, MD. Before joining Stuckey's in 1993, worked for Contenova Gifts in British Columbia and Ontario as territorial sales rep, national marketing manager, vice president/marketing, executive vice president, and chief executive officer. Joined SMEI in 1977 and held various offices. Certified sales executive (CSE) and certified marketing executive (CME); graduated from SMEI Graduate School of Sales Management and Marketing at Syracuse University.

Bobbie Oglesby Manager, small and medium business marketing at Apple Computer, Jacksonville, OR. Previously developed new products for Philips Consumer Electronics. Marketing responsibilities have included developing segmentation strategies, positioning, communications/advertising programs, new-product development and introduction, distribution strategy, and marketing research management. Phi Beta Kappa, magna cum laude B.S., business administration; M.S., marketing, University of South Carolina.

Mark D. Oshnock CPA and Partner at Arthur Andersen-Atlanta. Areas of specialty include business and financial planning; operations improvement through business process reengineering; physician-hospital integration strategies; multihospital systems; mergers and acquisitions; financial and operational restructuring. Serves on Andersen's firmwide health care services core team, which sets direction for research & development efforts and educational plan; and on special firm task forces on operations reengineering and integrated health care delivery systems. Graduated Michigan State University.

Charles H. Sawyer Account executive for Metromail, Chicago. From 1985 to 1993 with Computerized Marketing Technologies (CMT) as account executive, regional sales manager, and vice president/database marketing. At CMT, worked with Grey Direct Advertising in new venture called Personal Media Corporation (PMC), creating household targeted magazines and relationship-driven media vehicles. Prior to CMT, worked with Colgate-Palmolive Company and James River Corporation in brand management. Experienced in marketing, targeted marketing applications, and database marketing. B.A., business administration, University of Oregon; M.B.A., international management, American Graduate School of International Management.

Mary E. Washington Buyer for Atmel Corporation, Colorado Springs, CO, purchasing products such as printed circuit boards, office supplies, and computer software. Previously was buyer for Honeywell Inc. in Colorado. Active in National Association of Purchasing Management. B.A., English, Doane College, Crete, Nebraska.

Acknowledgments

Writing a text requires a team effort, and we have enjoyed a collaboration with the best teammates imaginable. Cooperative, knowledgeable, creative, candid, and always encouraging—these are but a few of the positive things we found in our teammates. We are especially appreciative of the countless number of people involved in this project who time after time put forth the extra effort necessary to accomplish our mutual goals.

- The professionals at Richard D. Irwin led the way well before the first page of manuscript was produced. Steve Patterson, Bill McDowell, and Greg Patterson saw the opportunity to bring the author team together and convinced us that our plans could become reality. Rob Zwettler, a long-appreciated colleague, got us off to a good start, and Nina McGuffin later took overall responsibility for the project. Thanks to many others at Irwin, including Jim Lewis (marketing), Ethel Shiell (production), Mercedes Santos and Michael Warrell (designers), Mike Hruby (photo research), Harriett Stockaness (permissions), and many other Irwinites who worked long hours behind the scenes. A special thank you and much more to managing development editor Eleanore Snow, a champion of doing the right things right. Eleanore's knowledge, work ethic, persistence, and sense of humor kept us on course all the way.

- We appreciate the continuing efforts and support of the Irwin salesforce, who recommended their best marketing professors as reviewers for the text and helped us conduct research in the areas of ancillary items and other important issues. We especially thank the **BIL Task Force** members who followed and supported our progress through the various drafts of the manuscript. And we thank in advance the expert team of **Irwin Product Specialists** who will become our champions in marketing the finished product. The high esteem and respect the Irwin salesforce enjoys in the publishing world is well deserved.

The BIL Task Force	The Irwin Product Specialists
Barbara Anson	Bunny Barr
Cathy Bennett	Steve Bellochio
Beverly Dunn	Ginny Frazier
Garrett Glanz	Sam Hussey
Diane Hilgers	Julie Britt Jahn
Sam Hussey	Gordon Jepson
Julie Britt Jahn	Michelle LeBlanc
Jim Lewis	Jim Lewis
Mary Lucke	Denise Mariani
Denise Mariani	Brian Murray
Brian Murray	Greg Patterson
Greg Patterson	Gary Rodgers
Bruce Powell	Kas Salazar
Todd Strever	Rosalie Skears

- Our book has been improved by a long list of reviewers—both national and international—of three drafts of the manuscript. We were stimulated and encouraged by their comments and suggestions, and incorporated many of their ideas into the text. Our thanks to our marketing colleagues listed below and to additional reviewers who prefer to remain anonymous. Several people reviewed multiple manuscript drafts; we owe them a special thanks for their patience and diligence. Because of length considerations we were not able to incorporate every good suggestion; but we considered all of them carefully and appreciate the reasoning behind them. We believe **MARKETING: PRINCIPLES & PERSPECTIVES** comes much closer to meeting your teaching needs and the learning needs of your students because of your efforts.

Ronald J. Adams
University of North Florida

Ramon Avila
Ball State University

Joe Ballenger
Stephen F. Austin University

Connie T. Boyd
University of Tennessee–Martin

John R. (Rusty) Brooks
Houston Baptist University

Phyllis Campbell
Bethel College

Lyndon Dawson
Louisiana Tech University

Oscar DeShields
California State University–Northridge

John Doering
Minot State University

Casey Donoho
Northern Arizona University

Michael Drafke
College of DuPage

Ralph Gallay
Rider College

William G. Glynn
University College Dublin, Ireland

Robert F. Gwinner
Arizona State University

Fleming Hansen
Copenhagen Business School, Denmark

Fredric Kropp
University of Oregon

Priscilla A. La Barbera
New York University

J. Ford Laumer, Jr.
Auburn University

Dale Lunsford
University of Tulsa

H. Lee Meadow
Northern Illinois University

Carla Millar
City University Business School, London

Linda Morris
University of Idaho

Erik B. Ness
Norwegian School of Management, Oslo, Norway

Linda Pettijohn
Southwest Missouri State

Marie A. Pietak
Bucks County Community College

Andrea Prothero
Cardiff Business School University of Wales

Daniel Rajaratnam
Baylor University

Glen Riecken
East Tennessee State University

Nick Sarantakes
Austin Community College

Charlie Schwepker
Central Missouri State University

C. David Shepherd
University of Tennessee–Chattanoga

Carol Soroos
North Carolina State University

Michael J. Swenson
Brigham Young University

Ronald D. Taylor
Mississippi State University

Sushila Umashanker
University of Arizona

David J. Urban
Virginia Commonwealth University

Rockney G. Walters
Indiana University

Terrence H. Witkowski
California State University–Long Beach

Helen R. Woodruffe
University of Salford, England

Sherilyn Zeigler
University of Hawaii–Manoa

• Very early on we conducted a survey of marketing principles teachers about which supplements were critical to their teaching success—and how these items should be constructed. We incorporated many of their good suggestions into the ancillary package. Our special thanks to the colleagues who offered their suggestions:

Maria Aria
Camden County Community College

Noel Bennett
Metropolitan Community College

William Bonwich
St. Louis University

Connie T. Boyd
Southern Illinois University–Carbondale

Jeffrey L. Bradford
Bowling Green State University

V. Carter Broach
University of Delaware

James Butts
American University

Gerri Chaplin
Joliet Junior College

Michael Cicero
Highline Community College

Susan Cisco
Oakton Community College

Robert Collins
University of Nevada–Las Vegas

William Crandall
College of San Mateo

Richard Cummings
College of Lake County

Donald Dalton
*St. Louis Community
College–Meramec*

Martin Decatur
Suffolk Community College

Michael Drafke
College of DuPage

Chaim Ehrman
Loyola University

Herman Floyd
Catonsville Community College

Fred Folkman
*Queensborough Community
College*

Blaine Greenfield
*Bucks County Community
College*

Matthew Gross
*Moraine Valley Community
College*

Roy Grundy
College of DuPage

Robert Gwinner
Arizona State University

Timothy Hartman
Ohio State University

Salah Hassan
George Washington University

James Healey
Chabot College

Sanford Helman
Middlesex Community College

Richard Immenhausen
College of the Desert

Robert Jones
*California State
University–Fullerton*

Herbert Katzenstein
St. Johns University

Charles King
University of Illinois–Chicago

Maryon King
*Southern Illinois
University–Carbondale*

Joseph Kissan
Purdue University

Lawrence Knight
Indiana State University

Fredric Kropp
University of Oregon

Ford Laumer
Auburn University

William Leahy
St. Joseph's University

Gary McCain
Boise State University

Lee Meadow
Northern Illinois University

Joan Mizis
St. Louis Community–Florissant

Joseph Moutran
*Miami Dade Community
College*

Robert O'Keefe
De Paul University

Marie Pietek
*Bucks County Community
College*

Nick Sarantakes
Austin Community College

Raj Sethuraman
University of Iowa

Jack Sheeks
Broward Community College

Robert Snyder
Roosevelt University

Michael Swenson
Brigham Young University

Jan Taylor
Miami University

Frank Titlow
St. Petersburg Junior College

Hope Torkornoo
Kennesaw State University

John Wagle
Northern Illinois University

Donald Walli
Greenville Technical College

Kathy Walton
Salt Lake Community College

Alan Weintraub
Tulsa Junior College

Robert Witherspoon
Triton College

Joyce Wood
*North Virginia Community
College–Alexandria*

Paul Zinser
Syracuse University

• Our ancillary coauthors are top-notch, and it has been our privilege to work with each of them: Ron Weir (East Tennessee State), Nick Sarantakes (Austin Community College), Scott Inks (The University of Memphis). Thanks also to Bob Gwinner of Arizona State University for preparing the Color Print Acetates to accompany the text. Brad Brooks (Queens College) was especially helpful in developing several of the cases.

• We also appreciate the support from our institutions: At the University of South Carolina, doctoral student Ken Manning and administrative specialists Edie Beaver and Jennie Smyrl; at The University of Memphis, doctoral students Victoria Bush, Ed Bashaw, and Charlie Schwepker; undergraduate student Lee Mabie and administrative assistant Pat Fulton; and at the University of Louisville, student assistance from Kelly Vincent and, as always, executive secretary Charlotte Ford.

• Finally, with love and respect, we offer special recognition to our families, who have contributed in countless ways from proofreading to pep talks over the past three years—we could not have done it without you. Thanks for your understanding and support. ∎

Brief Table of Contents

Contents

PART 2

Buying Behavior   102

chapter 4

Marketing's Role in the Organization   78

chapter 5

Consumer Buying Behavior and Decision Making   104

PART 5

Pricing Concepts and Strategies   278

chapter 12

Pricing Concepts   280

Snapple: Grapples with premium price and premium value   281

chapter 13

Price Determination and Pricing Strategies   304

Swatch watches: Prices don't change over time   305

Where to find . . .

PART 1

Marketing in a Dynamic Environment

Marketers today need new perspectives to operate effectively in a fast-changing global environment.

*T*he exciting field of marketing is introduced in Part 1. Chapter 1, "An Overview of Contemporary Marketing," defines marketing, discusses the evolution of marketing practice, and introduces a contemporary marketing framework. Chapter 2, "Ten Key Marketing Perspectives," examines ten key marketing perspectives that are increasingly important to marketers. Chapter 3, "The Global Marketing Environment," discusses important relationships among marketing and the global social, economic, competitive, technological, legal/political, and institutional environments. Chapter 4, "Marketing's Role in the Organization," investigates the role of marketing in multibusiness, multiproduct organizations operating in a global marketplace.

An Overview of Contemporary Marketing

After studying this chapter you should be able to:

1. Discuss what marketing is and why it is important to organizations and individuals.

2. Distinguish between marketing as an organizational philosophy and a societal process.

3. Understand the components of a marketing strategy and the different activities involved in marketing goods and services.

4. Be aware of the various marketing institutions and the different marketing positions available in these institutions.

5. Appreciate how marketing has evolved from earlier times to the present.

6. Understand the basic elements and relationships in the contemporary marketing framework.

Domino's Pizza: Pizza delivery and freebies

*T*om Monaghan pioneered the idea of pizza delivery when he established Domino's Pizza in 1960. Domino's strategy of delivery within 30 minutes rocketed the company to success in the 1980s. Company sales are now around $2.2 billion annually, with about 5,200 US stores and 700 restaurants in 36 foreign countries.

Why has Domino's strategy been so successful? Tom Monaghan identified and responded to an unserved market need. Pizza businesses of the time were either unaware that consumers wanted the convenience of pizza delivery or were not willing to offer the service. He saw the market need and developed a company to satisfy it. Identifying and responding to market needs is the essence of successful marketing.

Domino's success did not go unnoticed. Other pizza places began to offer delivery as a way to compete with Domino's. Even Pizza Hut, the pizza restaurant market leader, introduced delivery and has captured almost 25 percent of the $6.4 billion pizza delivery market.

Increased competition dropped Domino's market share to about 45 percent. Domino's is responding to the competition in several ways. It is introducing new products and expanding into new markets. Bread sticks and garden salads have been added to the menu. Chicken wings, submarine sandwiches, and other items are being tested at some stores. Domino's is also emphasizing international markets, with a focus on Southeast Asia, South America, and Europe.

Competitors have attacked the quality and variety of Domino's pizzas. Domino's is reacting by introducing pizzas with more toppings and extras and by increasing expenditures on advertising. Much of the advertising promotes the flavor of Domino's pizzas and the firm's leadership in home delivery by offering satisfaction or a new pizza or a refund. Even though the 30-minute guarantee had to be dropped due to safety concerns, the company still emphasizes its delivery capabilities. One campaign is "Nobody knows like Domino's—How you like pizza at home." Another campaign, dubbed "Somethin' for Nothin'," offers freebies, such as bread sticks or hats, with each pizza ordered. This campaign also introduces Donny Domino, the company's animated character.

Even though these marketing changes are important, Domino's basic advantage is still pizza delivery, so the company is experimenting with new technologies to make it easier for customers to order. The most promising is the use of one telephone number by which customers can order a Domino's pizza from anywhere in the United States. The service, if introduced as expected, would give Domino's a strong advantage in maintaining customer relationships. As a Domino's spokesperson says, "The main thing is the convenience of the customer. If they move, if they're at the office, if they're at home, if they live in Michigan and are visiting relatives in California, they just have to call that one number."

Sources: "Domino's Tests National Number for Pizza Orders," *Marketing News,* October 14, 1991, p. 21; Lisa Driscoll and David Woodruff, "With Tom Monaghan Back, Can Domino's Deliver?" *Business Week,* October 28, 1991, pp. 136–40; "Domino's, Pizza Hut Make a Run for the Border, Continue Their War," *Marketing News,* November 11, 1991, p. 5; Michael O'Neal, " 'Pizza Pizza' and Tigers, Too," *Business Week,* September 14, 1992, pp. 108–9; "Menu Is Being Expanded to Offer Bread Sticks, Salads," *The Wall Street Journal,* December 2, 1992, p. C12; John P. Cortez, "The New Direction for Domino's," *Advertising Age,* January 3, 1993, pp. 33–34; Krystal Miller and Richard Gibson, "Domino's Stops Promising Pizza in 30 Minutes," *The Wall Street Journal,* December 22, 1993, pp. B1 and B5; and Jeanne Whalen, "Domino's Turnaround Master Exits," *Advertising Age,* January 24, 1994, p. 4.

The Domino's example illustrates a basic principle of successful marketing: identify market needs and respond by developing and executing marketing strategies that satisfy these needs better than competitors. In Domino's case, the market need was convenience. The response was the development of a business based on making it as easy as possible to get pizza delivered.

In a dynamic and turbulent marketing environment, marketers must continually adapt their strategies to maintain or gain market share. The success of the Domino's strategy, for example, led to fierce competition from new and existing pizza marketers. But Domino's constantly looks for ways to improve its service and to combat competitors. It has added new products, expanded internationally, improved the quality and assortment of pizzas offered, and communicated to customers through extensive advertising and sales promotions. It also plans to use recent advances in telephone technology to strengthen its position in the delivery market by making it even easier for customers to order pizza.

Domino's is actively involved in marketing. The most accepted definition of **marketing** is that adopted by the American Marketing Association:

Marketing is the process of planning and executing the conception, pricing, promotion, and distribution of ideas, goods, and services to create exchanges that satisfy individual and organizational goals.[1]

This definition views marketing as a process involving marketing exchanges, strategies, activities, positions, and institutions. Before discussing each of these areas in detail, we examine the importance of marketing to different organizations and individuals, the involvement of people in marketing activities, and different views of marketing.

The importance of marketing

Marketing is usually associated with business organizations. Most people are probably familiar with the marketing activities of Domino's and other consumer product firms such as Procter & Gamble, Sony, Nike, McDonald's, General Motors, and Kmart. They also may be aware of marketing efforts by firms that market to other organizations such as Xerox, Monsanto, Caterpillar, Boeing, and Allied-Signal.

Marketing also plays an important role in a wide variety of situations. Consider the following:

- *Gifts in Kind America*—This nonprofit organization matches donated goods with groups that can use them. It also operates a shipping service to help other nonprofit organizations reduce their shipping costs. Marketing these services is what this organization does.[2]

- *First Interstate Bancorp*—The 12th largest commercial bank in the US has improved its financial performance by reducing nonperforming assets. It has launched a program entitled Revenue Rev-Up to increase fee and interest income from retail customers. Many of the bank's executives participate in sales training programs every six months and spend time making sales calls to small- and medium-sized companies. Their slogan is "We're Addicted to Sales."[3]

- *President Clinton*—President Clinton used marketing research throughout his campaign for the presidency and continues to use it to help develop policies. Focus groups and surveys are employed to assess potential public reaction to policy alternatives. Once policy decisions are made, President Clinton tries to market them to the public through appearances at town meetings and on call-in television shows.[4]

Marketing is important to the success of Roger Williams Park Zoo and many other non-profit organizations.

- *Southern California Gas*—The largest gas utility in the country, Southern California Gas rarely considered how consumers felt about its services. Now, with deregulation producing a number of competitors, the utility regularly evaluates customer satisfaction and provides extensive training to customer service and field representatives. The results have been impressive, with both customer satisfaction scores and financial performance improving substantially.[5]

- *Mecklenburg Community Church*—Mecklenburg Community Church is nondenominational and was established to appeal to baby boomers not currently attending a church. Marketing research identified over 6,000 potential church members in Charlotte, North Carolina. Direct mail was used to promote the church and specific programs developed to meet the needs of the baby-boom generation.[6]

- *Jewish Hospital*—Jewish Hospital used an integrated marketing communications strategy to establish itself as the premier heart care provider in the Louisville, Kentucky, area. The hospital effectively integrated television, radio, newspaper, magazine, and billboard advertisements with a direct-mail campaign and telemarketing program. The different communication tools educated consumers about the warning signs of heart disease and the capabilities of Jewish Hospital to treat all types of heart disease.[7]

These examples illustrate marketing's importance to a nonprofit organization, financial services firm, politician, utility, church, and hospital. Today, more organizations and individuals realize that effective marketing is a critical determinant of success.

The people dimension

It is important to understand that an organization's marketing activities are performed by people. Although we talk about Domino's "marketing strategy," one person, Tom Monaghan, identified the market need for convenience and developed the pizza delivery strategy. He and many of the Domino employees at the Ann Arbor, Michigan, headquarters, and at the more than 5,000 company-owned or franchised outlets in the US and 36 foreign countries, remain involved in planning and executing marketing strategies.

To highlight the people aspects of marketing, we'll spend a day with a marketer. Roger Dow is vice president, general sales manager, for Marriott Hotels, Resorts, and Suites. He is extremely busy and logs more than 300,000 air miles per year. We catch up with him on a day in June:[8]

8:23 AM—Lands at Chicago's O'Hare airport on flight from Washington, DC.

9:35 AM—Meets with a dozen of Marriott's account executives to develop plans to improve relationships and increase business with the company's largest customers.

12:25 PM—Has lunch and meeting with six meeting planners from Marriott's largest accounts. The meeting focuses on obtaining feedback from these customers about the Marriott Masters event held last year. The feedback is used to improve this year's event.

4:40 PM—Meets with Marriott's sales managers to develop plans to increase convention business.

6:30 PM—Gives talk on service quality to Chicago meeting planners group.

8:00 PM—Calls home to talk with family.

9:05 PM—Leaves for airport and flight to Los Angeles.

This glimpse of Roger Dow's day shows that much of marketing involves interacting with people. Dow spent most of his day talking with colleagues at Marriott, customers, and members of a trade group to develop and execute marketing plans.

Executive Roundtable

Because of the importance of the people dimension in marketing, we assembled a group of marketers into an Executive Roundtable for this text. You can get to know the Executive Roundtable members by turning to the preface at the beginning of the book, where we present a photo and a short biographical sketch of each member. They represent a diverse group of people actively involved in different types of marketing activities for various organizations and industries. The Executive Roundtable members share their experiences and knowledge by commenting on specific marketing topics throughout the book. The objective is to offer insights from people currently performing marketing activities for their organizations.

The remainder of this chapter provides an overview of contemporary marketing. We begin by defining marketing and discussing how it has evolved. The chapter concludes with a contemporary marketing framework that serves as a structure for examining marketing practice throughout the remainder of the text.

Views of marketing

Most of the emphasis in this book is on marketing as the process defined at the beginning of the chapter. Nevertheless, marketing can also be viewed as an organizational philosophy and as a societal process.

Marketing as an organizational philosophy

An organization typically has some type of philosophy that directs the efforts of everyone in it. The philosophy might be stated formally, as in a mission statement, or it might become established informally through the communications and actions of top management. An organizational philosophy indicates the types of activities the organization values. Three different philosophies deserve mention.

Exhibit 1.1

The marketing concept

A **production philosophy** exists when an organization emphasizes the production function. An organization following such a philosophy values activities related to improving production efficiency or producing sophisticated products and services. Production drives the organization. Marketing plays a secondary role, because the organization thinks the best-produced products can be easily marketed. High-technology companies often follow a production philosophy.

A **selling philosophy** predominates where the selling function is most valued. The assumption here is that any product can be sold, if enough selling effort is given to it. Marketing's job is to sell whatever the organization decides to produce. Although selling is one component of marketing, organizations driven by a selling philosophy emphasize selling efforts to the exclusion of other marketing activities.

A **marketing philosophy** suggests that the organization focuses on satisfying the needs of customers. This focus applies to people in the marketing function as well as to those in production, personnel, accounting, finance, and other functions. Production and selling are still important, but the organization is driven by satisfying customer needs.

As illustrated in Exhibit 1.1, marketing as an organizational philosophy is based on the **marketing concept**.[9] This concept consists of three interrelated principles: an organization's basic purpose is to satisfy customer needs; satisfying customer needs requires integrated and coordinated efforts throughout the organization; and organizations should focus on long-term success.

Many firms have a marketing philosophy and the marketing concept is evidenced by the following statements from various top executives:[10]

- *"Customers must be the center of your management philosophy"*—Yutaka Kume, president of Nissan Motor.

- *"The winners of the nineties will be those who can develop a culture that allows them to move faster, communicate more clearly, and involve everyone in a focused effort to serve ever more demanding customers"*— John F. Welch, Jr., CEO of General Electric.

- *"The winners in the 1990s will listen to the customer. . . . How are we so smart? The customer! . . . You just listen to the customers and then act on what they tell you"*—Charles Lazarus, CEO of Toys " Я " Us.

- *"In an age when business success depends on staying close to customers, my experience—without exception—has been that successful companies spend time in conversation, in close touch, with what is going on in the marketplace"*—Kenichi Ohmae, managing director of McKinsey & Company in Japan.[11]

Johnson Controls follows a marketing philosophy because the satisfaction of customers drives company operations around the world.

MANY
COMPANIES
TEST THE
WATERS OF
CUSTOMER
SATISFACTION

FEW
MAKE IT
THEIR
PASSION

JOHNSON CONTROLS, A GLOBAL MARKET LEADER IN FACILITY SERVICES AND CONTROL SYSTEMS, AUTO-MOTIVE SEATING SYSTEMS, PLASTIC PACKAGING, AND AUTOMOTIVE BATTERIES, IS DEDICATED TO EXCEEDING CUSTOMER EXPECTATIONS.

JOHNSON CONTROLS

Although the marketing concept was first articulated in the 1950s, it seems to be receiving attention from more firms as we move through the 1990s. This emphasis is prompted by the increasing evidence of a positive relationship between implementing a market orientation and business performance.[12]

And firms that do not satisfy customer needs are paying the price. For example, Northern Telecom neglected its key US customers while expanding business outside North America. Several US customers became dissatisfied with Northern Telecom and reduced their purchases substantially, producing a quarterly loss that got the attention of top management and the board of directors. A number of changes were made to keep the US customers happy.[13]

Marketing as a societal process

Marketing as a societal process can be defined as a process that facilitates the flow of goods and services from producers to consumers in a society. At this level, the emphasis is on issues such as:

- What institutions are involved in the societal marketing system?
- What activities do these institutions perform?
- How effective is the marketing system in satisfying consumer needs?
- How efficient is the marketing system in providing consumers with desired goods and services?

As a society's marketing system becomes more effective and efficient, more choices are available to better satisfy the consumption needs of citizens. Take, for example, the situation of Hu Zhiyi, a music teacher in Shanghai, China. Only 18 months ago, Hu and the 114 million residents of Shanghai and the surrounding region could choose between two government channels. Now, Shanghai Television offers Hu and fellow citizens a cable system of over 30 stations, 30 percent of which are foreign stations. Hu now might watch a Virginia Slims tennis championship, episodes of "Falcon Crest" or "Dynasty," the Oscars, or even the Super Bowl. He is, however, also exposed to a great deal of advertising,

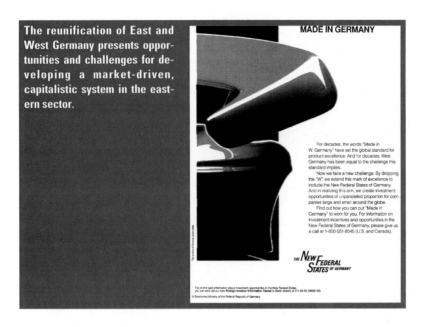

The reunification of East and West Germany presents opportunities and challenges for developing a market-driven, capitalistic system in the eastern sector.

MADE IN GERMANY

For decades, the words "Made in W. Germany" have set the global standard for product excellence. And for decades, West Germany has been equal to the challenge this standard implies.

Now we face a new challenge. By dropping the "W," we extend this mark of excellence to include the New Federal States of Germany. And in realizing this aim, we create investment opportunities of unparalleled proportion for companies large and small around the globe.

Find out how you can put "Made in Germany" to work for you. For information on investment incentives and opportunities in the New Federal States of Germany, please give us a call at 1-800-551-8545 (U.S. and Canada).

THE NEW FEDERAL STATES OF GERMANY

For on-the-spot information about investment opportunities in the New Federal States, you can also call our new Foreign Investor Information Center in Berlin directly at 011-49-30-39665-100.
© Economics Ministry of the Federal Republic of Germany

since Shanghai Television generates 90 percent of its revenue from ads. Shanghai Television reviews ratings closely to provide viewers the shows they want to watch. Consumers are signing up for the cable service in droves, and the television company is expanding its facilities and services. These developments are fueling other improvements in the Shanghai marketing system.[14]

A society's marketing system is closely related to its political and economic system. These close relationships are vividly illustrated by the tremendous changes that continue in Eastern Europe. Countries that operated under a communist political system with centrally planned economies did have some sort of marketing system, because products and services were provided to consumers. The marketing systems, however, were woefully ineffective and inefficient, largely because most "marketing" decisions were made centrally by government bureaucrats. With little consideration of customer needs, these officials decided what to produce, in what quantities, how products were to be made available to consumers, and at what prices.

Ineffective marketing systems contributed to the overthrow of the communist regimes in Eastern Europe, and these countries continue to struggle with developing democratic political systems and market-based economies. A

Colgate-Palmolive is taking advantage of the opportunities offered in countries such as Poland and Malaysia that are emphasizing economic growth through a market-driven system.

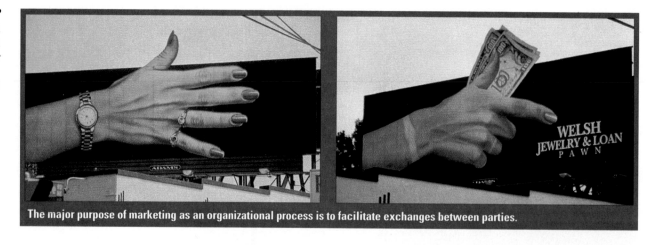

The major purpose of marketing as an organizational process is to facilitate exchanges between parties.

market-based economy requires an effective and efficient marketing system that can identify and satisfy consumer needs for products and services. Although transforming political, economic, and marketing systems is painful and difficult in the short run, the changes promise to improve the standards of living in these countries in the long run.

Important relationships exist between marketing at the organizational and societal levels. People moving from a planned to a market-based economic system must learn and implement basic marketing practices. The success of a society's marketing system depends on the ability of individuals in organizations to identify and respond to consumer needs effectively and efficiently. These individuals face the following problems, as expressed in a study of managers in several Eastern European countries:[15]

- Becoming more market-oriented and consumer-responsive.
- Improving product quality.
- Changing product design, assortment, finishing, and packaging.
- Increasing communications efforts such as personal selling and point-of-purchase sales.
- Increasing merchandising efforts.
- Using competitive pricing.
- Instituting promotional pricing and price discounts.

Marketing as a process

Marketing as an organizational philosophy and a societal process are related to the way marketing is performed by organizations and individuals. We are now ready to discuss the major aspects of marketing as a process.

Marketing exchanges

Exchange is generally viewed as the core element of marketing.[16] **Exchange** has been defined as the "transfer of something tangible or intangible, actual or symbolic, between two or more social actors."[17] Thus, the basic purpose of marketing is to get individuals or organizations to transfer something of value (tangible

| Exhibit 1.2 | Marketing exchanges |

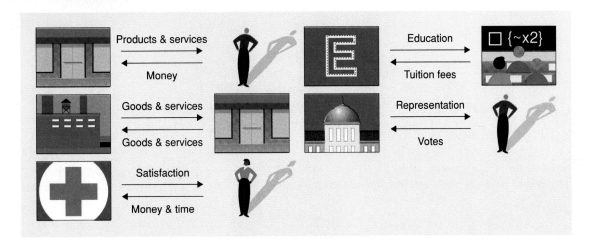

or intangible, actual or symbolic) to each other. The most familiar type of exchange occurs when a customer exchanges money with a retail store for a product. Every time a customer pays the Domino's pizza delivery person and receives a pizza, a marketing exchange takes place.

Marketing exchanges are not confined to transactions of money for products, as shown in Exhibit 1.2. Businesses engage in barter where they exchange their goods and services for the goods and services of another firm. Nonprofit organizations, colleges and universities, politicians, and many other "social actors" are also involved in exchanges. Volunteers and contributors to nonprofit organizations, for example, exchange their time and money for the satisfaction derived from helping a good cause. Or consider the tuition students pay a university or college in exchange for the education they receive. Even politics involves exchanges, with people trading their votes for the promise of representation from a political candidate.

An interesting example of marketing exchanges is the gun buyback program used by some businesses and government units. These programs get guns off the street by allowing people to exchange their guns for something else of value. One business swapped toys-for-guns and took 3,000 weapons off the street. Denver traded sporting events tickets, California cities exchanged concert tickets, and in St. Louis guns were swapped for gas.[18]

According to the marketing concept, the major objective of marketing exchanges is to satisfy the needs of the individuals and organizations involved. For an exchange to take place, each party must be willing to give up something to get something. What each party gets must be as satisfying as what it gives up. If someone decides to buy a delivered pizza from Domino's, the pizza must be as important as the money exchanged to get it. Similarly, Domino's must think the money it receives from the customer is as important as the delivered pizza it exchanges.

Creating exchanges that satisfy customer needs requires that marketing strategies be developed and marketing activities performed. The process involves people in various marketing positions who determine what is to be done (they plan) and then do it (they execute). Some people in marketing positions are employed by the firm that produces the product and some by other organizations that specialize in specific marketing activities.

| Exhibit 1.3 | Marketing mix decisions |

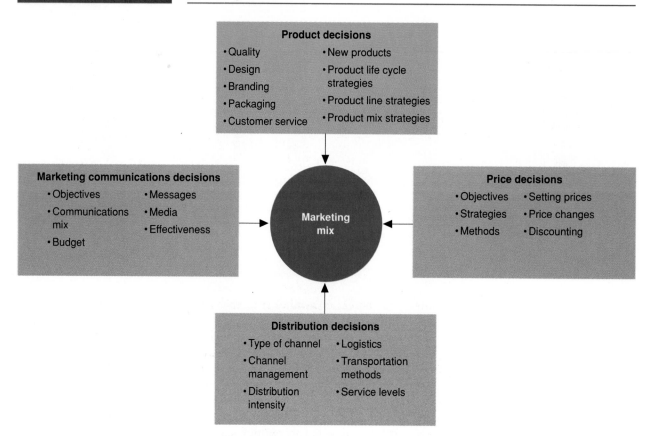

Product decisions
- Quality
- Design
- Branding
- Packaging
- Customer service
- New products
- Product life cycle strategies
- Product line strategies
- Product mix strategies

Marketing communications decisions
- Objectives
- Communications mix
- Budget
- Messages
- Media
- Effectiveness

Marketing mix

Price decisions
- Objectives
- Strategies
- Methods
- Setting prices
- Price changes
- Discounting

Distribution decisions
- Type of channel
- Channel management
- Distribution intensity
- Logistics
- Transportation methods
- Service levels

Marketing strategies

Marketing strategies consist of selecting a target market and developing a marketing mix to satisfy that market's needs. A **target market** is a defined group of consumers or organizations with whom a firm wants to create marketing exchanges. A **marketing mix** is the overall marketing offer to appeal to the target market. It consists of decisions in four basic areas: product (development of a product, service, or idea to exchange), pricing (what to charge for the exchange), communications (how to communicate with the target market about the possible exchange), and distribution (how to get the product, service, or idea to the target market to consummate the exchange). As is evident from Exhibit 1.3, many marketing decisions must be made within the product, pricing, communications, and distribution areas.

One key to marketing success is developing a consistent, integrated marketing mix that satisfies the needs of the target market better than competitors. Take Domino's, for example. Its competitive advantage is in distribution through pizza delivery. Yet this single advantage will not lead to success unless the quality and variety of pizzas satisfy customer needs, pricing is appropriate, and all these various features are communicated effectively to the target market.

The cosmetics industry is a good place to look for examples of different marketing strategies. Note in Exhibit 1.4 that Maybelline, Mary Kay, and Clinique all market a variety of cosmetic products to defined target markets. Brands differ, as do the prices charged, the method of distribution, and the type of marketing communications. Each company effectively blends product, price, distribution, and communications decisions into a different marketing mix designed to serve its target market.

Exhibit 1.4   **Marketing strategies**

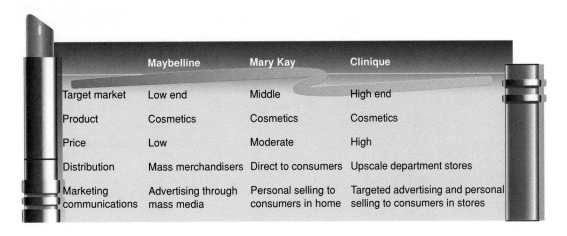

	Maybelline	Mary Kay	Clinique
Target market	Low end	Middle	High end
Product	Cosmetics	Cosmetics	Cosmetics
Price	Low	Moderate	High
Distribution	Mass merchandisers	Direct to consumers	Upscale department stores
Marketing communications	Advertising through mass media	Personal selling to consumers in home	Targeted advertising and personal selling to consumers in stores

Marketing activities

Regardless of an organization's specific marketing strategy, a number of different marketing activities must be performed to move products from producers to end-users. Exhibit 1.5 illustrates these important activities schematically.

Buying and selling activities are required to finalize an exchange. The product assortments desired by buyers must be transported to appropriate locations and stored in inventory. The inventories must be financed and the risk associated with holding the inventory assortment assumed. Quality and quantity of product assortments must be standardized and graded. Finally, marketing information about buyers and competitors is needed to make marketing decisions.

Say you want to buy a video camera. A number of producers of video cameras—Hitachi, RCA, JVC, Sony—would like to sell you their brand. But it would be inefficient if you had to contact each producer to examine its product and then purchase directly from the factory. To facilitate the exchange process, the producers market their video cameras through various types of retailers, such as Circuit City.

So now you can go to Circuit City, try out different video camera brands, and easily purchase the one best suited to your needs. Circuit City has performed

Exhibit 1.5

Marketing activities

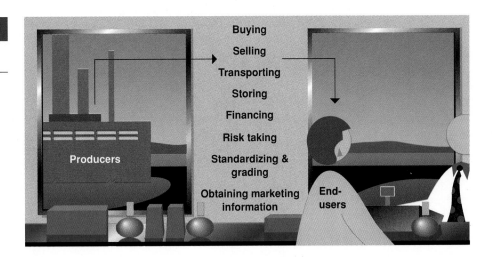

Exhibit 1.6	Marketing positions

Position/Alternative titles	Duties
Marketing manager Vice president of marketing, director of marketing	Directs all company's marketing activities, including planning, organizing, staffing, directing, controlling, evaluating performance
Product manager Brand manager	Develops goals, objectives, plans, strategies, marketing mixes for product line or brand
Advertising manager Advertising director, director of communications	Devises advertising policy & strategy, selects advertising agencies, develops promotional campaigns, selects media, allocates advertising expenditures
Distribution manager Logistics manager, traffic manager, transportation manager	Manages distribution system, including storage, transportation, for all products, services
Purchasing manager Director of purchasing, director of procurement	Manages all purchasing activities, including buying product ingredients or components, supplies, equipment, needed materials
Marketing research manager Director of commercial research, director of market research	Develops research designs for specific problems, collects, analyzes, interprets data, presents results to top management
Public relations manager Director of public relations, director of communications, public affairs officer	Manages all communications with media & company stakeholders to present favorable public image
Customer service manager Director of customer relations	Provides customer service, handles customer complaints
Sales manager Vice president of sales, director of sales, national sales manager, regional, district, or branch sales manager	Organizes, develops, directs, controls, evaluates salesforce

many of the marketing activities shown in Exhibit 1.5 that are required to complete an exchange between you and the producer of video cameras. Circuit City buys an assortment of video camera brands, transports them to its retail outlets, and stores them there in inventory. It assumes the expense and risk of holding this inventory. It standardizes and grades the product quality and quantity. Because it wants to move the video cameras from inventory to end-users, it advertises and promotes the brands it carries and the price at which it is willing to exchange each brand. Buyers come to the stores, talk with salespeople, and purchase desired brands.

One way or another, certain marketing activities must be performed for exchanges to occur between producers and end-users. In some cases, marketing institutions, such as retailers like Circuit City, perform many of the marketing activities for producers. In others, most activities are performed by individuals within the producing firm. Sometimes consumers perform some of the required marketing activities.

Marketing positions

There are a variety of marketing positions within most organizations. Examples are shown in Exhibit 1.6. Some of these positions, such as advertising manager, distribution manager, or sales manager, indicate specialization in one area of

These job announcements illustrate the variety of marketing positions available and the potential excitement and rewards they offer.

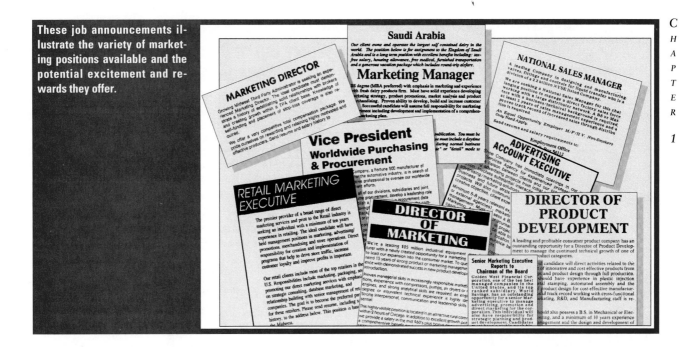

marketing. Others suggest working across marketing areas (marketing manager, product manager, marketing research manager). The reality is that most marketing positions require close working relationships among different marketing and business functions. For example, advertising, sales, product, marketing, production, and accounting managers typically work together to develop and execute marketing plans for specific products.

Marketing positions are most prevalent in business firms, although similar positions exist in nonprofit organizations, hospitals, government agencies, museums, accounting firms, and other organizations. For organizations that follow a marketing philosophy, many employees are involved in marketing activities even though they may not hold formal marketing positions.

EXECUTIVE ROUNDTABLE COMMENT | **Mark Oshnock, partner at Arthur Andersen, suggests how important marketing is in a major public accounting firm:**

Marketing became a formal function in public accounting beginning in the early 1980s. Today, most offices of any size in international, national, regional, and local firms emphasize marketing activities to support their practice. Only a few employees at Arthur Andersen have *marketing* in their titles, but an in-depth understanding of marketing is vitally important to everyone in our firm. The successful professional employs a targeted marketing plan to satisfy the needs of current clients and to generate new clients.

Marketing institutions

Some organizations specialize in specific marketing activities and become experts in performing them. Thus, a firm may work with several of these organizations to handle the required marketing activities.

We have already discussed the important role that retailers, such as Circuit City, play in making a variety of different products and brands available to consumers. Sometimes wholesalers also undertake specific marketing activities for producers and retailers. Wholesalers engage in exchanges with producers and subsequently exchange these products from their inventory to meet the needs of retailers. They might also perform specialized services for producers and retailers. Some of the leading wholesalers are McKesson Corporation (health care products), Fleming Co. (food), Produce Specialties (exotic fruits and vegetables), and United Stationers (office supplies).

Marketing research firms and advertising agencies also provide specialized services for client firms. Some firms emphasize specific types of marketing research, but the largest firms offer a full array of research services, including focus groups, concept tests, customer interviews, mail surveys, experiments, or other types of marketing research. The largest US marketing research firms include Nielsen Marketing Research, IMS International, Information Resources, Inc., and the Arbitron Co. The top 50 US research firms generate over $3.1 billion in revenues annually.[19]

Advertising agencies also provide various services to help firms develop and implement marketing communications campaigns. Again, some of these firms specialize in specific areas, while others provide full services, often including marketing research. The leading advertising agencies in the US are Young & Rubicam, Saatchi and Saatchi, BBDO Worldwide, DDB Needham Worldwide, and Ogilvy & Mather Worldwide.

EXECUTIVE ROUNDTABLE COMMENT | Tom Kapella, vice president of product development, Gibson Greetings, Inc., indicates the important role that marketing research firms and advertising agencies play:

We are experts in the greeting cards business, not in marketing research or advertising. It makes sense to work with companies specializing in these activities. Professionally prepared studies by Nielsen or Gallup help us learn about our target market and tailor our marketing strategies toward satisfying market needs. Ad agencies help us develop effective communication programs that set us apart from the competition. Gibson is a creative company. Relying on outside experts allows us to spend our time on what we do best—marketing greeting cards.

| How has marketing evolved? |

Traditionally, the roots of "modern" marketing have been traced to the 1950s, when the marketing concept was first articulated. Before then, according to this view, most firms were driven by either production or sales philosophies, even though they engaged in marketing activities. So in the 1950s, leading firms presumably embraced the customer-oriented marketing concept. However, recent historical analysis provides strong evidence that marketing activities and customer orientations were commonplace in firms much earlier than the 1950s in the US, Germany, and England.[20]

The early years

In the early 1500s in Germany and England and the 1600s in North America, most of the population was rural and largely self-sufficient. Production and transportation were primitive and capitalism was not well developed. Some astute marketers emerged nevertheless. Typically they marketed luxury goods to the nobility and the growing urban middle class, armaments to governments, or textiles and basic staples to selected elements of the population. Important marketing institutions and activities originating during this period include fixed-location retail shops, advertising, wholesale trade, warehouses, and traveling salespeople.

Modern marketing begins

The Industrial Revolution, from about 1750 in England and 1830 in the US and Germany, produced tremendous changes in marketing. Production methods and transportation systems greatly improved. A substantial migration from rural areas to urban centers created potentially large markets. Marketing became a pervasive and central activity as firms tried to serve these developing markets. Because of intense competition, firms targeted particular population groups, developed products specifically for them, and promoted the products vigorously. The important marketing activities that we know as market segmentation, target marketing, and promotion were carried out by many firms during this period.

Modern marketing develops

Beginning with the Industrial Revolution, institutions and activities associated with modern marketing became more widespread. Here are some ways firms implemented a customer orientation in the 19th century:

• During the 1880s, Waltham Watch Co. moved from marketing whatever the factory decided to produce to producing exactly what customers wanted.
• Hampshire Paper Co. gave its salesforce extensive training in the philosophy that salespeople were expected to help customers solve their problems.
• Parker Pen Co. realized that all customers did not want the same type of pen; its 1899 catalog included 40 pens priced from $1.50 to $20.

Even though the marketing concept was not formally articulated until the 1950s, some firms were clearly practicing it much earlier, as shown by a business text published in 1916:

Today the progressive business man makes careful, intensive studies not merely of the consumer's recognized wants but of his tastes, his habits, his tendencies in all the common activities and relations of life. This he does in order to track down unconscious needs, to manufacture goods to

These ads were popular around 1900. Marketing has changed greatly since then, yet many firms have been practicing basic marketing concepts for a long time.

satisfy them, to bring these products to the attention of the consumer in the most appealing ways, and finally to complete the cycle by transporting the goods to him in response to an expressed demand.[21]

Modern marketing evolves

Marketing has built on past accomplishments as it evolved. Many firms for many years have taken a customer orientation and performed basic marketing activities. What has changed most in recent years is the way marketing activities are performed. For example, the practice of dividing the market for a product into segments with different needs (market segmentation) has been used by at least some firms for over two centuries. However, segmentation procedures have changed drastically from simple, judgmental approaches to the use of sophisticated statistical techniques and large databases today. Much of this book discusses changes that have taken place in recent years and suggests marketing changes for the future.

A contemporary marketing framework

The contemporary marketing framework that underlies the focus for this book is presented in Exhibit 1.7. The framework has three major elements: marketing, the marketing environment, and marketing perspectives.

Marketing

The inner circle represents marketing as an organizational philosophy and organizational process. Most of this book expands on topics that fit within this circle: the marketing concept and marketing exchanges, strategies, activities, positions, and institutions. The marketing circle contains the largely controllable decision areas for marketers in all types of organizations. For example, Domino's decisions to deliver pizza, the types of pizza to offer, the prices to charge, where to locate outlets, and how and where to advertise are all part of the marketing circle.

Exhibit 1.7

A contemporary marketing framework

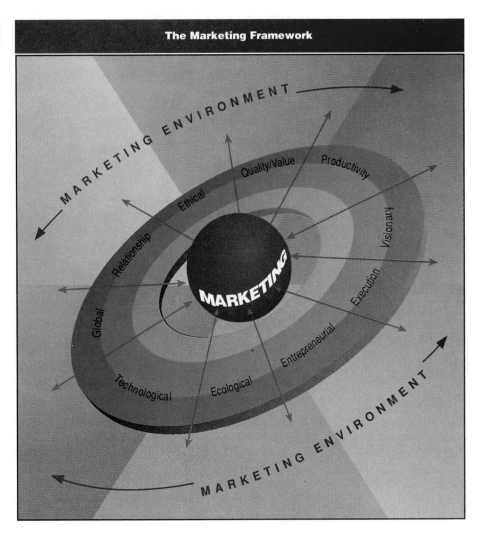

The Marketing Framework

Marketing environment

The larger circle represents the uncontrollable environment within which marketers must operate. The marketing environment is categorized further into social, economic, competitive, technological, legal/political, and institutional environments. Each of these categories is examined in detail in Chapter 3.

Marketing is largely concerned with identifying market opportunities and responding to these opportunities by developing and executing effective marketing strategies. Market opportunities are typically the result of conditions or changes in the marketing environment. For example, many of the marketing decisions made by Domino's were precipitated by existing or expected conditions in the marketing environment. Changes in people's lifestyles (social environment) produced an opportunity for pizza delivery to satisfy consumers' need for convenience. Actions by competitors (competitive environment) to enter the pizza delivery business in response to Domino's led to improvements in the quality and variety of Domino's pizzas and more aggressive advertising. Technological advancements (technological environment) present opportunities to use the latest telecommunication advances to simplify pizza ordering by consumers.

Thus, successful marketing requires constant assessment of the marketing environment to identify opportunities and to determine the best way to capitalize on them. The difficulty is that the marketing environment is complex, turbulent, and uncertain.

Key marketing perspectives

We have identified ten key marketing perspectives to guide marketers in responding effectively to opportunities offered by the marketing environment. (See Exhibit 1.7) These perspectives provide links between marketing and the marketing environment. The ten key marketing perspectives are:

 A global perspective

 A technological perspective

 A relationship perspective

 An ecological perspective

 An ethical perspective

 An entrepreneurial perspective

 A quality/value perspective

 An execution perspective

 A productivity perspective

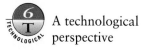 A visionary perspective

---

EXECUTIVE ROUNDTABLE COMMENT | **Bob Kyle, international marketing manager, Diebold, confirms the value of the perspectives:**

These perspectives are all extremely important for success in the marketplace of today and of the future. Marketers who incorporate these perspectives into their thinking will be in a good position to identify and capitalize on market opportunities. At Diebold, the perspectives help us assess and respond to opportunities that vary from country to country because of different cultures and business methods.

We discuss each perspective in detail in Chapter 2. Moreover, believing that these perspectives are important considerations in all aspects of marketing, we also integrate them throughout the remaining chapters in several ways.

First, the appropriate perspectives are discussed in relevant places in each chapter. Italicized bold type or icons in the margin indicate when a specific perspective is being discussed.

Second, each remaining chapter contains sidebars entitled "The Technological Edge" and "The Entrepreneurial Spirit." These sidebars present examples of a technological and entrepreneurial perspective toward the material covered in the chapter.

Third, many chapters conclude with a section entitled "Ethical Issues" to identify and discuss important ethical issues relevant to the chapter topics.

Finally, our Executive Roundtable members address the perspectives in various ways through their comments in each chapter.

From chemistry to candy bars, more global companies choose Citibank than any other bank.

BECAUSE Citibank forges solid, long-term relationships with its customers—over 70 years each with Dow and Nestlé. **BECAUSE** Citibank has established an extraordinary record in foreign exchange, ranked number one by customers worldwide for 15 consecutive years. **BECAUSE** no other bank can match Citibank's expertise and experience in emerging markets—over 90 years in Asia, and 75 years in Latin America. **BECAUSE THE CITI NEVER SLEEPS.** CITIBANK

Many of the key marketing perspectives are interrelated. Citibank helps clients implement a *global perspective* in emerging markets through its expertise in foreign exchange.

Summary

1. *Discuss what marketing is and why it is important to organizations and individuals.* Marketing "is the process of planning and executing the conception, pricing, promotion, and distribution of ideas, goods, and services to create exchanges that satisfy individual and organizational goals." Marketing is important to all types of organizations, because it focuses on satisfying the needs of customers. Individuals, such as politicians, also engage in marketing during campaigns for election and when developing and implementing policies. Marketing activities are performed by people in various positions at different organizations. Interacting with people is a major component of most marketing positions.

2. *Distinguish between marketing as an organizational philosophy and a societal process.* Marketing can be defined in different ways. As an organizational philosophy, marketing is an orientation where everyone in the organization is driven by the marketing concept to satisfy customer needs. At the societal level, marketing is the process that determines the flow of goods and services from producers to consumers in a society.

3. *Understand the components of a marketing strategy and the different activities involved in marketing products and services.* A marketing strategy consists of the selection of a target market and the development of a marketing mix to appeal to that target market. The marketing mix is an integration of product, price, communications, and distribution decisions to serve a target market better than competitors.

   Implementing marketing strategies to facilitate exchanges requires many activities, including buying, selling, transporting, storing, financing, risk taking, standardizing and grading, and obtaining marketing information.

4. *Be aware of the various types of marketing institutions and the different marketing positions available in these institutions.* The necessary marketing activities are performed by different institutions and various positions within these institutions. Although some producers can perform all required marketing activities, organizations specializing in specific marketing activities are often used. Typical marketing institutions are wholesalers, retailers, distributors, marketing research firms, and advertising agencies.

Important marketing positions include marketing managers, product managers, advertising managers, purchasing managers, sales managers, marketing research managers, and individuals who report to these managers. Marketing activities are also performed by people in nonmarketing positions.

5. *Appreciate how marketing has evolved from earlier times to the present.*   Marketing has evolved substantially. This evolution moved from the origins of retailing to improved production and transportation methods brought about by the Industrial Revolution, to the consumer-orientation of modern marketing.

The biggest change in marketing today is the way in which marketing activities are performed, for instance, segmenting markets by using statistical technology and databases.

6. *Understand the basic elements and relationships in the contemporary marketing framework.*   The contemporary marketing framework depicts the important relationship between marketing and the marketing environment. Ten key marketing perspectives are presented as orientations that drive marketing's interactions with the external environment.

Key terms & concepts

marketing   6
production philosophy   9
selling philosophy   9
marketing philosophy   9

marketing concept   9
marketing as a societal
    process   10
exchange   12

marketing strategies   14
target market   14
marketing mix   14

Review & discussion questions

1. How can top management in an organization ensure that all employees are driven by the marketing concept?

2. What is an example of barter as a marketing exchange?

3. How would you describe the major target market and marketing mix for your college or university?

4. What are the marketing activities required to get toothpaste from a producer, such as Colgate-Palmolive, to a consumer, such as yourself?

5. What marketing activities can wholesalers perform for retailers?

6. What are the relationships between marketing as a societal process and the economic and political systems in a country?

7. What do you think is the most innovative development in marketing practice during the past few years? Why?

8. What types of marketing positions interest you? Why?

9. What role do the ten key marketing perspectives play in the contemporary marketing framework?

10. How does the marketing environment affect marketing?

Application exercises

1. Pick a retail store where you frequently shop. Identify and discuss the store's target market and the specific product, price, communications, and distribution decisions the management has made to develop a marketing mix.

2. Interview someone in a marketing position. Ask him or her about the activities involved in the position,

about any expected changes in the position during the 1990s, and about career opportunities.

3. Identify a nonprofit organization in your community. Determine the role of marketing in this organization by reading promotional materials and talking with someone in the organization.

Case 1.1   *Coca-Cola: What happened to the US market?*

Soft-drink sales growth in the US has slowed to 2 percent annually from the more than 4 percent yearly growth experienced during the late 1980s. The Coca-Cola Company has felt this trend. Coke's international sales have been increasing about 31 percent per year, while domestic sales

are only growing about 7 percent yearly. Despite its many growth opportunities in international markets, Coke wants to increase its domestic business. The domestic business is important to Coke because it provides a base on which the company builds its business around the world.

Sergio Zyman has been appointed to the top marketing job at Coke and given the task of reviving domestic sales. This is a formidable task for several reasons. First, the total cola market itself has been shrinking. Cola sales accounted for 70 percent of all soft-drink sales in 1990, but only about 68 percent in 1992. This downward trend is expected to continue.

Second, Coke and Pepsi have almost identical market shares in the important supermarket business, although Coke maintains about a 6 percent advantage over Pepsi in all cola sales. In addition, private-label brands have been capturing an increasing share of cola sales. Royal Crown Cola is becoming much more aggressive in producing private label cola brands as well as in marketing the firm's RC and Diet Rite brands. All these activities translate into an extremely competitive marketplace.

Third, diet colas and diet Coke are also experiencing declining sales. Some consumers have tired of the taste of diet colas and are switching to other soft drinks. And the growing older market has never been strong for diet colas. Thus, there are limited growth opportunities in the diet cola market.

Despite these problems, Zyman is expected to increase Coke's domestic business. One approach being considered is to focus marketing efforts on new products such as clear colas, iced teas, fruit drinks, and sports drinks.

Another idea is to introduce a midcalorie cola to the market. The expected name would be Coke Light. Coke

Light would use less artificial sweetener than the diet colas and, therefore, taste more like the regular colas.

Coke executives are also concerned whether the "Always Coca-Cola" advertising campaign is really tapping into the important youth market. Developing a new slogan and advertising plan is another option open to Zyman.

Questions:

1. Do you think Coca-Cola is driven by a production, selling, or marketing philosophy? Why?

2. Why is the domestic market important to Coke? Why does Coke not focus most of its attention to growth opportunities in international markets?

3. What marketing activities and marketing institutions are required to get cola products from producers to consumers?

4. If you were Mr. Zyman, what would you do to increase Coke's domestic business?

Sources: Michael J. McCarthy, "Zyman Confronts Classic Coke Problems," *The Wall Street Journal,* July 23, 1993, p. B1; and Nikhil Deogun, "Royal Crown Bubbles with Revival Plans," *The Wall Street Journal,* July 22, 1993, pp. B1, B5. Reprinted by permission of *The Wall Street Journal.* © 1993 Dow Jones & Company, Inc. All Rights Reserved Worldwide.

Case 1.2   *Texaco: Gasoline, hamburgers, donuts, and . . . ?*

The gasoline retail business has been stagnant for the past five years. US service stations sold 115 billion gallons of gas in 1989 and about the same amount in 1992. The competitive situation is also tough. Chevron, Mobil, Texaco, Amoco, Exxon, and Shell all have about 7 percent gasoline market share. Despite these conditions, Texaco is trying to increase sales and profits.

Texaco's strategy is to increase retail traffic at its gas stations and to generate more sales from this traffic. One approach the company is taking is expansion of many of the 6,000 convenience stores at its stations. These stores will offer a wider selection of food and beverages. Fast-food franchises, such as McDonald's and Dunkin' Donuts, are also being added to many locations.

Although the expanded convenience stores are helping to increase retail traffic and sales, the company is also aggressively pursuing the gasoline business. The gasoline business is very competitive, with even a penny-per-gallon price difference causing some consumers to switch brands. Texaco is trying to differentiate its gasoline products. Its CleanSystem3 brand is a high-performance gasoline that improves engine performance, lowers emissions, and increases gas mileage. Competitors can deliver on one or two of these, but no other gasoline brand does all three. Some consumers are willing to pay a higher price for CleanSystem3 because of the value they receive.

Another option is to focus on ways to keep gasoline prices low. Although crude oil prices have a direct effect

on gasoline prices, transportation costs are also important. Texaco has been buying, selling, and swapping retail gas stations to build retail networks near one of its seven refineries in the United States. Lowering transportation costs in this manner can shave a penny or more off the price of a gallon of gasoline.

Texaco's US strategy is also being exported overseas. CleanSystem3 products are being introduced in Europe and Asia. For example, it opened Europe's largest gas station in Britain in November 1992 and will serve the Asian market from a $1.8 billion refinery in Thailand.

Questions:

1. Why is Texaco adding franchises, such as McDonald's and Dunkin' Donuts, to its convenience stores?

2. What is the basic marketing mix that Texaco offers to target customers?

3. What other products or services might Texaco offer to increase retail traffic and sales?

4. What is Texaco's approach for expanding its retail business internationally? What suggestions do you have to improve this strategy?

Sources: Tim Smart, "Pumping Up at Texaco," *Business Week,* June 7, 1993, pp. 112–13; and Leah Rickard and Gary Levin, "Texaco Tanks Up on Marketing Tactics for New Detergent Gas," *Advertising Age,* February 28, 1994, pp. 3, 42.

chapter | *2*

Ten Key Marketing Perspectives

After studying this chapter you should be able to:

1. Define ten key marketing perspectives.

2. Understand the importance of these perspectives for marketing success.

3. Appreciate the interrelatedness of the perspectives.

IBM: Big changes at Big Blue

*I*BM was once the envy of the global business world as it annually reported sales and profit increases. Recently, however, the company has suffered in an intensely competitive business environment. Since reaching a peak in 1987, sales have been stagnant, profits turned into losses, and market share eroded.

IBM is responding to its problems by making many changes to improve future performance. One major thrust is to make itself more productive. The company has lowered costs by reducing the number of employees, improving the efficiency of existing processes, and doing many things differently. For example, IBM now sells PCs through direct marketing in an effort to increase sales and reduce costs.

Another aim of IBM's restructuring is to improve relationships with customers, suppliers, distributors, and other business partners. A key to enhancing these relationships is improvement in the quality and value of IBM products and services. Quality programs aimed at producing 100 percent customer satisfaction have been established. To provide value, IBM has lowered prices, extended warranties, and improved service delivery.

A key to improving quality and increasing value is the adoption of new and emerging technologies. IBM has been slow to introduce new products using the latest technologies and has not used core technologies throughout its product line. It lagged behind its competitors, for example, in launching a laptop computer for this fast-growing segment of the market. Changes since then have halved the time IBM takes to introduce the latest technological advances to the marketplace.

Successfully implementing these changes is a formidable task for a company the size of IBM. Even though employment has been reduced by more than 100,000 in recent years, IBM still employs more than 200,000 people scattered throughout the world. Its size and perhaps complacency over its perennial success combined to make the company a massive, inflexible bureaucracy unable to respond quickly enough to changes in the business environment.

IBM attacked this problem by restructuring operations. From one mammoth IBM with a centralized orientation, the company divided into autonomous groups with decision-making authority and profit responsibility. The objective of this restructuring is to stimulate an entrepreneurial orientation within each business group. However, a top-level executive committee is used to coordinate relationships across business units.

Whether these moves can turn IBM around remains to be seen. Management is intent on executing these changes in the short run. For the long run, IBM will need to establish an overall vision for how its different technologies and products fit together.

Sources: Catherine Arnst, Judith H. Dobrzynski, and Bart Ziegler, "Faith in a Stranger," *Business Week,* April 5, 1993, pp. 18–21; "IBM's Search for Yesterday's Glory," *Sales & Marketing Management,* July 1993, pp. 10–11; Catherine Arnst and John Verity, "IBM: A Work in Progress," *Business Week,* August 9, 1993, pp. 24–26; Jan Jaben, "Customer Time for Big Blue," *Business Marketing,* May 1993, pp. 22–23; Leslie Scism, "Gerstner Moves to Coordinate IBM Businesses," *The Wall Street Journal,* September 14, 1993, p. A4; and Ira Sager and Amy E. Cortese, "Lou Gerstner Unveils His Battle Plan," *Business Week,* April 4, 1994, pp. 96–98.

Exhibit 2.1   **Ten key marketing perspectives and IBM**

Marketing perspectives		IBM
Global	**1 G** GLOBAL	Compete effectively all over the world with particular emphasis on increasing business in Asia
Relationship	**2 R** RELATIONSHIP	Develop effective relationships with customers, suppliers, distributors, other organizational partners & within functions at IBM
Ethical	**3 E** ETHICAL	Operate in an ethical & socially responsible manner throughout the world
Quality/Value	**4 QV** QUALITY/VALUE	Continue to improve product quality & reduce prices to satisfy customers
Productivity	**5 P** PRODUCTIVITY	Increase marketing productivity to return to profitability, with major focus on reengineering the salesforce to cut costs
Technological	**6 T** TECHNOLOGICAL	Translate new technologies into successful products, expand the use of core technologies throughout the product line & use technologies to improve marketing
Ecological	**7 E** ECOLOGICAL	Ensure that operations are sensitive to environmental considerations
Entrepreneurial	**8 E** ENTREPRENEURIAL	Replace bureaucratic stagnation with creativity, risk-taking & innovation
Execution	**9 E** EXECUTION	Successfully execute new strategic themes & reorganization changes
Visionary	**10 V** VISIONARY	Develop a vision of what IBM should be in the future

The changes under way at IBM illustrate the dynamic nature of marketing in a complex and uncertain business environment. The globalization of markets, spread of information and communication technologies, adoption of Total Quality Management (TQM) programs, and massive corporate restructuring are some of the revolutionary trends affecting marketing.[1] The marketing world in which IBM and other companies operate is changing dramatically. To be successful in such an environment, marketers must be ready to do things differently.

We have reviewed the major business trends and identified ten key perspectives to guide marketers in responding to changes in the environment. These perspectives are illustrated in the contemporary marketing framework presented in Chapter 1. The perspectives provide important vantage points for marketers in a volatile business world.

Exhibit 2.1 relates these ten perspectives to the demands on IBM today. Applying these perspectives requires major changes in the way IBM does business. However, viewing marketing this way should help IBM better identify and respond to market opportunities and improve marketing decision making.

We discuss all these key marketing perspectives in this chapter and explore many of the important interrelationships among them. Each *perspective* is printed in italicized bold type or is represented by an icon in the margin to identify its discussion throughout the text.

A global perspective

The marketplace in the 1990s is global. Few marketers operate in isolation. Advances in technology make it possible to communicate practically instantaneously throughout the world. Former Citicorp chairman Walter Wriston uses

Exhibit 2.2	**A global marketing quiz**

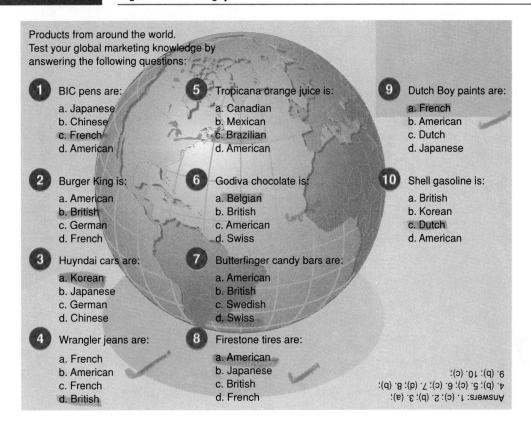

Products from around the world.
Test your global marketing knowledge by
answering the following questions:

1 BIC pens are:

a. Japanese
b. Chinese
c. French
d. American

2 Burger King is:

a. American
b. British
c. German
d. French

3 Huyndai cars are:

a. Korean
b. Japanese
c. German
d. Chinese

4 Wrangler jeans are:

a. French
b. American
c. French
d. British

5 Tropicana orange juice is:

a. Canadian
b. Mexican
c. Brazilian
d. American

6 Godiva chocolate is:

a. Belgian
b. British
c. American
d. Swiss

7 Butterfinger candy bars are:

a. American
b. British
c. Swedish
d. Swiss

8 Firestone tires are:

a. American
b. Japanese
c. British
d. French

9 Dutch Boy paints are:

a. French
b. American
c. Dutch
d. Japanese

10 Shell gasoline is:

a. British
b. Korean
c. Dutch
d. American

Answers: 1. (c); 2. (b); 3. (a);
4. (b); 5. (c); 6. (c); 7. (d); 8. (b);
9. (b) 10. (c):

the term *global conversation* to indicate the world "is tied together in a single electronic market moving at the speed of light." He estimates that, every hour, over 100 million telephone calls are completed worldwide and that this volume will triple by the year 2000.[2]

Products and services are produced and marketed throughout the world. Most firms market products and services in international markets, face international competitors, deal with international suppliers, work with international partners, or have international employees. The magnitude of international marketing is evident by the growth in world trade from $200 billion to over $4 trillion during the past two decades.[3]

To understand the scope of a global marketplace, answer the questions in Exhibit 2.2. How many did you get right? Few students (or professors for that matter) answer these questions correctly. It is surprising to many Americans that many brands common in the US are actually marketed by internationally based firms.

What about companies such as Gillette, Colgate, IBM, Coca-Cola, Dow Chemical, Xerox, Caterpillar, Hewlett-Packard, and Johnson & Johnson? They are American companies, right? Well they may be American-*based* companies, but 50 percent or more of their sales and a substantial proportion of their assets are in international markets.

It should be clear from these examples that marketers operate in a global marketplace and must view their marketing operations from a global perspective. A *global perspective* means that marketers should view the world as the potential marketplace in order to compete successfully against firms from many countries. The essence of a true global perspective is expressed by Percy Barnevik, president of Asea Brown Boveri:

There is a tendency in the Western world to talk about only one region at a time. Ten years ago, people talked about Latin America as a great

AIG emphasizes a *global perspective* in the insurance business.

THE RULES, REGULATIONS AND CUSTOMS OF 130 COUNTRIES AROUND THE WORLD AREN'T FOREIGN TO US. *Most of AIG's 34,000 people are native to the lands in which they work. So they have a deep understanding of local laws, practices and traditions. They know how to design insurance products specifically for their own markets* and can respond quickly to changing conditions and customer needs. Together they form a unique network of service capabilities. Because the quality of our services to clients is a product of the number and experience of our people. And that is something no one else can match in this fast-changing world. AIG WORLD LEADERS IN INSURANCE AND FINANCIAL SERVICES. American International Group, Inc., Dept. A, 70 Pine Street, New York, NY 10270.

opportunity. Now everyone talks about Eastern Europe. Instead, we should look everywhere, including the fast-moving Far East, the forgotten Africa and Latin America, all of Europe, and the subcontinent of India. To meet global competition, you have to be global yourself and meet your competitors on their home ground.[4]

To achieve this type of global perspective, many marketers must expand their horizons when identifying growth opportunities, developing marketing strategies, and evaluating world events.

Identifying growth opportunities

Many US firms operate in mature markets that provide only limited opportunities for future growth. These firms often find potential growth opportunities in international markets. Two examples are illustrative.

- Growth in the US soft-drink market has slowed, with the average American drinking 770 soft drinks per year. The 290 million citizens of the former Soviet Union, on the other hand, consume an average of only 39 soft drinks annually. Pepsi and Coke have moved rapidly to take advantage of the tremendous market opportunities for soft drinks in the former Soviet Union.[5]

- Duracell International holds 79 percent of the US battery market. Because opportunities for further growth in the US market are very limited, the company is expanding marketing efforts into Eastern Europe and Asia.[6]

Firms in many other industries face similar constraints. Limited growth opportunities at home mean that many US marketers must scan the globe to identify opportunities in international markets. Taking a broadened perspective may be new and difficult for established firms that so far have operated only domestically. Many of the 2,000-odd start-up firms backed by venture capitalists each year are global from the beginning, however. For example, Aspen Technology, a software manufacturer, had over half of its customers from outside the US from day one, and now 80 percent of its sales are to international customers. In fact, most of US export growth is now being generated by smaller firms.[7]

Developing marketing strategies

Firms operating in international markets expect to face international competitors from both the host country and other countries. Even firms that limit operations to US markets, however, must compete effectively against international firms. Think about the automobile industry, for example. US automobile dealers market cars in limited geographic areas. Nevertheless, the dealers are involved in global competition, because different dealers carry cars from different international firms.

The number of product and service categories in which firms from different countries compete against American firms in the US is large and continually increasing. And more and more American firms are entering international markets. Thus, marketers must take a global perspective when assessing the competitive landscape and developing marketing strategies.

Evaluating world events

A global perspective also requires an understanding of how events around the world can affect the markets in which a firm operates. As the economies of countries throughout the world become increasingly interlinked, events in different parts of the world are rapidly communicated around the globe and have potential impacts in all business areas. Political, economic, and social changes in Eastern Europe, the former Soviet Union, Central and South America, the Middle East, the Far East, and elsewhere may affect not only companies operating in these areas but also marketers in domestic markets.

The situation in South Africa is illustrative. Because of political developments, the UN lifted the trade embargo on South Africa. Firms from around the world are increasing marketing efforts in South Africa. In addition, South African companies are expanding their international trade and investment. Although the situation is uncertain, the political changes in South Africa have an impact on companies in the US and around the world.

A relationship perspective

The increasingly complex business environment drives companies and marketers to work together for their mutual benefit. No longer can one individual or one company have all of the knowledge, skills, or resources necessary for marketing success. Instead, networks of relationships offer the most productive route to marketing success in a global environment. As John F. Welch, Jr., CEO of General Electric, puts it, "The lines between the company and its vendors and customers must be blurred into a smooth, fluid process with no other objective than satisfying customers and winning in the marketplace."[8] A *relationship perspective* consists of building partnerships with firms outside the organization and encouraging teamwork among different functions within the organization to develop long-term customer relationships.

Customer relationships

Marketing has traditionally been viewed as the sales-generating business function. Its importance is reflected in the adage "nothing happens until a sale is made." This sales orientation can mean that a marketer focuses entirely on generating sales in the short run, with little consideration for profitability or the long-term impact of the activities used to produce sales. The stereotype of a salesperson is a lone-wolf, fast-talking manipulator who will do anything to close a sale.

Fortunately, this view of marketing and salespeople does not represent many successful marketers today. The emphasis on producing sales in the short run at any cost, or **transaction marketing,** is being replaced by an emphasis on developing, maintaining, and enhancing long-term, profitable relationships with customers, or **relationship marketing.** Exhibit 2.3 presents the major differences between the transaction and relationship marketing orientations.

EXECUTIVE ROUNDTABLE COMMENT | **Paul Casey, vice president, branch manager,**

Smith Barney, emphasizes the importance of relationship marketing:

Our business has traditionally focused on short-term transactions—our brokers emphasized the buying or selling of securities. We make money both ways. Smith Barney is now changing to relationship marketing. Our current objective is to develop profitable relationships by managing customer assets over the long term. The change from a transaction to a relationship orientation is difficult, but essential to our continuing success.

Customer relationships are often critical in international markets, particularly in Asia. Often, firms must invest a great amount of time in developing relationships before any business can be conducted. This can be expensive and frustrating for many American firms. The Grass Valley Group (GVG) division of Tektronix was able to speed up this process in the professional video hardware market in Japan. Although GVG manufactures all its products in the US, the company staffed its Japanese office with Japanese nationals who already had good relationships with prospective customers. GVG built on these relationships to successfully market customized products to savvy Japanese customers.[9]

Organizational relationships

Few firms can themselves perform all the necessary marketing activities productively and profitably. They may work with specialist firms to carry out many marketing activities. Examples include hiring marketing research firms to perform marketing studies, employing advertising agencies to develop advertising campaigns, and distributing products through wholesalers and retailers.

A firm's success in developing long-term customer relationships typically requires close working partnerships with the organizations that perform marketing activities for them. Three examples illustrate different types of organizational relationships.

- Procter & Gamble (P&G) used to treat retailers as adversaries. Now, given that the 100 largest grocery and department store chains account for 80 percent of P&G's US grocery sales, the firm treats them as partners. Teams of P&G people work with their largest customers, such as Wal-Mart and Kroger, to help improve inventory, distribution, and sales promotion.[10]
- Colgate-Palmolive once worked with 13 different advertising agencies. It fired all of them, formed a partnership with two worldwide agencies, and told them: "You set up wherever we do business. You don't have to worry about losing our business. It's a long-term relationship."[11]
- Many marketing programs take the form of partnerships among different firms. Frequent flier programs, such as United Airlines Mileage Plus or

Exhibit 2.3   **Transaction marketing versus relationship marketing**

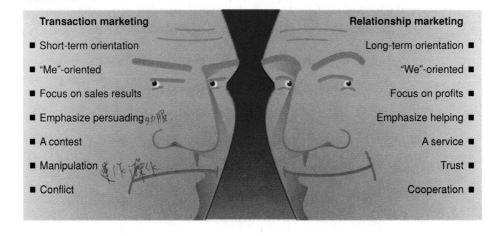

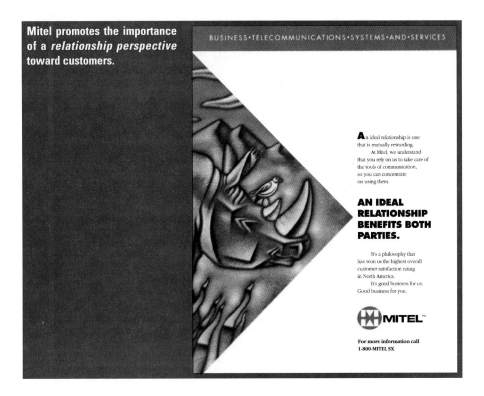

Mitel promotes the importance of a *relationship perspective* toward customers.

American Airlines AAdvantage, consist of partnerships with different airlines, hotels, rental car companies, and even telephone companies such as MCI. Travelers earn and use travel awards by doing business with any of the firms in the partnership.

The development of different types of relationships with a variety of organizations produces firms called **network organizations.**[12] Partnerships may include strategic alliances, joint ventures, vendor partnering, and other arrangements. IBM, for example, has partnership arrangements with Toshiba, Mitsubishi, Intel, Motorola, Apple Computer, Sears, Lotus, Novell, Wang, Siemens, Borland, and many other firms.[13]

Functional relationships

The day when marketing managers operated in isolation from other business functions is over. Success in the current business environment requires that all company members work as a team toward common objectives. No one individual or function performs effectively as an independent entity. Cooperation and teamwork are necessary to succeed in an increasingly complex and changing business environment.

The movement toward a teamwork approach is best exemplified in the area of new-product development. At one time, the typical new-product development process was a step-by-step procedure, with a specific function performing each step. For example, say the research and development people came up with an idea for a new product. They passed the idea on to the engineering people to design the product. Product specifications were then handed to manufacturing to produce the product, and the finished product given to marketing people to sell. In this process, each function performed specific tasks independently and then passed its work to the next function in the chain.

The teamwork approach to new-product development requires multifunctional teams working together throughout all stages of the process. Take, for example, the approach Ford used in developing the Taurus.[14] Ford organized employees from all relevant functions into a product development group called *Team Taurus.* The manufacturing people worked with the designers and engineers, the legal staff, and people from sales, marketing, purchasing, and service

P
A
R
T

1

Johnson & Johnson's credo expresses the firm's *ethical perspective*.

Our Credo

We believe our first responsibility is to the doctors, nurses and patients,
to mothers and fathers and all others who use our products and services.
In meeting their needs everything we do must be of high quality.
We must constantly strive to reduce our costs
in order to maintain reasonable prices.
Customers' orders must be serviced promptly and accurately.
Our suppliers and distributors must have an opportunity
to make a fair profit.

We are responsible to our employees,
the men and women who work with us throughout the world.
Everyone must be considered as an individual.
We must respect their dignity and recognize their merit.
They must have a sense of security in their jobs.
Compensation must be fair and adequate,
and working conditions clean, orderly and safe.
We must be mindful of ways to help our employees fulfill
their family responsibilities.
Employees must feel free to make suggestions and complaints.
There must be equal opportunity for employment, development
and advancement for those qualified.
We must provide competent management,
and their actions must be just and ethical.

We are responsible to the communities in which we live and work
and to the world community as well.
We must be good citizens — support good works and charities
and bear our fair share of taxes.
We must encourage civic improvements and better health and education.
We must maintain in good order
the property we are privileged to use,
protecting the environment and natural resources.

Our final responsibility is to our stockholders.
Business must make a sound profit.
We must experiment with new ideas.
Research must be carried on, innovative programs developed
and mistakes paid for.
New equipment must be purchased, new facilities provided
and new products launched.
Reserves must be created to provide for adverse times.
When we operate according to these principles,
the stockholders should realize a fair return.

Johnson & Johnson

throughout the entire product development process. Dealers, insurance companies, and government officials were also consulted throughout the project. This teamwork approach resulted in the development cost of the extremely successful car being $400 million less than expected.

The trend toward teamwork relationships among different functions is expected to increase dramatically in the future. Marketers will play a key role in this approach, being directly involved in the networks of firm teams, organizational partnerships, and customer relationships.

An ethical perspective

Because marketers work at the interface between the company and its customers, distributors, and other groups, ethical and social responsibility considerations are important and often complex. Most decisions made by marketing managers have ethical and social consequences. An ***ethical perspective*** involves addressing the morality of marketing decisions, and practicing social responsibility.

Consider the following:

• A major automobile manufacturer advertises rebates that are inflated by 25 percent because dealers do not pass their proportion of rebates back to customers.

- A major health exercise chain pretends to do telephone marketing research but actually conducts telephone selling.

- Various organizations market products that are unsafe for sale in this country, according to US government regulations, to developing countries where no regulations exist.[15]

These examples of misleading advertising, selling under the guise of marketing research, and selling unsafe products in developing nations do not represent the proper ethical perspective needed in today's marketplace. A company must project a high level of morality to develop trust between itself and its customers and other stakeholders. Trust provides the foundation for long-term relationships with customers and organizational partnerships.

Social responsibility refers to ensuring that marketing actions have a positive impact on society. This includes minimizing social costs, such as environmental damage, as well as taking positive actions that benefit society. For example, Von's, Dollar General, Ben & Jerry's, and The Body Shop have opened retail operations in inner-city neighborhoods and made positive contributions to these communities. These companies measure success as both the profit generated and the benefits provided to the community from their operations.[16]

Fortunately, many organizations are working to promote social responsibility and ethical behavior. Some see business playing an increasingly important social role in the future. Instead of a narrow focus on profit maximization, enlightened companies are acting as global stewards, promoting economic and social justice, and becoming involved in global, national, and local affairs. The efforts of Xerox in education and Du Pont in the environmental area are illustrative.[17]

Efforts to promote ethical behavior are also increasing. The American Marketing Association updated its Code of Ethics for marketers with guidelines for ethical behavior (see Exhibit 2.4). Companies such as United Technologies, Colgate-Palmolive, Chase Manhattan Bank, Harris Corp., and many others

| Exhibit 2.4 | American Marketing Association Code of Ethics |

Members of the American Marketing Association (AMA) are committed to ethical professional conduct. They have joined together in subscribing to this Code of Ethics embracing the following topics:

Responsibilities of the Marketer
Marketers must accept responsibility for the consequences of their activities and make every effort to ensure that their decisions, recommendations, and actions function to identify, serve, and satisfy all relevant publics: customers, organizations, and society. Marketers' professional conduct must be guided by:
- The basic rule of professional ethics: not knowingly to do harm;
- The adherence to all applicable laws and regulations;
- The accurate representation of their education, training, and experience; and
- The active support, practice, and promotion of this Code of Ethics.

Honesty and Fairness
Marketers shall uphold and advance the integrity, honor, and dignity of the marketing profession by:
- Being honest in serving consumers, clients, employees, suppliers, distributors, and the public;
- Not knowingly participating in conflict of interest without prior notice to all parties involved; and
- Establishing equitable fee schedules including the payment or receipt of usual, customary, and/or legal compensation for marketing exchanges.

Rights and Duties of Parties in the Marketing Exchange Process
Participants in the marketing exchange process should be able to expect that:
- Products and services offered are safe and fit for their intended uses;
- Communications about offered products and services are not deceptive;
- All parties intend to discharge their obligations, financial and otherwise, in good faith; and
- Appropriate internal methods exist for equitable adjustment and/ or redress of grievances concerning purchases.
It is understood that the above would include, *but is not limited to*, the following responsibilities of the marketer:

In the area of product development and management,
- disclosure of all substantial risks associated with product or service usage;
- identification of any product component substitution that might materially change the product or impact on the buyer's purchase decision;
- identification of extra-cost added features.

(continued)

Exhibit 2.4   **American Marketing Association Code of Ethics (concluded)**

In the area of promotions,
• avoidance of false and misleading advertising;
• rejection of high pressure manipulations, or misleading sales tactics;
• avoidance of sales promotions that use deception or manipulation.
In the area of distribution,
• not manipulating the availability of a product for purpose of exploitation;
• not using coercion in the marketing channel;
• not exerting undue influence over the reseller's choice to handle a product.
In the area of pricing,
• not engaging in price fixing;
• not practicing predatory pricing;
• disclosing the full price associated with any purchase.
In the area of marketing research,
• prohibiting selling or fund raising under the guise of conducting research;
• maintaining research integrity by avoiding misrepresentation and omission of pertinent research data;
• treating outside clients and suppliers fairly.
Organizational Relationships
Marketers should be aware of how their behavior may influence or impact on the behavior of others in organizational relationships.
They should not demand, encourage, or apply coercion to obtain unethical behavior in their relationships with others, such as
employees, suppliers, or customers.
• Apply confidentiality and anonymity in professional relationships with regard to privileged information;
• Meet their obligations and responsibilities in contracts and mutual agreements in a timely manner;
• Avoid taking the work of others, in whole, or in part, and represent this work as their own or directly benefit from it without
  compensation or consent of the originator or owner;
• Avoid manipulation to take advantage of situations to maximize personal welfare in a way that unfairly deprives or damages the
  organization or others.
Any AMA member found to be in violation of any provision of this Code of Ethics may have his or her Association membership
suspended or revoked.

promote ethical behavior throughout their organizations by developing codes of ethics, policies on ethics, and ethics boards, and holding out termination for unethical behavior.[18] An example of these efforts is the ethical philosophy of Procter & Gamble presented in Exhibit 2.5. This statement addresses both ethical behavior between specific constituent groups, and responsible behavior to society as a whole.

An approach for integrating an ethical perspective into marketing decision making is suggested in Exhibit 2.6. This approach incorporates ethical and social responsibility concerns at each stage of the decision process. For every marketing decision option, management evaluates who might be affected, how they might be affected, potential moral and social consequences, and ethical and social values. Once a decision has been made, the company develops a specific course of action to implement the decision.

A quality/value perspective

A *quality/value perspective* consists of continually improving the quality of products and services and offering this quality at lower prices to customers. The basic idea is to give customers "more for less." Understanding the quality/value perspective requires a separate discussion of the quality and value components.

What is quality?

Quality can be defined in a number of ways. In one accepted definition, **"quality is the totality of features and characteristics of a product or service that bear on its ability to satisfy stated or implied needs."**[19] The important aspect of this definition for marketers is the focus on satisfying the needs of customers. Thus, quality means offering customers product and service features that satisfy their needs, as the customers define them.

Exhibit 2.5

Procter & Gamble's ethical philosophy

Constituent groups	Company responsibilities to each group
Customers	• To provide products with superior benefits • To listen & respond to customer opinions • To ensure products are safe for intended use & anticipate accidental misuse
Suppliers, wholesalers & retailers	• To strive for fair & open business relationships • To help business partners improve performance • To reject illegal or deceptive activities anywhere in the world
Employees	• To provide a safe work place • To show concern for the well-being of employees • To create opportunities for individual achievement, creativity & personal reward
Shareholders	• To provide a fair annual return to the owners • To build for the future to maintain growth
Society	• To safeguard the environment • To encourage employees to participate in community activities • To be a good neighbor in communities in which business is done

Marketers must assess how each activity related to a product or service affects quality and customer satisfaction. The driving force is continual improvement as the means to increasing customer satisfaction. Simply stated, marketers must constantly increase customer satisfaction by providing products and services that better satisfy their needs. Notice how similar quality is to the marketing concept presented in Chapter 1.

Firms such as Xerox, Motorola, and P&G realize the importance of quality for being an effective, world-class business competitor. Companies that improve quality are more likely to develop long-term relationships with satisfied customers. Satisfied customers are more likely to be loyal customers, and retaining loyal customers is important for company profitability. An often quoted axiom is that "it costs at least five times as much to get a new customer as it does to keep an existing customer." Continuous improvements in product and service quality are effective ways to keep existing customers.

Exhibit 2.6   **An ethical perspective for marketing decision making**

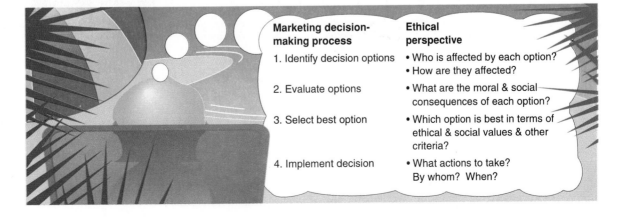

Ford provides an example of *quality/value perspective* by offering a high-quality Escort at a lower price.

ESCORT IS AMERICA'S
BEST-SELLING SMALL CAR.

PEOPLE LIKE GETTING THEIR
MONEY'S WORTH.

FOUR ESCORTS FOR THE SAME LOW PRICE—AND IT'S THOUSANDS LESS THAN THE LEADING IMPORTS.

HAVE YOU DRIVEN A FORD LATELY?

There are two major reasons quality improvements lead to increased profitability. First, firms that successfully implement quality improvements increase their productivity substantially. These gains in productivity translate into reduced costs and more profits. For example, Xerox achieved the highest product-quality rating in five out of six market segments. It also reduced the time it takes to bring a product to market by 60 percent and increased revenue per employee by 20 percent. The improved quality led to lower costs, higher sales, and more profits.[20] Second, empirical evidence suggests that firms perceived as providing high-quality products and services can charge prices 10 percent higher than competitors.[21] The combination of lower costs due to increased productivity and the ability to charge higher prices creates a powerful formula for improving profitability.

Adding value to quality

As we move through the 1990s, more consumers base their purchasing decisions on value rather than on image or prestige. These consumers demand higher quality at lower prices, that is, more value for the dollars they spend. Thus, successful marketers must reduce prices at the same time they improve quality. This value imperative is expressed by Jack Welch, CEO of General Electric: "If you can't sell a top-quality product at the world's lowest price, you're going to be out of the game."[22]

Companies that provide value to their customers have performed well in recent years:[23]

- Toyota's Lexus and Nissan's Infiniti cars hold a substantial market share because they provide quality similar to European imports, such as BMW and Mercedes, but at substantially lower prices ($42,000 versus $55,000).

- Wal-Mart is the nation's largest retailer largely because it offers name-brand products at lower prices than competitors.

- Church and Dwight enjoys a significant share of the toothpaste market with products containing its Arm & Hammer baking soda. These toothpaste products are priced almost 25 percent higher than competitors, but provide more value because they are much more beneficial to gums than competitive products.

On the other hand, some companies seen as not providing value to customers suffered in recent years. For instance, Kellogg lost market share when it charged premium prices for cereals that consumers perceived to be of similar quality to the lower-priced store brands. Compaq Computer maintained 35 percent price premiums when its products were technically superior to competitor products. As the quality of IBM-compatible clones improved, however, Compaq lost sales and had to lower prices. Campbell Soup introduced soup in a disposable microwave container with a price of 99 cents for 7.5 ounces. The product did not sell well, because consumers considered the regular soup, which they could microwave in their own container, a better value at 69 cents for 7.5 ounces. These examples illustrate the link between quality and prices as an important determinant of value and ultimately sales.

The concept of value is being expanded by many consumers. Instead of just low price for the initial product cost or just high quality for basic product features, more consumers consider the convenience of the purchase, after-the-sale service, dependability, and other factors in assessing value. One study found three basic types of value consumers:[24]

- Consumers who want acceptable quality, but are most concerned with making the purchase at the lowest possible price and with the most convenience. Discount stores and membership warehouse stores provide value to these consumers.

- Consumers who demand high quality and are willing to pay a higher price and spend more time in getting exactly what they want. Specialty retailers and specialized catalog companies offer value to this group.

- Consumers who purchase new, different, and unusual products. These consumers derive value from products that represent the latest fashion, state-of-the-art technology, and innovation.

How do marketers integrate a quality/value perspective into marketing operations? The basic approach is to examine all the activities involved in the exchange process (see Exhibit 1.5) for ways to add value. In some cases, activities are performed more efficiently, with the savings passed on to consumers in the form of lower prices. In other cases, more quality is added to the activity without an increase in price.

The effectiveness of a quality/value perspective is illustrated by the success of Nissan's Altima. The Altima is Nissan's recent entry into the biggest and most competitive segment of the automobile industry: the four-door, mid-sized sedan. Nissan designed a car equal in quality to the Toyota Camry and Honda Accord, but priced at $1,500 to $2,000 less. The advertising slogan emphasized the quality of the car: "It's time to expect more from a car." This combination of high quality and low price provided the value many consumers desired. First year sales of the Altima ran 10,000 units ahead of projections.[25]

A productivity perspective

During the 1980s, US marketers blitzed consumers with various types of communications. Collectively, these communication expenditures amounted to more than $6 a week for every man, woman, and child in the US, almost 50 percent more per capita than in any other nation.[26]

What were the results of these expenditures? For many firms, they did produce small increases in sales, although those increases often did not cover the high marketing expenses. As a result, high marketing costs reduced profits for many firms. A typical comment from a marketing manager is, "I spend millions of dollars each year promoting our products to consumers, but see only small increases in sales. Much of my communications expenditures seem to be wasted."

This situation forces firms to view their marketing activities from a productivity perspective. A *productivity perspective* requires getting the most output

This Mita ad promotes the productivity that can be achieved using its office equipment.

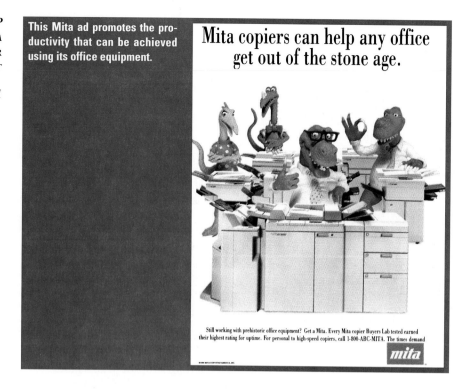

for each marketing dollar spent. Productivity is defined in terms of output per input ratios. For marketers, a typical output is sales or market share. Inputs might include dollars spent on advertising, sales promotions, salespeople, or any other marketing activity. Therefore, sales per advertising dollar or sales per salesperson are examples of important productivity ratios for marketers.

One way to increase marketing productivity is to perform current activities more efficiently. This is extremely difficult when many marketing costs have increased steadily for years. For example, in 1980 the average 30-second commercial on prime-time network television cost $57,900. By 1990, the cost had risen to $122,200, and the prime-time network viewing audience had decreased. The same situation exists in magazine advertising, where the cost to reach 1,000 readers with a full-page color ad increased from $9.72 to $18.44 during the 1980s.[27]

Marketers can also increase productivity by doing some things differently. One way is to develop communication programs that cost less and reach their target audiences more effectively. For example, AT&T spends less on network advertising and personal selling and more on lower-cost telemarketing. McDonald's reduced expenditures on national television advertising and increased them on local promotions by franchisees. B. F. Goodrich spends an increasing portion of its marketing dollars on events such as auto races.[28]

Rising marketing costs squeeze profits and force marketers to examine the bang they get for their marketing buck. The typical approach is expressed by Brian Ruder, vice president for consumer products marketing at H. J. Heinz Co.'s US unit: "I'm telling my people that every dollar they spend has to work 25 percent harder than it did in the good old days of endless supplies of money."[29]

The need to view marketing activities from a productivity perspective is likely to become even more important as we move through the 1990s into the 21st century. This may lead to radical changes in the way some businesses operate. For example, Chiat/Day is creating a new type of advertising agency. Employees will work out of their homes or clients' offices. Chiat will provide personal computers and telephones for everyone and keep a few meeting rooms and study carrels for employee use. The aim is to improve Chiat's productivity by reducing office space costs by more than 40 percent and to increase sales by having employees in the field with clients more often.[30]

Exhibit 2.7	**New-technology products**

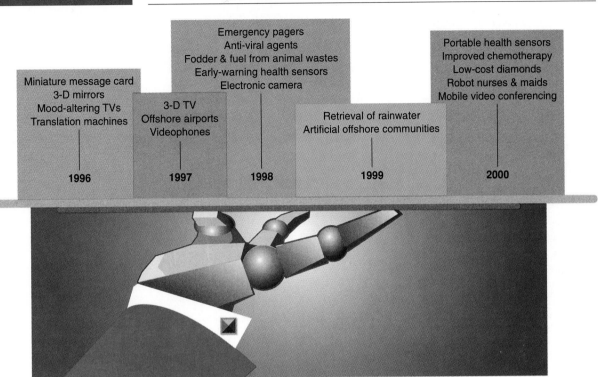

Miniature message card
3-D mirrors
Mood-altering TVs
Translation machines

3-D TV
Offshore airports
Videophones

Emergency pagers
Anti-viral agents
Fodder & fuel from animal wastes
Early-warning health sensors
Electronic camera

Retrieval of rainwater
Artificial offshore communities

Portable health sensors
Improved chemotherapy
Low-cost diamonds
Robot nurses & maids
Mobile video conferencing

1996   1997   1998   1999   2000

A technological perspective

Technology is advancing at a tremendous pace. New developments in artificial intelligence, biotechnology, optoelectronics, and many other areas are reported daily. The dizzying pace of technological change challenges marketers to embrace a ***technological perspective*** so they can translate new and emerging technologies into successful products and services and use technology to improve marketing practice.

Developing new products

Technological developments provide the foundation for many new products. Although the US remains the world leader in many new technologies, Japan and other countries often surpass the US in translating new technologies into successful products. For example, a study of technological and new-product development for 12 emerging technologies found the US ahead of or even with Japan in technology development in all 12 areas, but behind Japan in developing new products in 5 of those areas.[31]

The critical task for many marketing managers is to translate new technologies into successful new products. This requires establishing an environment that promotes innovation, risk taking, and a long-term perspective. Many Japanese firms possess these characteristics and produce a constant stream of new products that incorporate the latest technologies. One study of Japanese firms produced the calendar for new-product introduction presented in Exhibit 2.7.

Improving marketing practice

Many marketing managers start the day by examining electronic messages from the marketing staff and checking on-line reports from distributors and manufacturing plants. They spend the rest of the day on the telephone and manipulating databases to assist in marketing planning. John Kennedy, president of Marketing and Information Systems, predicts "In the future there will be two kinds of

Global marketing electronically

*A*dvances in videoconferencing technology are changing the way companies do business around the world. Videoconferencing allows even small companies to interact globally with customers, suppliers, distributors, and other organizational partners. The cost of videoconferencing is decreasing, and when the savings from reduced business travel are included, videoconferencing becomes a very productive way for marketers to communicate. A study by Arthur D. Little suggests that by the year 2010 videoconferencing centers will be available in almost all company locations and that videoconferencing may replace up to 23 percent of business travel.

One example of the use of videoconferencing is by Philips Medical, a manufacturer of sophisticated medical equipment. Headquartered in Holland, the company has 52 offices in the US. In the past, a representative from the US flew to Holland each month to discuss marketing plans for the US. Now, videoconferencing allows marketing planning meetings involving key decision makers from all 52 locations. Sometimes the company brings in customers to talk with executives in Holland. The result is a better communication process and better marketing planning.

Source: Bryan Batson, "You Really Can Be in Two Places at One Time," *Export Today*, May 1993, pp. 58–59.

companies. One will be using computerized sales and marketing systems. The other will be out of business."[32]

Today, marketers are accustomed to using information and communication technologies. Cellular telephones, fax machines, notebook microcomputers, desktop publishing, multimedia technology, and other technologies offer marketers important competitive advantages. New technologies are routinely used in almost every area of marketing:

- Research results suggest that sales managers using territory-mapping software can improve territory designs sufficiently to produce sales increases of 2 to 7 percent.[33]

- Frito-Lay uses a sophisticated decision-support system to gather sales data daily from supermarkets, scan it for important clues about local trends, and notify executives about problems and opportunities in all markets. The system has substantially increased Frito-Lay's speed in responding to market changes.[34]

Zenith *executes a technological perspective* with state-of-the-art assembly equipment in its Matamoros, Mexico, TV tuner plant.

- Wal-Mart uses satellite networks linking point-of-sale terminals in each store to distribution centers and headquarters in Bentonville, Arkansas. This information is used to manage inventory effectively.[35]

These examples illustrate the wide use of new technologies in marketing. **The Technological Edge: Global Marketing Electronically** provides another example. The challenge for marketers is to keep abreast of new technological developments and determine the best ways to use them to improve marketing practice.

An ecological perspective

Consumers all over the world are increasingly concerned about the environment. Ecological concerns can have important effects on purchasing behavior. Studies in the US found that:[36]

- Eight of 10 Americans consider themselves environmentalists.

- Consumers are more concerned now about the environment than they were in the past.

- Consumers change their purchasing decisions on the basis of environmental concerns.

- Consumers consider a company's environmental reputation before deciding to do business with it.

- Consumers refuse to buy products with bad environmental reputations.

- Consumers consider improvements in packaging the best way for finding environmental solutions.

Although many express concern about the environment, consumers vary considerably in how much they actually alter their purchasing behavior because of this concern. One study segments the US market into three environmental groups:

- *Visionary greens*—Representing 5 to 15 percent of the population, these are the hard-core environmentalists whose buying behavior is very ecologically oriented.

- *Maybe-greens*—The largest group at 55 to 80 percent of the population, these consumers express environmental attitudes but do not always purchase in an environmental way.

Lever Brothers implements an *ecological perspective* with its Double Power refills. The refills, made with recycled unpigmented plastic, save packaging and lower retailers' direct product costs while increasing profits.

- *Hard-core browns*—This group, representing 15 to 30 percent of the population, is antienvironmentalist in its purchasing behavior.

Even though environmental considerations do not currently motivate all consumers, it is wise for marketers to adopt an *ecological perspective* by considering the environmental impacts of all marketing decisions. Astute marketers can find many profitable opportunities in satisfying the needs of environmentally concerned consumers. **Green marketing,** the popular term for implementing an ecological perspective, is likely to increase in importance in the US and throughout the world. Some firms are already addressing the environmental situation. Du Pont pulled out of a $750-million-a-year business that may harm the earth's atmosphere, and entered the toxic-waste cleanup business, where it expects sales of $1 billion per year by 2000. McDonald's actively recycles materials and spends a great deal of time and money educating consumers about environmental issues. Retailers such as Wal-Mart and Kmart press suppliers for more recycled or recyclable products.[37]

The expectation is that ecological considerations will become increasingly important to consumers around the world as we move into the 21st century. Marketers who adopt an ecological perspective can take advantage of the market opportunities offered by these consumers. Marketers who do not will certainly lose customers in the future.

An entrepreneurial perspective

A dynamic business environment creates a need for firms to be flexible and responsive to marketplace demands. Slow and rigid business bureaucracies need to be replaced by streamlined organizational structures and procedures. Success often hinges on being able to do some things differently, sooner, or better than competitors. This requires that marketers bring an entrepreneurial perspective to their work.

An *entrepreneurial perspective* has three basic dimensions: innovation, risk taking, and proactiveness.[38] Marketers adopting an entrepreneurial perspective

The Indiglo watch is an example of how Timex uses an *entrepreneurial perspective* to turn new ideas into innovative products.

Being entrepreneurial in Russia

*H*ow do you stage a direct-mail campaign in a country that does not have telephone directories or mailing lists, and whose post office is not accustomed to direct-mail marketing? The answer is that you have to be a little entrepreneurial.

AT&T faced this situation in a direct-mail program intended to replace Russia's antiquated telephones with AT&T business systems. The problem of establishing a mailing list was solved by employing YAR Communications to search all possible sources for companies that had hard currency accounts. Then, YAR conducted focus groups to determine the best way to address the executives in these companies.

The 4,000-piece mailing included a one-page profile of AT&T, a color brochure on AT&T products, and step-by-step instructions on how to reply by mail. Training was also provided to AT&T's two Moscow distributors on handling telephone responses.

When the promotional material was sent, the Russian post office was suspicious of the mailing and impounded most of the pieces pending an investigation. YAR Communications cleared up the confusion and got the mail delivered. Response has been very good, with some Russian executives placing orders over the telephone without even seeing the equipment.

Source: Sue Kapp, "AT&T Reaches Out to Russian Execs," *Business Marketing*, May 1993, p. 70. Reprinted with permission. Copyright Crain Communications Inc.

attempt to do things in new and unique ways, to make decisions under uncertainty, and to be willing to be the first to try something different. An example of an entrepreneurial perspective is presented in **The Entrepreneurial Spirit: Being Entrepreneurial in Russia.**

The most dramatic effect of an entrepreneurial perspective is the creation of new companies. The story of Domino's Pizza in Chapter 1 illustrates how a completely new firm developed from the idea of pizza delivery. Even more innovative was the establishment of Apple Computer by Steven Jobs, who started a new company and new industry by translating an emerging technology into microcomputer products.

More often, an entrepreneurial perspective produces new products or ways of doing business for existing firms. Some companies are more entrepreneurial than others. A survey of US executives found that the most innovative companies were Microsoft, General Electric, 3M, AT&T, Motorola, Apple Computer, Intel, Merck, Wal-Mart, and Chrysler.[39]

Whether starting new firms or innovating within established organizations, entrepreneurial marketers tend to possess certain marketing skills (see Exhibit 2.8). These skills emphasize an innovative, risk-taking, and proactive approach toward marketing.

EXECUTIVE ROUNDTABLE COMMENT | Tom Kapella, vice president of product development, Gibson Greetings, Inc., strongly favors taking an entrepreneurial perspective toward marketing:

At Gibson, the entrepreneurial spirit is part of the corporate culture. Being the smallest of the industry's top three companies gives us a tremendous advantage. Our product development cycles are shorter and we can react faster to trends or new concepts. We know we must capitalize on this by constantly encouraging the freedom to try different things, be more innovative, and take prudent risks. Our marketing team is rarely criticized for making mistakes with new products that don't quite live up to expectations. Creating a reason to buy Gibson is being first with the newest.

Exhibit 2.8	Entrepreneurial marketers

1. They possess unique environmental insight, which they use to spot opportunities that others overlook or view to be problems.

2. They develop new marketing strategies that draw on their unique insights. They view the status quo & conventional wisdom as something to be challenged.

3. They take risks that others, lacking in vision, consider foolish.

4. They live in fear of being preempted in the market.

5. They are fiercely competitive.

6. They think through the implications of any proposed strategy, screening it against their knowledge of how the marketplace functions. They identify & solve problems that others do not even recognize.

7. They are meticulous about details & are always in search of new competitive advantages in quality & cost reduction, however small.

8. They lead from the front, executing their management strategies enthusiastically & autocratically. They maintain close information control when they delegate.

9. They drive themselves & their subordinates.

10. They are prepared to adapt their strategies quickly & to keep adapting them until they work. They persevere long after others have given up.

11. They have clear visions of what they want to achieve next. They can see farther down the road than the average manager can see.

An execution perspective

Developing marketing strategies to improve product quality and increase customer value is one thing; effectively implementing them is another ball game. Formulating a marketing strategy consists of determining what to do; execution consists of doing it on a day-to-day basis. Lawrence Bossidy, CEO of Allied Signal, emphasizes the importance of execution: "The competitive difference is not in deciding what to do, but in how to do it. Execution becomes paramount."[40]

Firms that promise quality and value as their strategy (what to do) do not succeed unless they actually produce the promised quality and value (do it). In fact, promising customers more than can be delivered can turn a seemingly effective strategy into a disaster. Successful marketers, therefore, must focus on an *execution perspective* to ensure their marketing strategies are implemented correctly.

We can illustrate with examples of both poor and good marketing strategy execution.[41] Leading Edge Products developed a strategy of low price, coupled with the longest service guarantee in the industry. The strategy generated substantial sales, but Leading Edge could not fill the orders or deliver the promised service and ultimately filed for Chapter 11 bankruptcy. Marriott Corporation, on the other hand, developed a strategy to increase room-service business by guaranteeing delivery of breakfast within 15 minutes or providing it free. The company devised specific procedures (such as having deliverers carry walkie-talkies to receive instructions more quickly) to ensure that the promised level of service would be achieved. Room-service revenues jumped by 25 percent.

Both Leading Edge Products and Marriott Corporation developed sound marketing strategies based on quality and value. Marriott delivered on its promise and was successful; Leading Edge did not and was unsuccessful.

DHL suggests the importance of an *execution perspective* in a global marketplace.

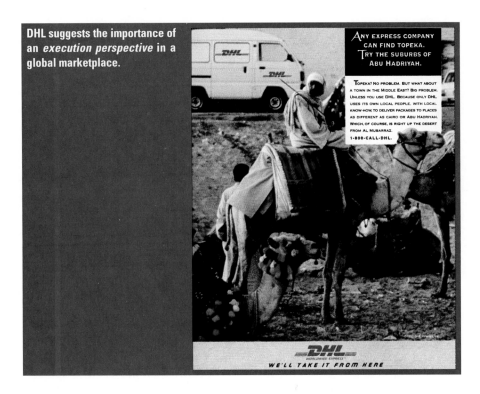

Successful implementation of marketing strategies often requires teamwork within the firm and partnerships with other organizations. The execution problem also becomes much more complex as firms operate on a global basis. For example, Hewlett-Packard (H-P) developed its line of Vectra personal computers for the global marketplace. However, it executed the strategy by introducing the product in the US and Europe but delayed introduction into Asia and other countries. Although the product was successful in the US and Europe, by the time H-P entered the Asian market it had been beaten badly by competitors. Based on this experience, H-P introduced its new line of graphics terminals simultaneously in 15 different languages and successfully beat competitors to the punch worldwide.[42]

A *visionary perspective*

Marketers are often caught up in the day-to-day business of marketing products and services. Much of their time is spent making quick decisions in response to the constant changes in the environment. They may find they "don't see the forest for the trees."

Nevertheless, it is important to operate from a visionary perspective. A *visionary perspective* consists of maintaining a well-articulated picture of how everything fits together to produce what an organization wants to become. This vision can then help guide marketers toward better day-to-day decisions. Marketers can examine how well each decision contributes to achieving the organization's vision. A visionary perspective is especially important for entrepreneurial marketers (see Exhibit 2.8).

IBM illustrates how important a visionary perspective can be. IBM now focuses most of its attention on improving its short-term situation. This is probably appropriate at this time because of the need to increase financial performance quickly. Yet, the company must develop some type of guiding vision of what it is and wants to be over the long haul. This type of vision is important to IBM employees and its customers, suppliers, distributors, organizational partners, and investors.

MagneTek emphasizes the importance of a _visionary perspective_.

A visionary perspective helps marketers focus on the long run. It often leads to actions that are unprofitable in the short run, but necessary steps in realizing the organization's ultimate vision. Rupert Murdoch's Fox Network is a case in point. The company outbid CBS for television rights to National Football Conference games from 1994 to 1997. Analysts expect Fox to lose as much as $155 million per year from televising the National Football League games. Murdoch was ecstatic at winning the contract, not because it would lose so much money, but because it "makes us a network in the real sense of the word. It is all part of a long-term strategy. You can have 500 channels, but no one will have this but Fox."[43] The short-term losses are a minor setback in Fox's vision to become a major network with important advantages in an increasingly competitive environment.

EXECUTIVE ROUNDTABLE COMMENT | **Jack Kennard, executive director of spirits marketing, Brown-Forman Beverages Worldwide, emphasizes the importance of a visionary perspective:**

If a firm's employees could ask top management only one question it would likely be "What is our future?" Every company needs to be driven by a vision of where it wants to be in the future. The vision must be realistic yet challenging and "alive," even passionate, to provide a clear sense of direction based solidly on core values. At Brown-Forman, we recently developed a vision statement for the North American Beverage Company. The vision we adopted was the product of considerable teamwork and lively debate. At the end of the debate, our CEO, William M. Street, took responsibility for writing the final statement. This way, the vision had both broad ownership and leadership commitment.

Conclusions

These are exciting times for marketers. The ten key marketing perspectives discussed in this chapter illustrate the complexity and challenges of modern marketing. Productively competing in a global marketplace requires developing long-term relationships with customers by providing the highest-quality products and services at the best value. Organizational partnerships, teamwork, and an entrepreneurial orientation are often needed to translate new technologies into new products or new approaches for improving marketing practice. Firms must also address ethical and ecological considerations throughout the entire marketing process. And developing plans that incorporate all of these perspectives is not enough. Success requires that these plans are executed effectively within the framework of an overall organizational vision.

Summary

1. *Define ten key marketing perspectives.* A global perspective involves viewing the world in terms of potential market opportunities and competition. A relationship perspective consists of building partnerships with other firms and encouraging teamwork within the organization to initiate and develop long-term customer relationships. An ethical perspective means considering the moral and social implications of all marketing decisions. A quality/value perspective focuses on offering consumers higher levels of quality at lower prices. A productivity perspective is an emphasis on getting the most output for each marketing dollar spent. A technological perspective consists of translating emerging technologies into new products and using new technology to improve marketing practice. An ecological perspective entails a sensitivity to the potential environmental impact of marketing decisions. An entrepreneurial perspective is an emphasis on innovation, risk taking, and proactiveness in all marketing activities. An execution perspective means that marketers focus on the implementation of marketing strategies. A visionary perspective is developing a picture of what an organization wants to be.

2. *Understand the importance of these perspectives for marketing success.* The increasingly complex and turbulent business environment requires marketers to employ these perspectives to be successful. The global marketplace produces intense competition from companies offering increasingly higher levels of quality and value. Successful marketers must view operations from a global perspective and offer quality and value to be able to hold their own against global competitors.

Networks of relationships are often necessary to provide quality and value to customers productively. Firms must consider the environment and ethical behavior to succeed in a global environment. An entrepreneurial approach that often includes the use of emerging technologies is a critical success requirement in many industries. Finally, an overall vision and the execution of marketing strategies is crucial for marketing success.

3. *Appreciate the interrelatedness of the perspectives.* The ten key marketing perspectives are interrelated in a number of ways. For example, providing what consumers need at increasingly lower prices (quality/value perspective) to establish long-term customer relationships (relationship perspective) in a profitable manner (productivity perspective), wherever these customers may be in the world (global perspective), often requires working with other organizations (relationship perspective), employing new technologies (technological perspective) in new and different ways (entrepreneurial perspective), and being sensitive to the environment (ecological perspective) and ethical considerations (ethical perspective). All of these perspectives must fit within the organization's vision (visionary perspective).

Key terms & concepts

global perspective *29*
relationship perspective *31*
transaction marketing *31*
relationship marketing *31*
network organizations *33*
ethical perspective *34*

social responsibility *35*
quality/value perspective *36*
quality *36*
productivity perspective *39*
technological perspective *41*

ecological perspective *44*
green marketing *44*
entrepreneurial perspective *44*
execution perspective *46*
visionary perspective *47*

Review & discussion questions

1. Why does a small retailer in your hometown need to take a global perspective toward marketing?

2. How can marketers improve the productivity of their operations?

3. Select a product or service that you think is a particularly good value, and discuss why it is such a good value.

4. Identify companies that you think employ a relationship marketing approach, and discuss what they do to develop long-term customer relationships.

5. Refer to **The Entrepreneurial Spirit: Being Entrepreneurial in Russia.** How does this example illustrate innovativeness, risk taking, and proactiveness?

6. Why is an ethical perspective important in today's environment?

7. What is meant by the term *green marketing?*

8. Refer to **The Technological Edge: Global Marketing Electronically.** What are some other marketing uses for videoconferencing?

9. Why is an execution perspective increasingly important?

10. Select any three of the ten perspectives, and discuss how they are interrelated.

1. Find the most recent annual report of a company that interests you. Review the report for evidence of how the company focuses on any of the ten key marketing perspectives. Summarize your findings.

2. Identify one successful and one unsuccessful product based on the latest technology. Discuss why one was successful and the other unsuccessful.

3. Go to a grocery store, and identify as many examples of green marketing as you can. Discuss each of these examples.

Case 2.1   *Procter & Gamble: More for less*

Procter & Gamble is one of the world's most well-known marketers. Many of its brands, such as Tide, Pampers, Crisco, and Folgers, have been consumer favorites for years. Today, tough economic times and more knowledgeable, value-conscious consumers are forcing P&G to modify its marketing approaches. The company aims to provide consumers with more value and, at the same time, to become more productive so that the changes will increase profits.

One major change is to simplify product lines. For example, P&G is cutting the colors, flavors, and sizes of its 100 US brands by 15 to 25 percent. Some brands will be killed, others combined. Fewer new products that are only marginally different from existing products will be introduced.

Another marketing change is a drastic reduction in the use of cents-off coupons to encourage purchase of P&G brands. The plan is to use free samples to get consumers to try new products, but then to offer the products at a consistent low price, instead of burying consumers with a blizzard of coupons.

P&G is also reducing the promotions it offers to retailers and wholesalers. Instead of using a mixture of discounts, allowances, and other incentives, P&G is lowering the list prices of its brands. This helps to cut costs, stabilize production scheduling, and maintain consistency in brand pricing.

These changes appear to be paying off so far. Cost reductions have allowed P&G to reduce prices to wholesalers and retailers, and ultimately to users. For example, trade and consumer price promotions have been cut by 40 percent or almost $1 billion per year. During the past few months, these cost savings have been translated into price reductions. List prices for Tide and Cheer have been reduced by 9 percent, Pampers and Luvs reduced by 12 percent, and Folgers by over 10 percent. Consumers have responded by increasing their purchases, and this has strengthened P&G's market position in many product categories.

Questions:

1. Which of the ten key marketing perspectives are driving the changes at P&G?

2. How are these key marketing perspectives interrelated?

3. Should P&G introduce these same programs in international markets? Why or why not?

4. What is your evaluation of these marketing changes?

Sources: Zachary Schiller, "Procter & Gamble Hits Back," *Business Week*, July 19, 1993, pp. 20–22; and Jeanne Whalen, "Coupon Marketers Felt Chill in '93," *Advertising Age*, January 17, 1994, p. 26.

Case 2.2   *Fidelity Investments: People, technology, and service*

Fidelity Investments is the largest mutual fund company in the US and a leader in the international financial services marketplace. This success has been achieved under the leadership of Edward C. Johnson III, chairman since 1972. Johnson's philosophy is an unwavering devotion to meeting customer demands by nurturing a spirited environment that encourages employees to continuously create innovative ways to satisfy customers.

Technology plays a key role in executing this philosophy. Fidelity has integrated the most advanced computer and communications technology into every aspect of its business. For example, customers can contact Fidelity in person at one of its 70 investor centers, by phone to a Fidelity representative who can answer questions 24 hours a day, 365 days a year, by telephone to automated telephone services, by personal computer through an investment software package called "Fidelity On-Line Express," or by mail. All of Fidelity's telephone, mail, and printing services are highly automated.

These technologies have helped Fidelity improve the quantity and quality of its services and keep prices low. The challenge, according to Johnson, is to "listen to what customers say they need and then provide them with extra value—the best service in the industry for the same fees charged by most of our competitors. Our quality initiatives help us maintain this balance by making us more efficient."

But technology is only as good as the people using it. Fidelity fosters an atmosphere that allows employees to be creative and innovative. These employees receive continuous training that emphasizes hands-on learning. Experimentation is encouraged to get new ideas tried and implemented.

Everything at Fidelity revolves around the customer. Phone and mail surveys, focus groups, reading customer letters, visiting branch offices, and informal conversations are all used to identify customers' needs and gauge how well Fidelity's services are satisfying those needs.

Questions:

1. Which of the ten key marketing perspectives do you see illustrated in the Fidelity situation?

2. How are these perspectives interrelated?

3. Why is a technology perspective so important to Fidelity?

4. How would you evaluate Fidelity as a company driven by a marketing philosophy?

Source: Karen Bemowski, "The Secret to Fidelity's Success," *Quality Progress,* June 1993, pp. 25–28.

The Global Marketing Environment

After studying this chapter you should be able to:

1. Understand the nature of the marketing environment and why it is important to marketers.

2. Describe the major components of the social environment and how trends in the social environment affect marketing.

3. Understand how the economic environment affects marketing.

4. See how the political/legal environment offers opportunities and threats to marketers.

5. Appreciate the importance of the technological environment to marketers.

6. Understand differences in the competitive environment.

7. Know how changes in the institutional environment affect marketers.

General Motors: Facing a tough marketing environment

General Motors is the largest manufacturing company in the world. Despite this distinction, the company experienced disappointing performance in recent years. The low point occurred with a $4.5 billion loss in 1991. During the 1980s, General Motors fell from a 46 percent share of a 14 million US car market to a 35 percent share of a 13 million car market. GM is now taking drastic action to turn its performance around.

Achieving a turnaround, however, is difficult because of the complex environment within which the automaker operates. Some of these complexities are:

- Governments around the world are passing legislation requiring car manufacturers to improve miles-per-gallon standards and to produce cars that use alternative fuels. California, for example, will require automakers to sell 1 million electric cars a year there by 2003.

- The push for better mileage and alternative fuels involves a costly technological battle. GM is working feverishly to develop the Impact as the first mass market electric car. Ford, Chrysler, and automakers in Europe and Japan are also working on electric cars.

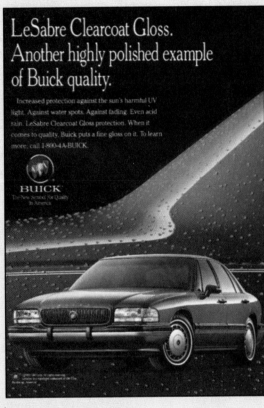

LeSabre Clearcoat Gloss.
Another highly polished example of Buick quality.

Increased protection against the sun's harmful UV light. Against water spots. Against fading. Even acid rain. LeSabre Clearcoat Gloss protection. When it comes to quality, Buick puts a fine gloss on it. To learn more, call 1-800-4A-BUICK.

BUICK
The New Symbol For Quality In America

- The economy in the US and throughout many other parts of the world has been stubbornly sluggish for several years. Consumers bought fewer cars during this period. The US economy improved in late 1993, fueling record new-car sales during the first quarter of 1994.

- Even as the overall US market for cars has declined, competition from foreign carmakers has increased. The Japanese share of the US car market, for example, fluctuates between 21 and 27 percent.

- Demographic trends, such as the aging of the population, change the types of cars consumers want. As the baby boomers grow older, they want to move up to comfortable, roomier cars that have more features. Changing tastes constantly pressure carmakers to respond quickly by designing the desired types of cars.

- Unexpected political events can also create havoc. As one example, when Iraq invaded Kuwait in 1991 and the Gulf War followed, Kuwait canceled an order for 10,000 Chevrolets.

These are only some of the trends in the environment that affect General Motors. Its ability to improve performance depends on how well it can address the key factors in this complex environment. Although the company does not expect a complete turnaround until 1996, it reported modest profits in 1993 and expected higher profits in 1994. GM is trying to become a company that is responsive to changes in the marketing environment.

Sources: David Woodruff, Larry Armstrong, and Resa King, "A Sudden Embrace Sweeps Detroit Off Its Feet," *Business Week,* April 25, 1994, p. 33; Robert L. Simison and Joseph B. White, "Strike Fears Imperil GM's Bid to Rev Up Its Turnaround," *The Wall Street Journal,* January 7, 1994, p. B3; David Woodruff, John Templeman, and Neal Sandler, "Assault on Batteries," *Business Week,* November 29, 1993, p. 39; Joseph B. White, "GM Is Overhauling Corporate Culture in an Effort to Regain Competitiveness," *The Wall Street Journal,* January 13, 1993, pp. A3, A5; Kathleen Kerwin, James B. Treece, and Zachary Schiller, "GM Is Meaner, but Hardly Leaner," *Business Week,* October 19, 1992, pp. 30–31; Alicia Hills Moore amd Wilton Woods, "Can GM Remodel Itself?" *Fortune,* January 13, 1992, pp. 26–34; and David Woodruff, Thane Peterson, and Karen Lowry Miller, "The Greening of Detroit," *Business Week,* April 8, 1991, pp. 54–60.

The General Motors example illustrates how changes in the marketing environment profoundly affect a firm's marketing operations. Legislative requirements, new technological developments, economic conditions, increased competition, the aging of the population worldwide, and political events around the world are some of the factors affecting GM's current and future marketing efforts. The long-term performance of GM or any organization depends, in large part, on its ability to identify and respond effectively to the key changes in its marketing environment.

The **marketing environment** consists of all factors external to an organization that can affect the organization's marketing activities. These factors are largely uncontrollable, although marketers can influence some of them. For example, GM cannot control population trends, economic conditions, or laws once passed, but it can have some influence on political processes, technological developments, and competitive situations.

All marketers face the difficult task of identifying the important elements of the marketing environment for their organization, assessing current and likely future relationships between these factors, and developing effective responses to the changing environment. This task has become increasingly difficult in recent years as many elements of the marketing environment change rapidly and unpredictably. The objective of this chapter is to help you understand the important elements and relationships in the marketing environment.

The marketing environment

In the contemporary marketing framework diagrammed in Chapter 1 (Exhibit 1.7), the marketing environment appears in the outer circle. We now expand that framework by describing the major elements of the marketing environment. Exhibit 3.1 presents the addition of the social, economic, political/legal, technological, competitive, and institutional environments to the original diagram.

The best way to understand the marketing environment is to place yourself in the middle of the marketing circle. You are now a marketer for some organization and must make decisions about the marketing exchanges, strategies, activities, positions, and institutions employed by your organization. However, the decisions you *can* control depend on factors and trends in the marketing environment that you *cannot* control. Thus, your task as a marketer is largely to identify opportunities or threats in the marketing environment and then make marketing decisions that capitalize on the opportunities and minimize the threats.

Creation of market opportunities and threats

The marketing environment creates opportunities or threats in two basic ways. First, changes in the marketing environment can directly affect specific markets. A **market** is a group of people or organizations with common needs to satisfy or problems to solve, with the money to spend to satisfy needs or solve problems, and with the authority to make expenditure decisions. Specific markets can be defined at many different levels. For example, GM's overall car market includes the new-car, the sports car, the luxury car, and the minivan markets. Customers in each of these markets desire a specific type of car and have the money to spend to satisfy that need and the authority to make the purchase decision.

Changes in the marketing environment can make markets larger or smaller or sometimes create new markets. Market opportunities typically arise when markets increase in size or new markets are created. For example, population growth, increases in income, and lower interest rates should present market opportunities for GM by expanding the pool of people who need some type of car and have the money to purchase one. Social changes, such as more women in

Exhibit 3.1

Expanding the contemporary marketing framework

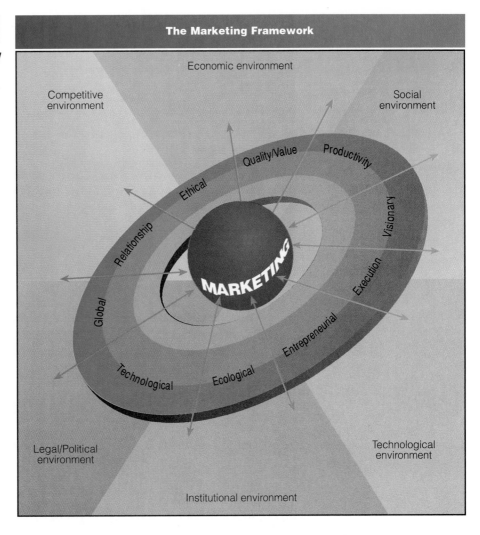

The Marketing Framework

Economic environment

Competitive environment

Social environment

Quality/Value Productivity

Ethical

Relationship Visionary

Global MARKETING Execution

Technological Ecological Entrepreneurial

Legal/Political environment

Technological environment

Institutional environment

the workforce and as heads of households, can affect who makes the car buying decision, thus creating market opportunities. These and other trends also might produce new-market opportunities because of developing needs for different types of cars. Conversely, slow population growth, reduced incomes, and higher interest rates would present threats to GM in some car markets, because there would be fewer people with the financial ability to purchase cars.

The second way the marketing environment produces opportunities or threats is through direct influences on specific marketing activities. Legislation requiring automakers to improve gas mileage is an example. The law can be viewed as a threat, at least in the short run, because it limits the number of current models carmakers can sell and forces them to design new models with better gas mileage. This adds to the cost of making a car, which can either reduce sales, if car prices are raised to cover the additional costs, or reduce profits, if prices are not raised. The legislation, however, might also be viewed as an opportunity to create new markets for cars with extremely good gas mileage or those that use alternative fuels, such as the electric car. Changes in the technological environment similarly provide opportunities to produce these high-mileage or alternative-fuel cars.

The critical point of this discussion is that marketers need to understand the marketing environment to be able to make good decisions. Changes in the marketing environment may create opportunities or threats either by affecting markets or directly influencing marketing activities. Often, short-term threats might offer opportunities in the long run for astute marketers.

EXECUTIVE ROUNDTABLE COMMENT | **Dick Bohy, vice president, professional services,**
Sioux Valley Hospital, indicates the problems marketers face in a turbulent environment:

What a time to be in the health care industry! We've got pressures from everywhere. Patients, physicians, insurance companies, competitors, technological developments, and all types of possible legislation at the federal and state levels. There is no shortage of challenges. At Sioux Valley Hospital we are trying to synthesize what is going on and develop a vision of the future for the health care industry and our hospital. Then, we must execute this vision.

Identifying market opportunities and threats

Many firms use **environmental scanning** to identify important trends and determine if they represent present or future market opportunities or threats. As illustrated in Exhibit 3.2, this procedure consists of identifying relevant factors and assessing their potential impact on the organization's markets and marketing activities. This is simpler to say than do, because many of the potentially important environmental factors are interrelated, and many of them change constantly.

One way to deal with a volatile marketing environment is to use the ten key marketing perspectives discussed in Chapter 2. As shown in Exhibit 3.1, these perspectives are at the interface between the controllable marketing circle and the uncontrollable marketing environment. They thereby provide important orientations for viewing the marketing environment, assessing market opportunities and threats, and determining the best marketing responses to the changing environment. The perspectives work both ways: they guide both a marketer's outward evaluation of the environment and inward response to the environment through marketing decisions.

Social environment

The **social environment** includes all factors and trends related to groups of people, including their number, characteristics, behavior, and growth projections. Since consumer markets have specific needs and problems, changes in the social environment can affect markets differently. Trends in the social environment might increase the size of some markets, decrease the size of others, or even help to create new markets. We discuss two important components of the social environment: the demographic environment and the cultural environment.

Demographic environment

The **demographic environment** refers to the size, distribution, and growth rate of groups of people with different characteristics. The demographic characteristics of interest to marketers relate in some way to purchasing behavior, because

Exhibit 3.2	**The environmental scanning approach**

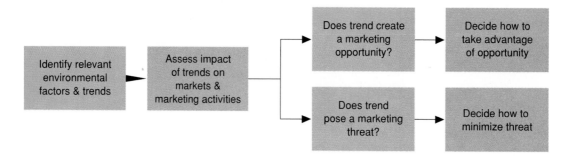

people from different countries, cultures, age groups, or household arrangements often exhibit different purchasing behaviors. A *global perspective* requires that marketers be familiar with important demographic trends around the world as well as within the United States.

Global population size and growth

Population size and growth rates provide one indication of potential market opportunities. The world population is now more than 5.3 billion, and almost 100 million people will be added each year during the 1990s. Thus, the world population is expected to grow by 1 billion during the decade of the 1990s. Approximately 95 percent of that growth will take place in developing countries in Asia, Africa, and Latin America.[1] Population in the developed countries will grow at a much slower rate. For example, the US population grew by approximately 1 percent per year during the 1980s, a low rate expected to persist throughout the 1990s.

There is a tremendous disparity in population size and growth rates across countries, as shown in Exhibit 3.3. China currently has the largest population, followed by India, with the US a distant third. The rapid growth of the Indian population is expected to make it the world's most populous nation by the year 2100. Other countries with large and growing populations are the developing nations of Indonesia, Brazil, Pakistan, Bangladesh, and Nigeria.

The world population situation can be summarized as follows. About every two seconds, nine babies are born and three people die, for a net increase of three people each second. This leads to a growth rate of 10,600 people per hour, 254,000 per day, 1.8 million per week, 7.7 million per month, and 93 million per year. Of this annual increase, developing countries will have 87 million new

Exhibit 3.3	**The most populous countries**

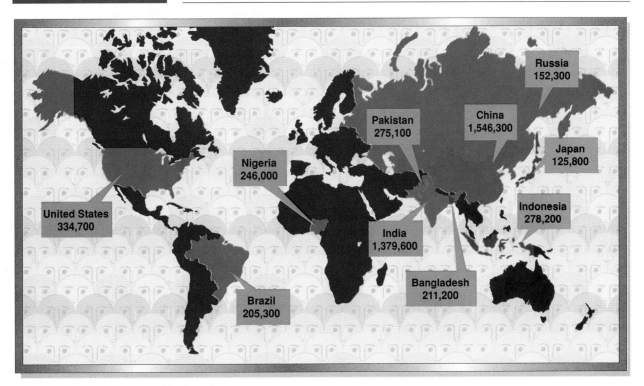

Population in thousands — Year 2025 (estimated)

people, and developed countries, 6 million. Annual growth will increase to 94 million by the year 2000; by 2020 it will be 98 million, with 98 percent occurring in developing countries.[2]

These world population statistics make it clear that marketers cannot rely on population growth in developed countries alone for general increases in market size. The largest growth markets, measured by population size, are in the developing countries. Yet, lower income levels in developing countries may limit the actual market size for many products. Thus, marketers will have to look hard to find attractive growth markets in developed and developing countries.

Global demographic characteristics and trends

Overall world and country population statistics are important, but most marketers target subgroups within these large populations. Trends in population subgroups are therefore typically the most useful to marketers.

An important trend in many countries is growth of the urban population. Current and projected populations for the world's largest cities are presented in Exhibit 3.4. In general, the largest cities and the highest city growth rates are in developing countries such as Mexico, Brazil, and India; however, growth in urban population is evident in many developed countries. For example, in 1900 the US population was 39.6 percent urban and 60.4 percent rural; in 1990 the figures are 75.2 percent urban and 24.8 percent rural.[3] This means the largest and fastest-growing markets for many products are located in the urban areas of most countries.

Another interesting trend is the aging of the population in many countries. Current and projected median ages for selected countries are presented in Exhibit 3.5. The aging of the population is especially evident in Italy, Japan, Britain, and the United States. Notice, however, the relatively young populations in the developing countries, such as Nigeria, Mexico, Brazil, and China.

Age distribution trends in the US are presented in more detail in Exhibit 3.6 (p. 60). The largest percentage of growth is occurring in the 45–64 and 65+ age

| Exhibit 3.4 | | | **The world's largest cities** | | |

City	1991 (000)	2000 (est.) (000)	City	1991 (000)	2000 (est.) (000)
Tokyo–Yokohama, **Japan**	27,245	29,971	Osaka–Kobe–Kyoto, **Japan**	13,872	14,287
Mexico City, **Mexico**	20,899	27,872	Bombay, **India**	12,109	15,357
São Paulo, **Brazil**	18,701	25,354	Calcutta, **India**	11,898	14,088
Seoul, **South Korea**	16,792	21,976	Rio de Janeiro, **Brazil**	11,688	14,169
New York, **US**	14,625	14,648	Buenos Aires, **Argentina**	11,657	12,911

brackets, with slight to moderate decreases in all younger age categories. These trends have important implications for marketers; older consumers have different needs and purchasing habits than younger consumers. Marketers are responding to different age markets in a number of ways. For instance,

| Exhibit 3.5 | **Median age in selected countries** |

Whose population is aging fastest?

COUNTRY	MEDIAN AGES PAST & PROJECTED	
	1990	2010
Italy	36.2	42.4
Japan	37.2	42.2
Britain	35.7	40.0
US	32.9	37.4
Korea (North & South)	25.7	34.4
China	25.4	33.9
Brazil	22.9	29.2
Mexico	20.0	26.5
Nigeria	16.3	18.1

Exhibit 3.6

**Age distribution of US
population**

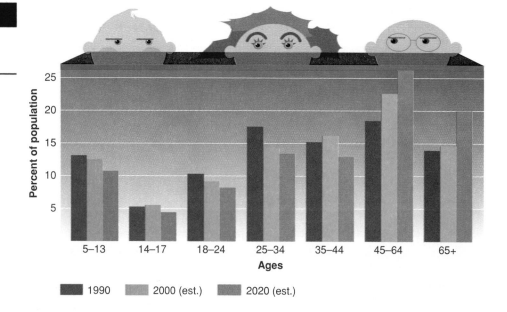

Percent of population

| | 5–13 | 14–17 | 18–24 | 25–34 | 35–44 | 45–64 | 65+ |

Ages

■ 1990   ■ 2000 (est.)   ■ 2020 (est.)

- Financial institutions have increased marketing efforts to attract mature
  Americans. Mutual fund giants, T. Rowe Price and Vanguard, offer software
  programs to help older consumers plan for retirement. Merrill Lynch hired
  a gerontologist to understand mature consumers better and to develop
  products to suit their goals.[4]

- Consumers aged 18 to 29 (generation X) and those aged 30 to 49 (baby
  boomers) respond differently to marketing efforts. Mazda capitalized on
  these differences when marketing the Mazda 929. The ad directed toward
  boomers used extremely conservative cues and emphasized the luxury and

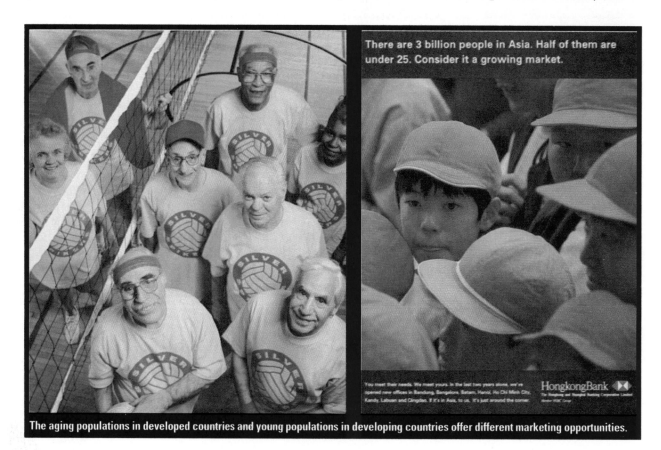

The aging populations in developed countries and young populations in developing countries offer different marketing opportunities.

safety of the car. The ad for Xers contained bright colors and loud music and emphasized the exciting aspects of the car. The company is now designing a car specifically targeted to Xers.[5]

• Sega of America spends a great amount of time trying to understand teens. The company's advertising agency visits the homes of 150 teens and goes shopping with them at the malls. This information helps Sega introduce new video games successfully.[6]

Yet another relevant demographic trend is the declining number of household units consisting of the "typical" family: married couples with children living at home. Only 26 percent of US households fall in this category, down from 31 percent in 1980. People living with nonrelatives is the fastest-growing household type, up 46 percent during the 1980s.[7] In addition, 23 million Americans live by themselves. This is an increase of 91 percent for women and 156 percent for men during the 1980s.[8] The needs and purchasing behaviors of different household arrangements represent important trends affecting marketers.

Cultural environment

The **cultural environment** refers to factors and trends related to how people live and behave. Cultural factors, including the values, ideas, attitudes, beliefs, and activities of specific population subgroups, greatly affect consumers' purchasing behavior. Thus, marketers must understand important cultural characteristics and trends in different markets.

Cultural diversity

Cultural differences are important in both international and US markets. A cultural group's characteristics affect the types of products it desires and how it purchases and uses those products. Different cultural groups in international markets often require marketers to develop strategies specifically for them. One company, Ramsey Popcorn, found this out when it tried to market popcorn globally. Popcorn, an American product, was new to international markets. Consumers in Japan, Taiwan, the Netherlands, and Canada were willing to purchase the same Cousin Willie's microwave brand sold in the United States.

Magazines for new brides capitalize on the cultural and regional diversity in the US market.

Product adaptations had to be made for other cultural groups, however. For example, the Swedes like more butter on their popcorn, the Germans and French prefer it sprinkled with sugar, and the Mexicans want it jalapeño-flavored. Ramsey succeeded by adjusting the product to different tastes and providing consistent quality.[9]

Much of the population growth in the US is and will be accounted for by immigration. During the 1980s, for example, immigration was responsible for 39 percent of the total population growth; about 35 percent of the immigrant population came from Asia and 35 percent from Mexico, Central America, and South America.[10] Many of these immigrants are maintaining important elements of their native culture, leading to increasing cultural diversity throughout the United States. This trend has important implications for marketers insofar as cultural characteristics affect purchasing behavior.

Maybelline, Revlon, Cover Girl, and L'Oreal are adapting their marketing strategies to appeal to different cultural groups. Cover Girl introduced 72 new products for "women of color," while Revlon targets a specific cosmetic line toward each market. The companies are also changing their advertising by featuring entertainers such as Cuban-born Gloria Estefan, African-American Angela Bassett, and Asian-American Tia Carrere in ads.[11]

Marketers can use a ***technological perspective*** to locate different cultural groups in the United States. For example, the market research firm Claritas offers *Rezide,* a CD-ROM with 122 statistics for the 42,496 US ZIP codes. So a marketer wanting to locate the greatest concentration of German-Americans with incomes over $45,000 can do a search on the *Rezide.* The answer: ZIP code 95242, Lodi, California.[12]

Changing Roles

As more women enter the workforce and household compositions change, typical household roles are altered. No longer are financially supporting the household and developing a career solely the responsibility of men. No longer are household chores, child care, or grocery shopping solely the responsibility of women. In many households, roles have shifted and distinctions have become blurred. More men spend time on household and shopping chores, while many women are involved in career development and provide much or most of the financial resources for a household. Tremendous market opportunities exist for firms that can develop effective strategies for appealing to these changing roles.

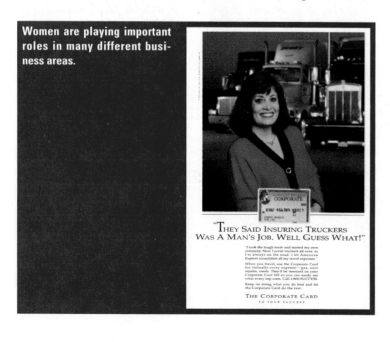

Women are playing important roles in many different business areas.

"THEY SAID INSURING TRUCKERS
WAS A MAN'S JOB. WELL GUESS WHAT!"

THE CORPORATE CARD
TO YOUR SUCCESS

Emphasis on health and fitness

Another cultural trend is an increased emphasis on health and fitness. The pursuit of a healthier lifestyle includes eating more nutritious foods, exercising regularly, participating in various sports activities, and focusing on wellness. This translates into potential market opportunities for firms that provide products and services geared toward improving health and fitness. One firm taking advantage of this trend is Snapple Beverage Corp. Snapple has doubled its sales every year since 1988 by marketing noncola, nonalcoholic, and preservative-free drinks to health-conscious consumers. Some people are willing to pay more than twice as much for a bottle of Snapple than for a regular cola.[13]

Desire for convenience

Changes in household composition, increases in the number of working women, and a general shortage of time underlie an increased desire for convenience. Two-paycheck households often have more money than time. And they are willing to spend this money to avoid spending time doing undesirable chores, such as cooking, cleaning, or auto maintenance. Thus, many consumers buy products and services to minimize time devoted to such chores, opening new-market opportunities for marketers able to meet these needs.

   Firms specializing in home shopping and individual retailers are taking advantage of this need for convenience. QVC and Home Shopping Network dominate the $2.5 billion televised home shopping business. Macy's, Spiegel, and Fingerhut have announced plans to launch 24-hour home shopping channels.[14] In Japan, consumers are purchasing US products through World Shopping Network (WSN). WSN is available 24 hours a day as an on-line computer service.[15]

Consumerism

Consumerism is the movement to establish and protect the rights of buyers. Some say the consumerism movement will intensify as we move through the 1990s. Consumers are more educated, knowledgeable, and organized. They will demand better consumer information, quality, service, and dependability,

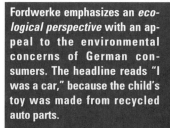

Fordwerke emphasizes an *ecological perspective* with an appeal to the environmental concerns of German consumers. The headline reads "I was a car," because the child's toy was made from recycled auto parts.

ICH WAR EIN AUTO.

Ford-Automobile sind in hohem Maße aus wiederverwertbaren Teilen gefertigt. Da kann es vorkommen, daß manche dieser Teile in einem völlig anderen Produkt wieder auftauchen.

   Wichtiger ist uns jedoch die umfassende und sinnvolle Wiederverwendung aller eingesetzten Werkstoffe im Automobilbau. Deshalb untersucht Ford in einer Pilot-Demontageanlage die optimale Zerlegung von Altfahrzeugen.

   Mit den dort gewonnenen Erkenntnissen verbessern wir ständig die Recyclingfähigkeit neuer Ford-Modelle. So können wir bereits seit Oktober 1991 die kostenlose Rücknahme aller ab diesem Zeitpunkt vom Band gelaufenen Fahrzeuge der Escort-/Orion-Baureihe garantieren.

   Wenn Sie mehr über Recycling oder andere umweltentlastende Maßnahmen beim Produktionsprozeß bei Ford wissen möchten, rufen Sie uns einfach an: 01 30 42 42.

FORD. BEI UNS DREHT SICH ALLES UM SIE.
Die Ford-Werke AG Ösnamierma seit 1987 des Wettbewerb des Europäischen Umweltpreises und siften der Preisgelder.

and fair prices.[16] The consumerism movement is one reason marketers need to adopt *quality/value* and *ethical perspectives.* Giving consumers products that work, charging fair prices, and being honest are the best ways to respond to consumerism.

One increasingly important consumer issue is environmentalism. As consumers worldwide become concerned with environmental issues, their purchasing behavior will change. Successful marketers can respond by taking an *ecological perspective* that emphasizes development of environmentally safe products and communication of the environmental contributions of their firm. Wal-Mart is capitalizing on this trend by merchandising environmentally safe products at its new Eco-Mart. The prototype store was built with environmentally safe materials and uses less energy than traditional stores.[17]

Popular culture

The final cultural trend we note is the popularization of the US culture throughout much of the world. Movies, television shows, and commercials typically express a culture's values and attitudes, and US food, fashion, and entertainment trends are becoming increasingly popular worldwide. Technological advances and globalization of the media allow the export of this popular culture, resulting in a variety of market opportunities. One firm taking advantage of these opportunities is MTV, which beams music videos into 210 million households in 71 countries. Revenues are increasing at the rate of 20 percent per year as MTV establishes or expands operations in Europe, Australia, Latin America, Russia, China, Korea, and Taiwan.[18]

Economic environment

The **economic environment** includes factors and trends related to the production of goods and services and income levels. While demographic and cultural trends generally affect the size and needs of various markets, economic trends affect the purchasing power of these markets. Thus, it is not enough for a population to be large or fast growing, as in many developing countries, to offer good market opportunities; the economy must provide sufficient purchasing power for consumers to satisfy their wants and needs.

Economic trends in different parts of the world can affect marketing activities in other parts of the world. For example, changes in interest rates in Germany affect the value of the dollar on world currency markets, which affects the price, and subsequently sales, of American exports and imports. Several important global economic statistics are presented in Exhibit 3.7.

Market opportunities are a function of both economic size and growth. The **gross domestic product (GDP)** represents the total size of a country's economy measured in the amount of goods and services produced. Changes in GDP indicate trends in economic activity. Column 2 of Exhibit 3.7 shows that the US has the largest economy in the world, followed by Japan, Germany, France, Italy, and Britain. Yet, column 3 shows that the US ranks relatively low on economic growth in recent years, surpassed by much higher growth in Hong Kong, Japan, and some countries in Western Europe.

Another important economic factor is the level of economic activity per person. Per capita data integrate population and economic data to provide an assessment of the purchasing power of individual consumers in a country. The US ranks at the top of the pack in per capita GDP, followed by Switzerland,

| *Exhibit 3.7* | **Global economic statistics** |

	Per capita GDP adjusted for purchasing power (US dollars, 1990)	GDP ($ billions, 1992)	Percent annual growth rate (1987–92)	Population (millions, 1992)
US	$21,571	$5,954.0	1.6%	255.5
Switzerland	20,893	241.5	1.6	6.8
Canada	20,694	568.1	1.2	27.4
Luxembourg	19,205	9.6	2.6	0.4
Germany	18,122	1,928.1	2.9	80.7
Japan	17,792	3,674.3	4.2	124.3
Sweden	17,320	247.9	0.3	8.7
Australia	17,144	286.7	2.1	17.6
Belgium	16,739	219.6	3.0	10.0
France	16,681	1,336.8	2.6	57.3
Denmark	16,679	142.8	1.2	5.2
Norway	15,967	112.9	1.3	4.3
Netherlands	15,543	323.2	2.9	15.2
Austria	15,475	186.0	3.5	7.9
Britain	15,374	1,051.3	0.8	57.6
Italy	15,062	1,237.7	2.3	58.0

Canada, Luxembourg, Germany, and Japan. Notice that Exhibit 3.7 does not include the developing countries that have the largest or fastest-growing populations (China or India) or smaller countries with high per capita income (United Arab Emirates or Kuwait).

Some smaller countries have large GDPs relative to their small populations, although their overall level of economic activity is small in comparison to the larger countries listed in the exhibit. Consumers in these countries may have a lot of purchasing power, but there are not that many of them. These countries typically offer attractive market opportunities for luxury products.

Conversely, many developing countries have large populations relative to their economic strength; that is, individual consumers do not have much purchasing power. However, subgroups within these countries may have substantial

The 250 million middle-class consumers in India offer Frito-Lay a market opportunity larger than the total US market.

purchasing power, or economic growth may offer substantial opportunities in the future. India, for example, has a large and growing population but a low per capita income. Within this relatively poor country, however, are 250 million middle-class consumers. This is larger than the total US market. Coca-Cola, Walt Disney, Kentucky Fried Chicken, Frito-Lay, and many other companies have recently started Indian operations to take advantage of this opportunity. Motorola estimates 40 to 50 million middle-class families there have the buying power to purchase a telephone or pager. It considers India one of the largest untapped markets in the world.[19]

China is an example of a country whose economic growth has been increasing at a rapid pace over the past few years, offering substantial opportunities. As incomes rise in China, so too does the demand for consumer products and the heavy machinery, agricultural and medical equipment, power plants, and communication equipment needed by business and government organizations. US firms responded to these opportunities by increasing exports to China and other developing nations by almost 14 percent in 1992. This compares to a less than 2 percent increase in exports to developed countries.[20]

EXECUTIVE ROUNDTABLE COMMENT | Bob Kyle, international marketing manager, Diebold, is enthusiastic about the market opportunities offered by developing countries, especially China:

The market opportunities in China and other developing nations are almost unbelievable. The Chinese are currently upgrading 100,000 branch banks. Each bank will likely need an automated teller machine, vault door, safe-deposit boxes, and a security alarm system. Diebold has a joint venture for automated teller machines in Shanghai and is developing other joint ventures in China. We achieve the most success when we work with in-country people.

Political/legal environment

The **political/legal environment** encompasses factors and trends related to governmental activities and specific laws and regulations that affect marketing practice. The political/legal environment is closely tied to the social and economic environments. That is, pressures from the social environment, such as ecological or health concerns, or the economic environment, such as slow economic growth or high unemployment, typically motivate legislation intended to improve the particular situation. Regulatory agencies implement legislation by developing and enforcing regulations. Therefore, it is important for marketers to understand specific political processes, laws, and regulations, as well as important trends in each of these areas.

Global political trends

In today's world economy, international political events greatly affect marketing activities. One significant trend is a move from government-dominated economies and socialist political systems toward free-market economies and, in many countries, democratic governments. The republics in the Commonwealth of Independent States and former communist countries in Eastern Europe, such as Hungary, Romania, and Poland, are moving in this direction at various rates. China is taking a different tack: trying to promote a free-market economy within its socialist political system. This objective may be difficult to achieve, as rapid economic growth is generating pressure for a more democratic political system.

These historic developments offer potentially huge market opportunities for many firms, given that these populations need many different types of products and services. Creating effective free-market economies is likely to take a long time and considerable effort. Poland is the only Eastern European country that produced economic growth in 1992 and expects continued growth in the future.[21] The other countries are still struggling with new political and economic systems.

Elimination of trade barriers in Europe should reduce traffic jams like this between France and Spain.

A second important political trend is movement toward free trade and away from protectionism. One approach is the development of trading blocs throughout the world. The largest trading bloc is the European Economic Area (EEA). It consists of 17 European countries from the Arctic to the Mediterranean, representing 372 million consumers and a combined GDP of $6.6 trillion.[22] The next largest is the North American Free Trade Agreement (NAFTA). It consists of the US, Mexico, and Canada and includes 360 million consumers and $6 trillion GDP.[23] The aim is to eliminate trade barriers and to promote easier access to the markets in each participating country. As this development continues, trading blocs have the potential to generate many opportunities for marketers.

The free-trade trend goes beyond trading blocs and encompasses a *global perspective.* The best example of this perspective is the General Agreement on Tariffs and Trade, or GATT. This agreement is the result of long and ongoing negotiations among 117 countries to eliminate trade barriers worldwide. These negotiations are slowly beginning to open world markets for many products. Estimates are that the latest GATT agreement will expand the US economy by $1 trillion over the next decade and increase world trade by $750 billion a year.[24]

A final trend is the use of embargoes or sanctions by the UN or individual governments to limit trade to specific countries, a popular political weapon in recent years. For example, the US participated in embargoes against Iraq, South Africa, Libya, and Vietnam. An embargo, of course, eliminates many potential market opportunities. In contrast, the lifting of trade sanctions, as in the case of South Africa, can release pent-up demand and produce tremendous opportunities.

Unilateral embargoes are especially difficult for affected firms. A case in point involves Vietnam, against which the US had a near total economic embargo for 18 years. When the embargo was lifted in February 1994, Boeing, Marriott, Johnson & Johnson, Coca-Cola, Kodak, Du Pont, Kellogg, and American Express initiated efforts to enter the Vietnamese market. This is an attractive market because of its size (72 million people) and movement toward a market-based economy. However, American firms are at a competitive disadvantage. Firms from Asia, Australia, and Europe have invested over $7.5 billion in Vietnam since 1987. Sanyo, Toshiba, and Honda are among the firms that have already established strong competitive positions. US firms will have to work hard to overcome the problems caused by the embargo.[25]

Exhibit 3.8   **Key US laws affecting marketing**

A. Promoting competition	
Act	Purpose
• Sherman Act (1890)	Prohibits monopolistic practices
• Clayton Act (1914)	Prohibits anticompetitive activities
• Federal Trade Commission Act (1914)	Establishes regulatory agency to enforce laws against unfair competition
• Robinson–Patman Act (1936)	Prohibits price discrimination
• Lanham Trademark Act (1946)	Protects trademarks & brand names
• Magnusson–Moss Act (1975)	Regulates warranties
• U.S.–Canada Trade Act (1988)	Allows free trade between US & Canada

B. Protecting consumers & society	
Act	Purpose
• Food, Drug, and Cosmetics Act (1938)	Regulates food, drug & cosmetic industries
• Fair Packaging and Labeling Act (1966)	Regulates packaging & labeling
• Child Protection and Toy Safety Act (1969)	Prevents marketing of dangerous products to children
• Consumer Credit Protection Act (1968)	Requires full disclosure of financial charges for loans
• Fair Credit Report Act (1970)	Regulates reporting & use of credit information
• Fair Debt Collections Practice Act (1970)	Regulates methods for collecting debts
• Child Protection Act (1990)	Regulates advertising on children's television programs
• Americans with Disabilities Act (1990)	Prohibits discrimination against consumers with disabilities

Legislation

Organizations must deal with laws at the international, federal, state, and local levels. US laws directly affecting marketing typically fall into two categories: those promoting competition among firms and those protecting consumers and society. Exhibit 3.8 presents examples of each type.

Laws promoting competition focus on outlawing practices that give a few firms unfair competitive advantages over others. The specific impact of these laws depends on court rulings that may change over time or differ at the state and national levels. An interesting example is in the area of pricing. A federal court ruled that American Airlines was not guilty of trying to drive weaker competitors out of business when it slashed fares in 1992. In contrast, a state court in Arkansas found Wal-Mart guilty of predatory pricing by selling pharmacy products below cost to drive out competitors.[26] Although Wal-Mart is appealing this verdict and may get it reversed, these examples illustrate the complexity of the political/legal environment.

Consumer protection laws generally indicate what firms must do to give consumers the information they need to make sound purchasing decisions or to ensure that the products they buy are safe. For example, the Fair Packaging and Labeling Act requires packages to be labeled honestly, while the Child Protection Act regulates the amount of advertising that can appear on children's television programs.

Laws typically affect marketing activities by indicating what can or cannot be done. Such constraints might be interpreted as general threats, because they either limit what an organization can do or require an organization to do things that are costly. Although many marketers see most laws and regulations as

Responding to opportunities

*T*he Americans with Disabilities Act (ADA) was enacted in 1990 as the most sweeping antidiscrimination law since the Civil Rights Act of 1964. It gives civil rights protection to individuals with disabilities by guaranteeing equal opportunity in employment, public accommodations, transportation, government services, and telecommunications. Various ADA requirements were phased in through 1994.

Although some companies complain about some of the law's requirements, other firms are capitalizing on the marketing opportunities promoted by the legislation. Consider the following. IBM is marketing eight new products for people with disabilities. Developed at its Special Needs Systems facility, these are part of the IBM Independence series of products. AT&T is aggressively marketing a text telephone (TT) for use by the hearing impaired. Xerox is modifying its machines to assist people with various disabilities.

The potential market for these types of products is huge. Estimates are that 43 million Americans, or 16 percent of the population, have some type of disabling condition.

Source: Adapted from Jan Jaben, "Enabling the Disabled," *Business Marketing,* July 1992, pp. 24–26. Reprinted with permission from *Business Marketing.* Copyright Crain Communications, Inc.

threats, those taking an *entrepreneurial perspective* can often identify attractive market opportunities arising from them. An example of the way one law produced marketing opportunities for many firms is described in the **The Entrepreneurial Spirit: Responding to Opportunities.**

Some laws are directed at providing marketing opportunities. Syria, for example, in trying to open its economy to the private sector and foreign investment, passed a law that exempts investors in approved projects from taxes for five to nine years, waives customs duties on certain imports, and removes regulations that made it difficult to do business in Syria. Known as No. 10, it has contributed to a 7 to 8 percent growth in the Syrian economy.[27]

Regulation and regulatory agencies

Most legislation in the US is enforced through regulations developed by a variety of agencies, and marketers must often work with regulatory authorities at the federal, state, and local levels. Often, regulations are not the same at different governmental levels. For example, the Federal Trade Commission (FTC) enforces guidelines for how firms promote the environmental advantages of their products, but these guidelines do not supersede state laws or regulations. Now, 12 states regulate environmental claims in some way, with more states likely to follow in the future. Sorting through different regulations is a complex task for marketers.[28]

Several of the most important federal agencies are described in Exhibit 3.9. Some of these regulatory agencies cut across industries (FTC, CPSC, EPA), while others focus on specific industries (FDA, ICC, FCC). The impact of these regulatory agencies is especially evident in the pharmaceutical industry. The FDA must approve a new drug before it is marketed and can place limitations on its use. For example, the FDA approved Warner-Lambert's anticonvulsant, Neurontin, but only as an add-on therapy for patients taking other epilepsy medications. This stipulation limits Warner-Lambert's marketing efforts for Neurontin.[29]

The degree of development and enforcement of regulations is related to the national political situation. Recent changes in the US political situation suggest the development of new regulations in many areas and tougher enforcement of

| Exhibit 3.9 | Important US regulatory agencies |

Agency	Responsibilities
• Federal Trade Commission (FTC)	Regulates business practices
• Consumer Product Safety Commission (CPSC)	Protects consumers from unsafe products
• Environmental Protection Agency (EPA)	Protects environment
• Food & Drug Administration (FDA)	Regulates food, drug & cosmetic industries
• Interstate Commerce Commission (ICC)	Regulates interstate transportation industry
• Federal Communications Commission (FCC)	Regulates interstate communications industry

existing ones. Examples include stepping up antitrust enforcement, scrutinizing the pricing practices of airlines, and increasing regulations for the cable television industry.[30]

As more firms participate in the global marketplace, the need for international regulations is emerging. One example is the International Standards Organization's 25-page set of quality standards called *ISO 9000*. These standards apply to 20 different functions within a company, such as product design, process control, purchasing, customer service, inspection and testing, and training, and are being incorporated into laws of the European Community to regulate trade in Europe. A company must go through a long and expensive process to become ISO 9000–certified, which would indicate it meets world standards in many areas. Companies not ISO 9000–certified may not do business in Europe or many other countries. Even individual companies, like General Motors and Siemens, require their suppliers to be ISO 9000–certified.[31]

Regulations in different countries also change and present market opportunities or threats. One example is Japan's Ministry of Posts & Telecommunications (MPT) deregulation of the cellular telephone market in April 1994. Consumers can now purchase cellular telephones instead of leasing them from a few firms at high prices. New cellular products are also being authorized for sale. These regulatory changes represent a threat to Nippon Telegraph and Telephone, but offer promising opportunities for foreign firms such as Motorola, Nynex, Ericsson, and Nokia.[32]

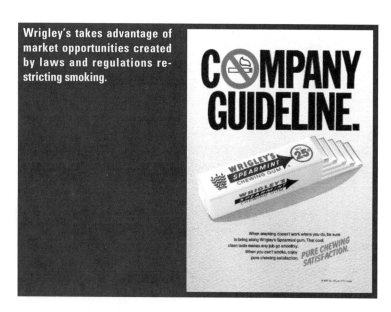

Wrigley's takes advantage of market opportunities created by laws and regulations restricting smoking.

Another example is China's ban on new joint ventures in carmaking for a three-year period. This change is favorable for firms already involved in automobile joint ventures. It is, however, a severe setback for carmakers planning joint ventures in the near future.[33]

Technological environment

The **technological environment** includes factors and trends related to innovations that affect the development of new products or the marketing process. Rapid technological advances make it imperative that marketers take a *technological perspective.* These technological trends can provide opportunities for new-product development, affect how marketing activities are performed, or both. For example, advances in information and communication technologies provide new products for firms to market, and the buyers of these products often use them to change the way they market their own products. Using these technological products can help marketers be more productive. Fax machines and cellular telephones are illustrative.

New technologies can spawn new industries, new businesses, or new products for existing business. Firms at the leading edge of technological developments are in a favorable position. Thus, marketers need to monitor the technological environment constantly to look for potential opportunities that will improve their positions.

In general, the level of R&D expenditures and patents provides an indicator of technological development. Although US-based companies rank high in many overall measures, firms in other countries are increasing R&D expenditures and receiving patents at a higher rate than US firms. This situation has placed many US firms at a severe technological disadvantage when trying to compete globally.[34]

To compete successfully, firms must monitor developments in specific technologies. Important technological developments through the 1990s will likely include those in computers, robotics, and computer-aided design and

The partnership among France, Germany, United Kingdom, and Spain acquires technology from and markets aircraft to firms in the US and around the world.

To earn 30% of the commercial aircraft market, we've spent over $5 billion in the United States.

The United States plays a vital part in Airbus Industrie's long-term global business strategy. Some 500 companies in 35 states manufacture a significant proportion of vital components for our constantly evolving Airbus family of aircraft: a clear demonstration of the massive scale of our commitment to America, and the importance we place on our continued co-operation. Airbus orders from US airlines, including most major carriers, have made a valuable contribution to our worldwide sales success.

AIRBUS INDUSTRIE
TAKING THE WORLD VIEW

The imagination machine

*P*hilips Electronics, the Dutch consumer electronics giant, has successfully developed new-technology products, such as the VCR and the compact disc player. Its marketing efforts, however, have been much less successful, and Japanese firms have achieved market leadership in those product categories using technologies Philips developed.

Philips hopes to change this situation with introduction of the Imagination Machine. The Imagination Machine is a compact disc-interactive (CDI) player that hooks into a TV. CDI programs stored on optical discs mix stereo sound, graphics, photos, text, and video. The product initially retailed for around $800, with programs costing between $19 and $59 each. Since its introduction, some retailers have lowered the price for the CDI player, and improved but more expensive programs have been developed.

Philips has the opportunity to lead the market with this new product. However, Sony, Apple, IBM, and other companies are devising strategies to enter the market. Philips hopes to maintain its lead by motivating outside producers to develop a large variety of CDI programs and by aggressively marketing the product through selected retailers. Philips' position in the global consumer electronics industry is at stake.

Sources: Adapted from Jonathan Levine, Catherine Arnst, and Neil Gross, "Will Philips Sell the World on the VCR of the Future?" *Business Week,* August 17, 1992, pp. 44–45; and Philips *1992 Annual Report,* p. 18.

---

manufacturing (CAD/CAM), and their potential impact on how people live and work; in artificial intelligence and expert systems, and how they are used to solve problems; in superconductors and potential applications for new products; in transportation technologies, such as magnetically levitated trains, supersonic aircraft, and "smart" cars; and in communication technologies and their effects on individuals and organizations.[35]

The key for many companies is to not only have access to the latest technologies, but to be able to market them effectively. An interesting example of the difficulties involved in marketing emerging-technology products is presented in **The Technological Edge: The Imagination Machine.**

Competitive environment

The **competitive environment** consists of all the organizations that attempt to serve similar customers. Two types of competitors are of major concern: brand competitors and product competitors. **Brand competitors** provide the most direct competition, offering the same types of products as competing firms. For example, Nike is a brand competitor of Reebok, LA Gear, and other firms that market different brands of the same types of sport shoes. These firms target the same markets and typically try to take customers away from each other.

Product competitors offer different types of products to satisfy the same general need. Domino's Pizza, McDonald's, and Kentucky Fried Chicken are product competitors. They attempt to satisfy a consumer need for fast food, but they offer somewhat different menus and services. Domino's, McDonald's, and KFC also have brand competitors, which market the same types of fast food to the same customers. Brand competitors of Domino's, for example, are Pizza Hut, Godfather's Pizza, and Little Caesar's Pizza.

The competitive environment for most firms is fierce and often global. Marketers must identify their relevant brand and product competitors in order to

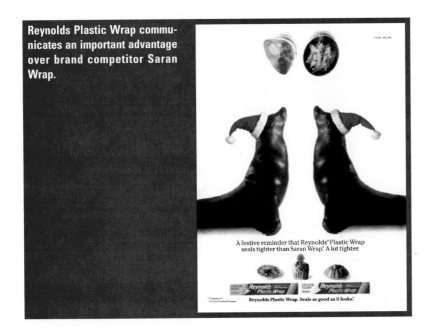

Reynolds Plastic Wrap communicates an important advantage over brand competitor Saran Wrap.

identify market opportunities and develop marketing strategies. One trend affecting many industries is the changing competitive landscape. Some product competitors have become brand competitors by expanding their product offerings.

EXECUTIVE ROUNDTABLE COMMENT | Paul Casey, vice president, branch manager, Smith Barney, describes the competitive changes in the financial services industry:

It used to be that banks offered savings accounts, insurance companies sold insurance, brokerage firms traded stocks, and savings and loan associations made mortgages. Now, everybody is offering everything. Smith Barney competes with many different financial institutions in the brokerage area and for other financial services. It is an extremely tough competitive environment.

Institutional environment

The **institutional environment** consists of all the organizations involved in marketing products and services. These include marketing research firms, advertising agencies, wholesalers, retailers, suppliers, and customers. Specific trends and characteristics of these institutions are discussed in detail in subsequent chapters.

Many organizations are changing how they are structured and managed. These trends in the institutional environment include reengineering, restructuring, the virtual corporation, horizontal organizations, and empowerment. An organization's adoption of any of these concepts means that it is changing some elements of its structure and processes. These changes are likely to affect the amount and types of products the firm needs as well as the purchasing processes it uses. The potential marketing implications of organizational changes are illustrated by the total quality management (TQM) and downsizing trends.

Many organizations are implementing TQM programs. These programs typically emphasize long-term relationships with selected suppliers instead of short-term transactions with a large number of suppliers. Xerox, for example, has cut its supplier base from several thousand to several hundred. This trend means that the pool of potential customers for many marketers is becoming limited. Success in this type of environment requires that marketers take a *relationship perspective* and focus on doing more business with fewer customers.

The downsizing of organizations is commonplace. Sometimes entire departments are eliminated; in other cases, the number of employees within departments is reduced. The major purpose of downsizing is to lower costs and make the organization "leaner and meaner."

When it eliminates departments, the organization typically hires outside firms to replace them. This can offer market opportunities for accounting firms, advertising agencies, personnel firms, and other businesses that can perform the needed functions. When department personnel are reduced, fewer people are available to do the work. For example, many firms have downsized their purchasing departments, and purchasing managers at these companies are responsible for purchasing more products and services than in the past. Marketers employing *relationship* and *quality/value perspectives* can take advantage of this situation. Professional salespeople can work closely with these busy purchasing managers to help purchase quality products that add value to their businesses.

Consolidation throughout industries is another important trend. In the future, many industries will consist of a few large firms enjoying most of the market share, plus many small firms, each with limited market share. One source makes specific predictions illustrating this trend.[36] It reports that nine domestic US airlines currently account for 80 percent of the market, with smaller carriers getting only 20 percent. By 2001 there will be only four major domestic carriers. Also, there are now 20 major auto firms around the world, with market shares ranging from 1 to 18 percent. By 2001, only five will be left. As a final example, by 2001 only three firms will dominate the US computer hardware industry: IBM, Digital, and Apple. Whether these specific predictions become true or not, the overriding trend toward consolidation is clear.

Consolidation has two important implications for marketers. First, organizations must develop marketing strategies to hold their own in a competitive environment consisting of a few large firms and many small firms. Second, they must develop effective marketing strategies to serve both very large and very small customers.

These and other institutional trends affect the way organizations operate. Marketers that serve organizational customers must examine these trends to identify market opportunities and develop effective marketing strategies. Moreover, these trends affect the competitive structure for all marketers and have important implications for the types of marketing strategies likely to be effective.

Megatrends

Although we discussed the different components of the marketing environment separately, they interact in a variety of complex ways. The challenge facing marketers is to understand how these trends interact and how they ultimately affect markets and marketing activities. The Naisbitt Group, a futures consulting firm, identified ten key megatrends that are related to this interaction and have broad effects on many organizations. Exhibit 3.10 presents megatrends for the 1980s and 1990s.

Although the general nature of these trends makes it difficult to assess the accuracy of any prediction, many of those identified for the 1980s and 1990s seem to represent reality. Occurring to at least some extent are the movements from an industrial to an information society, from a national to a world economy, and from a short-term to long-term orientation. The emergence of free-market socialism and the rise of the Pacific Rim countries are also evident.

The value of the megatrends lies not so much in absolute accuracy, but in the attempt to integrate many important trends in the social, economic, political/legal, technological, competitive, and institutional environments. This helps marketers take a *visionary perspective* toward the future.

Exhibit 3.10	Megatrends

Megatrends for the 1980s		Megatrends for the 1990s
1. Industrial society → Information society		1. Booming global economy of the 1990s
2. Forced technology → High tech/high touch		2. Renaissance in the arts
3. National economy → World economy		3. Emergence of free-market socialism
4. Short term → Long term		4. Global lifestyles & cultural nationalism
5. Centralization → Decentralization		5. Privatization of the welfare state
6. Institutional help → Self-help		6. Rise of the Pacific Rim
7. Representative democracy → Participatory democracy		7. Decade of women in leadership
8. Hierarchies → Networking		8. Age of biology
9. North → South		9. Religious revival of the new millenium
10. Either/or → Multiple option		10. Triumph of the individual

Astute marketers will benefit from examining these megatrends. They may be able to identify potential opportunities and threats and devise effective marketing responses. Visionary thinking is valuable in helping marketers understand the complex marketing environment. Those engaging in this type of analysis and thinking will be better prepared to meet the challenges that will certainly confront them in a dynamic marketing environment.

Summary

1. *Understand the nature of the marketing environment and why it is important to marketers.* The marketing environment consists of all factors external to an organization that can affect its marketing activities. Elements of the marketing environment are largely uncontrollable, although marketers have influence over some factors. Environmental factors can affect the size and growth rate of markets and can influence marketing activities. Thus, changes in the marketing environment offer opportunities and threats to marketers. Identifying and responding effectively to these opportunities and threats is a major challenge.

2. *Describe the major components of the social environment and how trends in the social environment affect marketing.* The social environment comprises all factors and trends related to groups of people, including their number, characteristics, behavior, and growth projections. Its major components are the demographic and cultural environments. The demographic environment refers to the size, distribution, and growth rate of people with different characteristics. The cultural environment refers to factors and trends related to how people live and behave. Demographic factors typically relate to the number of people in different markets, while cultural factors generally influence the needs of these markets.

3. *Understand how the economic environment affects marketing.* The economic environment includes factors and trends related to the production of goods and services and the relationships between this production and income levels. The economic environment affects the purchasing power of consumers, which is an important determinant of the size of a market.

4. *See how the political/legal environment offers opportunities and threats to marketers.* The political/legal environment, encompassing factors related to governmental activities and laws and regulations, directly affects marketing activities. Laws and regulations normally present constraints within which marketers must operate. These laws and regulations are closely related to current political trends. Some marketers, however, can identify market opportunities arising from these laws and regulations.

5. *Appreciate the importance of the technological environment to marketers.* The technological environment includes factors and trends related to innovations that affect the development of new products or improving marketing practice. Technological advances are happening so rapidly that marketers must constantly monitor the technological environment to keep abreast of latest developments.

6. *Understand differences in the competitive environment.* The competitive environment consists of all the organizations that attempt to serve the same customers. Brand competitors compete directly by offering the same type of product to the same market. Product competitors compete more indirectly by offering different types of products to satisfy the same basic need.

7. *Know how changes in the institutional environment affect marketers.* The institutional environment consists of all the organizations involved in marketing products and services. These include marketing research firms, advertising agencies, wholesalers, and retailers. As the characteristics of these and other institutions change, so will the marketing strategies necessary to serve different customers and to compete effectively in different industries.

Key terms & concepts

Review & discussion questions

1. How do changes in the marketing environment generate opportunities and threats for marketers?

2. What are the major differences between the demographic and cultural environments?

3. Why are trends in the institutional environment important to marketers?

4. Why is the competitive environment so important to marketers?

5. Look at **The Technological Edge: The Imagination Machine.** How does the technological environment relate to the marketing of this product?

6. How do political changes affect regulations and regulatory agencies?

7. What are the most important social trends facing marketers in the 1990s?

8. Refer to **The Entrepreneurial Spirit: Responding to Opportunities.** What are some other opportunities or threats this legislation poses for marketers?

9. How are the social and economic environments interrelated?

10. Why are the megatrends discussed in this chapter important?

Application exercises

1. Identify several marketing environment trends that you think might affect enrollment at your college. Discuss whether each trend represents an opportunity or a threat. What strategy might your institution use to take advantage of the opportunity or minimize the threat?

2. Compare and contrast the megatrends for the 1980s and 1990s. What are the similarities and differences? Which megatrends for the 1980s were accurate? Inaccurate? Which are continuing in the 1990s? Which

megatrends for the 1990s do you view as the most important? Why?

3. Contact a marketing executive at a local company and ask how he or she assesses changes in the marketing environment. Identify who in the company is involved in what types of environmental scanning. Ask the executive to identify the key trends affecting his or her company and what the firm is doing to respond appropriately to these trends.

Case 3.1   *Nike: Sneakers go European*

Philip Knight is the billionaire founder of Nike, Inc. While continuing to focus on sneakers, the company has expanded into outdoor footwear and apparel and even into sports licensing. Growth has slowed somewhat, but 1993 results indicate a sales increase of 15 percent and a profit increase of 11 percent.

The sneaker business in Europe is experiencing fast growth. Marketing efforts have expanded that market to

$4.5 billion annually, twice the 1985 level. And Nike is getting a larger share of this growing market. Sales in Spain, Britain, and Italy, for example, are increasing nicely.

A few years ago, many Europeans looked at sneakers with disdain, wearing them only in gyms and on tennis courts. When government official Josef Fisher wore sneakers to his German office 15 years ago, he was featured on the evening news! The sneaker situation has changed dramatically since then. Chanel models now stroll down fashion runways in Paris wearing canvas high-top sneakers. A standard outfit for Austrian Prince Karl von Hapsburg is a coat, tie, black denim pants, and sneakers.

These changes are due to several factors. One is that the US image, especially as it relates to sports, has become much more popular in Europe. US professional basketball, especially, is surging in popularity in Europe. Nike has built on and fueled this interest by featuring National Basketball Association stars in advertising. The company has also sent Michael Jordan and Charles Barkley to Europe to participate in basketball clinics and to sign autographs.

Nike has also improved the quality and design of its sneakers. The company introduces about 800 different styles a year, so almost everyone can find some type that is acceptable. Nike spends around $100 million a year on advertising in Europe to promote both the quality image and the variety of designs available.

Nike expects to generate much of its future growth from Europe. Although there are about 130 million more people in Europe than in the US, European sneaker sales are only a third of current US sales, indicating the potential for substantial growth. Nike plans to take advantage of this opportunity, but will face fierce competition from

Reebok, Adidas, and other firms. Europe's lingering recession has limited sales growth as well, as many Europeans perceive sneaker prices to be high. In addition, Nike must adapt to cultural nuances in sneaker distribution and purchasing behavior.

Questions:

1. What trends in the marketing environment have produced the increases in the size of the sneaker market in Europe?

2. What has Nike done to take advantage of the opportunities offered by these marketing environment trends?

3. What types of cultural nuances in sneaker distribution and purchasing behavior might Nike face?

4. What is your assessment of Nike's marketing strategy in Europe?

Sources: Joseph Pereira, "Nike and Reebok Sell Sneakers to Europe," *The Wall Street Journal,* July 22, 1993, pp. A1, A8; Fleming Meeks, "Be Ferocious," *Forbes,* August 2, 1993, pp. 40–41; and Dori Jones Young, Michael O'Neal, Charles Hoots, and Robert Neff, "Can Nike Just Do It?" *Business Week,* April 18, 1994, pp. 86–90.

Case 3.2   *Gerber Products: Where have all the babies gone?*

Gerber Products, the baby-food giant, recently watched the overall market for baby food decline by about 6 percent, as its sales dropped by about 3 percent. The baby-food market is expected to continue this decline as the population ages and growing numbers of women move out of the childbearing years. Although Gerber maintains a 71 percent market share, the company is looking for ways to increase sales in the baby-food market and to seek growth opportunities in other areas.

One approach has been to introduce Gerber Graduates, a line of products aimed at toddlers. The product line features small, microwavable dishes such as chicken stew with noodles, finger foods like meat sticks, and snacks such as animal crackers. The basic idea is to build on the relationship established when the toddlers ate Gerber's baby food. Despite an aggressive introductory marketing campaign, sales of Gerber Graduates were initially disappointing. However, sales in 1993 increased 40 percent to $47 million. The company is trying to increase growth through a $30 million marketing communications campaign and the introduction of new products in 1994.

Gerber is also trying to target population subgroups that have higher birthrates than the national average. Hispanic-Americans, for example, have an above average birthrate and also feed their children more prepared baby foods than other ethnic groups. Gerber introduced its Tropical line, with fruits such as papayas and mangoes, to appeal to this Hispanic-American group. Market tests in New York and Miami were successful, but sales have not met expectations after a national rollout.

The company has considered offering organic baby food, but has not taken action. The growing concern for pesticides by some consumers has generated successful products in other food lines. Organic baby food might meet the needs of these consumers, but it would be a high-cost product, which might limit its sales. Gerber is also concerned that the introduction of organic baby foods might signify there is something wrong with its regular baby food. This would be disastrous.

Clearly, the rapidly changing marketing environment offers opportunities and threats to Gerber. Although the company has considered a number of different approaches, it has not yet developed an effective strategy to ensure future growth.

Questions:

1. What environmental trends affect the baby-food market and Gerber's position within this market?

2. Do you think the introduction of Gerber Graduates was a good strategy? Why or why not?

3. Should Gerber introduce a line of organic baby food? Why or why not?

4. What other opportunities does the marketing environment offer to Gerber that are not discussed in the case?

Sources: Carl Quintanilla, "Gerber Stumbles in a Shrinking Market," *The Wall Street Journal,* July 6, 1993, pp. B1, B7. Reprinted by permission of *The Wall Street Journal,* © 1993 Dow Jones & Company, Inc. All Rights Reserved Worldwide; and Leah Rickard, "Gerber Trots Out New Ads Backing Toddler Food Line," *Advertising Age,* April 11, 1994, pp. 1, 48.

Marketing's Role in the Organization

After studying this chapter you should be able to:

1. Discuss the three basic levels in an organization and the types of strategic plans developed at each level.

2. Understand the organizational strategic planning process and the role of marketing in this process.

3. Describe the key decisions in the development of corporate strategy.

4. Understand the different general business strategies and their relationship to business marketing, product marketing, and international marketing strategies.

5. Realize the importance of teamwork in executing strategic plans.

Blockbuster Entertainment Corp.: Exploding into new markets

Blockbuster Entertainment began business as a video-rental retailer. Based in Fort Lauderdale, Florida, the company grew from 238 stores in 1987 to more than 3,400 stores, with total revenues in excess of $2.2 billion. Its closest competitor is West Coast Video with around $120 million in annual sales.

Blockbuster started as a relatively simple company following a relatively simple strategy: renting videos to consumers at retail store locations. Initial growth came about through effective marketing at existing stores and the establishment of new retail outlets. Although Blockbuster continues with this strategy, top management has crafted different strategies to take advantage of opportunities in the global entertainment industry. One strategy is to increase its share of the video-rental market through aggressive marketing. Another is global expansion. The company's objective is to have international operations account for 25 percent of revenues by 1995 with stores in Britain, Canada, Chile, Austria, Mexico, Japan, Australia, Spain, Italy, and Venezuela. Blockbuster is also expanding its product offerings at video-rental stores. A strategic alliance with Philips Electronics, for

example, offers the possibility to market Philips' new Imagination Machine (see *The Technological Edge: The Imagination Machine* in Chapter 3). This compact-disc interactive (CDI) product should appeal to many consumers who rent videos.

Blockbuster is also diversifying into new business areas. It is moving into music and videogame retailing; considering mini-amusement parks, with computers producing special effects for the rides; and searching for other opportunities in the entertainment business. An example of this diversification is a joint venture with Virgin Retail Group for megastores in Europe, Australia, and the US. The megastores offer music, video, and game prod-

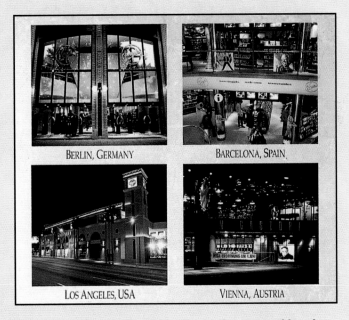

BERLIN, GERMANY

BARCELONA, SPAIN

LOS ANGELES, USA

VIENNA, AUSTRIA

ucts, and special-interest departments, interactive entertainment facilities, personal listening posts, video viewing posts, information centers, and cafes.

These strategies have transformed Blockbuster into a complex firm that sees itself as an entertainment company, not merely a video-rental company. With its moves into new products and markets, the corporation reorganized operations into six divisions: domestic and international home video, domestic and international music retailing, new-technology ventures, and other entertainment venues. Each division is managed as a separate business within the Blockbuster corporate family.

The company made two major moves in 1994. First, it announced a merger with Viacom subject to approval by Blockbuster's shareholders. This merger would create a multimedia powerhouse by combining Blockbuster's entertainment businesses with Viacom's strengths in the television industry. Second, Viacom won the takeover battle for Paramount, adding additional capabilities in television, movies, and publishing. Although it is too early to determine exactly how all these pieces will fit together, it is clear that Blockbuster will be involved in even more new areas of the global entertainment industry.

Sources: John Greenwald, "The Deal That Forced Diller to Fold," *Time,* February 28, 1994, pp. 50–53; Thomas McCarroll, "A Blockbuster Deal for Beavis and Butt-Head," *Time,* January 17, 1994, pp. 41–42; Jeffery D. Zbar, "Blockbuster Thinks Big in Videogames," *Advertising Age,* January 10, 1994, pp. 1, 40; Gail DeGeorge, Jonathan B. Levine, and Robert Neff, "They Don't Call It Blockbuster for Nothing," *Business Week,* October 19, 1992, pp. 113–14; Eleena De Lisser, "Blockbuster's Baczko Quits Two Posts amid Reorganization and Expansion," *The Wall Street Journal,* January 5, 1993, p. B7; and Blockbuster Entertainment *1992 Annual Report,* p. 29.

Exhibit 4.1   **Organizational changes at Blockbuster**

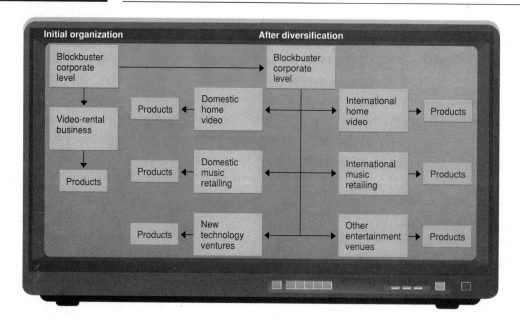

The Blockbuster experience exemplifies a typical success scenario. First, a small company markets a few products to a well-defined market. Although this sort of marketing is not easy, the company directs all its efforts toward the initial products and market. If the firm succeeds and grows, competitors enter with similar products. Over time, the company's opportunities for marketing the same products to the same market decline. To continue growing, the firm must develop new strategies. Typically, it must either market different types of products to its current market, the same products to different markets, or new products to new markets. The relatively simple single-business, few-product firm becomes a complex multibusiness, multiproduct company.

The organizational changes at Blockbuster prior to the Viacom merger are illustrated in Exhibit 4.1. At the left is the initial Blockbuster structure. The corporation consisted of one business: marketing video rentals from retail stores in the United States. Marketing efforts focused on increasing video rentals at existing stores and on opening new retail stores.

Over time, Blockbuster moved to the position shown at the right of the exhibit. The corporation now consists of six major businesses, each marketing various products to various markets. Blockbuster no longer markets just video rentals from just US retail stores; it opened video-rental stores throughout the world (new markets); it markets CDI products (new products) at its stores; and it has entered new types of businesses such as music retailing, video-game retailing, and mini-amusement parks (new products and new markets).

Changes like these dramatically increase the complexity of the marketing task. Blockbuster's marketers must evaluate new business areas, consider new products for the video-rental stores, and look into global market opportunities. In short, they have the responsibility of developing and executing marketing strategies for all the company's businesses and products.

Although these changes are new for Blockbuster, many of the most familiar firms around the world are complex organizations that market many different products in many different business areas. Take, for example, Asea Brown Boveri (ABB), the worldwide heavy-industry giant. The ABB corporation consists of eight major business segments, 65 business areas, 1,300 independently incorporated companies, and about 5,000 autonomous profit centers.[1] Marketing

The University of Chicago Graduate School of Business can be considered a business unit of the university.

efforts require planning and implementation across all the various business segments, business areas, incorporated companies, and profit centers.

The complexities facing ABB, Blockbuster, and other firms produce many of the key challenges for today's marketers. In this chapter we examine the important role of marketing in the contemporary multibusiness, multiproduct firm. We classify organizations into corporate, business, and functional levels, and discuss strategic planning and strategic decision making at each level. Our focus is on the role of marketing. The chapter concludes with a discussion of teamwork in the execution of strategic plans.

Organizational levels

The **corporate level** is the highest in any organization. Corporate managers address issues concerning the overall organization, and their decisions and actions affect all other organizational levels. The corporate management and staff positions at Blockbuster are located at this level.

The **business level** consists of units within the overall organization that are generally managed as self-contained businesses. The idea is to break a complex organization into smaller units to be operated like independent businesses. This is the level at which competition takes place; that is, business units typically compete against competitor business units, not corporate levels versus corporate levels. Blockbuster consists of six business units: domestic home video, international home video, domestic music retailing, international music retailing, new-technology ventures, and other entertainment venues.

The **functional level** includes all the various functional areas within a business unit. Most of the work of a business unit is performed in its different functions. Marketing, accounting, finance, and other areas within each of Blockbuster's business units constitute the functional level.

A typical university provides a good illustration of different organizational levels. The president, vice presidents, and other central administration positions represent the corporate level. The different colleges within the university, such as the college of business or college of arts and sciences, can be considered business units. There are also different functions performed within each college. The typical functions are teaching, research, and administration carried out by faculty, staff, and administrators.

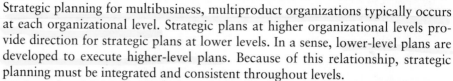

Organizational strategic planning

Strategic planning for multibusiness, multiproduct organizations typically occurs at each organizational level. Strategic plans at higher organizational levels provide direction for strategic plans at lower levels. In a sense, lower-level plans are developed to execute higher-level plans. Because of this relationship, strategic planning must be integrated and consistent throughout levels.

A study of US and South African firms provides a general description of strategic planning.[2] These firms reported that the major benefits of strategic planning are improved performance relative to objectives and a better organizational focus and vision. Most of the firms prepare formal strategic plans at the corporate, business, and product levels, with different functional managers participating in the planning process. These include sales managers, product managers, marketing researchers, production managers, and financial managers. Many firms also incorporate customers into the process. Over 75 percent of the firms said their strategic planning was well coordinated.

Types of strategic plans

The different types of strategic plans and important strategic decisions are illustrated in Exhibit 4.2. A **corporate strategic plan** provides guidance for strategic planning at all other organizational levels. Important corporate strategy decisions concern development of a corporate vision, formulation of corporate objectives, allocation of resources, determination of how to achieve desired growth, and establishment of business units. These decisions determine what type of company the firm is and wants to become.

Business strategic plans indicate how each business unit in the corporate family expects to compete effectively in the marketplace, given the vision, objectives, and growth strategies in the corporate strategic plan. Different businesses within the same organization are likely to have different objectives and business strategies. For example, the Hilton Hotels Corp. emphasizes growth of its gambling casino business by expanding throughout the US and into foreign markets such as Egypt, Turkey, and Uruguay. Hilton is selling some downscale hotels to concentrate on ritzy resort hotels. These changes in corporate strategy influence

Exhibit 4.2	Organizational strategic plans	

Organization level	Type of strategic plan	Key strategic decisions
Corporate	Corporate strategic plan	• Corporate vision • Corporate objectives & resource allocation • Corporate growth strategies • Business-unit composition
Business	Business strategic plan	• Market scope • Competitive advantage
Marketing	Marketing strategic plan	• Target market approach • Marketing mix approach
	Product marketing plan	• Specific target market • Specific marketing mix • Execution action plan

the company's business strategies and are turning Hilton into more of a gaming than a hotel company.[3] Each business needs to make decisions concerning the scope of the market it serves and the types of competitive advantage to emphasize. Decisions in these areas contribute to a general business strategy.

Each business consists of different functions to be performed, and strategic plans may be developed for each major function. Thus, many organizations will have marketing, financial, R&D, manufacturing, and other functional strategic plans. **A marketing strategic plan** describes how marketing managers will execute the business strategic plan. It addresses the general target market and marketing mix approaches.

Each business unit has its own **product marketing plans** that focus on specific target markets and marketing mixes for each product. Product marketing plans typically include both strategic decisions (what to do) and execution decisions (how to do it).

It is extremely important that organizations integrate their strategic plans across all levels. Coordination of business, marketing, and product plans is especially critical. For example, P&G has a general strategic plan for its detergent business and specific product plans for the different brands such as Tide and Cheer. Brand managers for each of P&G's detergent products must clear marketing strategies for their individual brands through the detergent business marketing manager. Without this coordination, P&G would find itself competing more against its own brands (Tide versus Cheer) than against those of other companies (P&G versus Dial versus Unilever).[4]

The strategic planning process

Although individual organizations will differ in the way they approach strategic planning, a general process is illustrated in Exhibit 4.3. This process applies to strategic planning at every level. We present it as a step-by-step approach to make it easier to understand strategic planning. In the business world, most organizations are involved in different stages of the process simultaneously and do not necessarily follow such a definite, lock-step approach.

Examine the current situation

First, the managers evaluate the existing situation for the corporate, business, marketing, or product level. They typically analyze historical information to describe current strategies, assess recent performance, and evaluate the competitive situation. The objective is to develop a picture of the present position, as when Blockbuster identified the maturation of the video-rental business. This background information provides a benchmark for the remainder of the strategic planning process.

Identify potential threats and opportunities

Next, the focus changes from what has happened to what might happen. Managers identify key trends in the marketing environment, assess the possible impact of these trends on the current situation, and classify them as either threats or opportunities. Threats represent potential problems that might adversely affect

Exhibit 4.3

General strategic planning process

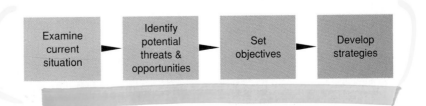

the current situation; opportunities represent areas where performance might be improved. For instance, Blockbuster saw new technological developments, like Philips' Imagination Machine, as opportunities. Managers typically rank potential threats and opportunities, addressing the most important ones first in the next strategic planning stage.

Set objectives

Managers must now establish specific objectives for the corporate, business, marketing, and product levels. Typical objectives involve sales, market share, and profitability. The specific objectives should be based on the analysis of the current situation and the marketing environment. As we discuss later, objectives at the different organizational levels must be consistent. For example, the sales objectives for all businesses must be set so that meeting them means meeting the corporate level sales objectives.

Develop strategies

Finally, managers develop strategies for achieving the objectives. These strategies will indicate how the organization will minimize potential threats and capitalize on specific opportunities. The strategies developed at this stage represent what an organization plans to do to meet its objectives, given the current situation and expected changes in the marketing environment. An example product marketing plan is presented in Appendix B at the end of the text.

The role of marketing

Marketing plays an important role in the strategic planning process for many organizations. Although some marketing positions are represented at the corporate level, most are at the functional level within the business units of an organization. As shown in Exhibit 4.4, however, marketing is involved in strategic planning at all organizational levels.

Strategic marketing describes marketing activities that affect corporate, business, and marketing strategic plans. Strategic marketing activities can be classified into three basic functions. First, marketers help orient everyone in the organization toward markets and customers. Thus, they are responsible for helping organizations execute a marketing philosophy throughout the strategic planning process.

| *Exhibit 4.4* | **Role of marketing in strategic planning** |

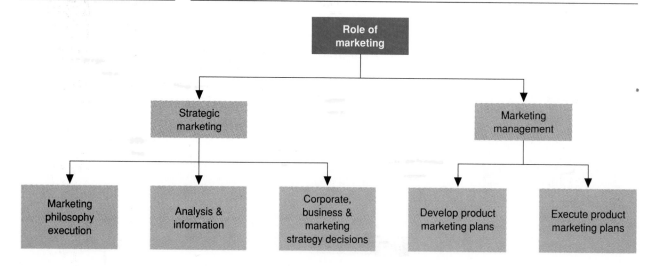

Second, marketers help gather and analyze information required to examine the current situation, identify trends in the marketing environment, and assess the potential impact of these trends. This information and analysis provides input for corporate, business, and marketing strategic plans.

Third, marketers are involved in the development of corporate, business, and marketing strategic plans. Marketing's influence varies across organizations. For organizations driven by a marketing philosophy, marketing necessarily plays a key role in strategic decision making. The trend toward pushing strategic planning responsibility further down the organization is increasing marketing's clout in an organization's strategic planning process.[5]

Marketing management relates to specific product marketing strategies. It differs from strategic marketing in its basic orientation. Strategic marketing focuses on broad strategic decisions at the corporate, business, and functional levels. Marketing management is concerned, by contrast, with specific strategic decisions for individual products and the day-to-day activities needed to execute these strategies successfully.

Our discussion of organizational strategic planning provides an overview of different types of strategic plans, a general strategic planning process, and marketing's basic role in these areas. With this background, we are now ready to examine the major strategic decisions at the corporate, business, marketing, and product levels.

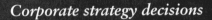

Corporate strategy decisions

The key corporate strategy decision areas defined in Exhibit 4.2 are corporate vision, corporate objectives and resource allocation, corporate growth strategies, and business-unit composition.

Corporate vision

A **corporate vision** represents the basic values of an organization. The vision specifies what the organization stands for, where it plans to go, and how it plans to get there. As indicated in Exhibit 4.5, a comprehensive vision should address the organization's markets, principal products and services, geographic domain, core technologies, objectives, basic philosophy, self-concept, and desired public image.[6] Blockbuster, for example, addresses many of these areas in a short description of its corporate vision: "We want to be the source for family fun and entertainment. Our vision is to be a global entertainment company, building on the strength of our core business—video."[7]

Exhibit 4.5	Corporate vision components

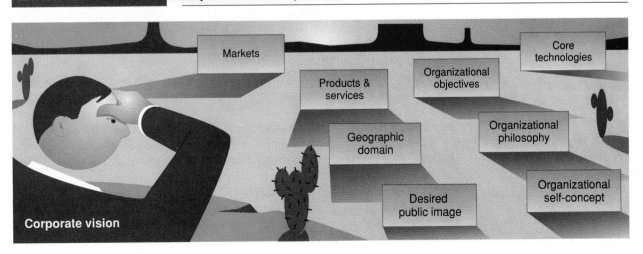

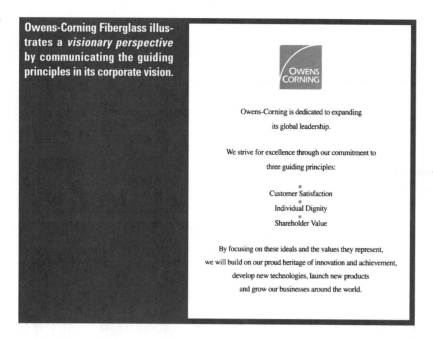

Owens-Corning Fiberglass illustrates a *visionary perspective* by communicating the guiding principles in its corporate vision.

Sometimes organizations develop a formal mission statement to communicate the corporate vision to all interested parties. A mission statement can be an important element in the strategic planning process, because it specifies the boundaries within which business units, marketing, and other functions must operate.

Consider the mission statement for the Bread Loaf Construction Co., a general contractor in Middlebury, Vermont:

We are Bread Loaf, a family of building professionals dedicated to and empowered by the strength of our people. We seek challenges to create innovative solutions which make statements demonstrating our commitment to excellence. As we grow into the 21st century, we shall continually focus upon employee wellness, community responsibility, and a sensitive balance between personal and professional fulfillment.[8]

In developing this statement, Bread Loaf solicited input from all its employees to help ensure that they agree with the firm's vision. Although the statement does not specify markets, products, geographical domain, or core technologies beyond its reference to building professionals, it does express the company's basic values: the importance of people, an emphasis on innovation, and a commitment to excellence. This vision motivates marketers and other employees to work together in developing and implementing company strategies.

Increasingly, companies are emphasizing a *visionary perspective*. One study found that companies with a formal vision outperformed similar companies without a formal vision by more than six to one. Marriott illustrates what some companies are doing. After management developed mission statements for the corporation and hotel division, each of the company's 250 hotels crafted its own mission statement. Staff members at each hotel spent three days participating in "visioning" exercises to develop the mission statements.[9]

Corporate objectives and resource allocation

The second major corporate strategy decision area involves setting objectives for the entire organization and assigning objectives and resources to business units and products. Although the corporate vision provides general overall direction for the organization, corporate objectives specify the achievement of desired levels of performance during particular time periods. Corporate objectives are established for many areas, but the most visible tend to be financial objectives. Typical financial objectives concern sales, sales growth, profits, profit growth, earnings per share, return on investment, and stock price.

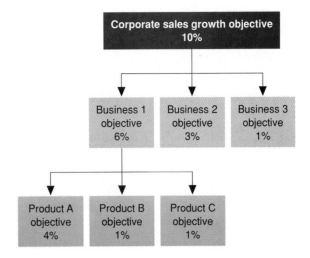

Exhibit 4.6

Hierarchy of sales growth objectives

Sales and sales growth objectives are of most direct concern to marketers. Although sales-related objectives are set at the corporate level, actual sales are achieved by marketing individual products to individual customers. Therefore, corporate sales objectives influence marketing activities throughout the organization, as illustrated in Exhibit 4.6.

Suppose the corporate sales growth objective is to increase this year's sales by 10 percent over the previous year's total. To achieve the desired results, management must break down this objective into goals for each business unit and product. If all products and business units meet the assigned objectives, the organization will achieve the desired growth.

In Exhibit 4.6, 6 percent of the desired sales growth is assigned to Business 1, 3 percent to Business 2, and 1 percent to Business 3. The sales growth objectives for each business unit are then further assigned to the specific products marketed by each business. Again, the sales growth objectives are not equally divided across products, because the various products have different opportunities for increasing sales. But if each product achieves the desired sales increase, the business unit will meet its sales growth objective. And, if each business unit does so, the organization will meet its 10 percent objective.

This hierarchy of objectives represents the organization's sales growth plan. Now, corporate resources are allocated to the business units and business-unit resources are allocated to products. A ***productivity perspective*** is necessary to ensure that resources are allocated efficiently. Thus, Business 1 receives more corporate resources than the two other business units, and Product A receives more of the resources from Business 1 than the other two products it markets. The more sales growth required from a business unit or product, the more resources it typically needs to achieve the desired increases.

Corporate objectives and resource allocation affect marketers in two basic ways. First, marketers are involved in setting the objectives for different organizational levels. Although the amount of marketing participation varies across firms, setting realistic objectives requires the market information and analysis that marketers can provide. Assessments of trends in the size and growth rates of markets and the potential actions of competitors are inputs for setting objectives and allocating resources.

Second, corporate objectives and resource allocation decisions provide guidance for the development and implementation of business and marketing strategies. For example, the marketing managers for Products A and C in Business 1 have different objectives and receive different levels of resources to achieve them. Therefore, they are likely to develop and implement different marketing strategies for their products.

Exhibit 4.7   **Corporate growth strategy options for Blockbuster**

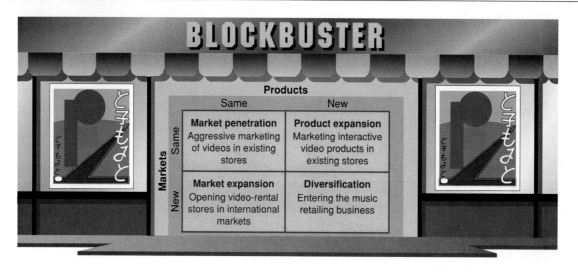

Corporate growth strategies

Corporate growth strategies describe the general approach for achieving corporate growth objectives. The basic strategic alternatives involve limiting corporate operations to the same products and markets or expanding into new ones. Exhibit 4.7 presents four general options, with examples from Blockbuster.

A **market penetration strategy** represents a decision to achieve corporate growth objectives with existing products within existing markets. The organization needs to persuade current customers to purchase more of its product or to capture new customers. This typically necessitates an aggressive marketing strategy, which means increasing marketing communications, implementing sales promotion programs, lowering prices, or taking other actions intended to generate more business. Blockbuster, for example, follows a market penetration strategy as it attempts to increase the video-rental business in existing stores.

A **market expansion strategy** entails marketing existing products to new markets. The new markets might be different market segments in the same geographic area or the same target market in different geographic areas. Much of Blockbuster's recent growth, for example, came from opening new stores in new areas throughout the United States. With saturation of the US market, however, Blockbuster plans to establish more video-rental stores in international markets.

A **product expansion strategy** calls for marketing new products to the same market. The organization wants to generate more business from the existing customer base. Blockbuster employs this strategy by marketing interactive video products to customers in its existing video-rental stores.

A **diversification strategy** requires the firm to expand into new products and new markets. This is the riskiest growth strategy, because the organization cannot build directly on its strengths in its current markets or with its current products. There are, however, varying degrees of diversification. **Related diversification** occurs when the new products and markets have something in common with existing operations. Blockbuster's move into music retailing has some relationship to video-rentals, since both are retailing operations in the electronic entertainment business. **Unrelated diversification,** in contrast, means that the new products and markets have nothing in common with existing operations. Blockbuster might pursue unrelated diversification by moving into a completely new business area, such as financial services, health care, or manufacturing.

A *global perspective* often results in a firm entering different international markets as part of a market expansion strategy.

A sound corporate growth strategy is important to an organization's long-term performance. Some firms pursue one basic corporate growth strategy. Tootsie Roll Industries, for example, has remained in the candy business for 97 years. The company produces 37 million Tootsie Rolls and 16 million Tootsie Pops annually from factories in the US and Mexico City. Although the company emphasizes market penetration, it has purchased 17 different candy brands to generate some growth from new products.[10] Many firms, such as Blockbuster, employ several growth strategies simultaneously.

EXECUTIVE ROUNDTABLE COMMENT | **Jack Kennard, executive director of spirits marketing, Brown-Forman Beverages Worldwide, describes the use of various corporate growth strategies:**

Brown-Forman uses several different strategies to achieve corporate growth objectives. New products are developed for existing and emerging beverage markets. Global business growth is accelerated by marketing current products to more countries, especially Japan and other Far Eastern countries. Brown-Forman has also diversified into consumer durable goods business areas by purchasing premium brands such as Lenox china, Gorham silver, and Hartmann luggage. While different corporate growth strategies always pose new challenges and sometimes result in painful learning experiences, the company emerges more poised to seize future market opportunities.

Business-unit composition

In pursuing its corporate growth strategy, an organization may operate in a number of different product and market areas. It does so through business units designed to implement specific business strategies. A strategic business unit (SBU) focuses on "a single product or brand, a line of products, or mix of related products that meets a common market need or a group of related needs, and the unit's management is responsible for all (or most) of the basic business functions."[11]

SBUs are sometimes separate businesses from a legal standpoint. Sears at one time, for example, consisted of Dean Witter Reynolds (investments), Coldwell Banker (real estate), Allstate Insurance, and the basic retailing business, Sears Merchandise Group. In other cases corporate management establishes SBUs to facilitate planning and control operations. And they can change these SBU

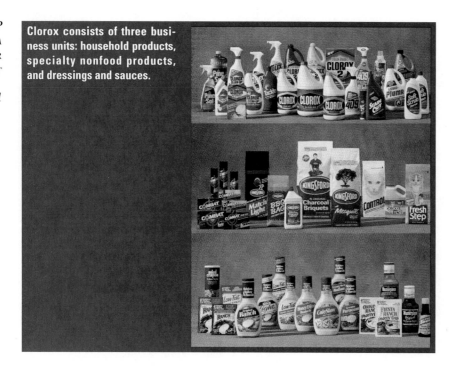

Clorox consists of three business units: household products, specialty nonfood products, and dressings and sauces.

designations when conditions warrant. For example, Digital Equipment once organized itself into 150 SBUs. With recent cost cutting, however, management consolidated the 150 into 9 SBUs that focus on specific industries. Now, management looks at the company as if operating in only 9 separate businesses, rather than the previous 150.[12]

Changing a firm's business composition is not unusual these days. Corporate downsizing often causes a firm to exit from some business areas. Sears, for example, sold all or parts of its investment, real estate, and insurance businesses to concentrate on its retail business.[13] Whether the corporate decision is to increase or decrease the number of SBUs, once a given business composition is established, separate strategies are developed for each business unit.

Business strategy decisions

The basic objective of a business strategy is to determine how the business unit will compete successfully—that is, how the business unit's skills and resources can be translated into positional advantages in the marketplace. Management wants to craft a strategy difficult for competitors to copy so the business can sustain any advantages it has. For example, some retailers achieve sustainable advantages by selecting the best locations for their retail stores, effectively shutting out competitors from those areas. Other retailers try to gain advantages by offering the lowest prices. Price advantages are often difficult to sustain, however, because competitors can usually match them.

A business strategy consists of a general strategy as well as specific strategies for the different business functions such as marketing. The general strategy is based on two dimensions: market scope and competitive advantage.

Market scope

Market scope refers to how broad the business views its target market. At one extreme, a business unit can select a broad market scope and try to appeal to most consumers in the market. The business might consider all consumers part of one mass market, or more likely, divide the total market into segments and

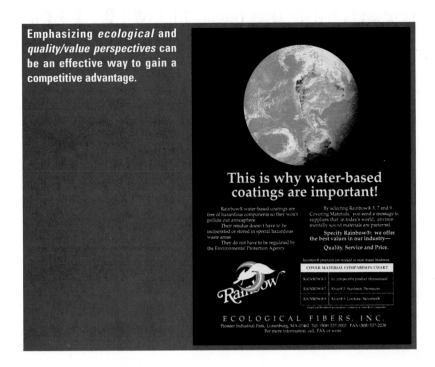

Emphasizing *ecological* and *quality/value perspectives* can be an effective way to gain a competitive advantage.

target all or most of those. An example of a broad market scope strategy in the on-line computer service industry is discussed in **The Technological Edge: Prodigy Goes after Everybody** (p. 92).

At the other extreme, a business unit can focus on only a small portion of the market. An example of a focused market scope strategy, again in the online computer service industry, is discussed in **The Entrepreneurial Spirit: America Online Targets a Few** (p. 93). While Prodigy appeals to the mass market for its services, America Online focuses on a few specific and well-defined segments of the market.

Competitive advantage

Competitive advantage refers to the way a business tries to get consumers to purchase its products over those offered by competitors. Two basic strategies are again possible. A business can try to compete by offering similar products and services as competitors, but at lower prices. Succeeding in a low-price strategy typically requires the business unit to have a lower cost structure than competitors. Wal-Mart is a good example of a business that prospers with a low-price strategy. It offers the same brands as many other retailers, but at lower prices. Wal-Mart can sustain this advantage and be profitable, because it has a very low cost structure and constantly looks for ways to reduce costs.

A business may also compete through differentiation, that is, offering consumers something different from and better than competitors' products. If it is successful in achieving the desired differentiation, the business can typically charge higher prices than competitors. Neiman Marcus, for example, offers a unique product mix and exceptional service to differentiate itself from competition. Consumers are willing to pay higher prices to receive these benefits.

EXECUTIVE ROUNDTABLE COMMENT | **Tony Donnan, general manager, European government affairs, Avon, comments on how quality and value can differentiate a business from its competition:**

In a world awash in consumer goods, the need to distinguish your products in terms of quality and value is no luxury; it is the norm! Avon maintains a competitive advantage through constant quality and value improvements. Our products and sales representatives differentiate us from the competition. Failure to do this will result in withdrawal from the future business arena.

Prodigy goes after everybody

Prodigy is the most popular online computer service today. Established in 1984 as a joint venture between IBM and Sears, Prodigy has about 2 million subscibers. Prodigy's marketing strategy is to offer online computer users a variety of services that have widespread appeal. Subscribers select from different pricing plans that consist of mixtures of monthly fees and charges for service usage. The company announced its first profit in 1993.

The use of emerging information and communication technologies allows Prodigy to make strategic changes to improve the service and increase profitability. It is testing new ways to enhance the service with photos, video, and sound to increase its home shopping business. It is also considering transmitting to TVs, in addition to PCs, and sending CD-ROM disk catalogs to Prodigy members. Changes Prodigy has made include more extra-cost options, the use of faster modems to speed things up, more bulletin boards for members, better financial information and services, and improved interface with users. Even though Prodigy is struggling for profits, the company is a major factor in the on-line computer industry.

Sources: Walter S. Mossberg, "Dialing Up Details on New and Improved On-Line Services," *The Wall Street Journal,* January 6, 1994, p. B1; Jim Carlton, "Apple Plans to Offer 'On-Line' Service in Bid to Gain Steady Revenue Stream," *The Wall Street Journal,* January 5, 1994, p. B6; and Evan I. Schwartz, "Prodigy Installs a New Program," *Business Week,* September 14, 1992, pp. 96–100.

General business strategies

Combining the market scope and competitive advantage decisions produces the four general business strategies presented in Exhibit 4.8. The exhibit provides examples of each strategy for the airline industry.[14]

Kiwi Airlines targets the small-business or leisure traveler on routes between Newark, Chicago, Atlanta, and Orlando. Thus, its market scope is focused on only two segments and a few routes. Kiwi achieves competitive advantage by offering low fares with no purchase or travel restrictions.

Destination Sun Airways focuses on flights from the Eastern seaboard to Florida destinations such as Fort Lauderdale and West Palm Beach. It flies only routes abandoned by the major carriers. Therefore, it maintains an advantage by providing airline service not available from other carriers.

Most of the major airlines, such as American, United, and Delta, employ broad, differentiated strategies. These global carriers compete on many of the same routes,

Exhibit 4.8   **General business strategies**

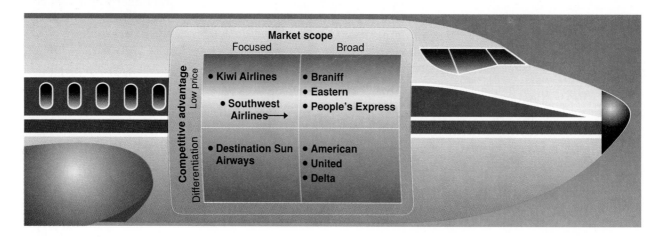

America Online targets a few

In contrast to Prodigy, which serves a broad market for computer online services, America Online successfully uses an entirely different strategy. America Online created a number of small, but profitable, niche markets for online information services. Cofounder and president Stephen M. Case describes the company as "a series of specialized magazines catering to specific interests." Prodigy, on the other hand, is more like *Time* magazine or *USA Today*.

One reason for America Online's profitability is that it charges fees based on actual time connected to the service. But because its services are geared to the specific needs of specific customer groups, consumers are willing to pay these charges, and they use the service often. For example, America Online made a deal with SeniorNet, a group that encourages older consumers to use computers. SeniorNet markets the service to its members, and America Online has introduced a number of services that appeal directly to older consumers. With about 500,000 subscribers, America Online is not likely to grow as large as Prodigy or some other services, but its focused strategy should deliver continued profitability.

Sources: Walter Mossberg, "Dialing Up Details on New and Improved On-Line Services," *The Wall Street Journal*, January 6, 1994, p. B1; *America Online 1993 Annual Report*; and Mark Lewyn, "For America Online, Nothing Is as Nice as a Niche," *Business Week*, September 14, 1992, p. 100.

but try to differentiate themselves through service, frequent flier programs, and other benefits. These airlines must be price competitive, but their major strategic focus is to find ways to differentiate themselves on nonprice factors.

Although a strategy of broad scope and the lowest price has been seen in the airline industry, several carriers have been unsuccessful in implementing it. Examples are People's Express, Braniff, and Eastern Airlines. These carriers all failed, largely because none could reduce its cost structure enough to be profitable at the low fares.

One airline that might succeed with this strategy is Southwest Airlines. Southwest began as a narrow-scope, low-price airline in 1971, and the company has posted profits for 20 consecutive years. The airline now serves 36 different

Southwest Airlines is successful with a focused, low-price business strategy.

Exhibit 4.9

Business and product marketing strategies

Decision area	Business marketing strategy	Product marketing strategy
Target market	Segmented or mass approach	Specific definition of target market to be served
Product	Number of different products	Specific features of each product
Price	General competitive price level	Specific price
Distribution	General distribution policy	Specific distributors
Marketing communications	General emphasis on marketing communications tools	Specific marketing communications program

cities and is expanding into several others. Thus, its market scope is broadening. Southwest may be able to do what other airlines have not: make its no-frills approach work even with a broad market scope.[15]

As Southwest expands its market scope, many major carriers have announced plans to go after the short-haul market. Continental has already entered the short-haul business with CALite. USAir, Delta, and United have similar plans. The major carriers are trying to borrow from the strategies that have made Southwest successful.[16]

Marketing strategy decisions

Recall from Chapter 1 that a marketing strategy addresses the selection of a target market and the development of a marketing mix. The remaining chapters in this book discuss these areas in great detail. Our purpose here is to overview the two basic types of marketing strategy and to discuss international marketing strategy.

Marketing strategies are developed as functional strategies at the business-unit level and as operating strategies at the product level. The two strategies differ in specificity of decisions. Business strategy decisions are relatively general, intended to provide direction for all business-level marketing activities. Product strategy decisions are very specific, because they guide the actual execution of marketing activities for individual products. Exhibit 4.9 compares the decisions for the two types of marketing strategy.

Business marketing strategies

A business marketing strategy must be consistent with the general business strategy. For example, if the general business strategy includes a focused market scope, the target market strategy must concentrate on only a few market segments, perhaps only one. If the general business strategy is low price, the price strategy must be low price. Aside from these obvious constraints, several strategic options are typically available in each marketing strategy area.

Saturn Corporation provides a good illustration of a business marketing strategy.[17] General Motors established its Saturn business unit to develop new approaches for manufacturing and marketing cars, and the unit reported its first profit in 1993. Saturn's general business strategy is a broad market scope and a differentiated competitive advantage. The strategy includes a segmented target market, a relatively narrow product line, value-based pricing, selective distribution, and balanced marketing communications.

Saturn focuses on the broad market, but divides it into specific segments and develops strategies for each. It offers a relatively narrow product line with many

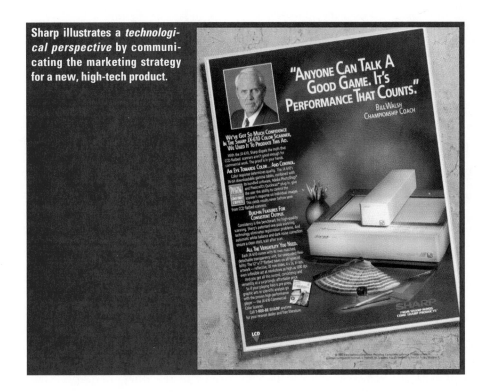

Sharp illustrates a *technological perspective* by communicating the marketing strategy for a new, high-tech product.

options available for each product. Pricing is based on value, and dealers typically do not negotiate. Distribution is selective, with only certain dealers chosen to market the Saturn vehicles. Marketing communications are balanced between advertising to inform consumers and get them into the dealers, and personal selling to sell the cars.

Product marketing strategies

Product marketing strategies require very specific decisions (see Exhibit 4.9). The target market is defined in detail, the product features and options specified, exact prices established, actual dealers identified, and a detailed communications program developed.

These decisions must be consistent with both the general business and the business marketing strategies. For example, Saturn's target market for each product fits within the market scope of the general business strategy. The unit decides on each product within the business product line, sets prices within the business product guidelines, uses appropriate dealers, and develops a communications strategy similar to the business communications strategy.

International marketing strategies

Marketers must address two key areas when developing international marketing strategies: selecting an entry strategy and deciding on a strategic orientation. An **entry strategy** is the approach used to market products in an international market. The basic options include exporting, joint ventures, and direct investment. Each option has advantages and disadvantages in level of investment and amount of control.

Exporting is a method of selling products to buyers in international markets. The exporter might sell directly to international buyers or use intermediaries, such as exporting firms from the home country or importing firms in the international country. Exporting typically requires the lowest level of investment, but offers limited control to the marketer. Carrier (commercial air conditioners), Caterpillar (construction equipment), and Chrysler (cars) are firms actively engaged in exporting.[18]

P
A
R
T

1

This ad is part of the product marketing strategy for the Saturn coupe.

SUZANNE STEHLIK bought a Saturn coupe because she didn't have enough excitement in her life.

Like some kind of comic book superhero, Suzanne seems to lead two lives. During the week, she's a mild-mannered property tax analyst for a large corporation. Come the weekend, though, you could say it's a different story.

This is Suzanne at her current favorite, skydiving, but it might have been something else. She scuba dives. She skis. She'd like to go sailing, but she gets seasick. Oh, and she owns two Rottweilers, and a cockatiel that can whistle half of the Flintstones' theme.

Anyway, she'd been driving a humdrum sort of econobox, and she came to feel she needed something else. Something more like her weekend, less like her week.

The Saturn SC2

Why is our SC2 so fun to drive? For some, it's the 124 horsepower engine. For others, it's the sport-tuned suspension. But for you, all we can say is "Here's the key."

What Suzanne bought was a Saturn coupe. She says it was like finding the shoe that fits—it has the styling, the handling, the performance and all the other fun-to-drive stuff her freefall/underwater/cartoon self wants.

And, funny thing, the price didn't bother her property tax analyst side one bit.

A DIFFERENT KIND of COMPANY. A DIFFERENT KIND of CAR.

At the other extreme is *direct investment,* where the marketer invests in production, sales, distribution, or other operations in the foreign country. This normally requires the largest investment of resources, but gives the marketer the most control over marketing operations. Wang Laboratories, for example, emphasizes direct investment by operating 175 sales and distribution offices worldwide.[19] United Kingdom's Cadbury Schweppes PLC purchased Industrias Dulciora SA to give Cadbury the second-largest market share in Spain's confectionery market.[20]

In between these extremes are various joint venture approaches. *Joint ventures* include any arrangement between two or more organizations to market products in an international market. Options are licensing agreements, contract manufacturing deals, and equity investments in strategic partnerships. Investment requirements and marketing control are usually moderate, although this depends upon the details of each joint venture. Examples of joint venture strategies include Apple Computer's licensing of its new PowerPC chip to Asian firms such as Taiwan's Acer; the joint venture for pesticides, named Qingdao Ciba Agro Ltd., between Switzerland's Ciba-Geigy AG and China's Qingdao Pesticides Factory; and the marketing partnership between Delta Airlines and Virgin Atlantic Airways to coordinate flights and give access to London's Heathrow Airport.[21]

Firms often engage in different entry strategies in different countries. For example, Japan's Nissan Motor Co. used direct investment to establish Nissan Iberica SA in Spain. The Spanish subsidiary now exports cars to other European countries and even recreational vehicles to Japan.[22]

Firms operating in international markets can use two different orientations toward marketing strategy. With a **standardized marketing strategy,** a firm develops and implements the same product, price, distribution, and promotion programs in all international markets. With a **customized marketing strategy**, a firm develops and implements a different marketing mix for each target market country.[23] Most international marketing strategies lie somewhere between these extremes, leaning toward one or the other.

Coca-Cola, for example, uses a largely standardized marketing strategy, where the brand name, concentrate formula, positioning, and advertising are virtually the same worldwide, but the artificial sweetener and packaging differ across countries.[24] TGI Friday's restaurants are successful in the Far East using the same concept as in the United States. The mix of American memorabilia and chatty, high-fiving waiters produces high sales per store. In fact, the TGI

1
G
GLOBAL

Coca-Cola uses a standardized marketing strategy around the world. Here Cameroon street vendors pose with their carts of iced, bottled Coke.

Friday's in Seoul generates double the sales volume of an average restaurant in the United States.[25]

Nissan, in contrast, uses a more customized marketing strategy by tailoring cars to local needs and tastes. One success has been the Nissan Micra, designed specifically to negotiate the narrow streets in England.[26] Similarly, Campbell Soup gets higher sales by adapting its products to local tastes. For example, sales accelerated when it introduced a cream of chile poblano soup to the Mexican market.[27]

Some companies are moving from customized to standardized marketing strategies. Appliance marketers traditionally customized products for each country. But Whirlpool, through extensive research, found that homemakers from Portugal to Finland have much in common. It now markets the same appliances with the same basic marketing strategy in 25 countries.[28]

Executing strategic plans

As we discussed in Chapter 2, developing strategic plans is one thing; executing them effectively is another. An *execution perspective* is a requirement for successful marketing. One route to effective execution of strategic plans is encouraging individuals within an organization to work together to achieve organizational objectives, reflecting a *relationship perspective.* Two forms of teamwork are important: across the different functional areas and within the marketing function.

Cross-functional teamwork

Traditionally, the different functions within an organization worked largely in isolation. Manufacturers "manufactured," engineers "engineered," marketers "marketed," and accountants "accounted." With little direct communication between these functions, their orientations were often more adversarial than cooperative, especially since each function has somewhat different objectives and operates from a different vantage point.

Exhibit 4.10 presents the different orientations between marketing and the other organizational functions. The potential difficulties in getting different functions to work together as a team are clear. Why should production care about marketing's interests, when it is supposed to produce as much as possible as cheaply as possible? There was no reason for one function to care about another in this type of situation, and typically they did not.

Exhibit 4.10

Business function orientations

Function	Basic orientation
Marketing	To attract & retain customers
Production	To produce products at lowest cost
Finance	To keep within budgets
Accounting	To standardize financial reports
Purchasing	To purchase products at lowest cost
R&D	To develop newest technologies
Engineering	To design product specifications

The problem is that if an organization does not produce products that consumers will purchase, it does not matter how low production costs are. More and more organizations are realizing this and adopting a marketing philosophy—which means that everyone within the organization focuses on satisfying customer needs. And satisfying customer needs requires teamwork within an organization.

Many organizations have overcome differences in functional objectives and orientations by communicating the importance of teamwork. They reward the meeting of organizational goals such as customer satisfaction instead of merely functional goals such as low-cost production.

An interesting example of cross-functional teamwork is in the use of multifunctional teams to work with organizational customers. Companies such as Hewlett-Packard, Du Pont, Polaroid, and CIGNA send multifunctional teams from marketing, manufacturing, engineering, and R&D to visit specific customers regularly. The objective is to promote teamwork among employees from different functional areas, to develop a customer focus in all functional areas, to collect useful marketing information about customers, and to improve customer relationships. The value of these multifunctional customer visits is expressed by an R&D manager:

In the past, engineering and marketing would argue about a product . . . Instead, now we have marketing, manufacturing, and engineering all together deciding on the goal from the beginning. It's more of a trust and team-building kind of thing. We traveled together and went to all of these customers together. And we had conversations following it so that we trust each person's opinion more.[29]

Hallmark emphasizes a *relationship perspective* by promoting teamwork across the different business functions.

Marketing teamwork

Even within marketing functions, teamwork is not universal. Different marketing functions often operate somewhat independently—advertising people perform advertising activities, salespeople sell products, brand managers manage their brands, and marketing researchers engage in marketing research. Many firms have little coordination among the different marketing functions. Today, however, the leading organizations are coordinating their marketing efforts and requiring close contact among the different marketing functions.

Many consumer product manufacturers, for example, foster close coordination among brand managers, salespeople and sales managers, and marketing researchers to execute tailored marketing programs for individual retail stores. Working as a team, they uncover information about the customers of each store. The sales and brand managers then work together to execute specific marketing programs for each store to improve sales and profits.

Kodak's reorganization illustrates the importance of marketing teamwork. In changing from a product-driven to a marketing-driven philosophy, the company established a group to integrate marketing functions that had been run separately, such as advertising, sales promotions, public relations, sales, and marketing research. The integrated group will work together in developing and executing all marketing plans.[30]

EXECUTIVE ROUNDTABLE COMMENT | **Bob Kyle, international marketing manager, Diebold, emphasizes the importance of organizational teamwork in global marketing:**

There is no way you can be successful today without being able to work with people throughout your organization. This is especially true when operating in international markets. I cannot develop long-term relationships with my customers unless I have developed strong relationships with individuals throughout my company—both in marketing and in other functions. I need their help to ensure success. Diebold has been emphasizing a teamwork approach for several years. The approach has produced significant improvements in business and customer relationships.

Summary

1. *Discuss the three basic levels in an organization and the types of strategic plans developed at each level.* Organizations can be defined at three basic levels. The corporate level is the highest and responsible for addressing issues concerning the overall organization. The business level is the basic level of competition in the marketplace. It consists of units within the organization that are operated like independent businesses. The functional level includes all the different functions within a business unit. Strategic plans are developed at each level. Corporate and business strategic plans provide guidelines for the development of marketing strategic plans and product marketing plans.

2. *Understand the organizational strategic planning process and the role of marketing in this process.* The general strategic planning process consists of examining the current situation, evaluating trends in the marketing environment to identify potential threats and opportunities, setting objectives based on this analysis, and developing strategies to achieve these objectives. Strategic marketing describes marketing activities at the corporate and business levels. Marketing management emphasizes the development and

implementation of marketing strategies for individual products and services.

3. *Describe the key decisions in the development of corporate strategy.* The key corporate-level decisions include establishing a corporate vision, developing corporate objectives and allocating resources, determining a corporate growth strategy, and defining the business-unit composition. Corporate strategy decisions affect strategic planning at all lower organizational levels. And, strategic plans at lower organizational levels are designed to execute the corporate strategy.

4. *Understand the different general business strategies and their relationship to business marketing, product marketing, and international marketing strategies.* General business strategies require decisions concerning market scope and competitive advantage. Market scope can range from focused to broad, while competitive advantage might be based on pricing or differentiation. Combining the market scope and competitive advantage options produces four general business strategies. A firm's business marketing strategy must be consistent with its general business

P
A
R
T

1

strategy. Decisions on market scope and competitive advantage directly affect business marketing strategies. Product marketing strategies must also be consistent with and serve to execute business marketing strategies. International marketing strategies require decisions about entry method and strategic orientation.

5. *Realize the importance of teamwork in executing swtrategic plans.* The complexity of today's business environment requires cooperation both across different business functional areas and within the marketing function itself. Cross-functional and marketing teamwork are necessary to execute strategic plans effectively.

Key terms & concepts

corporate level   *81*
business level   *81*
functional level   *81*
corporate strategic plan   *82*
business strategic plan   *82*
marketing strategic plan   *83*
product marketing plan   *83*
strategic marketing   *84*

marketing management   *85*
corporate vision   *85*
market penetration strategy   *88*
market expansion strategy   *88*
product expansion strategy   *88*
diversification strategy   *88*
related diversification   *88*
unrelated diversification   *88*

strategic business unit (SBU)   *89*
market scope   *90*
competitive advantage   *91*
entry strategy   *95*
standardized marketing
   strategy   *96*
customized marketing strategy   *96*

Review & discussion questions

1. How does a firm's corporate vision affect its marketing operations?

2. How does marketing differ for a new, single-product venture and a large, multiproduct corporation?

3. What are the basic options for a corporate growth strategy?

4. Look at **The Technological Edge: Prodigy Goes after Everybody.** How might Prodigy grow through related diversification?

5. How do business marketing strategies and product marketing strategies differ?

6. What are the keys to effective execution of strategic plans?

7. Refer to **The Entrepreneurial Spirit: America Online Targets a Few.** How might America Online grow through related diversification?

8. How does an understanding of the marketing environment, as discussed in Chapter 3, help in the development of strategic plans?

9. Why do firms change their business composition?

10. How do corporate objectives affect marketing operations?

Application exercises

1. Read an annual report for any company. Using only the information in the report, describe the firm's corporate, business, and marketing strategies.

2. Pick a recent issue of *Business Week*, *Fortune*, or any other business publication. Review it to identify examples of corporate growth strategies used by different firms.

3. Interview a marketing executive at a local firm. Ask the executive what types of strategic plans the firm develops and what is included in each strategic plan. Also, inquire about the firm's strategic planning process.

Case 4.1   *Chubb: Targeting the upscale consumer*

The property and casualty insurance business is extremely competitive. Most companies have a difficult time differentiating themselves from competitors. Thus, price competition is typical. This emphasis on price has reduced the average return on shareholder's equity to less than 5 percent.

But Chubb has been racking up more than a 20 percent shareholder return in its property and casualty business. How has it been able to do this?

Part of the reason for Chubb's success is its business marketing strategy. Instead of taking a shotgun approach,

Chubb focuses on a few specific target markets. Rather than compete on price, Chubb differentiates itself by providing superior service to customers. For example, Chubb dominates the market for insuring expensive homes. Policyholders include more than half of the CEOs in the Fortune 500 and Service 500. These individuals are willing to pay a high price, if they receive good value.

Chubb also differentiates itself by providing personalized attention to customers. Appraisers visit policyholders to discuss coverage and offer advice on storing and valuing expensive items. When a customer has a claim, Chubb settles it fairly and fast. This high level of customer service drives the company, as evident from the comments of Kevin Day, claims manager:

> The foundation of our claim philosophy is to be responsive to the insured at a time of misfortune. We view a Chubb insurance policy as not just a commercial transaction, but as a relationship of trust between ourselves and the policy holder.

Chubb also uses a focused market scope and differentiated business strategy in other insurance areas. For example, it has strong positions in directors' and officers' liability and fidelity insurance markets. In both areas,

Chubb targets specific markets and customizes marketing strategies. Chubb has also built its expertise to become the largest insurer of other insurance companies.

The success of Chubb's organizational strategies is reflected in 1993 revenues of over $5 billion and net profits in excess of $635 million. Competitors have been trying to copy Chubb's approach, but with little success to date.

Questions:

1. How would you describe Chubb's corporate, business, and marketing strategies?

2. What are the keys to effective execution of these strategies?

3. What types of teamwork do you think are required to provide the personalized customer service delivered by Chubb?

4. Why have competitors not been able to copy Chubb's strategies?

Sources: Mark D. Fefer, "How to Win in a Land of Losers," *Fortune*, August 23, 1993, p. 80; and Kevin Day, personal conversation, January 17, 1994.

Case 4.2   *KinderCare: Getting back to basics*

KinderCare Learning Centers is the nation's only publicly traded company devoted entirely to child care. This was not always the case for the company. In the late 1980s, it moved into the retailing, banking, and insurance businesses with funding provided by high-risk junk bonds. Problems with these businesses forced the company into bankruptcy in 1992. In April 1993, the company emerged from bankruptcy with a new strategy.

The new strategy emphasizes a marketing philosophy and focuses KinderCare on child care, with existing and new child care businesses. The basic child care business consists of 1,160 centers in 39 states. Increased training of teachers is under way to help reduce teacher turnover, the biggest complaint of parents. There are also plans for international growth in Great Britain, and possibly New Zealand and Australia.

A new business area is the KinderCare at Work division, which caters to commuters. These centers are located close to commuter train stations. Hours are longer, and amenities such as free coffee are provided. The basic idea is to provide convenience to commuting parents.

Another new business area is the Kid's Choice division. These centers accept only children six years and up. The older children like this because they are not together with babies. Kid's Choice centers provide computers to use for homework and big screen TVs for movies. The centers are

located in shopping strips and malls, reducing facility costs substantially. Employee costs are also lower, because the centers need full staffing only before and after school.

Although these new business moves look promising, KinderCare is also considering building child care centers for large employers and running existing facilities for a fee. This offers tremendous growth potential and builds on the basic strengths of the company.

Regardless of the future growth strategies used, KinderCare is committed to a marketing philosophy of listening to customers and acting on what they say.

Questions:

1. How would you describe KinderCare's corporate, business, and marketing strategies?

2. What type of corporate growth strategy is KinderCare pursuing?

3. What trends in the marketing environment offer threats or opportunities for KinderCare?

4. What is your evaluation of KinderCare's new organizational strategies?

Source: Adapted from Susan Caminiti, "New Lessons in Customer Service," *Fortune*, September 20, 1993, pp. 79–80. © 1993 Time Inc. All rights reserved.

PART

Buying Behavior

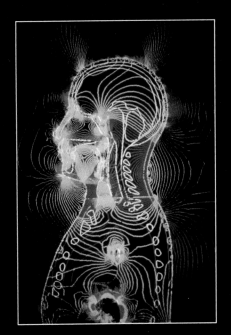

Buying behavior involves

simple and complex

decision processes.

*B*uying behavior includes the actions taken and decisions made by individual consumers for purchases for their personal and family needs, and the decisions and actions taken by buyers in business-to-business markets. How do consumer and business buyers make purchase decisions? What influences affect those decisions? How does consumer buying behavior differ from business buying behavior?

Chapter 5, "Consumer Buying Behavior and Decision Making," explores many of the key issues in consumer decision making and the major influences that affect consumer behavior. Key individual, social, and situational factors are discussed. Chapter 6, "Business-to-Business Markets and Buying Behavior," introduces the business buying process and describes the major business markets. The chapter focuses on business buying behavior and how it differs from consumer buying behavior.

chapter 5

Consumer Buying Behavior and Decision Making

After studying this chapter you should be able to:

1. Discuss the importance of consumer behavior.

2. Understand consumer decision making and some of the important influences on those decisions.

3. Distinguish between low-involvement and high-involvement consumer behavior.

4. Understand how attitudes influence consumer purchases.

5. Appreciate how the social environment affects consumer behavior.

6. Recognize many of the individual consumer differences that influence purchase decisions and behavior.

7. Recognize the outcomes of consumers' decisions to purchase or not to purchase and how they affect marketing success.

Hush Puppies: An old dog learns new tricks

*F*ew US industries have been hit harder by foreign competition than shoe manufacturers. Imports now account for more than 85 percent of US shoe sales. One success story in this industry involves Wolverine World Wide, Inc., and its Hush Puppies brand. Sales of Hush Puppies have grown dramatically and the company now operates worldwide with a licensing program that serves more than 60 countries, from Australia to Japan to Bulgaria. Hush Puppies is the number-one shoe brand in the world, selling 35,000 pairs per day in 65 countries.

For years, consumers associated Hush Puppies with a single, unexciting product: the brushed pigskin shoe. When it decided to expand the Hush Puppies line, Wolverine's challenge was to convey an image that appealed to many consumer lifestyles. With the help of Maggi Mercado, a renowned shoe designer, the company expanded its line to include men's and women's comfort dress, career casual, everyday casual, and outdoor. To support this expansion and to obtain needed cash, Wolverine sold its line of athletic shoes. The company plans to focus upon offering a variety of casual and work or outdoor footwear, appealing to the varied needs of price-sensitive consumers.

Wolverine continues to expand its international operations, as well. Efforts are under way to introduce the Hush Puppies brand into the Moscow market through the opening of specialty stores. Demand among Russian consumers for cheap, casual footwear is predicted to be great. The Moscow venture is based upon a licensing agreement in which Wolverine will receive royalties from sales paid part in hard currency and part in barter of raw pigskins. The latter will be used in future shoe production. Investment in specialty stores is unusual for companies entering Eastern markets. However, the anticipated demand among Russian consumers, who traditionally have had few limited value alternatives from which to choose, warrants the risk.

How has an understanding of consumer behavior enabled Wolverine to succeed? First, Wolverine expanded the image of the shoes to being more than a cheap footwear alternative. Second, the company recognized the global trend toward casual lifestyles and the increasing value orientation among consumers. Third, it understood the product attributes and benefits consumers now seek (cushioned comfort, excellent fit, superior quality, real value) and how beliefs about those attributes affect consumer purchase decisions.

Sources: Julie A. Cohen, "Footwear and the Jet Set," *Management Review*, March 1990, pp. 42–43; John P. Cortez, "Wolverine Seeks Agency to Run with Hush Puppy," *Ad Age*, February 22, 1993, p. 12; Beth Heitzman, "An Old Dog Learns New Tricks," *Adweek*, August 2, 1993, p. 2; Rita Koselka, "The Dog That Survived," *Forbes*, November 9, 1992, pp. 82 and 84; and "President's Letter," *1992 Wolverine World Wide Inc. Annual Report*, p. 3.

In the Hush Puppies example, an existing brand was successfully changed to appeal to different consumer segments. The success of these changes depended on an understanding of consumer behavior and the many influences that affect consumer decision making.

In this chapter, we define and explain the importance of consumer behavior. Then we use a model of consumer decision processes to explore consumer problem solving and decision making. Next, we describe important environmental, individual, and situational influences that affect consumer behavior. The chapter concludes with a discussion of the primary outcomes that can follow the purchase and use of products and services, as well as ethical issues and the rights of consumers.

The nature of consumer behavior and decision making

Consumer behavior can be defined as the mental and emotional processes and the physical activities that people engage in when they select, purchase, use, and dispose of products or services to satisfy particular needs and desires. Identifying and understanding consumer needs and preferences and their determinants is critical in the pursuit of profitable business opportunities.

Today a number of factors make it all the more important to understand consumer markets and individual consumer behavior: the mere size of the consumer market, changes in consumer shopping habits and purchase decisions, and the continuing emphasis on consumer-oriented marketing.

Size of the consumer market

The US consumer market consists of all individuals in the United States. In 1992, the consumption expenditures for this market were huge: $4.39 trillion out of a total gross domestic product of $6.37 trillion, or 69 percent.[1] Demand of this magnitude is well worth understanding. Moreover, competition for consumer dollars will increase as populations in the US and other countries age, resulting in declining expenditures for some products. Firms that understand consumer behavior will be best able to compete effectively.

Changes in the consumer market

Of equal importance are changes occurring in the consumer market. Some important trends affecting consumer buying behavior are detailed in Exhibit 5.1. They include consumers' concern for quality at reasonable and fair prices, for

Exhibit 5.1	A sampling of trends affecting consumer behavior and consumer marketing

- Shoppers increasingly economizing or downscaling to less expensive brands, searching for deals, waiting longer to rebuy, balancing quality & price consciousness.
- Consumers increasingly factoring environmental considerations of brand & company reputation into buying decisions.
- People finding shopping more distasteful, frustrating, time-consuming.
- Nontraditional methods of selling & buying—direct mail, catalog, home shopping, videotext—growing at remarkable rate; changes supported by improving communications technology.
- In-store selling evolving rapidly—as seen in product appeals on shopping carts, electronic ads above aisles, coupon dispensers attached to shelves.
- Consumers moving from conspicuous consumption to rational consumption & cautious use of finances.
- Consumers altering behaviors & diets to reflect greater concern for health & physical fitness.
- The aging of the population, longer life expectancies & lower birth rates making the over-50 segment a dominant force in society.
- Changes in family & workforce composition making men & women increasingly similar in choices of products & services.

the effects of their purchases on the environment, and for health and diet. Many of these trends offer opportunities, especially for firms pursuing the *quality/value* and *ecological perspectives.*

Nowhere are the complexities more obvious than in the food industry. The paradox here is that consumers may want low-fat, low-cholesterol salads for lunch and fish for dinner, but many also choose a hot fudge sundae for dessert. This means that some old-fashioned, middle-of-the-road products like ordinary ice cream are being squeezed by low-cal frozen yogurts on one side and extra-luscious, superpremium ice creams on the other.[2]

McDonald's and other restaurants reacted to consumer demands by offering new products with less fat and fewer calories, such as lean chicken sandwiches and salads, and by focusing on wholesomeness in ads. In addition, themes of value and high quality/low price are widely trumpeted to consumers.

Consumer-oriented marketing

To become more consumer oriented and to build long-lasting relationships with their customers, companies need to understand what motivates buyers. Ford Motor Company, for example, focuses on increased customer satisfaction and employee commitment. The company

- Is dedicated to being customer driven.

- Makes carefully thought-out decisions about the customers each product is to appeal to.

- Studies potential customers and what they most want.

- Develops detailed product attributes to fulfill customer wants; doesn't copy what someone else is doing.

- Follows up with customers to confirm that products and marketing programs meet objectives.[3]

To consistently deliver high-quality products and services, marketers must understand and respond to continually changing consumer needs and expectations.[4] And marketers with the best understanding and the least-biased perceptions of consumer needs will be the most competitive.[5] This constant striving to understand and better serve consumers reflects the pursuit of Total Quality Management (TQM) principles. **The Entrepreneurial Spirit: The Midas Touch** describes how one company succeeded by responding to consumer needs.

Häagen-Dazs targets chocolate lovers with its Triple Brownie Overload flavor. The company also targets health-conscious consumers with its line of frozen yogurt products.

The Midas touch

Carolee Designs offers an example of how an entrepreneur can become successful by anticipating consumer needs and providing innovative products that enhance consumer confidence. Carolee Designs, begun in 1972 in Carolee Friedlander's kitchen and backyard, is now a force in the fashion jewelry industry. Carolee's operations include headquarters and a product-development center in Greenwich, Connecticut; manufacturing plants in Connecticut and Rhode Island; retail outlets in New Jersey and New York; 12 in-store boutiques and 150 miniboutiques at upscale department stores; and 2,000 additional retailers that carry her products. The company's annual revenues are at $30 million and growing, achieved through tremendous effort and constant innovation.

Trained in ad design, Carolee Friedlander began making jewelry for her friends. However, her selling efforts began with her need for more family income. After many phone calls and days of standing in line to see buyers, in 1976 she finally obtained an order from Bloomingdale's. This helped establish her business.

In 1985, she ran a national ad campaign in magazines such as *Vogue*. These efforts involved considerable risk, for her funds were limited and the advertising was expensive. Yet, the campaign improved her image with both consumers and retailers. She also offered innovative display ideas to retailers and introduced the very successful Duchess of Windsor Jewel collection. Recently, she appeared on the QVC shopping network. Carolee advises potential entrepreneurs to take chances because competitors probably will not. However, successful innovation depends upon a thorough understanding of consumer decision making and the role that product beliefs and interpersonal influences play in determining those decisions.

Source: Gayle Sato Stodder, "The Midas Touch," *Entrepreneur,* February 1994, pp. 114–19. © 1994 by *Entrepreneur.* Reprinted with permission.

Consumer decision making

A general model of consumer decision making and influences on these decisions is presented in Exhibit 5.2. The consumer decision process, shown in the center of the model, assumes a conscious and logical decision-making process: from recognition of a need or problem to information search to evaluation of alternatives, and purchase. This sequence can be affected by the social environment, individual differences, and situational factors. All have implications for the design and implementation of successful marketing strategy.

The consumer decision process

A consumer's recognition of a *need* or *problem* may come out of an internal desire, the absence or failure of a product, or some external influence such as advertising. It can be as simple as getting thirsty and wanting a soda or having to replace a used or an outdated product or one that has lost its appeal. Advertising may also trigger the consumer's perception of a need or serve as a reminder.

After recognizing a problem, the consumer engages in search for information. An *internal search* involves a review of information stored in memory. Although readily available, internal information may be incomplete or inaccurate. An *external search* involves gathering information from marketing sources such as advertising or from nonmarketing sources such as friends or *Consumer Reports*. Nonmarketing sources of information may be particularly useful because they are likely unbiased.

After searching for information, the consumer evaluates possibilities (products, brands). This *evaluation of alternatives* is based on the individual's beliefs about the products and their features or characteristics. These beliefs form the basis for the consumer's attitudes, which influence intentions to buy and purchase

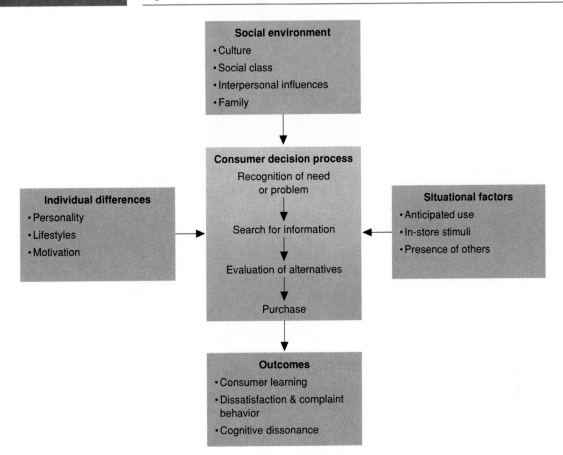

Exhibit 5.2   **A general model of consumer decision making and influences**

behavior. Following purchase, outcomes such as feelings of satisfaction or dissatisfaction and the development of brand loyalty may occur.

Consumer behavior is a complex phenomenon, and many internal and external factors may influence an individual decision. Many decisions are motivated by specific needs and values; some involve a conscious and logical decision process; others are made with little or no thought.

EXECUTIVE ROUNDTABLE COMMENT | Bobbie Oglesby, manager of small and medium business marketing for Apple Computers, comments upon the importance of understanding consumer decision-making processes:

Consumer awareness of our computers has always been high. However, we have encountered problems at the evaluation stage of consumer decisions. Apple was sometimes dropped from consumer consideration because buyers did not know Apple products were MS-DOS compatible. Now, we continue to promote compatibility as a major message in our promotions and in marketing events. As awareness of our products' compatibility increases, the evaluation of our computers also increases.

High- and low-involvement decisions

Involvement represents the level of importance or interest generated by a product or a decision. It varies by the situation or the product decision at hand and is influenced by the person's needs or motives. Frequently, involvement is affected by how closely the purchase decision is linked to one's self-concept and how personally relevant the product is to the consumer.

High-involvement decisions are characterized by high levels of importance, thorough information processing, and substantial differences between alternatives.

This Saturn ad promotes the value of consumer search. Here, a testimonial is offered regarding the benefits of search and the evaluation of alternatives.

The choice of a college to attend, the purchase of a home or vehicle, or the purchase of a bike for a sports enthusiast are all examples of high-involvement decisions. As such, high-involvement decisions are consistent with the logical and thoughtful sequence shown in the center of the consumer behavior model in Exhibit 5.2.

High involvement may be caused by a number of personal, product, and situational factors.[6] Again, importance of the purchase to one's self-concept increases involvement. If financial or performance risk is high, the decision is more likely to have high involvement. High involvement is also more likely when a gift is purchased or social pressures occur.

Low-involvement decisions occur when relatively little personal interest, relevance, or importance is associated with a purchase. These decisions involve much simpler decision processes, and little information processing, than the sequence described in Exhibit 5.2. For low-involvement decisions, consumers do not actively seek large amounts of information. Low-involvement purchases

This New York State Lottery ad uses a simple message and funny theme to encourage consumers to imagine the benefits of Lotto loot. Would the purchase of lottery tickets be a high-involvement or low-involvement decision for most consumers?

may include soft drinks, fast foods, toothpaste, and many snack foods. In these instances, repetitive purchase behavior may develop. Since these decisions involve little risk, trial purchases are often the consumer's major means of information search and product or brand evaluation.[7]

Consumer problem solving

Consumer decisions are often described as involving one of three types of problem-solving effort: routinized response behavior and limited or extensive problem solving. The type of decision is important to marketers because it influences the nature of the communications they should use to market their products, and hence, affects the productivity of their expenditures.

In **routinized response behavior,** some need results in a quick, habitual decision with limited search for information: if you are out of your favorite shampoo, you buy some more. The decision process is quite simple and results in a purchase from the consumer's set of acceptable brands. Generally, the consumer requires information only about price and availability. These decisions are relatively automatic, with minimal mental effort and little related search for alternative brands. Routinized response behavior, then, is often reflected in low-involvement decision making and in brand-loyal purchase patterns.

At the other extreme, **extensive problem solving** involves considerable mental effort and substantial search for information. Many high-involvement decisions result in extensive problem solving. The first purchase occasion for many complex and expensive products, for example, typically involves extensive problem solving. Even the criteria on which the choice will be made (the product attributes) must be learned. In the first purchase of a computer or a stereo system, unless the decision is turned over to someone else, the buyer may obtain much information about features, makes, models, and prices. He or she must then process this information and consider the alternative brands.

Limited problem solving reflects an intermediate situation. Here the consumer encounters an unfamiliar brand in a familiar product class. For instance, a sports enthusiast may see a new brand of running shoes or golf clubs. Although understanding the relevant product attributes, the consumer must obtain sufficient information to evaluate the new brand on these criteria.

Types of consumer choices

Actually, the acquisition of goods and services is made up of many choices. At least six generic choices may be involved in consumer behavior: product, brand, shopping area, store type, store, and, to an increasing degree, nonstore source (catalogs, PC and TV shopping).[8] The decision-making processes and the influences on those decisions discussed in this chapter apply to all six of these choices. Later, the chapter on retailing addresses the last four decisions directly.

EXECUTIVE ROUNDTABLE COMMENT | **Bobbie Oglesby, manager of small and medium business marketing for Apple Incorporated, points out that consumers' decision processes affect what and where they buy:**

Today, as more computer purchases are made by experienced, repeat buyers, the decision process is becoming less complex. As a result, *where* the customer is buying has changed. New forms of distribution are flourishing—primarily computer superstores and mail order. These outlets are appealing to the knowledgeable buyer more interested in price and availability than the traditional support offered by the computer specialty store. Apple recognizes these changes in consumer behavior and has adapted its distribution strategies appropriately.

Attitudes

Attitudes and attitude formation are related to the evaluation stage of the consumer decision process. **Consumer attitudes** are learned predispositions to respond favorably or unfavorably to a product or brand. Most of us take for granted our attitudes toward our favorite restaurant or soft drink. However, attitudes are instrumental in determining which alternative products and brands will be purchased and used.

An understanding of consumer attitudes has very basic implications for marketing, for two reasons. Attitudes are based on beliefs consumers hold about the attributes or features (price, level of service, quality) of the products being evaluated. In many instances, these attributes form the basis for the development of marketing strategies. And attitudes are primary causes of behavior, which makes them very relevant to marketers who want to understand why consumers buy—or do not buy—their products.

Influence of the social environment

A number of external influences affect consumer behavior and purchase decision processes. The social environment directly affects sources of information consumers use in decision making and product evaluations. In many instances, personal sources, such as family and friends, may be more credible and influential to consumers than any other source of information.

The most important social influences are culture, subculture, social class, family, and interpersonal or reference group influences. These flows of influence within the social environment are summarized in Exhibit 5.3.

Cultural influences

Culture refers to the values, ideas, attitudes, and symbols that people adopt to communicate, interpret, and interact as members of society. In fact, culture describes a society's way of life. Culture is learned and transmitted from one generation to the next. It includes abstract elements (values, attitudes, ideas, religion), and material elements (symbols, buildings, products, brands). The process of absorbing a culture is called **socialization**. It continues throughout one's life and produces many specific preferences for products and services, shopping patterns, and interactions with others. Applied to marketing and consumer behavior, it is referred to as *consumer socialization*.

The concept of culture has two primary implications for marketing: it determines the most basic values that influence consumer behavior patterns, and it

Exhibit 5.3   **Flows of influence within the social environment**

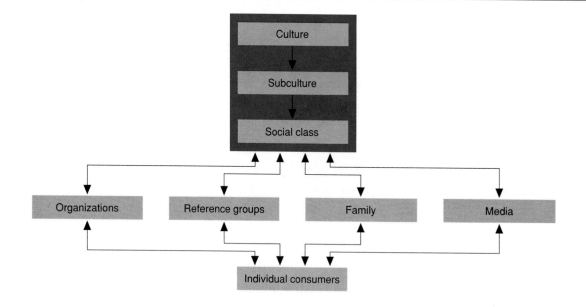

can be used to distinguish subcultures that represent substantial market segments and opportunities.

Values

Values are shared beliefs or cultural norms about what is important or right. Values, such as the need to belong or to succeed, represent important goals to which consumers subscribe. A society's values are transmitted to the individual through the family, through organizations (schools, religious institutions, businesses), and through other people (the community, the social environment).

Cultural values directly influence how consumers view and use individual products, brands, and services. One typology of values used by consumer researchers is the List of Values (LOV).[9] It includes nine basic values:

- Self-respect
- Warm relationships with others
- Self-fulfillment
- Respect from others
- Excitement

- Security
- Sense of accomplishment
- Sense of belonging
- Fun and enjoyment in life

Values influence the goals people pursue and the behavior used to pursue those goals. Many marketing communication campaigns recognize the importance of values as advertising themes and justification for purchase. For example, the desire for recognition and self-fulfillment is frequently used by companies selling self-improvement and exercise products. Or, the sense of belonging forms the basis for marketing many personal and gift products.

Subcultures

The norms and values of specific groups or subcultures within a society are called **ethnic patterns.** Ethnic groups or subcultures may be formed around national, religious, racial, or geographic factors. Members of a subculture share similar values and patterns of behavior, making them attractive marketing targets for specific products and brands.

Porsche targets upscale drivers with ads that appeal to self-fulfillment and excitement.

Exhibit 5.4

Class distinctions: You are what you choose

		Lower Middle	Middle	Upper Middle
Car	1980s	Hyundai	Chevrolet Celebrity	Mercedes
	1990s	Geo	Chrysler minivan	Range Rover
Business shoe (men)	1980s	Sneakers	Wingtips	Cap toes
	1990s	Boots	Rockports	Loafers
Business shoe (women)	1980s	Spike-heel pumps	Mid-heel pumps	High-heel pumps
	1990s	High-heel pumps	Dressy flats	One-inch pumps
Alcoholic beverage	1980s	Domestic beer	White wine spritzer	Dom Perignon
	1990s	Domestic lite beer	California Chardonnay	Cristal
Leisure pursuit	1980s	Watching sports	Going to movies	Golf
	1990s	Playing sports	Renting movies	Playing with computers
Hero	1980s	Roseanne Barr	Ronald Reagan	Michael Milken
	1990s	Kathie Lee Gifford	Janet Reno	Rush Limbaugh

Unique subcultures often develop in geographic areas of a nation. The Southwest US is known for casual lifestyles, outdoor living, and active sports.[10] The Southeast is associated with a conservative lifestyle and friendly atmosphere. One system divides North America into "nine nations": the Foundry (industrial Northeast); Dixie; Ectopia (northern Pacific Rim); Mexamericana (Southwest area); the Breadbasket (Kansas, Nebraska, Iowa, etc.); Quebec (French-speaking Canada); the Empty Quarter (Northwest Canada); the Islands (tip of southern Florida, Caribbean Islands, some Latin American influence); and New England.[11] Each region contains many individuals who share similar values and lifestyles.

The black and Hispanic subcultures, while diverse themselves, are the largest ethnic subcultures. The black subculture is growing in size and spending power. ispanics make up the second-fastest-growing subculture, behind the Asian subculture. Many Hispanics share a common language and a strong family orientation. Conservative Christian areas and Jewish centers also represent subcultures of influence.

Social class influences

Social classes are relatively homogeneous divisions within a society that contain people with similar values, needs, lifestyles, and behavior. One approach for consumer analysis describes four social classes: upper, middle, working, and lower class, each of which can be further subdivided.[12] Identification with a social class is influenced most strongly by level of education and occupation. Social class is also affected by social skill, status aspirations, community participation, cultural level, and family history.[13] Social classes are relatively stable, but educational experiences and career moves enable individuals to shift from one class to another. Today, the middle class is declining in size. Economic conditions have limited upward mobility of the working class and caused many borderline families to fall into poverty.[14]

Social class influences the types of purchases consumers make and the activities they pursue. Who goes to wrestling matches and who goes to the opera? Who plays polo and who goes bowling? Exhibit 5.4 summarizes some of the differences among subclasses of the middle class. Although preferences do change within

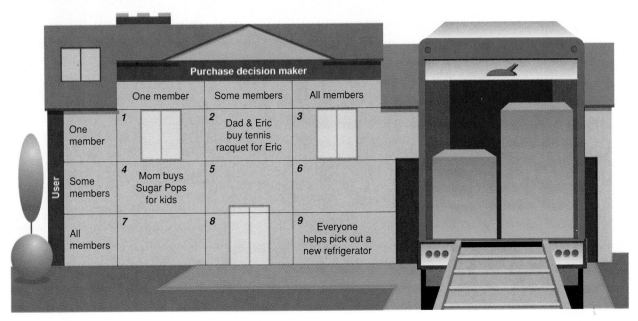

Exhibit 5.5 **Family buyer and user differences across purchase categories**

Family purchases fall into nine categories, depending on who makes
the purchase decision & who uses the item purchased.

classes over time, as evidenced by the differences between the 1980s and 90s, significant differences in purchases and behaviors occur between classes.

Family influences and the family life cycle

Family influences play two important roles: in the socialization of people and in affecting individual purchase decisions. Families are the most influential factor on an individual's behavior, values, and attitudes. Patterns of behavior and values learned early in life are not easily changed. Lifestyles (athleticism, fondness for outdoors) are usually learned from parents through **childhood consumer socialization**—the process by which young people acquire skills, knowledge, and attitudes relevant to their functioning as consumers in the marketplace.[15]

Individual family members also influence purchase decisions through their performance of different roles within the family. Members of a family or household may assume different roles—and roles may change, depending on the situation. In the choice of toys, for example, parents often determine the acceptable set of brands children may select from. The parents make the decision to buy, yet the child makes the brand choice. In other cases, all family members may influence decisions to purchase large-ticket items such as homes and automobiles. Increasingly, men and teenagers are doing the grocery shopping; and marketers target these shoppers with ads in the magazines they buy.

Today, the role of children and teenagers within a family, and even as a market themselves, cannot be underestimated. One estimate is that 4- to 12-year-olds influence purchases valued at more than $130 billion annually.[16] These influences affect choices of food items, clothing, restaurants, entertainment, and even automobiles. A grid showing how family influences relate to different product decisions appears in Exhibit 5.5. It crosses the number of decision makers with the number of users, identifying nine categories of family influence, depending on who makes the purchase decision and who uses the item. Cereal, as shown in cell 4, might be consumed by multiple members of the family but selected by the primary grocery shopper.[17]

Family life cycle is also relevant to consumer behavior. It describes the sequence of steps a family goes through, from young, single adults to the married

Exhibit 5.6

Changing shares of household types

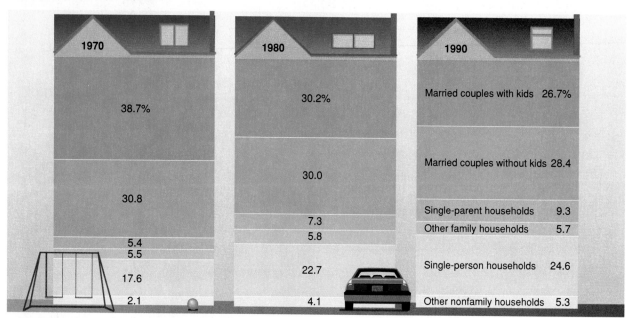

Note: Totals for 1970 and 1980 are 100.1% due to rounding.

couple whose children have left home to, possibly, the retired survivor. The family life cycle suggests ways to develop marketing strategies and design products and services. Household consumption patterns vary dramatically across the family life cycle. Appliances and insurance are bought for the first time during the early stages, for instance. Luxury products, travel, and recreation are typical expenditures for middle-aged adults with no children at home. Product variations are tailored for specific stages of the family life cycle, such as Campbell's soups or Chef-Boy-R-Dee pasta packaged in smaller sizes for households of single or older consumers.

Changing family life cycles also have implications for product needs and buying behavior. Dramatic increases in age associated with first marriages, women working outside the home, single parents, premarital births, single-person households, childless couples, divorces, remarriages, alternate forms of living arrangements, and lower fertility rates have produced striking changes in families and households.[18] Exhibit 5.6 shows the decline in the number of households comprising married couples with children at home and the increase in single-parent and single-person households. These trends may decrease demand for large dining room tables, but they are good news for businesses that sell smaller tables, refrigerators, televisions, cleaning products, and other one-to-a-household items.[19]

Interpersonal influences

Marketers also recognize interpersonal influences beyond the family, including friends, co-workers, and others. These sources of influence are often referred to as **reference groups,** or those others look to for help and guidance. They may be groups a person belongs to and ones he or she admires or wants to join.

Interpersonal influence processes

Three types of interpersonal processes—informational, utilitarian, and value-expressive—form the basis for interpersonal influences. **Informational influence** is based on the consumer's desire to make informed choices and reduce uncertainty.

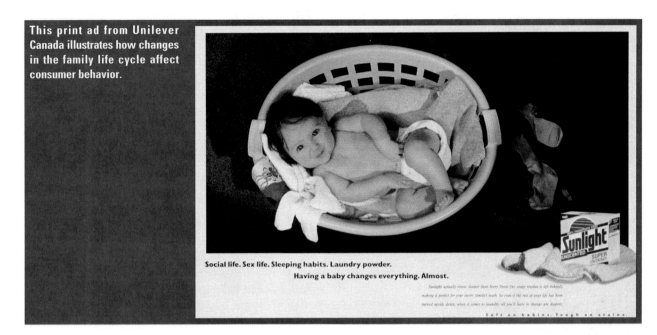

This print ad from Unilever Canada illustrates how changes in the family life cycle affect consumer behavior.

When we need to buy a complex product or face a new decision, we often seek information and advice from others we trust.

Utilitarian influence is reflected in compliance with the expectations, real or imagined, of others. These expectations are referred to as *norms*. Compliance to norms occurs in efforts to achieve rewards or avoid punishments. Rewards and punishments in day-to-day consumer behavior involve acceptance and peer approval and disapproval. These normative influences are particularly acute for young people. Sometimes these can be negative influences, such as peer pressure to use drugs, alcohol, or tobacco.

Value-expressive influence stems from a desire to enhance self-concept through identification with others. These influences are seen in the frequent use of popular spokespersons and attractive models in much consumer advertising. Celebrity endorsements from Olympic medalist Nancy Kerrigan, actor Bill Cosby, and model Cindy Crawford are intended to encourage identification with these figures through brand purchases. In other instances, products or brands are purchased in support of one's real or desired image.

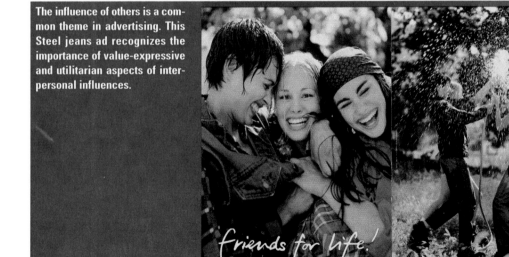

The influence of others is a common theme in advertising. This Steel jeans ad recognizes the importance of value-expressive and utilitarian aspects of interpersonal influences.

Exhibit 5.7	Reference group influence on product and brand purchase decisions	
Product ⟍ Brand	Weak reference group influence (−)	Strong reference group influence (+)
Strong reference group influence (+)	**Public necessities** *Influence:* Weak product & strong brand *Examples:* Wristwatch, automobile, business suit	**Public luxuries** *Influence:* Strong product & brand *Examples:* Golf clubs, snow skis, sailboat
Weak reference group influence (−)	**Private necessities** *Influence:* Weak product & brand *Examples:* Mattress, floor lamp, refrigerator	**Private luxuries** *Influence:* Strong product & weak brand *Examples:* Video game, pool table, CD player

Opinion leaders and market mavens

Some people, traditionally labeled **opinion leaders,** influence consumer behavior through word-of-mouth communications. Opinion leaders were originally viewed as intermediaries between sources of information, such as advertising and other media, and the consumer. Their influence often stems from their involvement and interest or expertise in particular products. Marketers now recognize that communication flows both from and toward opinion leaders.

Market mavens are another type of information diffuser. These are consumers who know about many kinds of products, places to shop, and other facets of the market, and they like to share this information with other consumers.[20] Market mavens are similar to opinion leaders in that their influence is based on general marketplace knowledge and expertise. They do not necessarily adopt new products or even use the products they are knowledgeable about; but they influence other people's choices and diffuse information on new products.

Word-of-mouth influence operates in other ways as well. For example, MCI uses relationship marketing in its "friends and family" campaign by mentioning the names of current customers to targeted individuals. MCI customers thus become spokespeople through their own networks of interpersonal relationships.[21]

Luxuries and necessities

Interpersonal influences on buying behavior vary across product types and depend on two conditions: whether a product is a luxury or a necessity and whether it will be used largely in public or in private.[22] If the product is consumed visibly, social approval and the effects of others' opinions may be important. Necessity products are owned by virtually everyone; hence the influence of others for necessities is on the brand purchased, not on product ownership.

Exhibit 5.7 gives an overview of the effects of public versus private consumption. Note that interpersonal influence on product *and* brand decisions is weak in the case of private necessities. In the case of public luxuries, interpersonal influence is thought to be strong for both product ownership and brand selection decisions. The strength of interpersonal influence varies for other combinations of luxury/necessity and public/private buying behavior.

Individual differences

A vast number of individual differences can influence consumer behavior. Some of the most important include personality, lifestyles and psychographics, and motivation.

Personality

Personality reflects a person's consistent response to his or her environment. It has been linked to differences in susceptibility to persuasion and social influence and thereby to purchase behavior. General personality traits related to consumer behavior include extroversion, self-esteem, dogmatism (closed-mindedness), and aggressiveness. For example, dogmatism might limit product trial or the adoption of product innovations for some consumers; aggressiveness may be related to the purchase of certain types of sporty cars and to consumer complaint behavior in reaction to unsatisfactory purchases. Self-esteem is thought to be inversely related to persuasibility—the more self-esteem, the less subject to persuasion—and has implications for the effectiveness of marketing communications.

The use of general personality measures to explain purchase behavior has been disappointing. Researchers need to develop marketing or consumer-related measures to determine the role of personality in the consumer decision process and explore whether findings can be generalized across product and service classes. Such consumer-related measures would help in identifying market segments and creating and sustaining effective promotional campaigns.

The notion of *self-concept* is one idea used to explain the products consumers buy and use. Self-concept is the overall perception and feeling that one has about herself or himself. Consumers buy products and brands that are consistent with or enhance their self-concept.[23]

Marketers try to create relationships between their products or services and consumers. Marketers can affect consumers' motivation to learn about, shop for, and buy the sponsored brand by influencing the degree to which people perceive a product to be related to their self-concept. This objective is clear in the many ads that emphasize image enhancement and personal improvement through use of the advertiser's brand of product or service.[24]

Lifestyles and psychographics

An outgrowth from attempts to use personality measures to explain consumer behavior are the concepts of lifestyle and psychographics. *Lifestyle* describes a person's pattern of living as expressed in activities, interests, and opinions (AIOs). Lifestyle traits are more concrete than personality traits and more directly linked to the acquisition, use, and disposition of goods and services.[25]

Psychographics divide a market into lifestyle segments on the basis of consumer interests, values, opinions, personality characteristics, attitudes, and demographics.[26] Marketers use lifestyle and psychographic information to develop marketing communications and product strategies. For example, responses to questions about the frequency of outdoor activity, cultural arts viewing, and opinions on social issues can be related to product use and then used as the basis for advertising themes and other marketing communications.

Motivation

Motivation refers to a state or condition within a person that prompts goal-directed behavior. Motivation generally occurs with recognition of some need or problem and can affect information search, information processing, and purchase behavior.[27] For example, washing machine owners are not routinely motivated to evaluate washing machine ads. But if their Maytag bites the dust, they will be motivated to evaluate washing machine brands. Motivation involves both energy and focus. Motives themselves may be obvious or hidden.

Researchers frequently cite the classification of motives proposed by Abraham Maslow.[28] In this approach, individuals evolve in their personal growth, with higher-level needs (esteem, self-actualization) becoming important only after lower-level needs (physiological, safety) are satisfied. Any unfulfilled needs

Appeals to safety and love needs are illustrated in this Honda ad.

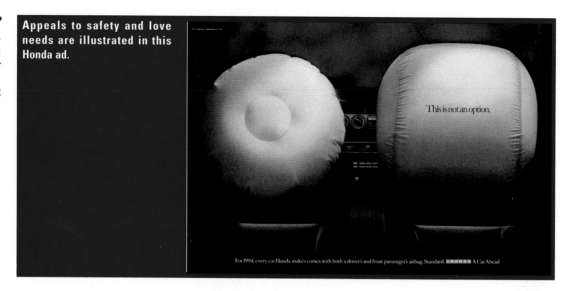

This is not an option.

For 1994, every car Honda makes comes with both a driver's and front passenger's airbag. Standard. HONDA A Car Ahead

are assumed to be "prepotent" and provide the most immediate motivation for behavior. Levels of needs in Maslow's hierarchy and examples of associated product purchases include:

Self-actualization needs—Art, books, recreation.

Esteem needs—Clothing, home furnishings.

Love and belonging needs—Mementos, gifts, photographs.

Safety needs—Burglar alarms, seat belts.

Physiological needs—Food, heat, shelter.

Motives that drive consumer behavior are affected by an individual's environment, including marketing communications and reference group influences. The productivity of marketing communications is enhanced when marketers position products to satisfy consumers' needs and the motivations that generate them.

Situational factors

In addition to the social environment and individual consumer characteristics, situational influences also affect consumer behavior.[29] Situational influences can involve purchases for anticipated situations, such as special occasions, and unanticipated occurrences, such as time pressures, unexpected expenses, and changed plans. In-store sales promotions and advertising can exert situational influences on consumers as they often make buying decisions while shopping. A common in-store situational factor is music, long considered an effective means for triggering moods. One study reveals that grocery store sales volume was significantly higher with slow rather than with fast music.[30]

Situational determinants of consumer behavior can be summarized as follows:

• Consumers purchase many goods for use in certain situations, and the anticipated use influences choice. Gift giving and social occasions are often important determinants of purchase behavior.

The ultimate sell

Some people entering the grocery store do not know the exact brands or even the products they will purchase—they decide among brands while they are in the store. Sometimes, product purchase decisions have not been made as well. How often do you go to the store in search of "something to eat" for the evening or weekend? In these cases, little planning precedes the consumer decision. Some retailers believe that up to 80 percent of consumer decisions are made in-store.

This is pretty alarming to consumer-goods companies that spend more than $70 billion annually on advertising and distribute over 300 billion cents-off coupons, of which only 7 billion ever get cashed in. Now, however, VideOcart brings brand advertising right to the supermarket, exposing consumers to advertising as they walk the aisles. The device, which includes a video screen on the shopping cart, is activated by infrared "triggers" placed throughout the store. Ads pop up at precisely the moment the buyer is confronted with the products on the shelves.

VideOcart, Inc., has already managed to get some of the biggest names in the packaged-goods business to participate. Companies such as Procter & Gamble, PepsiCo, Nabisco, and Ralston Purina pay about $4 to reach 1,000 consumers, compared to $7 for a newspaper coupon insert and $10 to $12 for a prime-time network commercial. Initial tests revealed that VideOcart shoppers bought more in total and that promoted-brand sales exceeded other brands from 5 percent to 60 percent.

Source: Joshua Levine, "The Ultimate Sell," *Forbes,* May 13, 1991, p. 108; "VideOcart Shopping Cart with Computer Screen Creates New Ad Medium That Also Gathers Data," *Marketing News,* May 9, 1988, p. 2; Terence A. Shimp, *Promotion Management and Marketing Communications,* 2nd ed. (Chicago: The Dryden Press, 1990), p. 365; Larry Stevens, "Front-Line Systems," *Computerworld,* March 2, 1992, pp. 61–63; William H. Bolen, "Shopper Takes VideOcart for Test Drive, Finds It a Pleasant Experience," *Marketing News,* March 16, 1992, p. 6; and Kate Fitzgerald, "Paper Coupons Losing Lure in High-Tech Store," *Ad Age,* March 21, 1994, pp. 5–14.

- Situational factors can be inhibitors as well as motivators. Inhibitors that constrain consumer behavior include time or budget constraints.

- The likely influence of situations varies with the product. Consumers buy clothing items, books, and many food products with anticipated uses in mind.

Situational store factors within the retail environment are also important. These store conditions include physical layout, atmospherics, location, the presence of others, the assistance of salespeople, and in-store stimuli. For example, **The Technological Edge: The Ultimate Sell** discusses an in-store technique that is emerging as an important situational determinant of the brands consumers select in the grocery store. Other merchandisers also try to capitalize on situational factors in developing their marketing plans. Gas stations have evolved into multiline convenience stores, for instance, and fast-food chains cater to situational needs with drive-through services.

Advertising often incorporates situational use into its message themes. For example, consider the well-known message "use Arm & Hammer Baking Soda as a refrigerator deodorant." This ad suggests the target brand (Arm & Hammer) as a reasonable choice for the target situation. In contrast, some ads compare the target brand with another product already associated with that situation ("Eat Orville Redenbacher Popcorn instead of potato chips as an afternoon snack"). Other situation comparison ads associate the use of the target brand in a new situation with its use in a more familiar situation ("Special K breakfast cereal is as good at snack time as it is at breakfast").[31]

Consumer behavior outcomes

The study of consumer behavior does not end at purchase. Other phenomena or outcomes may and often do occur. These include consumer learning; consumer satisfaction, dissatisfaction, and complaint behavior; and cognitive dissonance.

Consumer learning

When marketers set out to influence consumers, they typically try to implant knowledge through advertising, product labels, and personal selling appeals—methods that are efficient and can be controlled by the marketer. Marketers hope consumers will attend to, comprehend, and then remember these messages. Yet, consumers also learn by experience. Experiential learning is highly interactive, and consumers often give it special status—"experience is the best teacher."

Consumer learning happens when changes occur in knowledge or behavior patterns. Learning as knowledge gained is consistent with the decision process we have described.[32] Learning as behavior is also a critical outcome. Because successful marketing depends on repeat purchase behavior, providing positive reinforcement for the desired behavior is crucial.[33]

EXECUTIVE ROUNDTABLE COMMENT | Bobbie Oglesby, manager of small and medium business marketing for Apple Computers, notes the importance of consumer learning:

Steve Jobs, one of Apple's founders, recognized the power of behavior learned early in life. Large donations of Apple products to schools nationwide exposed students to Apple products. This influenced family purchases and continues to influence business purchases today. IBM later recognized the impact of this strategy and began a similar program.

Consumer satisfaction, dissatisfaction, and complaint behavior

Consumer satisfaction, dissatisfaction, and complaint behavior are also important outcomes of consumer purchase decision processes. *Satisfaction* and *dissatisfaction* describe the positive, neutral, or negative feelings that may occur after purchase; *consumer complaints* are overt expressions of dissatisfaction.

Judgments of satisfaction and dissatisfaction result from comparisons between a person's expectations about a purchased product and the product's actual performance.[34] Purchases that turn out worse than expected result in **negative disconfirmation** and negative feelings. Purchases that turn out better than expected, or **positive disconfirmation,** are evaluated positively.

A simple model of consumer satisfaction-dissatisfaction relationships is depicted in Exhibit 5.8. First, the consumer's prior experiences with products and brands establish expectations. When you take your car to be serviced or repaired, what expectations do you have? Consumers thus develop expectations about what a product or service should be able to provide. Comparison between the buyer's expectations and the product or service performance levels results in the confirmation or disconfirmation of expectations and the outcomes of satisfaction or dissatisfaction. These positive or negative feelings serve then as input into the formation of future attitudes and expectations. Although disconfirmation is generally considered the most important determinant of satisfaction, expectations and performance directly influence satisfaction also. This is consistent with research showing that consumers with higher expectations experience higher levels of satisfaction and that performance, independent of positive or negative disconfirmation, exerts a direct effect on feelings of satisfaction.[35] Similarly, research on cars shows that consumers with high product involvement tend to be more satisfied with their purchases than less-involved car owners.[36] Regardless, however, firms adopting a *quality/value perspective* must employ marketing communications that convey realistic expectations.

Exhibit 5.8

A model of consumer satisfaction

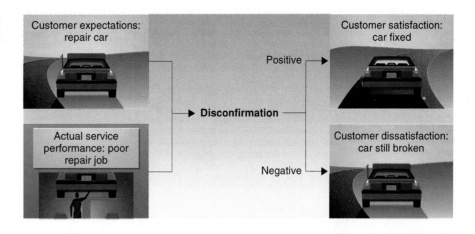

Customer expectations: repair car

Actual service performance: poor repair job

Disconfirmation

Positive

Negative

Customer satisfaction: car fixed

Customer dissatisfaction: car still broken

Besides influencing subsequent expectations and purchase behavior, dissatisfaction can result in several forms of consumer complaints: **voice responses** (seeking satisfaction directly from the seller), **private responses** (bad-mouthing to friends), and **third-party responses** (taking legal action, filing complaints with consumer affairs agencies).[37] Remember that word-of-mouth personal communications are very credible and influential.

Complaints are customer feedback about products, services, and company performance that marketers should never take lightly. Dissatisfied customers talk to more people than satisfied customers; but most dissatisfied customers never make a complaint to the company.[38] Because new customers are harder to find, maintaining satisfaction among existing customers should be paramount.

Consistent with the *relationship perspective,* to gain feedback some companies even encourage their customers to complain. Companies that know what is bothering their customers have a better chance of correcting problems, retaining sales, and preventing further damage.[39] At Dell Computer Corporation, the mail-order PC marketer, staff and managers meet every Friday morning to review customer complaints. The Dell vision is that every customer must be pleased, not merely satisfied.[40] In the same way, Coca-Cola wants to hear from its customers when they have a problem. According to its consumer affairs department, "Consumers who have a good experience with our company tell an average of five other people; but those who have a bad experience will tell twice as many people."[41]

Cognitive dissonance

The final consumer behavior outcome we consider is **cognitive dissonance,** a form of postpurchase doubt about the appropriateness of a decision.[42] Cognitive dissonance may occur over major choices, such as college decisions and purchases of homes and expensive furniture, stereo systems, and appliances. Most students remember some uneasiness about whether they made the best choice of a college to attend. This uneasiness is caused by an imbalance of information because each alternative has attractive features. Cognitive dissonance is most likely to occur when the purchase is important, perceived risk is high, the purchase is visible, and the decision involves a long-term commitment.

Dissonance can affect postpurchase attitudes, change behavior, and cause additional information seeking. Strategies marketers can use to reduce postpurchase cognitive dissonance include regular programs of follow-up communications with buyers to discourage doubt and reinforce convictions about product strengths; solid service and maintenance plans to provide reassurance and increase postpurchase satisfaction; and warranty agreements arranged after purchase to protect buyers against problems that may occur.

This Audi ad targeted at French consumers is designed to inhibit dissonance by reminding them: *"Ten-year anti-corrosion guarantee. To handle those shocks an Audi 80 simply cannot avoid. There's no room for chance with an Audi."*

Ethical and social issues

Some instances of consumer and business behavior raise ethical and social concerns.

Consumer behavior

Unethical consumer behaviors include shoplifting and abuse of return policies. Shoplifting losses represent a tremendous cost to retailers and eventually to other consumers as retailers pass on the costs. Abuse of a company's return policies is also unethical; returns should be made only for reasonable problems.[43]

On the positive side, consumers are increasingly incorporating social concerns into their buying decisions. Environmentally concerned consumers show high awareness of label information and product content. Companies maintaining an *ecological perspective* market their products with messages and product information that recognize these environmental concerns.

Other consumer behaviors driven by ethical and social motivations are less personal and more political. For example, 1970s boycotts of infant formula products sold in Third World countries, and suspended in the mid-80s, have reemerged because consumers believe the manufacturer failed to live up to its promise of ethical practice. Minority and gay rights groups use their buying power to express opinions about political issues.[44] "Buy American" campaigns recognize the effects of individual consumer behavior on jobs and local economies.

Business behavior

As discussed earlier in Chapter 2, business behavior must meet two standards: corporate social responsibility and business ethics. For example, firms are expected to provide safe products for reasonable prices. Their actions are not expected to detract from the general well-being of consumers. Efforts to monitor waste and the effects of production on the environment stem from these firm

Although this warning takes a humorous approach, shoplifting is a serious crime, and merchants pass its costs to consumers through price increases.

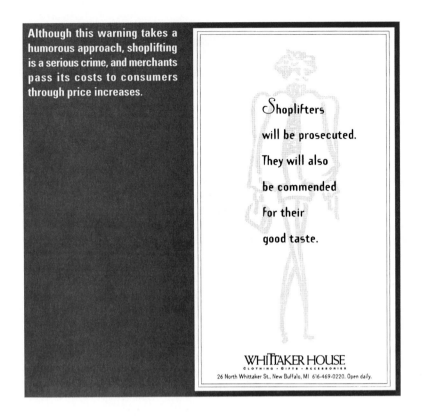

$\mathcal{S}$hoplifters will be prosecuted. They will also be commended for their good taste.

WHITTAKER HOUSE
CLOTHING · GIFTS · ACCESSORIES
26 North Whittaker St., New Buffalo, MI 616-469-0220. Open daily.

responsibilities. Likewise, marketing practices should not offend individuals or specific groups. Hence, liquor and tobacco advertising has moderated in recent years; and tobacco advertising has been banned from the networks. Many liquor companies, such as Coors and Budweiser, now emphasize responsible use of their products.

Consumer rights

In the early 1960s, President John Kennedy identified four inherent consumer rights:

- **The right to safety**—to be protected against products and services that are hazardous to health and life.

- **The right to be informed**—to be protected against fraudulent, deceitful, or misleading advertising or other information that could interfere with making an informed choice.

- **The right to choose**—to have access to competitive products that are priced fairly and are of satisfactory quality.

- **The right to be heard**—that consumer interests will be fully and fairly considered in the formulation and administration of government policy.[45]

Unfortunately, violations of these rights are not uncommon. Deceptive advertising and pricing practices and unsafe and poor-quality products exist; and there may be plenty of obstacles standing between policymakers and those who feel aggrieved by business practices.

Summary

1. *Discuss the importance of consumer behavior.*
Marketers must understand consumer behavior to develop successful strategies and identify target market segments. Furthermore, awareness of emerging trends in the consumer marketplace is essential for quick recognition of and response to problems and opportunities with sound marketing strategies.

2. *Understand consumer decision making and some of the important influences on those decisions.* Consumer behavior describes the mental and physical activities that people engage in when they select, purchase, use, and dispose of products and services purchased to satisfy needs and desires. The traditional view of consumer decision making is sequential: recognition of problem, search for information (either internal or external), evaluation of alternatives, purchase, and postpurchase evaluation.

3. *Distinguish between low-involvement and high-involvement consumer behavior.* Involvement represents the level of importance or interest generated by a product or a decision. A person highly involved in a decision (the purchase is personally relevant) will likely go through the entire decision-making sequence, from problem recognition to postpurchase evaluation. High-involvement decisions are characterized by thorough information processing, significant personal relevance of the decision, and substantial differences between alternatives.

   Consumers with low involvement will probably not engage in an extensive information search. Low-involvement decisions have minimal personal relevance and are likely routine or habitual. Consequently, they require less mental or physical effort than extended or limited problem solving.

4. *Understand how attitudes influence consumer purchases.* Consumer attitudes, which are learned predispositions to respond favorably or unfavorably toward a product or service, are important primary causes of behavior. They are important for both explaining consumer behavior and designing marketing communications for changing consumer behavior. One useful view depicts attitudes toward purchase behavior as a combination of beliefs about the product's attributes and the relative evaluation of those attributes.

5. *Appreciate how the social environment affects consumer behavior.* Social influences on behavior must be understood prior to the development of sound marketing strategies. Social class and family influences affect consumer behavior and can be used to identify market segments.

   The culture in which consumers are raised is also critical in determining the values that matter to them; culture may be used to identify segments with unique needs (subcultures). A great deal of learning also comes from observing and interacting with others (informational interpersonal influence). Some behavior occurs with the expectations of others in mind (utilitarian influences) and some with how they will react to our own behavior (value-expressiveness). The latter two are normative social influences. Consumers are also influenced by the situations in which behavior occurs or is expected to occur.

6. *Recognize many of the individual consumer differences that influence purchase decisions and behavior.* Individual consumer differences affect consumer decision making and behavior. These include personality differences; lifestyle differences, which are often measured as consumer activities, interests, and opinions; and differences in motivation.

7. *Recognize the outcomes of consumers' decisions to purchase or not to purchase and how they affect marketing success.* Some of the more important outcomes that occur after purchase are consumer learning, feelings of satisfaction or dissatisfaction, and cognitive dissonance. Learning may result from experience and knowledge gained through advertisements and marketing communications.

   Feelings of satisfaction and dissatisfaction occur when product performance exceeds or falls short of expectations. Dissatisfaction may lead to consumer complaints and loss of future business. Cognitive dissonance is postpurchase doubt about the appropriateness of a decision. It is most likely to occur when the purchase is important or involved, perceived risk is high, the purchase is visible, and the decision involves a long-term commitment.

Key terms & concepts

consumer behavior *106*
involvement *109*
high-involvement decisions *109*
low-involvement decisions *110*
routinized response behavior *111*
extensive problem solving *111*
limited problem solving *111*
consumer attitudes *111*
culture *112*
socialization *112*

values *113*
ethnic patterns *113*
social classes *114*
childhood consumer
  socialization *115*
family life cycle *115*
reference groups *116*
informational influence *116*
utilitarian influence *117*
value-expressive influence *117*

opinion leaders *118*
market mavens *118*
psychographics *119*
consumer learning *122*
negative disconfirmation *122*
positive disconfirmation *122*
voice responses *123*
private responses *123*
third-party responses *123*
cognitive dissonance *123*

Review & discussion questions

1. Describe the importance of understanding consumer behavior. How does this understanding relate to the identification of target markets?

2. Outline and discuss the steps involved in the consumer decision-making process. How might this sequence differ for routinized response behavior and limited problem solving?

3. What is meant by low-involvement consumer behavior?

4. Why are consumer attitudes important? What role do consumer beliefs about product attributes play in consumer decision making?

5. Outline the three types of interpersonal influence, and explain how each may affect purchase behavior.

6. Explain how understanding social class and the family life cycle can enhance marketing effectiveness.

7. How does culture affect consumer behavior, and what are the implications for marketers?

8. Explain the success of the VideOcart described in **The Technological Edge: The Ultimate Sell** in terms of consumer decision making and grocery store shopping.

9. Contrast cognitive dissonance with consumer dissatisfaction. What determines feelings of satisfaction and dissatisfaction?

10. Refer to **The Entrepreneurial Spirit: The Midas Touch.** What role do social influences play in the purchase of these products?

Application exercises

1. Contrast the decision sequence you made for two recent purchases—one expensive or complex decision, and one simple decision.

2. Discuss two examples of the way marketers could use interpersonal influence to their advantage. Under what conditions would you consider using interpersonal influence as a marketing tool to be unethical?

3. Find examples of ads that exemplify the following consumer behavior concepts: safety needs, consumer satisfaction, family influences, and subcultures.

P
A
R
T

2

Case 5.1
Burger King: Now serving dinner

The Burger King Corp., a unit of Grand Metropolitan P.L.C. of London, is the second-largest competitor in the fast-food industry with annual worldwide sales between $6 and $7 billion. Fast-food sales are characterized by ups and downs throughout the day, with sales after 4:00 PM typically being the lightest. For years, the major fast-food chains have explored ways to increase late-day sales. McDonald's Corp., the industry leader, considered several dinner options, particularly centered on pizza, but has moved slowly in implementing any specific new dinner-time strategy. Wendy's International successfully expanded its menu by offering entrée-and-salad superbars.

Research by Burger King indicated that, although fast-food consumers desire quick and inexpensive lunches, they prefer different "end benefits" for dinner. Prompt service is still an important feature, but consumers prefer a more relaxed dinner atmosphere. Restaurant chains such as Chili's and Applebee's are more appealing to dinner consumers than the fast-food restaurants because they offer a chance to sit down and relax at only a slightly higher price.

To capitalize on this situation and improve evening sales, Burger King began serving dinner baskets after 4:00 PM. Customers could choose a Whopper (hamburger), chicken fillet, fried shrimp, or steak sandwich served with their choice of a baked potato or french fries, salad or cole slaw, and a roll to go with the chicken or shrimp. The customer ordered at a counter, but a server brought the food directly to the table. Meanwhile, popcorn was provided to make the wait seem shorter. The lights were dimmed and music played during dinner hours to enhance the relaxed atmosphere.

Burger King recognized, however, that the move entailed a certain amount of risk. Consumers' pre-existing perceptions and attitudes toward fast-food restaurants were inconsistent with a relaxing sit-down dinner; breaking that mind-set would be no easy task.

To predict the results of making such an innovation, Burger King tried the sit-down dinner strategy in diverse markets for about a year and a half. A strong consumer response led to significant rollout in October 1992. The initial national results were extremely positive, with dinner sales increasing as much as 20 percent in some markets.

Dinnertime sales did not stay at such high levels, however. After the initial bounce, Burger King's dinner menu failed to maintain its increased sales levels. Franchise owners explained that their customers came to Burger King for good, quick food at a low price, and dinners such as steak or shrimp may have confused some of them. Even with the expanded menu, customers primarily purchased the Whopper basket over the other baskets. Meanwhile, the revitalized approach slowed down the food-serving system with increased requirements on each Burger King's cooking facilities.

In June 1993, the company decided to let franchisees choose for themselves whether they wanted to continue the new approach. Since then, most Burger King restaurants have dropped the innovation altogether.

Questions

1. What do you think were the biggest challenges to Burger King's implementation of this strategy? Why?

2. How do the choice criteria and their importance differ between lunch and dinner location decisions?

3. How could this change in dinner strategy affect consumers when considering where to go for lunch?

4. What external influences affect consumers' dinner restaurant decisions?

Sources: Alva Marilyn, "Franchisees Can BK's Dinner Program," *Restaurant Business*, September 20, 1993, p. 22; Michael McCarthy, "The Heat Is On: D'Arcy's Burger King 'TeeVee' Ads in Jeopardy as Franchisees Revolt," *Adweek*, April 12, 1993, pp. 1, 4; Gretchen Morgenson, "Look Who's Coming to Dinner," *Forbes*, March 1, 1993, pp. 104–5; Charles Bernstein, "Dinner at Burger King: Overshooting the Mark," *Restaurants and Institutions*, March 1, 1993, p. 14; "Burger King's Dinner Exploration: Bold Move in Treacherous Territory," *Nation's Restaurant News*, October 19, 1992, p. 21; and Richard Gibson, "Guess Who's Coming to Dinner Now: It's Burger King," *The Wall Street Journal*, September 18, 1992, p. B1.

Case 5.2   *Calyx and Corolla: Selling hedonic benefits*

In the late 1980s, Americans spent about half as much as Europeans on flowers per capita. Now in the mid-1990s, Americans want to learn more about flowers and how to best enjoy them. This increase in consumer interest in flowers led entrepreneur Ruth Owades to pioneer her company, Calyx and Corolla.

Calyx and Corolla offers flowers and plants by catalog. Conceived in 1988, the company reached annual revenues of $10 million by 1990 with a mailing list of over 8 million. What led to such tremendous growth? The company capitalized on two key phenomena. First, American consumers' interest in flowers is increasing. Second, flowers offer emotional benefits that exceed their tangible properties, and Calyx and Corolla found a way to further enhance these benefits.

Eighty percent of a florist's customer orders are placed by telephone, and the customer doesn't see what the order will actually look like. The Calyx and Corolla catalog lets buyers see orders in advance. Each selection is pictured in the catalog against a subdued background that draws attention to the flowers themselves, and only two or three selections are displayed on a page.

Additional catalog sections include factual information on flowers and other decorative plants with suggestions on different arrangement styles. The information is designed to educate consumers, while simultaneously keeping their attention on the catalog. With each flower shipment, Calyx and Corolla includes detailed information on caring for that particular order. Also available is a toll-free service line that provides advice on related decisions, such as the appropriate arrangements for different occasions.

The allure of flowers is not only in their aesthetic beauty and pleasant fragrance, but also in the positive feelings associated with a statement of caring from one individual or group to another. Calyx and Corolla ships orders directly from the grower, via Federal Express; so flowers are delivered to the consumer with 72 hours of picking. Flowers purchased through traditional florists may have taken 5 to 10 days to reach the florist, let alone the consumer. Therefore, Calyx and Corolla can offer much fresher flowers than their competitors, a strong benefit for the customer asking for forgiveness or expressing affection. Calyx and Corolla has become an attractive option for consumers looking for the right arrangement to convey the right sentiments.

How long Calyx and Corolla can continue to increase or even maintain sales levels remains to be seen. By building on the still-increasing consumer interests and offering fresher flowers that elicit strong hedonic responses, the company sees the continuing potential for growth.

Questions

1. What do you see as the strengths and weaknesses for Calyx and Corolla in addressing desired consumer benefits? How are these benefits related to developing positive attitudes?

2. What social trends are likely to affect Calyx and Corolla's future performance?

3. How do floral decisions made in catalog shopping differ from those made in stores?

Sources: Lynn Hayes, "1992 American Catalog Awards—Gifts under $75: Expertise Abounds in Calyx and Corolla," *Catalog Age,* September 1992, pp. 71–73; Everett Martin, "Ruth Owades—A Budding Entrepreneur," *Sales & Marketing Management,* June 1992, pp. 32–33; Ellie Winninghoff, "Growing a New Market Niche," *Working Woman,* February 1991, pp. 42, 44, 46; and Paul Miller, "Business Is Blooming," *Catalog Age,* January 1991, pp. cover, 32–33.

6

Business-to-Business Markets and Buying Behavior

After studying this chapter you should be able to:

1. Define the nature of business-to-business buying behavior and markets.

2. Explain the differences between business-to-business buying and consumer purchase behavior.

3. Recognize the different types of buying decisions.

4. Define the different stages of the business buying process.

5. Describe the buying-center concept and the determinants of influence within the buying center.

6. Understand the nature of government, reseller, and other institutional markets.

Whirlpool: Wringing profits from business buying

Whirlpool, the giant appliance maker, is changing the way it buys from suppliers. These changes in purchasing are expected to lead to higher profits.

According to Robert Hall, corporate vice president for purchasing, Whirlpool looks for four things from its suppliers. First, Whirlpool wants to work more closely with fewer suppliers. Second, the company is interested in buying from companies that offer new technologies or innovative approaches for doing things. Third, superior quality is a must. Fourth, Whirlpool looks favorably on suppliers that give it some type of cost advantage.

Instead of buying small amounts from many suppliers, Whirlpool wants to develop strategic alliances with a few companies. These alliances are long-term, mutual dependency relationships. Whirlpool depends on each selected supplier for most of its purchases of a particular product. In turn, a selected supplier depends on Whirlpool for a large portion of its sales. For example, Wollin Products is a plastics manufacturer with about $50 million annual sales. More than a third of those sales, around $19 million, are products for Whirlpool washing machines.

Since Whirlpool is forming relationships and not just buying products, more factors are considered in selecting suppliers. Quality and cost of a product are still important. But now, Whirlpool also looks closely at specific characteristics of the supplying company. It is interested in the supplier's financial situation, its ability and willingness to expand to meet Whirlpool's growing needs, and the continuity of the supplier's management team.

Trust is also an important factor. The strategic alliances require that Whirlpool and its suppliers share a great deal of information—often sensitive—with each other. Both parties must trust that the shared information will not be disclosed to competitors.

Whirlpool is focusing on other ways to reduce costs through improved purchasing. One interesting example is in the corporate travel area. Along with other major companies, including General Motors, Bell Atlantic, and Merck, Whirlpool is investigating a proposal that would lower travel costs by wiping out travel agent commissions from airlines and eliminating frequent flier miles for employees. Air fares would be negotiated directly with the airlines through Business Travel Contractors. The high marketing and administrative air travel costs would be replaced by a low negotiating fee to Business Travel Contractors. Although this proposal had not been implemented yet as of June 1994, the trend toward lowering costs through improved purchasing is likely to continue and intensify.

Sources: Barry Rehfeld, "How Large Companies Buy," *Personal Selling Power,* September 1993, pp. 31–32; and James S. Hirsch, "Big Companies Band Together to Cut Air Travel Costs," *Dow Jones/News Retrieval,* June 8, 1994.

Companies like Whirlpool spend enormous amounts on products and services for business operations, and then market products and services to other consumer or business buyers. As indicated in the Whirlpool situation, these firms are making many changes to improve purchasing performance. Companies marketing to businesses and other organizations need to understand purchasing behavior to develop and execute marketing strategies successfully.

In this chapter, we define business-to-business buying, discuss its importance, identify emerging trends, examine important business purchasing concepts, describe government, reseller, and other institutional buying practices, and address relevant ethical considerations. Our objective is to understand what these buyers do and want, so we can market to them effectively.

The nature of business-to-business buying

Business-to-business buying behavior defined

Business-to-business buying behavior refers to decision making and other activities of organizations as buyers. It involves transactions between buying and selling organizations. A primary element in business-to-business buying is the selection of **suppliers, sources, or vendors.** These are interchangeable terms for companies or individuals who sell products and services directly to buying organizations. In practice, industrial or manufacturing firms distinguish between two kinds of purchases: those involving production and operational products routinely needed in ongoing production or maintenance (raw materials, fasteners, bearings, paint) and those involving capital products (milling machines, power-generating devices, computers and telecommunication systems).

Characteristics of business-to-business buying behavior

There are some similarities but many differences between consumer and organizational buying behavior and decision making. Principally, consumers buy for their own use and for household consumption. Business buyers purchase for further production (raw materials, components), for use in their firm's operations (office supplies, insurance), or for resale to other customers.[1] Major distinguishing characteristics of business-to-business buying behavior are presented in Exhibit 6.1.

Demand for business-to-business products is often dependent on demand in consumer markets. This phenomenon is referred to as **derived demand.** For example, the demand for many products is derived from consumer demand for new automobiles. When demand for new autos goes up, the demand for products used to make them, such as steel, plastic, and textiles also goes up. The reverse is also true.

Exhibit 6.1   How business-to-business buying behavior differs from consumer buying

1. Business-to-business buyers are fewer in number, larger & more concentrated geographically than consumer buyers. This necessitates heavy emphasis on personal selling and trade advertising in business-to-business marketing.

2. Business purchase decisions often involve a more deliberate or thorough product evaluation & are subject to influence from multiple sources (purchasing, engineering) within a firm.

3. The demand for consumer products drives the purchases made by product manufacturers. Business purchase behavior is thus closely tied to economic fluctuations in the consumer market.

4. The demand for some products is related to the purchase of other products (joint demand). For example, if the demand for business personal computers declines, the demand for software applications and business computer printers may decline also.

5. Purchased industrial products are often complex, expensive & bought in large quantity. Thus, many purchase decisions are based on detailed product specifications or choice criteria. Business markets also make greater use of leasing.

6. There is much more interdependence between business buyers and sellers. This underlies the need to build long-term buyer-seller relationships and leads to greater emphasis on after-sale service.

Evaluating business-to-business markets

Marketers can evaluate the size and growth rates of consumer markets using demographic characteristics. Many information sources report population statistics by characteristics like age or income level for different geographical areas. These demographic characteristics are not useful for evaluating business markets.

The federal government has developed a numerical scheme called the **Standard Industrial Classification (SIC) system** for categorizing businesses. SIC codes range from two to seven digits to classify businesses from general industry groupings to specific product categories. Of most interest to marketers are the two- and four-digit SIC codes illustrated in Exhibit 6.2. The two-digit code identifies major industry groups. In this case the SIC code is 25 and the major industry group is furniture manufacturing. The four-digit code breaks the major industry group into more specific industries. In our example the furniture manufacturing group is divided into 13 specific industries. One specific industry is SIC code 2514—metal household furniture manufacturing.

Statistics about business markets are presented according to SIC codes. So, once marketers identify the SIC codes of their business target markets, they can often use available statistics to evaluate the size and growth rates of these markets. Notice the statistics provided in Exhibit 6.2 for each of the 13 specific furniture industries.

The importance of business-to-business buying

Business-to-business markets and purchasing behavior are important for two basic reasons. First, the size of business markets offers many opportunities for astute marketers. Second, many firms are trying to increase profits by improving purchasing practices.

Just how important is business purchasing, anyway? About half of all manufactured goods made in the US are sold to business buyers. The total value of these manufactured goods is now over $1 trillion annually. Moreover, businesses are the prime buyers of raw materials, such as minerals and farm and forest products; used for further processing and manufacturing, adding at least $275 billion more to the annual purchase total. Finally, business buyers purchase

Exhibit 6.2   **US totals for 4-digit SIC industries**

SIC 25 Furniture	Establishments Total	Large	Employ-ment	Shipment receipts ($ millions)	% in large estab.
2511 Unupholstered wood household furniture	4,271	279	128,408	$6,808.6	68%
2512 Upholstered household furniture	1,857	245	100,333	5,523.6	73
2514 Metal household furniture	546	70	25,250	1,979.8	70
2515 Mattresses & bedsprings	1,090	71	29,288	2,326.0	39
2517 Wood TV & radio cabinets	129	24	7,784	478.2	82
2519 Household furniture n.e.c.	661	31	15,944	1,077.7	57
2521 Wood office furniture	1,429	101	45,861	2,894.8	59
2522 Office furniture, except wood	491	92	45,238	4,105.4	83
2531 Public building & related furniture	637	89	31,032	2,104.8	71
2541 Wood partitions & fixtures	2,690	76	44,894	2,936.1	32
2542 Partitions & fixtures	1,165	125	47,547	3,954.5	61
2591 Drapery hardware & blinds & shades	982	51	27,143	1,924.2	60
2599 Furniture & fixtures n.e.c.	904	41	24,547	1,692.0	52

more than products; they buy services from advertising agencies, accountants, lawyers, railroads, airlines, and so on.[2]

One of the biggest spenders is Ford Motor Company, at around $58 billion.[3] The purchasing budgets of General Electric, Du Pont, GMC, Ford, and other companies exceed the gross national product of many countries. It is easy to see that businesses represent potentially lucrative markets for the products and services of many companies.

Organizations fall into four general categories: *business firms,* including manufacturers of tangible goods and firms that provide services such as health care, entertainment, and transportation; *government markets,* federal, state, and local; *reseller markets,* such as the many wholesalers and retailers; and other *institutional markets,* such as hospitals (profit and nonprofit), educational and religious institutions, and trade associations. Each of these categories includes organizations that purchase from other organizations. One study found many of the purchasing activities in these types of organizations to be similar—more so than was reported in a study done three years earlier. Thus, much of our discussion on business buying applies to other types of organizations.[4]

Lowering the cost of purchased products can be an effective way to increase profits. Consider this simple example. Assume a firm has annual sales of $100 million and a net profit margin of 5 percent. If this firm wanted to increase profits by $1 million, it would have to increase sales by 20 percent ($20 million sales increase × .05 net profit margin = $1 million profit increase). This type of sales increase may be difficult to accomplish in the slow growth markets facing many firms. But if the company reduced costs by $1 million through improved purchasing, it would achieve the profit growth objective. This may be more doable in many situations.

The reality is that most firms are trying to increase profits by both increasing sales and reducing costs. However, more and more firms realize the powerful impact that purchasing improvements can have on profits. As business buyers change purchasing practices, marketers need to be aware of the changes and adapt marketing efforts appropriately.

Trends in business-to-business buying

The purchasing operations at many firms are undergoing substantial changes. The results from a study of current and future purchasing trends are presented in Exhibit 6.3. There are only a few differences in the rankings of the current and future trends, and the trends are expected to continue into the foreseeable future.

A synthesis of the Whirlpool example at the beginning of this chapter, the purchasing trends in Exhibit 6.3, and other information indicates that purchasing is driven by many of the ten key marketing perspectives. It is important for marketers to understand how these perspectives affect business buyers so they can respond effectively to the changing needs of purchasers.

Productivity improvement

Productivity improvement is emphasized throughout many companies. This affects purchasing in at least two major ways. First, firms find that it is often more productive to purchase products and services from other companies than to make the products or perform the services internally. This is called **outsourcing.** Outsourcing is increasing for both product components and various services. For example, purchased components represent 93 percent of the cost of sales of a typical Apple computer. The figure for overall manufacturing is about 52 percent.[5] Outsourced services include shipping, PC network management,

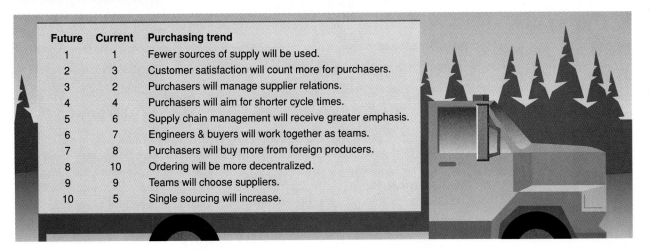

Future	Current	Purchasing trend
1	1	Fewer sources of supply will be used.
2	3	Customer satisfaction will count more for purchasers.
3	2	Purchasers will manage supplier relations.
4	4	Purchasers will aim for shorter cycle times.
5	6	Supply chain management will receive greater emphasis.
6	7	Engineers & buyers will work together as teams.
7	8	Purchasers will buy more from foreign producers.
8	10	Ordering will be more decentralized.
9	9	Teams will choose suppliers.
10	5	Single sourcing will increase.

Exhibit 6.3 **Purchasing trends**

telecommunications, copier and printing services, nursing services, and payroll administration.[6] The trend is likely to continue, as one study indicates that 70 percent of responding firms found outsourcing to increase productivity.[7]

The net effect of outsourcing is that buyers have to buy more products and services than in the past. And, as indicated in Exhibit 6.3, buyers are taking a *global perspective* by purchasing more from foreign producers. Companies are outsourcing products and services to suppliers around the world.

Second, as firms downsize to reduce costs, fewer buyers are being asked not only to purchase more products, but to perform more activities. Purchasing personnel are now often involved in strategic planning, new product development, relationship management, and other diverse activities. A *productivity perspective* is driving both companies and buyers to do more with less.

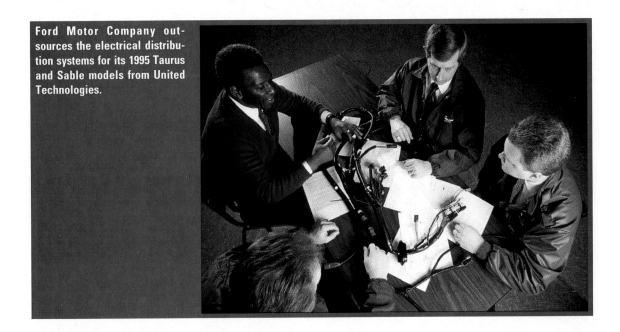

Ford Motor Company outsources the electrical distribution systems for its 1995 Taurus and Sable models from United Technologies.

P
A
R
T

2

EXECUTIVE ROUNDTABLE COMMENT | **Mary Washington, buyer for Atmel Corporation,**

describes how a *productivity perspective* is changing purchasing operations:

One of the biggest changes in purchasing is that there are fewer buyers doing more things. At Atmel, several buyers are taking on the role of planners as well. We have to maintain our purchasing responsibilities, but also plan and manage stockroom inventories. These increased responsibilities mean that buyers are extremely busy. We don't have any time to waste with sellers that cannot help our business or are not prepared.

A relationship perspective

Many of the purchasing trends reflect an emphasis on a *relationship perspective* (see Exhibit 6.3). These include supplier relationships (working with fewer suppliers, managing supplier relations, and an increase in single sourcing), organizational partnerships (emphasis on supply chain management), and teamwork within the firm (engineers, buyers, and other functions working as teams).

The focus on supplier relationships by buyers is driving the emphasis on relationship marketing by sellers. Business buyers want to work much more closely with many fewer suppliers. For example, 90 percent of Fortune 1000 companies expect to continue trimming suppliers through the year 2000.[8] Rubbermaid plans to reduce its suppliers base by 80 percent before 1996.[9] Some companies are trying to get to a single source for each product or service purchased. As firms engage in long-term relationships with fewer suppliers, the role of buyers changes from just making purchases to managing relationships with suppliers. Jesse Schook, senior buyer at the Ford Motor Truck Plant, considers his suppliers "an extension of the Ford family" and works with them as if they were Ford employees.[10]

An important element of supplier relationships is an *ethical perspective.* Successful relationships must be based on trust. As indicated in the Whirlpool example at the beginning of the chapter, buyers and sellers share a great deal of information and must trust that this information will remain confidential. Both parties must trust each is working for mutual benefit. Honest and open communication are necessary. Once developed, trust is a powerful asset in a supplier relationship. Once lost, it is very difficult—and maybe impossible—to reestablish. Jesse Schook emphasizes this point: "Trust is the whole ballgame. If we lose trust in a supplier, our response is quite simple. We find another supplier."[11]

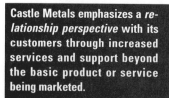

Castle Metals emphasizes a *relationship perspective* with its customers through increased services and support beyond the basic product or service being marketed.

Buyers are in a rather unique situation because they work directly with suppliers to purchase products for their firm (internal customers) that are used to produce products for external customers. They are involved throughout the supply chain. Although it is important for buyers to meet the needs of their internal customers, ultimate success depends upon contributing to the success of external customers. Buyers are spending more time with external customers to better understand how the products they purchase from suppliers affect the products purchased by external customers. This helps them make purchases that can both reduce costs and increase customer satisfaction.

An example from Cadbury Beverages, maker of Mott's applesauce, illustrates these relationships. Consumers indicated a preference for a bottle that had some etching on it to make it easier to grip. Allen Hagstran, director of world sourcing, worked with his bottle supplier, Owens Brockway, to design such a bottle and to make improvements in shipping and inventory practices. The net result was an increase in Mott's applesauce sales and a reduction in glass purchasing costs.[12]

The final aspect of a *relationship perspective* is teamwork within the firm. Buyers are working more as teams with engineers and other functions in the selection of suppliers. In many respects, buyers orchestrate the purchasing process within their firms. They coordinate the flow of information between the seller and buyer and rely on people within and outside their firm for expertise in evaluating different products and suppliers.

EXECUTIVE ROUNDTABLE COMMENT | Mary Washington, buyer for Atmel Corporation, emphasizes the importance of interacting with people inside and outside her firm to make the best purchasing decisions:

I cannot be an expert on all of the products I purchase. Therefore, it is important for me to work with a lot of people from different functions and companies. The test engineering people at Atmel and I work closely together. I also rely on marketing reps and trade publications for information about products and suppliers. Another useful source of information is to talk with other buyers in the area. We share information about specific companies, marketing reps, and products.

Quality/value considerations

One of the keys to successful supplier relationships is a *quality/value perspective.* Buyers are interested in suppliers that can add value to their business by continually increasing quality and lowering costs. Quality and cost considerations go beyond just the product being purchased to everything related to doing

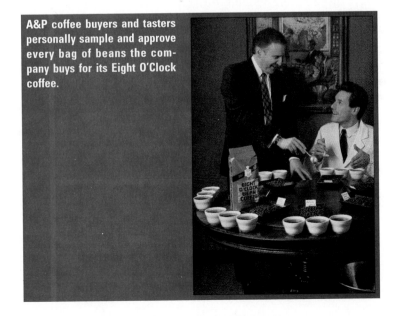

A&P coffee buyers and tasters personally sample and approve every bag of beans the company buys for its Eight O'Clock coffee.

AVO: Recently Du Pont announced that its energy unit would pioneer the use of

new double-hulled oil tankers. In order to safeguard the environment.

(MUSIC)

The response has been overwhelmingly positive

Du Pont

Better things for better living.

Consistent with the *ecological perspective,* Du Pont developed double-hulled transports for buyers of oil tankers.

business together. In fact, many buyers are willing to pay more for a product if they get added value from the relationship. Consider the example of Milliken, a large textile manufacturer that sells towels to industrial laundries, which in turn supply them to factories. Although Milliken's towels are similar to those of other companies, the laundries are willing to pay 10 to 15 percent more for them. Milliken tells its laundries: "If you buy from us, you're our Partner for Profit." To add value to this relationship, Milliken provides special software to help route laundry trucks, accounting assistance, salesforce training, and customer leads. Such benefits are worth much more to the laundries than the extra price paid for Milliken towels.[13]

Many buyers emphasize an *ecological perspective* by examining the costs associated with product disposal and looking for ways to recycle or reuse products. Suppliers can add value to relationships by helping buyers in these areas. Apple Computer and IBM have "take back" programs for customers to return used computers. Apple and IBM recycle or reuse the equipment or components.[14] Amana Refrigeration returns used foam packaging to its supplier.[15] These types of programs are likely to be more important in the future, as buyers become more actively involved in the environmental area.

Use of technology

Buyers are increasingly employing a *technological perspective* to improve the productivity of purchasing operations. Reducing cycle time is an important purchasing trend (see Exhibit 6.3). Because time is money, buyers are interested in ways to reduce the purchasing, product development, product delivery, manufacturing, and inventory cycles. Reducing cycle times increases productivity by lowering the costs of doing business and can help increase sales. The use of new technologies often leads to shorter cycle times. J. C. Penney, for example, uses a program called Quick Response Partnerships to get suppliers to help minimize the replenishment cycle for retail inventory. Computer links enable suppliers to replenish goods before shortages occur at retail stores. J. C. Penney stores have thus reduced inventory costs, while still providing the products desired by customers.[16]

Entrepreneurial emphasis

Buyers constantly look for creative and innovative ideas to improve purchasing and business operations. The purchasing department at Baxter Health Care, for example, used an innovative approach to make several improvements. Purchasing coordinated several on-site visits for hourly employees to different suppliers. After these visits, the employees came up with ideas to redesign shipping cartons and a packaging change that improved recyclability. The interaction of purchasing with Baxter and supplier employees generated the ideas for improvement.[17]

Suppliers can use an *entrepreneurial perspective* to add value to relationships and increase purchasing productivity. Wayne Whitworth, purchasing manager for Brown-Forman Beverages Worldwide, recalls how one supplier used an *entrepreneurial* approach to lower delivery costs substantially:

> *We were receiving 20 truckloads of a product from a supplier each week. The product contained 77 percent water. We were paying a great deal to ship water, because the product was not stable by itself. The supplier developed a new process to keep the product stable without water. Now, we only get 5 truckloads and save $30,000 a week. The water is added at our plant. This supplier developed an innovative process that saved us a lot of money.[18]*

Emphasis on execution

Because execution is extremely important to buyers, most buyers evaluate supplier performance on an ongoing basis. The evaluations include various aspects of quality, service, and price. For example, buyers might keep track of the days late or days early in delivering products. Or the number of times salespeople have provided service to the firm might be monitored. This information is usually kept for each supplier so comparisons can be made accross suppliers and over time.

Brown-Forman Beverages Worldwide instituted a unique approach that shifts some of the evaluation responsibility to the supplier. Buyers still track objective supplier performance data. But suppliers are now required to prepare a worksheet each year that shows how they helped Brown-Forman lower costs or improve business operations. Each supplier meets with the purchasing people at Brown-Forman to go over this report and support the cost savings and improvements. Wayne Whitworth thinks this approach is important because "it actively involves the supplier in the evaluation process and makes them aware of how they are doing."[19]

A visionary approach

A firm's purchasing operation should be driven by a vision of purchasing in the future. Some see dramatic changes; and the trends presented in Exhibit 6.3 support this view. As these trends become widespread, the term *purchasing* is less descriptive of what buyers actually do. Many see the name purchasing being dropped. One study found that 64 percent of the responding purchasing executives expect purchasing to have a different name by the year 2000. The most often mentioned new names were supply management, sourcing management, and logistics. Northern Telcom and Southern Pacific Transportation have already converted the purchasing name to supply management.[20]

Timken illustrates a *visionary perspective* and many of the trends we have been discussing. Purchasing at the $1.7 billion producer of roller bearings and alloy steel was a centralized function that tried to get what was needed at the

P
A
R
T

2

Type of buying decision	Newness of the problem	Information requirements	Consideration of new alternatives
New task	High	Maximum	Important
Modified rebuy	Medium	Moderate	Limited
Straight rebuy	Low	Minimal	None

Exhibit 6.4

The buying decision grid

lowest price. Buyers maintained an arm's-length relationship with suppliers and avoided contact with the company's manufacturing people. Then global competition motivated Timken to develop a coordinated sourcing vision for its purchasing function. Buyers teamed with internal users—engineers, production controllers, and manufacturing experts—and Timken began inviting suppliers into its plant. Today, buyers often visit suppliers. They know more about manufacturing operations and how purchases are put to use. Buyers now emphasize value—not just the lowest price, but the lowest total cost to use.[21]

Types of buying decisions

In Chapter 5, we classified consumer decisions on a continuum ranging from extensive problem solving (requiring development of criteria for a decision) to routinized response behavior (requiring only price and availability information). Business-to-business purchase decisions can be classed similarly: straight rebuy, modified rebuy, and new-task decisions.[22] These categories are described in a grid in Exhibit 6.4. Note that the classes are distinguished according to the newness of the purchase decision, the information required, and the need to consider alternatives in the purchase, such as different suppliers.

New-task decisions

In **new-task decisions,** as shown in Exhibit 6.4, the buying problem is new and a great deal of information must be gathered. New-task decisions are relatively infrequent for a company, and the cost of making a wrong decision is high. Suppliers must convince the buyer their product will solve the buyer's problem; they cannot count on merely offering a price advantage to win the sale. New-task decisions are generally consistent with the sequence of activities in the buying process (discussed later).

When NBC purchases new technology products for use in its studios, the purchase is considered from every angle. A nationwide team of television engineers, production staffers, and buyers is assembled. Major electronic corporations, generally about seven, from the US, Europe, and Japan are asked to submit proposals. Engineers evaluate their technical capabilities. Production people evaluate their ability to produce quality pictures easily. Then written evaluations from these examinations are used, along with input from NBC's buyers, to make a selection.[23]

Modified rebuy decisions

Modified rebuy decisions call for the evaluation of new alternatives for purchase decisions. A modified rebuy could involve considering either new suppliers for current purchase needs or new products offered by current suppliers. The amount of information required and the need to consider new alternatives are less than for new-task decisions but more than for straight rebuy decisions. More familiarity with the decision means less uncertainty and perceived risk

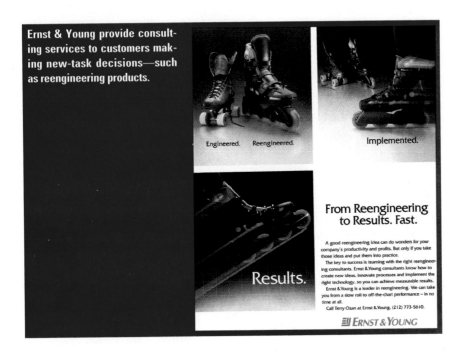

Ernst & Young provide consulting services to customers making new-task decisions—such as reengineering products.

than for new-task decisions.[24] Purchases of complex component parts from a new supplier are typical modified rebuy decisions. In these situations, the firm's buyer, often with some input from management, will make the decision.

Straight rebuy decisions

Straight rebuy decisions are the most common type. Products and services bought previously are simply repurchased. Delivery, performance, and price are the critical considerations in a straight rebuy. "Out suppliers," or suppliers not currently being used, are at a considerable disadvantage in this case because of the perceived costs of evaluating new alternatives.[25] Purchases of office supplies, raw materials, lubricants, castings, and frequently used component parts involve straight rebuy decisions. Business buyers typically make these decisions.

The buying process

The buying process is presented in Exhibit 6.5. Like many consumer decisions, the decision sequence begins with problem or opportunity recognition. Problem recognition may be triggered by the depletion of supplies, worn-out equipment, or the need for improved technology. It may arise in various departments: operations, production, purchasing, engineering, or planning. New business opportunities may also generate the need for purchases. Once the firm recognizes need to purchase, it determines the desired product characteristics and the quantity to buy. Then production, R&D, or engineering personnel determine specific details for each item. These "specs" are the needed levels of product characteristics.

Exhibit 6.5   **The business buying process**

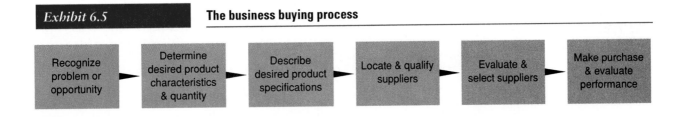

Recognize problem or opportunity → Determine desired product characteristics & quantity → Describe desired product specifications → Locate & qualify suppliers → Evaluate & select suppliers → Make purchase & evaluate performance

This Brown and Caldwell ad emphasizes meeting environmental criteria in the selection of a supplier.

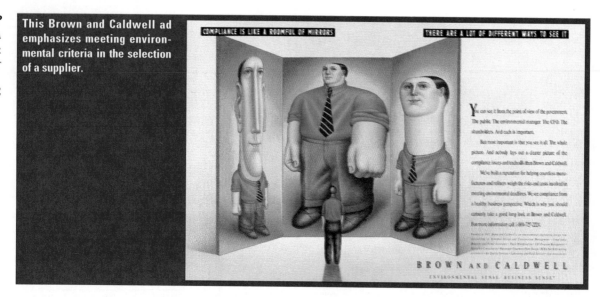

Next, the firm searches for qualified sources or suppliers. Information about potential suppliers may be available from salespeople, exhibitions and trade shows, direct-mail advertising, press releases, trade news and trade advertising, word-of-mouth, and professional conferences. Suppliers are evaluated to ensure they can produce and deliver the product as needed and provide service after the purchase. Surveys of business buyers indicate that product quality, delivery reliability, and price are often the most important factors in the decision to select one supplier over another.[26] A formal procedure for evaluating suppliers is presented in Appendix A.

EXECUTIVE ROUNDTABLE COMMENT | **Mary Washington, buyer at Atmel Corporation, indicates the factors she considers in making a purchase decision:**

I purchase products such as printed circuit boards, office supplies, and computer software for Atmel. My general approach is to try to get the best quality for the best value. For example, when purchasing printed circuit boards, I am concerned about a supplier's ability to meet product specifications and delivery schedules, and its overall technical capabilities. Once I am convinced a supplier can provide the desired quality, then I focus on getting the lowest total cost for my company.

Once a decision has been reached, the firm makes the purchase. Typically, buyers negotiate the final purchase. Buyers try to get the best deal for their company and often negotiate for better payment terms, delivery schedules, or other benefits. After the purchase is finalized, buyers continually monitor the suppliers' performance.

The business buying process varies according to the type of buying decision. New-task decisions are the most complex and typically follow the process we discussed. Modified rebuy situations are less complex, but normally include most of the stages in the buying process. Straight rebuys are usually a reorder from a current supplier. Some innovative firms are empowering employees to make some purchases on their own. The use of procurement cards to facilitate this type of purchasing is presented in **The Entrepreneurial Spirit: Empowering Employee Purchasing.**

The buying center

Sometimes one individual in a firm makes the buying decisions. These buyers have tremendous responsibilities in some industries. In the chemicals industry,

Empowering employee purchasing

Most of a company's purchases are for less than $2,500. The cost of processing a purchase order for these purchases is from $15 to $150. Some companies spend as much as $100 to process and manage a $300 purchase—a very high cost to administer the purchasing process.

Credit card companies, such as VISA and American Express, identified an opportunity to help firms reduce these purchasing costs by offering procurement cards for their employees. The cards are issued to designated employees with specific spending limits. These employees can then make needed purchases within their spending guidelines using the procurement cards.

The procurement cards benefit the company by lowering purchasing costs for many products. Statistics indicate a savings of 35 to 90 percent of purchasing costs. Employees also seem to like the ability to purchase what they need when they need it without all the paperwork. Jeff Egan, staff accountant at IBM, believes that the procurement cards give employees both empowerment and responsibility, but it is a responsibility they seem to enjoy.

Source: Jill Miller, "Purchasing Gets a New Charge," *NAPM Insights,* March 1994, pp. 50–51.

for example, Monsanto buyers are responsible on average for over $21 million in purchases. Decisions made by a single individual occur most frequently for casual, routine, low priority, and simple modified repurchase decisions.

In many instances, however, purchases are joint decisions of a buying center involving more than just a professional buyer. The **buying center,** a primary concept in business purchasing, includes more than the purchasing department or the purchasing function; it is made up of people throughout the organization at all levels. Moreover, the makeup of the buying center may vary as decisions change.

The number of people and departments represented and the levels of management involved are greater for new-task and complex modified rebuy decisions. The roles that people assume in influencing a purchase decision include initiator, decider, influencer, purchaser, gatekeeper, and user. These terms are largely self-explanatory, except for **gatekeepers,** those who control the flow of information and communication among the buying-center participants. Joint decisions made by these different individuals and departments involve some combination of problem solving, persuasion, bargaining, and politicking.[27]

Vendors selling to industrial firms must recognize these multiple roles. The potential supplier may have to reach everyone involved in the decision process. That is, the seller must go beyond engineering and purchasing and talk to the gatekeeper, influencer, and decider, for instance. Reflecting the *execution perspective,* IBM is a legendary example of how to do this well. IBM salespeople try to identify everyone involved in the purchase decision, the interrelationships among these individuals, the contribution of each, and the criteria each uses in making product or service evaluations.[28]

Firms pursuing a *global perspective* face additional challenges since international purchases can make buying decisions and processes even more complicated. Most firms prefer to use overseas purchasing offices, typically staffed with foreign nationals with both purchasing and technical training. Some companies hire import brokers to handle their international purchases.[29]

Buying-center members, connected by both workflow and communication networks, receive information from several sources.[30] These sources of information may be personal or impersonal, commercial or noncommercial. Commercial

P A R T 2

In this example of a commercial source of information, Konica promotes quality and performance capabilities of its copiers to buyers of office equipment.

sources come from some *sponsor* that advocates purchase of a particular product or service. Noncommercial personal sources, such as professional contacts, are influential because they include actual users of the product. They also have more credibility because of their likely unbiased perspective. Noncommercial personal sources are the most frequently used source of information, along with trade journal advertising, about foreign suppliers.[31]

Marketing efforts targeted toward businesses depend heavily on personal selling. However, commercial nonpersonal advertising through trade publications and other sales literature can stimulate customer leads, enhance a vendor's image, and generally support personal selling efforts.

Government markets

The **government market** includes federal, state, and local government organizations that purchase goods and services for use in many activities. In 1991, total government expenditures exceeded $1.1 trillion.[32] This level of expenditure makes governments the largest of buyers.

The *Commerce Business Daily (CBD)* publishes notices of government procurement needs, contract awards, sales of government property, and other procurement information for the federal government. A new edition of the *CBD* is issued every business day. Each edition contains approximately 500 to 1,000 notices, and each notice appears only once. All federal procurement offices are required to announce in the *CBD* all contracts or subcontracts involving expenditures over $25,000.[33]

Harsco Corporation successfully made the conversion from defense products to commercial, civilian products to meet the changing needs of the government market.

Competing for government business is a complex, time-consuming, and often frustrating endeavor. Government purchase decisions are subject to legislative direction and, in the case of the federal government, monitored by outside agencies such as the Office of Management and Budget (OMB). Most governments, whether national, state, or local, purchase through open bids or negotiated contracts. **Bids** are written proposals from qualified suppliers in response to published governmental requirements or specifications. The lowest bidder is typically selected. In some instances, small business suppliers get preferential treatment in bid evaluations. A negotiated contract is reached when a government unit works with a company to determine contract terms.[34]

The federal government spends close to $200 billion yearly on purchases of goods and services, exclusive of salaries and operating expenses. The Department of Defense represents the largest organizational purchaser.

Governments often seek to award contracts to businesses owned by women or minorities. These efforts have been less than completely successful, however. In 1990, for example, woman-owned firms were awarded only 5.8 percent of contract funds set aside for small businesses. And during economic downturns, many local governments give up minority-business programs in efforts to reduce costs. In fact, there are pros and cons to promoting a business as a minority- or woman-business enterprise. Some observers argue that positioning the firm merely as a small business is a more successful approach for gaining government contracts than is competing for those set aside for minority business.[35]

Reseller markets

The **reseller market** is made up of firms that purchase goods and in turn sell them to others at a gain. This market includes nearly 416,000 wholesaling establishments employing 6.5 million people and nearly 2 million retailing establishments employing approximately 19 million people.[36] Retailers and wholesalers are covered in detail in Chapters 15 and 16.

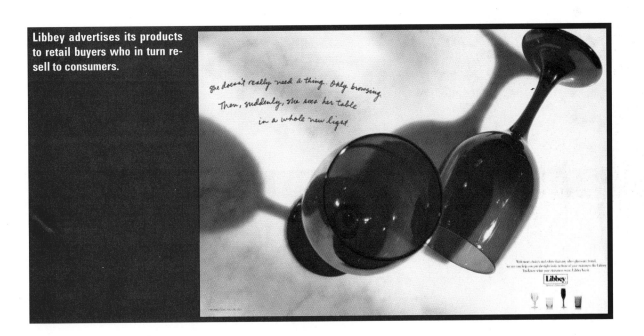

Libbey advertises its products to retail buyers who in turn resell to consumers.

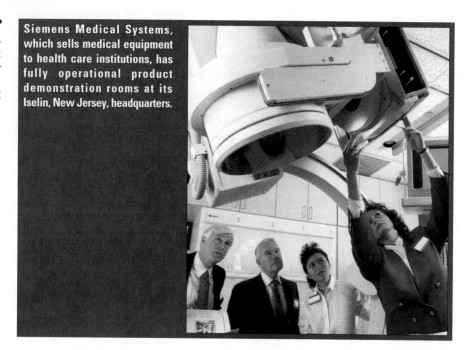

Siemens Medical Systems, which sells medical equipment to health care institutions, has fully operational product demonstration rooms at its Iselin, New Jersey, headquarters.

Retail businesses are everywhere. They make goods and services available to consumers at reasonable prices and in wide assortments. Most goods sold directly to consumers are first purchased by resellers. Wholesale firms tend to be more concentrated in trade centers surrounding larger population areas.

Retail establishments frequently use professional buyers to make their purchase choices. In many instances, say, for grocery chains, salespeople call on the buyers at central wholesale locations. Buyers at other retail firms, such as department stores, frequent trade shows where they place purchase orders directly with manufacturers.

Small retailers not part of large chain or franchise arrangements often band together to make purchases. Through buying-group memberships, these retailers get merchandise discounts or rebates they could not typically get on their own. For example, one appliance dealer in Sacramento, California, Filco Inc., obtained $100,000 in rebates from Amana and General Electric for purchases made through a buying group, Selective Consolidated Dealers Co-op.[37]

Assortment and quantity decisions are the cornerstones of retailing and wholesaling success. Resellers must be able to purchase products with significant consumer demand or appeal. Their success also depends heavily on their ability to purchase products that they can resell at prices above their purchase price. Competitive pressures and growing consumer price sensitivity have greatly increased the need to make correct decisions.

Other institutional markets

Nonprofit organizations must also purchase goods and services to support their activities. These organizations include educational institutions, public and private hospitals, religious and charitable organizations, and trade associations. As buyers, they represent viable marketing opportunities, and many specialized firms meet needs in these unique market niches. For example, some architects specialize in church or school design and construction. Other companies specialize

Helping hospitals cut costs

*H*ospitals are trying to find ways to cut costs. Evidence indicates that a 500-bed hospital spends $30 to $40 each time it places an order. Many hospitals have tried to lower this cost through electronic data interchange (EDI) that allows them to place orders electronically with many suppliers. Unfortunately, however, each supplier typically has a different system, forcing hospitals to order from different systems, often with a separate computer terminal for each supplier.

Baxter International, Eastman Kodak, Boise Cascade, and Bergen Brunswig are spearheading an initiative to establish a common data communications standard for both hospitals and suppliers. Hospitals will now have to deal with only one system that will run on a desktop computer with special software to automate the purchasing function. If successful, the system will be expanded to include electronic invoicing, online catalogs, and electronic payment.

Source: "Four Hospital Suppliers Will Launch Common Electronic Ordering Systems," *The Wall Street Journal*, April 12, 1994, p. B8.

in supplies for public and private schools. And of course, institutional buyers have standard business needs too. Many firms produce and sell health care equipment and supplies. Concerns about communicable diseases have given rise to an entire industry of protective health equipment such as disposable gloves. An example of using new technologies to improve the buying process for hospitals is presented in **The Technological Edge: Helping Hospitals Cut Costs.**

Ethical considerations

Ethics is a constant concern in business-to-business negotiations and transactions. The most frequently cited ethical issue is bribery.[38] Bribery can take many forms: gifts from vendors to people involved in decision making, "money under the table," and promises for the future. Suppliers offer these financial inducements to increase their chances of being selected by firms. Another related practice that may occur in purchase interactions between organizations is **reciprocity.** Reciprocity is when firm A purchases from supplier B who in turn buys A's own products and services. Such practices are illegal if they restrict competition and must not be used in decisions to select suppliers unless the arrangements can be made legally.

The important values of fairness, honesty, and trust are cornerstones of the *ethical perspective.* They should influence all negotiations between business purchasers and their suppliers, including the selection of suppliers or vendors. Judgments of suppliers should be made impartially and fairly. Unfair trade promises should not be extracted from companies that are in dire need of business or at some other disadvantage. This is the inverse of price discrimination, when firms unethically and illegally charge different prices to different customers for similar products and services. Purchasers should not unfairly require different suppliers to charge different prices for similar goods and services.[39]

Practices that are perfectly ethical in some countries may be frowned upon in others, as in the giving and accepting of business gifts. International companies must therefore establish policies based on the customs acceptable in the host countries.

General Motors is one large buyer that has been accused in the past of heavy-handed and questionable tactics in its dealings with suppliers. Examples include exaggerating rivals' bids to compel others to lower their own bids and exposing supplier technology in hopes of eliciting still lower supplier bids. Such behavior is not without cost. Lack of trust between business buyers and their suppliers is likely to undermine the quality of future interactions.[40]

For firms pursuing a *global perspective,* the possibility of encountering ethical dilemmas is multiplied many times. Practices in some countries differ dramatically from domestic expectations. In Japan, South Korea, and Taiwan, for example, failure to accept a business gift can imply insensitivity and disrespect. Many international companies have therefore had to develop well-defined policies that address the issue of receiving favors and gifts from overseas suppliers. Such policies should establish ethical standards of conduct on a country-by-country basis.[41]

Summary

1. *Define the nature of business-to-business buying behavior and markets.* Business-to-business buying behavior refers to the process through which organizations make purchase decisions involving other organizations as suppliers. The three broad business markets are business firms; federal, state, and local governments; and wholesale and retail firms that buy products and then resell them.

2. *Explain the differences between business-to-business buying and consumer purchase behavior.* Business buyers differ from consumer buyers in important ways. Overall, industrial and business buyers are more geographically concentrated, purchases are larger, decisions are subject to multiple influences and often approached more analytically, and demand is derived from consumer markets and trends in those markets. Organizational buying decisions typically rely on a number of choice criteria, including quality and reliability of performance, price, inventory service, reputation of supplier, and the ability to provide technical and service support.

3. *Recognize the different types of buying decisions.* Business-to-business purchase decisions can be classified into one of three categories, differentiated by complexity: new-task decisions, where the choice criteria must be determined and substantial information gathered; modified rebuys, where new sources of supply may be evaluated for situations previously encountered or the decisions are only moderately complex; and straight rebuys, where products and services bought previously are repurchased from known vendors.

4. *Define the different stages of the business buying process.* The most complex purchase decisions involve the sequence (1) recognize the problem or opportunity; (2) determine desired product characteristics and quantity; (3) describe desired product specifications; (4) locate and qualify suppliers; (5) evaluate and select suppliers; and (6) evaluate performance and feedback.

5. *Describe the buying-center concept and the determinants of influence within the buying center.* The buying center for an organization is responsible for selecting suppliers and arranging purchase terms. It is made up of people involved in routine and nonroutine purchase decisions. They may come from different departments (purchasing, engineering, production) and levels within the organization and may play one or more roles: initiator, decider, influencer, purchaser, gatekeeper, or user. Buying-center members vary in their influence on decisions, and a number of factors affect the relative power they hold in business-to-business purchases.

6. *Understand the nature of government, reseller, and other institutional markets.* The primary organizational markets include the government market, resellers, and other institutional firms. The federal government is the largest single purchaser. State and local governments make many purchases as well. Resellers are wholesale and retail firms that purchase goods to resell to other organizations or directly to consumers at higher prices.

Key terms & concepts

business-to-business buying
  behavior   *132*
suppliers, sources, or vendors   *132*
derived demand   *132*
Standard Industrial Classification
  (SIC) system   *133*

outsourcing   *135*
new-task decisions   *140*
modified rebuy decisions   *140*
straight rebuy decisions   *141*
buying center   *143*

gatekeepers   *143*
government market   *145*
bids   *145*
reseller market   *146*
reciprocity   *147*

Review & discussion questions

1. What are the distinguishing characteristics of business-to-business buying behavior?

2. What is the Standard Industrial Classification system? How can it be used to assist in marketing to business buyers?

3. Describe some of the current trends in business-to-business buying behavior.

4. Refer to **The Technological Edge: Helping Hospitals Cut Costs.** How will the common data communications standard affect relationships between suppliers and hospitals?

5. Refer to **The Entrepreneurial Spirit: Empowering Employee Purchasing.** What are the advantages and disadvantages of procurement cards?

6. What are the different types of buying decisions, and how do the information requirements vary across the decisions?

7. What is the general sequence of activities in new-task purchase decisions?

8. What is the buying center? Who are some of its typical members?

9. Contrast personal and impersonal sources of information. How might credibility differ across sources of information that are available to organizational buyers?

10. What is reciprocity? Why might it be illegal?

Application exercises

1. Assume you must purchase new personal computers for your medium-sized company. What decision criteria would be involved, and how might the decision be reached?

2. Assume your manufacturing company has made the decision to begin importing critical component parts from country X. It is common practice for companies in that country to offer their customers personal gifts and small amounts of cash for their business. These parts, which are critical to your company's success, can be purchased abroad in country X at a much lower price and at quality matching products of current US suppliers. What policies should be established for guiding the behavior and decision making of your company's purchasing personnel?

3. Describe the way the buying needs of a small retail clothier (the business owner and four employees) might differ from the needs of a manufacturer of industrial forklifts. The manufacturer makes purchases through its buying center. Discuss the likely differences in the decision processes involved for the two businesses.

Case 6.1   *General Electric: Streamlining its purchasing practices*

General Electric, along with Whirlpool, Frigidaire, Maytag, and Raytheon, dominate the white goods, or large appliance, market. GE spends in excess of $20 billion annually in buying from over 45,000 suppliers worldwide. That is, 45,000 companies are making, on average, about a half a million dollars in business from one company. GE spends $7 billion annually for appliance component parts and materials alone. Like many companies, GE is strengthening its global network of suppliers while reducing its number of suppliers.

GE's purchasing is both centralized and decentralized. Each of the company's 12 divisions does its own buying, unless what they need is required across divisional lines. The company now has a single computer supplier and travel agency. Such purchase decisions, which affect the whole company, are made by a "council of users," one representative from each of GE's divisions. Other purchases are made by professional buyers at the division level.

John D. Cologna, manager of planning and development for GE, oversees much of the company's purchasing activity. He emphasizes to potential suppliers that GE is not the end-user, and if suppliers can't provide GE with the best, GE can't give its customers the best. Cologna asks, "Does the vendor's management have the same objectives and goals as we do? Do they manage their suppliers as we manage ours?"

Questions:

1. What criteria are likely to be most important for a company that wants to sell appliance parts to GE?

2. What buying-center individuals are likely to be involved in decisions about the purchase of aluminum for one of GE's appliance divisions?

3. How will GE's goal to be competitive in the appliance market worldwide influence the selection of suppliers?

Sources: Barry Rehfeld, "How Large Companies Buy," *Personal Selling Power*, September 1993, pp. 26–33; Ernest Raia, "Top 100, 1992," *Purchasing*, November 19, 1992, pp. 43–67; and Shirley Layer, "'White Goods' Wars Continue," *Purchasing*, May 7, 1992, pp. 69–73.

Case 6.2   *General Motors: Cutting costs, not quality*

General Motors endorses a corporatewide commitment to increasing quality. Consumer perceptions of poor quality hurt GM's image in the 1980s, including its traditionally strong divisions such as Cadillac. GM heavily promoted a high-quality image in the late 80s and early 90s; it now must continue its dedication to quality, but with reduced production costs.

A sizable portion of GM's high cost structure comes from the costs of *materials* (belts, hoses, glass, plastics) used in production and *equipment* and *machinery* costs. Purchasing chief J. Ignacio Lopez de Arriortua demanded lower costs from GM's materials suppliers. He severed ties with long-standing materials suppliers that were underbid by competitors. Many suppliers were unhappy with GM and threatened to no longer develop research designed to benefit the company. Lopez's tough stance, however, has allowed GM to lower its costs of production materials.

GM knows it could further reduce equipment and machinery costs, but to do so might affect the quality of its finished automobiles. Such a strategy would destroy the gains it has made in customer perceptions of the company. GM could also maintain its current level of equipment costs *and* maintain desired quality standards. But this strategy would mean increased prices for finished products or reduced profits for GM, neither of which GM finds ideal. Another option is for GM to take the same approach with its machinery suppliers that it took with its materials suppliers: simply demand lower prices. This approach risks alienating some of these suppliers as well.

Equipment does represent a significant portion of operations costs. GM hopes its equipment suppliers can help determine a strategy that would allow the company to produce automobiles of the current high quality but at lower costs. Suppliers should be interested in this endeavor since they have a large stake in whatever decision GM makes. Some specific concerns GM hopes to address

are: Can current suppliers provide cheaper models of the same equipment? Are there ways GM can use its current equipment more efficiently, and if so, would suppliers be willing to offer training classes to GM employees for operating their equipment? Would suppliers willingly reduce their prices of the equipment? And are there ways to reduce other equipment-related costs such as transportation expenses?

The equipment suppliers know that if they cannot answer these questions to GM's satisfaction, Lopez may simply demand lower prices from them as he did earlier with materials suppliers.

Questions:

1. Evaluate Lopez's earlier strategy of demanding lower prices from the materials suppliers. Which is more important from GM's perspective as a business-to-business buyer, costs or quality?

2. What, if any, are the ethical issues that might arise?

3. Propose a specific strategy that would allow GM to maintain its high quality at reduced cost. Be specific in your recommendation and its implementation.

4. What strategy should business marketers use in trying to get or maintain GM's business? That is, how should suppliers of equipment used in automobile manufacturing market products to GM?

Sources: John Templeman, "It's Getting Tougher to Untangle the Lopez Imbroglio," *Business Week*, July 26, 1993, pp. 32–34; John Templeman, "How Many Parts Makers Can Stomach the Lopez Diet," *Business Week*, June 28, 1993, pp. 45–46; Richard Downs, "Cut Costs or Else: Companies Lay Down the Law to Suppliers," *Business Week*, March 22, 1993, pp. 28–29; Jane Easter Bahls, "Managing for Total Quality," *Public Relations Journal*, April 1992, pp. 16–20; and General Motors *Annual Report 1990*.

PART 3

Marketing Research and Market Segmentation

7. Marketing Research and Decision Support Systems

8. Market Segmentation and Targeting

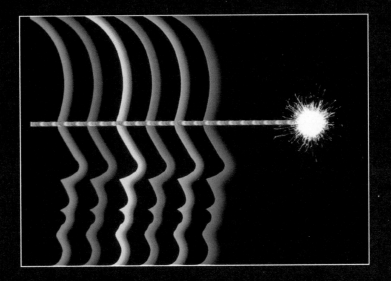

Marketers today must appeal to diverse and highly fragmented markets.

Marketing research involves the generation of useful information to improve managerial decision making. Market segmentation is the division of a market into subsets of customers with similar needs or behaviors.

How are useful data collected and analyzed to shed light on marketing problems? How does a firm develop and use a market segmentation philosophy? How does it target segments with the appropriate messages and products? The two chapters in this part of the text address these and related topics. Chapter 7, "Marketing Research and Decision Support Systems," discusses the nature of marketing research and the ways research can be used to improve marketing decisions. Chapter 8, "Market Segmentation and Targeting," explains the process of segmenting markets and targeting products and services to appeal to those segments.

Marketing Research and Decision Support Systems

After studying this chapter you should be able to:

1. Understand the purpose and functions of marketing research.

2. Be familiar with the stages of the marketing research process.

3. Discuss different types of research designs, data collection methods, and sources of secondary and primary marketing research data.

4. Understand many of the major issues involved with survey design and sampling.

5. Appreciate the role of marketing research within decision support systems.

G.I. Joe and Barbie—or Pick Up 'n Go: Marketing to kids

Toy makers constantly race to develop the next irresistible product for children. Outstanding successes include Cabbage Patch dolls, laser tag, G.I. Joe, Rubik's cube, Barney, and the super water pistol. Because most successful toys are not unisex but are aimed at either the girls' market or the boys' market, gender-specific marketing has become a fact of life for toy marketers. Mattel, for example, has been incredibly successful in the girls' market, with Barbie-related products so consistently dominant it is difficult for new entries to capture market share. Action figures are the most popular toys for the boys' market, with the Turtles (launched in 1988 by Playmates) the most successful line in US toy history.

Currently, marketing research indicates that parents want more unisex or gender-neutral toys to avoid teaching stereotyping and sexism to their children. But research with kids reveals that many children still prefer gender-specific toys. For example, when Fisher-Price introduced a unisex-designed Pick Up 'n Go Dump Truck that sweeps blocks into its bed, the truck was purchased primarily for boys. Facing this disappointment, Fisher-Price redesigned the concept and introduced Pick Up 'n Go Vacuum—and found it was purchased largely for girls.

To combat the gender dilemma and to lure both boys and girls to their products, toy companies are trying to broaden the appeal of their offerings. Mattel launched a tie-in with cable TV network Nickelodeon to create activity toys aimed at both girls and boys. And Strombecker's Tootsie brand Bubble Sword seems to appeal to both boys and girls. It is an uphill battle, though. Focus groups indicate that many parents become upset if their boys play with stereotypical "girls' toys," and vice versa.

Younger children are more open to different types of products, but marketing research reveals that when kids begin school they split into very distinct gender play patterns, and the best bet for gender-blind products seems to be action-oriented toys and games.

When you're expecting company, everything has to be perfect.

The Fisher-Price Magic Vac is the best way to keep all your housekeeping from feeling like a chore.

It's a lot more fun than Mom's vacuum cleaner. Just as sturdy. And it's a lot easier to use.

The Magic Vac not only looks real, it sounds real, too. It even lights up when you push it. Of course, it must be magic, because it does all of that without any batteries.

The Magic Vac from Fisher-Price. It's just one of over 300 toys we make that make childhood a little more special.

Fisher-Price
Because you're only young once.

Sources: Kate Fitzgerald, "Toyland's Elusive Goal—Win Over Both Sexes," *Advertising Age,* February 8, 1993, pp. S1, S18; Kate Fitzgerald, "Domestic Life Fun for Tots Eager to Emulate," *Advertising Age,* February 8, 1993, p. S1; and Selinda S. Gruber, "Sugar and Spice and Everything," *Advertising Age,* February 8, 1993, p. S4.

Marketing research is used in planning to identify the needs of product users and in problem solving to evaluate the types of products to offer.

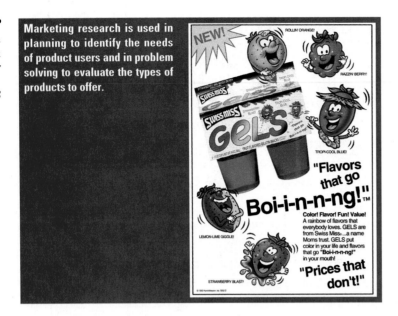

The problems encountered by toy manufacturers in developing unisex toys will not be easily solved. However, this is a situation in which marketing research offers some promise. Using the approaches described in this chapter, marketing researchers are beginning to assist manufacturers in understanding the purchase decisions made by children and parents. Marketers anticipate improvements in managerial decision making in marketing to kids.

The overall objective of marketing research is to help a firm's management understand its uncertain and changing marketplace and the consumers and competitors that make up its markets. The marketing research process involves the collection, interpretation, and use of data to make decisions. Such understanding makes the firm better able to provide products and services that meet customer expectations and needs. Marketing research enhances communication between the firm and its markets with the aim of improving managerial decision making. The aim of research is not to confirm that decisions already made are correct, but to identify alternative choices and to support the decision-making process.[1]

What is marketing research?

In its definition of **marketing research,** the American Marketing Association recognizes the complexity of the process and the different activities that may be performed.

> *Marketing research links the consumer, the customer, and the public through information used to:*
> * *Identify and define marketing opportunities.*
> * *Generate, refine, and evaluate marketing actions.*
> * *Monitor marketing performance.*
> * *Improve understanding of marketing as a process.*
>
> *Marketing research:*
> * *Specifies the information required to address these issues.*
> * *Designs the methods for collecting information.*

Exhibit 7.1	Kinds of questions marketing research can help answer

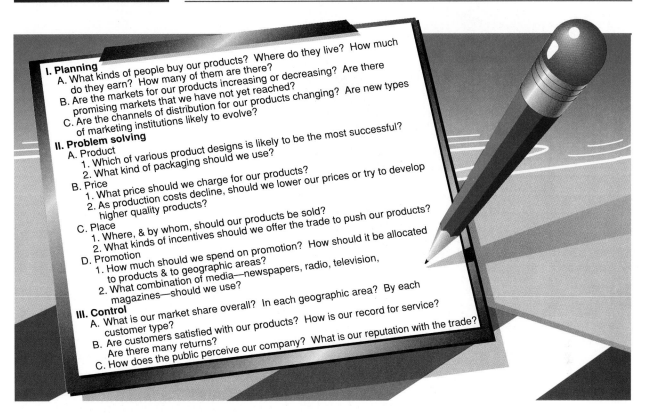

I. Planning
  A. What kinds of people buy our products? Where do they live? How much do they earn? How many of them are there?
  B. Are the markets for our products increasing or decreasing? Are there promising markets that we have not yet reached?
  C. Are the channels of distribution for our products changing? Are new types of marketing institutions likely to evolve?

II. Problem solving
  A. Product
    1. Which of various product designs is likely to be the most successful?
    2. What kind of packaging should we use?
  B. Price
    1. What price should we charge for our products?
    2. As production costs decline, should we lower our prices or try to develop higher quality products?
  C. Place
    1. Where, & by whom, should our products be sold?
    2. What kinds of incentives should we offer the trade to push our products?
  D. Promotion
    1. How much should we spend on promotion? How should it be allocated to products & to geographic areas?
    2. What combination of media—newspapers, radio, television, magazines—should we use?

III. Control
  A. What is our market share overall? In each geographic area? By each customer type?
  B. Are customers satisfied with our products? How is our record for service? Are there many returns?
  C. How does the public perceive our company? What is our reputation with the trade?

- *Manages and implements the data collection process.*
- *Analyzes the results.*
- *Communicates the findings and implications.*[2]

EXECUTIVE ROUNDTABLE COMMENT | **Bill Neal, senior executive officer, SDR, Inc., Atlanta, and past American Marketing Association chair, comments:**

This definition gives the marketing researcher several professional roles—the role of consultant, of designer, of analyst, and of information communicator. For this definition to have impact, we as marketing research professionals must take responsibility for promoting it throughout corporate America.

This definition emphasizes the generation of information that assists in managerial decision making. We adapted the second half of the definition as an outline for discussing the stages of the marketing research process in this chapter.

Marketing research is useful in planning, problem solving, and control as shown in Exhibit 7.1. Marketers following a *productivity perspective* use marketing research to provide guidance in decision making. This enables them to spend their resources more effectively. Researchers must understand the research process, the marketing process, and the industries in which the firm operates.[3] Take the research team for Stouffers, a national organization that manages private restaurants and clubs, for example. Stouffer researchers must understand the growth and image objectives of the organization, besides identifying new-market opportunities and conducting customer satisfaction surveys. Only by knowing the club management business can meaningful research be conducted to support the Stouffer organization.

Ford finds it useful from the *re-lationship* and *quality/value perspectives* to obtain input from customers in designing new products.

Marketing research is often used to evaluate the characteristics and potential of markets prior to making decisions about product introductions and new-market entry. Research is helpful in evaluating new-product concepts and advertising campaigns under consideration. It is also used to monitor market performance and competitive reaction. Nielsen Inc., one of the oldest and largest marketing research firms, provides data to packaged goods manufactures like Coca-Cola and Nabisco about their product sales. Research is also used to identify and solve problems. Municipalities, for example, frequently conduct marketing research to identify citizens' needs and methods for attracting shoppers to the area.

The marketing research process

Exhibit 7.2 presents the stages of the **marketing research process.** The sequence begins with an understanding of the problem and ends with analysis and interpretation.[4] The overall objective should be to generate useful, timely, and cost-effective information. That is, the resulting reduced risk and improved decision making should justify the research costs involved. Even a small study involving 500 local telephone interviews can cost more than $10,000 when researcher time and other costs are considered. Consequently, the cost/benefit trade-off of doing research is always an issue for a firm.

EXECUTIVE ROUNDTABLE COMMENT | **Bill Neal, senior executive officer, SDR, Inc.,** emphasizes the *visionary perspective* of marketing research:

Research oriented toward market segmentation, product/service positioning, market forecasting, and customer retention is strategic in nature. Major corporate failures can usually be traced to failures in at least one of these strategic areas—and often to a lack of information that could have been provided by good marketing research.

Exhibit 7.2

The marketing research process

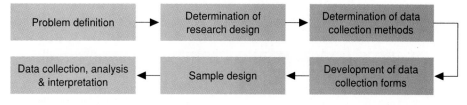

Problem definition → Determination of research design → Determination of data collection methods →

Data collection, analysis & interpretation ← Sample design ← Development of data collection forms ←

Problem definition

Problem definition is the first step in any marketing research project and is critical to its success. Problems in a business are often defined as differences between the way things should be and the way they are. Both researchers and management (the users of the research) need to understand the research problem clearly.

The problem definition stage is often difficult, for the expectations and desires of the manager and the researcher frequently differ. Researchers generally take an exploratory perspective, while managers may prefer research that confirms their expectations and provides few surprises. An *execution perspective* is critical to ensuring that the problem is defined properly.

For best results, all parties involved must take a constructive stance in defining the research problem. They must focus on the real problem and not the symptoms; anticipate how the information will be used; and avoid prescribing a specific study until the problem is defined.

Research designs

Marketing research designs are general strategies or plans of action for addressing the research problem and the data collection and analysis process. The problem definition stage is likely to suggest approaches for determining which marketing research design to use. Research generally has three purposes: exploration, description, or explanation.[5] They result in three general types of research designs: exploratory, descriptive, and causal. Common methods and example studies for each of these designs are shown in Exhibit 7.3.

This ad is part of a South Seas Plantation campaign developed from focus groups of guests and resort prospects who helped in decisions about themes, logos, TV spots, and brochures.

NOT ALL OUR GUESTS ARRIVE IN RANGE ROVERS.

At South Seas Plantation, some of our guests actually sail oceans to visit us. But no matter what method of transportation you choose, you'll be welcomed by a Resort and Yacht Harbour that *Motorboating and Sailing* magazine named among the dozen most spectacular cruising grounds in North America.

Located at the end of a private channel at Intracoastal Mile Marker 39, with a 6 ft. low tide depth, our full-service marina can easily accommodate craft up to 110 feet and offers more than 3,600 feet of berthing space. Amenities include fuel, electricity, water, complimentary pumpout facilities, telephone, ice, and cable TV. And the Ship's Store is stocked with supplies, marine charts, groceries, and packaged goods.

So next trip, set your course for South Seas Plantation. Because no matter how you arrive, we promise you'll leave with more wind in your sails. For more information, call your travel agent or 1-800-237-3102.

South Seas Plantation
Captiva Island, Florida

Exhibit 7.3   **Three general research designs**

Type	Common methods	Example studies
Exploratory designs	Literature reviews Case analyses Interviews with knowledgable persons In-depth interviews, focus groups	Evaluation of new-product concepts, environmental trend analysis, identification of product attribute importance
Descriptive designs	Cross-sectional surveys Panel studies Product movement surveys Store audits Telephone, mail, personal interviews	Market potential, image studies, competitive positioning analysis, market characteristic examinations
Causal designs	Experimental designs (lab & field studies) Market tests	Evaluation of alternative marketing mix combinations, (varying price levels, changing promotional appeals, reallocation of salesforce efforts)

Exploratory designs

Exploratory research is typically carried out to satisfy the researcher's desire for better understanding, or to develop preliminary background and suggest issues for a more detailed follow-up study.

As shown in Exhibit 7.3, exploratory research can be conducted using literature reviews, case analyses, interviews, and focus groups.[6] Better understanding of a problem might begin with a review of prior research. A researcher working for a bank would not begin a study of the bank's image, for example, without some review of the banking literature on what determines a bank's image. In-depth interviews with individuals who already have some knowledge of the problem may shed some light on the issue.

Descriptive designs

Descriptive research is normally directed by one or more formal research questions or hypotheses. Typically, a survey or questionnaire is administered to a sample from a population of interest to the firm, such as female household heads or purchasing agents in an industry. Examples include consumer surveys to estimate market potential, segmentation research to identify demographic consumer segments, attitude and opinion surveys, and product usage surveys.

Descriptive studies may be cross-sectional or longitudinal, depending on the timing of the observation. For example, a survey of customers administered at a given time to assess perceived satisfaction with service is a *cross-sectional study*. Consumers who participate in panel studies of purchase behavior over a period of time are involved in *longitudinal research*.

Causal designs

Exploratory and descriptive studies can help answer certain questions, but identification of cause and effect relationships require **causal research.** Causal designs call for *experiments,* in which researchers manipulate independent variables and then observe or measure the dependent variable or variables of interest.

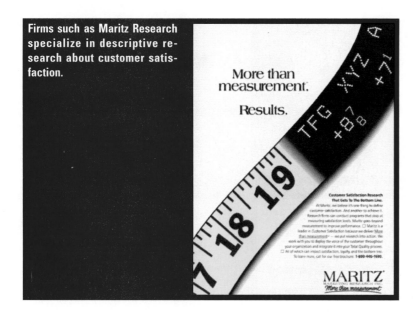

Firms such as Maritz Research specialize in descriptive research about customer satisfaction.

Suppose a direct marketing company wants to see the effect on sales of increasing its 50-cents coupon to $1. To test this, the company matches two markets, using key variables such as product sales, consumer demographics, and market size. In one market, consumers receive the $1 coupon; in the other market, they receive the 50-cents coupon. At the end of the experiment, the company compares sales in the two markets and learns that the $1 coupon generates more sales. When it incorporates the cost/profitability of each coupon value into the analysis, however, the company finds the $1 coupon results in a loss, while the 50-cents coupon is profitable. This analysis convinces the company to continue its 50-cents coupon promotion.

Data types

Marketing research information is categorized as either primary data or secondary data. Interrelationships among the different types of data and the various data collection methods are summarized in Exhibit 7.4.

Exhibit 7.4 **Data collection methods and examples**

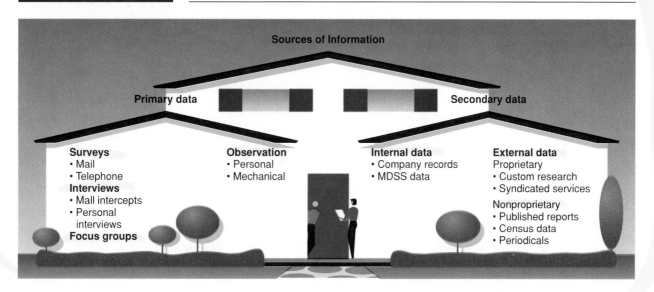

CF Motor Freight developed a new service—Guaranteed Pickup—using primary data obtained from a study of CF customers.

Primary data

Primary data are collected specifically for a particular research problem. This is the type of information most frequently associated with marketing research, such as survey data from a sample of customers about satisfaction with services. Polls on the standing of political candidates prior to elections are another example. Primary data have the advantage of currency and relevance for a specific research problem. Their primary disadvantage is cost.

Secondary Data

Secondary data are those already collected for some other purpose and are available from a variety of sources. As a rule, researchers should consult secondary data before collecting primary data. Corporate libraries and outside vendors (firms that specialize in providing research data) provide secondary data. Some public and private universities offer secondary research services. Japanese firms have long recognized the value of secondary data within their firms and regularly use it to compare product movement.[7]

Internal secondary data are collected within a firm and include accounting records, salesforce reports, or customer feedback reports. *External secondary data* may be nonproprietary or proprietary. *Nonproprietary* secondary data are available in libraries and other public sources. For example, information from the *Sales & Marketing Management's* "Survey of Buying Power" about population, income, and age groups can help managers estimate market potentials and identify likely market segments.

Online computer databases using CD technology are often free or available in libraries for minimal fees. Many companies now purchase demographic and geographic census data on CD-ROM for use in selecting store sites, mapping sales territories, and segmenting markets.[8]

Proprietary secondary data are provided by commercial marketing research firms that sell their services to other firms. Commercial firms can establish *diary panels* of representative households that record product and brand purchases. These data can help companies evaluate market share and purchase patterns. *Scanner data* obtained from Universal Product Code (UPC) information read in grocery stores provide timely information on actual purchase behavior.

Advances like these enable retailers to monitor product movement and to assess the effectiveness of advertising and in-store promotions. Several firms, including Nielsen and Information Resources, Inc., developed proprietary systems

THE TECHNOLOGICAL EDGE

CATS *provide single-source data*

*S*ingle-source marketing data is a hot advance in marketing research. This is information from a single group of households about the consumption of goods and the group's exposure to advertising and sales promotion. The single-source concept was developed for packaged-goods manufacturers seeking reliable information about brand sales and market share, retail prices, consumer and trade promotion activity, TV viewing, and household purchase behavior.

In response to the growth of single-source data, Research Systems Corp. and Nielsen Marketing Research developed the Comprehensive Advertising Tracking System (CATS), which measures a TV campaign's quality and the effects of advertising on sales performance. CATS can also examine the relative weight of advertising versus sales promotions (coupons, in-store price discounts). Nielsen's Monitor-Plus system provides commercial ratings for each TV spot by brand. Research Systems' ARS Persuasion system pretests an ad's selling power by measuring a group's brand preferences before and after exposure to a series or block of commercials. The data can also be combined with Nielsen's ScanTrack data, which track sales and promotions in product categories at the household level.

NPD/Nielsen has a representative sample of over 15,000 households equipped with a bar-code reader, or "wand," that contains prices from stores participating in its Scantrack program. As purchases are put away at home, the reader records purchase information. The bar-code reader prompts for additional information if products are bought from any nonparticipating stores. This information can then be combined with demographic data and other information already known about the household's characteristics.

Sources: Scott Hume, "Power of Persuasion," *Advertising Age,* March 11, 1991, p. 24; Howard Schlossberg, "IRI, Nielsen Slug It Out in 'Scanning Wars,' " *Marketing News,* September 2, 1991, pp. 1, 47; and Carol Hildebrand, "A Wave of a Wand Tracks Buying Habits," *Computerworld,* June 10, 1991, p. 31.

that combine information on product purchasing behavior with TV viewing behavior to produce **single-source data.**[9] **The Technological Edge: CATS Provide Single-Source Data** describes an advanced program that enables marketers to evaluate the movement of products and the effectiveness of their marketing strategies.

Computer technology is used in novel ways to combine US census data with internal customer data. For example, *geographic information systems (GIS),* provide digitized maps that can be displayed on color computer terminals.[10] There

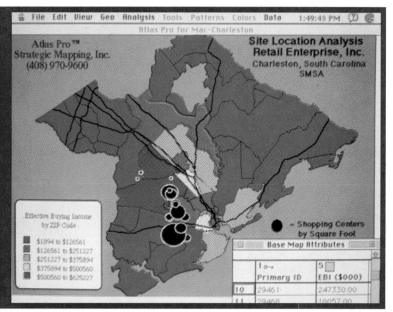

This geodemographic map, developed by Strategic Mapping, Inc., assists a retailer's sight selection decision in Charleston, SC, with a view of the area's buying income by ZIP code.

Exhibit 7.5	Advantages and disadvantages of frequently used data collection methods	
Method	**Advantages**	**Disadvantages**
Focus groups	• Depth of information collected • Flexibility in use • Relatively low cost • Data collected quickly	• Requires expert moderator • Questions of group size & acquaintanceships of participants • Potential for bias from moderator • Small sample size
Telephone surveys	• Centralized control of data collection • More cost effective than personal interviews • Data collected quickly	• Resistance in collecting income, financial data • Limited depth of response • Disproportionate coverage of low-income segments • Abuse of phone by solicitors • Perceived intrusiveness
Mail surveys	• Cost effective per completed response • Broad geographic dispersion • Ease of administration • Data collected quickly	• Refusal & noncontact problems with certain segments • Limited depth of response • Difficult to estimate nonresponse biases • Resistance & bias in collecting income, financial data • Lack of control following mailing
Personal (in-depth) interviews	• More depth of response than telephone interviews • Generate substantial number of ideas compared to group methods	• Easy to transmit biasing cues • Not-at-homes • Broad coverage often infeasible • Cost per contact high • Data collection time may be excessive

is a huge difference between a stack of printed customer names and addresses and a color-coded map showing where the customers are located. GIS systems save marketing researchers hours of tedious plotting. GIS maps were used in the Clinton/Gore presidential campaign to improve volunteer and media efforts.[11]

Geographic displays have significant potential for marketing research use in the next decade. The Bureau of Census now sells street maps with economic and population data detailed to city blocks on compact discs. Programmers can mesh customer data with these spatial databases, allowing display of three-dimensional plots of customers. Consistent with the *ethical perspective,* Chemical Bank uses GIS to ensure the bank acts in a socially responsible manner and lends money fairly in poor neighborhoods. And PepsiCo uses GIS to pinpoint the best locations for new Pizza Huts and Taco Bells.[12]

Data collection methods

Some of the more popular methods of primary data collection include focus groups, telephone surveys, mail surveys, personal interviews, and mall intercepts. Their principal advantages and disadvantages are summarized in Exhibit 7.5.

Focus groups

The most common exploratory procedure is the **focus group.** Focus groups usually comprise 8 to 12 individuals led by a moderator in a focused, in-depth discussion on a specific topic. Usually lasting no more than two hours, the sessions are designed to obtain participant feedback on a particular subject. Focus groups of consumers are well suited for examining new-product concepts and advertising themes, investigating the criteria underlying purchase decisions, and generating information for developing consumer questionnaires.[13]

	Exhibit 7.5	**Continued**

Method	Advantages	Disadvantages
Mall intercepts	• Flexibility in collecting data, answering questions, probing respondents • Data collected quickly • Excellent for concept tests, copy evaluations, other visuals • Fairly high response rates	• Limited time • Sample composition or representativeness is suspect • Costs depend on incidence rates • Interviewer supervision difficult
Projective techniques	• Useful in word association tests of new brand names • Less threatening to respondents for sensitive topics • Can identify important motives underlying choices	• Require trained interviewers • Cost per interview high
Observation	• Can collect sensitive data • Accuracy of measuring overt behaviors • Different perspective than survey self-reports • Useful in studies of cross-cultural differences	• Appropriate only for frequently occurring behaviors • Unable to assess opinions or attitudes causing behaviors • May be expensive in data collection time costs

Marriott, in an attempt to strengthen relationships with its customers, conducts ongoing focus groups with its customers and its service personnel. The focus groups used to develop Tylenol's new cough medicine revealed that the brand symbol, an elongated "C," reminded them of cough and care. In focus groups for Crayola, consumers were asked to draw the product's package from memory. The results revealed the green and yellow colors are synonymous with the product and demonstrated the importance of keeping these colors in the package design.[14] Focus groups have even been asked to watch movies (*WarGames* and *The Firm*) and then provide endings.

Telephone surveys

Telephone interviews are relatively cost effective; a large number of them over a wide geographical area can be conducted quickly and efficiently. Many firms use telephone interviews as their primary means of conducting survey research.

Telephone interviews also enable centralized control and supervision of data collection. *Random digit dialing* and *plus-one dialing* methods have become increasingly popular in the telephone interview process. In one popular version of random-digit dialing, four random digits are added to three-digit telephone exchanges. In plus-one dialing, a telephone number is randomly selected from the local directory, and a digit or digits added to it. This enables the inclusion of unlisted numbers in the sample and increases the likelihood of sampling a working number.

Technology has both positive and negative effects on telephone interviewing. On the positive side, the availability of computer-assisted telephone (CAT) interviewing has enhanced sampling, data entry, and data processing. Interviewers can read questions from a computer screen and record answers directly on the computer. This process results in instantaneously updating data. Moreover, WATS services have lowered the cost of telephone surveying. Yet technology has some negative effects on the use of telephone interviews too. Answering machines and voice-mail responses inhibit both consumer and business-to-business telephone research.[15]

Surveys on a budget

Caravan is a unique service offered by Opinion Research Corporation (ORC) and targeted for smaller companies with entrepreneurial interests. Caravan provides a slot for a number of clients on the same telephone survey. If a firm gets its questions to ORC by Wednesday afternoon, the results are back by Tuesday. For surveys of five or more questions, ORC charges $525 per question. The responses are based on 1,000 randomly dialed telephones—a method that can reach any market. Although the research is not a large customized study, the costs do not approach the $50,000 to $80,000 often required for some marketing research surveys.

The service can produce insightful research that is timely and cost effective. For example, Jacques Borisewitz, marketing manager for GlassBlock products of Pittsburgh Corning, used the Caravan to assess the reasons underlying the unusual growth of its building products in a slow-growth industry. For Borisewitz, the responses to the 14 questions he included on the Caravan survey were unexpected. Fully one-third of the respondents said they would likely buy glass block for their homes, an eye-popping figure, considering that market penetration was only 10 percent. This research led to subsequent consumer research intended to evaluate alternative consumer advertising themes.

Source: "Marketing Research: Surveys on a Budget," *Sales & Marketing Management,* November 1991, p. 29.

Problems with the use of telephone interviews limit their effectiveness. Questionable ethical practices, such as the use of marketing research as a sales ploy, hurt the research industry. Both the European Society for Opinion and Marketing Research (ESOMAR) and Council of American Survey Research Organizations (CASRO) have called for self-regulation among companies doing telephone interviews to stem the growing backlash against researchers.[16] Many states are contemplating legislation to restrict telephone survey research. In addition, the breadth and depth of information that can be obtained from telephone interviews is limited.[17]

Mail surveys

Mail surveys can obtain broad geographical market coverage, are generally less expensive per completed survey than other methods, and can be used to collect data rather quickly. Surveys can address a range of issues in a single questionnaire. Studies based on mail questionnaires, and to lesser degrees those using telephone and personal interviews, suffer from nonresponse. Inaccurate mailing lists, questions about who exactly answers the survey, and the inability to handle respondent questions are additional shortcomings of mail surveys.

Although mail questionnaires are relatively inexpensive, conducting a mail survey can involve investments that may be prohibitive for smaller firms. **The Entrepreneurial Spirit: Surveys on a Budget** describes the attempts of one company to serve smaller firms or those without a research department.

Costs can be reduced by other means as well. For example, Plymart Company, a large southeastern building supply company, chose a university professor over an independent marketing research contractor to design and administer a survey of customer perceptions. The results persuaded management to add framing supplies, which increased sales by 22 percent. For less than $5,000, the company received $100,000 worth of information.[18]

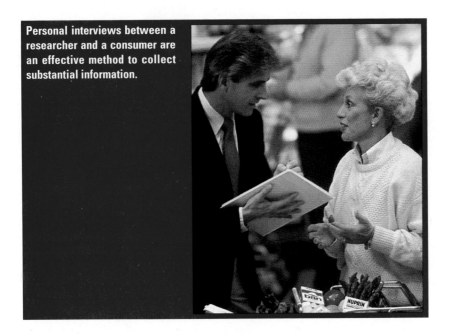

Personal interviews between a researcher and a consumer are an effective method to collect substantial information.

Personal interviews

Personal interviews involve one-on-one interactions between a consumer, customer, or respondent and the researcher or some field interviewer paid to conduct the interviews. Personal interviews have relatively high response rates. In addition, they can collect substantial in-depth information and provide visual stimuli such as products and advertisements. Some researchers believe personal interviews are even more flexible than focus groups in that questioning adjustments can be made between interviews if necessary.[19] In addition, shy respondents can have their say, and sensitive topics can be more easily covered than in focus groups.

Disadvantages of personal interviews include the time and travel costs, concerns of personal safety of the interviewer, and inability to cover a wide geographical area. Personal interview response rates average 70 percent, but participation varies widely over types of neighborhoods. People living in metropolitan areas tend to be the least responsive.[20]

Mall intercepts

The shortcomings of personal interviews have led to increased use of **mall intercept interviews**—the fastest growing method of data collection. In a mall intercept, consumers are approached and interviewed while on shopping trips. One-on-one interaction provides the chance to show visual cues, while overcoming many of the time, travel, and safety concerns associated with door-to-door personal interviewing. Research has shown mall intercept interviewing to provide findings and quality of responses similar to other data collection methods.[21]

Technological advances have enhanced the productivity of mall intercept research. MarketWare Corporation solicits participants for their "virtually real shopping" simulation: "strolling" through store aisles via computer screen. Research can be conducted on any number of variables simultaneously, such as price, package information, and shelf location.[22]

Projective techniques and observation

Marketing researchers sometimes use projective techniques and observation for data collection. **Projective techniques,** such as word association or sentence completion, allow a researcher to elicit feelings that normally go unexpressed. They may be particularly useful in eliciting honest opinions about sensitive subjects. They can be used effectively in focus groups, mall intercepts, and personal interviews. In one application, consumers are asked to react to different forms of an advertisement or pictures without any brand or product information included in the mock-up. Reactions are reassessed when brand names are added.[23]

Observation research monitors customer behavior by a researcher or by video camera. Much can be learned by unobtrusively observing how customers use a firm's or its competitor's products. In some instances, observation may provide more accurate information than survey data.[24] Observation research is also useful when traditional survey methods may not reveal the process by which goods and services are bought and used.

In another form of observation research, mystery shoppers evaluate the consistency and quality of services offered. Banks frequently use this practice to evaluate the service quality provided by their tellers and service personnel.

Ethnographic research attempts to record how consumers actually use products, brands, and services in day-to-day activity. This form of direct observation—called *ethnography*—is based on techniques borrowed from sociology and anthropology. For example, a researcher may actually enter the consumer's home, observe consumption behavior, and record pantry and even garbage content. This method of collecting more realistic data and richer descriptions of consumer behavior is expected to increase dramatically.[25]

Data collection instruments

The collection of marketing research information typically involves construction of a data collection instrument called a *survey* or *questionnaire*. Once a survey has been drafted, the instrument should be pretested on a representative sample and revised accordingly. The final instrument should consist of unambiguous, concise, and unbiased questions that respondents will be able and willing to answer.

Data collection instruments vary in structure. The degree of structure is influenced both by the research design (exploratory versus descriptive) and the method of data collection (focus group versus mail survey). Questions may take an open-ended, multiple choice, or scaled response format. Examples of questions and response formats are shown in Exhibit 7.6.

Exhibit 7.6	Types of questions used in survey research

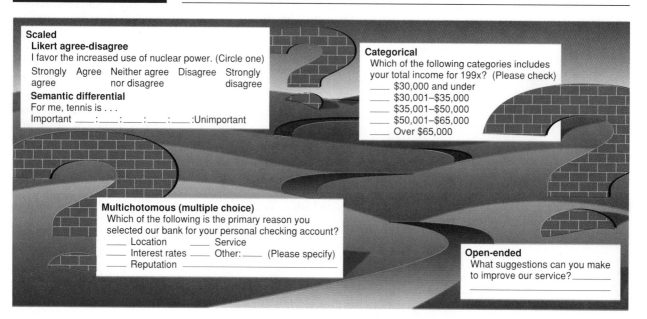

Scaled
Likert agree-disagree
I favor the increased use of nuclear power. (Circle one)
Strongly   Agree   Neither agree   Disagree   Strongly
agree   nor disagree   disagree
Semantic differential
For me, tennis is . . .
Important ____:____:____:____:____:Unimportant

Categorical
Which of the following categories includes your total income for 199x? (Please check)
____ $30,000 and under
____ $30,001–$35,000
____ $35,001–$50,000
____ $50,001–$65,000
____ Over $65,000

Multichotomous (multiple choice)
Which of the following is the primary reason you selected our bank for your personal checking account?
____ Location   ____ Service
____ Interest rates ____ Other:____ (Please specify)
____ Reputation _____

Open-ended
What suggestions can you make to improve our service?_____
_____

Sample design

The decisions and sequences involved in sampling are presented in Exhibit 7.7. The particular purpose of any research greatly influences the nature of the sampling process; of course, the population or group to be studied is determined by the issue of interest. If a wholesale bakery experiences declining product sales at the store level, it would want to sample individual purchasers and users of bakery products. Researchers might decide to sample household heads who regularly purchase bakery products.

Sampling saves money and time in that a smaller subgroup (or sample) is assumed to represent a larger population. Inferences from sample responses are then made to the population. The quality of these projections depends largely on how representative the sample is.

Probability sampling

In **probability sampling**, each person or unit in the population has a known, nonzero chance of being selected by some objective procedure. Probability samples are desirable, because the use of an objective, unbiased selection technique enhances the representativeness of the sample. There are several probability sampling approaches. In *simple random sampling*, each unit has an equal chance of being selected, such as the use of a random number table to select phone numbers. *Stratified sampling* occurs when the population is divided into mutually exclusive groups, such as consumers with different income levels, and random samples are taken from each group. *Cluster sampling* consists of organizing units into smaller groups or clusters, such as similar neighborhoods or census tracks, then selecting clusters randomly and including each house in the selected clusters in the sample.

Nonprobability sampling.

In **nonprobability sampling**, the selection of a sample is based on the judgment of the researcher or field worker. When funds or time are limited, or when only preliminary insight into a problem is needed, nonprobability samples may be appropriate. Nonprobability samples include convenience samples: for instance, the use of student samples in academic research; quota samples, in which a sample is selected to conform to some known distribution such as half female or 30 percent minority; and judgment samples, in which sample members are selected because researchers believe they bring some unique perspective to the research problem.

Exhibit 7.7	Sampling decisions and data collection issues

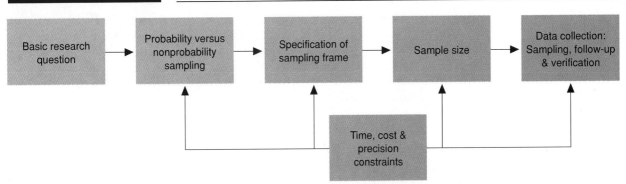

FREEZE FRAME

"Margaret, I want to know the real you . . . subject to a sampling error of plus or minus three percentage points, of course."

Sampling frame

Once the type of sample and the target population have been determined, the **sampling frame** is specified. The sampling frame is the outline or working description of the population used in sample selection. A frequently used sampling frame is the telephone book. For business-to-business marketing research, customer or firm lists might serve as the sampling frame. Today, firms often purchase sample lists from companies that specialize in providing them. Care must be exercised in selecting a sampling frame (say, a telephone listing) to minimize the exclusion of relevant population members. Telephone directories do not include unlisted households and households without telephones.

Sample size

The desired **sample size** is based on a combination of factors: the anticipated response rate, the variability in the data, cost and time considerations, and the desired level of precision.

In practice, a sample size is often some even number (500; 1,000) large enough to give the user confidence in the results, on which he or she will base decisions. As a rule, researchers may benefit by taking smaller samples selected by more rigorous but possibly more expensive probability sampling procedures. That is, research users will be more confident in the representativeness of samples selected by some unbiased selection process.

Fieldwork

Fieldwork is the process of contacting respondents, conducting interviews, and completing surveys. In the case of mail surveys, field workers must prepare mailing labels, develop introductory and follow-up letters, and carry out the mailings. Telephone surveys, personal interviews, and mall intercepts require the recruitment and training of interviewers to collect the data from the designated sample.

In many instances, the data collection process, and perhaps data analysis, will be subcontracted out to a supplier or field service firm. That is, the actual interviews may be performed by a company that specializes in collecting marketing research data. Under these circumstances, the subcontractor supervises the data collection process and verifies the quality of the information collected. This should include verifying that the interviews were indeed conducted and that the responses to certain key questions are valid or correct.

LEA & PERRINS GIVES YOUR CHICKEN AN ENGLISH FLAVOUR.

ALL CHINESE FOOD NEEDS IS AN ENGLISH DIP.

Implementing the *global perspective*, Lea & Perrins used marketing research to investigate cultural differences prior to positioning this new product in Singapore.

Analysis and interpretation

There are a variety of techniques for analyzing marketing research data, ranging in complexity from straightforward frequency distributions, means, and percentages to complex multivariate statistical tests. Statistical analyses typically look at group differences (males versus females, users versus nonusers) or the strength of association between marketing variables (advertising and sales, prices and sales). The most frequently used statistical tests include those of mean differences (*t*-tests, analysis of variance) and correlation tests (chi-square cross classification tests, Pearson correlations, regression).

The types of analysis to be performed on the data should be anticipated at the design stage so the appropriate data collection forms are developed. As a rule, managers prefer simple understandable presentations of findings. Reports should focus on the original problem and objectives of the research.

International considerations

Rote application of US research practices to other countries is not likely to be appropriate. Firms following a *global perspective* must understand that cultural and economic differences between countries add a layer of complexity. One researcher identifies eight common errors in conducting an international research project:[26]

1. *Selecting a domestic research company to do international research*—It is best to choose a company with experience in conducting global research.

2. *Rigidly standardizing methods across countries*—In certain countries postal problems present unique difficulties; and in many countries, communications systems are inadequate for telephone interviews.

3. *Interviewing in English around the world*—Depth of responses is greatest when the local language is used.

4. *Implementing inappropriate sampling techniques*—Probability sampling designs are difficult to implement in many foreign countries.

Exhibit 7.8		Evaluating the research design		
Will the design provide information that addresses the research problem and needs of the decision maker?	Are the anticipated implications from the research actionable?	Will the value of the information justify the research cost?	Will the findings be limited by questions about the validity and generalizability of the results?	Are all aspects of the proposed research process and the use of the research ethically sound?

5. *Failing to communicate effectively with local research companies*—Everything should be put in writing and all deadlines should be specified exactly to avoid delays.

6. *Lack of consideration given to language*—For some research studies, measurement instruments should be "back translated" to ensure equivalence in meaning.

7. *Misinterpreting data across countries*—Cultural and ethnic differences can affect response, the meaning of concepts, and even responses to measurement scales. For example, Asians may use the midpoints of scales, while the English tend to understate responses.

8. *Failing to understand preferences of foreign researchers regarding the effective conduct of qualitative research*—For example, Europeans expect focus group moderators to have training in psychology; Asian mixed-sex group discussions do not yield useful information.

Conducting research using Japanese participants in particular requires some adjustment of American and European methods. The moderator or interviewer must repeatedly reassure the Japanese respondent that negative statements are acceptable. Open-ended questions, lacking some illustration, will not elicit adequate responses from Japanese consumers. Nonverbal responses, such as body movement and facial expressions, often yield more information than verbal answers.[27]

Evaluating the research design

A research proposal is often developed prior to conducting a research study. These proposals outline the purpose of the research, the activities of the project, the costs and time constraints, and the likely implications or outcomes. Once such a proposal or plan of research has been designed, it should be reviewed from a *quality/value perspective*. The most important questions to ask in evaluating a research design are presented in Exhibit 7.8.

Ethical issues in marketing research

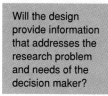

Research ethics are increasingly debated. The American Marketing Association (AMA), the Advertising Research Foundation (ARF), and the Council of American Survey Research Organizations (CASRO) are collaborating on a code of ethics. Self-regulation among firms conducting research is increasingly being called for in efforts to improve the practice of marketing research. If these efforts are not successful, respondent cooperation will continue to erode.[28]

Questionable tactics in marketing research that are frequently criticized include excessive interviewing, lack of consideration and abuse of respondents, and delivering sales pitches under the guise of marketing research.[29] The latter is particularly important for the research industry, as two-thirds of Americans consider survey research and telemarketing to be the same thing.[30] Legislation that now addresses only unsolicited commercial telephone calls could easily be extended to cover survey research.[31] Legislation already exists in most European Community nations that restricts the research industry by protecting privacy rights of consumers.

Ethical considerations are involved in the researcher's relationships with all parties in the process, including respondents, the general public, and clients. First, marketers have the responsibility to treat respondents fairly by being candid about the nature and purposes of the research, by not using research as a sales ploy, and by not violating the confidentiality of respondents' answers. Researchers' obligations to the general public include being unintrusive, being considerate, and protecting the rights of privacy.

At the same time, researchers have a responsibility to gather accurate and reliable data for their clients.[32] Researchers should not manipulate findings to present a more favorable image of themselves or the firm. The significance of results should not be overstated. Questionable research practices, such as incomplete reporting of results, misleading reporting, and nonobjective research, can bring the integrity of the entire research process into question. For example, a cigarette ad once claimed that "an amazing 60 percent" of a sample said Triumph cigarettes tasted "as good as or better than Merit." Although this statement was technically correct, the results also indicated that 64 percent said Merit tasted as good as or better than Triumph—which was not reported to the public.[33]

A final issue is the subsequent use of data and the confidentiality of information collected for a client by a firm specializing in marketing research. Consistent with the *relationship perspective,* data collected for one client should not be made available to other clients.

EXECUTIVE ROUNDTABLE COMMENT | **Bill Neal, senior executive officer of SDR, Inc.,**
suggests:

  We must do everything possible to preserve and expand the trust relationships that exist in this profession between the purchasers and providers of research. The alternative to developing partnership relationships between providers and users of research will be increasingly rigid guidelines that restrict our behavior.

Marketing decision support systems (MDSS)

Glaxo Inc., a pharmaceutical maker in Research Triangle Park, North Carolina, spends about $2 million a year on its sales and marketing decision support system for hardware, software, user training, and personnel. Donald Rao, manager of market analysis and decision support at Glaxo, claims a return on investment of 1,000 percent, since the system's development in 1987. The system provides detailed data on physician locations within sales territories, which allow managers to fine-tune marketing plans and product sample allocations. In addition, it allows substantial savings in managerial time.[34]

Like Glaxo, many firms view all marketing data and information as part of a larger entity called a **marketing decision support system (MDSS).** All activities and computerized elements used to process information relevant to marketing decisions are components. These systems are now commonplace in many Fortune 500 business-to-business giants in industries such as airlines, banking, insurance, and pharmaceuticals.

A schematic overview of an MDSS is shown in Exhibit 7.9. Such systems represent a comprehensive perspective allowing a combination of different sources of information from different departments. MDSSs are useful for both manufacturing and services companies.

Marketing decision support systems are generally designed to:[35]

• Support but not supplant management decision making.

• Apply to semistructured decisions of middle and upper management, such as pricing, promotion, and location decisions.

Exhibit 7.9   **Marketing decision support system**

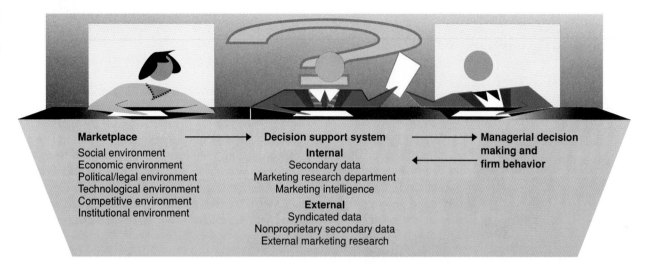

Marketplace	Decision support system	Managerial decision making and firm behavior
Social environment	**Internal**	
Economic environment	Secondary data	
Political/legal environment	Marketing research department	
Technological environment	Marketing intelligence	
Competitive environment	**External**	
Institutional environment	Syndicated data	
	Nonproprietary secondary data	
	External marketing research	

- Provide interaction between and among people and systems.
- Center on a segment of related decisions (the allocation of marketing effort and resources).
- Be user-friendly.

An MDSS is designed to enhance managerial decision making and firm performance by providing relevant and timely internal and external information. Input comes from many sources: the economic environment, social trends and changing consumer tastes, and the legal environment. Data from consumers, customers, and competitors are relevant. Prior experiences and decisions are also fed back into the system. Even permanent linkages with customers are now included in some MDSS systems. For example, a system linking Levi Strauss and Milliken, a textile manufacturer, significantly reduced costs for both companies, while enabling Levi Strauss to respond to fashion changes and bring new products to market more quickly.[36]

External marketing research data may come from syndicated sources or various nonproprietary sources of secondary data. Syndicated market databases are useful for comparison with internal sales data to gauge market penetration. Internal data normally come from the marketing research department's own input, accounting records, and salesforce reports.

Computer *technology* now enables a variety of outputs from an MDSS. Output might include forecasts of sales, comparison of sales relative to forecasts, analysis of competitor performance, estimation of market potentials, evaluation of advertising effectiveness, and monitoring of consumer expectations and satisfaction.

Database marketing

A significant technological innovation is **database marketing,** the collection and use of individual customer-specific information to make marketing more efficient. The term *database* refers to customer/prospect information stored in a computer with software to process the information. Computer technology provides the ability to pull apart and recombine information in ways previously impossible. Knowing which customers are more predisposed to which products allows a firm to tailor marketing efforts to individual customers.

Database marketing is used by Kay-Bee Toy Stores to build a customer base within the neighborhood of its stores. It distributes the *Goodtimes* magazine to all families who live within a 10-minute drive of a Kay-Bee store and have children between 4 and 14 years old.

Vipoint Pharmaceutical, a Fort Collins, Colorado, marketer of oral hygiene products, grew from start-up sales of $13,000 to $37 million in 10 years. The company credits its success to its relationships with its customers, both consumers and dentists, which the compilation of individual information files helped establish.[37] Similarly, relationship marketing has been strengthened for the Bank of A. Levy, of Ventura, California, by its implementation of a system that catalogs and sorts marketing customer information files. Manipulation of individual customer files through some database marketing program is becoming increasingly important to relationship marketing.[38]

Summary

1. **Understand the purpose and functions of marketing research.** The function of marketing research is to generate information that assists the firm's managers in making decisions. Marketing research helps managers respond to the ever-changing environment in which businesses operate. It is useful in problem solving, planning for the future, and controlling or monitoring ongoing performance. Marketing research links the marketer, the customer, and the public through information used to identify and define marketing opportunities; generate, refine, and evaluate marketing actions; monitor marketing performance; and improve understanding of marketing as a process.

2. **Be familiar with the stages of the marketing research process.** There are six stages of the marketing research process, through which primary data are generated to address a specific marketing problem or issue. In the first stage, problem definition, both the researcher and the user develop a clear conception of the problem that the research is intended to address.

   The second stage is specification of the appropriate research design, which is then used in the third stage, determination of the types of data to be collected and the methods of collection.

   In the fourth stage, researchers develop a data collection form, often called a survey or questionnaire.

In the fifth stage researchers design the sample, specifying the fieldwork required to collect the data. Finally, the data collected are analyzed, summarized, and presented to the users or firm management.

3. **Discuss different types of research designs, data collection methods, and sources of secondary and primary marketing research data.** Exploratory research designs are used to obtain general familiarity with a topic or problem. Focus groups, literature reviews, case analyses, interviews with knowledgeable individuals, and convenience sampling are examples of exploratory research.

   Descriptive designs are typically guided by some specific research question or hypothesis. Cross-sectional designs involve surveys administered at a given time. Longitudinal designs examine research questions over time through repeated measures of a common sample. Causal designs involve experiments, in which researchers manipulate independent variables of interest, such as price or advertising.

   Marketing data can be primary or secondary. Secondary data may be either internal, coming from within the firm, or external. External secondary data may be either nonproprietary (noncommercial) or proprietary.

4. *Understand many of the major issues involved with survey design and sampling.* Each survey method has its advantages and disadvantages. The different survey methods include telephone interviews, mail questionnaires, personal interviews, and mall intercepts. Researchers must carefully construct items or questions in a survey to ensure that the data collected are reliable (yield consistent responses) and valid (reflect the concepts being studied).

Researchers can use probability or nonprobability samples, depending on the objectives, characteristics, and budget of the research. Probability samples are selected by some objective, unbiased process. Simple random samples are the most typical example.

To assemble a nonprobability sample, the judgment of the researcher enters into the selection. Examples of nonprobability samples are convenience samples and quota samples. The researcher must decide on the population to be sampled, the sample size, and the sampling frame.

5. *Appreciate the role of marketing research within decision support systems.* Within the firm, the marketing decision support system (MDSS) consists of all activities and the hardware and software regularly used to process and provide marketing information relevant to marketing decisions. The firm may also employ outside agencies to provide marketing input.

Key terms & concepts

marketing research   *156*
marketing research process   *158*
problem definition   *159*
marketing research designs   *159*
exploratory research   *160*
descriptive research   *160*
causal research   *160*
primary data   *162*

secondary data   *162*
single-source data   *163*
focus group   *164*
mall intercept interviews   *167*
projective techniques   *167*
observation research   *168*
ethnographic research   *168*
probability sampling   *169*

nonprobability sampling   *169*
sampling frame   *170*
sample size   *170*
marketing decision support system (MDSS)   *173*
database marketing   *174*

Review & discussion questions

1. How might a concert organizer develop a research program for evaluating customer satisfaction? Refer to **The Entrepreneurial Spirit: Surveys on a Budget.**

2. What is the purpose of marketing research? What are the primary stages of the marketing research process?

3. Explain differences among exploratory, descriptive, and causal designs, and give examples of each.

4. Differentiate these pairs of concepts:
   a. Cross-sectional versus longitudinal designs.
   b. Secondary versus primary data.
   c. Field market tests versus simulated market tests.

5. Describe the primary advantages and disadvantages of mail surveys, telephone interviews, personal interviews, and mall intercepts. What is the primary advantage of

single-source data as discussed in **The Technological Edge: CATS Provide Single-Source Data.**

6. What are the different types of probability and nonprobability samples? Give examples of each.

7. What is the difference between projective techniques and observation research? What is enthnographic observation?

8. What factors determine sample size? What is involved in fieldwork?

9. What is an MDSS? Describe its primary advantages.

10. Identify three ethical issues in marketing research. Cite some concerns faced by firms conducting marketing research.

Application exercises

1. Develop a sampling plan to conduct a telephone survey of residents in the county where your university is located. Assume you want to investigate opinions about the construction of a nuclear power plant in a nearby county. Who should be interviewed? How will the sample be drawn?

2. A manufacturer of roller blades is interested in assessing the satisfaction of its retailer customers. What are the advantages and disadvantages of the alternative data collection methods in gathering customer satisfaction data for the firm?

3. Research Incorporated, a regional marketing research firm that does tailored primary research projects in California, has been contacted by ABC Company for what appears to be a very profitable research project involving the demand for catalog shopping services. Research Incorporated recently completed a similar project for XYZ Company, a competitor of ABC. Both ABC and XYZ are large retail discount chains with over 50 stores in the Southwest. Should Research Incorporated accept the project? Should the information obtained for XYZ be given or sold to ABC?

Case 7.1   *White Castle: Expanding to Castle Meals and frozen sliders*

The Ohio-based White Castle hamburger chain began in the 1920s when the idea of fast-food hamburgers was just a novelty. Edgar W. "Billy" Ingram began the company with a $700 loan he repaid in 90 days. This conservative financial philosophy prevails at White Castle today. It has earned this company the respect of many and has enabled it to expand strongly, albeit rather slowly, to gross sales of over $300 million and nearly 300 stores in 1992. One secret of White Castle's success has been its highly effective marketing strategies.

White Castle has always enjoyed a loyal customer base; in fact, its strength has been in repeat business—loyal customers who buy the two-inch steamed "sliders" by the dozens. However loyal, this customer base is also aging, and White Castle was not reaching younger consumers.

In the 1980s, White Castle made some significant marketing moves to counter this trend. It test-marketed a packaged children's meal called the "Castle Meal" in Cincinnati and Dayton, Ohio, and in Louisville, Kentucky. Initial results were so positive these stores could not meet customer demands. By the late 1980s, the Castle Meal was offered in all White Castle restaurants, and its appeal to younger consumers is now much stronger as a result.

White Castle also discovered customers were purchasing bulk orders of hamburgers to freeze at home. White Castle's steam process leads to high moisture in the hamburgers, making them well suited for freezing and microwaving. This discovery inspired the company to test-market frozen, microwavable hamburgers in Chicago, Columbus, Denver, Indianapolis, and Portland, Oregon, grocery stores. Television advertising and coupon promotions were introduced in the Portland area test markets, while discount coupons only were used in Denver. No other promotional support was offered in Chicago, Columbus, or Indianapolis. The results were so encouraging that the company began large-scale distribution. White Castle's frozen hamburgers now give the company a presence in markets in which it had never before competed.

White Castle's test-marketing practices proved worthwhile. Successful results led the company to expand its product line and therefore reach new markets both within the restaurants and through additional outlets. Except for these innovations, White Castle maintains its conservative approach to marketing. In the late 1980s and early 1990s, most of its larger competitors in the fast-food industry branched out into numerous product offerings. White Castle, however, has remained faithful to its original niche. The company's staple product is still the two-inch square hamburgers. White Castle is not yet willing to offer new products that might conflict with its image built around that hamburger.

White Castle's slow but sure marketing promotions effectively reach its customers. Although not a national chain, the company is expanding. New stores opened in Cleveland in the late 1980s, and the company is researching potential sites in Atlanta, Denver, Philadelphia, Baltimore, and throughout Florida. But don't look for any White Castle outlets to drift too far from the niche it has filled for decades.

Questions

1. Explain the benefits of establishing different levels of promotional support for test markets in different cities.

2. What other types of research might White Castle find helpful?

3. Given your knowledge as a consumer, what strategies should White Castle consider for the future? How might the company use marketing research to evaluate these strategies?

Sources: William R. Dillon, Thomas J. Madden, and Neil H. Firtle, *Marketing Research in a Marketing Environment,* 2nd ed. (Homewood, IL: Richard D. Irwin, Inc., 1990), pp. 84–87; Bill Carlino, "Burger Chains Find It's a Hit to Be Square," *Nation's Restaurant News,* September 17, 1990, p. 12; and "White Castle: It's Like Nothing Else. Nothing," White Castle Public Relations Brochure (Columbus, OH: White Castle System, Inc., 1992).

Case 7.2   *Kellogg's Frosted Flakes: Rejuvenated and repositioned*

Like people, brands have a life span. They are born, they grow, they mature, and they die. To delay the end process, marketers may give a brand a makeover or reposition it in the minds of consumers. Another way to continue its lifespan is to capitalize on a successful brand name by applying it to other products, as brand extensions. As the financial risk and promotional costs escalate for introducing new brands, firms increasingly use the goodwill associated with existing brands to launch new brand extensions. The danger in introducing brand extensions, however, is in going too far. Levi Strauss succeeded when it introduced looser-fitting jeans; it failed when it introduced a line of dress suits.

Kellogg's Frosted Flakes suffered declining sales in the face of rising consumer health consciousness and avoidance of sugar-coated foods. Kellogg's responded to this threat by repositioning Frosted Flakes as something fun to eat, but also healthful. Its humorous new commercials

show adults secretly admitting they love the cereal. The advertising targeted the adult cereal market and successfully repositioned a well-known but aging brand.

Questions

1. What kinds of research could be used to measure the success of this repositioning strategy?

2. How could research be used to determine whether or not a new brand should have been introduced instead of repositioning the old brand?

3. What are the advantages and disadvantages that could result from this repositioning?

Sources: Diane Crispell and Kathleen Brandenburg, "What's In a Brand?" *American Demographics,* May 1993, pp. 26–32; Barbara Loken and Deborah Roedder John, "Diluting Brand Beliefs: When Do Brand Extensions Have a Negative Impact?" *Journal of Marketing,* July 1993, pp. 71–84.

Market Segmentation and Targeting

After studying this chapter you should be able to:

1. Define and explain market segmentation, target markets, and product differentiation and positioning.

2. Understand the criteria used for evaluating the likely success of a segmentation strategy.

3. Know the role of market segmentation in the development of marketing strategies and programs.

4. Describe the issues involved in product and brand positioning.

5. Understand the alternative bases for segmenting consumer and business-to-business markets.

6. Evaluate alternative approaches for pursuing segmentation strategies.

Levi Strauss: A "stitched niche" strategy

*L*evi Strauss relies on a true "stitched niche" strategy—the jeans maker mounts more than a dozen different campaigns for its different markets, both in the US and internationally. Maintaining a brand's core identity across different languages, cultures, ages, and incomes requires marketers to innovate. Levi Strauss & Company of San Francisco established a niche-market segmentation strategy in the late 1980s to respond to a diverse market for its products. Markets range from baseball-card-collecting youth to fashion models to balding Grateful Dead–heads.

Some recent Levi Strauss advertising campaigns to support its core business of men's jeans products, including the 501 Button-Fly Report for 14- to 24-year-olds, feature Spike Lee interviewing spelunkers and others on what they do while wearing their jeans. For men 25 and up, Levi's uses a different campaign, with ads on sports TV programs and in magazines showing men in more moderate activities such as touch football and outings with kids. A Hispanic campaign on TV and outdoor advertising follow two men through their day, from work

to teaching softball to a young boy. These ads convey the message, "Levi's always fits well." Silver Tab jeans, a Levi's fashion jeans line, is supported with a transit campaign in New York City, involving ads in buses and trains. "The Levi's 501 Guarantee" runs on TV and outdoor billboards in 10 regional markets the jeans maker has targeted for growth. The Loose jeans campaign uses some print ads but relies heavily upon advertising placed in TV programs targeted toward young adults.

None of these strategies is independent, however. Teenagers, for example, watch televised football games and see the Levi's ads for older buyers. The firm, as a result, is careful about the way it presents itself to its different markets. "We have to make sure our ads for jeans for men don't turn off our teenage audience, and vice versa," states Levi's marketing manager Dan Chew.

Levi's approach to marketing men's jeans is to offer multiple product versions for different consumer groups, defined largely by age and lifestyle differences. The company now follows a similar approach in its successful Dockers campaign, targeted initially to baby boomers and recently to 21- to 35-year-olds. Product offerings are supported by different messages designed specifically for segments the company wants to reach.

Sources: Pat Sloan and Marcy Magiera, "Rustling Up Jean Ads: Major Marketer Gallops into Fall on New Campaign," *Advertising Age,* July 29, 1991, p. 3; Stuart Elliot, "Levi and Spike Return in ZButton Your ZFly," Part 2, "*The New York Times,* July 22, 1991, p. D7; Sid Astbury, "Levi's Back in the Saddle," *Asian Business,* June 1992, pp. 46–48; Marcy Magiera, "Basic Jeans Shine for Levi's, Lee," *Advertising Age,* February 17, 1992, p. 22; Cyndee Miller, "Levi's, Espirit Spin New Cotton into Eco-Friendly Clothes," *Marketing News,* April 29, 1992, pp. 11–12; Marcy Magiera and Pat Sloan, "Levi's, Lee Loosen Up for Baby Boomers," *Advertising Age,* August 3, 1992, p. 9; Marcy Magiera, "Levi's Dockers Looks for Younger, Upscale Men with Authentics," *Advertising Age,* January 18, 1993, p. 4; "Levi to Market Upscale Dockers," *Marketing News,* August 16, 1993, p. 1; and Nina Munk, "The Levi Straddle," *Forbes,* January 17, 1994, pp. 44–45.

P
A
R
T

3

Procter & Gamble segments the laundry detergent market by performance needs and then offers products and promotional communications for each segment.

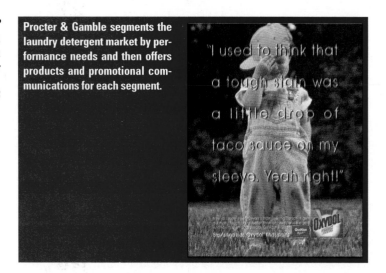

"I used to think that a tough stain was a little drop of taco sauce on my sleeve. Yeah right!"

The Levi Strauss story highlights many of the decisions firms face in developing market segmentation strategies, including identifying which markets to pursue and determining how best to reach and then appeal to buyers in those markets. A prime decision is the extent to which a marketer will vary product offerings for the different segments.

Market segmentation is among the most popular and important topics in the entire field of marketing.[1] Furthermore, market segmentation strategies are necessary both for consumer goods and services marketers and for firms operating in business-to-business markets. In this chapter, we explore the concept of market segmentation and how firms develop their market segmentation strategies. We define target markets and product differentiation and positioning, and we discuss the stages involved in developing a segmentation strategy.

Market segmentation, target markets, and product differentiation

Mass markets and widespread brand loyalty, once taken for granted in business, have given way today to market segments of widely varying tastes and needs and sensitivity to competing products. The emergence of these fragmented markets plus new economic demands, changing technology, and intense international competition have altered the ways firms must compete.

Market segmentation

Firms often pursue a market segmentation approach to meet today's market realities. As discussed in Chapter 1, a market is a group of consumers or organizations with which a firm desires to create marketing exchanges. **Market segmentation** divides a market into subsets of customers who behave in the same way, have similar needs, or have similar characteristics that relate to purchase behavior. The overall market for a product consists of segments of customers who vary in their responses to different marketing mix offerings. Market segmentation attempts to explain differences among groups of consumers who share similar characteristics and to turn these differences into an advantage.[2]

A segmentation strategy can be pursued through variations in some or all aspects (product, marketing communications, price, distribution) of the marketing mix elements. For example, many widely purchased products such as soft drinks, computers, and clothing involve variation in both product and marketing communications to reach market segments and increase sales. In other instances, a single product may be marketed to different segments, but by different marketing communication campaigns. For example, a pharmaceutical manufacturer may promote the same new drug product to physicians, pharmacists, and hospitals using a different communication program for each.

Firms taking a *visionary perspective* recognize the factors that make understanding market segmentation more important:

- Slower rates of market growth, coupled with increased foreign competition, have fostered more competition, increasing the need to identify target markets with unique needs.

- Social and economic forces, including expanding media, increased educational levels, and general world awareness, have produced customers with more varied and sophisticated needs, tastes, and lifestyles.

- Technological advances make it possible for marketers to devise marketing programs that focus efficiently on precisely defined segments of the market.[3]

- Marketers now find that minority buyers do not necessarily adopt the social and economic habits of the mainstream. As one market researcher observes, America is no longer a melting pot, but more of a mosaic or "salad bowl."[4]

Market segmentation is appropriate not just for firms marketing tangible products; nonprofit and service organizations also find it useful. For example, realizing that it had many different types of donors and volunteers, the Arthritis Foundation looked for an effective way to reach the right person, at the right time, with the proper request amount, and with the right message. To address the diversity in possible donors and volunteers, the foundation identified 12 categories of individual households defined by location, housing type, and income. The foundation found the segment labeled "urban gentry" (upper-income city dwellers) four times more likely than any other group to contribute both money and time.[5]

International marketing may be based on the cultivation of **intermarket segments,** which are well-defined, similar clusters of customers across national boundaries. This view of segmentation allows firms to develop marketing programs and offerings for each identified segment on a global basis.[6] Reliance on a single standardized global strategy can cause a firm to miss important target markets or to position products inappropriately. Similarly, customizing marketing strategy only to individual countries may result in a firm losing either potential economies of scale or opportunities for exploiting product ideas on a wider scale.[7]

Some consumer-product businesses, such as McDonald's, Coca-Cola, and Colgate-Palmolive, use globally standardized products and marketing themes for some of their products. For most consumer products and brands, however, international marketing benefits from segmentation principles. In these instances, customized strategies may be developed for different countries or groups of countries. One recent study of soap and toothpaste preferences, for example,

Patek Phillipe's multinational campaign emphasizes *global perspective* by recognizing the existence of segments across country lines. The ads are included in women's magazines in Switzerland, Japan, France, Spain, Singapore, Italy, Austria, Hong Kong, Germany, the United Kingdom, and the United States.

revealed four segments across consumers in the US, Mexico, the Netherlands, Turkey, Thailand, and Saudi Arabia. The largest segment comprised substantial numbers of consumers from Saudi Arabia, Mexico, and the Netherlands. These people all shared preferences for selected product benefits.

Target markets

Market segmentation lets a firm tailor or develop products and strategies to appeal to the preferences and unique needs of specific groups of customers. These groups are typically referred to as target markets: groups of consumers or organizations with whom a firm wants to create marketing exchanges.[8] Examples of target markets include the elderly, the Hispanic, or the college student markets—each of which can be targeted for specific products and reached through specific marketing programs. **Targeting** involves selecting which segments in a market are appropriate to focus on and designing the means of reaching them. Appealing to an entire market is often too costly. Moreover, a focus on certain markets can increase the efficiency and effectiveness of marketing efforts.

As we shall see later in this chapter, segmentation may be appropriate for businesses of all sizes—not just for large firms with many products. Many small- and medium-sized companies find it better to concentrate on gaining a large share of one segment or a few, rather than small shares of all possible segments in a product market. For example, Liberty Bank of Philadelphia generates a profitable business from a market segment overlooked by many of its competitors: small businesses. Liberty Bank exhibited an *entrepreneurial perspective* through its efforts to establish itself as the bank for small-business customers, thereby increasing its share of an important target market.[9]

Product differentiation

Related to market segmentation is **product differentiation**. Product differentiation exists when a firm's offerings differ or are perceived to differ from those of competing firms on any attribute, including price. A product differentiation strategy positions a product within the market. Consistent with the *execution perspective,* marketers attempt to position a product or service in customers' minds—to convince customers the product has unique and desirable characteristics. By developing these perceptions, marketers seek to establish a competitive advantage relative to competing firms that offer similar products or brands.

In the mid-1980s, for example, brands in the frozen entrée market were differentiated on convenience, and consumers traded taste for that convenience.

AT&T USADirect Service ad targets US residents visiting Mexico.

Stouffer's changed that balance by introducing a line of entrées positioned on taste, but offered at a premium price. By focusing on a key benefit previously missing from other frozen dinners, Stouffer's expanded the market and became the category leader. Product differentiation and positioning are explained in more detail later in this chapter.

When is market segmentation appropriate?

Market segmentation can be useful for both new ventures and mature brands. In the case of new products, marketers target segments likely to respond positively to the introduction. Products that have been on the market for a while face an increasing number of competitive offerings, making it more difficult for any mass marketer to dominate in its product categories. Some frequently used approaches include: develop brand-line extensions, reposition the product for additional uses, or identify the needs of a particular segment, or segments, and develop marketing strategies for each.[10]

The frozen entrée category again provides an example of a combined approach. Once Stouffer's successfully introduced its line of frozen entrées, the competitors came running. Stouffer's built on its success by extending its product line, tapping another key segment in the marketplace: the weight-conscious consumer. Stouffer's Lean Cuisine frozen entrées offered this segment low-calorie, tasty meals and the convenience of quick preparation. The frozen entrée category continues to be one of the most competitive in the grocery store, but Stouffer's maintains dominance through its target marketing approach.

A market segmentation strategy is not always appropriate, however. Advertising and marketing research practitioners suggest segmentation may not be useful when the overall market is so small that marketing to a portion of it is not profitable, or when the brand is dominant in the market and draws its appeal from all segments.[11]

Criteria for effective segmentation

Successful execution of a market segmentation strategy depends on the presence of several characteristics in the overall market and its various segments. In determining strategies to pursue, a firm should consider five criteria for effective segmentation: measurability, accessibility, substantialness, durability, and differential responsiveness.

Acme-McCrary and its ad agency Trone Advertising directed its Essence Hosiery campaign toward African-American women, reflecting the five criteria for effective segmentation—measurability, accessibility, substantialness, durability, and differential responsiveness.

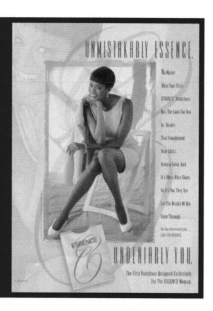

five criteria for effective segmentation

Measurability

Measurability reflects the degree to which the size and purchasing power of segments can be assessed. Measurability is enhanced if segments are defined by concrete variables enabling easily obtainable data. Demographic characteristics, such as income and age, are examples. Firms can use such data to reach segments and to estimate the size and potential of target markets.

Accessibility

Accessibility describes the degree to which a firm can reach intended target segments efficiently. That is, the selected market segments must be reachable with unique marketing communications and distribution strategies. The Hispanic market is an example of a growing segment reached by specific media (newspapers, radio, television). In another example, previously successful albums now available on CDs, such as Led Zeppelin albums, are marketed to middle-aged consumers by ads on ESPN and Arts and Entertainment cable channels.[12]

Substantialness

Substantialness refers to the degree to which identified target segments are large enough or have sufficient sales and profit potential to warrant unique or separate marketing programs. The growing Hispanic population is a sizable market that merits specifically designed products, advertising campaigns, and even distribution approaches. African-Americans make up another important demographic segment. With annual earnings over $275 billion, the segment has buying power well worth targeting.[13]

Durability

Durability has to do with stability of segments—whether distinctions between segments will diminish or disappear as the product category or the markets themselves mature.[14] The development of differentiated products, communication campaigns, or distribution strategies often involves considerable financial

Hartmarx Corporation applies the *quality/value perspective* in offering multiple product lines to various price-sensitive segments.

and time commitments. Segments selected for targeting should offer reasonably enduring business opportunities. The Hispanic market meets this criterion, as it is a significant and, perhaps more important, growing segment of the population. Current population trends indicate the Hispanic population will be a key segment for marketers for many years to come. Another is the aging US population. By the year 2000, there are expected to be 59 million people over 55 years of age. This segment is ripe for targeting products and services oriented toward health and conservation of income.[15]

Differential responsiveness

Differential responsiveness refers to the degree to which market segments exhibit varying responses to different marketing mix combinations.[16] This is a key aspect of the *productivity perspective* and the use of market segmentation. If segments do not respond differently to varying marketing communications or product offerings, there is little need to segment. People interested in price will respond differently to low prices from people who seek high quality and assume price and quality are related.

Hartmarx Corporation provides a good example of the way a manufacturer segments target markets by price sensitivity. Pursuit of the *quality/value perspective* enabled Hartmarx, a national producer and marketer of men's and women's fashions, to develop brands and strategies to fill unique market voids.[17] Once Hartmarx acknowledges that different groups of consumers are sensitive to different price levels, it designs marketing strategies to differentiate variations in product (quality), communications (types of ads), and distribution (types of retail outlets). The company targets Hickey-Freeman clothing to the upper market segment and Hart Schaffner & Marx to the upper-moderate segment. Jaymar dress slacks and Sansabelt slacks are sold to the moderate segment. Kuppenheimer Men's Clothiers and Allyn St. George are included in the popular offerings. Each brand name provides a product designed for different price-sensitive segments. Exhibit 8.1 is an example of how a retailer might segment men's clothing by price range.

Exhibit 8.1   **Hypothetical retail market segments and price points**

Retail market segments	Business clothing			Furnishings		Casual wear	
	Suits	Jackets	Dress slacks	Dress shirts	Neck–ties	Sport shirts	Casual slacks
Upscale	$600 & over	$475 & over	$150 & over	$55 & over	$45 & over	$47.50 & over	$95 & over
Upscale moderate	$450–$600	$350–$475	$100–$150	$39.50–$55	$37.50–$45	$37.50–$47.50	$65–$95
Moderate	$375–$450	$250–$350	$75–$100	$30–$39.50	$25–$37.50	$32.50–$37.50	$45–$65
Value conscious	Under $375	Under $250	Under $75	Under $30	Under $25	Under $32.50	Under $45

Satisfying the segmentation criteria

By satisfying these various criteria, a company can choose market segments that can be described in managerially useful terms (measurability); that can utilize its communication and distribution channels (accessibility); that are sufficient in profit potential (substantialness); that will persist for some reasonable period (durability); and that vary in their reactions to different marketing efforts (differential responsiveness).

The Hispanic market provides a good example of combining segmentation criteria to evaluate a market. Although there are subsegments within it, the overall Hispanic market possesses unique cultural characteristics that make it an attractive target segment. The unique language and cultural characteristics of this market clearly make the segment *measurable* and *responsive* to appeals designed directly for it. Hispanic-Americans will account for over one-fourth of the population by the year 2000; the market thus represents both a *substantial* and *durable* opportunity. The market is also *accessible*—both broadcast (radio, television) and print (newspapers, magazines) media reach the Hispanic community efficiently with specialized ads.

Marketing to Hispanic consumers has international implications as well. Wal-Mart, Sears, McDonald's, Ford, General Motors, and PepsiCo target Mexico for expanded export and local operations. McDonald's earmarked $500 million to open 250 new restaurants in Mexico by the year 2000, while relaxed trade restrictions have opened opportunities for Ford and GM to export luxury automobile models.[18]

Stages in developing market segmentation strategies

Stages required in the development of a market segmentation strategy are summarized in Exhibit 8.2. The organization's core business determines the product or service market in which it operates, be it the restaurant industry, computer software, lawnmowers, cleaning services for office buildings, or whatever. Given its overall product or service market, a firm identifies the distinguishing characteristics, or **bases of segmentation** for the segments within that market. After

Exhibit 8.2	Developing a market segmentation strategy

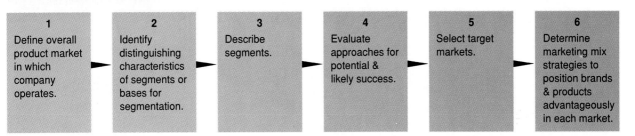

1	2	3	4	5	6
Define overall product market in which company operates.	Identify distinguishing characteristics of segments or bases for segmentation.	Describe segments.	Evaluate approaches for potential & likely success.	Select target markets.	Determine marketing mix strategies to position brands & products advantageously in each market.

describing these segments, the firm evaluates them for potential and likely success, then selects the key segment or segments to target. Finally, the firm develops marketing mix strategies, including various product and service forms, and price and distribution strategies and communication appeals for each segment.[19]

Bases for segmentation

Logical bases to define market segments have to do with characteristics of the firm's customers or their behaviors. Exhibit 8.3 describes some of these bases for both consumer and business-to-business marketing situations.[20] The Levi Strauss strategy in the opening example uses some of the most easily identified consumer segmentation bases, including age, race, and gender. For business-to-business marketing, computer companies provide an example. They frequently organize their selling efforts around different industries, such as banking, insurance, and educational institutions.

Exhibit 8.3	Frequently used consumer and business-to-business segmentation bases

Consumer marketing

User-related:

Demographics: age, gender, race, income, education, family size, family life cycle stage
Social class: lower, middle, upper
Culture: religion, nationality, subculture
Geographic: region, state, metropolitan location & size, urban versus rural
Lifestyles & psychographics: quiet family person, traditionalist attitudes, progressive, conservative

Behavioral:

Benefits: desired product attributes
Usage: users versus nonusers, light versus heavy
Price or promotional sensitivity: high versus low
Brand loyalty: loyal versus nonloyal
Buying situation: kind of store, gift giving (kind of shopping)

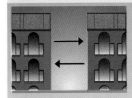

Business-to-business

User-related:

Customer size: annual sales
Geographic location: Northeast versus West Coast
Organizational structure: centralized versus decentralized
Stage of buying process: decision at hand versus initial stages of decision making
Attitude toward vendor: current purchaser versus new account
Buying decision criterion: price versus quality
Type of product: installations, supplies, services, raw materials, component parts
Type of organization: manufacturing, government, public utility

Behavioral:

End use: resale versus production component
Usage: users versus nonusers, light versus heavy
Product/service application: insurance versus banking

PRIZM+4 *clusters customers*

Marketers around the country are using a new generation of segmentation techniques for customer profiling, analysis, and direct mail. One new tool is PRIZM+4, the lifestyle cluster system for ZIP+4 areas, or nine-digit ZIP codes. PRIZM, which stands for potential rating index by ZIP markets, groups neighborhoods in the US into one of 40 distinct cluster types. The procedure matches census data with ZIP code information. Each cluster, such as "Blue Blood Estates" or "Shotguns and Pickups," has a unique multidimensional profile detailing its product, media, and leisure preferences as well as demographics. The Blue Blood Estates group, for example, has a median income over $75,000 and a median home value over $200,000 and is predominantly college graduates. PRIZM+4 allows even greater detail by allowing PRIZM codes to be assigned to each ZIP+4 area in the US.

   PRIZM+4 is built from four different types of individual consumer data covering individual demographics, individual credit usage records, model-specific auto registration records, and purchase behavior data obtained from private sources. A number of companies now use PRIZM+4 to guide their direct mail more efficiently.

Sources: "PRIZM+4 Offers Precise Targeting, Analysis," *The Claritas Target Marketing Newsletter*, Summer 1991, p. 1; Paula Munier Lee, "The Micro-Marketing Revolution," *Small Business Reports*, February 1990, pp. 71–82; and Patricia Strand, "Count on Cartography: Researchers Plot Maps to Survey Census Data," *Advertising Age*, December 10, 1990, p. 46.

Demographics

For consumer marketing, demographic segments are particularly significant. Some products are targeted for teenagers and others for the elderly, while still others are designed for young couples just beginning a family. Vacation decisions are uniquely related to family life cycle characteristics, with children having significant input even at young ages. Marketing researchers often rely heavily on occupation and education to form social class segments.

   Ethnic and racial characteristics are also important segment descriptors. According to the 1990 census, there are now 29.8 million African-Americans in the US, up 13.2 percent from 1980; 22.3 million Hispanics, up 53 percent; and, 7.3 million Asian-Americans, up 108 percent.[21]

Geographics

Geographic differences are sometimes important in the development of marketing strategies. Consider the ways Detroit automakers are fighting foreign imports in California, for example. Analysis of California's uniqueness has resulted in a chromeless Buick California Regal and ads promoting Cadillac Seville as a "perfect rodeo drive" in recognition of the luxury Beverly Hills shopping district.[22]

   One method of categorizing geographic differences uses census data to identify metropolitan areas. There are three types: **metropolitan statistical areas** (MSAs), **primary metropolitan statistical areas** (PMSAs), and **consolidated metropolitan statistical areas** (CMSAs). MSAs must have a city with a population of at least 50,000 or be an "urbanized area" with 50,000 people that is part of a county of at least 100,000 residents. The largest designation is CMSA. These are the approximately 20 largest markets in the US that contain at least two PMSAs. PMSAs are major urban areas, often located within a CMSA, that have at least one million inhabitants. New York, Los Angeles, and Chicago are among the largest CMSAs. Populated areas within these markets, such as Marietta near Atlanta and Ventura near Los Angeles, represent PMSAs.

Exhibit 8.4		**Tomorrow's wealthiest metros and their average household income in 1996**

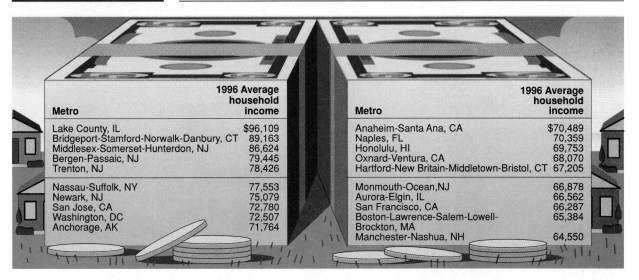

Metro	1996 Average household income
Lake County, IL	$96,109
Bridgeport-Stamford-Norwalk-Danbury, CT	89,163
Middlesex-Somerset-Hunterdon, NJ	86,624
Bergen-Passaic, NJ	79,445
Trenton, NJ	78,426
Nassau-Suffolk, NY	77,553
Newark, NJ	75,079
San Jose, CA	72,780
Washington, DC	72,507
Anchorage, AK	71,764

Metro	1996 Average household income
Anaheim-Santa Ana, CA	$70,489
Naples, FL	70,359
Honolulu, HI	69,753
Oxnard-Ventura, CA	68,070
Hartford-New Britain-Middletown-Bristol, CT	67,205
Monmouth-Ocean, NJ	66,878
Aurora-Elgin, IL	66,562
San Francisco, CA	66,287
Boston-Lawrence-Salem-Lowell-Brockton, MA	65,384
Manchester-Nashua, NH	64,550

The combination of geographic information and demographic characteristics is called **geodemographics.** Much published geodemographic data are available that firms can use in evaluating the size of potential market segments. Products are often directed toward geographic markets, particularly when tastes differ between regions. Further, it is important for marketers to know which areas are the fastest growing and represent the greatest future opportunities. Exhibit 8.4 lists tomorrow's wealthiest metropolitan areas based on forecasts of household buying income data.[23]

Firms employing a *technological perspective* use geodemographic data systems to integrate geographic information with census data. The fundamental premise in such geodemographic systems is that households in neighborhoods share similar lifestyles and that such neighborhoods repeat themselves, allowing similar neighborhoods to be classified into market segments.[24] Southwestern Bell Corporation (SBC) uses geodemographic analysis to develop marketing strategies for its European cable operations in the United Kingdom. The company uses the data to identify neighborhoods susceptible to sales through direct marketing campaigns and to screen bad-debt areas.[25] One geodemographic system is described in **The Technological Edge: PRIZM+4 Clusters Customers.**

Psychographics and lifestyles

Psychographic or **lifestyle research** attempts to segment customers according to their activities, interests, and opinions.[26] Such research uses survey responses to items concerning individual *activities, interests,* and *opinions*—called **AIO statements**—to develop in-depth profiles of consumer groups or segments. Examples of AIO statements are:

- "A person can save a lot of money by shopping around for bargains." (*price conscious*)

- "An important part of my life is dressing smartly." (*fashion conscious*)

- "I would rather spend a quiet evening at home than go to a party." (*homebody*)

- "I am uncomfortable when my house is not completely clean." (*compulsive housekeeper*)[27]

Some ads appeal to the lifestyles of the rich and elegant.

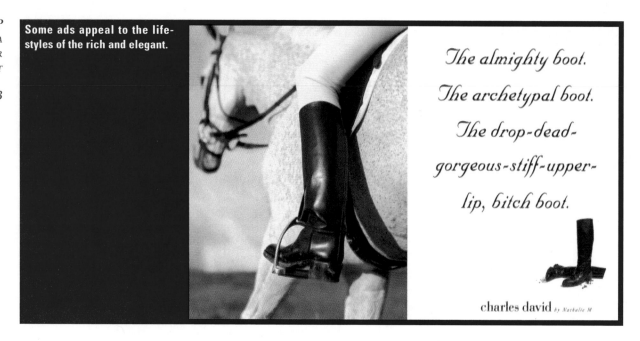

The almighty boot.

The archetypal boot.

The drop-dead-

gorgeous-stiff-upper-

lip, bitch boot.

charles david *by Nathalie M*

Psychographic research has been used successfully in a variety of segmentation applications. As an example, one study of women over 65 combined psychographic research with an analysis of segments identified by media
preferences. This study of the growing over-65 market described the following
media consumption patterns:[28]

- *The Engaged*—High levels of newspaper readership, and high viewing levels
  of television news programming.

- *The Autonomous*—Moderate levels of newspaper readership, and low use of
  media in general.

- *The Receptive*—High viewing levels of television comedy programs, and
  moderate levels of newspaper readership.

A follow-up study using responses to a series of AIO agree-disagree statements
provided a richer description of lifestyles within these segments. For example,
women in the engaged segment were heavier users of cosmetics, considered
cooking and baking extremely important, and were quite negative toward large
companies and business practices.

A popular application of the lifestyle and psychographic approach to segmentation is the **Values and Lifestyles Program (VALS2)** of SRI International.
VALS2 segments consumers into eight groups: actualizers, fulfilleds, believers,
achievers, strivers, experiencers, makers, and strugglers. Firms pursuing the *execution perspective* can use this system to effectively develop advertising and promotional campaigns, including the selection of media and the design of message
content. As shown in Exhibit 8.5, the groups are arranged along two dimensions: self-orientation and resources. Self-orientation refers to the attitudes
and activities people use to maintain their social self-image and self-esteem.
Resources include attributes such as education, income, age, energy, self-
confidence, and even health.[29] For example, the actualizers, the smallest segment
at 8 percent of the US population, have the highest incomes and self-esteem.
The remaining seven segments each represent from 11 to 16 percent of the
population.[30]

Exhibit 8.5

VALS2: Eight values and lifestyles segments from SRI International

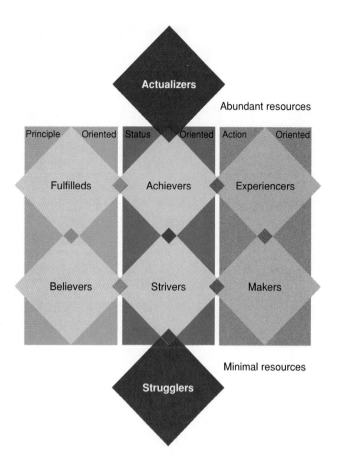

Benefit segmentation

Many firms segment markets according to the particular attributes or benefits that consumers want.[31] **Benefit segmentation** enhances the design and marketing of a product to meet expressed consumer needs for quality, service, or unique features. For example, Apple targeted a segment that wanted easy-to-use computers, consumers put off by what they saw as complications in operating other PCs. Defining this niche and simplifying the process of learning built Apple into a major factor in this market.

Benefit segmentation is consistent with the *quality/value perspective* and the marketing concept, that is, to be customer-oriented and to provide consumer benefits to generate long-term customer satisfaction. The belief underlying benefit segmentation is that true segments are best described in terms of the causal factors or basic reasons for purchase.[32]

Benefit segmentation works in marketing services as well as products. Through its novel promotional messages, Andersen Consulting markets itself as a provider of much-needed benefits to many companies—information systems that do not threaten the firm's employees and that make computer technology a real contributor to the firm's performance.

International segmentation

Segmentation is an important part of international marketing as well. Firms can employ one—or some combination of—three approaches. First, companies may use a single standardized strategy in all international marketing. Second, customized strategies may be developed for different countries or groups of

Great pieces don't always make a masterpiece.

Consider the landscape of your business. Your strategy may be inspired. Your technology cutting edge. Your people top notch. But unless all these elements share a common perspective, the result will almost certainly be less than beautiful. Andersen Consulting has the experience and discipline to stand back and see the whole picture. By taking a wider view, we can help synchronize your business processes with your business strategy. We can help integrate your technological resources with your human resources. Thereby enabling technology to move the entire enterprise forward. Over half of the Fortune 500 are already using our panoramic approach. Because they realize what artists have always known. It takes more than great pieces to make a masterpiece.

ANDERSEN CONSULTING
ARTHUR ANDERSEN & CO., S.C.

Andersen Consulting combines a benefit segmentation strategy with its business-to-business services marketing efforts.

countries. In these cases, the countries represent different segments. Third, and as explained earlier, intermarket segments, comprising similar clusters of consumers across national boundaries, may be identified. Variables typically used to form country segments include income and GNP per capita, telephones and TV sets per capita, percent of population in agriculture, and political stability. Taking the *global perspective,* a company considering the sale of durable electronic products (VCRs and CD players) identified two important segments formed by combining countries: (1) Holland, Japan, Sweden, and the UK; and (2) Austria, Belgium, Denmark, Finland, France, Norway, and Switzerland. Those segments were found to share similar patterns of new-product adoption and, hence, were addressed with similar marketing efforts.[33]

Combining bases for market segmentation

Exhibit 8.6 diagrams one way a firm might combine consumer characteristics to decide on a market segmentation strategy. Here a two-stage process begins with research designed to identify the heavy users of a product or service. If the heavy-user segment has unique or consistent demographic characteristics, such as income or education, the firm's decisions about how to reach that segment are easier: that is, which magazines or television programs can be used efficiently.

Exhibit 8.6	**A two-stage segmentation example**

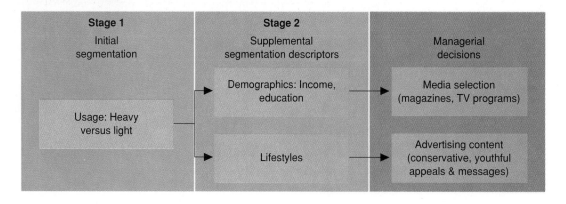

| Exhibit 8.7 | Segmentation bases and related product purchases: A lifestage analysis |

Lifestage segment: new, unmarried householders
Predicting variables:
Income $0–$24,999
Head of household age 18–24
Unmarried
Renters
No children present

Products of interest:
Credit
Basic household supplies, furnishings
Consumer electronics
Appliances
Career clothes, materials

Lifestage segment: upscale, married, new children
Predicting variables:
Income $75K+
Head of household age 35–44
Married
Homeowner
Children present, age 0–5

Products of interest:
Insurance
Financial planning
Toys
Education plans
Vehicles with high safety ratings
Home entertainment products (cameras, film)

Lifestage segment: preretired, upscale, empty nesters
Predicting variables:
Income $75K+
Head of household age 50–64
Married, widowed, divorced (3 distinct subsegments)
Homeowners or renters (additional subsegments)
No children present, only 1 or 2 adults present

Products of interest:
Remodeling services
Real estate services
Travel services, equipment, clothes
Retirement planning
Healthcare planning
Upscale vehicles
Recreational items (golf, tennis, sailing)

Similarly, identifying certain lifestyle characteristics of the heavy-user segment gives the firm additional insight about which product configuration or advertising theme is likely to be successful.

Exhibit 8.7 gives another approach for combining different variables to describe segments of consumers. Here, five demographic and household characteristics describe segment membership: income, age of head of household, marital status, home ownership, and presence of children in the household. Marketers can add these variables to their data files of current and potential customers and tailor products and services according to this analysis. For example, target products relevant to the "preretired, upscale, empty nester" segment include remodeling services, real estate services, health care planning, upscale vehicles, and recreational equipment.[34]

EXECUTIVE ROUNDTABLE COMMENT | **Sheila Burroughs, assistant vice president for quality planning at NationsBank, notes:**

The demographic variables that most accurately segment the financial services NationsBank offers are age and income. When we combine these variables with psychographic lifestyle information, such as a customer's attitude toward risk, we are better able to develop and offer products that appeal to our customers.

Basically then, firms identify and combine distinguishing buyer segment bases to:

• Help them design product or service offerings to market to targeted consumer segments.

• Help them choose media vehicles.

• Help them develop marketing themes for use in communicating to a particular segment or segments.

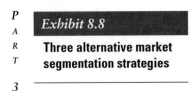

Exhibit 8.8

Three alternative market segmentation strategies

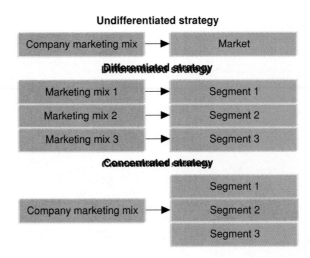

Undifferentiated strategy

| Company marketing mix | → | Market |

Differentiated strategy

Marketing mix 1	→	Segment 1
Marketing mix 2	→	Segment 2
Marketing mix 3	→	Segment 3

Concentrated strategy

Company marketing mix	→	Segment 1
		Segment 2
		Segment 3

Segmentation strategies

Strategies for engaging in segmentation are often categorized as undifferentiated, differentiated, or concentrated. These approaches provide firms alternative methods for enhancing the execution of their marketing programs. Exhibit 8.8 is a schematic view of the three approaches.

Undifferentiated strategy

A company adopts an **undifferentiated strategy** when it markets a single product using a single communication and distribution mix for the entire market. Neither the product nor the promotional theme is varied or differentiated. Undifferentiated approaches are most often used early in the life of a product category. Initial product introductions, such as the early introduction of the automobile, often use a single mass-marketing approach. The undifferentiated strategy offers some advantages because of economies of scale but opens the firm to competition. Today, even water is marketed in brands to different segments.

Differentiated strategy

At the other end of the scale is the **differentiated strategy**, under which a firm uses different strategies for different segments. In some cases, a unique product and communications campaign may be developed for each segment. In other instances, a common product may be marketed to different segments with varying communication strategies. The Hartmarx and Levi Strauss approaches, with their multiple product versions and advertising campaigns, are examples of complex segmentation schemes. Differentiated strategies are often the choice of companies such as soft-drink manufacturers and life insurance firms, which offer many product versions to meet different preferences. McDonald's for example, embodies segmentation principles in its offerings. Happy Meals and playgrounds are offered for children, while nutritional information on trays and commercials showing parent/child interactions are targeted toward adults. Likewise, traditional burgers are offered along with healthier salads and sandwiches. Although a differentiated strategy is often useful for increasing sales and profits, continual adjustments to segmentation programs may prove expensive.

Concentrated strategy

A firm pursues a **concentrated strategy** when it seeks a large share of just a few profitable segments, perhaps only one, of the total market. With such a strategy, a company concentrates more on serving segments innovatively and creatively

This Purina Hi Pro Ad for high-performance dog food is targeted for readers of *Field and Stream Magazine.* In a differentiated segmentation scheme, Ralston Purina, maker of Purina dog food, has products and promotional campaigns aimed at different market segments.

than on pricing.[35] American Express, for example, has traditionally sought upscale instead of middle-income customers. Thus, the company concentrates its advertising resources in pursuit of a large share of the higher-income consumer market.

Countersegmentation strategy

Countersegmentation is an alternative strategy to traditional segmentation approaches. It involves combining market segments and assumes an increasing consumer willingness to accept fewer product and service variations for lower prices. Countersegmentation is seen in the move toward generic brands and retail superstores and warehouse stores. Sam's outlets and Toys " Я " Us, in their pursuit of the *quality/value perspective,* appeal to a broad range of consumers and do not emphasize finely focused target segments. Countersegmentation is seen also at IBM and Chrysler, which have streamlined their product lines by combining operations and eliminating some brands.

Factors influencing segmentation strategy

A number of market, product, and competitive factors may influence a firm's choice of segmentation strategy. They include size and type of the market, and a variety of competitive factors.

If consumers are not particularly sensitive to product differences, an undifferentiated strategy may be appropriate. But if the firm sells to an overall product market with many different segments, a differentiated or concentrated approach is the better choice. Two product-related factors are also relevant: stage in the product life cycle, and the degree to which the product may be varied or modified. If the product is new, a concentrated segmentation strategy may be best, that is offering only one product version, or a few at most. If the firm's interest is to develop primary demand, an undifferentiated strategy may be appropriate. In the later stages of a product's life, large firms tend to pursue a differentiated segmentation strategy.

For example, consumer product giant Procter & Gamble pursues a differentiated strategy in the laundry detergent category. P&G markets powdered laundry detergents such as Cheer and Tide to different segments of the product market. The company constantly differentiates its products within and across brands to address the segments vital to its success. Potential growth segments are prime candidates for differentiated products. When the liquid detergent segment was growing, P&G introduced a liquid version of Tide; later, the company addressed another potential growth segment with Concentrated Tide.

Competitive factors are particularly important in a firm's market segmentation strategy. If its major competitors pursue an undifferentiated approach, a firm may decide to engage in a differentiated or concentrated approach. If a firm has many competitors, its best strategy may be to concentrate on developing strong brand loyalty and buyer preferences in one target segment or perhaps a few. Finally, a firm's size and financial position can influence the choice of strategy. Smaller firms with relatively limited resources often find it necessary to pursue a concentrated segmentation strategy.

A firm adopting an undifferentiated approach or pursuing only the largest segments may well invite substantial competition. This is the **majority fallacy:** although large "majority" segments may appear to offer a firm potential gains, pursuing only them may involve confronting overwhelming competition. In this case, it is better for a firm to pursue a concentrated strategy, focusing on one segment, or a few, to obtain larger shares of markets in which it can compete effectively.

Targeting market segments and positioning products

Once a firm has chosen its overall market segmentation strategy, it then must select specific segments and position products for effective appeal to those segments. Factors that affect the choice of a segmentation strategy also influence which specific segments should be targeted.

Estimating segment potentials

To estimate market potential and likely sales, the firm should distinguish between firm and industry potentials and between forecasts of the best possible results and expected results. As Exhibit 8.9 shows, **market potential** is the maximum amount of industry sales possible for a product or service for a specific period. The **market forecast** for that same period is a function of the amount of marketing effort (expenditures) put forth by all companies competing in that market. Total market potential then represents an upper limit on total sales. **Sales potential** is the maximum amount of sales a specific firm can obtain for a specified time period.

To produce a sales forecast, a company should screen out market segments that represent insufficient potential sales and analyze further the remaining segments. Company forecasts must consider competitive activity and the availability of channels of distribution and marketing media. What brands are already in the

Exhibit 8.9   **Firm and market potentials and forecasts**

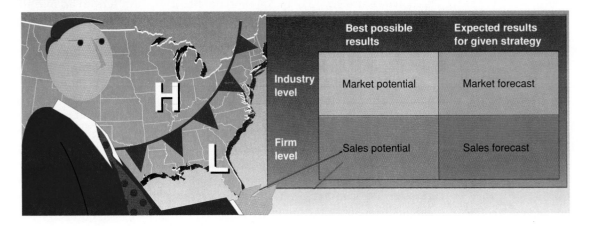

	Best possible results	Expected results for given strategy
Industry level	Market potential	Market forecast
Firm level	Sales potential	Sales forecast

market? What are the strengths and weaknesses of the competition? What distribution outlets and supporting channels of distribution are available? What is the cost of access to the appropriate media? One set of steps firms can use to estimate potential for a segment is:

1. Set time period of interest.
2. Define product level.
3. Specify segment characteristics or bases.
4. Identify geographic market boundaries.
5. Make assumptions about marketing environment (uncontrollable factors such as competitive activity).
6. Make assumptions about company's own marketing efforts and programs (controllable factors).
7. Make estimates of market potential, industry sales, and company sales.[36]

Exhibit 8.10 sets out data on market potential for golf shoes across four age groups in Pennsylvania. Population information of this sort is obtainable from US census or state records. The product purchase percentage data can be obtained from an annual "Survey of Buying Power" in *Sales & Marketing Management*.

Developing forecasts

Forecasts represent the amount the company expects to sell in a market over a specific time period. The period will vary by company and use of the forecast. Forecasts are used to evaluate opportunities, to budget marketing efforts, to control expenditures, and to evaluate subsequent sales performance. High forecasts can lead to excessive investment and expenditures, while low forecasts can result in lost opportunities.

There are a number of methods for forecasting sales, some of which are explained below. These methods can be grouped into *qualitative* procedures, which employ judgmental opinion and insight, and *quantitative* methods, which use historical data to make trend extensions or numerical estimates of forecasted sales. The primary qualitative forecasting methods are a survey of buyers' intentions, expert opinion, and a composite of salesforce estimates. The primary quantitative methods are trend analysis, market tests, and statistical demand analysis.

Exhibit 8.10   **Estimating market potential for golf shoes in Pennsylvania**

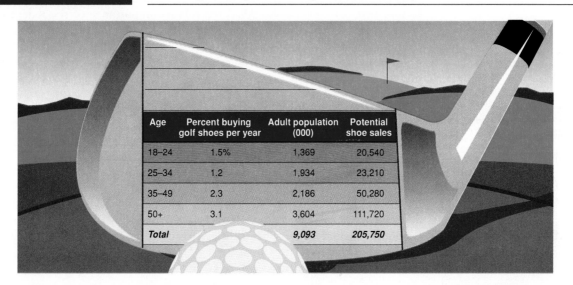

Age	Percent buying golf shoes per year	Adult population (000)	Potential shoe sales
18–24	1.5%	1,369	20,540
25–34	1.2	1,934	23,210
35–49	2.3	2,186	50,280
50+	3.1	3,604	111,720
Total		**9,093**	**205,750**

A **survey of buyers' intentions** is useful in certain situations. Under this method, forecasts are based on surveys of what consumers or organizational buyers say they will do. First, the buyers must have well-formed intentions and be willing to follow those intentions. In addition, they must be willing to disclose their intentions accurately. These conditions are most often satisfied for durable consumer goods and for large purchases in business-to-business marketing.

Expert opinion represents another qualitative or judgmental approach to forecasting. Using this approach, analysts ask executives within the company or other experts to provide forecasts based on their own judgments or experiences. This can be a quick and perhaps inexpensive method; however, the forecast accuracy depends on the knowledge of the executives or experts involved and their ability to provide realistic estimates.

A **composite of salesforce estimates** provides another means of forecasting sales. Under this method, sales representatives give forecasts for their individual territories, which can then be combined across territories. Sales reps have unique exposure to the competition and market trends. Plus, these estimates can be obtained cheaply and regularly. However, reps may give low forecasts in efforts to keep their own sales quotas low.

Trend analysis, a quantitative forecasting approach often referred to as *time-series analysis,* examines historical sales data for predictable patterns. If the environment is reasonably stable, extrapolating past sales data can provide a quick and efficient means of making forecasts. Often the firm will identify trend, cyclical (economic cycles), and seasonal effects in its past sales pattern. Exponential smoothing is a frequently used form of trend analysis in which the most recent sales data are weighted the heaviest in determining each new forecast. The major problem with time-series or trend analysis is that the firm is assuming that what happened in the past will continue in the future, making no attempt to determine what caused the sales.

When the firm is uncertain about its subjective judgment, or the ability of past data to forecast the future, a market test may be necessary. Market tests are particularly useful for evaluating the likely success of new-product introductions. **Market tests** involve marketing the product in test locations using the planned communications, pricing, and distribution strategies. Forecasts for other areas can then be obtained from sales in the test markets.

Statistical demand analysis involves developing forecasts from the factors thought to be most important in determining sales. Under this method, sales are forecasted from equations in which price, advertising and sales promotion, distribution, competitive, and economic factors serve as independent variables. Regression analysis is the most frequently used estimation procedure. Statistical demand analysis is advantageous in that it forces the firm to consider the causal factors that determine sales. Also, the relative importance of the independent factors can be evaluated. Although computers have made demand analysis readily available to forecasters, the usefulness of the method depends on appropriate application. Some sophistication in data analysis procedures is clearly a prerequisite to their use.

Targeting market segments

To select target segments, the firm must consider a combination of factors, including the segment's potential sales volume and profits, competition currently selling to the segments, and the firm's abilities and objectives.

Although large segments with a substantial number of buyers seem to promise high potential sales volume and profits, smaller segments served by a unique marketing mix may also provide lucrative business opportunities. Specialty stores in large malls serve many of these segments. For example, General Nutrition Center targets health-conscious people, and Lady Foot Locker, women sports enthusiasts.

Nintendo builds a database

*S*egmentation depends on knowing who your customers are and being able to reach them effectively. How does Nintendo build a database for targeting communications to its most loyal patrons? Through its *Nintendo Power* magazine. The full-color, monthly magazine, which began as a newsletter for members of Nintendo's Fun Club, reached a 2 million circulation and yielded a database of 6 million names in 1990, according to Gail Tilden, director of publications.

Names get into the database four ways: players mail back scores on games for a top-30 monthly listing; players list their favorite games; players ask to have games reviewed; and players tell what games they plan to buy, all on mail-back cards generated in a monthly sweepstakes competition. *Nintendo Power* has an estimated "pass along" readership of its magazine of over 8 million. Its key objective is to target the heavy-user segment with product endorsements and marketing communications. It also enhances satisfaction by helping customers make informed decisions about software purchases.

Source: Howard Schlossberg, "How Five Companies Targeted Their Best Prospects," *Marketing News*, February 18, 1991, p. 12. © 1991 by the American Marketing Association. Reprinted with permission.

The larger markets may also attract the greatest number of competing firms (the majority fallacy). In general, a firm will have to assess market potential in light of competitive issues. If the firm has a competitive advantage that cannot be easily copied, it may attempt to approach the larger market segments.

The selection of target markets has a lot to do with the firm's objectives and distinctive competence. A firm specializing in innovative technological products, for example, may compete on total value, rather than on price alone, focusing on one segment or a few segments where high-quality, innovative products appeal.

Targeting also requires designing advertising and promotional mixes to reach the intended segments. Resources are wasted if the advertising results in duplication of audience or reaches nontarget market consumers. Accurate identification of the marketing segments appropriate for a particular product is critical if firms are to target efficiently to reach those segments.

Technology brings new precision to both the selection of specific target segments and the ability to reach them. When Buick's analysis of the large station wagon segment revealed that upscale suburbs, particularly in the Midwest and Northeast, were potentially lucrative markets, it targeted consumers with ads in magazines sent to the relevant ZIP codes. Targeted ads promoting the Roadmaster station wagon ran in issues going to 4,940 of the more than 40,000 US ZIP codes. That was 20 percent of US households—but those households represented 50 percent of the buyers of large wagons.[37] **The Entrepreneurial Spirit: Nintendo Builds a Database** describes how another company targets its customers.

EXECUTIVE ROUNDTABLE COMMENT | **Sheila Burroughs, assistant vice president/quality planning at NationsBank, underscores the differences in needs that form market segments:**

Target marketing and segmentation are the ultimate in being customer-focused. They allow the service provider to more deeply understand the differing needs of customers—to recognize that all customers are not the same. Even customers from differing segments using the same product probably do so for different reasons—your loan is needed to pay for books and keep a roof over your head. Someone from another market segment would use the same loan to add a pool room to their home or buy a luxury yacht. Obviously, the strategy for appealing to these segments must be different.

Nick Jr. television programs are targeted at preschoolers, but ad campaigns in family-oriented magazines are targeted at parents.

Positioning

Once segments have been selected and targeted, the firm must position its products and services in the minds of its customers. **Positioning** a product or service involves designing a marketing program, including the product mix, that is consistent with how the company wants its products or services to be perceived. The strategy a firm adopts is driven then by the desired positioning. Positioning aims to influence or adjust customer perceptions of a product or brand. An effective position lets a brand occupy a preferred and unique position in the customers' minds while being consistent with the firm's overall marketing strategy.[38]

Positioning a new brand requires distinguishing it from other brands. Customers must perceive it as sharing important attributes with other brands in the product category but as being superior on differentiating attributes.[39] **Repositioning,** called for when a firm wants to shift consumer opinions about an existing brand, requires development of new marketing programs.

Schwinn is attempting to reposition itself as an aggressive and youthful company with its campaign entitled "Established 1895. Re-established 1994."

Exhibit 8.11   **General Motors car markets**

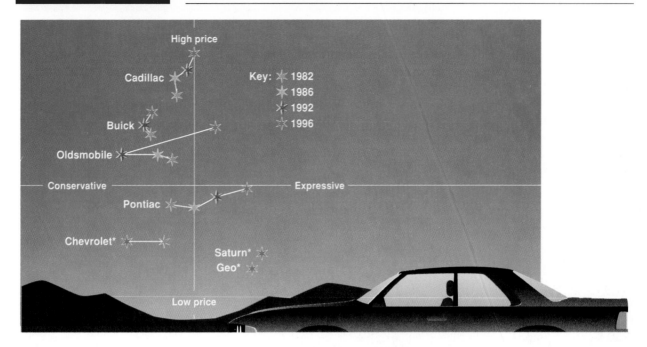

Product attributes, price, and image enhancements are major components in positioning. **Perceptual maps,** spatial representations of consumer perceptions of products or brands, are often used to evaluate brand positions in a market. Exhibit 8.11 is a perceptual map for the automobile market. Cars are positioned on the map according to consumer perceptions of price and brand expressiveness. Note that over time, a brand's market position can shift. Perceptual maps often show positions for competitors' brands.

Micromarketing

The ultimate in target marketing is **micromarketing,** which frequently combines census and demographic data to identify clusters of households that share similar consumption patterns. The PRIZM market segmentation system described earlier is one example. Demographic descriptions of county, ZIP code, and census tract locations combined with information about area values, preferences, and purchasing habits enable companies to pinpoint likely or desired customers. Firms pursuing the *execution perspective* use micromarketing to increase the productivity of their marketing expenditures. Micromarketing enhances the effectiveness of marketing efforts by enabling marketers to:

- Identify potential markets for direct selling through mail and telemarketing campaigns.
- Profile their customers by matching them to demographic and lifestyle clusters.
- Learn which areas offer the greatest potential in site selection for new stores or offices.
- Tailor their advertising themes and plan their media.[40]

As an example of the latter, *Reader's Digest* will soon print 40 different versions of their monthly editions. The advertising in each version will be designed for different areas of the country. This will enable advertisers, who provide much of the publication's income, to reach high-potential market segments.[41]

Market segmentation and ethics

Targeting selected market segments can provide substantial benefits to both marketers and consumers: the marketer gains sales and the consumers receive the particular products and services they most want and value. Yet, segmentation practices can be so effective that they are fraught with opportunities for exploitation. Marketers must consider the *ethical* issues associated with some segmentation and targeting practices.

Advertising to children

Advertising to children, a large and influential market segment, can stimulate demand for expensive and unnecessary products. Such advertising has been criticized for developing unrealistic expectations and demands for some youthful consumers who can least afford unnecessary expenditures. Demand for expensive athletic shoes or certain kinds of jackets or jewelry is easily fostered. Further, very young children sometimes have difficulty differentiating between program content and commercial messages.

Gender-role stereotyping

To capture universalities among members of market segments and to simplify messages, marketers often resort to stereotypes. Portrayals of women in advertising are frequently criticized. For instance, some have argued that the "traditional housewife," occupied primarily in her kitchen or laundry room, and the bikini-clad model in beer ads are inaccurate stereotypes that negatively influence gender-role formation for both men and women.[42]

Harmful products

Marketing harmful products, such as cigarettes and alcohol, to young people raises important ethical issues. Some brands of cigarettes, such as Dakota, Virginia Slims, or Eve, are positioned to attract young women. Models in cigarette and beer ads are youthful, active, and attractive individuals. Messages for these products often emphasize the social acceptability of smoking and drinking, minimizing the impact of package warnings of the negative effects of their use.

Privacy issues

As marketers are increasingly able to target precise consumer segments, concerns about privacy arise. Consumer purchase histories, credit histories, and telephone numbers can be combined for use in developing and targeting direct marketing campaigns. Care must be exercised in the use of this information.

Summary

1. *Define and explain market segmentation, target markets, and product differentiation and positioning.* Market segmentation is used when consumer groups (segments) share needs or preferences that differ from other segments. Market segmentation strategies attempt to take advantage of these differences and to meet each segment's demands. The segments served by firms are often called *target markets.*

   Product differentiation exists when customers perceive that a firm's product offerings differ from those of competing firms on any physical or nonphysical attribute. Positioning a product within a market is the process of exercising a differentiation strategy to convince consumers that the product has unique desirable characteristics.

2. *Understand the criteria used for evaluating the likely success of a segmentation strategy.* Five criteria are relevant in the design of a market segmentation strategy. Measurability refers to the extent to which the size and purchasing power of segments can be defined. Accessibility is the degree to which firms can efficiently reach intended target segments. Substantialness addresses the size of the target segment and its potential sales and profits. Durability refers to a persistence—the extent to which segments will persist over time as good business opportunities. Differential responsiveness is the degree to which market segments differ in their response to varying marketing mix combinations.

3. *Know the role of market segmentation in the development of marketing strategies and programs.* Market segmentation can be useful for both new and mature products or services. New products can be targeted to segments promising opportunities for introduction and growth. Mature brands can be repositioned, extended, or marketed to appeal to specific segments. An appropriate market segmentation strategy can help marketers focus on growth and expansion opportunities in an increasingly competitive marketplace.

4. *Describe the issues involved in product and brand positioning.* After determining the segmentation strategy, the marketer must take care in selecting the appropriate segments and positioning the firm's brands for those segments. Positioning refers to consumers' perceptions of the particular product or brand in relation to its competitors. Overall, the firm must identify the existing competitive products and brands within a market. It then must assess which attributes determine product preferences for the brands in that market. An examination of the fit between existing preferences and beliefs, ideal preferences, and

brand capabilities will assist the firm either in positioning a new brand or in repositioning an already available brand.

5. *Understand the alternative bases for segmenting consumer and business-to-business markets.* Variables used to develop segmentation schemes may be either user- or behavior-based, and they may apply in either consumer or business-to-business marketing situations. User-related characteristics include demographic and psychographic variables for consumers, and customer size and geographic location for business-to-business applications. Behavior-related characteristics include benefits desired and extent of usage for consumers, and product application for business-to-business markets.

6. *Evaluate alternative approaches for pursuing segmentation strategies.* Segmentation strategies are of three types—undifferentiated, differentiated, and concentrated. An undifferentiated strategy involves the use of only one combination of marketing mix variables to meet the demands of the entire market. This strategy is appropriate if consumers are insensitive to product variations, if the competition is light, or if the product itself cannot be easily varied.

A differentiated strategy involves the use of different marketing mix combinations to meet all or many of the segments constituting a market. A concentrated strategy aims to achieve a large share in just one or a few segments.

In practice, many firms evolve from using an undifferentiated or concentrated strategy to adopting a differentiated approach, either as the firm can produce variations of the product or as the product develops beyond its introductory stage. An alternative approach, countersegmentation, combines market segments to provide consumers lower-priced products with fewer product variations.

CHAPTER 8

Key terms & concepts

market segmentation *180*
intermarket segments *181*
targeting *182*
product differentiation *182*
measurability *184*
accessibility *184*
substantialness *184*
durability *184*
differential responsiveness *185*
bases of segmentation *186*
metropolitan statistical areas *188*
primary metropolitan statistical areas *188*
consolidated metropolitan statistical areas *188*

geodemographics *189*
psychographic or lifestyle research *189*
AIO statements *189*
Values and Lifestyles Program (VALS2) *190*
benefit segmentation *191*
undifferentiated strategy *194*
differentiated strategy *194*
concentrated strategy *194*
countersegmentation *195*
majority fallacy *196*
market potential *196*

market forecast *196*
sales potential *196*
surveys of buyers' intentions *198*
expert opinion *198*
composite of salesforce estimates *198*
trend analysis *198*
market tests *198*
statistical demand analysis *198*
positioning *200*
repositioning *200*
perceptual maps *201*
micromarketing *201*

Review & discussion questions

1. What is market segmentation, and how does it differ from product differentiation?

2. How might a marketer attempt to differentiate a product from competing products?

3. What are the criteria for segmenting a market, and what is meant by each one? Contrast differential responsiveness with segment accessibility.

4. Describe the different bases for segmentation. In doing so, explain the differences between user-related and behavior-related characteristics. How does the PRIZM+4 described in **The Technological Edge** example make use of these bases?

5. What bases might be used to define segments for these products: cassette recorders, hand calculators, personal computers, and public universities?

6. What is benefit segmentation? How does demographic segmentation differ from psychographic segmentation?

7. Define the different segmentation strategies. Compare and contrast each strategy with the others, and explain the conditions under which each may be appropriate.

8. What implications does the majority fallacy hypothesis have for the pursuit of a concentrated segmentation strategy?

9. How might Nintendo use its databases to strengthen its marketing efforts?

10. Why is the practice of market segmentation and targeting now more important than ever?

Application exercises

1. Compare the audiences of *Time* and *Rolling Stone* magazines. How does advertising in these magazines relate to market segmentation?

2. A large US manufacturer of heavy-duty carpet for use in office buildings is considering expanding its marketing efforts to include European countries. The company has segmented its marketing efforts geographically and by company size. What market segmentation decisions does the company face as it expands its efforts to include both Eastern and Western European countries?

3. Bicycle manufacturers pursue a benefit segmentation strategy to address the US adult market. Using this method, they can market essentially the same product for exercise, for leisure, or for just plain fun. Bicycles are also popular worldwide. How would you go about segmenting the bicycle market in, say, the Netherlands and Egypt?

Case 8.1   *Toyota: Picking up a new market*

Japanese automakers gained a foothold in the US by offering small, energy-efficient, and low-priced cars to American consumers. At first, US automobile manufacturers were unconcerned about yielding some of this market segment to Japanese firms because they mistakenly did not see it as very profitable. But faced with the energy crisis of the 1970s, American car owners turned increasingly to less expensive, highly efficient autos such as those offered by the Japanese—and eventually Japanese firms captured more than 30 percent of all US car sales.

Still, prior to 1993, the Big Three US automakers (Ford, General Motors, Chrysler) had no real Japanese competition in the full- and mid-sized pickup truck market segment. The Big Three now see a threat in Toyota's 1993 introduction of a midsized pickup into the US market. As truck sales have now surpassed car sales in the US, Toyota's move has the Big Three worried about again losing market share and profits to Japanese competitors.

Toyota contends its midsized truck is not designed to compete with the leaders of the full-sized pickup truck market such as the Ford F-series or the Chevrolet C/K-series.

Instead, Toyota claims to target its truck, the T100, toward pickup users who want trucks for personal transportation. Both the F-series and the C/K-series are built for transporting heavy loads and are designed for buyers who use their pickups for heavy work. Toyota's T100, on the other hand, is designed to offer a smoother ride and smoother handling. The T100 is smaller than the F-series or C/K-series, but larger than a compact-size pickup. It therefore meets the needs of a different segment of consumers from the Ford or GM full-sized pickup users. The closest-sized American pickup on the market is the Dodge Dakota. In size, the T100 falls between the larger F-series and C/K-series and the Dakota.

The Big Three are uncomfortable with Toyota's entry into the pickup market. Ford plans to introduce a new model of pickup truck, smaller in size and aimed at pickup owners who use their trucks more for personal use. Likewise, Chrysler, perhaps fearing that many potential Dakota customers may now consider a T100, will also market a redesigned pickup truck aimed at this segment.

The American companies seem to agree that this new Japanese competition is a legitimate factor in the industry. When the Japanese began marketing new compact automobiles in the US, many consumers considered their product superior. These perceptions may not hold for larger vehicles such as pickups, however. Recognizing its strong competition in the full-sized pickup market, Toyota opted to position its product in a different segment to avoid direct competition with the full-sized segment.

Questions

1. Will the new Toyota T100 compete either directly or indirectly with the American Big Three automakers' current pickup trucks? Why or why not?

2. What benefits underlie the different pickup truck industry segments?

3. What must Toyota do to pursue its segmentation approach?

4. Explain how the outcomes of Toyota's strategy would likely be different if it had offered a new full-sized pickup that would compete with the Big Three on some attribute such as price.

Sources: Jim Mateja, "Toyota's Pickup Plans Get Bigger," *Chicago Tribune*, August 11, 1992, p. 3–3; Neal Templin, "Japan, Detroit to Clash over Pickup Trucks," *The Wall Street Journal*, August 11, 1992, p. A3; Jim Mateja, "Toyota Picking Up the Size of Its Trucks for '93 Models," *Chicago Tribune*, March 11, 1992, p. 3–1; "Toyota Motor Corp.," *The Wall Street Journal*, March 8, 1991, p. A1; Joseph B. White, "Toyota to Decide within 60 Days on Large Pickup," *The Wall Street Journal*, January 10, 1991, p. A10; and Larry Armstrong, Kathleen Kerwin, and Bill Spindle, "Try to Rev Up," *Business Week*, January 24, 1994, pp. 32–33.

Case 8.2 — *O'Doul's: What beer drinkers drink when they're not drinking beer*

Stricter legal constraints against drinking and driving have left many consumers with a dilemma. They want to enjoy beer—for its taste or simply to join in the fun with other beer drinkers—yet they want to avoid the costs associated with overindulging. These social pressures have led to a surge in one segment of an overall flat beer market—the nonalcoholic beer segment.

Nonalcoholic beers (beers that contain less than 0.5 percent alcohol, approximately the amount found in orange juice) are certainly not new. They have been produced in this country since the colonial days, and their existence predates that period. Before the 1990s, however, the nonalcoholic beer segment was a very small part of the beer industry in America. In 1989, both Anheuser-Busch and Philip Morris' Miller brewing began heavily marketing their O'Doul's and Sharp's brands of nonalcoholic beers. With heavy promotion from these two industry giants, the nonalcoholic beer segment began growing. Though it still accounts for less than 1 percent of the overall beer market, the nonalcoholic segment grew 32 percent in 1991 alone. (By contrast, the light beer market rose just 6.7 percent and the regular premium beer market fell 6 percent.) Some industry analysts predict this segment could reach as much as 5 to 10 percent of the industry before the end of decade.

As of 1992, Sharp's was the leading brand (in market share by volume) of nonalcoholic beer, with O'Doul's closing the gap in second place. In part, O'Doul's market share growth may be related to a change in strategy consistent with industry findings that nearly all nonalcoholic beer drinkers are also regular or light beer drinkers, and not nondrinkers as might be expected. This fact disappointed some nonalcoholic beer manufacturers that hoped to appeal to nondrinkers as one way to increase the overall beer market.

Anheuser-Busch promotes O'Doul's accordingly—associating O'Doul's with its highly successful Budweiser brand. The campaign appeals to the segment of beer drinkers who want to avoid drinking alcohol when the occasion calls for sobriety, yet still wish to enjoy beer. Thus, the ads for O'Doul's feature the slogan, "What beer drinkers drink when they're not drinking beer."

Although nonalcoholic beer sales generally appear positive, beer manufacturers cannot be certain their product will continue its rapid growth as the experts have projected. Brewers remember only too well the initial promise low-alcohol beer displayed before falling flat in the mid-1980s. Furthermore, the failure of nonalcoholic beers to attract non–beer drinkers is disappointing. At the same time, however, some brewers view nonalcoholic beers as an opportunity to steal overall sales from the competition. By positioning its brand to the appropriate usage segment, O'Doul's has closed in on Sharp's in a fast-growing segment of a slow-growth industry.

Questions

1. Evaluate O'Doul's positioning strategy. Is it wise, given the flat market for the overall beer industry?

2. How would you define O'Doul's target segment? Be sure to include the base or bases used to define that segment.

3. How does this segmentation strategy satisfy the criteria for effective segmentation?

Sources: Ben Giliberti, "Taking the Measure of Nonalcoholic Beers," *Washington Post*, July 15, 1992, p. E1; Marj Charlier, "Big Beer Makers Go After the Sober Set with Assortment of Nonalcoholic Brews," *The Wall Street Journal*, March 30, 1992, p. B1; Stuart Elliot, "Anheuser Promotes Alternative to Bud," *The New York Times*, March 2, 1992, p. D10; Karen Blumenthal, "Coors Sets Rollouts of New Dry Beer, No-Alcohol Brew," *The Wall Street Journal*, July 29, 1991, p. B3; and Gerry Khermouch, "The Beer to Have When You're Having Little More than None," *Brandweek*, November 22, 1993, pp. 10–11.

Product and Service Concepts and Strategies

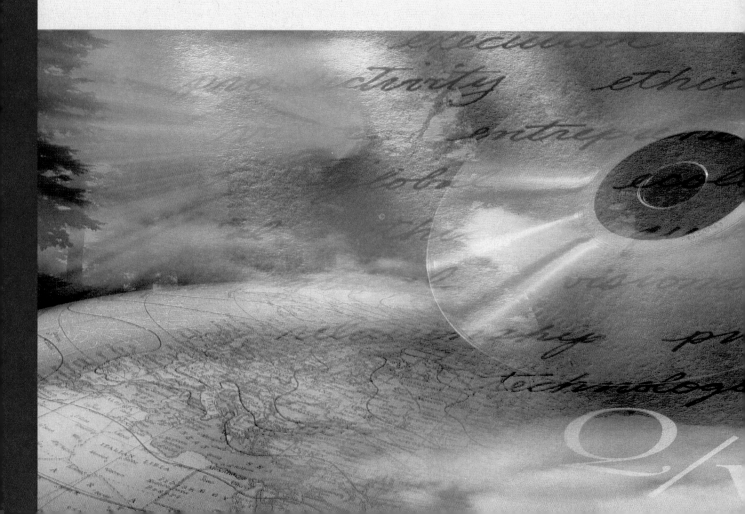

Marketing quality products and services

requires organizational teamwork.

*T*he chapters in Part 4 address the important concepts and strategies for the product portion of the marketing mix. Chapter 9, "Product and Service Concepts," introduces the key concepts that must be understood. The term *product* is defined, different types of products discussed, and the major product components examined. Chapter 10, "Developing New Products and Services," explores the key issues in new-product development. The types of new products and their sources are disussed. A new-product development process is presented, and each stage in the process is examined in detail. Chapter 11, "Product and Service Strategies," discusses the concepts of product life cycle and product mix. The focus is on investigating marketing strategies for individual products, product lines, and product mixes.

chapter 9

Product and Service Concepts

After studying this chapter you should be able to:

1. Understand the differences between goods and services.

2. Differentiate between consumer and business products and discuss the different types of each.

3. Recognize that marketers need to appreciate the perspective of the consumer.

4. Define and discuss the importance of product quality, product design, branding, packaging, and customer service.

5. Explain how the different product components need to be integrated to meet the needs of customers.

MCI Communications: Commodities or brands?

MCI Communications began as an upstart competitor to AT&T in the long-distance phone market in 1968. The company through its wholly owned subsidiary, MCI Telecommunications Corp., now holds 20 percent of the $65 billion US long distance market compared to AT&T's 65 percent. However, MCI's share is growing about 1 percent a year with AT&T's market share decreasing around 2 percent annually.

MCI's success is largely due to effective and entrepreneurial product decisions. The long-distance market used to be boring, but MCI has changed that. The company provides customers with value by offering a variety of telecommunications services, including quality long-distance service at low prices. Specific services packages are designed to meet the needs of different consumer and business markets. These products are then marketed aggressively.

MCI's entrepreneurial nature was evident when it began branding its products in 1972. Long-distance service had been considered a commodity business. But not at MCI. Over the years it developed brand names for specific services and used them to differentiate itself from competitors. Successful brand names include Friends & Family and 1–800–COLLECT for the consumer market and Proof Positive and Network MCI for the business market.

The aggressive marketing of these branded products generated substantial business. For example, over 12 million consumers subscribe to Friends & Family and 1–800–COLLECT produces around $200 million in annual revenues. Keeping this business in a competitive marketplace requires continued attention to customer service. An example is the Proof Positive brand for businesses. MCI evaluates a company's calls every 90 days to make sure it is getting charged the lowest rate for the type of service being used.

The company is using similar marketing approaches to grow in several areas. MCI and British Telecom have established a joint venture called Concert to penetrate the global business market. Products that appeal to all sizes of businesses using various combinations of voice, fax, and data transmissions have been developed. These brands include MCI Preferred Worldwide, MCI Global Vision Worldwide, and Vnet Worldwide.

Other plans call for a move into local telephone service to take advantage of opportunities on the expected information superhighway. MCI also announced an alliance with Nextel Communications to enter the wireless communication market. Under the terms of the proposed deal, Nextel's wireless phone, data, and dispatch services would be marketed as MCI Brand Wireless Services.

Sources: Patricia Sellers, "Yes, Brands Can Still Work Magic," *Fortune,* February 7, 1994, pp. 133–34; James G. Kimball, "MCI Shooting for Business," *Business Marketing,* May 1994, p. 14; Peter Coy and Mark Lewyn, "Nextel Keeps Making the Right Connections," *Business Week,* March 14, 1994; Kate Fitzgerald, "MCI Zips onto Superhighway," *Advertising Age,* January 10, 1994, pp. 3, 38; and company sources, June 1994.

Du Pont executes an *entrepreneurial perspective* by developing fire-resistent fibers used in state-of-the-art firefighting clothing worldwide.

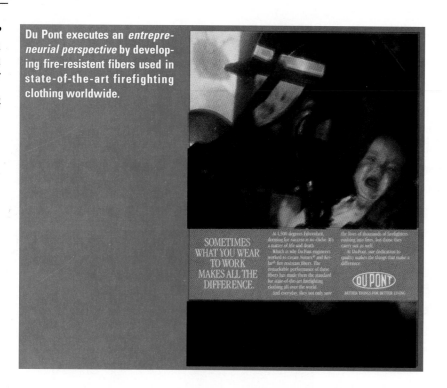

The MCI example illustrates how an *entrepreneurial perspective* can lead to marketing success. The company understood that long-distance phone service was not a commodity. Different customers have different needs. MCI developed products to meet the needs of defined markets, branded these products, and marketed the brands aggressively. These innovative approaches changed the long-distance marketplace and positioned MCI to expand into other telecommunications areas.

Much of MCI's success can be attributed to the important product decisions the company has made. This chapter explores some of these key concepts. We define different types of products and discuss the important components of a product: quality, design, branding, packaging, and customer service.

What is a product?

The term **product** is defined as an idea, a physical entity (a good), a service, or any combination of the three that is an element of exchange to satisfy individual or business objectives.[1] From a marketing viewpoint, the key element of this definition is "to satisfy individual or business objectives." Individuals and businesses purchase products to solve problems or satisfy needs. That is, products provide benefits. Successful marketers focus on the benefits products supply to consumers.

Let's examine the term *product* from a consumer's viewpoint. Say a consumer bought some product—maybe a notebook for a course, or lunch at a local restaurant, or perhaps picked up some dry cleaning. Why did the consumer make each purchase? The major reason is the consumer wanted the benefits offered by the purchased product. The notebook, the lunch, and the dry cleaning provided benefits, in the ability to take notes in class, to satisfy hunger, to have clean clothing. The specific features of each product (the type of notebook, specific restaurant and meal, characteristics of the dry cleaner) are important only insofar as they are translated into the specific benefits the consumer wants.

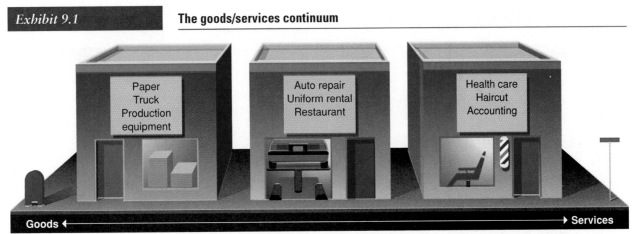

Exhibit 9.1   **The goods/services continuum**

While reading these three chapters in Part 4, it is helpful to think about products from a customer's viewpoint. Customers purchase products for their benefits, and astute marketers emphasize product benefits in their marketing efforts. For example, focusing on customer benefits is the basic marketing philosophy of Hewlett-Packard: "Many companies build a product and look for a market. We listen to our customers, research their needs, and build products that provide solutions for their problems."[2]

Types of products

Marketers often classify products into specific categories. We focus on the categories of goods and services, and consumer and business products. We then discuss different types of consumer and business products.

Goods and services

Goods are usually defined as physical products such as cars, golf clubs, soft drinks, or other concrete entities. **Services,** in contrast, are normally defined as nonphysical products such as a haircut, a football game, or a doctor's diagnosis.

Products, however, do not necessarily fall into one category or the other. Almost all products incorporate some characteristics of both goods and services. A useful way to view goods and services is on a continuum as presented in Exhibit 9.1. Where a product lies on this continuum affects how it should be marketed, because services possess several unique characteristics.

As indicated in Exhibit 9.2, the more a product lies toward the services end of the continuum, the more it is intangible, perishable, inseparable, and variable in quality. The more a product lies toward the goods end, the more it is tangible, storable, separable from the producer, and standardized in quality.

The purchase of a soft drink such as Pepsi-Cola in a restaurant can illustrate these differences. The soft drink is a good. It is tangible; it can be touched when it is served from the can. The restaurant can stockpile cases of Pepsi-Cola to serve when needed. The companies manufacturing and distributing the Pepsi are separated from the customer when the product is consumed. Finally, the quality of the Pepsi is expected to be the same from can to can, because the manufacturing process is standardized.

The service provided by the restaurant, however, is different. The activity of serving the Pepsi is not tangible; it cannot be touched. The restaurant cannot store the service provided by a waiter; if there are no customers, the potential service of a waiter is wasted. The waiter's service cannot be separated from the restaurant, and it is performed in the presence of the customer. Consumers

| Exhibit 9.2 | Characteristics and strategies for services |

Service characteristic	Service strategy	Examples
Intangible	Associate the service with something tangible.	General Motors' Mr. Goodwrench; models of buildings prepared by architects.
Perishable	Manage demand to utilize supply.	Reduced prices for afternoon movies; lower rates for off-season accommodations at tourist attractions.
Inseparable	Capitalize on advantages of person providing the service.	Motivate service providers through compensation and recognition programs; continual training of all customer contact personnel.
Variable	Standardize service delivery as much as possible.	Use of technologies, such as automated teller machines, to provide service; implementation of quality improvement programs.

consider the waiter and the restaurant to be the same. And finally, the service provided by the same waiter to different customers, or by different waiters, is likely to vary in quality.

Because most products represent a blend of goods and services, we normally use the term *product* to include both categories. At the same time, we sometimes refer to products and services, because in popular speech *product* is most frequently associated with goods. Therefore, when we speak of product and service together, *product* refers to goods.

Tangibility

One of the most interesting differences between goods and services relates to tangibility. Because goods are tangible, marketing strategies typically emphasize the intangible benefits derived from consuming the product. For example, many ads for Coke convey an intangible excitement associated with drinking the product. On the other hand, because services are intangible, marketers often try to associate them with something tangible. This approach is evident in the insurance industry: consider the "good hands" of Allstate, the "rock" of Prudential, the "cavalry" of Kemper, and the "good neighbor" of State Farm.

Perishability

Perishability also has an important effect on the marketing of services. Services cannot normally be stored, so marketers of services use different strategies to manage demand. For example, higher prices are charged when demand is expected to be high, but prices are lowered when demand is expected to be low.

Airlines offer a good example of this type of strategy. Passengers flying to the same destination often pay very different fares, depending on flight schedule and time of booking. During holiday periods, fewer discounted tickets are available. Various types of discounted tickets are offered at other times to fill planes that would otherwise fly with empty seats not purchased at regular fares. The earlier customers make reservations and pay for tickets, the lower the fare. Low fares also go to those on standby, that is, customers willing to wait for an available seat after all reserved passengers are boarded. Airlines use standby to generate revenue for seats that have not been purchased in advance and would otherwise go to waste.

Singapore Airlines emphasizes the inseparability of the person and the company in the marketing of services.

Separability

Goods like tennis racquets or tuxedos or tomatoes can be produced, stored, and then sold to customers. Services, on the other hand, are typically produced and consumed simultaneously. For example, a dentist produces dental service at the same time the patient consumes it. The customer, then, tends to see the person and the business providing the service as one and the same. Thus, bank tellers are the bank, nurses or billing personnel are the hospital, and salespeople are the firm.

The close relationships between the production and consumption of services and between the person and the business providing the service have significant implications. Whether a business provides goods or services, it must be concerned with the management of service employees. Every employee who has contact with customers is part of the firm's service offering. Therefore, effective management and training of employees who see customers is critical for providing quality services. Training of executive-level managers is not enough; service employees at all levels need the appropriate attention if they are to "be" the company.

Standardization

The difficulty of standardizing services, especially when they are delivered by people, has important implications for marketers. Even well-trained and professional service providers have bad days. Therefore, there will always be some variability in service quality. Even so, leading firms analyze their service processes and develop standards and procedures to minimize variability to the extent they can.

Consumer and business products

Another important distinction is between consumer and business products. This categorization is based on the way a product is used, and not on the specific characteristics of the product. **Consumer products** are those purchased by consumers for their own personal use. **Business products** are those purchased by a firm or organization for its own use. Thus, the same product could be classified differently depending on the purchase and use. For example, if Elena buys a pencil to use at home, it is considered a consumer product. If Elena's employer purchases the same pencil for her to use at work, it is considered a business product.

Exhibit 9.3   **Consumer and business products**

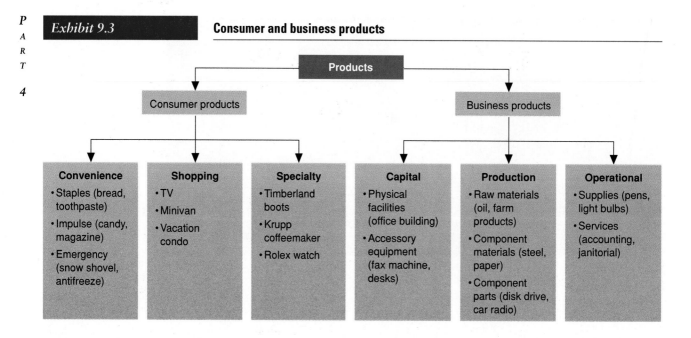

We have seen that the buying behaviors of consumers and businesses differ in important ways. These differences motivate different strategies, depending on whether a product is marketed to consumers or businesses. There are also different types of consumer products and business products, as Exhibit 9.3 demonstrates.

Types of consumer products

There are millions of consumer products, and they can be classified in a number of ways. One especially useful approach is to classify products according to how consumers shop. Such an approach is valuable because it suggests that specific marketing strategies are relevant for a particular consumer-product category. Relevant shopping behavior by category is described in Exhibit 9.4. Of course, the same product can be classified differently by different buyers.

Convenience products are items consumers do not want to spend much time shopping for. Buyers of convenience products typically want to make a quick purchase at the most convenient location. Although they may prefer a specific brand, they will buy something else if that brand is not available. Convenience products are normally low-priced, often-purchased goods. They might range

Exhibit 9.4   **Types of consumer products**

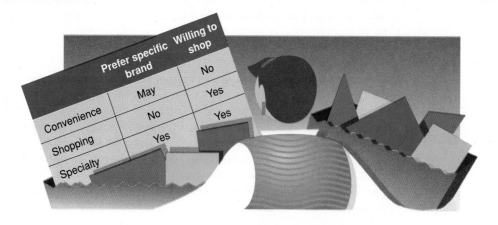

Caramello candy bars, Samsonite bags, and Bentley cars are examples of convenience, shopping, and specialty products, respectively, for most consumers.

from staples (toothpaste, bread, or mustard), to products bought on impulse (chewing gum, magazines, or candy bars) or in an emergency (umbrellas, antifreeze, or snow shovels).

A key to marketing convenience products is to obtain extensive distribution. Marketers should make such products available at all convenient locations so consumers will be able to find the brand they want and not have to switch to another. Widespread distribution is especially important for products bought on impulse, because consumers purchase them only when they see them during their shopping trip. Distribution is also important for products bought in emergencies.

Soft drinks are convenience products for most consumers. Although consumers might prefer Coke over Pepsi or vice versa, they tend to switch to the other if the preferred brand is not available. Coke and Pepsi marketing strategies are designed to ensure that their brands are readily available. Thus, the brands are marketed through all types of retail outlets, restaurants, vending machines, and now at the checkout counters in many grocery stores.

Shopping products, in contrast, are items consumers are willing to spend time shopping for. When consumers perceive all the product alternatives as similar, they often shop around for the best price. A family might shop at several electronics stores, for example, to get the best deal on a television. For other shopping products, consumers might see alternatives as differing in important ways and shop for the one that best meets their needs. A family might shop at Chrysler, Toyota, and Ford dealerships to determine which minivan suits them, as well as to obtain the best price.

Consumers are willing to spend time shopping if the purchase is important to them, particularly if the product is expensive. For marketers, the key strategic implication is to facilitate the shopping process. A shopping product needs to be readily available, but not as widely available as a convenience product. Distribution outlets for a shopping product should provide extensive information to help consumers in the purchase decision. This may be accomplished with knowledgeable salespeople and informative communications and promotional materials. Salespeople and printed brochures for car models at dealerships illustrate typical marketing approaches for shopping products. Locating several car dealers in the same general area also would help to facilitate the shopping process.

Rockwell emphasizes a *relationship perspective* by being responsive to the needs of its car and truck manufacturing customers.

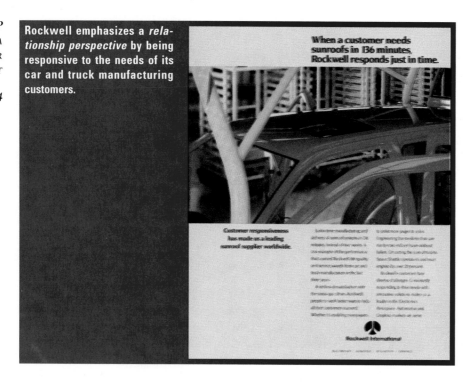

Specialty products are different yet, in that consumers both want to purchase a specific brand and are willing to look to find it. They are neither willing to switch brands, as they are for convenience products, nor shop to evaluate product alternatives, as for shopping products. They want one brand, and they will travel to buy it.

Marketers might limit distribution of specialty products to exclusive outlets and can typically charge high prices. Such marketing efforts should focus on maintaining the loyalty of customers and the image of the product. Certainly, most marketers would enjoy selling a brand considered a specialty product. These are rare circumstances, however, for few consumers are committed to only one brand in many product categories.

Types of business products

Classifying business products is difficult because a vast number of different products are used by for-profit firms, nonprofit organizations, and government agencies. Our categorization groups products according to the way they are used in the operation of a business (see Exhibit 9.3).

Capital products are expensive items used in business operations, but do not become part of any type of finished product. Because they are used over long periods of time, their cost is normally depreciated or spread over some useful life rather than expensed completely in the year of purchase. Capital products range from physical facilities such as manufacturing plants, office buildings, and major equipment, to accessory equipment such as desks, copy machines, fax machines, or forklifts.

The purchasing process for capital products may be long and involve many individuals. Marketers of capital products emphasize personal selling as the major communication tool. Prices are often negotiated, and sometimes businesses decide to rent or lease capital products rather than buy them outright.

Production products become part of some finished product. Raw materials, such as coal, oil, or farm products, are the basic type of production product. Component materials and component parts are also production products. Component materials are products that require further processing to be included in the finished product. Examples are steel, paper, and textiles. Component parts are fabricated for the finished product. They may require some minor processing or be used as is in the finished product. Thermostats and disk drives are examples.

The purchasing process for production products is extensive, but typically less involved than for capital products. Businesses want to receive quality production products when they are needed, otherwise the production process may be interrupted. Marketers of production products therefore must emphasize both product quality and reliability in meeting delivery schedules. A buyer does not necessarily select the supplier with the lowest initial price. Increasingly, the long-run cost of doing business with suppliers is more important to firms than the short-run price of the product.

Operational products are used in the firm's activities but do not become part of any type of finished product. Maintenance, repair, and operating supplies are considered operational products. These include light bulbs, cleaning materials, repair parts, and office supplies. Also included are services such as accounting, engineering, and advertising that are purchased from outside vendors rather than provided from within the business.

The purchasing process for many operational products is the least extensive for any business product. After an initial purchase, and assuming the business is satisfied, subsequent purchases may be straight rebuys; that is, the buyer merely places an additional order with the same supplier. Thus, it is important for a seller to get the initial order and to ensure that the buyer is satisfied with all aspects of the purchase. If this happens, it is almost impossible for a competitor to get its foot in the door.

As discussed in Chapter 6, many business products are purchased by professional purchasers. Purchasing managers typically set the rules for the business purchasing process and make the final purchasing decision for many products. As firms adopt a *productivity perspective,* purchasing managers become more important. They can improve productivity substantially by reducing the costs of purchasing capital, production, and operational products. Understanding this, effective marketers emphasize *quality/value* and *relationship perspectives* in their contacts with professional purchasing managers. The importance of these perspectives is reinforced in the comments of Wayne Whitworth, purchasing manager for Brown-Forman Beverages Worldwide:

> *I am constantly under pressure to reduce the total cost associated with the purchase and use of products for my company. World-class marketers are willing to work as partners by focusing on ways to add value to my business. We work together to continuously improve product quality and reduce total cost. If a supplier cannot improve quality and value through a long-term relationship, then I do not do business with it.[3]*

Product components

We have said that consumers purchase products to satisfy needs. Another way to say this is that people really want a "bundle" of benefits when they purchase a product, and different consumers are likely to want different benefits from the same type of product. To provide the benefits consumers want, marketers need to integrate the components that make up a product effectively. These consist of the product and customer service features illustrated in Exhibit 9.5. Product features include quality, design, branding, and packaging. Customer service encompasses various purchase and usage services. Different blends of product features and customer service provide different benefit bundles.

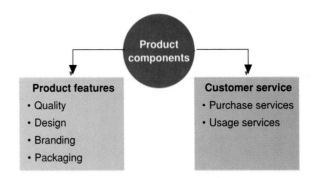

Exhibit 9.5

Product components

Credit cards offer a good example. Although all credit cards provide a basic benefit (credit), some offer a somewhat different mix of benefits to appeal to specific consumers. Credit cards differ in annual fees, rewards for use of the card, payment terms, design of the card, brand name, and services provided. All these components interact to produce the product, or the benefits, consumers purchase.

EXECUTIVE ROUNDTABLE COMMENT | **Dick Bohy, vice president/professional services,**
Sioux Valley Hospital, emphasizes the importance of providing the right mix of benefits to different customer groups:

As health care reform evolves, hospitals have to spend more effort in cultivating relationships with patients, their employers, physicians, our employees, and insurers. Each of these groups has different needs. Therefore, we have to tailor our hospital services to provide the benefits desired by each group. At Sioux Valley Hospital we look at our services from their viewpoints, not just ours. This is the key to developing the relationships needed for our success.

Product quality

In Chapter 2 we defined quality as all the features or characteristics of a product that bear on its ability to satisfy customer needs. We emphasized, moreover, that quality is defined by the *customer,* not the marketer. A *quality/value perspective* is defined as an effort to increase customer satisfaction by constant attention to improving product quality and lowering customer costs.

As a product component, product quality represents how well a product does what it is supposed to do as defined by the customer. Rational, a German manufacturer of computer controlled ovens that combine convection and steam heat, recognizes the importance of defining product quality from the customer's viewpoint. Everywhere in the plant, signs say, "Gut genug? Der Kunde entscheidet" ("Good enough? The customer will decide").[4]

Improving product quality as consumers define it can be an effective way to increase product sales. For example, most consumers probably consider a quality turtleneck to be one that looks good, fits well, and lasts a long time. J. C. Penney found that its turtlenecks were of lower quality than those offered by competitors like The Gap, Lands' End, and L. L. Bean. Penney's turtlenecks lost their fit and did not last very long, because they shrank and puckered at the seams upon washing. To improve the product's quality, the Penney company stiffened its specifications for fabric, fit, and construction, and added Spandex to the neck and cuffs. By introducing higher-quality turtlenecks and reducing the price to provide more value, the company saw sales triple in a year.[5]

Consumers define quality of turtlenecks in terms of looks, fit, and durability. In other markets, consumers define quality differently. In the prestige fountain pen market, for example, consumers consider utility along with glamour and

Parker emphasizes the factors used to produce quality writing instruments desired by consumers.

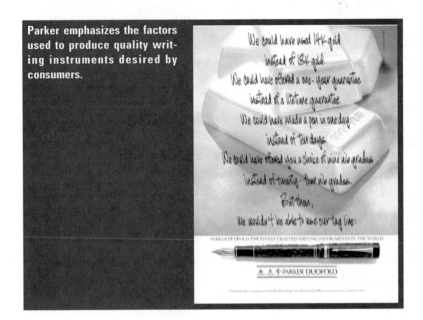

distinction. Cross, Waterman, Montblanc, and Parker compete in this market. All these products offer similar utility, but each provides prestige differently. Some makers emphasize glamour, citing the famous people who use their pens; others emphasize distinction, pointing to the historical documents signed with their pens. Consumers have responded to these pitches about quality by using as many as eight different pens during a year, with specific pens to match wardrobes or to sign different sorts of documents.[6]

Marketers, however, cannot always be sure consumers have accurate perceptions of the quality of their products. This is an especially difficult problem for the US automobile industry. Objective assessments of quality by trade observers or groups such as J. D. Power have consistently shown improvements in the quality of American cars. Yet, many consumers are not aware of these quality improvements. They typically base purchase decisions on personal perceptions of quality, not necessarily objective evaluations, and these perceptions may lag reality.

A recent compilation of objective quality evaluations for 313 product lines in 28 countries over a period of 30 years indicates there may be fewer differences in the actual quality of many competitive products than we typically think. Consider, for example, the global quality evaluations for selected 35 mm cameras for 1988–90 presented in Exhibit 9.6. Clearly, there are only minor quality

Exhibit 9.6

Global product quality evaluations

Brand	Australia	Europe	Japan	USA
Kodak	50	63	67	68
Minolta	76	80	68	76
Nikon	77	77	60	77

Note: These ratings are on a 100-point scale with 70 being average quality.

differences across the different products and countries. Most of the products cluster around average to high quality. "Contrary to conventional wisdom," concludes the author of the research, "there is little variation in the objective quality of most consumer products."[7]

Quality is what consumers consider it to be. Marketers should ensure that their products provide the desired level of quality, work to constantly improve this quality, and convey to consumers an accurate picture of the quality. These are difficult tasks, but they are essential for success in today's competitive marketplace.

EXECUTIVE ROUNDTABLE COMMENT | **Mark Oshnock, a partner at Arthur Andersen, discusses the importance of quality in marketing professional services:**

Constantly improving the quality of our services is critical for maintaining and enhancing relationships with clients. Arthur Andersen surveys all clients each year about the quality of the service we are providing them. The team serving each client uses this feedback to prepare an action plan to improve service quality to the client. The action plan is monitored by top management to ensure it is being executed effectively. We also recontact each client to make sure any problems have been corrected.

Product design

Product design includes the styling, aesthetics, and function of a product. How a product is designed affects how it works, how it feels, how easy it is to assemble and fix, and, from an *ecological perspective,* how easy it is to recycle.

Product design decisions can be pivotal in a product's success. Consider some examples: Reebok and Nike introduced basketball sneakers with inflatable air cushions for better ankle support. The Nike shoe required the wearer to carry a separate hand pump to inflate the shoe. The Reebok shoe design included a pump tucked neatly into the shoe's tongue. Reebok's Pump was successful; Nike had to drop its shoe from the market.[8]

Cannondale is a fast-growing manufacturer of high-tech bicycles. It dominates the high end of the market with the Super V bike that sells for $3,500 and

The exceptional design of the Cannondale Super V is a key factor in distinguishing it from other high-tech off-road bikes.

IF IT WERE HUMAN, THEY'D TEST IT FOR STEROIDS.

You don't steer it, you control it. For "it" is no ordinary suspension bike. This is Super V. A startling new breed of fully suspended mountain bike that attacks the terrain with such enormous power and innate grace, it seems almost alive. Part Brahma bull, part ballet dancer, Super V's strength emanates from its mega-large, yet surprisingly light, 4.40 pound aluminum frame. While its poise comes from an area Cannondale originated - the integrated suspension. Up front, there's the renowned Delta V fork. It eliminates stiction to soak up bumps of every size. And it's the only fork adjustable to the trail as you ride. In back, an oil-dampened, air-sprung shock absorber is attached to an efficient swingarm providing a luxurious three inches of rear-wheel travel. On the trail these systems work in concert. The frame transferring more of your energy to the rear wheel, and the suspension conserving that energy because it's taking the abuse instead of you. Call 1-800-BIKE USA to test drive Super V. Technically, it can't be called an animal. That term should be reserved for those who own it.

© 1993 Cannondale Corporation

Sony designs friendly products

Sony is probably Japan's best-known company, and possibly the world's most inventive consumer electronics firm. It is responsible for popularizing the pocket-sized transistor radio, battery-powered TVs, VCRs, camcorders, and CD players. According to Sony management, "Our basic concept has always been this—to give new convenience, or new methods, or new benefits, to the general public without technology."

The development of new technologies, and especially translating these into product ideas, is largely the responsibility of Sony's 9,000 scientists and engineers. The company backs their research and development efforts with over $1.5 billion a year.

Although engineers and scientists devise the electronic and mechanical heart of the products, product designers at the Sony Design Center give the products the distinctive Sony look and feel. The product designers use sophisticated computer workstations to help design the knobs, buttons, and packaging for each product. The objective is to make high-tech products stylish, but also easy to use.

Source: Adapted from Brenton R. Schlender, "How Sony Keeps the Magic Going," *Fortune,* February 24, 1992, pp. 76–84. © 1992 Time, Inc. All rights reserved.

draws raves because of its stylish and functional design. The success of the Super V is largely attributable to the bike's ability to smooth out bumps for off-road cyclists. The flexible aluminum frame, front and rear shock absorbers, and pivoting rear frame provide cyclists with control and comfort over various terrains.[9]

Toothbrushes are typically considered a commodity product that most consumers buy on price. Johnson & Johnson, Gillette, SmithKline Beecham, Procter & Gamble, and Colgate-Palmolive recently redesigned their toothbrush products. By changing shapes, adding handles with tiny shock absorbers, and incorporating rippled bristles, the companies have energized consumers. Toothbrush sales were up 30 percent in one year. The popularity of these products allowed the companies to raise prices and improve profits.[10]

Product design is becoming increasingly important. This is especially so for high-tech products, whose complex designs may present problems for consumers. User-friendly designs can increase the chances of success for high-tech products. **The Technological Edge: Sony Designs Friendly Products** shows how one company successfully designs consumer electronics products.

Branding

It is critical that a firm identifies its products to distinguish them from similar products offered by competitors. This is the **branding** process. Several key terms need defining for this discussion:

- **Brand**—A name, term, sign, symbol, design, or combination that a firm uses to identify its products and differentiate them from those of competitors.

- **Brand name**—The element of a brand that can be vocalized, such as IBM, Tide, Snickers, or Diet Coke.

- **Brand mark**—The element of a brand that cannot be vocalized, such as the MGM lion, the Buick symbol, or the Texaco star.

A number of different brand names and trademarks are illustrated for products offered by General Mills in this trade ad.

- **Trademark**—A brand or part of a brand that is registered with the US Patent and Trademark Office. This registration gives the owner exclusive right to use the brand and may even preclude other firms from using brand names or marks that are similar.

McDonald's provides an interesting illustration of these terms. The McDonald's brand consists of the name McDonald's and the golden arches symbol. Both of these are registered as trademarks to protect them from use by other firms. For instance, Quality Inns planned to develop a new economy hotel chain and wanted to name it McSleep. McDonald's went to court arguing that this name would lead consumers to believe that the hotel chain was part of McDonald's. The court agreed and made Quality Inns change the name. Interestingly, since McDonald's owns the trademark, it can use the brand name as it sees fit. For example, it named a chain of truck-stop–style operations McStop.[11]

Importance of branding

Branding is important to both consumers and marketers. From a consumer's viewpoint, branding facilitates buying. If there were no brands, consumers would have to evaluate the nonbranded products available every time they went shopping. They could never be sure they were purchasing the specific desired products and would have difficulty evaluating the quality of some. When selecting from among branded products, consumers can purchase specific ones and be reasonably certain of their quality.

Branding also provides psychological benefits to consumers. Some buyers derive satisfaction from owning brands with images of prestige. These brands convey status. Examples are Rolex watches, Mercedes-Benz automobiles, and Waterford crystal.

Exhibit 9.7

Important brand relationships

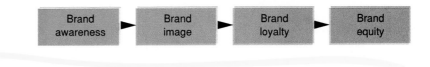

From a marketer's viewpoint, branding has considerable value. A brand differentiates a firm's product from competitors and helps to focus and facilitate marketing efforts. Marketing efforts are often designed to move consumers through the process depicted in Exhibit 9.7.[12]

The first step in brand marketing typically focuses on generating brand awareness. **Brand awareness** is achieved when target consumers know about a brand and call it to mind when thinking about the product category. For example, Procter & Gamble has achieved brand awareness with Tide, which many consumers automatically recall when thinking about buying laundry detergent.

Brand awareness must then be translated into a **brand image**, or the impression that consumers have about a brand. Marketers should ensure that consumers have accurate ideas of the brand's advantages and positive impressions of it. P&G is successful if consumers perceive that Tide gets clothes cleaner than competitive brands.

With a positive brand image established in their minds, some consumers will normally purchase Tide when shopping for laundry detergent. Such buyers exhibit **brand loyalty.** The most brand-loyal customers will select Tide on almost every purchasing opportunity.

The culmination of brand awareness, image, and loyalty is the development of **brand equity**, or the value that the brand has in the marketplace. Brand equity has a financial dimension, especially important in any merger or acquisition transaction. The financial value of P&G's Tide would be significant in any discussion of an acquisition price, for instance.

Brand equity also affects marketing efforts. The same marketing strategy and level of expenditures used for different brands are likely to have different results, depending on brand equity. Typically, marketing efforts built on an established positive brand awareness, image, and loyalty—or high brand equity—are more successful. Exhibit 9.8 presents examples of brands that have developed brand equity around the world.

The importance of the brand relationships shown in Exhibit 9.7 is illustrated in Russia. RJR Nabisco, Procter & Gamble, Colgate-Palmolive, Johnson & Johnson, Mars, and Coca-Cola are some of the companies trying to build brand loyalty and equity in Russia. The basic strategy is to generate brand awareness and positive images now, so that when Russia's 218 million citizens become more prosperous, the positive brand images will lead to sales and loyal customers. The initial success of this visionary approach is evident for the Snickers brand. In 1992, only 5 percent of Russians surveyed were aware of the Snickers brand. After substantial marketing efforts, brand awareness increased to 82 percent the next year.[13]

Types of brands

Marketers must decide early on whether to brand a product, and if so, which type of brand to use. **Generics** are products that are not branded. They are labeled instead by their generic name and may be of lower quality and cost less than branded competitors. Usually, plain black-and-white labels identify the product by its generic name, such as peas, aluminum foil, or tomato soup.

In the pharmaceutical industry, generic products must meet the quality standards set by the Food and Drug Administration. Many doctors specify generic

Exhibit 9.8   **Top world brands**

Interbrand, a branding consultancy, selected the top 10 brands in the world. Its evaluation was based on scoring each brand on leadership, stability, market, internationality, trend, support, and legal protection.

1. **Coca-Cola** — Brand introduced in late 1800s; has maintained strong brand identity through consistent imaging, packaging, advertising, promotion.

2. **Kellogg's** — Feeds high proportion of sales back into advertising cereals & concentrates heavily on brand management.

3. **McDonald's** — Operates approximately 11,500 restaurants in 52 countries. Brand success based on offering consistent quality & service & by controlling every step in the process.

4. **Kodak** — In 1887, George Eastman patented dry-plate process, bringing photography to the masses. Today, Eastman Kodak is world leader in photographic & related products.

5. **Marlboro** — Introduced in 1924 by Philip Morris, positioned as a woman's cigarette. In 1955, brand reintroduced as man's cigarette & marketed via the cowboy. Now the leading international cigarette brand.

6. **IBM** — Since 1911, has been making business-related products. Largest computer manufacturer in world. Differentiates brand with logo.

7. **American Express** — Card invented in 1958; succeeded immediately by conveying status for cardholders. Brand has maintained exclusiveness in competitive market.

8. **Sony** — Founded in 1946, became brand success by maintaining clear corporate image, focusing on electronics, quickly bringing new products to international market.

9. **Mercedes-Benz** — In 1909, logo was adopted to establish a visual identiy. Today, logo & name are central to this international brand.

10. **Nescafé** — Instant coffee introduced in 1938. Nestlé has focused on product development & brand support, consistently managed the brand, maintained the visual image.

TOP 10

drugs in an effort to reduce the patient's costs. Indeed, pharmaceutical companies that once marketed only branded products are hopping on the generic bandwagon. Merck, for example, has recently established its West Point Pharma division to market generic pharmaceuticals for brands no longer protected by patents. It will continue to market its branded products through other divisions.

If a firm decides to brand its products, it can choose one of two types of brands. The first and most familiar type is a **manufacturer brand.** Sometimes referred to as a **national brand** or **regional brand,** it is sponsored by the manufacturer of the product. The manufacturer is responsible for the product's quality and marketing. Many firms, such as P&G, IBM, Gillette, and Xerox, use manufacturer brands for their products.

The other type is a **distributor brand.** Also called **store brand, private brand,** or **private label,** it is sponsored by a distributor such as a wholesaler or retailer. Although the manufacturer's name may be indicated somewhere on the label, the distributor is responsible for the product's quality and marketing. Familiar store brands are Craftsman tools (Sears) and President's Choice soft drinks (Loblaw). Many distributors are introducing their own brands. The lower marketing costs for private-label brands make it possible for distributors to maintain high profit margins while charging lower prices than for manufacturer brands.

Intense competition today between manufacturer and distributor brands has been termed the *battle of the brands.* Initially, the mass-marketing power of large manufacturers gave them the edge in this battle. Recently, however, large retailers with tremendous amounts of consumer purchasing information have improved their position substantially.

The competition for market share involves the value provided to consumers. They typically perceive manufacturer brands as of higher quality than distributor brands. Yet, the quality and cost differences vary considerably. When consumers perceive large quality differences, manufacturer brands may provide the most value and are purchased. When consumers perceive small quality differences, then distributor brands may provide the best value and are purchased.

Spartan brand products are private-label brands.

Some examples will illustrate the importance of the quality, price, and value relationships between manufacturer and distributor brands. Kraft slowly increased the prices for its branded cheese products until they were 45 percent higher than private brands. This led to a loss of 3 percent in market share. When Kraft reduced prices by 8 percent, sales increased 5 percent. As another example, Frito-Lay lost 2 percent market share when it increased prices. Then it improved product quality and reduced prices by 15 percent. This increased value generated over a 1 percent market share increase in a $13 billion market.[14]

The battle between manufacturer and distributor brands is likely to intensify in the foreseeable future. Private label sales are increasing more than manufacturer brands in many US supermarket product categories. The situation is similar in Europe, where distributor brands have achieved over 20 percent of supermarket sales in Britain, Switzerland, Germany, and France.[15]

Choosing a brand name

Choosing an effective brand name is an important decision for both manufacturer and distributor brands. The brand name communicates a great deal, greatly affecting brand awareness and brand image. In general, an effective brand name suggests something about the product's benefits; is easy to pronounce, recognize, and remember; is distinctive in some way; and can be translated into other languages.

Ideally, a brand name should help to communicate to consumers the major benefits of the firm's product. If this is achieved, the brand name helps to link brand awareness with brand image. As consumers become aware of the brand name, they begin to associate it with specific product benefits. For example, Wal-Mart is introducing a line of 350 packaged food items under its own private label "Great Value." This name communicates the benefits of high quality and low price. And establishing value is critical for the success of distributor brands.[16]

A brand name that is easy to pronounce, recognize, and remember helps in establishing brand awareness. The name should also be distinctive. Brand names that meet these criteria are Mustang, Kodak, and Crest. Sometimes a brand name can be effective and not really mean anything in real words. Manfred Gotta develops brand names using "artificial nomenclature." Names he has created for companies include Vitek (fitness products), Tornac (umbrellas), Dogstix (dog snacks), and Ernty (baby food). For cars, his specialty, he has come up

Licensing booms at Starter

Starter Corporation's sales have soared in recent years. The company is a major player in the $12 billion team-licensed sportswear business. It acquires nonexclusive licenses from professional sports leagues to manufacture athletic apparel with team trademarks. Products range from New York Yankees caps to Washington Redskins parkas. Starter has kept ahead of an increasing number of rivals by expanding the types of products offered and designing high-quality clothing.

Its success has lead Starter to expand its own line of sportswear. These products will be branded with Starter's stylized "S" and star logo instead of professional team logos. This new sportswear will be supported by a $10 million integrated marketing communications campaign.

Starter is also trying to push into the European market. The company is an official sponsor of the 1996 Summer Olympic Games in Atlanta. It has recently obtained licenses to use the trademarks of well-known soccer teams in England and Italy. These moves should help in building a distribution network throughout Europe. It remains to be seen whether the use of licensed and company trademarks will be as successful overseas as it has been in the United States.

Sources: Tim Smart and Irene Recio, "A Sportswear House with Major-League Dreams," *Business Week*, April 5, 1993, p. 62; and "Starter's No. 1 Challenger Is the One with Keys to Tron," *Brandweek*, January 31, 1994, p. 27.

with the Opel Calibra, Mazda Xedos, and Volkswagen Corrado. None of these brand names is a real word, but each communicates an image and is distinctive and easy to pronounce, recognize, and remember.[17]

From a *global perspective* the brand name should be translatable into different languages. Many a firm has been embarrassed when introducing a brand name into a different language. Still others have been able to capitalize on effective brand names. For example, brands that translate well into Russian include Sony, Adidas, and Ford. As P&G introduces brands in Russia, it alters its usual names somewhat. Oil of Olay becomes Oil of Ulay, Tide becomes Ariel, and Pert Plus is Vidal Sassoon Wash & Go.[18]

An alternative to developing a brand name is licensing an existing name or logo. **Licensing** typically consists of the right to use a trademark in exchange for paying royalties on the sale of the licensed product. Licensing sales are in the range of $65 billion a year.[19] A familiar use of licensing is sportswear with an institution's name or seal on it. Sales of products with licensed university trademarks are brisk. The University of Louisville, for example, has licensing agreements with 260 different companies whose sales are at record levels.[20] Licensing offers opportunities for firms with an *entrepreneurial perspective.* An interesting example is presented in **The Entrepreneurial Spirit: Licensing Booms at Starter.**

Packaging

Packaging is an important component for many products. A *package* is the container or wrapper for a product. It typically includes a *label,* a printed description of the product on the package. Packaging is important to both consumers and distributors of a product. A product's package might perform a number of

New food labels give consumers detailed nutritional information on food packages.

Nutrition Facts

Serving Size ¾ cup (30g)
Servings Per Container About 11

Amount Per Serving	Whole Grain Total	with ½ cup Skim milk
Calories	100	140
Calories from Fat	5	10

	% Daily Value**	
Total Fat 0.5g*	1%	1%
Saturated Fat 0g	0%	0%
Cholesterol 0mg	0%	1%
Sodium 200mg	8%	11%
Potassium 100mg	3%	9%
Total Carbohydrate 24g	8%	10%
Dietary Fiber 3g	10%	10%
Sugars 5g		
Other Carbohydrate 16g		
Protein 3g		
Vitamin A	100%	110%
(10% as Beta Carotene)		
Vitamin C	100%	100%
Calcium	25%	40%
Iron	100%	100%
Vitamin D	10%	25%
Vitamin E	100%	100%
Thiamin	100%	100%
Riboflavin	100%	110%
Niacin	100%	100%
Vitamin B$_6$	100%	110%
Folic Acid	100%	100%
Vitamin B$_{12}$	100%	110%
Pantothenic Acid	100%	100%
Phosphorus	20%	30%
Zinc	100%	100%

*Amount in Cereal. A serving of cereal plus skim milk provides 1g fat, <5mg cholesterol, 260mg sodium, 300mg potassium, 30g carbohydrate (11g sugar) and 7g protein.

**Percent Daily Values are based on a 2,000 calorie diet. Your daily values may be higher or lower depending on your calorie needs:

	Calories:	2,000	2,500
Total Fat	Less than	65g	80g
Sat Fat	Less than	20g	25g
Cholesterol	Less than	300mg	300mg
Sodium	Less than	2,400mg	2,400mg
Potassium		3,500mg	3,500mg
Total Carbohydrate		300g	375g
Dietary Fiber		25g	30g

Calories per gram:
Fat 9 • Carbohydrate 4 • Protein 4

different functions, including protecting the product until consumed, storing the product until consumed, facilitating consumption of the product, promoting the product, and facilitating disposal of the product.

Because many retailers are self-service sellers, a product's package must communicate the brand's image and help to sell the product. Effective packages provide opportunities for marketers to gain competitive advantages. For example, Ty Nant is a brand of springwater from Lampeter, Wales. Although it does not taste better and is no more healthful than any other bottled water, sales increased from 1.8 to 8.5 million bottles in one year. The reason for the tremendous sales increase? The package. Consumers love the cobalt-blue bottle.[21]

Distinctive packages help capture the attention of consumers as they view competitive products. Both package and label also provide important information that consumers use in evaluating competing brands. Some labeling information is mandated by law. For example, the Nutrition Labeling and Education Act of 1990 required food manufacturers to disclose contents uniformly by May 1994. The purpose of the law is to help consumers compare fat content, vitamin content, or other nutritional characteristics before purchase.[22]

Innovations in packaging offer ways to differentiate brands that consumers might otherwise perceive as very similar. While once all toothpaste brands were packaged in tubes, they now come in pumps, squeeze containers, and stand-up tubes. This new packaging accounts for almost 20 percent of toothpaste sales.[23] It is normally hard to sustain an advantage with new packages, however, because competitors are quick to imitate successful innovations.

An *ecological perspective* is critical to packaging success in the current environment. Many consumers complain about packages that use too much material or material that is difficult to dispose of. Compact discs (CDs) were introduced with excessive packaging, and many people remember the flap over McDonald's Styrofoam containers. Today the CD industry has agreed on a new standardized package that is much smaller than the original versions, and McDonald's now

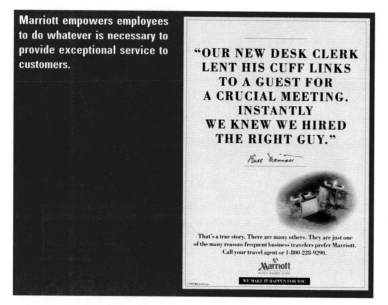

packages all its hamburgers in paper wrappers. L'eggs has replaced its plastic egg with a recyclable cardboard box; Kodak has eliminated its cardboard box. And P&G markets superconcentrated liquid detergents. There are many opportunities for marketers to develop innovative packages that help sell a brand, improve its function, and have environmental advantages.

Customer service

The final product component is **customer service,** which describes the assistance provided to help a customer with the purchase or use of a product. Customer service applies to both goods and services. For example, a consumer purchasing phone lines from South Central Bell for a new home is buying the basic service of being able to communicate by phone from specified locations within the home. These are the basic features of the phone service. However, customer service concerns all the contacts the customer has with South Central Bell employees. This includes the person taking the order and the employee installing the phone line. For instance, customers might evaluate the service according to how well the service options were explained, whether the installer arrived on time, and whether the work was completed as promised.[24]

For many products, especially business goods, customer service differentiates competitors. Providing exceptional customer service can give a firm a marketing advantage. For example, Packard Bell personal computers do not have any particular technological advantages over competitive products. However, by making it easy for consumers to buy and use its products, the company has an edge over competitors in customer service.

Since competitors can quickly copy changes in basic product components, the key to success in many industries is beating the competition in customer service. This approach requires *entrepreneurial* and *execution perspectives,* as the firm must develop and then effectively deliver innovative customer service. Few things hurt a firm more than not being able to deliver promised services. Few things can help a firm more than giving customers exceptional service, even under trying conditions.

An example will illustrate. The warehouse manager of Miller Business Systems received an order for 20 desks, 20 executive chairs, 40 side chairs, and 20 file cabinets that the customer wanted delivered and set up later in the afternoon. But there were no trucks or employees available to make the delivery. On hearing about the problem, the president had the warehouse manager rent a truck, and the two delivered and installed everything that afternoon as requested. It was an unusual situation, but what to do was clear: "If you promise a customer, deliver."[25]

Important elements of customer service during the purchasing process include providing information about product alternatives, training in product use, and credit and financing services. Exceptional customer service prior to a purchase can produce competitive advantages. Consider the case of Curry Hardware in Boston. This small hardware store is located next to a huge Home Depot store that offers much lower prices. Curry thrives in this situation because it has lots of salespeople available to answer customers' "how to fix it" questions. Customers are willing to pay more to receive this valuable service.[26]

Important elements of customer service after the purchase include fast and reliable delivery, quick installation, accessible technical information and advice, repair services, and warranties. Sometimes just employing a *relationship perspective* and showing concern for customers after the sale can do wonders. An interesting example is Yolanda Eijgenstein, head of Wie Mailt Wat? (Who's Mailing What?) in Rotterdam. Her company collects, categorizes, and reports on every piece of direct mail in the Netherlands. Clients are mostly banks and consumer product companies. After reports are sent to clients, she calls to see how they like the service. Most are astonished that she has called, and many place additional orders.[27]

EXECUTIVE ROUNDTABLE COMMENT | Tony Donnan, general management—External Affairs, Europe, at Avon, emphasizes the importance of customer service:

We market quality products. But what really differentiates us from competitors is the customer service provided by the independent Avon sales representatives. They bring our products directly to customers and help them determine what to buy and how to use our products in the best way; they also make sure the products are delivered promptly and respond to any questions that might arise.

The critical task facing marketers is to combine quality, design, branding, packaging, and customer service components into an effective product offering. A product must meet the needs of the target market and also have advantages over competitors on important product components. Moreover, businesses must constantly be ready to alter product components to adapt to a dynamic marketing environment.

Summary

1. *Understand the differences between goods and services.* Products can be viewed as a continuum, with goods at one end and services at the other. Goods are physical products; services are nonphysical products. Goods are more tangible, perishable, separable, and standardized than services. Most products represent a mixture of goods and services.

2. *Differentiate between consumer and business products and discuss the different types of each.* Consumer products are those purchased by consumers for their personal use. Business products are those purchased by a firm for its own use.

Different types of consumer products include convenience, shopping, and specialty products, which differ in the amount of shopping consumers are willing to undertake. Consumers are not willing to shop for convenience products, will shop to make the best purchase for shopping products, and will shop to purchase a specific product for specialty products.

Business products include capital, production, and operational products. Capital products are expensive goods that do not become part of a company's finished product. Production goods become part of a finished product; operational goods are used in a company's operations but do not become part of a finished product.

3. *Recognize that marketers need to appreciate the perspective of the consumer.* People purchase products to satisfy needs or solve problems. They perceive products as bundles of benefits that can help them satisfy needs or solve problems. To view products from the customer's perspective, marketers must focus on the benefits that product components provide to customers.

4. *Define and discuss the importance of product quality, product design, branding, packaging, and customer service.* Marketers need to look at products as consisting of various components that provide benefits to consumers. The major components are product quality, product design, branding, packaging, and customer service. Product quality could be described

as an assessment of how well a product does what it is supposed to do from the customer's viewpoint. Product design includes how the product looks and feels, and how easy it is to assemble and use.

Branding describes the way a firm identifies its products from those offered by competitors. Packaging addresses the container or wrapper for a product and any labeling that might be provided. Customer service refers to any activity intended to facilitate the purchasing or use of a product.

5. *Explain how the different product components need to be integrated to meet the needs of customers.* Marketers must integrate all product components to offer the bundle of benefits desired by customers. Marketers can achieve competitive advantages by skillfully mixing the different product components into an effective, complete product offering.

Key terms & concepts

product 210
goods 211
services 211
consumer products 213
business products 213
convenience products 214
shopping products 215
specialty products 216
capital products 216
production products 216

operational products 217
branding 221
brand 221
brand name 221
brand mark 221
trademark 222
brand awareness 223
brand image 223
brand loyalty 223
brand equity 223

generics 223
manufacturer brand 224
national brand 224
regional brand 224
distributor brand 224
store brand 224
private brand 224
private label 224
licensing 226
customer service 228

Review & discussion questions

1. What are the basic differences between goods and services?

2. Why is it important to differentiate between consumer and business products and among different types of each?

3. Refer to **The Entrepreneurial Spirit: Licensing Booms at Starter.** How has branding contributed to the company's success?

4. Refer to **The Technological Edge: Sony Designs Friendly Products.** How does Sony use technology in the product design process, and why is product design important for high-tech products?

5. Why is brand equity important?

6. Explain what product quality is. Why might it be important to your classmates?

7. Explain how firms can develop competitive advantages through customer service.

8. How does a global perspective affect product component decisions?

9. Why is it important to take an ecological perspective toward packaging?

10. Why is an executional perspective toward customer service important?

Application exercises

1. Go to a large chain supermarket. Select any one specific product and identify the manufacturer brands, distributor brands, and generics that this store stocks. List each specific brand under each type and compare the product components for each. Summarize your findings to report the results.

2. Assume you have developed a new type of microwave popcorn that tastes as good as competitive products but takes only half the time to prepare. Develop a

manufacturer brand name for this product. Compare the name you have chosen to brand names for other microwave popcorn brands. Discuss why you think your brand name will be effective.

3. Look through the ads in the local newspaper. Identify all the examples of customer service you find. Summarize your findings into a list of the ways marketers are using customer service to differentiate their products.

Case 9.1   *Fed Ex and UPS: Ships and planes*

Federal Express and UPS are major competitors in the express-delivery business. Each offers similar services to individual and business customers. Marketing strategies for both firms have focused on pricing and advertising in recent years. But the development of new technologies is changing the basis for competition.

Fed Ex developed PowerShip, and UPS followed with MaxiShip. PowerShip and MaxiShip are computer systems that the companies give to specific business customers. Both of the systems store addresses and shipping data, print handsome mailing labels, and help track where packages are in the delivery process. To date, Fed Ex has given out 26,500 PowerShips and UPS around 15,000.

The basic strategy is to provide customers with the computer system so that they will use more of the firm's express-delivery services. So far, the strategy seems to be working. For example, Disney Stores increased its use of Fed Ex for expedited delivery from 60 to 95 percent after it received a PowerShift system. UPS estimates that business increases by at least 20 percent when a customer receives a MaxiShip computer system.

Despite these results, some customers are disappointed with the systems. Although PowerShip and MaxiShip do track shipments made by the sponsoring delivery company, many customers want a system that will allow them to track their total freight activities at all locations and with all cargo carriers. Both shippers want to respond to this need. Technology staffs at both companies have been increased and are working hard to improve the computer systems and provide the data and reports customers want.

The stakes are high. Many customers ship huge volumes of packages. Lands' End, for example, ships over 12 million packages a year, while US West sends 10,000 packages by air each week. Increasing the amount of business with these and other customers offers any shipper tremendous opportunities to increase sales and profits. The computer systems are one way to increase business by enhancing relationships with customers.

Questions:

1. Describe the product components for Fed Ex and UPS.

2. Define the mix of goods and services in the product offerings of these companies.

3. What is your assessment of the use of the computer systems to strengthen customer relationships? What are the advantages and disadvantages of this strategy?

4. What other strategies could you suggest to help Fed Ex or UPS gain a competitive advantage in the express-delivery business?

Source: Laurie M. Grossman, "Federal Express, UPS Face Off on Computers," *The Wall Street Journal*, September 17, 1993, pp. B1, B6. Reprinted by permission of *The Wall Street Journal*. © 1993 Dow Jones & Company, Inc. All Rights Reserved Worldwide.

Case 9.2   *Butterfinger: Weird orange stuff*

Butterfinger is a chocolate candy bar with weird orange stuff in the middle. The brand has been around for 65 years, but Nestlé purchased it from RJR/Nabisco in 1990. Since the purchase, Nestlé successfully rejuvenated brand sales.

Butterfinger is targeted to the 12 to 24 age group, especially boys and men. Marketing research on chocolate candy bar purchasers indicates that most have four to eight favorite brands, but that they are not typically loyal to any one. Most purchases are made on impulse, with the candy bar normally eaten before the buyer returns home. Marketers based their strategy to increase sales of Butterfinger on this understanding of consumer buying behavior.

The marketing strategy emphasized two tactics: generating awareness and interest in Butterfinger and making the brand readily available. Awareness and interest were generated by using characters from the "Simpsons" in a promotional program. In the ads, Lisa, Homer, and the school bully plot to steal Bart's Butterfinger. The advertising campaign emphasized the theme: "Nobody better lay a finger on my Butterfinger."

Promotions were used to achieve widespread distribution of the brand. One was a tie-in with the movie *Dennis the Menace*. The promotion included prepacked retail display units in 75,000 stores nationwide, an offer for a Dennis the Menace watch, advertising on wrappers, full-page ads in *People* and *Entertainment Weekly*, 50 million freestanding newspaper inserts with a "buy two, get one free" coupon, and sneak previews for key buyers in 25 cities. Nestlé also paid to have a Butterfinger bar appear in a movie.

Nestlé's marketing strategy has been successful. Butterfinger became the fastest-growing established candy, outpacing industry average sales growth by 300 percent. Brand sales increased about 10 percent in 1991–92, with overall supermarket sales of $54.5 million in the year ending in April 1993. Nestlé is continuing the basic strategy but making some changes to maintain interest in the brand.

Questions:

1. What type of consumer product is Butterfinger? Why?

2. How would you evaluate the effectiveness of the Butterfinger brand name?

3. Why has Nestlé's marketing strategy for Butterfinger been so successful?

4. What changes would you suggest to Nestlé for the future?

Source: "Consumer Product: Nestlé," *Sales & Marketing Management*, August 1993, p. 40.

Developing New Products and Services

After studying this chapter you should be able to:

1. Recognize the different types of new products.

2. Discuss the different sources of new products.

3. Understand the stages in the new-product development process.

4. Describe the way marketing research is used in the new-product development process.

5. Appreciate the keys to new-product success.

General Mills: New restaurants on the new-product menu

General Mills reaps over $2.5 billion a year from its restaurant operations. Its 587 Red Lobster and 365 Olive Garden restaurants each gross about $2.7 million annually. A new restaurant concept called China Coast is now in test markets. If successful, China Coast would compete with more than 28,000 Chinese restaurants in the US for the $6.5 billion in sales produced by them each year.

General Mills is constantly looking to develop new products for its restaurant business. In recent years it has tested, but scrapped, Mexican restaurants, health food restaurants, steakhouses, pie shops, fern bars, and even another concept for a Chinese restaurant. The company follows a rigorous process in developing these products, as the China Coast case illustrates.

General Mills has been testing China Coast at eight prototype restaurants in Orlando, Indianapolis, and Fort Worth. Restaurants are open for lunch and dinner. The guiding concept is to offer an extensive, made-to-order menu with large servings. During planning and test-marketing stages, the company changed the basic menu 10 times with countless other variations. Current plans are to offer a basic menu, customized somewhat for local tastes.

China Coast restaurants are similar in appearance to each other. Each seats 260 people and has a turquoise pagoda roof, with bamboo rustling in the breeze outside. Touch-activated computer screens are available for servers to place orders.

The testing in Orlando indicated a large potential for take-out orders. The company is considering adding a special annex and parking lot to better serve take-out customers. The take-out portion of the business competes with rapidly growing Chinese fast-food chains.

General Mills continues to test and refine the China Coast concept. Although current test-market results have been very favorable, a highly publicized research report by the Center for Science in the Public Interest suggests that take-out Chinese food is fattier, more salt-laden, and higher in calories than most consumers thought. Sales of many Chinese-food products dipped sharply after the study results were reported, but they have rebounded to former levels. Terry Cheng, China Coast's director of menu planning, thinks the study is misleading and will have little effect on the expansion plans for China Coast.

Sources: Richard Gibson, "China Coast Restaurants May Mushroom," *The Wall Street Journal*, April 19, 1993, pp. B1, B5; and Julie Tilsner, "Pork, Sweat, and Tears," *Business Week*, September 20, 1993, p. 42.

Rubbermaid's success depends on the introduction of new products like the Little Tikes Rocking Rocket.

TO VENUS AND BACK BY SUPPER.

China Coast is an especially interesting example of new-product development. Each General Mills restaurant chain can be considered a different product. Moreover, each restaurant chain is a blend of goods and services. Thus, the development of a new restaurant concept is a complex type of new-product development. This is especially true for General Mills, which follows a rigorous multistep process for testing and refining new-product concepts.

In this chapter we examine new-product development. We begin by discussing the types and sources of new products. Then, we discuss the various stages of the new-product development process. Finally, we suggest several keys for successful new-product development.

New-product overview

Developing successful new products drives sales and profit growth for many companies. One study found that companies leading their industries in profitability and sales growth gain 49 percent of their revenues from products developed in the past five years. Companies at the bottom in sales and profit growth achieve only 11 percent of sales from new products.[1] Some companies set specific new-product goals. For example, Rubbermaid wants to enter a new product category every 12 to 18 months and expects to get 33 percent of sales from products introduced within the past five years.[2] Corporate goals like these establish a *visionary perspective* toward new products for all employees.

Despite the importance of developing new products, a large percentage of them fail. One study of 11,000 new products launched by 77 manufacturing, service, and consumer products companies reports that only 56 percent of these products were still on the market five years later.[3] Other studies suggest the failure rate is even higher, maybe up to 80 percent. Whatever the exact figure, new-product failures are costly. The failures of Ford's Edsel, Du Pont's Corfam, Polaroid's Polarvision, RCA's Videodisc, Cadillac's Allante, and IBM's PCjr cost each company millions.

These and other costly failures motivate companies to take a *productivity perspective* toward new-product development. The aim is to decrease the percentage of new-product failures, reduce the cost of development, and shorten the time required to get new products to market. These objectives drive most of the

Exhibit 10.1	Types of new products

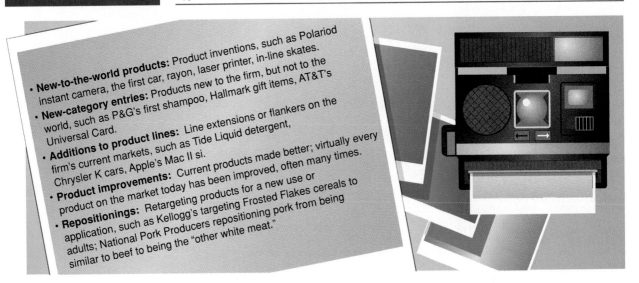

- **New-to-the-world products:** Product inventions, such as Polariod instant camera, the first car, rayon, laser printer, in-line skates.
- **New-category entries:** Products new to the firm, but not to the world, such as P&G's first shampoo, Hallmark gift items, AT&T's Universal Card.
- **Additions to product lines:** Line extensions or flankers on the firm's current markets, such as Tide Liquid detergent, Chrysler K cars, Apple's Mac II si.
- **Product improvements:** Current products made better; virtually every product on the market today has been improved, often many times.
- **Repositionings:** Retargeting products for a new use or application, such as Kellogg's targeting Frosted Flakes cereals to adults; National Pork Producers repositioning pork from being similar to beef to being the "other white meat."

changes companies are making in the new-product development process. Herman Miller, for example, incorporates customers, cross-functional teams, and computer software to develop new office furniture that satisfies customer needs. This approach shortened the new-product development cycle by 50 percent, lowered costs substantially, and led to an 11 percent sales increase in a sluggish market.[4]

EXECUTIVE ROUNDTABLE COMMENT | Tom Kapella, vice president/product development, Gibson Greetings, Inc., comments on the importance of improving the new-product development process:

New products are our lifeblood. We need a constant stream of successful new products and must get them to the market faster, even if costs are higher than projected. Gibson uses highly efficient marketing teams of people from the marketing, operations, finance, sales, and creative areas to develop new products. Teams are empowered to make decisions, move fast, and execute new ideas. They must work together as one or we will not meet our new-product objectives.

Types of new products

At first glance, defining a new product would seem to be easy. Yet, the term *new* can be defined from different vantage points and in a number of ways. The first issue is, new to whom? The first time a customer uses a product, it is a new product to him or her, even if it has been available and used by others for a long time. In this case, though the product newness affects the customers' purchasing behavior and the firm's marketing strategies, it does not have a major impact on an organization's new-product development process.

What does directly affect this process is how new the product is to the organization. And even from an organizational perspective, there are degrees of newness. Exhibit 10.1 presents several categories of new products, organized by how new they are to the company developing and marketing the product.

New-to-the-world products are the only ones that are new to both consumers and organizations. These products have never been offered before to any group of consumers; and if successful, they spawn a completely new industry.

When the automobile was introduced, it was truly a new-to-the-world product.

Obvious examples are the introduction of the first car leading to today's automobile industry, the first airplane and the aircraft and airline industries, and the first microcomputer and the personal computer industry.

The other types of new products in Exhibit 10.1 describe products new to the marketing firm, but not new to some other firms or to consumers. From the firm's point of view, the product could be a new-category entry, an addition to an existing product line, an improvement to an existing product, or a new use of an existing product. For General Mills, the China Coast restaurant chain is a new-category entry. Although General Mills currently operates several restaurants, the Chinese restaurant category is new to the company. Chinese restaurants are of course not new-to-the-world.

A large percentage of new products introduced each year are in the less innovative categories, particularly in many consumer product areas. Of the 15,866 health, beauty, household, food, and pet products introduced in 1992, nearly 70 percent were different varieties, formulations, sizes, or packages of existing brands. Through the first third of 1993, only 5.7 percent of new products in these categories represented breakthroughs in technology, formulation, packaging, or even positioning.[5]

Some companies are involved in all of the new-product categories. Sony, for example, introduces around 1,000 new products each year, about 4 every business day. About 800 of these are improved versions of existing products. Typically, improvements consist of new features, better performance, or a lower price. The other 200 Sony products are aimed at creating new markets. They may not all be completely new-to-the-world, but they are very innovative. Recent examples include Data Discman, PalmTop, and Mini Disc.[6]

Moving down the list of product types from new-to-the-world products to repositionings, the product is less new to the firm. This means that its development and introduction is less risky too, because the firm is building on areas of experience. Lower risk also typically makes the new-product development process shorter and less rigorous. General Mills is taking a long time to evaluate the China Coast product because the Chinese restaurant category is new to the company. There are important differences between that category and the other restaurant categories in which the company has experience. General Mills would likely follow a shorter and less rigorous process if it were merely introducing a new line of menu items at an existing restaurant.

The China Coast example is a good reminder that in our discussion of the new-product development process, we use the general term *product* to refer to

Ceremony luncheon hosted by AT&T to celebrate the formation of WorldPartners Company. John Petrillo, president of AT&T Business Communications Services, thanks KDD and Singapore Telecom for their leadership and commitment to the alliance.

both goods and services as well as to consumer and business products. The stages in the new-product development process generally apply to all types of products. Examples throughout the chapter include goods, services, and consumer and business products.

Sources of new products

Firms can obtain new products in a number of ways, with the two extremes being through external sourcing or through internal development. **External sourcing** is any approach by which a firm receives either ownership of another organization's products or the right to market the products of another organization. In such a case, products are new to the buying firm but not to consumers.

A number of alternative arrangements describe external sourcing. In an acquisition, the buying firm purchases another firm to obtain ownership of all the latter's products. The buying firm owns these products and may either merge them into its existing operations or allow the acquired firm to continue current operations. Hallmark Cards used this approach to get into the production of family-oriented TV movies and miniseries. It purchased RHI Entertainment, the producer of the award-winning "Lonesome Dove" miniseries.[7]

Sometimes a firm purchases only specific brands from another firm. This approach is often used to enter international markets. For example, Colgate-Palmolive purchased all of S. C. Johnson's liquid hand-and-body soap brands in Europe and the South Pacific. Sales of these brands were about $75 million. The purchase was viewed as a quick means for Colgate-Palmolive to add new products for the European and South Pacific markets.[8]

Other arrangements can be classified as some type of **collaborative venture**. **Collaborative ventures** allow two or more firms to share in the rights to market specified products. Often-used collaborative arrangements include strategic partnerships, strategic alliances, joint ventures, and licensing agreements. Although the specifics may vary considerably, in every case there is some agreement that allows a firm to market products new to it. For example, AT&T formed a strategic partnership with Kokusai Denshin of Japan and Singapore Telecom to introduce Worldsource, a global corporate network service.[9]

Internal development means that a firm develops new products itself. The firm may work with other firms for some parts of the process; it might subcontract product design, engineering, or test marketing to other firms. Or it might work in partnership with another firm throughout the entire process, as PepsiCo did in developing Splash. Splash is a new fruit-flavored sparkling water developed through a partnership arrangement between PepsiCo and Ocean Spray Cranberries.[10] The key point is that in internal development the firm is directly involved in the development of a new product, even though it may not accomplish every step by itself.

Internal development is riskier than acquiring new products from external sources. A firm developing new products assumes all or most of the costs and risks involved. When acquiring through external sources, a firm purchases or receives the rights to sell products that have a history in the market. External sourcing requires a firm to identify products of other firms, make the necessary agreements to obtain the desired products, and market them. Many firms use both external sourcing and internal development for new products.

EXECUTIVE ROUNDTABLE COMMENT | **Jack Kennard, executive director of spirits marketing, Brown-Forman Beverages Worldwide, discusses the use of external and internal sources for new products:**

New products are a great way to achieve profitable growth and build share of market. Knowing the odds for new-product success are less than 30 percent, Brown-Forman uses both external and internal new-product development approaches. We learned two lessons from the internal initiatives at Brown-Forman: (1) to be successful, new products must offer the consumer a real point of difference versus competition; (2) multidisciplined new-product teams led by experienced managers increase chances for success. Externally, Brown-Forman has nurtured long-term alliances to market products in the US with the Irish (Bushmills), Scottish/English (Glenmorangie), French (Noilly Prat), Chileans (Carmen Wines), and Italians (Bolla Wines).

New-product development process

The new-product development process can be conceived as consisting of the seven stages presented in Exhibit 10.2.[11] The process is presented as a logical series of steps for discussion purposes. In reality, the lines between each step are often blurred as companies are involved in different stages at the same time; sometimes they eliminate specific stages. Also, the specific process for any one product will vary by company, industry, and type of new product.

Two issues related to the new-product development process deserve some discussion. First, as a firm moves from one step in the process to the next, costs increase substantially. From a *productivity perspective,* a major objective is to weed out potential failures as early as possible without eliminating products that might be successful. This is a difficult balancing act, but one that cannot be avoided. Rigorous analysis to evaluate products at each stage and to determine which warrant further attention can help firms be both productive and successful in developing new products. Because of this, each stage requires a "go" or "no-go" decision. And since approximately 46 percent of new-product development costs are wasted on products that ultimately fail, firms must make such decisions as early as possible.[12]

Exhibit 10.2	New-product development process

Idea generation → Idea screening → Concept development & testing → Business analysis → Prototype development → Test marketing → Commercialization

The second issue of note is that the traditional approach to new-product development has been a functional, linear process as shown in Exhibit 10.3. Typically each functional area works on specific stages of a process in isolation. When one step is concluded, the results go to the following functional area for the next step. For example, R&D might conceive a product idea and give it to the design function, which would design the product. Design passes it to engineering, which develops engineering specifications and gives it to manufacturing to produce. Manufacturing produces the product and gives it to marketing to sell. Although this type of approach has resulted in some successes, the process can be very slow and costly.

Many firms have improved the new-product development process by adopting a multifunctional, simultaneous approach as shown in Exhibit 10.3. This *relationship perspective* toward new-product development requires all relevant functions to work together during all stages, with several steps typically performed simultaneously. Some firms benefit from including suppliers, distributors, customers, and other interest groups. We discussed this approach in Chapter 2; Ford's development of the Taurus is an example.

Ford expanded this approach in developing a world car called Mondeo. The company is spending $6 billion to develop one car to be marketed in Europe and North America. The typical approach would be to develop separate cars for these two markets. Instead, Ford is working on one car using one team consisting of more than 800 engineers, designers, and marketing and finance people on both sides of the Atlantic. The new approach costs less and is taking less time than if two cars were to be developed separately. Ironically, Ford seems to be back where it started many years ago. "We're back to the Model T again," as one Ford official observes. "We used to have one design [worldwide], and we've taken this big, long trip," to get back to the same point.[13]

Boeing is another company implementing a teamwork approach. After losing billions of dollars in recent years, the airline industry wants planes that cost less and operate more efficiently. Boeing is developing new planes with these characteristics by grouping experts from design, manufacturing, maintenance, finance, and marketing into new-product development teams. The 737X, a passenger jet scheduled for delivery in 1997, is one result of this teamwork approach.[14]

Exhibit 10.3   **New-product development approaches**

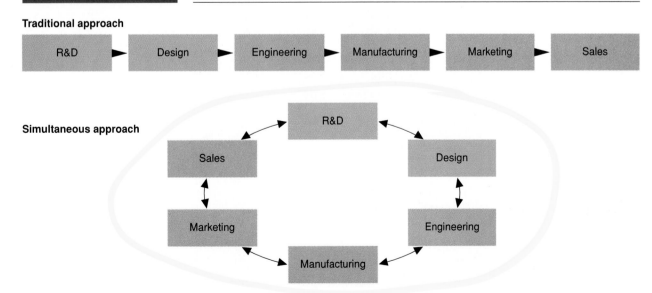

Driving on the information highway

*T*echnological advancements, such as the capacity to translate all audio and video communications into digital information and new methods for storing, compressing, and sending this information into homes, are producing an information highway that links video, telephones, and computers. Major telephone companies and cable operators are working together to make the information highway a reality.

Once established, the information highway is likely to give birth to a tremendous number of new products. The possibilities include interactive cable systems with 500 or more channels that deliver programs on demand. Viewers will be able to select what they want to watch from a computer menu on their TV screens. Also, specific ads targeted to individual homes may allow customers to take shopping trips over TV. For example, an individual could take a 15-minute trip around an auto showroom without leaving the couch. Or finally, videophones will transmit onto a TV screen the images of the people talking to each other.

Sources: Philip Elmer-Dewitt, "Take a Trip into the Future on the Electronic Superhighway," *Time,* April 12, 1993, pp. 50–58; and John Naisbitt, *Global Paradox* (New York: William Morrow and Company, Inc., 1994), pp. 53–102.

Idea generation

Idea generation is the initial stage of the new-product development process. A new product begins as someone's idea. Firms typically generate a large number of ideas relative to the number of successful products introduced. One study reported that 13 new-product ideas were needed for every successful new product.[15]

Ideas for new products can come from different methods and sources. Analyzing the products offered by competitors can generate ideas for new products or improvements in existing products. Typically, these ideas are ways to differentiate a firm's new product from competitive offerings. Ford used this approach in designing its new Mercury Mystique. The company evaluated the characteristics of the Honda Accord, Pontiac Grand Am, Mazda 626, Nissan Altima, and Mitsubishi Galant. As a result of this analysis, the Mystique is larger, roomier, and much easier to maintain than competing cars. Its engine needs a tune-up only every 100,000 miles.[16]

By watching customers use existing products, firms can generate ideas for new products. Employees at John Deere visit dealers and farmers to observe

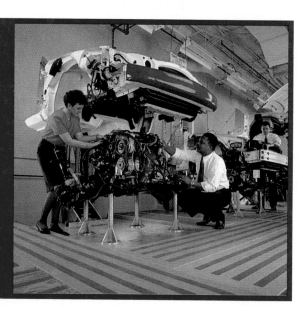

Ford's World Class Timing (WCT) process implements the *productivity* and *technological perspectives* in trimming product development time from design studio to showroom by 25 percent to bring its new high-quality cars and trucks to market more quickly.

America's greatest 18 holes

*T*hree golfing friends in Texas came up with the idea of developing a golf course called Tour 18 that consists of replicas of holes from the best courses in the United States. Their vision was first executed at a public country club in Houston featuring the holes:

Tour 18 holes	Original holes			Tour 18 holes	Original holes		
	Course	Hole	Location		Course	Hole	Location
1	Harbour Town	18	Hilton Head, SC	10	Desert Inn	10	Las Vegas, NV
2	Bay Hill	6	Tampa, FL	11	Disney	6	Orlando, FL
3	Pinehurst	3	Pinehurst, NC	12	Colonial	3	Ft. Worth, TX
4	Inverness	18	Toledo, OH	13	Pebble Beach	14	Carmel, CA
5	Augusta National	11	Augusta, GA	14	Oakmont	3	Oakmont, PA
6	Augusta National	12	Augusta, GA	15	Shinnecock Hills	8	Shinnecock, NY
7	Augusta National	13	Augusta, GA	16	Merion	11	Philadelphia, PA
8	La Costa	4	Carlsbad, CA	17	Oak Tree	8	Edmund, OK
9	TPC Sawgrass	17	Jacksonville, FL	18	Doral	18	Miami, FL

They took aerial photographs of each original hole and used computer graphics to get three-dimensional drawings of the contours of each. Green fees are $55 weekdays, $75 weekends. Golf architects and professionals who have played the original holes say the replicas are very good. Current plans are to expand the concept throughout the US and possibly move into Europe.

Sources: "Counterfeit Golf," *The Economist*, February 20, 1993, p. 94; and Peter Burrows, "Celebrity Fairways on the Cheap," *Business Week*, February 14, 1994, p. 8.

their products in use and to talk about potential problems. These visits often produce ideas for improved products for farmers or better ways to service John Deere dealers.[17]

In addition, technological developments can be a useful source of new-product ideas. A *technological perspective* can help firms think about ways that emerging technologies might be transformed into successful new products. Advances in technology are often responsible for the development of many new-product ideas; see **The Technological Edge: Driving on the Information Highway.**

Employees often suggest ideas for new products, and some firms reward them for doing so. Since salespeople have the most direct contact with customers, some companies motivate them through rewards for reporting new-product ideas to their managers.[18] Creative group methods, such as brainstorming, to stimulate thinking about new-product ideas are also useful. Rubbermaid introduces a new product almost every day. Most of the ideas for these products come from one of 20 teams made up of five to seven people from marketing, manufacturing, R&D, finance, and other departments. These teams take a product class, like mailboxes, garbage pails, or desk organizers, and identify ways for Rubbermaid to design new products that are better than those on the market. This *relationship perspective* toward idea generation is one reason 90 percent of Rubbermaid's new products meet company objectives.[19]

Because idea generation requires creativity and innovation, an *entrepreneurial perspective* can lead to the best ideas. The level of creativity and innovation needed depends on the type of new products being developed. As **The Entrepreneurial Spirit: America's Greatest 18 Holes** indicates, sometimes seemingly simple ideas can lead to new products that become the basis for a new business venture.

Exhibit 10.4

3M's idea-screening checklist

Factor	Scale						Rating
	0	1	2	3	4	5	
Customer need	Nice		Definite utility			Critical	5
Competition	Many		Limited			None	4
Technology	None in 3M		Within 3M			Within ISD*	4
Marketing	None in 3M		Tape Group			ISD	5
Manufacturing	None in 3M		Equipment modification			Existing equipment	4
Price versus competition	Competitive advantage		Neutral			Strong 3M	3
Performance versus competition	Strong competitive		Neutral			Strong 3M	5
* Industrial Specialties Division.						Total	30

Idea screening

Since the idea-generation stage is relatively inexpensive, the major objective is to create a large pool of ideas for potential new products. The purpose of **idea screening** is to evaluate the idea pool and reduce it to a smaller and more attractive set of potential new products. The ideas should be screened for consistency with company vision and strategic objectives, potential market acceptance, fit with firm's capabilities, and possible long-term contribution to profit. A major objective is to eliminate as early as possible ideas that have little chance of resulting in successful new products. Ideas that remain after screening move to the next stage in the new-product development process.

A popular idea-screening approach is to use a checklist. The basic procedure is to identify the factors that are important to a firm and to evaluate each new-product idea against each factor. Adding the individual factor scores for each idea produces an overall idea-screening score. The higher this score, the better the new-product idea. Sometimes firms have a cutoff score; they drop ideas scoring below the cutoff and retain those scoring above for further development. Or, companies might rank the idea-screening scores from highest to lowest and focus efforts on the ideas with the highest scores.

Exhibit 10.4 presents an example of a checklist used by 3M. 3M decided that customer need, competition, technology, marketing, manufacturing, price versus competition, and performance versus competition are important factors. The company rates ideas against each factor on a scale ranging from zero to five. The individual factor ratings are then summed to produce a total score. In the exhibit, the idea is evaluated very high on each factor, for a total score of 30. On the basis of this score, a go decision is likely. If the score had been very low, say 15, the new-product idea would not have been developed any further.

Concept development and testing

Concept development is the process of shaping and refining the idea into a more complete product concept. In the generation and screening stages, the product idea is typically very general, perhaps a soft drink with added nutrients for health-conscious consumers or a direct-mail service for marketing textbooks to students. The evaluation of product ideas to this point is generally done by people within the firm, with little if any assessment by potential customers.

Exhibit 10.5	Product concept test

NEW HEALTHFUL SOFT DRINK

This new drink is as refreshing & thirst-quenching as a normal soft drink, but much more healthful. It contains only natural ingredients. Three 12-ounce cans contain the normal vitamin & mineral daily requirements for an average adult. The drink will be available in several fruit flavors, will be clear in appearance & will be packaged in recyclable aluminum cans. The cost of a 12-ounce can will be 69 cents.

1. How likely are you to buy this product?
    Definitely would buy   _____
    Probably would buy   _____
    Might or might not buy   _____
    Probably would not buy   _____
    Definitely would not buy   _____

2. What do you like the most about this product?

3. How could this product be improved?

The major objective of concept development and testing is to formalize product concepts and have them evaluated by potential customers. Formalizing the product concept means describing the basic product idea in detail. This usually entails describing all of the product's components, including its projected price. If possible, a picture of the product is included with the concept description. A product concept for a new healthful soft drink is presented in Exhibit 10.5.

Concept tests are then used to get potential customers to evaluate the product concept. Sometimes multiple variations of the basic product concept are provided, so consumers can indicate which they like best. In other cases (see Exhibit 10.5), consumers are asked to respond to various questions about only one product concept. Besides assessing the concept provided to them, consumers are usually given an opportunity to suggest improvements. Concept tests are most often conducted as personal interviews, but they can be performed through mail surveys.

If the concept tests indicate a low level of consumer acceptance and low likelihood of purchase, the firm makes a no-go decision. If the tests indicate a high level of consumer acceptance and high probability of purchase, the firm makes a go decision. The results of the tests may also provide ideas for revising the concept to better meet the needs of consumers.

Business analysis

Ideas that survive concept development and testing are subjected to detailed business analysis. The **business analysis** stage of the new-development process calls for preparing initial marketing plans for the product. This requires developing a tentative marketing strategy and estimating expected sales, costs, and profitability for the product. A product idea reaching this point has passed general company screening criteria and been accepted by consumers. The purpose of the business analysis is to determine if it makes business sense to introduce the product.

The firm must assess whether it can market the new product profitably. This requires estimating costs, which is difficult but easier than forecasting sales.

Several types of sales estimates may be necessary. For infrequently purchased products, such as appliances, production equipment, or personal computers, the firm must estimate initial sales and long-term replacement sales. For frequently purchased products, like toothpaste, business supplies, or cookies, it must forecast both first-time sales and repeat sales over time.

The firm must attempt to predict sales over several purchasing cycles, because the ultimate success of a new product depends on consumers trying the product and then repurchasing it. Pillsbury's experience with Oven Lovin' Cookie Dough shows what can happen. Within months of introduction, the product was available in 90 percent of supermarkets and sales were growing. In less than two years, however, sales crumbled. After using the product, consumers did not think it was much different from the dough they were using previously, so they switched back to their old product.[20]

Because it is so difficult to estimate new-product sales and costs, the real value of the business analysis is in identifying products that are not likely to succeed commercially. Consumers might like the product, and it might meet the firm's general criteria, but the market might be too small or the marketing costs too high for the new product to have a reasonable chance of long-term profitability. If this is the case, the firm makes a no go decision. Although a no go decision at this point has some costs, it can save the firm the very high costs associated with the remainder of the new-product development process. A go decision means that the new product offers the potential profitability to warrant continued development.

Prototype development

Prototype development means converting the concept into an actual product. The objective is to use the information obtained from the concept tests to design an actual product that can be further tested. New-product costs begin to escalate at this stage, because developing a prototype normally requires a considerable investment. Product ideas that make it to this stage should have a high probability of succeeding. Firms are doing a better job of weeding out poor product ideas earlier in the development process, as evidenced by a decrease in the number of new products that make it to the prototype stage from about 50 percent to 20 percent.[21]

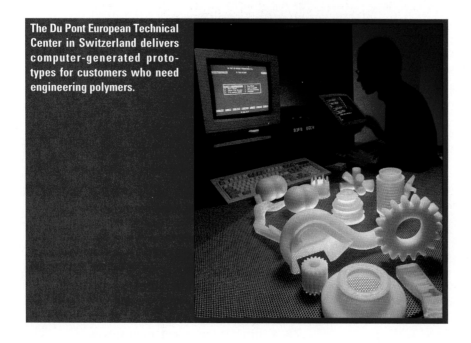

The Du Pont European Technical Center in Switzerland delivers computer-generated prototypes for customers who need engineering polymers.

Firms following a *quality/value perspective* focus on two areas during prototype development. The first is to design the product to satisfy the needs expressed by consumers in the concept tests. One approach is through **quality function deployment (QFD)**, a procedure that links specific consumer requirements with specific product characteristics. A simplified QFD matrix for a new copier product to be marketed to business users is presented in Exhibit 10.6. In this example, each product characteristic is designed to provide one or more benefits desired by customers. This approach directly links product features to customer requirements.

The second area is to build quality into the product. In the past, a product would be designed and then given to manufacturing to produce. Sometimes it would be difficult and costly to produce the product to the design specifications. Now, many firms include people from product design, engineering, and manufacturing in designing the prototype. Manufacturing considerations are incorporated directly into product design. This approach ensures not only that the prototype will satisfy customer needs on paper, but that it can be produced to the desired quality level.

Test marketing

Once a product prototype is developed, it can be tested. **Test marketing** involves testing the product prototype and marketing strategy in simulated or actual market situations. Test marketing can be both expensive and risky. Full-scale test marketing can cost over $1 million and last up to 18 months. Competitive reactions have taught even savvy marketers like Procter & Gamble to be cautious in their testing. Several years ago, P&G was testing a ready-to-spread frosting brand. Taking note of the test, General Mills rushed to introduce its own Betty Crocker brand, which now dominates the market.[22] The two primary methods for testing are simulated test marketing and standard test marketing.

Simulated test marketing refers to evaluating the new product in situations contrived to be similar to how consumers would purchase and use the product. A typical simulated test involves intercepting shoppers at a high-traffic location

---

Exhibit 10.6　　　**Product function deployment matrix**

Customer requirements	NEW COPIER PRODUCT Product characteristics					
	Multiple-size paper tray	Touch controls	Energy-efficient	Slip-in toner cartridges	Long-term warranty	High speed
Fast copies						X
Versatile	X					
Durable		X	X		X	
Low maintenance		X	X	X		
Easy to operate	X	X		X		X
Low operating cost			X			

X = Specific product characteristics designed to meet specific customer requirements

Campbell's uses simulated test marketing in its Hong Kong kitchen, while Nestlé uses its Cool-Out Caravan for standard test marketing in the US to obtain product evaluations from customers.

in a mall. Surveyors ask them about their use of various products and expose them to a concept or commercial for a new product. Respondents then participate in a shopping exercise during which they can purchase the new product. After the exercise, they are asked about their purchases. They are then contacted at a later date about their use of and intentions to repurchase the product.[23]

In **standard test marketing,** the firm tests the new product and its marketing strategy in actual market situations. The size and number of test markets depend on the need for reliable information, the costs associated with test marketing, and the potential reactions from competitors. Selected test markets should be representative of the characteristics of the target market for the new product. A typical approach is to execute the marketing strategy for the new product in the selected test markets and to carefully track results. Sometimes firms vary elements of the marketing mix in different test markets to identify the most effective marketing strategy. For example, General Foods test marketed the China Coast restaurant concept in Orlando, Indianapolis, and Fort Worth. Test-market results have led to several changes in the initial marketing strategy for the China Coast restaurants.

Test marketing represents the final exam for a new product. If the new product passes this exam, a go decision will lead to the commercialization stage. If the new product fails this exam, a no go decision will lead to dropping the new product or going back to the drawing board to make significant changes. Even though test marketing is expensive, it is typically much less costly than commercializing the product. So, a firm is much better off stopping an unsuccessful product at this stage than during the commercialization stage.

Commercialization

During the **commercialization** stage, the firm introduces the product on a full-scale basis. The level of investment and risk is generally the highest at this stage. Investments in production, distribution, and marketing support can be extremely high. However, the firm can reduce some of this risk by performing the other stages of the new-product development process appropriately. Successful commercialization requires understanding consumer adoption, timing decisions, and coordinating efforts.

Consumer adoption

The **adoption process** describes the steps consumers follow in deciding whether or not to use a new product. The stages in the adoption process are presented in Exhibit 10.7. Marketing strategies must be designed to move consumers through these stages to achieve the adoption of new products.

Sony illustrates an *entrepreneurial perspective* in the unique approach used to introduce its new MiniDisc.

Research suggests two important considerations about the adoption process. First, consumers differ in their rates of adoption. There is usually a small group of consumers who are the most willing to adopt new products. Typically called **innovators,** they normally represent the first 2.5 percent of the adopters. Identifying the innovators and targeting marketing efforts to this group are one key to successful commercialization of a new product.

Second, the characteristics of a new product affect its rate of adoption. The more complex the product, the slower the rate. The rate of adoption is facilitated, however, when the new product is compatible with existing products, has clear and readily observable advantages over those products, and can be tried on a limited basis. Marketing strategies should capitalize on the characteristics that facilitate adoption and minimize the characteristics that slow adoption.

The microcomputer software industry provides an example of how understanding the adoption process can improve marketing strategies. New software products are often complex. Software marketers also have difficulty convincing consumers the new product has major advantages over existing products. The typical approach has been for each firm to offer a demo product for consumers to try. This can be effective, but it is very costly. A more recent approach is to include new software products from many different firms on one CD-ROM.

Exhibit 10.7

Consumer adoption process

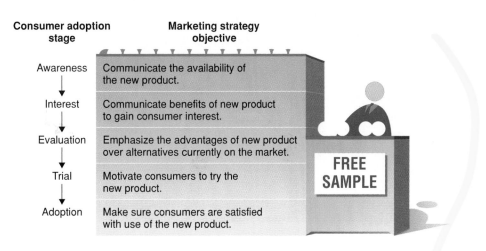

Consumer adoption stage	Marketing strategy objective
Awareness	Communicate the availability of the new product.
Interest	Communicate benefits of new product to gain consumer interest.
Evaluation	Emphasize the advantages of new product over alternatives currently on the market.
Trial	Motivate consumers to try the new product.
Adoption	Make sure consumers are satisfied with use of the new product.

Potential adopters can now easily try out and compare different software products. Marketers have the advantage of lower cost, since costs are spread among many firms. In addition, consumers with CD-ROM capability tend to be innovators for software products. Thus, CD-ROM technology offers software marketers a cost-effective way to facilitate the adoption process by making it easy for innovators to try new software products.

Timing

In most cases a firm can introduce a new product on its own timetable. A threat of competitive entry, however, can pressure a firm to launch the product quickly. The first entry in a market can often establish a long-term advantage. One study found that for technology-based companies, the profitability of new products is related more to getting to the market on time than to staying within the product development budget.[24]

Late entry can be advantageous if competitors have entered the market and developed interest and demand for the new product. Later entrants may be able to reduce the costs of market entry, avoid some of the mistakes made by the early entrants, or introduce better products. Compaq did this with its subnotebook computer. After many competitors were in the market, Compaq introduced a subnotebook similar to what was available but priced $1,000 below the competition. This entry appealed effectively to the home market.[25]

Coordination

As the new-product development stages have progressed, a marketing strategy for commercialization has evolved. A firm needs a coordinated *execution perspective* to implement this strategy effectively. Production, distribution, and all other marketing and company efforts must ensure that sufficient product is produced and available to satisfy the demand generated from the commercialization strategy.

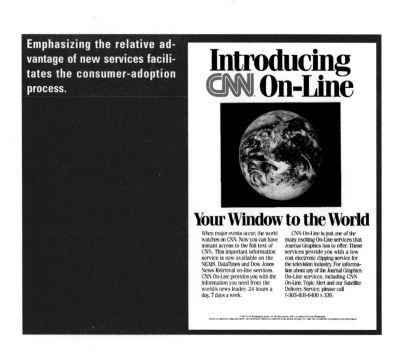

Emphasizing the relative advantage of new services facilitates the consumer-adoption process.

EXECUTIVE ROUNDTABLE COMMENT | Tony Donnan, general management/external affairs, Europe, at Avon, emphasizes the importance of coordinating all marketing efforts when introducing a new product:

We spend a great deal of time and money developing and evaluating new products before introducing them to the market. This is necessary to ensure that the new product will meet customer needs. However, none of this matters very much if we do not execute a coordinated and effective marketing strategy when the product is introduced. Nothing can hurt us more than having Avon representatives motivated to sell a new product and then have glitches in getting the product to customers.

Keys to new-product success

Studies of new-product introductions identify a number of reasons for failures and successes. A synthesis of these studies provides the keys for new-product success, as presented in Exhibit 10.8.[26]

Many of these keys to new-product success are consistent with the perspectives emphasized throughout this book. New-product development should be market-driven and customer-focused, aimed at developing superior products that offer consumers unique benefits and exceptional value. The predevelopment efforts, such as idea screening, concept development and testing, and business analysis, appear to be critical to new-product success. In fact, establishment of a disciplined and rigorous new-product development process, effectively executed at each step of the process, is an important determinant of success.

Organizational approaches

The use of cross-functional teams working simultaneously on different steps helps shorten the new-product development process and increases chances for success. Three organizational arrangements have been found to work well. A **balanced matrix organization** calls for a project manager to oversee the project and to share responsibility and authority with functional managers. Decision making and approval are a joint process.

Exhibit 10.8 **Keys to new-product success**

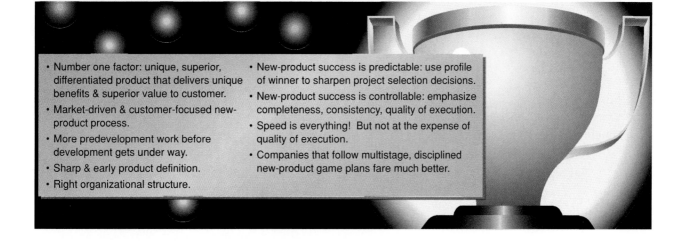

- Number one factor: unique, superior, differentiated product that delivers unique benefits & superior value to customer.
- Market-driven & customer-focused new-product process.
- More predevelopment work before development gets under way.
- Sharp & early product definition.
- Right organizational structure.

- New-product success is predictable: use profile of winner to sharpen project selection decisions.
- New-product success is controllable: emphasize completeness, consistency, quality of execution.
- Speed is everything! But not at the expense of quality of execution.
- Companies that follow multistage, disciplined new-product game plans fare much better.

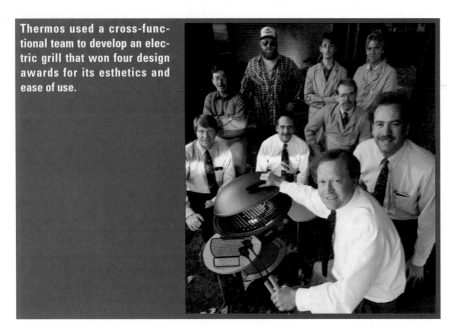

Thermos used a cross-functional team to develop an electric grill that won four design awards for its esthetics and ease of use.

A **project matrix organization** assigns a project manager to take primary responsibility and authority for the process. Functional managers then assign personnel as needed to perform various activities throughout the process.

In a **project team organization,** a project manager heads a core group of people selected from various functional areas. Managers from the different functional areas are not formally involved in the process.

Teamwork across functional areas is essential for new-product success. The emphasis throughout the process should be on producing products that offer the quality and value desired by consumers. In many cases, this means constant awareness of how new technologies may be used to solve customer problems. Although many of the keys to success seem obvious, the majority of new products still fail. The reason for many of these failures may be that firms did some of the obvious things wrong or failed to do them at all.

Marketing research support

Marketing research can make important contributions to the new-product development process. Concept tests and test marketing were discussed earlier in this chapter, and other marketing research approaches were covered in Chapter 7. Exhibit 10.9 highlights some of the types of marketing research that might be used throughout the new-product development process.

Prelaunch activities refer to marketing research studies prior to commercialization. These types of studies typically introduce consumer input into the decisions made at each stage of the new-product development process. *Rollout studies* are performed after the product has been introduced in the commercialization stage. These studies assess consumer response to the new product and its marketing strategy.

An example

Black & Decker (B&D) provides an example that illustrates many of the new-product success characteristics.[27] B&D was in the process of designing a pricey line of tools aimed at professional craftsmen and contractors. Marketing research indicated that there was a large group of nonprofessional do-it-yourselfers who, although price sensitive, wanted good-quality power tools. These findings were confirmed in conversations with retailers like Home Depot, Lowe's, and Hechinger.

B&D identified 50 consumers in this potential market. Marketing executives visited these consumers at their homes, watched how they used their tools,

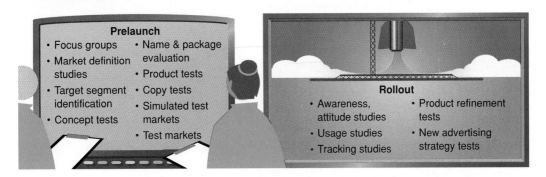

Exhibit 10.9 — Marketing research support for new products

asked them about problems, and even went on shopping trips with them. The company also interviewed hundreds of customers who had returned warranty cards. These marketing research approaches generated considerable information about the types and characteristics of power tools desired by consumers.

B&D then assembled Team Quantum to develop a line of power tools and introduce them to the market in August 1993. The team consisted of 85 employees from different functional areas and countries. The team members reviewed the marketing research and worked to design power tools with the characteristics desired by consumers. The prototypes were taken to retailers for evaluation. On the basis of the positive response from the retailers, B&D exhibited the tools at the National Hardware Show. Again, the response was very positive.

B&D began shipping the Quantum tools to retailers in August 1993 as scheduled. The new-product introduction was supported by a $10 million advertising campaign using the theme "serious tools for serious projects." Sales are expected to reach $30 to $40 million during the first year. Even though sales have been good, B&D spent three days telephoning 2,500 people to get their evaluation of the Quantum tools.

Summary

1. **Recognize the different types of new products.** Products differ in how new they are to customers or to the firm introducing them. From a firm's perspective, new products can be classified as new-to-the-world products, new-category entries, additions to product lines, product improvements, or repositionings.

2. **Discuss the different sources of new products.** New products can come from external sources or be developed internally. External sourcing includes acquisitions or various types of collaborative arrangements allowing a firm the right to market the products of another firm. Internal development is when a firm is directly involved in the development of new products. The firm might work with other firms on some new-product activities, but it is actively involved in the process.

3. **Understand the stages in the new-product development process.** The new-product development process consists of the interrelated stages of idea generation, idea screening, concept development, business analysis, prototype development, test marketing, and commercialization. As a firm moves through this process, costs rise substantially. A prime objective is

to eliminate potential product failures as early as possible and to spend time and resources on the ideas with the largest chances for success.

4. **Describe the way marketing research is used in the new-product development process.** Marketing research goes on throughout the new-product development process. Specific types of marketing research are valuable in the prelaunch stages. These studies help to assess market acceptance of the product and the likely success of particular marketing alternatives. Different marketing research approaches are used to monitor and evaluate results during the commercialization stage.

5. **Appreciate the keys to new-product success.** A synthesis of new-product research suggests the nine keys to new-product success presented in Exhibit 10.8. In general, the keys to success are market orientation, customer focus, effective execution of a rigorous new-product development process, adoption of a multifunctional new-product organizational approach, and development of products that deliver the benefits and value desired by consumers.

Key terms & concepts

Review & discussion questions

1. How does the new-product development process differ for different types of products?

2. What are the advantages and disadvantages of using external sources for new products?

3. Look at **The Technological Edge: Driving on the Information Highway.** Suggest five new-product ideas using the new technologies discussed.

4. Should all new products be test marketed? Why, or why not?

5. What should be included in a business analysis for a new product?

6. Reread **The Entrepreneurial Spirit: America's Greatest 18 Holes.** What type of new product is this? Why?

7. Describe the use of marketing research throughout the new-product development process.

8. What factors should be considered during the idea-screening stage of the new-product development process?

9. How is the development of new services likely to differ from the development of new goods?

10. How is the development of consumer products likely to differ from the development of business products?

Application exercises

1. Assume that students are complaining about how hard it is to get information about scheduled school events. Being entrepreneurially oriented, you would like to develop a product to solve this problem. Go through the idea-generation, idea-screening, and concept-development stages of the new-product development process. Bring one or more new-product concepts to class for testing.

2. Contact a local firm in your area that is active in new-product development. Interview people at the firm, and find out as much as possible about the company's new-product development process.

3. Identify a recent new product that you think has been very successful. Select a product that allows you to obtain information from both published sources and company officials. Evaluate how well the firm introducing this product followed the keys to new-product success presented in Exhibit 10.8.

Case 10.1 — *Polaroid: Captivating consumers with the Captiva*

Polaroid created the instant photography market in 1948 and still receives 90 percent of its revenues from instant cameras and film. Instant photography has suffered in recent years with the introduction and increasing popularity of video cameras, one-hour film developers, and easy-to-use 35mm cameras. Only about 10 percent of US households use instant cameras. These developments have caused Polaroid's instant film sales to drop from 205 million packs in 1978 to around 180 million packs today.

Polaroid has responded to these changes in several ways. The company has expanded into the 35mm camera arena, achieving a 4 percent US market share in 35 mm film sales. It has also introduced a disposable camera and is a leading marketer of videotapes. In addition, Polaroid is using its technological prowess to diversify into the high-resolution and electronic imaging markets. These moves are expected to produce 50 percent of the company's sales within the next decade.

Even though instant photography will be a less dominant part of Polaroid's future, the company spent hundreds of millions of dollars to introduce a completely new instant camera called the Captiva. The Captiva is intended to be Polaroid's last effort to design a completely new instant camera. The current strategy is to reduce R&D spending, focusing efforts on updating existing cameras and not designing new ones.

Polaroid used a long, rigorous, and expensive process to develop the Captiva. Researchers talked to over 15,000 people who currently didn't own a Polaroid camera. These respondents found existing Polaroid cameras to be "big and bulky"; they had difficulty catching the pictures "spit out" by the camera, especially when shooting multiple pictures.

The Captiva was designed to eliminate these problems. It is 40 percent smaller than other Polaroid cameras and looks like a 35mm camera when not in use. To take pictures, the user must open the camera. Once taken, the picture slides into a clear pocket on the camera's back where the user can watch it develop or continue to take more pictures. The camera comes with automatic focus, exposure, flash, and aperture control, and produces photographs that are 3-by-2 inches.

Polaroid is targeting the amateur photographer between the ages of 25 and 54. More than $30 million in introductory advertising will be spent to reach this target market. Captiva will be available at retail stores for $119 to $139. The camera will be sold in Europe as the Vision and in Japan as JoyCam.

Questions:

1. What role does the Captiva play in the corporate strategy of Polaroid?

2. How would you describe the new-product development process Polaroid used to design the Captiva?

3. How is the new-product process likely to be different in the future, when Polaroid will be only updating existing cameras and not developing new ones?

4. What type of marketing strategy would you suggest to Polaroid for introducing the Captiva?

Sources: Chris Swingle, "Polaroid's Photo Finish," *USA Today,* July 21, 1993, p. 5B; Chris Swingle, "Small Instant Camera Is a Big Gamble," *USA Today,* July 21, 1993, p. 5B; and "Compact Polaroid," *Fortune,* August 9, 1993, p. 95.

Case 10.2   *Send-a-Song: Musical messages*

Send-a-Song Corp. is a fast-growing business based on the relatively simple idea of sending digitized popular tunes over telephone lines as gifts for all occasions. Dan and Tim Price started the company in 1991. Projected sales of $875,000 in 1993 are expected to increase to $56 million in 1995. The path these entrepreneurs followed was up and down, typical of the process needed for success in the development and execution of new-product ideas.

Tim began working on the idea in early 1990; by the end of the year he had developed a prototype capable of sending songs from his personal computer to friends over the telephone. Friends could also send songs to their friends through his system.

The brothers then examined the sentiment-conveyance market to assess the potential of their idea. They found that 17 million greeting cards, 1.7 million bouquets, and millions of dollars of balloons are sent every day in the United States. The send-a-song idea seemed to have several convenience advantages over many of the available products. Also, no one offers a service to send songs by telephone, so the Prices could trademark the name, copyright the software, and patent the entire system.

After raising some initial capital, they asked a focus group of gift and greeting card store owners to evaluate the idea. The response was terrific. They then built prototype systems for retailers to test the system in their stores. The response was again very positive, but the need to expand beyond retail stores was identified. They decided to obtain a toll-free number for customers to place telephone orders. They tested this approach by getting some publicity in *USA Today* prior to Valentine's Day and evaluating the response. Although the day started slowly, eventually more than 3,000 calls came in.

On the basis of these results, the company raised more capital, increased spending on public relations and advertising, and made arrangements with a call service to handle the telephone calls. A membership club was also established to make it easier for customers to place orders. More than 10,000 members have joined; most use the system 3 to 6 times a year. There are, however, some heavy users who have placed more than 100 orders to send songs by telephone.

Send-a-Song is now evaluating different approaches to distribute the service and different pricing arrangements. The company is also developing and examining different promotional programs.

Questions:

1. How would you describe the process used to develop and introduce the send-a-song service?

2. How does this process differ from that typically used by an established firm?

3. How does this process differ from that typically used for a product instead of a service?

4. What suggestions do you have to improve the process used to establish Send-a-Song Corp.?

Source: Jay Finegan, "Sing to Me, Baby," *Inc.,* August 1993, pp. 90–99. Reprinted with permission, *Inc.* magazine, copyright 1993 by Goldhirsh Group, Inc., 38 Commercial Wharf, Boston, MA 02110.

chapter | *11*

Product and Service Strategies

After studying this chapter you should be able to:

1. Understand the different characteristics of a product mix.

2. Recognize the stages and characteristics of the product life cycle.

3. Identify appropriate marketing strategies for products in different life cycle stages.

4. Describe the limitations of the product life cycle concept.

5. Discuss different product mix and product line strategies.

Disney: Producing product magic

*E*veryone knows The Walt Disney Co. through its theme parks, resorts, or movies. Disney markets a number of different products and services in the entertainment industry. Many of these related products generate business for each other. For example, when people travel to Orlando to visit Walt Disney World, Epcot, and the Disney MGM Studios, they stay at Disney resort hotels, eat at Disney restaurants, and buy Disney products. The company is adept at developing and executing effective product and service strategies.

Disney's venture into videocassette sales illustrates this effectiveness. The company has many years' experience in producing successful movies. Examples are *Pinocchio, Beauty and the Beast, Aladdin,* and *Lion King.* Movies, however, cost a great deal to produce and market, but may generate sales and profits for only a short time.

With the introduction of videocassettes, Disney saw an opportunity to extend the life of its movie products. Its initial strategy was to develop videocassettes at a home video division and sell the tapes to video rental dealers. Typically, a rental tape is sold to retailers for $65. A hit rental movie will sell around 300,000 copies, for about $20 million in revenue. But the life cycle of a rental videocassette is also limited, and Disney receives no profits from the rentals.

Disney's latest strategy is to sell videocassettes to consumers through mass-merchandising retailers, such as Target, Wal-Mart, and Toys "Я" Us. The economics of this strategy are extremely favorable. For example, suggested retail price for the *Beauty and the Beast* videocassette is $24.99. Disney sells the product for $13.50 and has production and marketing costs of about $4. *Beauty and the Beast* sold about 20 million copies. Disney's profit—a whopping $200 million! The home video division generates about $1.1 billion in sales and $508 million in operating profit.

A number of factors are responsible for the success of this strategy. The Disney name is magic, especially to kids, who watch the videos as many as 30 times. Disney prices the videos low and focuses on sales through mass retailers, rather than video rental stores. Disney also uses cross promotions with such companies as McDonald's, Burger King, and Nabisco to reach its market at a low cost. It also uses rebates and other promotional tools.

Disney developed a sound product strategy and executed it superbly, capturing the largest market share in the videocassette sales market. This position appears to be secure, as the videocassette of *Aladdin* broke the previous sales record by selling more than 21 million copies.

Philip Morris markets more than 3,000 products around the world through different operating companies.

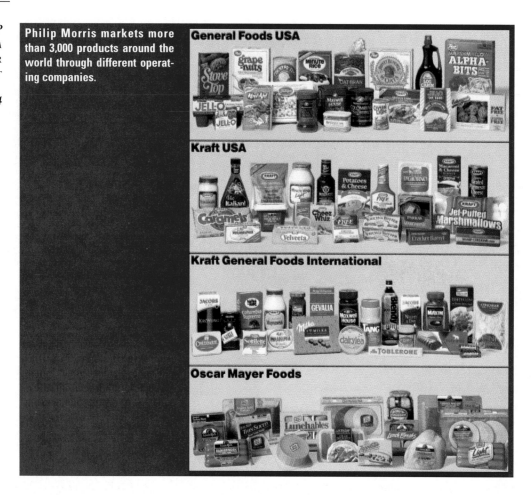

The Disney example illustrates effective product and service strategies for theme parks, movies, restaurants, hotels, and videocassettes. Strategies for the entire product mix, individual product lines, and specific products are developed and executed in an integrated manner.

Nowhere is this more impressive than in the movie and videocassette area. Disney movies are first shown at movie theaters. At the appropriate time they are then introduced to the video rental market, and finally offered for sale through mass-merchandising retailers. Disney uses specific marketing strategies at each step to maximize total sales and profits. This approach increases the return on an initial investment in the production of a movie.

Most firms market a mix of products and services. Even small, entrepreneurial firms based on a single product normally add new products to achieve growth objectives. One reason for this is that once a new product passes the commercialization stage and is introduced into the market, it typically goes through some type of life cycle. At the later stages of this life cycle, sales and profits decrease significantly. Thus, firms introduce new versions of existing products to extend this life cycle or new products in other areas to meet company growth objectives and take advantage of market opportunities. Smart companies, like Disney, employ effective product and service strategies to direct this growth.

In this chapter we introduce the product mix concept and discuss strategies for individual products, product lines, and the overall product mix. We emphasize the role of the product life cycle as a basis for strategy development.

J&J's changing product mix

Johnson & Johnson (J&J) was started more than 100 years ago as an entrepreneurial company marketing bandages. Since then J&J has added a host of products ranging from anesthetics and birth control drugs to baby powder and contact lenses. The firm has maintained its entrepreneurial orientation by organizing operations into 166 separate companies. Each company operates independently.

The growth of J&J is largely due to the company's entrepreneurial approach. It has been very successful in developing new products, with approximately 25 percent of sales generated from products introduced during the past five years. Some of the new products are new items for existing product lines. For example, Tylenol now comes in 20 different shapes and package sizes. Many of the new products represent completely new product lines, such as biotechnology, advanced surgical technology, and disposable contact lens products.

J&J also dropped products that have not performed well. Sometimes it has dropped an item—such as Medipren, an ibuprofen pain reliever—from a product line. Sometimes it has exited completely from product lines, such as kidney dialysis machines and magnetic resonance equipment. Willingness to abandon unsuccessful products and to continue to innovate with new products has been a key strength of J&J.

Sources: Joseph Weber, "A Big Company That Works," *Business Week,* May 4, 1992, pp. 124–32; and Elyse Tanouye, "Johnson & Johnson Stays Fit by Shuffling Its Mix of Businesses," *The Wall Street Journal,* December 22, 1992, pp. A1, A4.

Product mix

A **product mix** is the total assortment of products and services marketed by a firm. Every product mix consists of at least one product line, often more. A **product line** is a group of individual products that are closely related in some way. An **individual product** is any brand or variant of a brand in a product line. Thus, a product mix is a combination of product lines, which are combinations of individual products.

A product mix, relevant product lines, and individual products can be defined at different levels. In Chapter 4, we discussed organizational strategic planning at the corporate, business, and marketing levels. At the corporate level, the product mix would be defined as all products marketed by the entire corporate entity, with each business unit representing a product line. Each business unit, however, also has its own relevant product lines made up of related products.

This situation is illustrated in **The Entrepreneurial Spirit: J&J's Changing Product Mix.** At the corporate level, J&J consists of 166 product lines with multiple products within each line. Each of the 166 business units also has a product mix with individual products organized into product lines. For example, the Tylenol product line within the pain reliever business consists of 20 different shapes and package sizes of the Tylenol brand.

Any corporate or business-unit product mix can be defined in terms of width, length, and consistency. These characteristics are illustrated for the Charles Schwab Corporation in Exhibit 11.1. **Product mix width** refers to the number of product lines in the product mix. The more product lines, the wider the product mix. The Schwab product mix is relatively narrow, because it consists

Exhibit 11.1   **Product mix considerations**

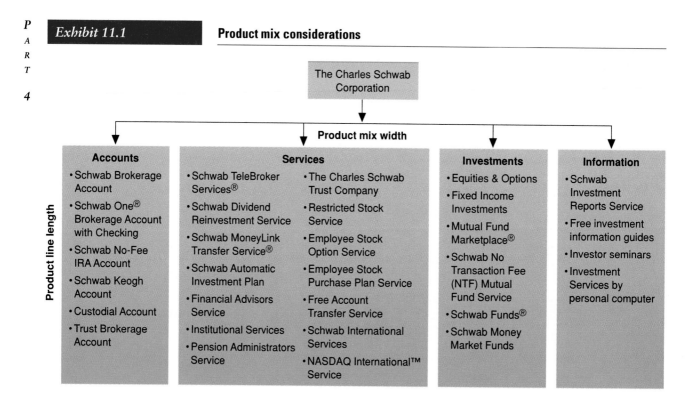

of only four product lines: accounts, services, investments, and information. Contrast this with the very broad product mix of J&J.

Product line length refers to the number of products in a product line. In the Schwab example, the services product line is the longest with 14 products. The information product line is the shortest with only four products. It is also sometimes useful to talk about the average product line length across a firm's product mix. For Schwab, the average product line length is 7.5, since there are 30 products organized into four product lines. J&J, in contrast, has longer product lines as evidenced by the 20 products in the Tylenol product line.

Product mix consistency refers to the relatedness of the different product lines in a product mix. Schwab has a very consistent product mix, because all of the product lines are closely related to investment products and services. J&J has product lines in very different areas such as contact lenses, biotechnology, pain relievers, and baby powder. However, the product mix is much more consistent within each of J&J's business units.

Firms marketing multiple products and services must devise strategies for individual products, specific product lines, and the overall product mix. Key strategies at each level are presented in Exhibit 11.2. Although we discuss each level separately, the strategies are interrelated. As indicated by the Disney example at the beginning of this chapter, effective firms integrate product and service strategies across these levels.

Individual product strategies

An important factor in the development of marketing strategies for individual products is the product life cycle. The **product life cycle (PLC)**, like the biological life cycle, describes the advancement of products through identifiable stages during their existence. The stages are introduction, growth, maturity, and decline,

Exhibit 11.2   **Product and service strategies**

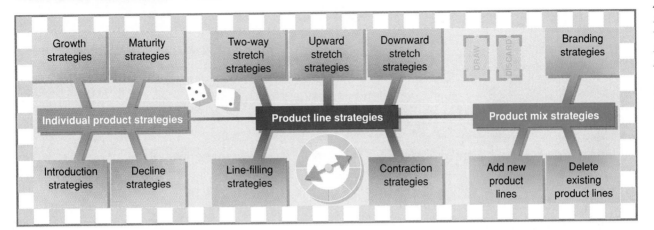

as shown in Exhibit 11.3. The product life cycle concept applies best to new product forms, but does not work as well to describe stages for general product classes or for the specific life of individual brands.[1] Thus, marketers at AT&T would find the product life cycle concept of most value for product forms, such as portable telephones, cellular telephones, or video telephones. The concept is less useful in analysis of the basic product class of telephones or of specific AT&T brands of telephones.

The product life cycle concept is based on four premises:

- Products have a limited life.
- Product sales pass through distinct stages, each with different marketing implications.
- Profits from a product vary at different stages in the life cycle.
- Products require different strategies at different life cycle stages.[2]

Before discussing relevant stages, characteristics, and marketing strategies, we should examine the diffusion process as a basis for the product life cycle concept.

Exhibit 11.3   **Stages in the product life cycle**

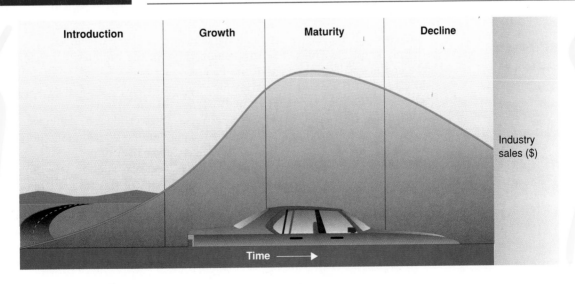

| Exhibit 11.4 | Diffusion process |

Innovators:
2.5%
Venturesome, higher educated, use multiple information sources

Early adoptors:
13.5%
Leaders in social setting, slightly above-average education

Early majority:
34%
Deliberate, many informal social contacts

Late majority:
34%
Skeptical, below-average social status

Laggards:
16%
Fear of debt, neighbors & friends are information sources

Diffusion process

When a new product form, such as the cellular telephone or compact disc, is first introduced to the market, consumers go through a process in determining whether or not to adopt it. We discussed this process and factors that facilitate adoption in Chapter 10. Research suggests that different groups of consumers adopt innovations at different rates. Some consumers adopt a new product when it is first introduced; others wait until the innovation has been on the market for some time. These different adoption rates mean that it typically takes time for an innovative new product form to diffuse throughout a market. The **diffusion process** describes the adoption of an innovation over time.

The general diffusion process is presented in Exhibit 11.4. The process is depicted as a bell-shaped curve with five different adoption groups. As discussed in Chapter 10, innovators are the first to adopt a new product; they represent about 2.5 percent of a market. The diffusion process then moves to the **early adopters** (13.5%), **early majority** (34%), **late majority** (34%), and finally the **laggards** (16%). The types of consumers in each group differ depending on the type of innovation. However, as shown in Exhibit 11.4, consumers within each category have several common characteristics.

The different categories of adopters in the diffusion process are one reason new products go through life cycles. As an innovative product diffuses through these adopter categories, competitors enter the market and marketing strategies change. The interaction of the diffusion process and firm competition means that marketers face a different situation at each stage of the product life cycle (see Exhibit 11.5).

PLC stages and characteristics

The **introduction stage** starts with the launch of a newly developed product into the marketplace. Thus, the introduction stage of the product life cycle extends the commercialization stage of the new-product development process discussed in Chapter 10. Sales growth in the introduction stage is often slow, because innovators typically represent a small portion of the market. Profits are low or nonexistent because of heavy expenses incurred in product development and intensive marketing to launch the product. There are no direct competitors for the first market entry, but competitors will likely enter over time.

Ideally, a new product would remain in the introduction stage for only a short time. However, some products never get out of this stage or remain in it for much longer than desired. A case in point is the introduction of personal digital assistants (PDA). Apple's Newton MessagePad was the first PDA, but other brands soon followed. Adoption was much slower than expected, because consumers did not perceive sufficient value from the initial product entries.

Exhibit 11.5	**PLC stages and characteristics**			
	Introduction	**Growth**	**Maturity**	**Decline**
Sales	Low	Rapid growth	Slow growth	Declining
Profits	Losses	Increasing	Decreasing	Low
Competition	Little	Increasing	Fierce	Changing

Industry sales ($)

Industry profits ($)

Time →

0

Apple responded by introducing a new model, the Newton MessagePad 110, with many new features. Competitors followed suit. If consumers find value in these new versions, then PDAs will move into the next stage of the product life cycle.[3]

The second phase in the product life cycle is the **growth stage**. During this time, sales and profits increase rapidly. Innovators, early adopters, and the early majority buy the product. Recognizing the potential for profits, additional competitors enter the market with different product versions. The number of competitors and rate at which they enter affect how long the growth stage will last. It will be shorter the faster competitors enter the market and the more aggressive their marketing strategies.

When the marketing efforts of all competitors begin to get adoptions from the late majority, the **maturity stage** begins. Profits peak, then begin to decline, reflecting intensified competition, especially on price. Competition becomes even more fierce during the latter part of the maturity stage when laggards adopt the product. The market gets saturated such that increased sales come more from taking business away from competitors than getting business from new adopter categories. Most companies market products in the maturity stage of the product life cycle.

When falling sales persist past the short run, a product enters the **decline stage**. Profits decline and competition is changing. A product can reach this stage for a variety of reasons. One, most consumers who could buy the product may have done so. Another reason may be a shift in consumers' tastes, which is common in the clothing industry. Sales can also decline because of technological advances. The rotary telephone, for example, has largely been replaced by touch-tone phones that make it easier and quicker to place a call. Compact discs and digital audiotape formats hastened the decline of long-playing (LP) records.

PLC length and shape

The length of a product life cycle depends on how well the product meets the needs of the marketplace. Products such as the basic household refrigerator have endured for a long time by offering consumers a good value. For less than $1,000, consumers can buy 20 years or more of convenient food storage.

In many industries, technology is advancing rapidly, which tends to shorten product life cycles. The life cycle for laptop computers was only a few years, as

Exhibit 11.6

PLC for styles, fashions, and fads

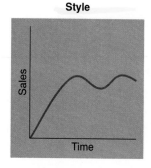

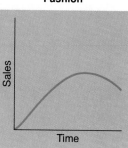

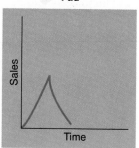

technology paved the way for introduction of equally powerful but smaller notebook computers. The product life cycles for styles, fashions, and fads are similarly shorter than for many other products.

Life cycle curves for styles, fashions, and fads differ from traditional product life cycle curves, as shown in Exhibit 11.6. A *style* is a unique form of expression defined by certain characteristics of the product. Decorating is a good example. There are different styles of furniture and home furnishings, such as early American, contemporary, and French provincial, and one style or another goes in and out of vogue over time. The Southwestern style, characterized by Native American and Mexican design and influence, is currently popular in home decorating. The product life cycle curve for a style fluctuates, reflecting periods of renewed and waning interest by consumers.

Fashion is a component of style. It reflects the more currently accepted or popular style. Fashions tend to follow the typical product life cycle curve. Here, a few consumers interested in differentiating themselves from the norm start a trend. Soon, more consumers follow the lead of these innovators in the desire to copy the latest fashion. The mass market adopts the popular fashion as the norm, and eventually the fashion goes into decline as the cycle starts all over with another new and different fashion. This is especially evident in the apparel industry.

Finally, *fads* are a subcategory of fashion. Fads have dramatic product life cycles. They capture attention and grow quickly, but last only a short time and attract a limited number of consumers. Fads do not last long because of their limited benefits. They merely satisfy the need to be different and interesting. Some examples of fads are Cabbage Patch dolls, high-power water pistols, and games such as Trivial Pursuit. The life cycle of a fad is thus a very steep curve over a short period.

Shortening lengths of product life cycles and their different shapes increase the complexity of marketing decisions. Firms respond to these trends by developing marketing strategies to take advantage of each life cycle stage. Some marketing strategies for each stage in a typical life cycle (Exhibit 11.5) are presented in Exhibit 11.7

Introduction strategies

The overall objective in the introduction stage is to increase awareness and stimulate trial of the new product. If there are no competitors, marketing efforts focus on generating **primary demand** or demand for the new product form. As competitive brands are introduced, the focus shifts to generating **secondary demand** or demand for the firm's specific brand. Thus, when Apple first introduced the Newton MessagePad, it emphasized the value of personal digital assistants. Any sales of PDAs would go to Apple, since it was the only brand available. When Sharp, Casio, and Tandy introduced PDA brands, Apple focused its marketing efforts on the Newton MessagePad.

Exhibit 11.7   **PLC marketing strategies**

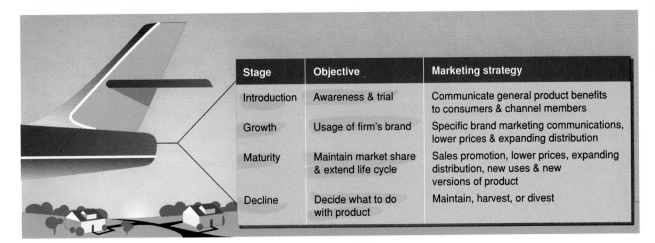

Stage	Objective	Marketing strategy
Introduction	Awareness & trial	Communicate general product benefits to consumers & channel members
Growth	Usage of firm's brand	Specific brand marketing communications, lower prices & expanding distribution
Maturity	Maintain market share & extend life cycle	Sales promotion, lower prices, expanding distribution, new uses & new versions of product
Decline	Decide what to do with product	Maintain, harvest, or divest

Two different pricing strategies are possible. Firms often set high introductory prices for new products to quickly recover the costs associated with development and introduction. Examples of this type of strategy are seen frequently in high-tech products. Most technologically advanced products start out at a high price that innovators are willing to pay. VCRs, home computers, and cellular phones, for example, were all introduced at a high price. Firms modified their pricing strategies as these products moved through the life cycle, making them much more affordable to the mass market.

Another strategy is to set a low introductory price. This approach is intended to generate faster market penetration. Because of the low price, it will take longer for a firm to recover new-product development costs. However, the low-price strategy can lead to a larger market share and long-term profits. Apple is following this strategy with the Newton MessagePad 110. The price of the 110 is $100 lower than the price of the original MessagePad. Apple thinks the lower price will speed up the diffusion process for its latest version.

Distribution in the introduction stage is typically limited. Marketing efforts must be targeted to channel members as well as final customers. Marketers use different communication tools to persuade resellers to stock the product and to get consumers to try it.

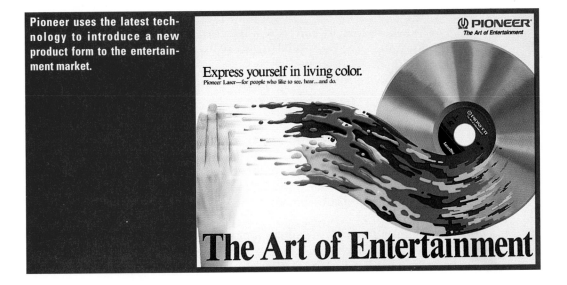

Pioneer uses the latest technology to introduce a new product form to the entertainment market.

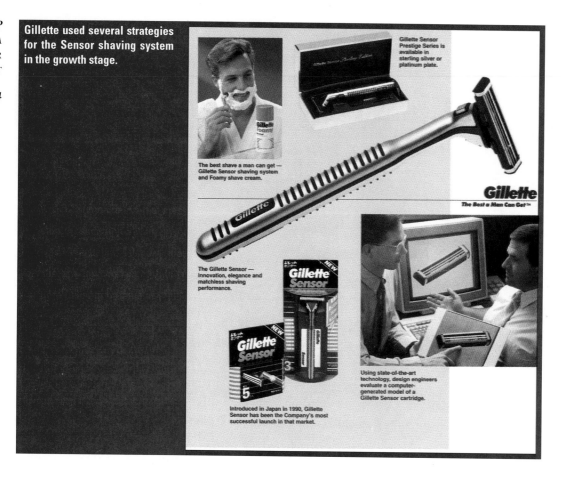

Gillette used several strategies for the Sensor shaving system in the growth stage.

The best shave a man can get — Gillette Sensor shaving system and Foamy shave cream.

Gillette Sensor Prestige Series is available in sterling silver or platinum plate.

The Gillette Sensor — innovation, elegance and matchless shaving performance.

Introduced in Japan in 1990, Gillette Sensor has been the Company's most successful launch in that market.

Using state-of-the-art technology, design engineers evaluate a computer-generated model of a Gillette Sensor cartridge.

Growth strategies

When a product enters the growth stage, the firm's basic objective is to build consumer preference for its brand. Because of the favorable characteristics of the growth stage, many competitors are likely to enter the market. These competitors usually challenge existing brands by offering improved versions of the product. Early fax machines, for example, were in the growth stage when they were challenged by plain-paper versions.

Increased competition often results in lowering of prices, especially toward the end of the growth stage. In addition, marketers usually expand distribution to make it easier for consumers to purchase the product. Communication efforts emphasize the competitive advantages of each firm's brand.

New Age beverages are currently in the growth stage, with sales expected to grow about 50 percent in 1994. Coca-Cola entered this market with its Fruitopia juice drinks. The company is spending $30 million on funky, kaleidoscopic ads to launch the brand. Referring to body, mind, and planet, the basic theme of the ads is "Welcome to Fruitopian life."[4]

Maturity strategies

The overall objectives at the maturity stage are to defend market share and extend the product life cycle. With the diffusion process nearing completion, opportunities to get new adopters are limited. Marketing efforts focus more on taking customers away from competitors than bringing new adopters into the market. But this is difficult and costly. Several strategies might be used during the maturity stage.

One popular strategy is to offer incentives to consumers for purchasing the firm's brand. These include lowering the brand's price relative to competitors or

Cheerios began as Cheerioats in 1941. Various strategies have successfully extended the Cheerios product life cycle for more than 50 years.

using sales promotions, such as coupons or rebates, to reduce the brand's price. Although incentives can produce more sales from existing customers and take sales from competitors, their cost reduces a firm's profit margins.

Another approach is to get consumers to use the product in different ways. This strategy can lead to more purchases from existing customers or might extend the product life cycle by bringing new consumers into the market. For example, Arm & Hammer successfully expanded the uses of its baking soda product. Originally used in cooking, baking soda now serves as a deodorizer for refrigerators, an element in carpet cleaning, an important ingredient in toothpaste, and an antiperspirant deodorant.

A final approach is to extend the life cycle by continually introducing new and improved versions of the product. Since these new versions are not new product forms, they do not start a new product life cycle. They do, however, help prevent the product from moving into the decline stage. Procter & Gamble uses this strategy often. For example, P&G has improved Tide detergent many times during its long history.

The sales, profit, and competitive characteristics of the maturity stage produce a difficult situation for marketers. Marketing strategies used in the introductory and growth stages are not normally successful in the maturity stage. Firms often try many different strategies to maintain market share and extend the product life cycle.

EXECUTIVE ROUNDTABLE COMMENT | Paul Casey, vice president, branch manager, Smith Barney Inc., discusses a *relationship perspective* toward marketing for a service in the maturity stage:

Merrill Lynch introduced its Cash Management Account as the first central asset account. We entered the market in the growth stage with our Financial Management Account (FMA). Now, everybody is in this mature market. Our strategy is to use the FMA as a central part of how brokers manage the total relationship with the client. We have added many services such as gain/loss analysis, year-end summary statements, and special coding of checks for tax purposes. Clients respond to these extra services by not only keeping their accounts with us, but by adding assets to these accounts.

Decline strategies

When a product reaches the decline stage, marketers must make tough decisions on what to do with their brand. Sales and profits are decreasing and competition is strong. However, the picture can change depending on what competitors do. If many competitors decide to leave the market, sales and profit opportunities increase. If most competitors stay in the market, opportunities are limited. Thus, the appropriate strategy depends a great deal on the actions of competitors.

Three basic strategic choices are available: maintaining, harvesting, or deleting the product. Maintaining refers to keeping a product going without reducing marketing support, hoping that competitors will eventually leave the market. Some people, for example, still prefer (or can only afford) black and white televisions. Similarly, rotary or dial telephones persist in some areas of the country for reasons of technology.

A harvesting strategy focuses on reducing the costs associated with a product in the decline stage as much as possible. Advertising, salesforce time, and research and development budgets are limited. The objective is to wring out as much profit as possible during the decline stage.

Finally, deleting refers to dropping a product altogether. A firm might withdraw the product from the market, ending its life cycle, or might be able to sell it to another firm. Deleting products is difficult for many firms. But it may be the best strategy from a *productivity perspective*. The resources expended on a product in the decline stage may produce only minimal returns. Productivity can normally be increased by allocating these resources to products that will produce higher returns.

Limitations of the PLC

The product life cycle is meant to be a tool to help analyze the characteristics of products and design marketing strategies. The concept, however, has limitations. Marketers should be aware of these before jumping to conclusions based solely on the product life cycle.

First, remember that the life cycle concept applies best to product forms rather than to classes of products or specific brands. If marketers look only at the brand and not the overall product form, they may not see the whole picture. Brand sales can fluctuate for reasons unrelated to the product life cycle.

Second, the life cycle concept may lead marketers to think that a product has a predetermined life, which may produce problems in interpreting sales and profits. A dip in sales, for example, may be taken to mean that a product is entering the decline stage. Managers could prematurely drop the product, when the dip represents only a temporary blip in the marketplace. Many products have survived for decades without decline because they were managed correctly. Ivory Soap (introduced in 1879) and Morton's Salt remain stalwart competitors. In other cases, declining products can experience a jump in sales with some new development in the environment, as was the case with cereals. When medical research seemed to show that oat consumption reduces cholesterol, sales of Quaker Oats Bran soared.

The final and most important limitation of the product life cycle is that it is merely a descriptive way of looking at the behavior of a product. There is no way the life cycle can predict the behavior of a product. That is, the product life cycle has limited relevance for forecasting future performance. Rather, marketing strategies help move a product along the life cycle. It is an interesting anomaly that the strategies marketers adopt are both a cause and result of the product's life cycle.

Product line strategies

Individual products that are related in some way form product lines. Firms must integrate strategies for individual products within the strategy for a product line. The basic strategic alternatives are to increase or decrease the length of a product line.

UPS filled its product line by introducing a service that takes more time than its overnight or second-day services, but less time than ground delivery.

Introducing 3 Day Select. Let's just say it's a more aggressive alternative to ground delivery.

At UPS, we've created a monster. And it's just the kind of thing that long-distance ground shippers have been waiting for.

With 3 Day Select, we guarantee delivery anywhere coast to coast in just three business days. While our state-of-the-art TotalTrack system monitors your shipment 24 hours a day, and confirms delivery in seconds.

In short, it's a service you can rely on to fine-tune manufacturing schedules. Streamline operations. Even improve customer service.

For your next shipment, try UPS 3 Day Select.™ After all, it's the road warrior of package delivery. **The package delivery company more companies count on.**™

Increasing the product line

Most firms have growth objectives, so they tend to adopt strategies that add products to a product line. Since few firms have product lines that cover all market segments, they focus on where to add products.

A **downward stretch strategy** is an attempt to add products to the lower end of the product line. The microcomputer industry offers an excellent example of this strategy. IBM, Compaq, and Apple traditionally operated at the upper end of the microcomputer market, with the clone marketers at the lower end. With sluggish sales and more value-sensitive consumers, the three companies introduced several low-priced microcomputers. This strategy has effectively revived sales for all three companies.

An **upward stretch strategy** is just the opposite: products are added at the higher end of a product line. This has been a favorite approach for Japanese companies in the US market. All the Japanese car marketers initially entered the US market at the low-priced end. As companies achieved success with these products, they gradually added higher-priced products. Now, most Japanese companies market products at all levels, even at the luxury end of the market with products such as Lexus and Infiniti.

A **two-way stretch strategy** entails adding products at both the high and low ends of the product line. Firms that have focused on the mass market might use this strategy to appeal to both price-conscious and luxury-seeking consumers. Marriott has used this strategy for its hotel product line, adding Marriott Marquis at the high end and Courtyard and Fairfield Inn at the low end. Marriott's product line now cuts across most segments of the lodging industry.

A **line-filling strategy** involves adding products in different places within a product line. A firm might use this strategy to fill gaps in its product line that are not at the high or low end. Candy marketers have used this approach with varying degrees of success. Hershey Chocolate successfully added Hershey's Hugs to its Hershey's Kisses product line. But it experienced disappointing results when Crunchy Peanut Butter Cups were added to the Reese's product line.[5]

A key concern in adding products to a product line is evaluating whether a new product will add new sales or take sales away from current products in the line. **Cannibalization** occurs when a new product takes sales away from existing products. If there is a great deal of cannibalization, sales shift from one product to the new product, with little overall gain for the firm. Strategies for

Product line strategies: Zenith was the first to offer StarSight Telecast's interactive on-screen program guide and one-button VCR record capability with its 1994 Advanced Video Imaging TV models *(left).* Mercedes-Benz introduced "24 Hour Service" for breakdown assistance around the clock throughout Europe *(right).*

adding products to a product line are typically most successful when cannibalization is low. For example, Kodak is investigating the possibility of adding private-label film to its product line. An important factor is determining how much the lower-priced film would increase the firm's total film sales versus taking sales from the company's higher-priced brands.[6]

Decreasing the product line

Firms must consider deleting products that are not successful or that have reached the decline stage of the life cycle, or because the costs of marketing long product lines are high. Such **product line contraction** is normally painful, but often necessary to improve performance. For example, because of intense price competition and decreasing consumer demand, ConAgra deleted breaded fish patties and breakfast sandwiches from its Healthy Choice product line.[7]

The more products a company sells in a product line, the higher its marketing expenses tend to be. Deleting products reduces expenses and can lead to improved profitability. For example, Borden reported disappointing financial results for several quarters. In examining strategies to turn performance around, the company realized it had 2,800 products in its snack-food product line, compared to 445 for industry leader Frito-Lay. The new strategy is to discard marginal products and eliminate product items so that the remaining products can be better supported.[8]

EXECUTIVE ROUNDTABLE COMMENT | **Dick Bohy, vice president/professional services, Sioux Valley Hospital, discusses the situation in the health care industry:**

Health care is dealing with the same market pressures as many other organizations. Sioux Valley Hospital's practice is to continually review our programs to measure their success and fit within our vision and strategic plan. We sometimes add programs, but often discontinue others. Recently, we closed a program serving people with eating disorders and consolidated several other programs. I suspect this type of contraction will continue at Sioux Valley Hospital and many other organizations.

Product line strategies are extremely important, and they are the result of complex and difficult decisions. The products in a product line represent a firm's offerings to its customers. As customer needs change or competitors introduce new products, a firm must be able to respond. One proper response might be to add products to a product line; another response, to delete some.

NEC emphasizes a *quality/value perspective* throughout its product mix.

Product mix strategies

The product mix consists of all product lines and individual products marketed by a firm. Strategies at all levels must be consistent for maximum effectiveness.

Strategic alternatives

The basic product mix strategic alternatives are to add new product lines or to delete existing ones. Many firms achieve growth objectives by expanding the product mix through the addition of new product lines. Successes are most likely when a new product line has some similarity to existing product lines. For example, Fidelity Investments is an established mutual funds marketer. When its business plateaued at 6.2 million accounts, Fidelity decided to expand its focus from mutual fund investment to serving all of a customer's financial needs. It added several new financial service product lines, from credit cards to insurance. Early indications are that the new strategy has been successful, as record revenues have been reported.[9]

Some similarities between product lines may not seem obvious at first glance. For example, Circuit City is considering adding used cars to its product mix. How are used cars similar to Circuit City's established consumer electronics and major appliance product lines? President and chief executive officer Richard L. Sharp comments: "We believe that automobile retailing offers opportunities to capitalize on Circuit City's strengths in customer service and big-ticket retailing."[10] As discussed in **The Technological Edge: AT&T at the Cutting Edge**, new and emerging technologies often provide opportunities for firms to add new product lines.

Although expanding into new product lines might seem to be an easy growth strategy, many firms find such success elusive. Adding new product lines can be risky. The more different a new product line is from existing lines, the more risk. This is especially true for firms that move into products outside their areas of expertise. The popular business press presents almost

P A R T 4

AT&T at the cutting edge

AT&T is best known for its telephone service. Today, however, it is positioning itself to be a major player in the global information and communication industries of the future. The convergence of communication, computer, and video technologies is leading toward the development of information highways, as discussed in Chapter 10. AT&T is involved in almost all aspects of the latest multimedia technology.

The company has added product lines in areas such as advanced microchips, computer software, electronic mail, and pocket communicators. Some of the new products have been developed internally through AT&T Bell Labs. AT&T has also used external sources, such as the acquisition of McCaw Cellular to add a cellular telephone product line. Strategic alliances with countries like China have helped the company move into international markets.

One element of AT&T's strategy is to promote the use of new communication devices, which would help build on its vast network of 80 million customers, accounting for $40 billion in telephone and data calls per year. AT&T expects the global multimedia industry to reach sales of $1.4 trillion by 1996. The company intends to be poised to compete throughout this industry.

Source: John J. Keller, "AT&T Is Trying Hard to Get a Major Role in Multimedia Future," *The Wall Street Journal*, April 22, 1993, pp. A1, A10. Reprinted by permission of *The Wall Street Journal*, © 1993 Dow Jones & Company, Inc. All rights reserved worldwide.

daily examples of firms that have downsized by dropping unrelated product lines. For example, Gerber's dropped trucking and furniture product lines to concentrate on its mainstay, baby-food.[11] Similarly, Coors is shedding diverse product lines, such as ceramic multilayer computer boards, dog food, and packages for soaps, to focus on beer.[12]

There are, however, many success stories of firms moving into new product and service areas. Texas Instruments, for example, has performed well with a product mix consisting of semiconductors, defense electronics, printers, notebook computers, productivity software, and consumer electronics products. And the company is capitalizing on recent technological advances to position itself to move into different areas of the emerging information highway.[13]

When Arthur Andersen added new service lines, clients had to be convinced the company was capable of providing these services.

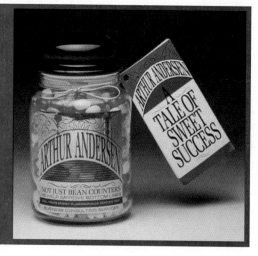

EXECUTIVE ROUNDTABLE COMMENT | **Mark Oshnock, partner at Arthur Andersen, indicates how the product mix at public accounting firms has changed in recent years:**

When I joined Arthur Andersen, our work consisted of financial audits, tax compliance, and tax strategy. Today our service lines have been expanded to include numerous new and nontraditional areas. One example is our Operations Consulting service line. With our Global Best Practices knowledge base, we help clients compare their processes to the best performers in the world and identify ways to improve their business. A concerted marketing effort was used to convince clients that Arthur Andersen could provide this type of service.

Branding strategies

Our discussion of branding in Chapter 9 focuses on branding decisions for a single product. As firms expand product mixes and extend product lines, brand decisions become more complicated. Companies marketing multiple products and services need a strategy to guide branding decisions. The basic options are presented in Exhibit 11.8.

One option is to use an **individual brand name strategy;** that is, the firm establishes specific brand names for each individual product in a product line. This approach allows a firm to choose what seems like an effective brand name for a particular product. The drawback is that because individual brand names are unrelated, products stand alone. Brand equity from one brand cannot benefit another. Procter & Gamble is probably the most famous user of individual brand names. P&G's objective is for all products to compete on their merits, so each product has its own brand name. For instance, P&G's detergent products have well-known individual brand names such as Tide, Cheer, Bold, Dash, and Oxydol.

The other basic option is to adopt a **family brand name strategy;** in this case, all brand names are associated with some type of family brand name. One approach is to brand all product items in the product mix with the company name, as Heinz and General Electric do. Another choice is to use different family brands for different product lines, with all items in a given product line bearing that same family brand name. Sears does this by using the Craftsman brand for tools, the Kenmore brand for appliances, and the Die Hard brand for batteries. A final alternative is to use both a family and an individual brand name for each product, for example, Kellogg's Rice Krispies and Kellogg's Raisin Bran.

Exhibit 11.8   **Branding strategies**

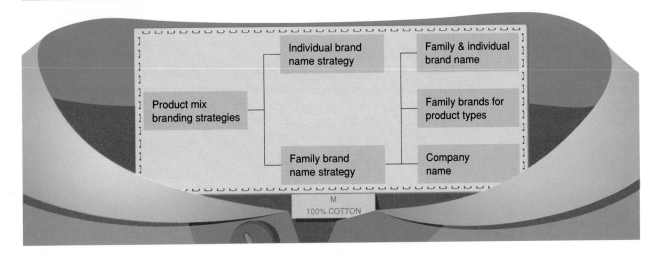

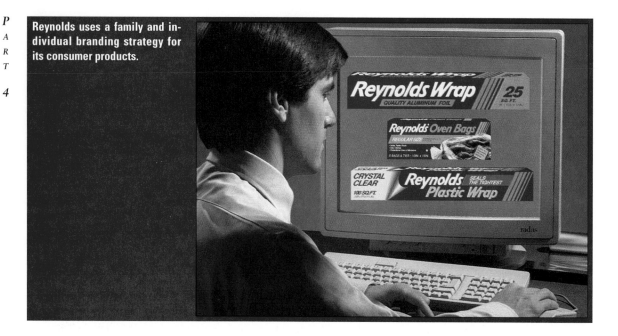

Reynolds uses a family and individual branding strategy for its consumer products.

Family brand name strategies can help firms increase product lines or add product lines. New products that build on the brand equity of an established brand are called *brand extensions*. Research indicates that the positive associations consumers have with a brand can be transferred to new products in the same category (increasing product lines) as well as to new products in different product lines (adding product lines). If successful, these extensions build additional brand equity.[14] Milky Way has used a family brand name strategy successfully in adding products to its candy bar line and establishing an ice cream product line.[15] There is some risk to using a family brand name strategy, however, because unsuccessful new products could weaken the brand equity of the established brand.

Ethical issues in product and service strategies

Marketers following an *ethical perspective* ensure that products are safe and not harmful, consumers receive relevant product information, there are meaningful differences among products in a product line, and if something goes wrong, there is a mechanism for redress.[16] It is important to continuously assess performance and safety issues from the new-product development process through production and marketing. Any identified problems should be corrected as soon as possible. Failure to do so can lead to dissatisfied customers, product recalls, and expensive lawsuits.[17]

Product recalls mean the marketer must allow customers to return the product to get the performance or safety defect corrected. This can be very expensive and harmful to a company's image. Companies can limit expenses and harmful effects by establishing a product recall procedure and recalling the product voluntarily. Without an established procedure, the process is likely to be inefficient and costly. If marketers do not proactively recall the product, they can be coerced to do so by various government agencies. For example, the National Highway Traffic Safety Commission forced Chrysler's three recalls of its new Neon car; and the Consumer Product Safety Commission recalled several brands of crayons containing hazardous lead levels.[18]

Potential harmful effects from products is a difficult issue. Should firms market products consumers want, but are harmful to them? Some observers argue that consumers should be allowed to decide through their purchasing practices; others think companies should not market products with harmful effects. The battle over the marketing of cigarettes is a current example of this issue. Another example is movie-theater popcorn. Most movie theaters prepare popcorn with coconut oil, which raises blood cholesterol more than any other fat or oil. Movie theaters could change to a more healthful way of preparing their popcorn, but consumers like the smell and taste of coconut oil–popped popcorn better. This issue will continue to receive attention, because it is being pushed by the Center for Science in the Public Interest.[19]

The issue of harmful effects goes beyond individual consumers to society at large. Products that are not harmful to consumers may create environmental problems for society as a whole, such as emissions from automobiles, non-biodegradable packaging, and polluting chemicals. Marketers emphasizing *ethical* and *ecological perspectives* act in a socially responsible manner by addressing the potential environmental problems associated with product use and disposal.

An increasingly important ethical and legal issue from a *global perspective* is product counterfeiting. *Product counterfeiting* occurs when a company copies another firm's trademark, copyright, or patent. Although this happens with US firms, product counterfeiting by foreign companies is a major problem. The US International Trade Commission estimates that counterfeit products by foreign companies cost US firms between $6 and $8 billion a year in sales.[20]

The problem is especially difficult in China. Chinese stores carry products that look like Colgate toothpaste, Del Monte canned food, or Kellogg's Corn Flakes. But the toothpaste is Cologate, the canned food made by a company called Jia Long, and the cereal is Kongalu Corn Strips. The damage from product counterfeiting in China is estimated to be $800 million a year. One company, Microsoft, says that Chinese software pirates cost it $30 million annually, and this amount is growing. The developing legal system in China makes it difficult to stop these infringements on property rights.[21]

To ensure they operate in an ethical manner, marketers need to conduct an ethical product analysis by answering the following questions appropriately:[22]

- Is the product safe when used as intended?
- Is the product safe when misused in a way that is foreseeable?
- Have any competitors' patents or copyrights been violated?
- Is the product compatible with the physical environment?
- Is the product environmentally compatible when disposed of?
- Do any organizational stakeholders object to the product?

US Customs agent in Miami drives a steamroller over 17,000 counterfeit designer watches smuggled in the country. Even as fakes, the watches were worth $620,000.

Conclusions

As this chapter clearly shows, product and service strategies are extremely important. These decisions must be integrated at different levels of the organization, and they provide direction for the other areas of the marketing mix. Pricing, distribution, and marketing communications decisions are all influenced by the product and service strategies of a firm.

Summary

1. *Understand the different characteristics of a product mix.* A product mix is the assortment of products marketed by a firm. It consists of individual products organized into product lines. The basic characteristics of a product mix are its width, length, and consistency. Product mix width refers to the number of different product lines in the mix; product line length to the number of different products in a product line; product mix consistency to how related the product lines are.

2. *Recognize the stages and characteristics of the product life cycle.* Products go through a life cycle similar

to a biological life cycle. The basic stages of the product life cycle are introduction, growth, maturity, and decline. Sales and profits change over the life cycle as competitors enter the industry and markets become saturated.

3. *Identify appropriate marketing strategies for products in different life cycle stages.* Marketing strategies differ for products as they move through different life cycle stages. In the introduction stage the firm emphasizes generating consumer awareness and stimulating trial of the product. During the growth stage it focuses on building consumer brand preference

to secure a strong market position. The maturity stage calls for a variety of strategies to maintain market share and extend the life cycle. During the decline stage the firm must consider options to maintain, harvest, or drop the product.

4. *Describe the limitations of the product life cycle concept.* The product life cycle concept applies mainly to product forms rather than product classes or specific brands. If, because of the concept, a marketer thinks a product has a predetermined life, it could adopt a marketing strategy that limits the product's life. The product life cycle concept is descriptive, not predictive.

5. *Discuss different product mix and product line strategies.* The basic product mix strategic alternatives are to add to or drop product lines from the mix. The similarity between product lines and use of a firm's strengths are key considerations in making these strategic decisions. Branding strategies are also important as firms add products to a product mix.

The basic product line strategies are to increase or decrease the length of a line. Downward stretch, upward stretch, two-way stretch, and line-filling strategies can be used to increase product line length. Product line contraction will decrease product line length.

Key terms & concepts

product mix   *257*
product line   *257*
individual product   *257*
product mix width   *257*
product line length   *258*
product mix consistency   *258*
product life cycle (PLC)   *258*
diffusion process   *260*
early adopters   *260*

early majority   *260*
late majority   *260*
laggards   *260*
introduction stage   *260*
growth stage   *261*
maturity stage   *261*
decline stage   *261*
primary demand   *262*
secondary demand   *262*

downward stretch strategy   *267*
upward stretch strategy   *267*
two-way stretch strategy   *267*
line-filling strategy   *267*
cannibalization   *267*
product line contraction   *268*
individual brand name
    strategy   *271*
family brand name strategy   *271*

Review & discussion questions

1. What are the major differences between the growth and maturity stages of the product life cycle?

2. What are the alternative marketing strategies firms might use for products in the maturity stage?

3. What are the major differences between style, fashion, and fad?

4. How do shortened product life cycles affect marketers?

5. Look at **The Entrepreneurial Spirit: J&J's Changing Product Mix.** Describe J&J's product mix and product line strategies.

6. How would you define the product mix for any firm?

7. Reread **The Technological Edge: AT&T at the Cutting Edge.** How do technological developments affect AT&T's product mix?

8. Why is product line contraction so difficult?

9. What is meant by the term *cannibalization*?

10. What are the risks associated with adding new product lines that differ greatly from a firm's existing product lines?

Application exercises

1. Go to a local supermarket, drug store, or discount store. Walk through the packaged-goods aisles, consider promotional and packaging information, and identify at least five examples of marketing strategies for mature products. Evaluate each marketing strategy example.

2. Obtain the annual report for any firm. Draw a chart that illustrates the product mix for this firm. Evaluate the firm's product mix.

3. Assume you have just invented a new-to-the-world product. Describe the product, and develop the marketing strategies you would use in the introduction and growth stages of the product life cycle.

P
A
R
T

4

Case 11.1   *Topps: Sports cards hit bottom*

The Topps Co. experienced rapid growth as the sports card market expanded from $50 million in 1980 to $1.4 billion in 1990. Card collectors were eager for new sports cards because the prices of some classic cards had soared. For instance, a Topps 1952 Mickey Mantle card sold at auction for $49,500. Typically, consumers bought cards when newly introduced and stashed them away until the price increased. Sports cards were viewed as a potentially attractive investment.

Topps and the other sports card manufacturers responded to this demand by flooding the market with dozens of new cards. But suddenly, consumers questioned whether these new cards would appreciate significantly in value. Many thought not and reduced their purchases, causing overall sales of sports cards to plummet to about $1.1 billion in 1993.

This devastated Topps, the market leader. The company experienced a 13 percent decline in sports card sales and a 65 percent reduction in profits for the 1992–1993 fiscal year. Investors soured on the company, causing Topps' stock price to decline by 35 percent. Several shareholders also sued Topps for understating the problems in the sports card market.

Topps responded in several ways. An aggressive television advertising campaign began in December 1993. The ads appealed to a young, hip audience with 30-second spots on network and cable broadcasts of basketball games. The corporation expanded its product mix from sports cards to broader entertainment. The new corporate strategy was to remain in the sports card business while introducing candy products and superhero comic books.

In the sports card business, Topps marketed cards tied to popular movies and TV shows that appealed to kids, an approach that had mixed initial success. The company dropped a line of cards tied to the *Last Action Hero* when the movie performed poorly. Better results were achieved with cards and other products tied to the movie *Jurassic Park*.

The new strategy is risky, because it has propelled Topps into some new business areas and changed the focus in the card business. Although sales have been flat, the company expects profits to increase during the next few years.

Questions:

1. At what stage in the product life cycle are sports cards? Explain.

2. What marketing strategies might Topps have used to prevent or slow the decline in the sports card market?

3. What is your assessment of the new strategy Topps has begun to execute?

4. What different strategies would you recommend?

Sources: Elizabeth Lesly, "A Burst Bubble at Topps," *Business Week,* August 23, 1993, p. 74; "Topps Second Quarter Net Fell 52%, Sending the Stock Price Down by 10%," *The Wall Street Journal,* September 16, 1993, p. B4; Kevin Goldman, "Rapid-Fire Topps TV Ads Ignore Nostalgia," *The Wall Street Journal,* December 10, 1993, p. B6; and "Find the Cardboard: Sports Trading Cards Pile on the High-Tech Gloss," *The Wall Street Journal,* March 31, 1994, p. A1.

Case 11.2   *Clearly Canadian: Clearly successful*

Clearly Canadian entered the North American beverage market in the late 1980s with a product intended to capitalize on increased interest in health and fitness. The company markets a line of beverages that are clear, contain no caffeine or artificial sweetener, incorporate only natural flavors, and are packaged in an attractive blue bottle. The beverages are positioned as a healthful and refreshing drink to upscale 18- to 34-year-olds. Marketing research, however, indicates that the beverages appeal to consumers of various age levels, social classes, and ethnic backgrounds.

Clearly Canadian beverages are made from spring water at company-owned locations. The basic natural flavors are Country Raspberry, Western Loganberry, Mountain Blackberry, Orchard Peach, Wild Cherry, Coastal Cranberry, and Summer Strawberry.

The beverages are marketed to retail stores through a network of independent bottlers. These distributors are an important element of Clearly Canadian's marketing strategy. They have helped the company obtain shelf space and promote the beverages in Canada, the US, Mexico, the Caribbean, England, and Ireland. In addition, the company is establishing distributor relationships to enter markets in Europe, Asia, Australia, Central America, and the Middle East.

The beverages were initially packaged in 23-ounce multiple-serving bottles and four-packs placed in display racks at retailers. An elegant 6-ounce bottle now is targeted at the business market, including airlines, cruise ships, health clubs, and fine restaurants.

Marketing communications efforts include regional ad campaigns on television, radio, and billboards to generate brand awareness and interest. Then, sampling and merchandising programs generate trial of the beverages. Attention-grabbing point-of-purchase displays are offered to retailers to help market the beverages.

The success of Clearly Canadian has not gone unnoticed, and the alternative beverage market is becoming much more competitive. For example, Seagram introduced 2 Calorie Quest to appeal to weight-conscious consumers. Clearly Canadian responded with Clearly 2, a 2-calorie version of its drink. Company executives are planning other moves to achieve desired growth in a complex, volatile, and competitive environment.

Questions:

1. At what stage in the product life cycle are alternative beverages? Explain.

2. Describe Clearly Canadian's basic marketing strategy.

3. What changes has Clearly Canadian made in this basic marketing strategy?

4. What strategic changes would you recommend Clearly Canadian make to continue growth in the future?

Sources: *Clearly Canadian Annual Report,* 1992; and Marcy Magiera, "Clearly Canadian in New Age Struggle," *Advertising Age,* January 31, 1994, p. 12.

PART

5

Pricing Concepts and Strategies

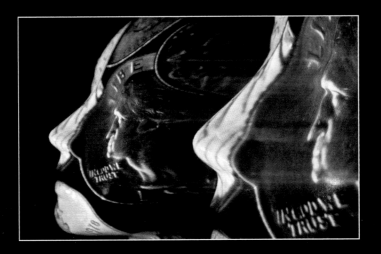

Pricing products and services is a complex process affected by many factors.

*P*ricing decisions are among the most important decisions marketing firms must make. Price is also a key influence on customers' reactions to products and services. How are prices established? How do a firm's pricing decisions affect the products it offers? And how are competitors and customers likely to react? What is the role of price in relation to the other elements of the marketing mix, such as advertising and distribution?

The next two chapters answer these and other questions. In Chapter 12, "Pricing Concepts," we discuss many issues associated with pricing products and services and with consumer evaluations of those prices. Chapter 13, "Price Determination and Pricing Strategies," describes the development of pricing strategies and practical issues involved in setting prices.

chapter 12

Pricing Concepts

After studying this chapter you should be able to:

1. Realize the importance of price and understand its role in the marketing mix.

2. Understand the characteristics of the different pricing objectives that companies can adopt.

3. Identify many of the influences on marketers' pricing decisions.

4. Explain how consumers form perceptions of quality and value.

5. Understand price/quality relationships and internal and external reference prices.

Snapple: Grapples with premium price and premium value

Snapple is one of the most successful "New Age" beverages. Company sales have risen by 1,300 percent in five years to over $180 million. Founded by Leonard Marsh and Hyman Golden, Snapple has demonstrated an entrepreneurial spirit and vision that others are now trying to emulate. Snapple offers 52 varieties of nonalcoholic and caffeine-free sodas, teas, juices, sports drinks, and seltzers. Competitors, including Coke and Pepsi, make favorable comparisons to Snapple, compliments that Snapple sincerely appreciates. Snapple already holds more than one-third of the bottled-tea market. The company's growth across the US has been unparalleled in the beverage industry.

This success comes largely from the sale of 16-ounce bottles priced at $1.25, which usually compete against 12-ounce cans of liquid refreshment that sell for around 75 cents. What are the reasons for Snapple's growth and popularity? First, cost minimization was not allowed to lower quality. Second, product taste is varied and excellent—people do not mind spending extra money if they receive good value. Third, distributors can charge a premium to retailers. Snapple insists on a premium price for its premium product. Hence, it can maintain relatively high prices with sizable profit margins, which help in obtaining distribution and retailer marketing support.

The situation may change for Snapple, however. In a joint venture, Pepsi-Lipton and Coca-Cola have begun marketing tea and sodas similar to those offered by Snapple. It remains to be seen how this new competition will affect Snapple's prices and other aspects of its marketing strategy. Snapple doubled its 1994 advertising expenditures to $65 million.

The best-selling iced tea from America's leading natural beverage company.

Sources: Elizabeth Lesly, "Does Snapple Have the Juice to Go National?" *Business Week,* January 18, 1993, pp. 52–53; Joshua Levine, "Watch Out Snapple," *Forbes,* May 10, 1993, pp. 142–46; Maria Mooshil, "Snapple Grapples with Rigors of Success: To Speed Production, Some Drink Flavors Are Put on Ice," *The Wall Street Journal,* August 20, 1993, p. A5; Greg W. Prince, "Snapple Comes of Age," *Beverage World,* February 1993, pp. 24–30; Gerry Khermouch, "Snapple's Ad Budget; Seeks Global Agencies," *Brandweek,* February 7, 1994, pp. 1, 6; and "Dino-mite Driven," *Advertising Age,* December 20, 1993, p. 12.

Many factors influence price, which in turn influences sales and profits. Snapple, for example, can charge premium prices because it offers a high-quality product that provides value to consumers in taste and health benefits. The premium prices enable distributors and marketers of the product to maintain sizable margins (the difference between price and cost of goods sold) and gain healthy profits. Perceptions of value at the consumer level allow higher prices, which can be used to maintain high quality in production and gain enthusiastic support by distributors and retailers.

Determining prices for companies like Snapple is an important task. Prices set too high will discourage sales; prices set too low may result in unprofitable business and a revenue stream that does not cover costs and expenses. Buyers in business-to-business markets, as well as individual consumers, often evaluate other factors, but price remains a primary choice determinant. And the interaction of prices with promotional activities often affects the firm's image.

In this chapter, we discuss the role of price and the major influences on pricing decisions. We explore the various pricing objectives governing marketers' decisions. Finally we discuss how advertised prices affect consumer perceptions of value and decision making.

The role of price

Price is the amount of money a buyer pays to a seller in exchange for products and services. It reflects the economic sacrifice a buyer must make to acquire something. This is the traditional economic concept of price, called the **objective price**. Where barter and exchanges pass for currency, prices may be nonmonetary. Much trade between developed and less developed countries involves barter. This practice, called *countertrade* by economists, holds particular promise as a means of helping Eastern European economies. Already, Mercedes-Benz trucks have been traded to Ecuador for bananas, while Russia has traded passenger aircraft to China for some consumer goods.

Prices frequently have other labels. The price of a university or college education is called *tuition*. The prices charged by professionals such as doctors and

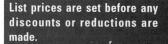

List prices are set before any discounts or reductions are made.

▼ **CAMSQUARES** are clear so you can tell what's inside at a glance. Shelf storage is maximized since these durable Cam-wear polycarbonate CamSquares take up 33% less space than round containers. List prices start at $4.65

lawyers are referred to as *fees*. Loans are paid for by *interest payments;* charges for meter violations and overdue books are paid as *fines;* apartment charges are called *rents*. Other terms used to describe prices include *premiums, taxes,* and *wages*. In nonprofit situations, *donations* and *time* represent prices to support charities and political candidates. In all cases, however, these terms reflect prices associated with the receipt of something of value.

List prices, set before any discounts or reductions, may differ from the actual market price or price paid. Price discounts, allowances, and rebates may make the market price different from the list price. Also a product's price may differ for particular uses or segments. In pharmaceuticals, for example, a drug might have a prescription price, a hospital price, and a Medicare price.[1]

Basic price mix versus price promotion mix

A recent view of the marketing mix (price, product, marketing communications, distribution) makes a distinction between the firm's basic price mix and the price promotion mix,[2] described in Exhibit 12.1. The **basic price mix** includes those components that define the size and means of payment exchanged for goods or services. Examples include the list price, usual terms of payment, and terms of credit. The **price promotion mix** includes supplemental components of price, which aim at encouraging purchase behavior by strengthening the basic price mix during relatively short periods of time. These include sale prices, end-of-season sales, coupons, temporary discounts, and favorable terms of payment and credit. For business-to-business marketers, a number of factors may reduce the invoice price to a final transaction price. The most common include prompt payment discounts, volume buying incentives, and cooperative advertising incentives.[3]

Examples of these mixes are common in the marketplace. Dry cleaners that reduce prices on certain days offer both standard and discounted prices. Automobile dealers vary dramatically in their price mixes. Many dealers offer temporary reductions and favorable credit terms to stimulate demand. Other auto dealers may offer fixed but low prices and terms to appeal to "negotiation haters."

The importance of price and pricing decisions

Price is the one aspect of the marketing mix that is most easily changed. Setting a price does not require the investment involved with advertising or developing products or establishing distribution channels. Price changes are certainly more easily implemented than distribution and product changes. Consequently, the fastest and most effective way for a company to realize its maximum profit is to get its pricing right.[4]

Price also affects customer demand. **Price elasticity,** or the responsiveness of demand to changes in price, is more than 10 times higher than advertising elasticity. That is, a certain percentage change in price can lead to 10 to 20 times stronger effects on sales than the same percentage change in advertising expenditures.[5]

Exhibit 12.1   **The basic price and price promotion mixes**

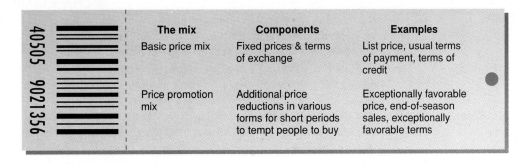

The mix	Components	Examples
Basic price mix	Fixed prices & terms of exchange	List price, usual terms of payment, terms of credit
Price promotion mix	Additional price reductions in various forms for short periods to tempt people to buy	Exceptionally favorable price, end-of-season sales, exceptionally favorable terms

Exhibit 12.2

Benefits of price promotions

- Stimulate retailer sales & store traffic.
- Enable manufacturers to adjust to variations in supply & demand without changing list prices.
- Enable regional businesses to compete against brands with large advertising budgets.
- Reduce retailer's risk in stocking new brands by encouraging consumer trial & clearing retail inventories of obsolete or unsold merchandise.
- Satisfy trade agreements between retailers & manufacturers.
- Stimulate demand for both promoted products & complementary (nonpromoted) products.
- Give consumers the satisfaction of being smart shoppers, taking advantage of price specials.

Price promotions or price reductions have become so common in some consumer product categories that sale prices represent the norm. Price reductions provide many benefits to consumers, manufacturers, wholesalers, and retailers. The primary benefits, illustrating the *productivity perspective,* are listed in Exhibit 12.2.

Both the importance and difficulty of pricing decisions have increased in recent years. These changes have arisen because of several environmental phenomena:[6]

- Introduction of look-alike products increases sensitivity to small price differences.
- Demand for services, which are labor-intensive, hard to price, and sensitive to inflation, has increased.
- Increased foreign competition has placed added pressure on firms' pricing decisions.
- Changes within the legal environment and economic uncertainty have made pricing decisions more complex.
- Shifts in the relative power within distribution channels from manufacturers to retailers, who are more price oriented, also has increased the importance of price decisions.
- A bottom-line emphasis places more pressure on performance. Price reductions boost short-term earnings more effectively than advertising.
- Technology that has reduced the time from new-product idea generation to production also shortens the average life span of products.

The general limits on prices are depicted graphically in Exhibit 12.3. Prices are limited on the high side by what the market will accept and competitive prices. On the low side, prices must cover costs plus some return on investment. Corporate objectives generally increase pressure toward higher prices to cover overhead and fixed costs and generate an adequate return or profit level. The exhibit depicts the limited latitude that managers may actually have in setting prices.

Global pricing considerations

Pricing in international markets is particularly difficult. Firms pursuing global opportunities find that prices for the same item can be extraordinarily different across countries, even within countries; prices seem to be driven by different dynamics in each situation. For example, in 1992 one brand of portable TVs was priced at 408 deutsche marks (DM) in the Netherlands, 434 DM in Germany, 560 DM in Italy, and 596 DM in Spain. Understanding price structures and managing prices internationally in these situations can be difficult.[7]

International pricing is also made difficult by exchange-rate differences and the need to present prices in foreign currency values. The **exchange rate** is the price of one country's currency in terms of another country's currency. Changes in exchange rates can affect the prices consumers in different countries have to pay for imported goods. For example, customers in Japan found prices for

Exhibit 12.3

Limits to price setting

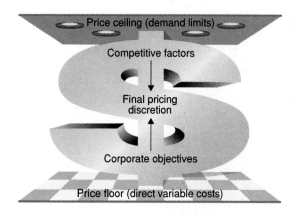

Brooks Brothers ties dropped recently from $84 to $69 due to the rising value of the Japanese yen; and Apple computers dropped over 25 percent.[8] Also, prices of goods are often driven up by taxes, tariffs, and transportation costs. *Protective tariffs* are taxes levied on imported products to raise the prices of those products in efforts to keep local prices competitive.

Pricing objectives

Pricing decisions are made to achieve certain objectives consistent with a firm's overall mission and marketing strategy. Five objectives commonly guide pricing decisions: ensuring market survival; enhancing sales growth; maximizing company profits; deterring competition from entering a company's niche or market position; and establishing or maintaining a particular product-quality image.[9]

Firms may pursue a combination of these objectives. The objective at Texas Instruments in pricing calculators is to achieve a cost advantage by virtue of growth in sales and dominant market share.[10] For Texas Instruments, large market share translates into competitive advantage through economies of scale from high-volume production and marketing operations. Kmart emphasizes low prices in efforts to generate sales growth and volume. Such objectives provide long-term direction to a company's pricing and promotion decisions.

Market survival

In some instances, a firm must set prices to ensure its short-term survival. That is, the firm adjusts prices so it can stay in business. Excess production capacity, for example, may require a firm to lower prices so it can keep plants open and maintain operations. In some instances, prices may be adjusted upward if increased revenues are required.

In 1992, the cruise industry's top two carriers, Carnival Cruise Line and Royal Caribbean Cruise Line, for example, broke all reservation records. To fill their rooms, however, they had to resort to deep price discounts. Increasing price consciousness and worries about the economy had led consumers to postpone trips, to trade down to less expensive accommodations, and to demand lower prices.[11]

Frequent end-of-season deals by retailers represent efforts to move inventory and thereby recoup cash for investment in continuing operations and for purchasing new merchandise. Similarly, manufacturers may reduce prices as new products are introduced in place of existing models. In some cases, even very successful companies like Procter & Gamble have lowered prices to lessen erosion in sales.[12] Pricing for survival is a short-term objective, however. At some point, profitability and return on investment must be satisfactory to ensure long-term success.

The Just Tires marketing concept provides Goodyear brand tires fast to price-conscious motorists.

Sales growth

Often companies set prices to stimulate sales growth, assuming that increased sales lower unit production costs, increase total revenues, and enhance profits at lower unit prices. **Penetration pricing** is often the strategy used to accomplish this objective. Firms following a *productivity perspective* set penetration prices low to encourage initial product trial and generate sales growth, often as part of market entry strategies. The assumption is that the market is sensitive to price differences and that low prices will drive up sales. In this case, short-term profits are sacrificed for future growth. Penetration pricing is also useful for deterring new competitors and reducing short-term costs through high-volume production runs. For international market entry, particularly for unknown companies or companies entering developing countries, a penetration approach is often useful. The initial success of Nissan, Toyota, and other foreign car manufacturers was due, in part, to the use of penetration pricing strategies.

Often firms set a high list price but then use a low introductory offer to generate initial sales. This approach is advantageous in that the high list price can signal product quality; otherwise, some buyers may question the quality if a low introductory price is used alone.[13]

Market share describes the firm's portion, or percentage, of the total market or total industry sales. Price setting to maximize market share is similar to price setting in pursuit of sales growth. Greater market share increases a firm's market power, which enables it to extract more favorable channel arrangements (price and distribution advantages with suppliers) and, in turn, to maintain higher margins.[14] For these firms, efforts to maintain market share are part of the *execution* and *productivity perspectives.*

Market share and firm profitability are often related. As in the case of Texas Instruments, greater market share leads to economies of scale. Economies of scale produce competitive advantages because of increased experience and efficiency; that is, companies learn to produce more efficiently with experience, and per unit costs decline as volume increases.

Even companies with high market shares can be affected by price competition. Gerber, for example, held 72 percent of the $1.1 billion baby-food market. When it raised prices by 5.5 percent, however, competitors Beech-Nut and Heinz began discounting their prices. Monthly sales for Gerber fell quickly by 16 percent.[15]

An increase in market share is a reasonable pricing objective, but not when competitors have lower unit costs. In such instances, it may be impossible to

Exhibit 12.4

Optimal pricing decisions

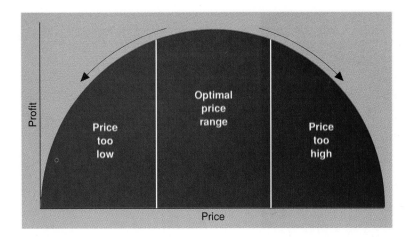

build market share by lowering prices. Similarly, it is foolish for a company to use pricing strategies to increase market share when customers are not price sensitive.[16] In this case, a firm may be better served by targeting particular market segments in which new products have a competitive advantage other than price.

Profitability

Maximization of profits is a frequently stated objective for many companies. Yet, this objective is difficult to implement. Profit maximization requires complete understanding of cost and demand relationships; and estimates of cost and demand for different price alternatives are difficult to obtain. As Exhibit 12.4 demonstrates, if prices are set too low, marketers' profits are insufficient; if set too high, no one will buy. Clearly, however, adequate profits are required, and companies are sensitive to changes in profits over time as indications of performance.

Increased prices can affect profitability three to four times more than increases in sales volume at constant prices. One consumer durable products company increased operating profits by nearly 30 percent with only a 2.5 percent increase in average prices. An industrial equipment manufacturer boosted operating profits by 35 percent by raising prices by only 3 percent.[17]

Price skimming is a strategy often associated with profit maximization. It includes setting prices high initially to appeal to consumers who are not price sensitive. In sequential skimming, the firm subsequently lowers prices to appeal to the next most lucrative segments.[18] This strategy allows companies to maximize profits across segments. Besides improving short-term profitability, price skimming lessens demand on production capacity, recoups R&D expenditures, and obtains profits before competitors enter the market. Moreover, consumers may associate product prestige and quality with the high introductory prices prevalent in a skimming approach. Du Pont and IBM are well known for using high introductory prices and skimming practices in marketing new products.[19]

Profitability is often related to **return on investment (ROI)**. ROI is the ratio of income before taxes to total operating assets associated with the product, such as plant and equipment and inventory. As for profitability objectives, the evaluation of the effects of alternative prices on ROI requires realistic estimates of cost and demand for a product or service at different prices. Firms attempting to obtain a desired ROI must take a longer-term, visionary view.

Competitive pricing

Prices may also be set in reaction to competition. As in penetration pricing, a firm may keep prices low to inhibit competition from entering. Or it may set prices close to those of lower-priced competitors to avoid losing sales. **Price competition** occurs most often when the competing brands are very similar, or when differences between brands are not apparent to prospective buyers.

Compaq emphasizes its warranty strength in this example of nonprice competition.

ITT Sheraton's simplified pricing system, modeled on the airlines' pricing approach, has been criticized by competitors as "rate cutting." The Sheraton pricing structure involves one room rate for business travelers, another for 14-day advance reservations, and a third for weekend rates. Sheraton also lowered its standard price. Not surprisingly, Hilton and Hyatt spokespeople warn that price competition will hurt the industry.[20]

Price competition may result in price wars, with prices spiraling downward in succeeding rounds of price cuts. They may lead to such low prices that all competitors operate at a loss in the short run. Price wars are frequent in the airline and computer software industries. Recent price wars over software in Europe may reduce the sizable margins US companies once obtained for their products, margins once justified by the costs of translation.

In **nonprice competition,** the firm attempts to develop buyer interest in benefits such as quality, specific product features, or service. For this to work, customers must view the distinguishing attributes as desirable.

EXECUTIVE ROUNDTABLE COMMENT | **Rich Kitaeff, district manager in the Marketing Research and Quality Measurements Group of AT&T, recognizes the importance of nonprice competition:**

AT&T continually stresses reliability and quality of service in our efforts to maintain a unique market position. This positioning is consistent with AT&T's technological strengths and eliminates the need to focus solely upon price. For example, our continual improvements in technology enable us to charge premium prices for some of our services.

Finally, focusing on unserved target markets in which competition is minimal may allow a firm to charge higher prices. **The Technological Edge: Charles Schwab and Discount Brokerage Marketing** presents an example. Schwab uses its technological communication advantages to offer low competitive prices for financial services.

Quality and image enhancement

Firms often keep prices at a premium to maintain an image of product-quality leadership. **Prestige pricing** is based on the premise that some buyers associate price with quality and avoid products or services for which they perceive prices as too low. The American Express Gold Card and Lexus are examples of

Charles Schwab and discount brokerage marketing

Charles Schwab, with 45 percent of the industry's business and 1992 sales of $909 million, is the leader in using computer technology to gain competitive advantage in the discount brokerage business.

To hold prices down while still offering excellent service, Schwab counts heavily on computer and telecommunications technology to provide service. This enables the firm to offer 24-hour service to its customers. Owners of personal computers can trade electronically via modem. Over 20 percent of Schwab's business comes through Telebroker, a service that lets investors get prices and enter trades by touch-tone telephone.

These technological capabilities do not replace other marketing efforts. Schwab advertises constantly through print and broadcast media. Over 160 branches are available in large and small cities. In each location, customer service is paramount. At the San Francisco and Miami offices, the service personnel speak several languages. Technology, emphasis on superior customer service, and advertising have helped Schwab create a strong market presence in the price-oriented brokerage industry.

Sources: Jason Zweig, "A Touch of Class," *Forbes,* February 3, 1992, pp. 82–84. Reprinted by permission of *Forbes* magazine. © Forbes Inc., 1992. David Baum, "It's All How You Slice and Dice It," *Computerworld,* February 14, 1994, pp. 101–3; and John Kimelman, "Schwab: Bear Food," *Financial World,* March 29, 1994, pp. 18, 20.

products that have images of exclusivity generated through premium prices. Professionals such as lawyers, doctors, and consultants often charge high fees for similar reasons. In these instances, low prices might imply lower-quality service or expertise. The reputations of these service providers allow the higher prices to be charged. The prestige associated with high-price–high-quality products and services is particularly important in gift-giving situations.

When the costs of malfunction are high, business buyers often purchase the highest-quality product available, regardless of price. They believe the risk of nonperformance, say, shutting down an entire production line or process, outweighs the risk of paying too much. Likewise, critical component parts that form the core of manufactured goods, such as electronic circuit boards, are likely to carry high prices.

Influences on pricing decisions: The five Cs of pricing

To ensure that pricing decisions are effective and consistent with its objectives, the firm should consider the **five Cs of pricing** shown in Exhibit 12.5: costs, customers, channels of distribution, competition, and compatibility.[21] These five elements represent the critical influences on pricing decisions.

Costs

Costs associated with producing, distributing, and promoting a product or service are instrumental in establishing the minimum price or floor for pricing decisions. Prices must cover, at least over the long term, the investment and support behind the product, as well as provide enough income and profit to the company. In some instances, costs must be reduced to maintain price competitiveness. This phenomenon is evident in the airline industry. Low-cost providers

P
A
R
T

5

Exhibit 12.5

Influences on pricing decisions

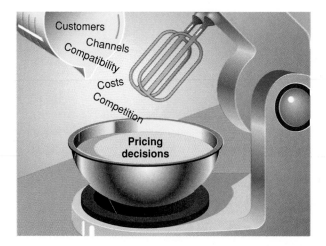

such as Southwest Airlines have forced full-service airlines, such as American, United, and Delta, to slash costs in efforts to maintain competitive prices. Thus, Southwest Airlines exemplifies the *execution* and *entrepreneurial perspectives.* These cost reductions have been forced by consumers who are willing to accept fewer extras in service for lower fares.[22]

Exhibit 12.6 details the various costs that must be covered by a $15 price for a CD. The largest of these costs are marketing related: retailer overhead, including operating expenses and profit margin, is 38 percent of the total price; record company overhead, including promotion, advertising, and profit, is 22 percent; and distribution is 13 percent. For this product, nonproduction costs far exceed the other sources of costs that must be covered by price.

Timex also bases its pricing and production decisions on cost considerations. Timex used to make most of its parts itself. Today, the company outsources its components (buys the parts from other manufacturers) so it can make production changes quickly. It is able to use its position as a dominant buyer of watch components to keep costs competitive and get faster payback on watches with shorter life cycles.[23] In industrial markets, Du Pont estimates its unit manufacturing costs early in the product development process to make sure costs allow enough profits to proceed with new-product ideas.

EXECUTIVE ROUNDTABLE COMMENT | **Rich Kitaeff, district manager in the Marketing Research and Quality Measurements Group of AT&T, comments on the relationship between costs and productivity:**

Imaginative and innovative applications of new technologies hold the promise of lowering costs, while simultaneously increasing the productivity of educational, health care, and social services at reasonable prices. At AT&T, we are continually searching for ways to reduce costs so that prices can be maintained or even reduced.

Customers

Customer expectations and willingness to pay are important influences on pricing decisions. Buyer reactions are primary determinants of demand. In some instances, customers may be willing to trade off increased prices for more benefits or enhanced product features.

The customer interest in value has not gone unnoticed. Many firms now emphasize value by offering lower prices and higher quality. Penney's returned to its original position as a moderately priced merchant. General Motors has seen substantial customer approval of its value-pricing approach that reduces the prices of its cars, including those models with attractive options.[24]

The health industry has also responded to price-conscious consumers. Today, prescription drug manufacturers like Miles Laboratories compete on

| Exhibit 12.6 | **Product prices as the mix of costs and profit** |

Retailers pay record companies $7 to $11 & more for the CDs they sell for $11 to $17. Who gets that money depends on contracts & market forces: big-name artists may get 20% or more royalties; when a CD goes gold (500,00 copies) or platinum (1 million), marketing costs drop & the record company's profits rise. Here's how the take on a typical $15 CD — one that's gone gold — is split:

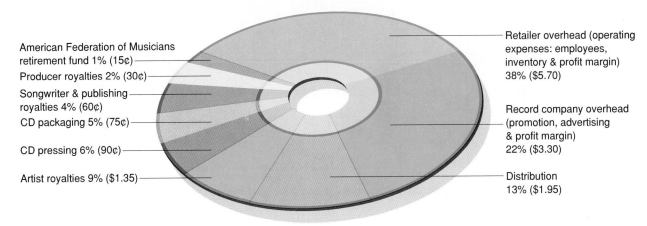

American Federation of Musicians
retirement fund 1% (15¢)

Producer royalties 2% (30¢)

Songwriter & publishing
royalties 4% (60¢)

CD packaging 5% (75¢)

CD pressing 6% (90¢)

Artist royalties 9% ($1.35)

Retailer overhead (operating
expenses: employees,
inventory & profit margin)
38% ($5.70)

Record company overhead
(promotion, advertising
& profit margin)
22% ($3.30)

Distribution
13% ($1.95)

price. Normally, new drugs are marketed on their medical advantages, and traditionally drug companies have used studies showing slight medical advantages as the basis for maintaining high prices.

Service companies occasionally use **value-in-use pricing** to factor customer input directly into pricing decisions. They base prices on customer estimates of the costs if the service could not be obtained. Such firms are responding to consumer perceptions of value. Computer repair services, for example, might be based on some percentage of the savings to the company from limiting computer downtime. This approach, while requiring some market research, satisfies customer needs and requirements for service at the price the customer defines as reasonable value.[25]

Channels of distribution

Prices must be set so that other members of the channel of distribution earn adequate returns on sales of the firm's products. Marketers must consider the margins that others in the channel can make. If channel intermediaries cannot

This Ralph Lauren men's fragrance is consistent with the need for distribution exclusivity for some high-priced products. The ad names Macy's as an outlet where the fragrances can be purchased.

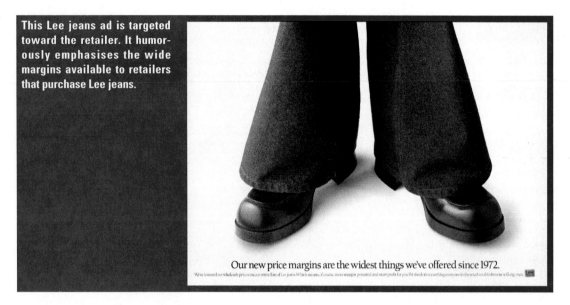

This Lee jeans ad is targeted toward the retailer. It humorously emphasises the wide margins available to retailers that purchase Lee jeans.

Our new price margins are the widest things we've offered since 1972.

realize a sufficient margin, they will not market the products adequately. Moreover, the product's image must be consistent with the channels of distribution. For a product that attracts buyers with a low price, the goal would be low-cost distribution. For a product that attracts buyers with its superior attributes despite a high price, distribution must complement those attributes.[26] For example, certain cosmetics are marketed only through exclusive-image departments. And some exclusive sportswear lines, such as Ellesse and Head, are marketed largely through restricted distribution networks.

Marketers give special sales promotion allowances and support to channel members to encourage purchase. These trade sales promotions now represent the largest of all marketing communications expenditures. Channel arrangements also involve restrictions on resale price, although manufacturers cannot require independent wholesalers and retailers to charge certain prices. Price guarantees stating that prices are the lowest available are also often given to retailers and wholesalers to encourage their patronage.

Competition

Prices charged by competing firms and the reaction of competitors to price changes also influence pricing decisions. Haggar cotton pants and Levi's Dockers are but one example of products that actively compete on price. As a rule, pricing decisions should not be made simply to make the next sale or to meet some short-term pricing objective. Companies that price successfully in competitive markets know that the goal is not just winning sales; they want to maintain those sales in the future. Firms taking a *visionary perspective* anticipate how pricing decisions will affect their long-term competitive position.

When competing products and services are very similar, the prevailing prices are a natural limit on the ability of the firm to adjust prices. Prices set significantly higher than the competition will attract only limited demand and cause buyers to switch brands, while low prices may result in heavy price competition or futile price wars. Burger King and Wendy's reacted to Checker Drive-In Restaurants by aggressive pricing of their "value" meals and products. Competitive prices also are a factor in the way consumers rate the fairness of a firm's prices.

Compatibility

Finally, the price of a product must be compatible with the overall objectives of the firm. Again, a firm's long-term image considerations will influence the prices it establishes. High brand equity enables the firm to launch brand extensions, to

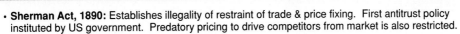

| Exhibit 12.7 | Significant US legislation influencing price decisions |

- **Sherman Act, 1890:** Establishes illegality of restraint of trade & price fixing. First antitrust policy instituted by US government. Predatory pricing to drive competitors from market is also restricted.
- **Federal Trade Commission Act, 1914:** Establishes Federal Trade Commission, which is charged with limiting unfair & anticompetitive practices of business.
- **Clayton Act, 1914:** Restricts price discrimination & purchase agreements between buyers & sellers; strengthens antitrust limits on mergers.
- **Robinson-Patman Act, 1936:** Limits the ability of firms to sell the same product at different prices to different customers. Price differentials can lessen or harm competition, particularly among resellers.
- **Wheeler-Lea Act, 1938:** Allows the Federal Trade Commission to investigate deceptive practices & to regulate advertising. Also ensures that pricing practices do not deceive consumers.
- **Consumer Goods Pricing Act, 1975:** Eliminates some control over retail pricing by wholesalers & manufacturers & allows retailers to establish final retail prices in most instances. Places limits on resale price maintenance agreements among manufacturers, wholesalers & retailers.

extract better arrangements from distributors and retailers, and to charge higher prices.[27] Dial soap, after 40 years, is still the category leader; Chips Ahoy, a 25-year-old brand, is still the leading chocolate chip cookie. These brands have strong brand equity and hence high prices and excellent margins. In both cases, the prices charged are compatible with the overall marketing strategy for the brand.

In pricing a product, the firm must also consider the prices of other products within its product line. The price of one product or brand should not cannibalize sales, that is shift sales from other brands within the same line of products. If a top-of-the-line model in a line of running shoes is priced at $150, a low-end model targeted to the novice runner should be priced so as not to steal sales from the higher-end model. Likewise, Boeing prices its line of commercial airliners so that low-end models do not detract from the larger, top-of-the-line airplanes.

Ethical and legal restraints on pricing

Marketers must consider more than the influences of the five Cs in price decisions. Pricing practices must also conform to laws and regulations and ethical expectations of customers and society in general. A variety of legislation affects the pricing decisions of firms. The objectives of this legislation are largely twofold: to protect competition among companies within markets and to protect the rights of consumers. The most important of these laws, summarized in chronological order of enactment in Exhibit 12.7, influence the ethical aspects of pricing decisions.

The Sherman Act (1890) inhibits price fixing and restraint of trade among competitors. Pricing practices designed to drive competitors from the market and conspiracy among competitors are limited by the case law established following this legislation. The act represents one of the government's first attempts to establish antitrust policies. A recent case involves allegations that 55 private educational institutions engaged in price-fixing agreements that resulted in overly high student fees. The Sherman Act was also used by the American Football League in its suit against the National Football League.

The Federal Trade Commission Act (1914) established the FTC as the administrative organization for monitoring unfair and anticompetitive business practices. The FTC is charged with limiting deceptive pricing and advertising practices.

The Clayton Act (1914) restricts price discrimination and purchase agreements between buyers and sellers and strengthened the antitrust limits on mergers and competitor arrangements of the Sherman Act. The act also limits requirements that a purchaser of one product must buy other products from the seller.

The Robinson-Patman Act (1936) places more stringent restrictions on **price discrimination** practices—selling the same product to different customers at different prices. Price discrimination can inhibit competition, particularly among resellers. It is legal to charge final consumers different prices (senior citizen discounts, student rates), because this does not impair competition. A manufacturer, however, may violate the law by charging different prices to different retailers. Quantity discounts are not an issue so long as all buyers can take advantage of uniform discount policies.

All price discrimination is not illegal, however. Under certain conditions, price discrimination may be permissible if the buyers are not competitors; the prices charged do not limit competition; the price differentials reflect differences in costs of serving the different customers; and the price differences occur because of efforts to meet competitor prices.

Acceptable price discrimination may reflect price differences based on time, place, customer, and product distinctions. For example, different prices are charged for telephone use and movies depending on the time of the day. Place differences account for differences in prices at hotels and entertainment events. Even individual customers may be charged different prices based on negotiations or differences in need.

Dumping—selling a product in a foreign country at a price lower than the price in the domestic country, and lower than its marginal cost of production—is a form of price discrimination. Most governments have antidumping regulations that protect their own industries against unfair foreign pricing practices. Typically, appeals for government assistance are based on the argument that offending firms are practicing **predatory dumping**—pricing intended to drive rivals out of business. A successful predator firm raises prices once the rival is driven from the market. One famous case involved Sony Corporation of Japan. Sony was selling TV sets for $180 in the US, while charging $333 in Japan for the same Japanese-made product. Threats of increased tariffs on Japanese TVs eventually forced increases in the prices of those exported to the United States.

The Wheeler-Lea Act (1938) expanded the FTC's role to monitor deceptive and misleading pricing and advertising practices. More recently, the Consumer Goods Pricing Act (1975) supported the right of retailers to determine final prices. The effect of the legislation is to limit the ability of manufacturers to control prices in their channels of distribution.

Implications for pricing decisions

Primary implications of legislation and case law for pricing include:

- Horizontal price fixing among companies at the same level of a distribution channel is illegal.

- In most cases, retailers are free to establish their own final selling prices. Prices charged by manufacturer- or wholesaler-owned retailers may still be restricted by the owner.

- Some states have enacted minimum price laws that prevent retailers from selling merchandise for less than cost.

Leading retailer and roaster of premium coffee

Only six years after buying the Starbucks Coffee Company, Howard Schultz transformed the Seattle-based gourmet coffee company into one of the fastest-growing businesses in North America. From being a small chain in 1987, the company has evolved into a national marketer of high-priced coffee. Starbucks now serves 13 million customers every week, with annual sales over $160 million. In addition to purchasing high-priced gourmet coffee, customers can purchase products ranging from stainless steel thermoses for $40 to $875 espresso machines.

How has this remarkable growth occurred in a market where total coffee sales are flat and the number of coffee drinkers has declined? First, gourmet coffee consumption is increasing among young, affluent adults—a market able to pay premium prices. Starbucks has aggressively increased the number of its outlets, which are modeled after European coffee cafes. The unique retail approach coupled with the sale of gourmet products enable Starbucks to charge premium prices. In addition, Starbucks views its employees as partners. Every Starbucks employee is eligible for health and dental benefits and is enrolled in at least 24 hours of instruction in an innovative training program. These programs enhance relationships with both customers and employees. Finally, the gourmet nature of espresso and specialty coffees enables Starbucks and other retail coffee bars to charge premium prices that yield signficant profit margins.

Sources: Ingrid Abramovitch, "Miracles of Marketing," *Success,* April 1993, pp. 22–27; Alice Z. Cuneo, "Starbucks' Word-of-Mouth Wonder," *Advertising Age,* March 7, 1994, p. 12; Carrie Goerne, "Coffee Consumption Down, but Sales of Exotic Blends Perk Up," *Marketing News,* July 20, 1992, pp. 1, 22; and John C. Maxwell, Jr., "Specialty Bars Brighten Lukewarm Coffee Market," *Advertising Age,* May 16, 1994, p. 16.

- Prices must not be presented in a way that deceives customers.
- Discrimination that reflects extremely low prices to eliminate competition, or that does not reflect cost differentials, may be illegal.
- In industries with a few large firms, it is generally acceptable for the pricing behavior of smaller firms to parallel that of larger firms.

International agreements and organizations

The prices charged for products and services are also affected by a number of international agreements or organizations. Among the more important agreements are the General Agreement on Tariffs and Trade (GATT); the Organization of Petroleum Exporting Countries (OPEC); the European Union (EU); and the North American Free Trade Agreement (NAFTA). All have wide-ranging effects on the prices charged in global markets.

For example, the Organization of Petroleum Exporting Countries (OPEC) is a loose federation of many of the oil-producing countries. This cooperative arrangement is designed to influence market prices and short-term profits for crude oil. The cartel has been affected by cheating on production among its own members as well as nonmembers' independent pricing actions. OPEC's effectiveness at controlling prices has been uneven in recent years.

The Entrepreneurial Spirit: Leading Retailer and Roaster of Premium Coffee describes how coffee cartels in South America actually enhanced the competitive positions of high-priced marketers of coffee, companies like Starbucks Coffee. Restrictions placed upon production of coffee, similar to those of OPEC on oil production, have hurt lower- and moderate-priced national brands by raising their costs and squeezing their already low margins. Starbucks and other high-priced sellers have greater margins to absorb the rising costs.

This nonprice ad subtly reinforces travelers' perceived value in choosing Motel 6 accommodations.

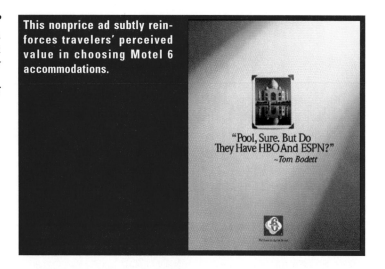

"Pool, Sure. But Do
They Have HBO And ESPN?"
~Tom Bodett

Customer price evaluations

We have talked so far about pricing from the perspective of the marketer or the seller. But how does the buyer judge prices? What determines a customer's evaluation of a product or brand?

The key to learning how prices influence purchase decisions lies in understanding how buyers perceive prices.[28] This **perceived monetary price** is the consumer's reaction that the price is high or low, fair or unfair. Further, consumers do not always remember prices even within the store and often encode or process them in personally meaningful ways.[29]

Judgments of perceived value

Perceived value describes the buyer's overall assessment of a product's utility based on what is received and what is given. It represents a trade-off between the "give" and the "get" components of a purchase transaction and plays a critical role in purchase decisions.[30] Some observers describe perceived value as "quality per dollar."[31]

The give is mainly the product's price. Increasingly, consumers base brand decisions on their notions of a "reasonable price" and compare prices regularly.[32] Exhibit 12.8 summarizes the effects of price on buyer judgments of value. Perceived value ultimately determines willingness to buy. Perceived value in turn is determined by a combination of the perceived benefits, or quality received, and the monetary sacrifice made. Higher benefits enhance value; higher monetary sacrifice detracts from it. These offsetting effects reflect the trade-off of the give and get components inherent in consumer perceptions of value. Understanding these consumer evaluations is essential to the *quality/value* and *execution perspectives.*

The power of consumer perceptions of value has not gone unnoticed by marketers. Well-known consumer companies whose stated primary emphasis is on consumer value include McDonald's, Wal-Mart, Sara Lee, Toyota, and Taco Bell. Business-to-business marketers now focusing on value through lower prices and enhanced quality include Emerson Electric, Electronic Data Systems (EDS), and 3M.

EXECUTIVE ROUNDTABLE COMMENT | **Rich Kitaeff, district manager in the Marketing Research and Quality Measurements Group of AT&T, recognizes the importance of consumer perceptions of value:**

Our strategy is to constantly enhance our own global networks and the networks of other service providers to add value to communications network services. This value-added approach strengthens our relationships with AT&T customers worldwide, and enables us to charge prices with profitable margins.

Exhibit 12.8

Relationships among price, perceived value, and willingness to buy

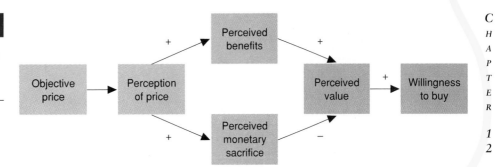

Price/quality relationships

Consumers trade off prices paid for benefits received, or product or service quality. The **price/quality relationship** describes the extent to which the consumer associates the product's price with higher quality. Higher prices do not always signal higher quality, however. Evidence suggests that, if there is a positive relationship, it is not very strong.[33] Sometimes uninformed consumers mistakenly use price to make quality judgments. When price and quality are not related, buying a higher-priced brand is a poor decision.

One study of *Consumer Reports* ratings reveals some interesting findings regarding the existence of actual price/quality relationships.[34] In tests across brands within nine product classes, prices and objective quality ratings were found to be positively related, negatively related, and not related, depending upon the products investigated. For example, positive relationships between price and quality existed for bicycles, washing machines, and frozen pizza. Negative relationships were observed for stereo speakers, blenders, and spray cleaners. Thus, consistently assuming higher prices mean higher quality does not always result in wise decisions.

Consumer use of price information

The effect of prices on consumers varies across people and situations.[35] Uncertainty about prices and quality can make purchase decisions difficult. The importance of quality and a buyer's previous experience determine the role of price in consumer evaluations. Ideally, consumers should use a **best-value strategy**, picking the lowest-cost brand available with the desired level of quality. In a **price-seeking strategy**, some consumers make a price/quality assumption and choose the highest-priced brand to maximize expected quality. Other consumers follow a **price-aversion strategy**, buying the lowest-priced brand simply to minimize risks from spending more than necessary.

Recognition that consumers use different purchase approaches can influence the firm's marketing strategies. If product quality is not obvious to the consumer but has high importance (imported wines, for example), firms often use a *price signaling strategy:* they set prices higher to imply higher quality. Where quality information is more readily available and the importance of quality is high (appliances, perhaps), firms often pursue a value-based strategy and use informative advertising. In this case, the firm keeps prices competitive and focuses marketing communications on the benefits and quality of the product. Firms market generic brands and brands competing largely on low price in recognition that some consumers are price-averse.

How are price judgments made?

How do people judge whether prices are too low, too high, or fair? Consumers compare product prices to internal and, in some cases, external reference prices. **External reference prices** include those charged by other retailers or comparison prices that a retailer provides to enhance perceptions of the published price.

Consumers have general expectations about market prices and a range of acceptable prices, as this ad suggests.

Internal reference prices are comparison standards that consumers remember and use to make their judgments. There are several internal reference prices. One is the expected price, a primary determinant of whether a buyer perceives a price as fair and reasonable. Another is the **reservation price,** an economic term for the highest price a person is willing to pay. Expectation of future prices is also a key internal reference, as the forward-looking consumer evaluates the costs and benefits of buying now versus buying at some future time.[36] Other internal reference prices include "the price last paid, the average retail price, and the price I would like to pay."[37]

A model of consumer evaluations of prices is presented in Exhibit 12.9.[38] It assumes that consumers have price information through past experiences with

Exhibit 12.9

**Consumer evaluations
of prices**

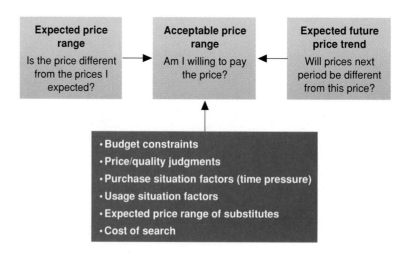

purchases of the same product or similar products.[39] Most people may be uncertain about specific prices but have some general expectations about market prices and a range of acceptable prices. They evaluate how the price of a product fits these expectations. They may interpret prices judged as too low as indicating suspect product quality; prices judged as too high are dismissed as out of the question or associated with a different product category.

Individual price evaluations may be influenced by external factors such as budget constraints, time pressure, anticipated use situations, or the cost of further search for lower-priced items. Consumers are generally less willing to pay higher prices for brands they perceive to have frequent price promotions.[40]

Advertised comparison prices

Advertisers often provide comparison prices (external reference prices) to persuade shoppers to buy. Comparison prices generally take one of three forms: prices previously charged by the retailer, prices charged by other retailers in the area, or manufacturer-suggested prices. Exhibit 12.10 summarizes the effect of

In this comparative pricing ad, Jennifer Convertibles temporarily reduces the price of its sofabed and loveseat from $1,199 to $599.

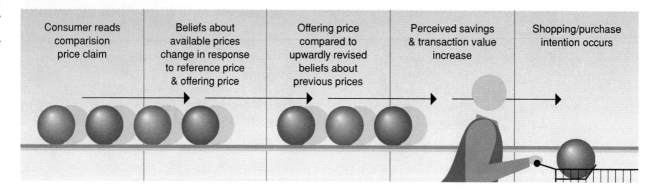

Exhibit 12.10   **A model of comparison reference price effects**

| Consumer reads comparision price claim | Beliefs about available prices change in response to reference price & offering price | Offering price compared to upwardly revised beliefs about previous prices | Perceived savings & transaction value increase | Shopping/purchase intention occurs |

comparison prices.[41] Comparison pricing increases the perceived **transaction value** of the purchase (the perceived merits of the deal) by raising the shopper's internal price standard, which makes the advertised price appear more attractive.[42] Basically, comparison pricing gives the buyer a higher reference price.

Summary

1. *Realize the importance of price and understand its role in the marketing mix.* For every good or service sold, the determination of price is critically important to the level of demand and the profits earned. A price set too high will discourage demand; a price set too low will result in less revenues; both lead to lower total profits. Determining an optimal price is becoming more difficult with changing marketplace trends, including faster technological progress, the proliferation of new products, increased demand for services, and growing global competition.

   Relationships between the determined price and the other marketing mix variables affect sales of the product and others the company offers. Price is only one aspect of the firm's marketing mix; other aspects, such as product and distribution, must be considered in pricing decisions. Further, price offers the selling firm a basis for competing whenever other differences among competing brands are not apparent to buyers.

2. *Understand the characteristics of the different pricing objectives that companies can adopt.* Common objectives that guide company pricing decisions include ensuring market survival, enhancing sales growth, increasing market share, maximizing profits, realizing a certain return on investment, deterring competition, and establishing or maintaining a particular quality image. Firms often pursue profitability objectives by a

price-skimming strategy and growth and competitive deterrence by a penetration-pricing strategy. Prestige pricing is consistent with quality and image-enhancement objectives.

3. *Identify many of the influences on marketers' pricing decisions.* Pricing decisions are influenced by the five Cs of pricing: costs, customers, channels of distribution, competition, and compatibility. Costs determine the minimum level of prices. Prices must at least cover costs in the long term, or insufficient profits and income result. Customer expectations, as well as perceptions of value and fairness, determine price acceptability.

   Price determination must also take account of other members of the channel of distribution. Intermediaries in the channel must be able to earn sufficient margins. Competitive factors also influence prices. When products are similar and price differences are important to consumers, prices will tend to move toward the going price.

   Pricing decisions must also be compatible with the overall marketing and communications objectives of the firm. Finally, national and international laws and agreements also influence price decisions.

4. *Explain how consumers form perceptions of quality and value.* Potential buyers, including individuals

and business buyers, form perceptions of value that influence their willingness to buy (purchase behavior). Perceived value is the overall assessment of the utility of a product, depending on what is received and what is given or paid. Price influences perceived value in terms of perceived benefits and perceived monetary sacrifice. Consumers vary in their reactions to price, but they typically adopt one of three strategies: a best-value strategy, a price-seeking strategy, or a price-aversion strategy.

5. *Understand price/quality relationships and internal and external reference prices.* Consumers frequently infer quality from prices. This reaction describes the price/quality relationship. These opinions, regardless of their accuracy, influence the buyer's decision; customers are more likely to pay a higher price if they believe a product to be of higher quality.

Many consumers compare advertised prices to expected prices—a frequently used internal reference price. If prices are above expectations, perceived value of a product declines; lower-than-expected prices may cause perceived value to rise. Companies often provide external reference prices by pairing an offered price with a higher comparison price designed to make the lower price more attractive. These comparison prices may be previously charged prices, manufacturer-suggested prices, or competitive prices.

Key terms & concepts

price 282
objective price 282
basic price mix 283
price promotion mix 283
price elasticity 283
exchange rate 284
penetration pricing 286
market share 286
price skimming 287
return on investment (ROI) 287

competition 287
nonprice competition 288
prestige pricing 288
five Cs of pricing 289
value-in-use pricing 291
price discrimination 294
dumping 294
predatory dumping 294
perceived monetary price 296

perceived value 296
price/quality relationship 297
best-value strategy 297
price-seeking strategy 297
price-aversion strategy 297
external reference prices 297
internal reference prices 298
reservation price 298
transaction value 300

Review & discussion questions

1. What is the meaning of price? Contrast the basic price mix with the price promotion mix.

2. Why are pricing decisions so important? What are the effects of setting prices too low? Too high?

3. What environmental conditions make pricing decisions so difficult? How might these effects influence estimation of costs and revenues?

4. How do these pricing objectives differ: quality enhancement versus market survival? Sales growth versus profitability?

5. Refer to **The Entrepreneurial Spirit: Leading Retailer and Roaster of Premium Coffee.** Use the Starbucks coffee example to summarize how each of the following can influence a product or service price: costs, customers, channels of distribution, competition, and compatibility.

6. Refer to **The Technological Edge: Charles Schwab and Discount Brokerage Marketing.** How does Charles Schwab compete with other brokerage houses such as Merrill Lynch? What influences Schwab's pricing strategy?

7. What are some of the primary legal restrictions on marketers' pricing decisions?

8. Contrast external reference prices with internal reference prices. Give several examples of each. How do reference prices affect consumer reactions to prices?

9. Define consumer perceived value and explain what determines it. How do price and perceived quality affect perceptions of value? Explain the relationship between price and quality.

10. Explain these purchase strategies that consumers use to evaluate prices: best value, price seeking, price aversion.

Application exercises

1. Interview a small retailer. Ask how prices are determined and how products put on sale are selected. Does support from the manufacturer influence the initial price of goods? What role does consumer demand play?

2. Find in your local newspaper reference price advertisements from two different retailers. What are the original prices and the sale prices? What are the percent reductions? To whom or to what is the sale price compared? What wording is used to make the reference price claim?

3. Interview a close friend or relative. Ask the question: "What comes to mind when you consider the purchase of a personal computer?" At what point does the person mention price? To what extent does the order of the attributes mentioned reflect their importance in determining the purchase?

Case 12.1   Silver Fox: Wily competitive pricing

For specialty stores such as Silver Fox in Columbia, South Carolina, pricing decisions take on some unique characteristics. Silver Fox is a small retail store offering tennis clothing and accessories. Near the store are a number of country clubs and a large high school, and there are many adult tennis teams in the area. Open six days a week, the store operates with four part-time employees and the owner, John Atkinson.

Silver Fox has annual sales of around $375,000. Tennis clothing, such as warm-up outfits, shorts and skirts, and T-shirts, constitutes 40 percent of the store's total sales, 50 percent including shoes. An additional 40 percent of sales is made up of tennis rackets and balls, while the final 10 percent comes from the store's racket-stringing service. Tennis clothing is a very important component of the store's business, as it sells these items at a 100 percent markup over cost during peak seasons. The store offers national brand names of clothing and, at least during the spring and summer, enjoys an acceptable sales level of tennis clothing.

As a small retailer in a suburban area, Silver Fox faces tough competition. Potential customers within the Columbia area may choose to purchase tennis-related items from Silver Fox or from several larger stores that typically carry more than just tennis accessories. The store competes both with large discount stores and local sporting goods chains. The competition provides Silver Fox with some distinctive problems.

During the spring and summer, demand for tennis supplies is much higher than during other months. This increased demand allows Silver Fox to mark up its clothing items a full 100 percent, a pricing strategy Atkinson believes is necessary to achieve the desired profitability. During these peak seasons, Silver Fox and its competitors charge comparable prices. With its convenient location the store is able to maintain a steady stream of sales.

During the fall and winter, however, demand for tennis clothes and accessories declines sharply, and the store's larger competitors really hold an advantage. By offering clothing and equipment for other sporting activities, these competitors can maintain overall high sales levels. Silver Fox does not offer any merchandise to offset slow tennis-related sales during these months, so it cannot compete on price with its competitors. Instead, the store is forced to come down considerably on its 100 percent markup just to maintain sales. Because the store purchases its merchandise directly from local sales representatives, costs for tennis clothing do not fluctuate during the year.

Reducing markup on clothing items during the fall and winter months provides some advantages. The store can increase its sales of tennis apparel during this otherwise slow period. Moreover, the lower clothing prices serve to increase the store's customer traffic flow during these months, although not as high as during the spring or summer. This increase in customer traffic serves to increase sales for nonclothing merchandise.

Questions:

1. Explain why Silver Fox's clothing pricing strategy seems to be cost-oriented during the spring and summer months, but more demand-oriented during other months.

2. Would you classify the demand for tennis clothing as elastic or inelastic? Explain your reasoning.

3. How would Silver Fox's pricing strategies be different if it did not face tough competition?

Source: Interviews conducted in Spring 1994 with store owners and Silver Fox manager.

Case 12.2   *The cable TV wars: Pricing in a regulated environment*

During the late 1980s and early 1990s, cable television consumers endured several price increases. These increases outraged many consumers who felt their cable services had not increased along with the rising prices. Finally, the Federal Communications Commission (FCC) investigated whether these industrywide price increases were truly necessary or if the cable TV suppliers were gouging consumers.

The cable TV industry is unique. Consumers typically do not have a choice of different cable operators to which they could subscribe, as each operator provides service to a particular geographical area, thereby holding a local monopoly. However, the cable industry should not be considered a purely natural monopoly since consumers can easily choose to cancel their subscriptions if rates get too high. Furthermore, the industry recognizes that it does compete with other forms of entertainment. Such obstacles prevent cable operators from charging overly excessive prices; however, the lack of competition between cable operators for any given household does set up the potential for prices being higher than they would otherwise be.

In October 1992, the FCC announced new pricing caps on cable operators nationwide, effective in 1993 or 1994. The regulations imposed maximum restrictions on how high companies could set rates for their "basic" cable (the package of channels bundled for consumers at a minimum rate). Cable suppliers screamed that the pricing caps were unfair, that they would severely limit their revenue and profit-earning abilities. The FCC, on the other hand, evaluated the cost and revenue structures of the industry and determined that the pricing caps would allow cable operators to recover their expenses and earn reasonable returns.

The local cable operators were not at all satisfied with the FCC's plans. During the months between the announcement of the price caps and their actual implementation, cable operators responded in a variety of ways, each of which led to consumers bearing the brunt of the industry's burdens from the caps. One of the local Los Angeles area cable operators increased its installation fees 91 percent

during this period. A Nashville, Tennessee, operator reduced the price of the basic service that only a few of its customers subscribed to, but imposed a fee of almost $40 for any subscriber who tried to switch to the new lower rates. Many other cable suppliers redefined basic cable. They removed popular channels, such as USA, MTV, and TNT, from the basic package, offering them as premium channels that would cost additional fees above those of the basic rates. For many cable suppliers, the redefinitions of basic and premium channels actually meant price increases instead of decreases.

For much of its existence, the cable industry went unchecked. Many industry analysts believe that the price caps implemented in 1993 were the first of many restrictions the FCC will impose. If the FCC determines that the cable operators' responses to the imposed caps have allowed them to continue achieving returns above "normal" profit levels, more legislation may come.

Questions:

1. How have the five Cs of pricing affected the price decision of cable operators?

2. Explain how the local cable operators could get away with setting prices so high that the FCC felt the need to step in and set controls.

3. Do you think that the FCC acted appropriately in setting the rate caps? Why or why not? Do you think that cable operators have responded appropriately to the rate caps? Why or why not?

Sources: "FCC to Enforce New Rates for Cable Starting September 1," *The Wall Street Journal*, July 21, 1993, p. B8; "FCC Plan on Cable-TV Fees Allows Reasonable Return," *The Wall Street Journal*, July 16, 1993, p. B3; Paul Farhi, "FCC Bid to Cut Cable Prices Might Push Them Higher," *The Washington Post*, May 14, 1993, p. D1; Mark Robichaux, "Premium Cable Channels Gain Viewers with Original Programs, Package Deals," *The Wall Street Journal*, March 24, 1993, p. B1; and Mark Robichaux, "Media: Cable Concerns Are Scrambling to Raise Rates," *The Wall Street Journal*, December 14, 1992, p. B1.

Price Determination and Pricing Strategies

After studying this chapter you should be able to:

1. Discuss the interrelationships among price, demand, demand elasticity, and revenue.

2. Understand methods for determining price.

3. Recognize the different pricing strategies and the conditions that best suit the choice of a strategy.

4. Recognize the importance of adapting prices under shifting economic and competitive situations.

5. Understand the ethical considerations involved in setting and communicating prices.

Swatch watches: Prices don't change over time

*S*watch watches retail for 50 francs in Switzerland and for $40 to $50 in the United States. This price has not changed in 10 years. Surprisingly, the watches are made in Switzerland, where the most junior secretary earns more than the most senior engineers in Thailand or Malaysia.

How is it possible to build and successfully mass-market products in countries like Switzerland? Nicolas Hayek, creator of the Swatch watch and acknowledged European business celebrity, emphasizes that Swatch must build its watches at home, at lower cost and higher quality than anywhere in the world. He argues that when a country loses its know-how and expertise to manufacture, it loses its ability to create wealth.

Swatch's secret is a manufacturing process that minimizes the number of parts in the watch and allows automated assembly, thereby enabling low-cost construction. By launching new limited collections of innovative designs twice a year, the company maintains high demand. Continuing innovation and strict cost control enable Swatch to produce and sell its watches at very affordable prices.

Hayek and his Swiss company, the SMH Group, is now moving into the luxury end of the watch industry. The company that created Swatch watches is revitalizing the Omega brand as a competitor to Rolex. The luxury watch industry—watches that typically sell for $3,000 to $5,000, but go as high as $500,000 for Patek Philippe's minute repeaters—has almost $3 billion in annual sales and is a highly profitable business. The success of this venture remains somewhat uncertain at this time. However, the remarkable strength of the trendy Swatch watch has restored faith in the Swiss watch industry, which suffered greatly in the 1980s from Japanese competitors. Industry observers predict that the makers of Swatch watches will also succeed in the upscale market. Interestingly, the differences in prices for these high-end products are due more to scarcity and snob appeal than to differences in production costs.

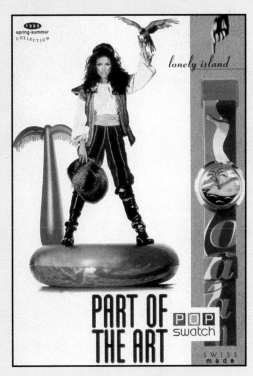

Sources: "Swatch: Ambitious," *Economist,* April 18, 1992, pp. 74–75; Peter Fuhrman, "Jewelry for the Wrist," *Forbes,* November 23, 1992, pp. 173–78; William Taylor, "Message and Muscle: An Interview with Swatch Titan Nicolas Hayek," *Harvard Business Review,* March–April 1993, pp. 98–110; and Elaine Underwood, "Time Runs Out: Zeitoum Watch Over at Swatch," *Brandweek,* March 14, 1994, pp. 1, 6.

The Swatch experience demonstrates the role of price in a marketing strategy. With its continuing innovations, low-cost structure, and competitive pricing, Swatch enjoys a profitable market niche. The example illustrates only one approach to pricing, however. In this chapter, we examine the processes companies use to select a specific pricing strategy. Additionally, we discuss some theoretical and practical issues affecting the determination of prices. Some of these issues involve ethical considerations. Price determination and evaluation of appropriate pricing strategies are a continual managerial challenge.

Price determination: An overview

The step-by-step procedure diagrammed in Exhibit 13.1 presents a logical approach for setting prices.[1] Execution of this process requires an understanding of the concepts described in Chapter 12. First, the firm must set pricing objectives consistent with its overall marketing and strategic efforts and with the product's image and quality. Common pricing objectives are to maximize profits or sales growth. Second, the firm must consider market demand and the responsiveness of demand to different prices. What will the level of sales be at different prices? How do sales change as prices vary?

Next, the firm determines the costs to manufacture products or provide services and the relationship of costs to volume. The company evaluates competitor prices and costs. If prices are set well above market prices, consumers will not purchase. If prices are too low, revenues and profits may be lost. Then the firm may use one of various methods for determining prices, including markup pricing, break-even analysis, and target-return pricing methods.

Exhibit 13.1   **The price-setting decision process**

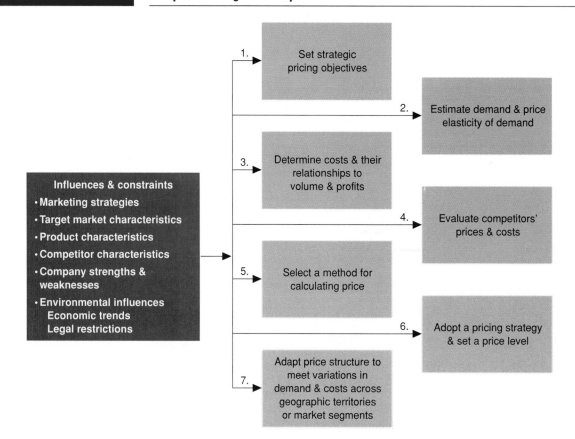

Finally, the firm must set specific prices, often using one of the common pricing strategies. After setting prices, the firm monitors and adjusts them to adapt to differences in demand and costs across market segments or to meet competitive reactions.

As Exhibit 13.1 shows, the stages in this pricing process are subject to several influences and constraints. These include product characteristics, company strengths and weaknesses, and legal constraints. Moreover, both costs and demand are difficult to estimate. Sometimes, price determination involves setting a price first, then revising in response to market performance.

Price and the quantity demanded

Demand curves

The relationship between prices and quantity demanded is expressed in the traditional market **demand curve** labeled D in Exhibit 13.2. Under normal conditions, customers buy more as prices drop; they buy less when prices rise. Price is only one determinant of demand, however. Others include household income, tastes and preferences, population growth, and prices of related products. For many business-to-business situations, demand is driven by general economic conditions and consumer demand, as well as by the preferences and needs of the firm's buyers. This is the concept of derived demand discussed in Chapter 6.

Price elasticity of demand

Price elasticity of demand is a basic business concept. The relationship between price and quantity varies; as one increases, the other decreases. Price elasticity of demand is computed as:

$$\text{Price elasticity of demand} = \frac{\text{Percent change in quantity demanded}}{\text{Percent change in price}}$$

Computational procedures and an example are shown in Appendix A.

Elastic demand exists when small price changes result in large changes in the quantity demanded. When demand is elastic, a small decrease in price increases total revenues. Elastic demand prevails in the motor vehicles, engineering products, furniture, and professional services industries.

Inelastic demand exists when price changes do not result in significant changes in the quantity demanded. Inelastic demand often occurs for books, magazines, newspapers, and clothing, as well as in the banking and insurance, beverage, and utility industries.[2] Exhibit 13.3 depicts elastic and inelastic demand situations. Overall, demand is likely to be inelastic to price changes when there are few or no product substitutes; when buyers do not readily notice the higher price and are slow to change their buying habits or to search for lower prices, or when they think higher prices are justified by product improvements or inflation; and when the product or service represents a small portion of the household income.[3]

Exhibit 13.2

Demand curve representing relationship between price and quantity demanded

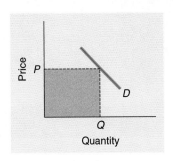

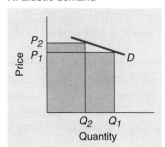

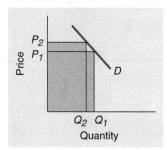

Exhibit 13.3

Elastic and inelastic demand

Where demand is price-elastic, marketers must carefully evaluate any proposed increases in price. Price changes may cause significant change in quantity demanded. Long-term elasticities may differ from short-term ones as customers become aware of changing prices and have time to search for alternative products or services.

Cross elasticity of demand relates the percentage change in quantity demanded for one product to percentage price changes for other products. For example, products are often part of a line of similar products; and changes in the price of one brand may affect the demand for other items in the product line. When products are close *substitutes,* such as cola beverages, a rise in the price of one will increase the demand for the other. For businesses, a sharp increase in prices of steel fasteners used in the construction of trucks would cause increased demand for less expensive plastic or aluminum fasteners.

Alternatively, when products are *complements,* a price increase of one may decrease the demand for the other. For example, large price increases for personal computers would cause a decrease in the demand for printers. And price reductions of taco shells may increase sales of taco sauce.[4]

Costs, volume, and profits

We have seen the trade-offs between prices and quantity demanded. Yet price determination must also consider the costs incurred in the production and sale of goods, as indicated in **The Entrepreneurial Spirit: Pricing to Cover Exporting Costs.**

Fixed costs (FC) such as plant and large equipment investments, interest paid on loans, and the costs of production facilities, cannot be changed in the short

Studies of what consumers can afford lead to lower-priced brands, like Pampers Uni in Brazil.

Pricing to cover exporting costs

One of the most serious mistakes companies make when entering overseas markets is to underprice products or services because they have underestimated the cost of going international. R&E Electronics, which exports integrated communications systems from its Wilmington, North Carolina, headquarters, wants the same profit margin on its overseas sales as on its domestic sales. But to achieve this objective, CEO Ed Mayorga calculates costs and price structure quite differently, so that all international-related costs are included in the final price. Additional costs that affect R&E's price structure include longer collection cycles, higher administrative overhead, insurance, and taxes.

Mayorga adds in a charge to cover the cost of borrowing while the company collects from export customers, who typically take longer to pay. To speed up collections, R&E offers discounts to international customers who pay on or before delivery. Because international sales require more personnel and administrative effort than domestic sales, a larger percentage of general and administrative costs is allocated to the costs of overseas jobs. Insurance costs are verified by the local country insurance firm prior to final pricing. Finally, estimates of foreign tax liability are added as well.

All firms, whether small entrepreneurial companies like Mayorga's or large multinational firms, must recognize the complexities of pricing for international situations. Estimated prices must take into account the additional hidden costs of doing business overseas.

Source: "International Business: Pricing to Cover Exporting Costs," *Inc.*, March 1992, pp. 103–4. Reprinted with permission, *Inc.* magazine. Copyright 1992 by Goldhirsh Group, Inc., 38 Commercial Wharf, Boston, MA 02110.

run and do not vary with the quantity produced. These costs would occur even if the quantity produced were zero. Many advertising costs are viewed as fixed costs, at least over a predetermined period.[5]

Variable costs (VC) such as wages and raw materials change with the level of output. Marketing variable costs include packaging and promotional costs tied to each unit produced.

Total costs (TC) are the sum of variable costs (VC) and fixed costs (FC). Variable costs are made up of the variable cost per unit times the number or quantity of units sold (Q):

$$TC = (VC \times Q) + FC$$

Marginal costs (MC) are incurred in producing one additional unit of output. They typically decline early over some level of production because of economies of scale, but eventually begin to increase as the firm approaches capacity and returns diminish.

Marginal revenue (MR) is the additional revenue the firm will receive if one more unit of product is sold. This amount typically represents the price of the product. **Total revenue** (TR) is total sales, or price times the quantity sold:

$$\text{Total revenues} = \text{Price} \times \text{Quantity}$$

To determine the price that maximizes profits, the firm combines cost information with demand or revenue information. Simply viewed:

$$\text{Profits} = \text{Total revenues } (TR) - \text{Total costs } (TC)$$

Jergens reduced costs and prices by using less plastic in its refill packaging. This approach is also consistent with an *ecological perspective* as the packages require much less landfill space.

This difference is greatest at the point where profits are maximized—where the firm's marginal revenue (MR) equals marginal cost (MC). When marginal revenue exceeds marginal cost, additional profits can be made by producing and selling more product. An example of these computations is presented in Appendix A.

EXECUTIVE ROUNDTABLE COMMENT | **Gene Martin, director of marketing and economic development for UtilCorp United, Inc., a large Western Electric utility, comments on costs and prices in the utility industry:**

Cost control and low market prices are now strategic imperatives for utilities, as deregulation has increased competitive pressures on electric service providers. Some of our large customers are now seeking long-term flat rates so that their costs (and our prices) are guaranteed over a period of time.

Price determination methods

A firm may choose from several methods of determining price. It may subjectively determine a price based on what management feels is appropriate at the time. Or, it may use a combination of methods or procedures. Some basic approaches are markup pricing, break-even analysis, target-return pricing, and price-sensitivity measurement.

Markup pricing

Retailers typically use some form of **markup pricing**, where markup is the difference between the cost of an item and the retail price, expressed as a percentage. A product's price is determined by adding a set percentage to the cost of the product. These percentages are often standardized across product categories. Formally:

$$\text{Price} = \text{Unit cost} + \text{Markup, or}$$
$$\text{Price} = \text{Unit cost} / (1 - k)$$

where k = desired percent markup.

Pricing your service for profits

A year after she founded the Delahaye Group, a $1 million Hampton Falls, New Hampshire, firm to track public relations effectiveness, Katherine Paine found her company in the black. But on closer inspection, she discovered that half her products lost money or barely broke even. Without an accurate reading of her costs, Paine was misquoting projects. To price profitably and to analyze time spent on projects, Paine began using Timeslips computer software. The software enables her to use cost and time estimates to make more reasonable price decisions.

To price profitably, she now asks:

- *How much time are we spending?* Paine asked her 15 employees to keep detailed time sheets. These sheets tell whether the company is spending more time on nonbillable tasks than anticipated.

- *What are my future costs?* Clients may ask for responses to proposals six months in advance. During that time, employees may get raises and costs may change, rendering a price quotation unprofitable. Improved forecasts were needed.

- *What's my billing rate?* Using analysis of sales and cost data for similar industries, Paine now incorporates a markup factor, derived by dividing the cost of direct labor into sales, to compute her billing rate. If on average, $40,000 worth of direct labor costs produce $100,000 in sales, for example, the markup factor would be 2.5. Paine can then multiply projected billable hours for a project by 2.5 to arrive at a price for a particular project.

Source: "Pricing Your Service for Profits," *Inc.*, June 1992, p. 107. Reprinted with permission, *Inc.* magazine. Copyright 1992 by Goldhirsh Group, Inc., 38 Commercial Wharf, Boston, MA 02110.

Assume, for example, that a retailer purchases a popular branded tennis racket at $80 and adds $40 to the cost, for a retail price of $120.

$$\text{Markup as a percentage of selling price} = \frac{\text{Markup}}{\text{Selling price}}$$

$$= \frac{\$40}{\$120} = 33\%$$

$$\text{Markup as a percentage of cost} = \frac{\text{Markup}}{\text{Cost}}$$

$$= \frac{\$40}{\$80} = 50\%$$

In some cases, the retailer may wish to know the markup charged for a product given the price and the original cost. This markup percentage can be computed simply as:

$$\text{Markup (\%)} = [(\text{Price} - \text{Unit cost})/\text{Price}] \times 100\%$$

Other procedures and examples for determining retail prices and markups are summarized in Appendix A.

The Technological Edge: Pricing Your Service for Profits describes how one company uses software to determine the markup necessary for profitability.

Exhibit 13.4

Break-even analysis

Break-even analysis

Break-even analysis is a useful guide for pricing decisions. It involves calculating the number of units that must be sold at a certain price for the firm to cover costs and, hence, break even. The approach is shown graphically in Exhibit 13.4. The *break-even point* (BEP) is determined by the intersection of the total revenue line ($TR = P \times Q$) and the total cost line ($TC = FC + VC \times Q$). The area between the two lines and to the right of the intersection represents profits. To make a profit, the quantity sold must exceed the BEP.

The slope of the total revenue line is determined by the price charged. A higher price would make the total revenue line steeper, and the BEP would be lower. Lower costs would also reduce the BEP.

The BEP in units is

$$Q\ (BEP) = FC/(P - VC)$$

where P = unit price and $Q\ (BEP)$ = break-even quantity. Once sufficient sales (or quantity sold) cover fixed costs, the quantity ($P - VC$) is typically referred to as the product's contribution margin.

Consider a case of plastic medical gloves priced at $7.25 and entailing $2.25 in variable costs. At total fixed costs of $200,000, the required break-even quantity would be 40,000 units. That is,

$$40,000 = \$200,000/(\$7.25 - \$2.25)$$

If the price were raised to $12.25, and assuming sufficient demand existed, the BEP would drop to 20,000 units.

BEP can also be expressed in dollars:

$$Q(BEP\$) = FC/(1 - VC/P)$$

Using the previous medical gloves example, the BEP in dollars would be:

$$\$289,855 = \$200,000/(1 - \$2.25/\$7.25)$$

Break-even analysis is useful for evaluating the effects of various price and cost structures on needed demand levels. And by adding a desired profit amount to the fixed cost portion of the equation, a firm can calculate the number of units that must be sold at a certain price to achieve a certain profit level.

Break-even analysis can be expanded to consider different price and quantity combinations. This modified break-even analysis (described in Appendix A) recognizes that the BEP can vary depending on the price chosen. Profits do not necessarily increase as quantity increases, as lower prices may be needed to generate the increased demand.

Exhibit 13.5	The role of cost in US and Japanese pricing

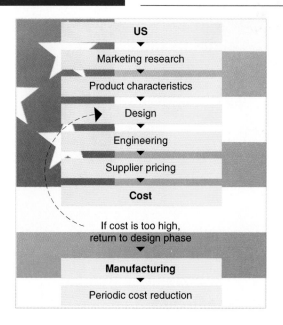

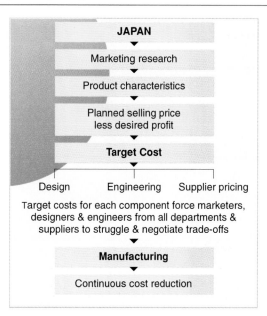

Target-return pricing

Target-return pricing is a cost-oriented approach that sets prices to achieve some desired rate of return. Cost and profit estimates are based on some expected volume or sales level. The price is determined using the equation:

$$\text{Price} = \text{Unit cost} + \frac{(\text{Desired return} \times \text{Invested capital})}{\text{Expected unit sales}}$$

Assume a national manufacturer of office supplies sells a computer-paper organizer. Average variable costs for the product are $8; total assets employed in the business are $4,500,000. The firm desires a 15 percent return and expects to sell 200,000 units. Therefore, the target-return price is:

$$\text{Price} = \text{Unit cost} + \frac{(\text{Desired return} \times \text{Invested capital})}{\text{Unit sales}}$$

$$= \$8 + (0.15 \times \$4,500,000)/200,000 = \$11.38$$

The firm would price the product at $11.38. Again, the success of the approach assumes the supplier can reach the expected sales volume of 200,000 units.

Target-return pricing forecasts a fair or needed rate of return. However, the effects of other variables in the marketing mix and competitive factors are not considered directly; and target-return pricing, like break-even analysis, is best used in combination with consideration of other determinants of demand.

Some Japanese firms use an approach to pricing that recognizes the effects of price on demand and the role of costs in determining demand. As Exhibit 13.5 shows, the Japanese specify a target cost based on the price they believe the market is most likely to accept. Designers and engineers then meet target costs. This approach, embracing the *execution perspective*, emphasizes the product's ability to achieve market acceptance by considering more directly the interface between the prices buyers are likely to accept and the costs necessary to produce products at those prices. Nissan, Sharp, and Toyota use this approach.

Some US and European companies design a new product first, and only then calculate the cost. If the cost is too high, the product must be redesigned or the company must settle for a lower profit level.[6] Generally, the Japanese worry less

Exhibit 13.6

Consumers' price sensitivity measurement for electric razors

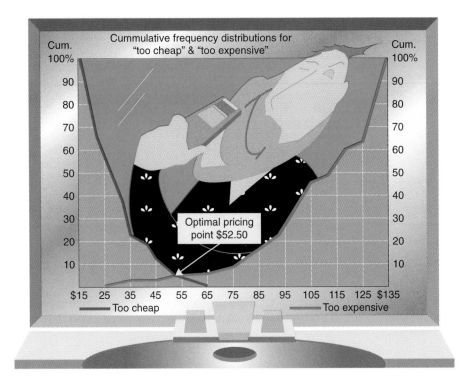

than American and European manufacturers about cost accounting. They work backward from a price and make sure the product can be produced with the quality demanded at that price.

Price sensitivity measurement

A useful approach for incorporating customer input into determination of prices is **price sensitivity measurement (PSM)**. Developed in the early 1970s, this procedure is still used today by many firms to estimate prices for new consumer and industrial products. First, a sample of potential buyers reads a product description and views any available pictures or diagrams. Then the buyers are shown a pricing scale that begins with $0 and includes up to 30 different price points. The scale measures the points at which buyers consider a price too expensive or so cheap they would question the product's quality. The PSM then yields price estimates high enough to reflect the product's perceived value and low enough to avoid sticker shock.[7]

A version of the PSM approach is shown in Exhibit 13.6, which plots the reactions of 249 European respondents to a new electric razor. The intersection between ratings of prices that are "too cheap" and "too expensive" provides an estimate of the price to charge. This approach considers consumer price sensitivity and perceptions of value as primary determinants of price, reflecting the *quality/value perspective.*

EXECUTIVE ROUNDTABLE COMMENT | Gene Martin, director of marketing and economic development for UtilCorp United, Inc., underscores the difficulty of pricing electric utility services:

A central issue for utility marketing is understanding the price elasticity of demand for electric utility services. How does demand vary by price and customer type? Some residential customers, who are in a survival mode, desire lower rates, even at the expense of consistent service. Other customers with special needs (say, important home computer usage) are willing to pay premium prices for excellent service.

Exhibit 13.7 **Alternative pricing strategies**	Differential pricing	Competitive pricing	Product-line pricing	Psychological pricing
	Second-market discounting	Penetration pricing	Bundling	Odd-even pricing
	Periodic discounting	Price signaling	Premium pricing	Customary pricing

Pricing strategies

Setting prices to achieve the firm's objectives requires the selection of a specific pricing strategy or a combination of strategies.[8] The eight pricing strategies shown in Exhibit 13.7 fall into four categories: differential pricing, where the same brand is sold to consumers under different prices; competitive pricing, where prices are set to take advantage of competitive market conditions; product-line pricing, where related brands are sold at prices to take advantage of interdependencies among brands; and psychological pricing, where prices are based on consideration of consumer perceptions or expectations.

The appropriateness of a particular pricing strategy depends on several circumstances: the variability of demand (the presence of different market segments), the competitive situation, the characteristics of consumers in the market, and the expectations or perceptions of consumers.

Several common sense assumptions about buyers underlie all pricing strategies. First, some buyers have search costs in taking time and effort to obtain information about which firms sell what products and at what prices. Second, some buyers have low reservation prices, the highest prices they are willing to pay. That is, some price-sensitive buyers do not need a product enough to pay the high price others pay. Third, all buyers face transaction costs besides search costs, such as the cost of money.

Differential pricing

Differential pricing involves selling the same product to different buyers under a variety of prices. This is price discrimination, or the practice of charging different buyers different prices for the same quantity and quality of products or services.[9] Differential pricing works because the market is heterogeneous or, more simply, differences in reactions to price exist among consumers or consumer segments in the market.

Second-market discounting

The most common form of differential pricing, **second-market discounting,** occurs when different prices are charged in different market segments. (Recall that this practice may be legal in retail, but illegal in wholesale if it harms competition.) Second-market discounting is useful when the firm has excess capacity and different market segments exist. Generic brands and some foreign markets often provide opportunities for second-market discounting. For example, if a firm can sell its product cost-effectively in a foreign market, it may be profitable to export even at a price below local prices. The exporting firm must have excess production capacity (so no new fixed costs are required), and the markets must be sufficiently separated so that transaction costs prevent interaction between markets.

RPS Air appeals to customers who have low reservation prices. The ad promotes low Roadway Package System charges compared to competing delivery service companies.

McDonald's uses differential pricing to the 60+ segment by offering 25-cent coffee and soft drinks and an invitation to "come in, relax, and stay a while."

Second-market discounting also occurs when the company sells a portion of its output as generic brands at lower prices to price-sensitive segments. Other examples include differences in student and senior citizen discounts for entertainment ticket prices.

For price discrimination to be successful, some rather restrictive conditions must be satisfied:

- The market must have segments that respond differently to price variations.
- Members of the market paying the lower price must not be able to resell the product to the people paying the higher price.
- Competitors should not be able to undercut the prices charged to the higher-price segment.
- The cost of segmenting and policing the market should not exceed the extra revenue derived from charging the higher prices.
- The practice should not cause consumer resentment.
- The form of price discrimination used should be legal.[10]

Periodic discounting

In some cases, it is advantageous for the firm to offer periodic or occasional discounts. **Periodic discounting** enables the firm to take advantage of the presence of consumer segments that differ in price sensitivity. This approach includes price skimming, where an initial high price is determined for new products to skim the market. Price skimming allows product development costs to be recovered when introductory sales are growing. People willing to pay the high price purchase first, and then prices are lowered, as sales slow, to attract the next-highest level of price-sensitive buyer. Du Pont, a well-known innovator of industrial products, frequently uses a price-skimming strategy.

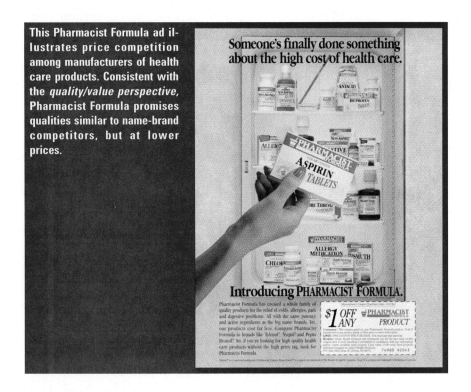

This Pharmacist Formula ad illustrates price competition among manufacturers of health care products. Consistent with the *quality/value perspective*, Pharmacist Formula promises qualities similar to name-brand competitors, but at lower prices.

Competitive pricing

Competitive pricing strategies, based on the firm's position in relation to its competition, include penetration pricing, limit pricing, and price signaling.

Penetration pricing calls for a low initial price to generate sales volume and take advantage of economies of scale (larger production runs at lower unit costs). It is often used when the marketer wants to maximize sales growth or market share.

Penetration pricing may be particularly beneficial when there are a significant number of price-sensitive consumers in the market (demand is price-elastic) or the firm fears early entry of a competitor if prices are set high and margins appear attractive. **Limit pricing** entails setting prices low to discourage new competition.

Price signaling puts high prices on low-quality products. This approach, although clearly not beneficial to buyers, can be pursued successfully if several conditions are satisfied. First, there must be a segment of buyers whose experience is consistent with a price/quality relationship, who believe firms spend more to provide higher quality, or who trust the market and assume a positive relationship between price and quality exists.[11] Second, information on the level of quality should be hard for buyers to obtain.[12] *Consumer Reports* regularly reports examples of successful brands that have high prices and suspect quality.

Product-line pricing

Firms often offer a line of multiple versions of the same product, such as Radio Shack stereo speakers priced from $59.99 to $149.99. Low- and high-end prices may influence buyer perceptions of quality and set standards for comparing items within the product line.

Low-end prices frequently influence doubtful or price-conscious buyers to purchase and are often used as traffic builders. The high-end price has considerable influence on the quality image of the entire product line. Marketers must be sensitive to price changes in the product line. A price change in one product can detract from sales of other products in the line, because they are often substitutes for each other.[13]

Pulsar Time prices its product line of watches from $50 to $300.

OBVIOUSLY, WE KNOW WHAT MAKES PEOPLE TICK.

PULSAR

Bundling

Increasingly, companies are realizing the value of combining separate products into bundles. **Bundling** is marketing two or more products or services in a single "package" for a single price.[14] The practice is seen frequently in the marketing of ski packages, hotel services, restaurant meals, and stereo and computer systems. Bundling also occurs in the purchase of health care equipment by hospitals. In these cases, the bundle price is typically less than if each item in the package is bought separately.

Pure price bundling occurs when the bundle includes a number of the *same* product, such as multiple candy bars or golf balls sold in a package for a single price. Two-for-one offers in travel packages or restaurant orders are price bundles often used to regulate demand levels. Product tie-ins or multiproduct bundles involve *different* products included in a single offering for a single price. The products may be complementary, as in the case of a personal computer and printer.[15]

Dunkin' Donuts combines a bundling strategy with price incentives to stimulate coffee sales.

Get our coffee canister for beans.

1 lb.

$7.99 Get our airtight coffee canister with a pound of our delicious coffee for one great price and you'll also get a coupon for a $7 rebate on one of the world's finest coffeemakers: the new Braun FlavorSelect. (Decaf extra. Canister is sold separately for $5.49.) At participating shops while supplies last. Plus applicable taxes.

DUNKIN' DONUTS

Premium pricing

When a firm offers several alternative models, it often uses a premium-pricing strategy. **Premium pricing** sets higher (premium) prices on more deluxe product versions. The various models are designed to appeal to different price-sensitive segments or to segments wanting different combinations of features. Typically the firm (the manufacturer or the retailer) makes most of its profits on the expensive models and less on lower-priced models in a product line. Premium pricing occurs often for beer, clothing, appliances, and automobiles. Hewlett-Packard successfully competed with IBM for corporate data-center business by aggressively promoting its top-line models in its HP9000 series.[16]

Psychological pricing

Psychological pricing recognizes that buyer perceptions and beliefs affect their price evaluations. Prestige or premium pricing and comparing competitors' prices to a firm's lower sale prices deal with the psychological aspects of consumer reactions to prices. Odd-even pricing and customary pricing are other applications of psychological pricing.

Odd-even pricing

Odd-even pricing presents prices at values just below an even amount, a common practice. Instead of pricing contact lenses at $200, for example, the price is set at $199.95. The marketer intends for consumers to associate the price with the $100 to $200 range, assuming that demand for the contacts will be less at $200 than at $199.95. In addition, the precision associated with the $199.95 price implies a bargain.

Customary pricing

In the past, consumers associated a **customary price** with a product; but frequent price promotions and price increases have made this practice less prevalent today. The classic example of customary price is the much dated five-cent candy bar; today's customary price might be 50 cents. Customary price beliefs

Wrigley gum, now also manufactured and sold in China, positions its products worldwide as a low-priced treat. Wrigley uses customary pricing, still offering five sticks for 25 cents.

represent consumers' strongly held expectations. Pricing strategies that set customary prices typically modify the quality, feature, or service of a product without adjusting the price. The many versions of Swatch watches, for example, are often set at the customary price of $40.

Adapting prices

Determining a pricing strategy and setting prices are only the beginning. Prices change as competition occurs, and as the firm's marketing and production expertise improve. The firm must react to competitive price changes as well, constantly considering how often and how much to change prices. Price discounts and geographical pricing decisions also require marketers to adapt their prices.

Price decreases and increases

Firms often must reduce prices to generate sales. Sometimes, lowering price improves profits through higher sales. When market share is declining or excess production capacity exists, the firm may lower prices. This may stimulate demand and allow greater use of production or plant investments. Depressed economic conditions may also necessitate price reductions.

Price reductions, however, are risky. Competitive retaliation to price decreases is particularly important. Firms may encounter three "traps" in reducing prices:[17]

- *Low-quality trap*—Buyers may question the quality of low-priced products.
- *Fragile market share trap*—Price-sensitive buyers may switch to the next lower-priced product that comes along.
- *Shallow pockets trap*—Higher-priced competitors that reduce prices also may have longer staying power due to higher margins.

Price decreases may be implemented in several ways, with direct reductions from the original price most common. Firms may also reduce prices by offering quantity discounts or rebates. Bundling additional products or services with the basic product, while maintaining the current price, is another tactic.

OshKosh reduced prices 6 to 8 percent for its line of clothing recently. Compaq reduced prices for its top-of-the-line PC by 23 percent. Boeing effectively froze the prices for its commercial airliners.[18]

Price increases are also common. A primary reason is inflationary pressure; increases in the costs of inputs and production force prices upward. Also, when demand is great, firms often raise prices. Moreover, they may do so indirectly by reducing or eliminating quantity discounts, cash discounts for prompt payment, and trade allowances. Services once included with a product may be unbundled so the buyer actually receives less for the same price. In effect, these tactics enable firms to adjust real prices upward without raising list prices.

Both price increases and decreases must be noticeable to affect purchase decisions. For example, a reduction from $5.75 to $5.45 may not influence demand, while a reduction to $5.15 might be meaningful. Buyers have **price thresholds** for products; and they notice when prices go under or above those limits. Thresholds depend on the average price of the product. A 10-cent reduction on a $10 product, for example, differs from the same reduction on a 50-cent product.

Ranges of acceptable prices also exist. The **acceptable price range** includes prices buyers are willing to pay. Buyers may react negatively when prices move outside the acceptable range, above or below. Prices raised too high may exceed buyer budgets or be judged as unfair. Marketers that gouge buyers by charging excessively high prices are often publicly criticized. Prices reduced below the acceptable range generate concerns about product or service quality, the low-quality trap.[19]

Reacting to competitive price changes

Competitive pressures affect pricing decisions of retailers and companies that sell to other businesses. Price competition among retail marketers is particularly acute with the advent of Wal-Mart, grocery superstores, and club warehouses. Recently, Target ads accused Wal-Mart of using misleading pricing tactics. Price comparisons by large retailers are likely to intensify as Wal-Mart, Kmart, Target, and others run out of territories to conquer.[20]

Brand managers should react to competitive price changes case by case. If price decreases among competitors do not increase total market demand, then price competition can hurt all competitors. The firm must try to determine the purpose of its competitive price change, its likely duration, and the reaction of other competitors in the market.

If buyers make decisions on nonprice characteristics, a reactive price decrease to meet the competition may not be necessary. Competitors instead might try to compete on service, quality, and features. When competition is based largely on price, however, a price decrease to match the competition may be required.

Examples of competitive price reactions are easy to find even among the most well-known companies. Pressures to reduce prices have been particularly strong in the computer software market, where competitors have undercut rivals by as much as six times. IBM reacted to the success of Toshiba and Compaq in the PC notebook market, by aggressively promoting the capabilities of IBM's line and offering competitive prices. In a similar move, Apple reduced its base price by more than $1,000 to stimulate sales of notebook computers.[21] Hertz cut its car rental rates to match competition from Alamo Rent-A-Car and Budget. Hershey Foods was forced to match price reductions by M&M Mars.[22]

Price discounts and allowances

The actual price a customer pays may differ from the market or list price, perhaps because of discounts from the original price. Discounts, which take many forms, occur in consumer and reseller transactions. They include cash discounts, trade promotion allowances, and quantity discounts.

Marketers often offer *cash discounts* for prompt payment by retailers. For example, terms of payment may be "3/10, net 30," indicating that the full amount of purchase is due in 30 days with a 3 percent discount available if the customer pays the bill in 10 days.

General Mills targeted this trade ad to retail buyers. The ad emphasizes advertising support and price discounts that retailers can use to appeal to their customers.

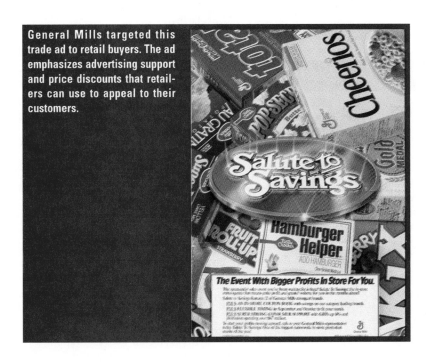

Trade sales promotion allowances are concessions a manufacturer pays or allocates to wholesalers or retailers to promote its products. The manufacturer or wholesaler may reduce prices on certain items so retailers can offer sale prices. Or the manufacturer may give additional marketing communications incentives to help the retailer pay for advertising. In fact, much of the newspaper advertising for grocery stores is actually supported by manufacturers' cooperative advertising payments.

Marketers give *quantity discounts* when the customer buys large quantities of a product. For example, full price might be charged for 500 or fewer reams of computer paper. For purchasing 501 to 1,000 reams, the customer receives a 3 percent discount per ream. For purchases over 1,000 reams, a 5 percent reduction off list price would be offered. A cumulative quantity discount entitles the purchaser to a larger discount as the sum of purchases within a specified time period, usually a year, exceeds a certain amount. Noncumulative quantity discounts apply to onetime purchases and are based on the size of the order.

Geographical pricing

Companies with geographically dispersed customers sometimes adjust prices because of costs resulting from distance. Shipping costs may be substantial and detract from profit if they are not included in the price. Marketers use geographical pricing approaches to address these issues.

One of the more commonly used methods is **FOB origin pricing.** FOB stands for free on board, meaning the goods are placed on a carrier (truck, train, barge) and shipped to the customer. FOB pricing requires customers to pay the unit cost of the goods plus shipping costs, which differ with location or market. An opposite strategy is to charge the same price and transportation charge to all customers. Using a **uniform delivered price,** the company charges each customer an average freight amount. A principal advantage of this method is ease of administration.

Zone pricing is an approach between FOB pricing and uniform delivered pricing. Customers within an area (say, the Northeast) are charged a common price. More distant zones or areas are charged higher freight amounts.

Freight absorption pricing is another form of geographical pricing. Here the seller absorbs freight costs—offers free or reduced costs of delivery—to attract more business. This practice occurs when competition among sellers is heavy.

Competitive bidding and negotiated pricing

In the US, retail prices for most consumer goods normally are not negotiable. However, outside the US, price negotiations for consumer goods occur regularly. Likewise, almost all business-to-business purchases are negotiated to some extent. In fact, many organizational buyers now view every aspect of their purchase transactions as negotiable. This trend exemplifies the *quality/value perspective* and the continuing search for lower prices and increased value. Negotiated pricing is the norm in marketing to the federal government, the largest purchaser of goods and services.

Sealed-bid pricing is unique in that the buyer determines the pricing approach and the eventual price. The buyer encourages sellers to submit sealed bids, or prices, for providing their products or services;[23] the sellers set prices on the basis of cost considerations and expectations about what competitors will bid.

Exhibit 13.8　　　**Alternative bid prices and expected values (in $000)**

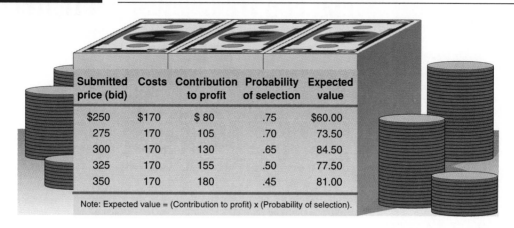

Submitted price (bid)	Costs	Contribution to profit	Probability of selection	Expected value
$250	$170	$ 80	.75	$60.00
275	170	105	.70	73.50
300	170	130	.65	84.50
325	170	155	.50	77.50
350	170	180	.45	81.00

Note: Expected value = (Contribution to profit) x (Probability of selection).

Sealed-bid pricing may be difficult for the seller. First, the seller must determine the costs involved in providing the product or service. And, as described in **The Entrepreneurial Spirit: Pricing to Cover Exporting Costs,** the firm must be careful to include hidden and unexpected costs. The seller must then set a price according to the prices it expects competing firms to submit. The price must cover costs, provide a reasonable return, and be low enough to be selected by the purchaser. Overall, the bidding company must be able to evaluate the chances of winning a particular contract at different prices; determine the profit potential under various bidding outcomes; and identify projects for which the expense of preparing and submitting a bid is economically justified.[24]

An example bidding situation is shown in Exhibit 13.8. This framework allows the seller to evaluate alternative bids in terms of the costs of the project, the contribution of each alternative to profits, and the probability of winning the job at each bid price. As the price or submitted bid increases, the probability of winning decreases.

Negotiated pricing is common for large investments, such as building or other installations, and for consulting arrangements, many professional services, or governmental work. Negotiation between vendor and supplier replaces evaluation of multiple bids. If these are long-term arrangements, or agreements likely to involve future negotiations, concern for developing and maintaining relationships is critical. In some smaller deals, sales reps may negotiate prices and margins for the company in the field on a transaction-by-transaction basis. Field salespeople can help identify situations when price quotes need to be more competitive to avoid losing profitable business.[25]

EXECUTIVE ROUNDTABLE COMMENT | **Gene Martin, director of marketing and economic development for UtilCorp United, Inc., points out that negotiated relationships are growing even for electric utility companies:**

Pricing options for large industrial customers are now negotiated based upon the nature of the customer's demand and their own operating processes. These negotiated arrangements are becoming increasingly important to our profitability. For example, we recently negotiated a special rate for one of our customers that purchases over $1 billion annually in electric services.

Pricing services

The unique characteristics of services—intangible, perishable, inseparable, and nonstandardized—make their pricing difficult. Price determination is influenced by the nature of the service involved. For professional services, such as those provided by attorneys and accountants, prices vary according to the complexity of the service and the amount of work or services provided. However, pricing decisions for services, as for tangible products, should consider expenses or costs involved with service delivery, price expectations of customers, management objectives of a reasonable return, and pricing for similar services by competitors.[26] Generally, the larger the share of the market held by a service provider, the higher the price it can charge relative to competition.

In some industries, pricing of services is extremely competitive. The airlines industry has wide differences in prices across markets, time periods, and competitors. The entry of competitive firms can influence prices dramatically. Recently, Morris Air, one of a handful of low-cost, low-fare airlines, forced Delta Airlines to cut its fares up to 80 percent and to offer double miles to frequent fliers in efforts to retain customers. Morris normally flies only short routes under 500 miles and offers no hot meals. Morris' discounted fares are more flexible than Delta's, and other large airlines'. In addition, prices are kept low by flying only Boeing 737s, which saves money on parts inventory and maintenance demands.[27]

Bundling of services into a single package and price is a common strategy. Hotels (lodging, meals), banks (large deposits yield free travelers' checks), physicians (exams, diagnostic tests), and airlines (travel, rental cars) are examples of services provided for a single bundle price.[28] Bundling increases demand by providing increased savings and convenience to the consumer.

Ethical issues and deceptive practices

Ethical problems associated with business pricing are not uncommon and are often the focus of much public scrutiny. A recent congressional investigation into the pricing practices of a national hospital company revealed significant bill padding. Patients were charged $44 for saline solutions (salt water) costing 81 cents and $103 for crutches costing $8.[29] Pharmaceutical companies have been cited for overpricing life-saving drugs, as in the case of AIDS vaccines.[30] Claims of price gouging have also been leveled against major airlines for their pricing during peak travel times or in geographic areas where a major carrier dominates. Following Hurricane Andrew, Florida's attorney general subpoenaed top plywood manufacturers for records justifying soaring prices. Evidence of profiteering and consumer gouging was found among sellers of batteries, chain saws, and flashlights. Similar accusations arose after the 1994 Los Angeles earthquake. In contrast, Home Depot, a national retailer of home building supplies, sold its products at cost immediately following Andrew.[31] Undoubtedly, Home Depot's positive response earned the company much goodwill.

FTC guidelines against deceptive pricing

Many advertised prices include comparison prices. These can enhance the attractiveness of the offer by making the price reduction appear lower than merely stating it alone. Comparison price advertising typically pairs the sale price with prices formerly charged by the retailer, competing retailer prices, or manufacturer-suggested prices.

Comparison price advertising is effective, and it provides useful information to the buyer. Unfortunately, the ease with which claims can be made and their influence on buyers increase the likelihood of deceptive pricing pratices. Federal Trade Commission (FTC) guidelines provide specific procedures for avoiding deceptive price advertising. The most common practices addressed by the guidelines include:[32]

- *Comparisons with former prices*—Prices claimed as former prices charged by the retailer ("Regularly $XX, Now Only $YY") must have been offered to the public on a regular basis for a "reasonable" period of time. Although sales are not required at the higher price, the former price must have been a genuine offer for some period.

- *Comparisons with other retailer prices*—When prices are said to be lower than those being charged by other retailers for the same merchandise in the advertiser's trade area, the advertised higher prices must be based on fact.

- *Comparisons with prices suggested by manufacturers or other nonretail distributors*—If prices are said to be reductions from the manufacturer's list price or suggested retail price, these comparison prices must correspond to the prices at which a substantial proportion of the product's sales are made.

Several years ago May Department Stores in Denver was cited by the attorney general of Colorado for "engaging in continuous and repeated patterns of deceptive price advertising and sales practices." Examples included houseware products "on sale" at the same sale prices for two years and luggage advertised as discounted from "regular" prices that never were May's prevailing prices and that were double the luggage prices for the same items charged by other local retailers.[33]

Bait and switch

Grocery stores and department stores advertise some brands at cost or near cost to attract consumers. These marketers hope that low-priced items or *loss leaders* will generate traffic and sales of other items in the store. A **bait and switch** occurs when the retailer advertises but does not actually offer a reasonable amount of the promoted product. If the product is not, or was not, actually available, consumers may trade up and buy a more expensive version of the advertised loss leader. This bait-and-switch practice is illegal and unethical.

Predatory pricing

In some instances, companies charge very low prices to drive competition from the market. Any losses incurred can be recouped later by charging higher monopoly prices once competition has been discouraged. This practice is called **predatory pricing.** A company that claims predatory pricing by a competitor must demonstrate that the low-priced firm, typically a larger firm, charges prices below its average total costs, with the *intent* to harm competitors.

Predatory pricing is difficult to prove in the courts, for juries are skeptical of these claims.[34] The company that sues must show not only that a rival firm prices below cost but also that it does so intending to raise prices later.

Unit pricing

The number of products, brands, and package sizes in the marketplace presents a bewildering array of choices. The potential to be misled or at least confused is likewise great. Many states have passed **unit pricing** legislation to help consumers

Unit pricing, shown here for Joan of Arc kidney beans, gives price information on a per-unit weight or volume basis to facilitate consumer price comparisons across brands and on sizes within brands.

process in-store price information. Unit pricing presents price information on a per-unit weight or volume basis to facilitate price comparisons across brands and across package sizes within brands. Unit pricing is intended to help low-income consumers and price-vigilant shoppers.[35] Although not an ethical issue per se, unit pricing is designed to improve consumer decision making and to reduce the potential for being misled or misinformed by the vast amount of in-store information.

Summary

1. *Discuss the interrelationships among price, demand, demand elasticity, and revenue.* Marketplace conditions influence prices. The higher the price of most goods or services, the lower the demand. These relationships are depicted in the familiar economic demand curve. The extent to which demand changes as price changes is the price elasticity of demand. Inelastic demand exists when a seller increases price and sees little decrease in sales. Demand is elastic when small changes in price cause large changes in the quantity demanded.

   The profit-maximizing price level is the point where total revenues minus total costs is highest. This point occurs at the price where marginal revenue equals marginal cost. This expression of profit maximization does not consider factors such as the seller's ability to influence demand through promotional activities.

2. *Understand methods for determining price.* Cost-oriented methods for determining price include markup pricing, where the price is set as a certain percentage increase above its cost; break-even analysis, which calculates the number of units required to be sold to cover costs at a certain price; and target-return pricing, where the price is set to provide some specific desired rate of return on investment. A competition orientation to determining price suggests firms charge prices similar to competitors' prices.

3. *Recognize the different pricing strategies and the conditions that best suit the choice of a strategy.* Four broad categories of pricing strategies are differential pricing, competitive pricing, product-line pricing, and psychological pricing.

   When differences exist across consumer segments, differential pricing is effective. Examples include second-market discounting, where different prices are charged to different segments, and periodic discounting.

   Competitive pricing includes penetration pricing, where a firm sets an initial low price to stimulate demand or deter competition, and price signaling, or offering a high price for a low-quality brand in hopes consumers will infer high quality.

   Product-line strategies are important for firms that sell a variety of brands of the same product, as the price set for one of the brands often affects sales of the entire product line. Some firms use bundling strategies, where separate products or services in a line are sold as a single bundle. Premium pricing, when the firm charges higher prices for deluxe brands within a product line, is most successful when market segments want different combinations of features. Psychological pricing includes the practice of odd-even pricing and customary pricing.

4. *Recognize the importance of adapting prices under shifting economic and competitive situations.* Prices are reduced under several circumstances: declining market share, changing customer preferences, or lower competitive prices. If competitors can easily detect price reductions and are willing to retaliate, price reductions are risky. Lowering prices may also affect consumer perceptions of quality, may work only until an even lower-priced product is available, and may be difficult to maintain in the presence of larger and stronger competitors.

   When products compete on attributes other than price (service, features), price changes in face of competitive price shifts may not be required. In homogenous markets, however, where products are similar and compete largely on price, price reductions by competitors will probably have to be matched. Inflation or excessive demand sometimes leads to price increases.

   For a price change to affect demand, the increase or decrease must exceed some minimal threshold so as to be noticeable. Buyers also have a range of acceptable prices. Prices reduced below the lowest acceptable price may generate perceptions of inferior quality; prices above the highest acceptable price will be rejected.

5. *Understand the ethical considerations involved in setting and communicating prices.* Ethical considerations are an issue in pricing decisions. Prices must not potentially mislead or take advantage of customers. The FTC offers guidelines that govern advertised price specials and comparison pricing. The most common aspects of comparison pricing governed by the FTC include comparisons with former prices, comparisons with other retail prices, and comparisons with prices suggested by manufacturers or distributors.

   Another unethical practice involves predatory pricing: pricing below average cost until competitors are forced out of the market. After driving out competitors, the firm raises its prices. Unit pricing is required in some states to provide information on prices on a per-unit or volume basis to enhance consumer decision making.

Key terms & concepts

demand curve 307
elastic demand 307
inelastic demand 307
cross elasticity of demand 308
fixed costs 308
variable costs 309
total costs 309
marginal costs 309
marginal revenue 309
total revenue 309
markup pricing 310
break-even analysis 312

target-return pricing 313
price sensitivity measurement
  (PSM) 314
differential pricing 315
second-market discounting 315
periodic discounting 316
competitive pricing strategies 317
limit pricing 317
price signaling 317
bundling 318
premium pricing 319
psychological pricing 319

odd-even pricing 319
customary price 319
price thresholds 320
acceptable price range 320
FOB origin pricing 322
uniform delivered price 322
zone pricing 322
freight absorption pricing 322
sealed-bid pricing 322
bait and switch 326
predatory pricing 326
unit pricing 326

Review & discussion questions

1. Define price elasticity, and explain its relationship to demand.

2. Briefly explain the steps that should be considered in determination of a price.

3. Why are pricing decisions so important, and why are these decisions becoming more difficult?

4. Refer to the situation faced by R&E Electronics, described in **The Entrepreneurial Spirit: Pricing to Cover Exporting Costs.** Why may pricing decisions involving international marketing be so problematic?

5. Contrast break-even analysis pricing with markup pricing. What are the shortcomings of each approach?

6. How might the pricing strategies for a line of low-calorie Chinese grocery items vary over time?

7. Contrast penetration pricing with price skimming.

8. Identify two examples of both pure price bundling and product bundling.

9. Consider **The Technological Edge: Pricing Your Service for Profits.** What will determine the prices charged by firms that provide accounting services to small businesses?

10. How does the Federal Trade Commission view reference claims for advertisements involving (a) former price comparisons and (b) comparisons with competing retailers?

Application exercises

1. Identify a new-brand entry in two different product categories. How do its prices compare with competing brands in each category? What factors might account for differences between prices within the categories?

2. Are the following practices ethical? Explain.
   a. John Doe is a retailer of brand X fountain pens, which cost him $5 each. His usual markup is 50 percent over cost or $7.50. Doe first offers the pens for $10, realizing he will be able to sell very few if any. This offer lasts for only a few days.

He then reduces the price to $7.50 and promotes as follows: "Terrific bargain: X Pens, Were $10, Now Only $7.50!"
   b. Retailer Doe advertises brand X pens as having "Retail Value $15, My Price $7.50," when only a few distant suburban outlets charge $15.

3. Explain why long-distance telephone suppliers charge different prices at different times of the day. Explain how the competition between AT&T and MCI influences their pricing behavior.

Case 13.1   *Sega versus Nintendo: A game of pricing technology*

In 1990, Nintendo held a 90 percent share of the US market for video game machines. Clearly, Nintendo held a dominant position in a lucrative and growing market that includes sales of both hardware and software. Led by

Thomas Kalinske, however, Tokyo-based Sega Enterprises cut drastically into Nintendo's position in just three years. Now, toy-retail analysts estimate Sega's market share at almost 50 percent, up from 7 percent in 1990. During that period, Sega's sales grew from $280 million to almost $1 billion in 1993, and Nintendo's market share dropped to around 50 percent.

What led to this dramatic turnaround? First, Sega's Japanese bosses let Kalinske and his top executives make decisions quickly and independently. Second, an integrated marketing communications plan supported by $250 million in 1993 was executed. This marketing effort included extensive advertising and product tie-ins with companies such as Coca-Cola and Lifesaver. Third, prices were slashed by 25 percent (around $50) and some of their best software was bundled with the basic machine. Consequently, market flexibility, heavy advertising and sales promotion, and aggressive pricing led to Sega's recent success.

Observers of the industry know that Nintendo will react. It plans to introduce an advanced machine in 1995. In technologically changing markets, firms like Sega and Nintendo must learn quickly and introduce new generations of machines. Interactive movie games and CD systems are also growing in popularity.

Questions:

1. Describe the role of price for the video machines and the software products that go with them.

2. What factors influence price determination for Sega? Is the demand faced by Sega for its basic machine elastic or inelastic?

3. Should Sega price its existing products the same in all markets? How might the introduction by Sega and Nintendo of new, technologically advanced products affect the prices of older existing products?

4. What should Nintendo do to combat Sega's successes?

Sources: "AT&T Goes Gaming," *AT&T Technology,* Summer 1993, pp. 18–19; Jonathan Durden, "To Get This Good Take a Look at New Media Angles," *Marketing,* November 25, 1993, p. 21; Kate Fitzgerald, "It's Game Time for the Sega Channel," *Advertising Age,* October 4, 1993, p. 28; Neil Gross and Richard Brandt, "Watch Out—Those Game Boys Are Growing Up," *Business Week,* November 22, 1993, p. 106; Nikhil Hutheesing, "Games Companies Play," *Forbes,* October 25, 1993, pp. 68–69; and Rick Tetzeli, "Videogames: Serious Fun," *Fortune,* December 27, 1993, pp. 110–16.

Case 13.2 — *Loctite: Securing a global grip*

Loctite Corp., the Hartford, Connecticut, maker and marketer of industrial sealants and adhesives used in manufacturing processes by other firms, has equity in companies in 24 countries, and its 1,000 products are sold in 80 nations. Loctite products are used in making motor vehicles, compact disc players, video cassette recorders, and other products. Because many of its customers produce with nonmetallic products, Loctite has developed adhesives for use on plastics, fiberglass, and ceramics.

Nearly 80 percent of Loctite's profits come from overseas sales. The company's growth strategy is to invest in developing nations and recently opened markets, ensuring a toehold in economies poised for rapid growth.

David Freeman president and chief operating officer, is optimistic that the North American Free Trade Agreement (NAFTA), the European Union (EU), the opening up of the Eastern bloc, and maybe China will give Loctite an even wider market to operate in. This global orientation is based on management's often-stated understanding that 95 percent of the world's population does not live in the United States.

Loctite's international strategy is straightforward. The company seeks local partners and gives them good margins that enable prices to be set at profitable levels. The company is patient in letting its subsidiaries develop. For

example, its Chinese operations took 10 years to turn a profit. Local managers make their own marketing and pricing decisions. Products are priced according to value in each of the company's markets. However, price decisions are subject to a wide variety of pricing situations, currency factors, and inflation rates in the numerous countries in which the company does business. In Brazil, for example, Loctite's subsidiary was subject to inflation over 1,000 percent during 1992.

Questions:

1. What cultural considerations must be considered in setting prices for Loctite's industrial products?

2. Despite the global recession in 1992, Loctite finished with growth in both sales and earnings. What strategies may have accounted for that success?

3. What are Loctite's major pricing objectives?

Sources: Bill Kelley, "Sticking to His Guns," *Sales & Marketing Management,* July 1993, pp. 54–57; Elizabeth S. Kiesche, "Loctite Secures a Grip in a Broader Market," CHEMICALWEEK, March 3, 1993, pp. 37, 40; Tim Smart, "Why Ignore 95% of the World's Market?" *Business Week,* October 23, 1992, p. 64; and *Managing through Recession,* Loctite Corporation 1992 annual report, p. 19.

PART

6

Marketing Channels
and Logistics

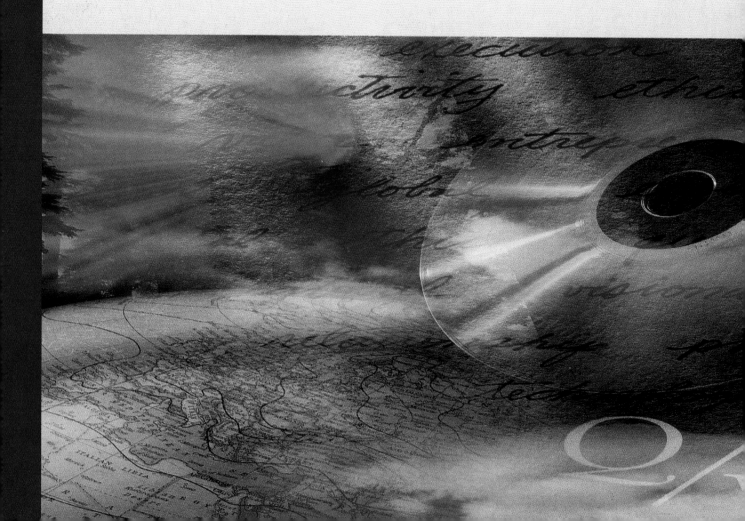

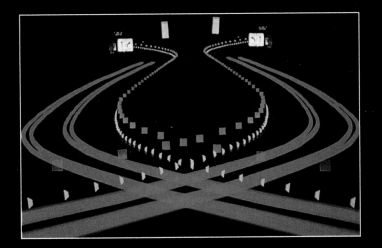

Because there are many ways to get there, marketing channels must be clearly chosen to ensure success.

The chapters in Part 6 deal with concepts, strategies, and tactics related to marketing channels and logistics. Chapter 14 provides an overview, explaining the functions and key activities of marketing channels. The role of channel intermediaries (wholesalers and retailers) is discussed. The relationship between channels and other marketing variables is illustrated in a discussion of the management of marketing channels. Chapter 15 examines retailing. Topics include types of retailers, trends in retailing, and retailing strategy. Chapter 16 considers wholesaling and logistics. It explains the functions and key activities of wholesaling and discusses how slow growth and globalization will affect wholesaling in the future. The discussion of logistics covers warehousing, materials handling, inventory control, order processing, and transporting. Ethical and legal issues are discussed in all three chapters of Part 6.

chapter 14

Marketing Channels

After studying this chapter you should be able to:

1. Explain the functions and key activities of marketing channels.

2. Discuss the role of intermediaries in marketing channels.

3. Distinguish between direct and indirect marketing channels.

4. Illustrate how some firms use multiple channels successfully.

5. See how marketing channel decisions are related to other key marketing decision variables.

6. Understand how power, conflict, and cooperation affect the operation of a marketing channel.

7. Give examples of ethical and legal issues encountered in the operations of marketing channels.

Lee Apparel Company: Lee's Riders on the move

*L*ee Apparel Company retailored its marketing approach to introduce the new Riders brand. Since the 1930s, Lee had used the "Rider" descriptor—as in Baggy Rider, Easy Rider, and Relaxed Rider. In the 1990s, however, Lee decided the time had come to split Lee Riders into two distinct brands. National chains would continue selling the Lee brand, and regional chains, including those based in Missouri (Venture), Wisconsin (ShopKo), Connecticut (Ames), and Massachusetts (Bradlees and Hills), would sell Riders.

The regional chains, though big-volume outlets, would no longer be allowed to carry the Lee brand. The basic problem was that while Lee's sales volume was growing with regional chains, it was declining with some of Lee's department store customers. Thus, Lee needed a strategy that could achieve growth in both distribution channels.

As expected, the regional retailers were upset at losing the Lee brand. Lee's director of advertising said, "When we initially told the regional retailers what we wanted to do, they were furious. In many cases, the Lee brand would bring customers into their stores, enhance the store image, and help to establish the value provided to their customers."

Lee carefully created Riders and a comprehensive marketing program to support it as an independent brand. Lee consulted regional retailers when formulating the program and convinced them that having a unique brand was in their best interest. The Riders brand has an identical fit to the Lee brand, but different pockets, finishes, and buttons. The packaging and labeling are different. A multimillion-dollar advertising effort, some of it done in cooperation with local stores, helped establish brand identity for Riders and build retail sales.

Lee supported both brands with its computerized Market Response System (MRS), which collects sales data at the retail checkout counter, then relays the information to Lee's manufacturing and shipping facilities. This allows Lee to replenish retailers' inventories quickly and minimize out-of-stock occurrences.

The MRS system is just one part of Lee's emphasis on relationships with customers and suppliers. Lawrence Pugh, president of Lee's parent company, VF Corp., says: "Adversarial relationships between retailers and manufacturers simply will not work. Partnerships are a necessity for the future." For Lee, this approach has resulted in healthy sales increases and ambitious plans to expand international sales efforts.

Sources: Beth Heitzman, "Lee's New Riders to Arrive in a Local Market Near You, *"Adweek,"* July 5, 1993, p. 2; Rosemary Cofasso, "Jean Genies," *Computerworld,* June 14, 1993, pp. 99–102; and Joseph Antonini and Lawrence R. Pugh, "Strategic Partnering," *Retail Business Review,* August 1992, pp. 4–10.

The Lee Riders example introduces several issues of interest in this chapter. First, the right product produced at the right time must be matched with the right means of distributing it to the marketplace. Second, the right means of distribution often changes over time. As Lee expanded its product offerings, regional retailers were dropped as sellers of the Lee brand, but chosen for the new Riders brand.

The Lee Riders scenario also reminds us that cooperation among different organizations can overcome ill feelings and help the marketing effort. Lee supports the retail sales effort with national advertising and by sharing advertising expenses with retailers in their local markets. The company further supports retailers with its MRS program, made possible with the latest communications technology.

In this chapter, we explore the **marketing channel,** or channel of distribution, defined as a combination of organizations and individuals (channel members) who perform the required activities to link producers of products to users of those products to accomplish marketing objectives.[1] In thinking about marketing channels, keep in mind that "products" can be goods, services, or ideas. Producers could be manufacturers, service organizations, or idea-generating groups or companies. Some alternative consumer and business-to-business channels are shown in Exhibit 14.1.

Different types of marketing channels require the services of **intermediaries,** often referred to as *middlemen,* which are directly involved in the purchase or sale of products as they flow from the originator to the user. Intermediaries include retailers, which sell to ultimate consumers, and wholesalers, which sell to retailers, other wholesalers, government buyers, manufacturers, and other business customers. Retailers and wholesalers are discussed in detail in subsequent chapters.

We introduce various types of marketing channels in this chapter. Some companies, such as Burger King, reach their customers through franchising. Computer producers, such as Tandy, may sell through their own retail stores (Radio Shack); others, such as Dell and Gateway, sell directly to the consumer via mail order. Decisions on marketing channels are prime elements in a firm's overall marketing strategy and a factor in pricing, product, and marketing communications considerations.

Importance of marketing channels

Since marketing channels determine how and where customers buy, the establishment of and any subsequent change in channels is indeed critical. Other marketing variables can be manipulated frequently, and changes are often easy

---

Exhibit 14.1	**Consumer and business-to-business marketing channels**

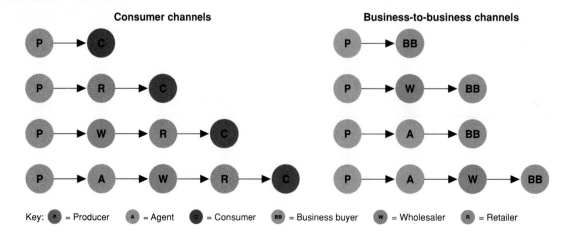

Key: (P) = Producer   (A) = Agent   (C) = Consumer   (BB) = Business buyer   (W) = Wholesaler   (R) = Retailer

to make. Marketers can raise and lower prices, vary advertising media and messages, and add and delete products from their market offerings without revolutionizing the way they do business.

Making major changes in marketing channels is not so easy. Marketing channels are harder to change because other parties, such as retailers and wholesalers, may play important roles in the channel. Royal Appliance, for example, receives 53 percent of its sales volume from only five retailers, of which 27 percent comes from Wal-Mart and 16 percent from Kmart.[2] Where would Royal Appliance make up the lost volume if the company decided not to sell through Kmart and Wal-Mart? Royal would require a marketing miracle to sell as many appliances without those two retailers.

Marketers are sometimes bound to their channels when significant sunk costs are involved. For example, McDonald's franchise system and company-owned outlets such as Exxon's convenience stores represent huge dollar investments. Such investments are made only after much forethought, and abandoning them is the last resort. For these reasons, marketing channels take on more of a sense of permanence—change is certainly an option, but one that is not so likely to be frequently exercised as with other marketing variables.

Functions of marketing channels

By performing five critical functions, marketing channels play an important role in accomplishing the key marketing activities discussed in Chapter 1 (Exhibit 1.5). These functions, shown in Exhibit 14.2, include the management of marketing communications, inventory, physical distribution, market feedback, and financial risk. It is important to note that none of these functions can be eliminated, but they can be shifted from one channel member to another.

Marketing communications

Channel members are frequently involved in marketing communications activities, which include advertising and public relations, sales promotion, personal selling, and direct marketing communications. Home Depot, for example, a

Exhibit 14.2   **Key functions performed in marketing channels**

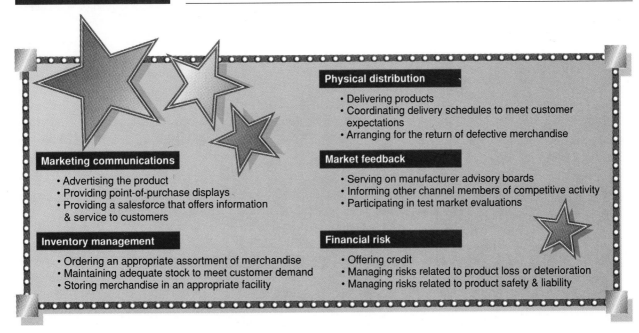

Physical distribution
- Delivering products
- Coordinating delivery schedules to meet customer expectations
- Arranging for the return of defective merchandise

Market feedback
- Serving on manufacturer advisory boards
- Informing other channel members of competitive activity
- Participating in test market evaluations

Financial risk
- Offering credit
- Managing risks related to product loss or deterioration
- Managing risks related to product safety & liability

Marketing communications
- Advertising the product
- Providing point-of-purchase displays
- Providing a salesforce that offers information & service to customers

Inventory management
- Ordering an appropriate assortment of merchandise
- Maintaining adequate stock to meet customer demand
- Storing merchandise in an appropriate facility

Personal touch pays off

*I*n the 1980s, Brenda French's French Rags label sold about $10 million (wholesale price) in upscale apparel through leading department stores such as Neiman Marcus, Bonwit Teller, and Bloomingdales. Yet, Ms. French was not happy with her chosen marketing channel.

A lack of personal selling attention in the large stores, along with dissatisfaction with how much of the profit went to the retailer, led to a withdrawal from the department store channel. French set up a direct salesforce of 45 women in high-income locales such as Grosse Pointe, Michigan, Kenilworth, Illinois, and Pasadena, California. These women show the French Rags line in their homes four times a year, mostly to friends and social contacts. They are paid a 15 percent commission.

Brenda French sells half as much now as she did through department stores, but makes more money with the new channel. French Rags now earns about $750,000 per year in net profit, compared to $200,000 per year in the past.

Source: Damon Darlin, "Rags to Riches," *Forbes,* March 28, 1994, p. 108.

leading retailer of home improvement products, demonstrates an *execution perspective* as it aggressively advertises and provides a trained sales staff to assist customers. Home Depot also uses in-store displays to demonstrate the mechanics of various home improvement projects such as building decks or installing ceiling fans. The importance to a producer of a marketing channel that provides adequate marketing communications support is seen in **The Entrepreneurial Spirit: Personal Touch Pays Off.**

Inventory management

Marketing channel members sometimes provide inventory management functions. For example, auto parts wholesalers must stock thousands of products, many of which sell for under a dollar each, to be a competitive supplier to the independent repair shop market. In contrast, a Corvette-only parts wholesaler may stock fewer products but offer virtually every part available for repairing Corvettes of all vintages.

Physical distribution

The actual movement of products and other physical distribution activities are important elements in a marketing channel. For example, it is not unusual for suppliers of raw materials and components to a high-volume, fast-paced manufacturing plant to be given windows of only a few minutes to make deliveries. The coordination of delivery times is thus a major issue in meeting customer expectations, and suppliers who cannot meet such operating demands will lose business.

Market feedback

The *relationship perspective* is illustrated when channel members provide valuable information to other channel members, leading to better performance in the channel. One company that uses feedback from its intermediaries is Specialized Bicycle Components, a California mountain-bike manufacturer.[3] Specialized decided to cut its product line from 40 to 26 models on the basis of input from a meeting with 15 of its dealers. Dealer assessments such as "the fluorescent colors don't match Specialized's image" were taken seriously. Such feedback can be invaluable. Specialized, which paid more than $800 per dealer to hold the meeting, considered this approach a good investment.

Financial risk

The last function performed in marketing channels relates to ownership of the products passing through the channel. With ownership, or taking title, come various forms of risk. Perishable products may deteriorate. Thefts may occur. Or nature may deal out a flood, fire, or some other disaster.

Another risk involves accounts receivable: who gets stuck if the customer doesn't pay the bill? For example, suppliers to Zale Corporation, a jewelry retailer, took a great risk in extending credit when Zale's sales volume, and thus cash flow, dropped significantly in the early 1990s. When Zale announced plans to close 500 stores in early 1992 and declared bankruptcy shortly thereafter, its suppliers lost at least 500 retail distribution outlets.[4] Their losses will take years to tabulate, and will depend on whether or not Zale, no longer protected by bankruptcy court, can settle its debts.[5]

The assumption of risk is part of the quest to make a profit. It is an essential part of the job for members of any marketing channel.

Contributions of intermediaries

It can be fashionable to rail about the perverse influence of channel intermediaries, or middlemen. Wholesalers and retailers in the grocery industry are sometimes portrayed as antiheroes, for example, while the farmer may be seen as the economic victim.

Those who take these views typically feel that intermediaries reap unfair profits. It is true that short-term imbalances in the economic system may allow opportunistic retailers and wholesalers to capture largely unearned windfall profits. For example, hotels may inflate prices for rooms, food, and beverages to maximize profits from a captive market, say, fans attending the Super Bowl.

In the long run, however, intermediaries must justify their existence on economic and societal terms to survive. An intermediary must be able to perform some marketing channel activity better than any other channel member. For example, Spiegel, Inc., a major intermediary for apparel and home furnishings manufacturers, has a catalog division and more than 275 stores in the US. Spiegel provides a wide range of marketing channel activities to boost sales in its stores, including sales and advertising support, store displays, inventory ordering and storage, delivery, and consumer credit. Manufacturers such as Sony, RCA, Calvin Klein, and Reebok benefit from the channel activities of Spiegel and other retailers. Without retail intermediaries, these manufacturers would

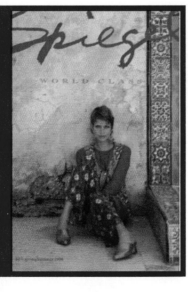

A retail intermediary, Spiegel performs a wide range of marketing channel functions, including advertising, selling, managing inventory, delivering merchandise, providing feedback to suppliers, and assuming financial risk.

have to build their own stores or sell directly to consumers through catalogs or some other means. If they could market more effectively and efficiently without Spiegel, good business sense says they would do so. Obviously, Spiegel is performing some of the marketing channel functions better than the manufacturers could.

Justifying their existence is painfully necessary for intermediaries in the highly competitive grocery products industry. Large supermarket chains following the *productivity perspective* continue to move away from independent wholesalers to their own distribution networks in an effort to control costs and improve product availability. In the early 1990s, for example, Fleming companies, the nation's largest food wholesaler, lost $700 million in sales volume when it was dropped by regional grocery chains such as Raley's and Albertson's.[6]

In the vast majority of cases, intermediaries are not profiteering parasites; they are simply businesses trying to compete by adding value to the market offering. Given far-flung global markets, intense competition, and specialized support services, intermediaries are likely to remain integral in most marketing channels.

EXECUTIVE ROUNDTABLE COMMENT | **Dave Moore, vice president of sales for Ruddell and Associates, Inc., a San Francisco–based wholesaler, indicates the importance of the *productivity perspective* as it relates to the use of intermediaries:**

Look at the cost of the alternatives. In the gift industry, roughly 98 percent of the 3,000 suppliers use the services of intermediaries, that is, independent manufacturers' reps to sell to retailers. Why? Because suppliers can gain distribution with manufacturers' reps for a lot less than the costs of having their own salesforces. Suppliers are well aware they have less control with independent reps, but most cannot afford to sink dollars into their own company salesforces.

Types of marketing channels

The major alternatives available for structuring a marketing channel include direct and indirect channels, single and multiple marketing channels, and vertical marketing systems.

Direct and indirect marketing channels

A marketing channel may be direct or indirect. A **direct channel** describes movement of the product from the producer to the user without intermediaries. An **indirect channel** requires intermediaries between the originator and the user to perform some functions related to buying or selling the product to make it available to the final user. A given company might employ both direct and indirect channels.

Direct channels

Direct channels frequently occur in the marketing of medical and professional services, where the use of an intermediary is often impractical. Direct channels are also frequently used in business-to-business markets, where production equipment, components, and subassembly manufacturers sell directly to finished-product manufacturers. Exhibit 14.3 gives some examples of direct marketing channels.

Some of the more spectacular marketing success stories come out of companies using direct channels of distribution. Dell Computer Corporation, a great example of the *entrepreneurial perspective,* sells over 75 percent of its products directly to consumers. Dell earned the coveted industrywide top spot in the

| Exhibit 14.3 | Companies using direct marketing channels |

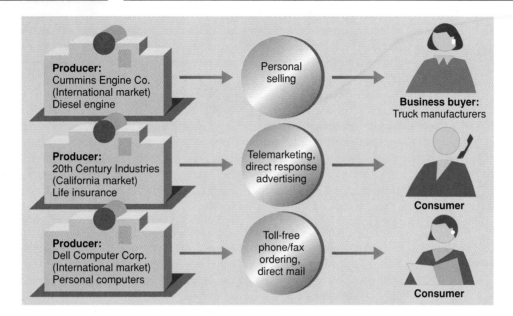

1993 J. D. Power & Associates customer satisfaction survey; its founder was dubbed entrepreneur of the year by *Inc.* magazine.[7] In less than a decade since its founding, Dell reached sales of nearly $3 billion. According to Dell, its "direct-relationship marketing approach" provides better value than traditional channels, such as retail stores.[8]

Direct channels can also be used to market services. Some insurance companies, such as California's 20th Century Industries, have dispensed with selling through agents and now sell directly to consumers. This eliminates the agent's commissions, which usually run about 15 percent of the policy's premium, and minimizes selling costs. 20th Century has been highly successful at selling low-cost insurance.[9]

Cummins Engine Company successfully uses direct channels in business-to-business markets. Cummins's salespeople must be knowledgeable about maintenance costs, engine operating costs, and other technical data to effectively sell directly to truck manufacturers such as Chrysler, Navistar, Kenworth, and Volvo-GM.[10]

Most consumers buy houses in an indirect marketing channel with the assistance of a real estate agent. Others may buy in a direct channel from producers such as Rocky Mountain Log Homes.

Indirect channels

Despite the increasing popularity of direct channels, most consumer purchases (homes, automobiles, groceries, appliances, clothing) are still made in an indirect marketing channel, where there is some intermediary between the producer and the end-user. Indirect channels are also important in some business-to-business settings.

Two examples of indirect marketing channels are shown in Exhibit 14.4. Orgill Brothers, one of the world's largest hardware wholesalers, is an important intermediary for thousands of manufacturers who want to reach small- and medium-sized retail hardware stores. It would not be economically feasible for most manufacturers to provide the sales support to individual hardware stores that Orgill Brothers provides. Example B is Beecham Products, which uses indirect channels to sell to ultimate consumers through retail intermediaries.

Single and multiple marketing channels

Some companies use a **single-channel strategy** to reach their customers; others rely on a **multiple-channels strategy.** Some companies with multiple products or brands may use a single-channel strategy in one situation and a multiple-channels strategy in another. A single-channel strategy is described as using only one means of reaching customers. Nexxus shampoo is distributed exclusively through hair care professionals, an example of a single-channel strategy. Prell shampoo, widely available at discount, drug, and grocery stores, is a product distributed through multiple channels. Liz Claiborne uses a multiple-channels strategy to reach different market segments. Its 16 Elisabeth stores serve large-size customers; 39 First Issue stores sell a full product line under the First Issue label; and 55 outlet stores market unsold inventory from past seasons. Liz Claiborne merchandise is also widely distributed in department and specialty stores.

As markets become increasingly fragmented, more firms use a multiple-channels strategy to appeal to as many potential buyers as possible. The basic idea is to allow customers to buy the way they want to and where they want to.

Exhibit 14.4	**Examples of indirect channels**

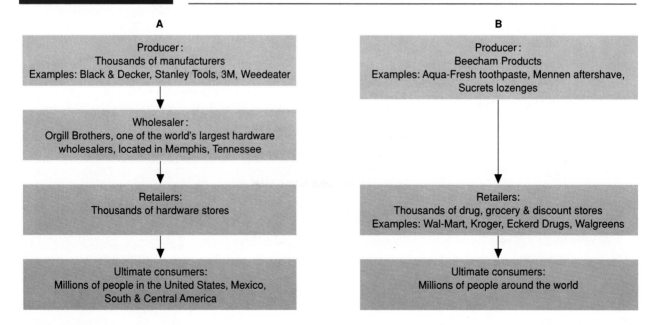

EXECUTIVE ROUNDTABLE COMMENT | **Dave Moore, vice president of sales for Ruddell and Associates, Inc., offers these thoughts on multiple channels:**

Mass-market operators such as Safeway and Raley's in northern California are gobbling up the lion's share of sales increases in the gift and greeting card industry. A manufacturer simply cannot be content to sell only through traditional channels (card and gift shops, specialty stores, independent pharmacies). The use of multiple channels is becoming the rule, not the exception. For most manufacturers, multiple channels are necessary for survival.

Vertical marketing systems

The *relationship perspective* recognizes the importance of strong bonds with other members of the marketing channel and teamwork within the company. Emphasis on this perspective has contributed to the growth of vertical marketing systems. These systems are centrally coordinated, highly integrated operations that work together to serve the ultimate consumer. The word *vertical* refers to the flow of the product from the producer to the customer. This flow is usually thought of as "down the channel" or "downstream," meaning that the product flows down from the producer to the customer.

Vertical marketing systems are now used in a sizable majority of the total sales of consumer goods. Exhibit 14.5 gives examples of the three basic types of vertical marketing systems: corporate, contractual, and administered channel systems.[11]

Corporate channel systems

Vertical coordination in a corporate channel system is achieved through ownership of two or more channel members on different levels of distribution. A corporate channel system in which one channel member owns one or more of its buyers downstream is called **forward integration.** Some of the companies that have used forward integration to open their own stores are Polo, Espirit, and Laura Ashley.

Business-to-business marketers also use forward integration. For example, Gulf States Paper Corporation, a manufacturer of assorted food service products such as paper plates, bowls, and serving trays, owns a chain of wholesale paper distributors in the southeastern United States.

| *Exhibit 14.5* | **Types of vertical marketing systems** |

Channel systems

Corporate
Forward integration:
  Polo, Laura Ashley, Gulf States
  Paper Corp.
Backward integration:
  Winn-Dixie grocery chain
Description
One channel member owns
one or more other channel
members

Contractual
Wholesaler-sponsored voluntary groups:
  Ace Hardware, Western Auto
Retailer-sponsored cooperative groups:
  Affiliated Grocers, Cotter & Company
  (True Value Hardware)
Franchise systems:
  McDonald's, Holiday Inns, Personnel
  Pool of America
Description
Channel members operate according to
contractual agreement

Administered
Abbott Labs, General Electric, Rolex
Description
Channel members operate
according to agreed-upon plan

S. C. Fang Brothers, a Hong Kong–based manufacturer, used forward integration in its marketing channel by opening its own Episode stores in the United States.

Other companies attempt to improve the efficiency and effectiveness of their marketing channels through ownership of one or more of their suppliers, not their buyers. This practice is called **backward integration.** The Winn-Dixie grocery store chain, for example, acquired its own cattle farms, coffee plantations, and ice cream manufacturing facilities for better control of the price and availability of key food products.

The global integration of marketing channels allows companies to take advantage of the strengths of various countries or regions of the world to maximize marketing efforts. For example, a company might manufacture its products in low-wage countries and use forward integration to establish retail distribution in more lucrative markets. This has been the channel strategy used by S. C. Fang Brothers, a Hong Kong textile manufacturing firm with a global sales base of more than $450 million. Fang Brothers was successful making T-shirts for The Gap and blouses for Calvin Klein, but it saw another retail opportunity. The company seized that opportunity in the late 1980s when it opened Episode stores in the United States. By 1996, Fang Brothers expects to operate 50 stores in the US and another 100 in Europe and Asia.[12]

Contractual channel systems

Contractual systems may allow some channel members to gain clout in the marketplace and compete effectively with large corporate systems. Coordination between independent firms is achieved through contractual agreements rather than through ownership of channel members upstream or downstream. In this way, contractual channel members try to improve their buying power, gain economies of scale, and realize greater efficiencies through the standardization of operating procedures. The three primary types of contractual channels are wholesaler-sponsored voluntary groups, retailer-owned cooperative groups, and franchise systems.

Wholesaler-sponsored voluntary groups consist of independent retailers that operate under the name of a sponsoring wholesaler. Examples of wholesaler-sponsored voluntary groups are Ace Hardware and Western Auto. The wholesaler (Ace Hardware) buys in quantity, makes deliveries to the individual stores, and offers a variety of services that benefit its retailers. These services may

| Exhibit 14.6 | Nonretail franchise channel systems |

Franchisor
Personnel Pool of America
Professional Polish, Inc.
Signs Now
Norrell Temporary Services
Jani-King
Padgett Business Services
Exectrain
TempForce
Voice-Tel
Dynamic Air Freight
Tempaco

Business category
Employment/personnel
Maintenance/sanitation
Business signs
Employment/personnel
Maintenance/sanitation
Accounting/credit/collections
Personal development/training
Employment/personnel
Voice messaging centers
Freight forwarding
Wholesaler

include merchandising, advertising, and pricing support based on quantities purchased. Ace Hardware retailers buy most of their merchandise from the group wholesaler and pool their funds for advertising.

Retailer-owned cooperative groups operate like wholesaler-sponsored voluntary groups, but the retailers actually own the wholesaler. Affiliated Grocers and Cotter & Company's True Value are two well-known examples of this type of system.

The third type of contractual channel system is the **franchise system.** One party, the **franchisor,** grants another party, the **franchisee,** the right to distribute and sell specified goods and services. The franchisee agrees to operate according to marketing guidelines set forth by the franchisor under a recognized trademark or trade name.

Franchise systems have been responsible for the growth of some of the most recognizable names in the business world, such as McDonald's and Holiday Inns. Nonretail franchise operations are also prominent, with companies such as Snelling & Snelling and Kelly Girls in the personnel placement business and the Coca-Cola bottlers at the wholesale level. Exhibit 14.6 lists some other examples of nonretail franchise organizations. Retail franchising is discussed in more detail in Chapter 15.

Administered channel systems

A system designed to control a line or classification of merchandise is called an **administered channel system.** Here, channel members agree on a comprehensive noncontractual plan, and no channel member owns another. The parties in an administered system may work very closely to reduce joint operating costs for advertising, data processing, inventory control, order entry, or delivery schedules.

  One example of an administered channel system is Abbott Lab's "physical and transactional" distribution to hospitals of products produced by several collaborative channel members.[13] Abbott provides bandaging materials and adhesives from 3M, urological products from C. R. Bard, and nonwoven disposable

Exhibit 14.7   **Managing marketing channels**

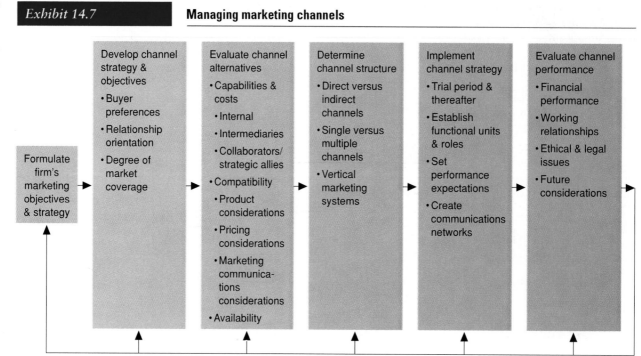

diapers and bedding materials from Kimberly Clark. The system integrates delivery, invoicing, and many other activities related to meeting the high expectations of the demanding hospital market.

In the retail sector, successful administered marketing channels include General Electric and Rolex. Both companies have reputations for quality products backed by highly effective marketing plans and activities. As a result, retailers are usually quite receptive to suggestions made by General Electric and Rolex for pricing and display practices.

Managing marketing channels

The management of marketing channels requires decision making and action in the six areas shown in Exhibit 14.7. First, the firm formulates its marketing objectives and strategy. Only then can managers develop marketing channel strategies and objectives. Various channel alternatives are then evaluated to determine capabilities, costs, compatibility with other marketing variables, and their availability to the firm. Next, the firm establishes its channel structure and implements the channel strategy. Finally, the firm must constantly evaluate channel performance—which may lead to adjustment in one or more of the other five management areas shown in the exhibit.

Formulate marketing objectives and strategy

Marketing channels often represent a significant dollar investment, and established channels can be difficult to change without risking lost sales volume. As a result, it is imperative that a firm develop marketing channel objectives and strategy only after formulating its overall marketing objectives and strategy. Famous Amos Chocolate Chip Cookie Company follows a marketing strategy that avoids direct confrontation with major brands like Nabisco and Keebler. The company does not advertise and sells through warehouse clubs and vending

The benefits of a *relationship perspective* can extend beyond economic advantage to the promotion of socially desirable results. For example, grocery retailer Kroger has an active program to develop close partnerships with minority suppliers.

EXCELLENCE THROUGH PARTNERSHIP & COMMITMENT

The Kroger Company's commitment to strengthen and support ties with present minority suppliers, and also establish partnerships with new minority owned firms is a very important part of our corporate mission.

Kroger will showcase this commitment to minority enterprise development at this year's MINORITY MARKET PLACE in Memphis, Tennessee.

We invite you to open the doors to one of the Nation's largest supermarkets and seek the possibility of developing future business opportunities.

Pictured (left to right): GEORGE DOBBINS, Owner, New Rise Products, Inc.; Chuck Shaffer, Merchandiser, The Kroger Co.; James Short, Buyer, The Kroger Co.

Kroger

rather than through the dominant channel, grocery chains. In this instance, the selection of the channel supports the overall marketing strategy—the company's 1992 sales were twice those of 1991.[14]

Develop channel objectives and strategy

Channel objectives should be specifically stated, measurable, and consistent with the firm's marketing objectives. Objectives are often stated in terms of sales volume, profitability, market share, costs, number of wholesale or retail outlets, or geographic expansion. Channel strategy then is an expression of a general action plan and guidelines for allocating resources to achieve the channel objective.

The development of channel strategy involves decisions in three key areas: buyer preferences, relationship orientation, and the degree of market coverage.

Buyer preferences

Buyer preferences are important in determining channel strategy. Understanding the logic behind letting customers buy the way they want to is a hallmark of both established marketing leaders and entrepreneurs who beat the odds by breaking into long-established markets. For example, Mike Williams, an Indiana distributor with a *visionary perspective,* has built a booming business selling seed corn via direct mail to part-time farmers, the fastest-growing segment of the farm market. Williams learned that part-time farmers don't like to buy through the traditional channel of agricultural dealers, primarily because they do not have time to talk to salespeople.[15]

Relationship orientation

Most successful organizations try to establish strong relationships with others in their channel—not only because it is profitable in the long run, but also because they believe that to do otherwise would be risky. That retailers and their suppliers understand the importance of catering to other channel members was reflected in a meeting of the Promotion Marketing Association of America. Among the comments from industry leaders: "End the cold war; turn away wrath, and work together to make the decade progressive and prosperous; marketers hoping to build relationships . . . should spend less time on their own promotions and ask how they can help with retailers."[16]

EXECUTIVE ROUNDTABLE COMMENT | **Dave Moore, vice president of sales for Ruddell and Associates, Inc., emphasizes the importance of the _relationship perspective_:**

Retailers in the gift industry are truly looking for partners in their business operations. They have a critical need to be linked with suppliers that can help manage significant footage in their stores and suggest meaningful ways to improve profitability. In the past, we could sell retailers on the basis of "this is hot." Those days are history—today we sell on return per linear foot, inventory turn rate, and annualized sales revenues.

Degree of market coverage

Market coverage has to do with the number of outlets used to market a product. Market coverage commonly takes one of three forms: intensive, selective, or exclusive distribution. With **intensive distribution,** the product or service is distributed through every available outlet. For example, PepsiCo has long used intensive distribution with its soft drinks, selling through all sorts of retail stores, vending machines, restaurants, and concessionaires. The company is now increasing the intensity of distribution for its fast-food companies—Taco Bell, Kentucky Fried Chicken, and Pizza Hut. All three have opened outlets in supermarkets to attract hungry shoppers.[17]

Selective distribution involves selling a product in only some of the available outlets. This is commonly used when after-the-sale service is necessary, as with home appliances. Maytag, for example, sells appliances via selective distribution, and the company is even more selective in designating certain dealers as authorized service centers. In a metropolitan area of a million residents, Maytag products might be sold through a dozen retail stores, only two or three of which are designated as authorized service centers.

Exclusive distribution occurs when only one outlet is used in a geographic marketplace. Honda's Acura division uses exclusive distribution to create distinctive dealerships for its upscale automobiles. At the wholesale level, personal computer manufacturers such as Compaq and AST Research often use this strategy in Western Europe. In certain countries, most computer distributors enjoy exclusive rights to sell the product. In return, each distributor typically handles all marketing activities for a computer manufacturer.[18]

Evaluate channel alternatives

As shown in Exhibit 14.7, the evaluation of channel alternatives requires analysis in three related channel areas: capabilities and costs, channel compatibility with other marketing variables, and availability.

Channel capabilities and costs

Marketers must determine exactly who will perform the various channel activities and at what cost. Establishing marketing channels can be expensive and difficult to reverse, so firms should carefully assess the costs and capabilities of each channel alternative.

General Mills and Nestlé are strategic allies outside the US and Canada. Nestlé provides the corporate name on the box, access to retailers, and the production capacity; General Mills provides the experience in cereal technology, its line of well-known brands, and its sophistication in marketing cereals to consumers.

The evaluation of channel alternatives often begins with an assessment of how the firm's internal resources might be used to accomplish channel activities. This naturally leads to subsequent examination of how intermediaries could fit in, if at all. Sometimes, firms join forces with others in the channel. For example, Nestlé, with long-standing experience in international markets, joined with General Mills to sell Cheerios in markets outside North America. Seiko's distribution partner in Japan handles Schick razors there and has become a market leader.[19]

Channel compatibility

Channel alternatives need to be compatible with other marketing variables affecting a firm's offering, including product, pricing, and marketing communications factors. For example, product perishability, consumer sensitivity to purchase price, and the nature of point-of-sale promotion could affect the compatibility of a particular marketing channel. Research suggests that channel variables such as amount and kind of shelf space and feature displays may interact with both price and perceived quality to affect purchase intentions or sales volume.[20]

Product considerations. A product-related consideration is the product's desired image. Consider the case of OshKosh B'Gosh Inc. OshKosh, a maker of children's clothing, traditionally relied on expensive department stores and specialty stores for retail distribution, in keeping with its high-quality image. In recent years, however, OshKosh expanded into Sears and J. C. Penney stores. The company made this decision after carefully analyzing how such a move would affect its image and, subsequently, sales in upscale department stores where image is important.

OshKosh hopes to avoid problems with the upscale department stores by offering them exclusive, higher-profit items such as a novelty denim line.[21] OshKosh is trying to minimize a possible product/channel incompatibility by differentiating its product offerings to two different types of retail customers.

To protect its high-quality image after expanding sales to Sears and J. C. Penney, OshKosh offered upscale department stores exclusive, profitable merchandise.

Pricing considerations.   Which marketing channels are appropriate can also depend on pricing strategies and tactics. One company that matches its marketing channel with its pricing strategy is Pitney Bowes, seller of high-end fax machines. Most fax machines are sold through discount office and general merchandise stores. Pitney Bowes, demonstrating an *execution perspective,* is careful to avoid the intense price competition in these outlets, targets the business user, and sells through a direct salesforce backed by a strong service network. The strategy works, for Pitney Bowes has captured almost half the fax market in large corporations.[22]

Marketing communications considerations.   Compatibility with marketing communications plans and strategies also determines the suitability of various marketing channels. Sony, in an attempt to showcase its full product line better, supplements its independent dealer network with its own Sony Gallery of Consumer Electronics in Chicago, New York, and Los Angeles.[23]

Reebok now sells directly to colleges and high schools while continuing to sell through its traditional retail channel.[24] Reebok took this action to address a lack of representation among American basketball players, a market dominated by Nike.

Availability

Another important issue in the evaluation of various channel alternatives is whether the channel is available under reasonable conditions. Quite often, new companies may have a hard time establishing an appropriate marketing channel. The right channel may simply be unavailable, or the desired channel is too expensive.

For large, powerful sellers, channel availability is less of a problem. Indeed, a firm with the financial wherewithal can simply purchase a channel of distribution. Such is the case with Nestlé SA, which followed a *global perspective* in acquiring Source Perrier SA. Perrier, the world's leading seller of mineral water, has long been established in the home-delivery market, a channel that Nestlé can now use to sell some of its products. In the US, Nestlé products that might be sold through the Perrier home-delivery network include coffee, milk, chocolate, and frozen foods.[25]

Determine channel structure

The fourth phase of managing marketing channels shown in Exhibit 14.7 is to determine channel structure. The major decisions here concern whether to use direct or indirect channels, a single channel or multiple channels, or one of the many forms of vertical marketing systems. Firms often mix direct and indirect channels, and many firms use multiple channels, especially to reach new markets.

Implement channel strategy

The first four phases of managing marketing channels concentrate on planning the appropriate channel strategy and structure. In the next phase, the *execution perspective* is the key, as the task now is to implement channel strategy. The full-scale implementation of a new channel strategy is often preceded by a trial period. Other important implementation tasks include setting performance expectations and creating communications networks.

Run a trial period

The results of a trial period may indicate that a change is warranted, or just the opposite—that an existing strategy should stay in effect. For example, Body Shop Plc., marketer of animal-fat-free lotions, creams, and shampoos, planned a new channel strategy in expansion of its 700 franchises worldwide. In the US, Body Shop decided to open company-owned stores rather than franchises. After a two-year trial period marked by slow growth, however, Body Shop reverted to its tried-and-true franchise strategy.[26]

Set performance expectations

As marketing channel members have become more interdependent, the setting of performance expectations has evolved into more of a joint decision process, rather than one party dictating standards to another. Procter & Gamble, one of the world's most powerful and effective marketing organizations, has learned the advantages of jointly setting performance standards with its wholesale and retail accounts. More than a hundred P&G key-customer marketing teams see reaching agreement on performance standards with their customers as an important part of their mission.[27]

Lack of agreement on performance standards could indicate that some other channel arrangement might be appropriate. If a channel is set up without advance agreement on performance standards, evaluation of channel performance becomes much more difficult.

Wal-Mart and Gitano link up with computers and satellites

Wal-Mart has invested more than $600 million in its Electronic Data Interchange (EDI) system in an effort to improve product availability in its retail stores and ultimately to improve profitability. The system links Wal-Mart with its key suppliers via computers and a communications satellite. It allows suppliers such as clothing manufacturer Gitano to access point-of-sale computer terminals in Wal-Mart's retail stores to track the sale of its jeans. Gitano can then plan production runs to keep retail inventories at the appropriate level.

Wal-Mart also uses EDI to communicate with suppliers upstream from the producer. In the case of Gitano, Wal-Mart communicates with the fabric maker that supplies Gitano, and even the fiber producer that supplies the fabric maker. According to a Wal-Mart executive, "We just tie everyone into the loop. You won't call the apparel manufacturer and have them say, 'Gosh, we'd like to make that for you, but we don't have any fabric.' "

By linking with its suppliers this way, Wal-Mart is acting as an agent for its customers, says president and CEO David Glass. According to Glass, "The name of the game is who can most efficiently deliver merchandise from raw materials to the customer."

Source: "Cutting Out the Middleman," *Forbes,* January 6, 1992, p. 169. Reprinted by permission of *Forbes* magazine. © Forbes Inc.

Create communications networks

Another crucial aspect of channel strategy implementation is to establish communications networks among channel members. Sophisticated computer and communications technologies have greatly enhanced the capabilities of channel members to share important information on a timely basis, maintain goodwill, and solve problems in the mutual interest of channel members. For an example of how a computerized network facilitates communications among channel members, see **The Technological Edge: Wal-Mart and Gitano Link Up with Computers and Satellites.**

The importance of ensuring adequate communications in the marketing channel, part of the *relationship perspective,* is seen in the case of Astor Restaurant Group, the parent company for almost 600 Blimpie franchise stores. When Anthony Conza, a cofounder of Astor, discovered he was losing the trust of his franchisees, he responded by making vast improvements in communications. He established a franchisee advisory council and launched "No Baloney News," a newsletter, and a toll-free hotline to improve communications. His increased attention to communications led to a dramatic improvement in sales growth and franchisee satisfaction levels.[28]

Evaluate channel performance

The evaluation of channel performance, the last area in Exhibit 14.7, can necessitate changes in any of the other decision areas. Evaluating marketing channels requires attention to four key areas: financial performance, working relationships with other channel members, ethical and legal issues, and future plans.

Financial evaluation

For the short run, channel members may be willing to operate at low levels of financial performance. Over time, however, financial results must be positive to sustain relationships in the channel.

Ferrara Pan Candy Company has expert power by virtue of its long history as a successful candy manufacturer. Market experience and continuous research enables Ferrara Pan to accurately forecast sales and plan promotions, thus stimulating retail sales.

An interesting example here involves Procter & Gamble. After years of offering significant discounts and costly promotions to retailers in the grocery trade, P&G concluded its marketing channel was too expensive. One step the company took was to drastically reduce discounts and other trade promotions. This angered some of P&G's retailer customers, but some analysts think the company may be deliberately shifting some of its distribution from grocery stores to discount stores, where the EDLP policy is more welcome. It will take years to see if P&G's *visionary perspective* pays off.[29]

Evaluate working relationships

Three related concepts—power, conflict, and cooperation—are important in evaluation of working relationships among channel members. A firm may gain power in a variety of ways and use it to enhance its position in the marketing channel. Conflict among channel members is natural and sometimes constructive; but it can become destructive if it rages out of control. As power is wielded and conflicts ensue, channel members often find cooperation is essential if they are to flourish and survive.

Channel power.   Channel members may gain **channel power** in many ways.[30] For example, a giant retailer like Kmart offers vendors the opportunity to sell their products in more than 2,500 stores in the United States. In effect, Kmart is in a position to use **reward power** when it agrees to buy from a vendor —the reward being widespread distribution and the high probability of large sales volumes. Other examples of reward power might be a manufacturer granting exclusive distribution rights to a wholesaler, offering special credit terms to deserving customers, or extending lenient returned-goods policies.

Another form of power is **legitimate power,** which lies in ownership or contractual agreements. Holiday Inns has a certain amount of legitimate power over its franchisees through contractual agreements, for example, while Polo controls one of its channels by ownership of its own retail stores.

Power developed through the accumulation of expertise and knowledge is called **expert power.** Large retailers have gained a tremendous amount of expert power using point-of-sale scanners to gauge product movements, price sensitivities, and trade promotion effectiveness. In fact, retailers can know more about how manufacturers' products are doing in the marketplace than the manufacturers. This expertise gives large retailers more power to negotiate favorably with their suppliers.

Power based on the desire of one channel member to be associated with another channel member is called **referent power.** For example, a jewelry store may wish to be selected as an exclusive dealer for Rolex watches. The store's desire would put Rolex in a powerful position with such a retailer.

Another form of power sometimes seen in channel relationships is **coercive power.** A manufacturer that threatens to cut off a distributor's credit unless the distributor pays its bills more promptly exemplifies coercive power. The use of coercive power can become abusive and even illegal. For instance, a distributor's coercing a manufacturer into dropping a competing distributor might be ruled a conspiracy in restraint of trade, a violation of federal antitrust legislation.

All channel members must develop some sort of power to survive. Some may build enough power to act as a **channel leader,** that is, a channel member with enough power to control others in the channel. Current channel leaders include Wal-Mart, Kroger, and Microsoft. While large, successful organizations can gain buying power and selling power by controlling economic assets and resources, smaller companies can also build power, especially by developing knowledge and expertise to gain expert power.

Channel conflict.   It is inevitable that channel members experience conflict with one another. **Channel conflict** may result from poor communications, a struggle over power in the channel, or incompatible objectives. For example, most buyers want to buy at as low a price as they can reasonably negotiate, while most sellers want to sell at as high a price as reasonably possible. Exhibit 14.8 provides several examples of routine channel conflict.

Channel conflict is commonplace in a competitive market where profitability is a requirement for survival, pointing up the importance of cooperation in resolving conflict to avoid senseless disagreements that can drain channel members' resources.

Channel cooperation.   A cooperative spirit among channel members can help to reduce the amount of conflict and to resolve conflicts once they do occur. Kellogg's response to the conflict in Exhibit 14.8 exemplifies **channel**

Exhibit 14.8	**Examples of channel conflict**

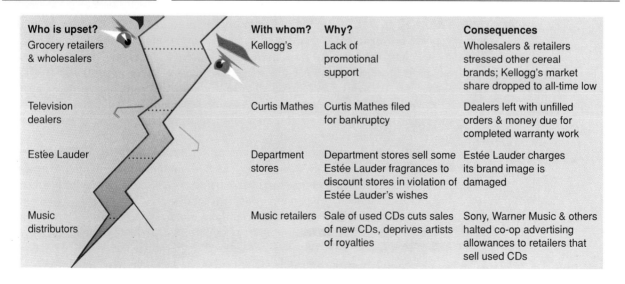

Who is upset?	With whom?	Why?	Consequences
Grocery retailers & wholesalers	Kellogg's	Lack of promotional support	Wholesalers & retailers stressed other cereal brands; Kellogg's market share dropped to all-time low
Television dealers	Curtis Mathes	Curtis Mathes filed for bankruptcy	Dealers left with unfilled orders & money due for completed warranty work
Estée Lauder	Department stores	Department stores sell some Estée Lauder fragrances to discount stores in violation of Estée Lauder's wishes	Estée Lauder charges its brand image is damaged
Music distributors	Music retailers	Sale of used CDs cuts sales of new CDs, deprives artists of royalties	Sony, Warner Music & others halted co-op advertising allowances to retailers that sell used CDs

cooperation. The company used a cooperative strategy that provided more marketing communications support and encouraged retailers to include special two-for-one coupons in their regular newspaper advertising. As a result, sales on targeted Kellogg's brands increased 10 percent.[31]

The incentive to cooperate with other channel members is clearly strongest if all parties agree on their functional roles, and if agreement on performance standards has been reached prior to or early in the business relationship. When channel members do not agree on these matters, conflicts may be settled according to where the power lies. But conflicts settled only by the exercise of power often resurface, especially if the loser in the prior conflict gains an edge in the power dimension. As we suggest frequently in this book, more and more companies are embracing cooperation and building relationships as a superior way to ensure lasting market strength.

Ethical and legal issues

The management of marketing channels calls attention to a number of ethical and legal issues, some of which are illustrated in Exhibit 14.9. Certainly, some channel conflicts have ethical and legal implications. And, strange as it might sound, cooperation taken to the extreme may also present problems, especially if agreements between channel members violate the key laws affecting marketing discussed in Chapter 3.

Because of the range of marketing activities that occur within any marketing channel, the potentially relevant legal issues for channels are numerous. Laws pertaining to pricing, product liability, and truth in advertising are a few examples of thousands of international, federal, state, and local regulations that might pertain to a given channel situation. Our discussion here focuses on the legal environment as it affects channel structure and selected buyer-seller interactions.

Producers may want to set up channel arrangements to ensure their products are given substantial market support by either wholesalers or retailers. One

---

Exhibit 14.9   **Examples of ethical and legal problems in marketing channels**

Situation	Ethical/legal problem
Large retailer threatens to stop buying unless supplier grants unreasonably low prices	Unfair use of coercive power (unethical)
Powerful producer of consumer goods dictates how its products will be displayed without regard for space constraints in smaller stores	Poor communications; unfair use of coercive power (unethical)
Large wholesaler demands supplier replace its male sales rep with a female because the purchasing agent does not like to deal with men	Unfair use of coercive power (unethical, potentially illegal)
Consumer goods producer offers toll-free hotline to resolve retailer complaints, then understaffs the hotline, resulting in a constant busy signal	Poor communications (unethical)
Desperate to sign up new franchises, franchisor's sales rep downplays financial risk of owning franchise	Poor communications (unethical, potentially illegal)
Wholesaler requests supplier stop selling to competing wholesaler; supplier grants request	Excessive cooperation among channel members (illegal)
Two manufacturing companies agree not to sell to a particular wholesaler in an effort to damage the wholesaler's business	Excessive cooperation among channel members (illegal)
Salesperson agrees to give retailer a lower price than competing retailers, based solely on friendship	Excessive cooperation among channel members (illegal)

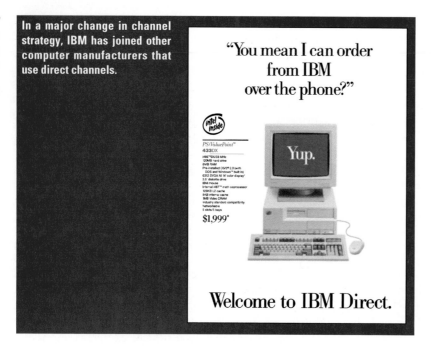

In a major change in channel strategy, IBM has joined other computer manufacturers that use direct channels.

"You mean I can order from IBM over the phone?"

intel inside

PS/ValuePoint
433DX

i486™DX/33 MHz
120MB hard drive
8MB RAM
Pre-installed OS/2® 2.0 (with DOS and Windows™ built in)
6312 SVGA NI 14" color display
3.5" diskette drive
IBM mouse
Internal i487™ math coprocessor
128KB L2 cache
8KB internal cache
3MB Video DRAM
Industry standard compatibility
Networkable
6 slots/5 bays

$1,999*

Yup.

Welcome to IBM Direct.

producer might wish to set up **exclusive territories,** so that no other reseller in a given geographic area sells a particular brand of a product. Another might enact **exclusive dealing agreements,** which would restrict a reseller from carrying a competing product line.

Another possibility is **tying contracts,** which require a reseller to buy products besides the one it really wants to buy. For example, a copier manufacturer may also require a customer to buy ink cartridges on the grounds that the printer can reach acceptable performance standards only if the specified cartridge is used.

Exclusive territories, exclusive dealing agreements, and tying contracts are legally acceptable unless they have anticompetitive effects or tend to create monopolies. A substantial reduction in competition through such arrangements is a violation of federal or state antitrust laws.

Future considerations

The final requirement in the evaluation of channel performance is to cast an eye to the future. Essentially, the firm should ask itself one key question: How well can this channel be expected to perform in the future? The answers can have far-reaching implications, as a *visionary perspective* requires that marketers make necessary changes in pursuit of their long-term goals.

Consider, for example, the computer industry. Dominated for a decade by IBM's dealer network, the industry has recently been revolutionized by intensified competition, changing customer preferences, and shifting marketing channel strategies and structures. Direct marketing channels are fast becoming a major factor in the computer industry, and now even IBM sells directly to consumers. Digital Equipment Corporation, the nation's second-largest computer manufacturer, has also modified its channel strategy to include direct marketing.[32] Compaq and Apple are also expanding their marketing channels beyond computer stores, which face increasing competition from both electronics superstores and department stores.[33]

None of these major computer companies would have modified its marketing channels had management believed that its "tried and true" channels were sufficient to get the job done in years to come. Strong competition from visionary direct marketing computer companies like Dell and Gateway convinced the industry leaders to make changes. The computer industry provides an excellent reminder that the management of marketing channels requires vigilance to respond to current and future marketplace threats and opportunities.

Summary

1. *Explain the functions and key activities of marketing channels.* A marketing channel, sometimes referred to as a *channel of distribution,* is a combination of organizations that perform the activities required to link producers to users to accomplish particular marketing objectives.

    The primary goal of a marketing channel is to allow companies to reach their customers with the right product at the right time, to meet customer expectations, and to stimulate profitable sales volume. The key functions of marketing channels are marketing communications, inventory management, physical distribution, market feedback, and the assumption of financial risk.

2. *Discuss the role of intermediaries in marketing channels.* Intermediaries, often called *middlemen,* provide key marketing channel functions. To survive in the economic system, an intermediary must perform its particular functions more efficiently than any other channel member.

3. *Distinguish between direct and indirect marketing channels.* Direct marketing channels use no intermediaries to move products from producers to end-users. Indirect marketing channels use at least one intermediary before the product reaches its final destination. Despite the dramatic growth of direct marketing channels, most products reach ultimate consumers through indirect marketing channels.

4. *Illustrate how some firms use multiple channels successfully.* As markets become increasingly specialized and companies seek to globalize their marketing efforts, the use of multiple channels is growing. Several examples of companies using multiple channels were presented in the chapter.

5. *See how marketing channel decisions are related to other key marketing decision variables.* Marketing channel strategies and objectives must be based on a firm's overall marketing strategies and objectives. After a channel strategy has been developed, different channel alternatives can be evaluated for capabilities, costs, and availability. Channel alternatives can also be evaluated for compatibility with product, pricing, and marketing communications variables.

6. *Understand how power, conflict, and cooperation affect the operation of a marketing channel.* Channel members develop power based on such factors as economic strength or market knowledge. In some instances, this power may be abused, leading to conflict between channel members.

    Conflict can also result from poor communications or incompatible goals among channel members. It is becoming increasingly necessary that channel members cooperate to resolve conflict and pursue mutually beneficial goals.

7. *Give examples of ethical and legal issues encountered in the operations of marketing channels.* The unfair use of power can raise ethical concerns. For example, a large buyer might try to force a small supplier to grant unreasonably low prices as a condition for continuing to be a supplier.

    If taken to the extreme, cooperation between channel members can be a violation of the law, as competition may be unfairly constrained. Certain arrangements between channel members may violate antitrust laws if they reduce competition. Exclusive territories, exclusive dealing agreements, and tying contracts are examples of potentially illegal channel arrangements.

Key terms & concepts

marketing channel *334*
intermediaries *334*
direct channel *338*
indirect channel *338*
single-channel strategy *340*
multiple-channels strategy *340*
forward integration *341*
backward integration *342*
wholesaler-sponsored voluntary
  groups *342*
retailer-owned cooperative
  groups *343*

franchise system *343*
franchisor *343*
franchisee *343*
administered channel system *343*
channel objectives *345*
channel strategy *345*
market coverage *346*
intensive distribution *346*
selective distribution *346*
exclusive distribution *346*
channel power *351*

reward power *351*
legitimate power *351*
expert power *351*
referent power *352*
coercive power *352*
channel leader *352*
channel conflict *352*
channel cooperation *352*
exclusive territories *354*
exclusive dealing agreements *354*
tying contracts *354*

Review & discussion questions

1. What are the key activities performed in a marketing channel?

2. How do indirect marketing channels differ from direct marketing channels? How do intermediaries contribute to marketing channels?

3. Review **The Entrepreneurial Spirit: Personal Touch Pays Off.** Which marketing channel functions did Brenda French take responsibility for after switching from sales through retail stores to a direct salesforce?

4. Explain the concepts of forward and backward integration.

5. How do franchisees and franchisors work together in a franchise system?

6. Describe the varying degrees of market coverage—intensive distribution, exclusive distribution, and selective distribution—and give examples of each.

7. Channels must be compatible with the other elements of the marketing mix. Give examples that reflect compatibility between channels and product, pricing, and marketing communications considerations.

8. How might channel members build their power bases relative to other members of the channel?

9. Review **The Technological Edge: Wal-Mart and Gitano Link Up with Computers and Satellites.** What are the advantages to Gitano of being electronically linked with Wal-Mart? Are there any disadvantages?

10. How can poor communication, abuse of power, and too much cooperation in marketing channels create ethical and legal problems?

Application exercises

1. Discuss the advantages and disadvantages to the consumer of buying these products in alternative channels as opposed to grocery stores:

Product	Alternative channel
Citrus fruit	Farmers' market
Rib-eye steaks	Specialty meat market
Milk	Home delivery
Popcorn	Movie theater
Bottled soft drink	Vending machine

2. Assume you own the concession rights for the Denver Broncos' home games in Mile High Stadium. What factors should you consider and what specific information would you need in deciding whether to buy soft-drink cups from a local distributor, who buys the cups from a Taiwanese manufacturer, or directly from the manufacturer?

3. Beth Norman is a sales rep for a leading manufacturer of commercial air-conditioning systems. She currently sells to three distributors in Dallas, who in turn sell exclusively to building contractors. One of Beth's distributors, Maverick Supply Company, has produced disappointing sales results for Beth during the past six months. Upon investigation, Beth discovered that Maverick bought heavily from one of her chief competitors. How might Beth use the five power bases discussed in this chapter to regain her lost position with Maverick?

Case 14.1   *Gateway 2000: New kid on the mail-order PC block*

Gateway 2000, a South Dakota–based company, surprised industry observers by becoming the largest mail-order computer seller in the US just seven years after its founding. In 1993, Gateway's sales exceeded $1.7 billion.

To distinguish its products from others in a market crowded by clones, Gateway president Ted Waitt uses creative packaging, unique advertising, and a value-added philosophy. Gateway computers are shipped in attention-getting black and white boxes inspired by the Holsteins of the Waitt family cattle business. The packaging contributes to a down-home, totally American image.

Even though PC buyers seem to focus on low prices when making buying decisions, Gateway focuses on what Waitt calls a "value equation." He says PC buyers are not really concerned with price per se but rather with value, or what they expect to get for the money. Gateway strives to differentiate itself from the majority of its potential competitors, which seemed to cluster at one of two extremes in the market. The competitors were either selling no-frills computers at rock-bottom prices or souped-up machines with a lot of extra features many buyers would never use.

Gateway does not rely on extensive marketing research to determine which features buyers really want. Instead, it uses in-house testing on component parts in an effort to make each generation of products "smaller, faster, and cheaper." Gateway also relies on customer feedback to refine its products.

Gateway's success, along with the success of other mail-order computer sellers like Dell, finally convinced the big computer manufacturers to enter the direct-mail business. Digital Equipment Corporation, IBM, Compaq, and Germany-based multinational Siemens have all become players in the direct-to-consumer computer game. Entrance of the industry giants has observers wondering just how long Gateway can sustain its spectacular success.

As Gateway continues to grow rapidly, some internal problems have developed. The company has had difficulty training enough new employees to handle the heavy flow of orders. At one point, delivery time for some products stretched from two weeks to six. Systems for processing and shipping orders simply had not kept up with the growth in sales volume. The company hired 1,500 new employees in 1993 in an effort to provide better service.

To maintain its market position, Gateway expanded its manufacturing capability and may stockpile more inventory to speed shipping times. Gateway also announced plans to install a communications system to allow major customers to place and monitor orders electronically.

Industry analysts point to Gateway's need to correct problems in customer service and technical support, functions particularly important to buyers whose only contact with the company is by telephone. Waitt acknowledges this crucial role, noting that while customers may first be attracted by low prices and unique advertising, they can be retained only if service is acceptable.

Questions:

1. Why have changes occurred in the marketing channels for personal computers?

2. Will Gateway have to perform activities traditionally performed by PC dealers to remain competitive in the future? In particular, will Gateway have to maintain more inventory and provide more technical and customer-service support to compete with PC dealers?

3. How should Gateway evaluate the benefits of direct marketing for its products to continue its market leadership? Should Gateway consider alternative marketing channels in the future?

Sources: *Gateway Monitor,* Winter 1993, pp. 1–4; Lois Therrien, "Why Gateway Is Racing to Answer on the First Ring," *Business Week,* September 13, 1993, pp. 92–94; Lois Therrien, "Computers by Mail: A Megabyte Business Boom," *Business Week,* May 11, 1992, pp. 93–96; Joshua Hyatt, "Betting the Farm," *Inc.,* December 1991, pp. 36–48; Michael Allen, "Gateway Appears to Pass Dell Computer as Leader of US Mail-Order Market," *The Wall Street Journal,* March 23, 1992, p. B3; Marilyn Much, "IBM Tips Its Hand with 800 Promo to Students," *Direct,* February 1992, p. 15; Laurence Hooper, "Siemens Unit Introduces Low-End PC; Company Plans to Try Direct-Mail Sales," *The Wall Street Journal,* March 12, 1992, p. B7; and Jacqueline Graves, "America's Smart Young Entrepreneurs," *Fortune,* March 21, 1994, pp. 34–48.

Case 14.2 — *Goodyear Tire & Rubber Company: Goodyear tires of independent channels*

Goodyear Tire & Rubber Company president Stanley Gault shocked the business world with his announcement that the company would begin selling tires through Sears stores. The 1992 announcement marked Goodyear's first distribution agreement with a mass retailer since the 1920s. Many of Goodyear's 2,500 independent dealers expressed anger and dismay, fearing that Sears would sell Goodyear tires at lower prices, which could cut into dealers' sales volume and profit.

The decision to sell tires through Sears was motivated by a number of factors. First, Goodyear's market share had declined, falling from 15 to 12 percent in 1992. Second, discount multibrand tire stores and wholesale clubs were growing faster as tire outlets than were traditional tire dealers. Using independent dealers loyal to its brand and company-owned stores, Goodyear's growth was flat during the five years preceding the surprise announcement.

According to industry analysts, Goodyear's outlets had developed a high-priced image that hurt sales volume. Basically, it did not look as if Goodyear was putting its tires where customers increasingly preferred to buy them.

Industry observers believe the move to Sears is simply one step in the evolution of a new marketing channel for Goodyear. They say other retailers, including giant discounters like Wal-Mart, may be in Goodyear's future. Goodyear already sells its Kelly-Springfield tires to Wal-Mart; and it might be tempted to try selling Wal-Mart the

Goodyear brand in the future. Goodyear has also begun selling through its own stores, Just Tires, and is experimenting with sales to multibrand discounters.

Gault has tried to reassure Goodyear dealers that Sears will not get top-of-the-line Goodyear products like the 1992 Aquatred tire. He also promised dealers Goodyear will not sell directly to Sears discount subsidiaries, Western Auto and Tire America. The dealers took a wait-and-see attitude before pledging continued allegiance to Goodyear.

Questions:

1. What risks does Goodyear face with its new channel strategy?

2. Did Goodyear make the right decision to expand its channels?

3. How can Goodyear minimize lost sales volume through its independent dealers?

Sources: Dana Milbank, "Goodyear Plans to Sell Its Tires at Sears Stores," *The Wall Street Journal,* March 3, 1992, p. B8; Zachary Schiller, "Goodyear Is Gunning Its Marketing Engine," *Business Week,* March 16, 1992, p. 42; Kate Ballen, "The Bounce Is Back at Goodyear," *Fortune,* September 7, 1992, pp. 70–72; and Gerhard Gschwandtner, "The Salesman Who Put the Go Back in Goodyear," *Personal Selling Power,* September 1992, pp. 21–28.

Retailing

After studying this chapter you should be able to:

1. Understand the economic importance of retailing and its role in the marketing channel.

2. Cite evidence of the globalization of retailing.

3. Discuss some of the advances in retailing technology.

4. Explain the reasons behind the growth of nonstore retailing.

5. Describe key factors in the retail marketing environment, and understand how they relate to retail strategy.

6. Cite important ethical and legal issues facing retailers.

Toys "Я" Us in Japan: The world's toughest retail market

What do Toys "Я" Us and McDonald's have in common? For one thing, both are interested in developing a market in Japan. They have joined forces there in an effort to pry open the world's toughest retail market. The plan calls for McDonald's to open restaurants on sites with Toys "Я" Us stores. The partnership provides Toys "Я" Us with McDonald's 20 years of experience in penetrating Japanese markets; for McDonald's, the relationship is a natural because both retailers attract similar clientele—families with small children.

Anticipating that the US toy market would someday become saturated, Toys "Я" Us moved into international markets in 1989 by opening stores in Canada. Since then, the company has expanded into Europe, Hong Kong, and Singapore. Japan, the world's second-largest toy market after the US, with annual toy sales of $6 billion, has long been a tempting market for the toy retailer.

In 1991, Toys "Я" Us opened its first store in Japan after overcoming Japanese bureaucracy, local small-business interests, confusing real estate practices, and the often-ferocious Japanese press. Future plans in Japan include the opening of 10 stores annually through the year 2000.

The Japanese retail toy market is served by a multitude of small shopkeepers who typically stock between 1,000 and 2,000 different items. Toys "Я" Us plans to open with 8,000 items, increasing to 15,000 over time. Although the Japanese shops may be small in comparison, they are protected by Japan's large-store law, which at one time delayed large retailers from opening new stores for up to 10 years. Since modification of the law, however, the big-store application process now takes no more than 18 months.

Despite the costs associated with entering the Japanese toy market, Toys "Я" Us appears to have the financial backing to make the enterprise successful. With projected minimum sales of $1.5 billion within Japan by the year 2000, Toys "Я" Us will earn substantial rewards from its successful penetration of the Japanese market.

Sources: Robert Neff, "Guess Who's Selling Barbies in Japan Now?" *Business Week,* December 9, 1991, pp. 72–76; "Retailing in Japan: Toy Joy," *The Economist,* January 4, 1992, p. 62; Cindy Kano and Thomas J. Martin, "Revolution in Japanese Retailing," *Fortune,* February 7, 1994, pp. 143–46; James E. Ellis, "Why Overseas? Cause That's Where the Sales Are," *Business Week,* January 10, 1994, pp. 62–63; and Mark Mason, "United States Direct Investment in Japan: Trends and Prospects," *California Management Review,* Fall 1992, pp. 98–115.

The Toys " Я " Us experience illustrates just a few of the many challenges a retailer encounters when entering a market. In Japan, Toys " Я " Us faces a multitude of strategic retail decisions related to location, merchandise mix, store atmosphere, marketing communications, and pricing—not to mention joint venturing in an international environment. In this chapter, we explore all these issues.

Retailing, an important part of many marketing channels, includes all the activities involved in selling products and services to the ultimate, or final, consumer. Despite the popular notion that all it takes to succeed in retailing is common sense, successful retailers exemplify the *execution perspective.* Approximately two-thirds of all new retailers fail within their first three years.[1] Common sense does not seem to be enough.

This chapter explains the importance of retailing in the US economy, discusses the functions retailers perform within the channel, and illustrates different types of retailers. Several trends in retailing are discussed: globalization, advances in technology, the focus on customer service, and nonstore retailing. We explore factors in the retail environment—both controllable and uncontrollable—that a firm must constantly monitor and coordinate to ensure a successful retail strategy. Finally, we examine some important ethical and legal issues in retailing.

The role of retailing

The role of retailing is to supply products and services directly to the final consumer. Retailers are differentiated from wholesalers according to the primary source of sales. **Retail sales** are sales to final consumers; **wholesale sales** are those to other businesses that in turn resell the product or service, or use it in running their own businesses. To be classified as a retailer, a firm's retail sales must equal or exceed 50 percent of its total revenues. Firms with less than 50 percent retail sales are classified as wholesalers. Wal-Mart was recently reminded of the distinction when its Sam's Wholesale Club was forced to change its name to Sam's Club in states where retail sales exceeded the 50 percent benchmark.

Economic importance

Retailing is a major force in the economy. Approximately 1.3 million retailers in operation in the US employ 19 million people, about one-eighth of the total US labor force.[2] Retailers generate an astonishing $1.8 trillion in annual revenues. This translates into a $5,000 retail expenditure for every man, woman, and child in the United States.[3] Leading retailers are shown in Exhibit 15.1.

Retailing also includes a diverse range of **service retailers.** Service retailers include dry cleaners, photo developers, shoe repair shops, banks, fitness clubs, movie theaters, game arcades, rental businesses (automobiles, furniture, appliances, videos), tourist attractions, hotels and restaurants, automotive repair shops, and some providers of health care services. Spending for services fuels increasing consumer-spending growth rates, as spending on products has underperformed the rest of the economy for quite some time.

Retailers' uniqueness in the channel

Retailers differ from other marketing channel members in that they handle smaller, but more frequent customer transactions, and in the importance of assortment. A pleasant shopping environment is also more important in most forms of retailing than at other levels in the channel. Creation of a pleasant shopping atmosphere entails additional expense, which contributes to higher prices.

| Exhibit 15.1 | | | | **Leading retailers, 1992** | | | |

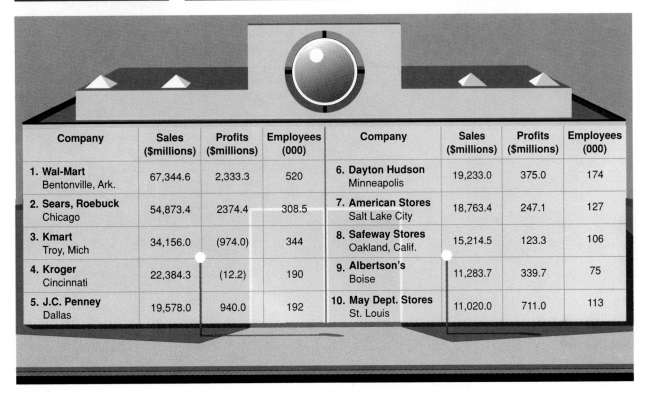

Company	Sales ($millions)	Profits ($millions)	Employees (000)	Company	Sales ($millions)	Profits ($millions)	Employees (000)
1. **Wal-Mart** Bentonville, Ark.	67,344.6	2,333.3	520	6. **Dayton Hudson** Minneapolis	19,233.0	375.0	174
2. **Sears, Roebuck** Chicago	54,873.4	2374.4	308.5	7. **American Stores** Salt Lake City	18,763.4	247.1	127
3. **Kmart** Troy, Mich	34,156.0	(974.0)	344	8. **Safeway Stores** Oakland, Calif.	15,214.5	123.3	106
4. **Kroger** Cincinnati	22,384.3	(12.2)	190	9. **Albertson's** Boise	11,283.7	339.7	75
5. **J.C. Penney** Dallas	19,578.0	940.0	192	10. **May Dept. Stores** St. Louis	11,020.0	711.0	113

Sell smaller quantities more frequently

Retailers offer products in the sizes suitable and convenient for household consumption. Besides buying smaller sizes, most consumers buy products frequently because they lack sufficient storage space and funds to maintain large inventories of products. The average convenience store transaction is for only a few dollars, for example, but the average convenience store handles thousands of transactions per week.

Provide assortments

Retailers assemble an assortment of products and services to sell. If retailers did not do so, shoppers would have to go to the bakery for bread, the butcher shop for meat, the dairy for milk, and the hardware store for light bulbs; and a simple shopping trip could take hours to complete. By providing assortments, retailers offer the convenience of one-stop shopping for a variety of products and services. The typical supermarket carries over 15,000 different items made by more than 500 different manufacturers.[4]

An assortment of items seen by the customer as reasonable substitutes for each other is defined as a **category.** Discount retailers that offer a complete assortment and thus dominate a category from the customer's perspective are called **category killers.** These include Toys " Я " Us, Home Depot, and Circuit City. Since category killers dominate a category of merchandise, they can negotiate excellent prices from suppliers and be assured of dependable sources of supply.

World Foot Locker stores offer a broad assortment of popular athletic footwear and apparel in a high-tech sports environment about six times the size of a conventional Foot Locker store.

Emphasize atmospherics

Atmospherics refers to a retailer's combination of architecture, layout, color scheme, sound and temperature monitoring, special events, prices, displays, and other factors that attract and stimulate consumers. Consistent with the *execution* and *productivity perspectives,* retailers spend millions of dollars to create the retail atmospheres that enhance their respective images and the products and services they offer for sale. Nike, F. A. O. Schwartz, and Express have created "environments that have customers oohing, ahhing, and buying."[5] Express stores, dubbed "tongue in chic" by some, imitate Parisian boutiques. Nike Town in Chicago provides 68,000 square feet of sight and sound (huge murals, sports videos, a miniature basketball court) to show off its athletic clothing line. And across the street, shoppers at F. A. O. Schwartz can chat with a talking tree or play a xylophone built into the floor.

The Mall of America near Minneapolis relies on a variety of dramatic atmospheric factors to attract and stimulate consumers, exemplifying an *execution perspective.*

The latest retail operation to gain headlines for its atmospherics is Mall of America, located in suburban Minneapolis. Opened in 1992, the Mall of America has a two-story miniature golf course, a 300-foot walk-through aquarium, Knott's Camp Snoopy (an amusement park with more than 20 attractions), and a Lego Imagination Center, complete with dinosaurs 20 feet tall. These features create an exciting atmosphere for shoppers who roam the 4.2-million-square-foot facility (2.5 million square feet of retail shopping space).

Atmospherics, though expensive to create, can generate considerable benefits for retailers. Atmospherics can boost the number of consumers who visit a retail location. Indeed, some retailers are trying to make their stores a "destination" for shoppers, a place a shopper will make a special effort to reach. Atmospherics can also boost the average time a shopper spends at the location and the average amount spent on each shopping trip. At the Mall of America, the average consumer spends $87 during a three-hour visit; the average consumer at US super regional malls spends $49 in an hour.[6] Atmospherics often allow retailers to charge higher prices. Compare the atmosphere of a discount store to that of a full-line traditional department store or an exclusive specialty shop, for example.

Types of retailers

Retailers can be classified according to the type of merchandise and services sold, location, various strategic differences, and method of ownership. Here we examine different ownership categories to provide an overview of several types of retailers.

Some significant retail enterprises, such as military exchange stores and public utility appliance stores, operate outside the realm of private enterprise. Within the private sector, there are several major retail ownership categories, including independent retailers, chains, franchising, leased departments, and cooperatives.

Independent retailers

Independent retailers own and operate only one retail outlet. Independent retailers account for more than three-fourths of all retail establishments, a testament to Americans' desires to own and operate their own businesses and a relative lack of barriers to entry. There are no formal education requirements, no specific training requirements, and few legal requirements to owning a retail business. This ease of entry likely accounts for the unpreparedness and the high failure rate experienced by new retailers. **The Entrepreneurial Spirit: sMall Shops Test Big Ideas** reveals how some shopping malls encourage new, independent retailers to start their own businesses.

Chains

A **retail chain** owns and operates multiple retail outlets. Examples are Nordstrom, Musicland, Pappagallo, The Gap, and J. C. Penney. Chains represent 20 percent of all retailers and account for 50 percent of all retail sales.[7] Their major advantage is the ability to service large, widespread target markets by selling a large assortment of products and services.

Franchising

Retail franchising is a form of chain ownership in which a franchisee pays the franchisor (parent company) fees or royalties and agrees to run the franchise by prescribed norms, in exchange for use of the franchisor's name. Well-known franchisors include McDonald's, Holiday Inn, Avis, Mrs. Fields', and Jiffy Lube. According to the International Franchise Association, about 3,000 franchise

sMall Shops test big ideas

*T*he Mall of Memphis targets specialty merchandisers with sMall Shops—tiny store-fronts ranging in size from 8-by-16 feet to 12-by-16 feet and equipped with shelving, spotlights, and rolling gates. Rents start at $1,000 per month, offering retailers a chance to test-market new products at minimum expense. Tenants of the first sMall Shops include We R the Magic Co. (Disney-licensed toys and clothing); Mother Made (children's clothing); and Family Entertainment (videotaped, animated Bible stories).

The sMall Shops are also a good concept for the mall. According to the mall manager, "On our side, we wanted to bring some exciting merchants to the property, to add a little flair and spice . . . Entrepreneurs provide these elements." Besides adding novelty to the mall, successful sMall Shop owners may become future tenants of larger store sites within the mall. In a sense, the Mall of Memphis may be investing in filling future mall store space.

Source: " 'sMall Shops' Target Specialties," *The Commercial Appeal,* July 12, 1991, p. B3.

companies operate in the United States. Franchising operations employ 7.2 million workers at approximately 542,000 separate establishments. In 1991, franchises generated $757.8 billion in revenues.[8]

US franchisors are taking a more *global perspective,* expanding operations around the world. Approximately 20 percent of US–based franchising companies also have overseas operations. Canada and the United Kingdom have long been favorite markets of US franchisors, but now the attention is shifting to other European countries. The vast untapped market and the continuing efforts toward economic unification encourage franchising in Europe.[9]

The arrangements between franchisors and franchisees illustrate the benefits of a *relationship perspective.* In return for fees or royalties, the franchisee may receive management training, participation in cooperative buying and advertising,

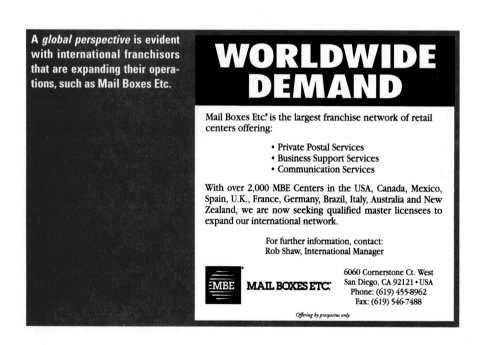

A *global perspective* is evident with international franchisors that are expanding their operations, such as Mail Boxes Etc.

WORLDWIDE DEMAND

Mail Boxes Etc.® is the largest franchise network of retail centers offering:

- Private Postal Services
- Business Support Services
- Communication Services

With over 2,000 MBE Centers in the USA, Canada, Mexico, Spain, U.K., France, Germany, Brazil, Italy, Australia and New Zealand, we are now seeking qualified master licensees to expand our international network.

For further information, contact:
Rob Shaw, International Manager

MBE MAIL BOXES ETC.®

6060 Cornerstone Ct. West
San Diego, CA 92121 • USA
Phone: (619) 455-8962
Fax: (619) 546-7488

Offering by prospectus only.

and assistance in selecting an appropriate location. The franchisor benefits in turn from a constant stream of income, fast payment for goods and services, and strict control over franchised operations that encourages consistency among outlets.

EXECUTIVE ROUNDTABLE COMMENT | **Don North, president of Stuckey's Family Favorites in Chevy Chase, Maryland, comments on the importance of the *relationship perspective* in franchising:**

Franchising at its best is all about cooperation and teamwork. The franchisor brings a lot to the table, as does the operator/franchisee. Neither party could succeed without the other. With the high cost of start-up capital, franchising is a great alternative for entrepreneurially oriented people.

Franchising systems are popular because they offer the franchisee a proven business and the franchisors the ability to establish a national presence with the funds provided by the sale of franchises. Overall, franchises are good examples of the *execution perspective,* in that they generally increase the odds of succeeding. Exhibit 15.2 presents some of the best-known franchise operations.

Leased departments

Leased departments are sections in a retail store that the owner rents to a second party. Typically, department stores rent their jewelry, shoe, hairstyling, and cosmetic departments. For example, Fox Photo leases space in Kroger grocery stores; travel agencies and hair salons often lease space in department stores; and cosmetics such as Esteé Lauder and Clinique are sold through leased space in clothing stores.

As with franchising agreements, a leased-department arrangement benefits both lessor (the department store) and lessee. The lessor receives rental fees, can reduce inventory investment and subsequent risk, gains expertise in a specialized area, and enjoys the benefits derived from the store traffic generated by the leased department. Lessees benefit by operating in an established location with the assurance of store traffic and advertising.

Cooperatives

Responding to competitive pressures exerted by the buying power of chain stores, independent retailers sometimes band together to form **retail cooperatives.** Although each store remains independently owned, the retail cooperative generally adopts a common name and storefront. By adopting a *relationship perspective,* the stores participate in joint purchasing, shipping, and advertising, which allows cost savings normally enjoyed by chain outlets. Retail cooperatives include Sentry Hardware, Associated Grocers, and Ace Hardware.

Trends in retailing

We have seen dramatic examples of change in retailing, such as the decline of Sears, the world's leading retailer since the turn of the century. Other major retailers continue to disappear from the scene, and observers predict that half the

---

Exhibit 15.2

America's best-known franchise companies

• AlphaGraphics	• Hertz	• Mrs. Fields'
• Arby's	• Holiday Inn	• Norrell
• Avis	• I Can't Believe It's Yogurt	• Packaging Plus
• Budget Rent-A-Car	• International House of Pancakes	• Pizza Hut
• Burger King	• Jiffy Lube	• Popeyes
• Century 21	• MAACO	• RE/MAX
• Domino's Pizza	• Mail Boxes Etc.	• Subway Sandwiches
• Dunhill Personnel	• McDonald's	• Super 8 Motels
• Dunkin' Donuts	• Meineke	• Wallpaper To Go
• Fosters Freeze	• Midas	• Wendy's

Independent retailers, such as the owners of True Value Hardware stores, sometimes form cooperatives to share the costs of advertising and other expenses. Cooperatives are examples of a *relationship perspective.*

nation's retailers in 1990 will be out of business by the year 2000.[10] In a widely circulated report, consulting firm Management Horizons predicts: "Structurally, financially, culturally, and competitively, retailing as a business will take on a whole new set of dimensions by the year 2000. It will change perhaps as much in one short decade as it has in the last hundred years or more."[11]

Notable current trends in the retailing environment include global retailing, the increasing use of technology, a renewed emphasis on customer service, and the rapid expansion of nonstore retailing.

Global retailing

With domestic markets becoming saturated and sales growth slowing, many retailers are exhibiting a *global perspective.* For example, the largest McDonald's in size and in daily sales is in Beijing, and 6 of the 10 busiest McDonald's are in Hong Kong.[12] Retailers Wal-Mart, Sears, J. C. Penney, and Radio Shack all plan further expansion in Mexico; and Home Depot, The Gap, and Talbot's are expanding in Canada.[13]

Other retailers appeal to international markets by locating in unique places. One highly profitable retailer, Duty Free International, is located between

British Petroleum has a *global perspective* for its retail operations. This outlet is in Dresden, a town in eastern Germany.

Target's bar-code scanning equipment provides up-to-the-minute information on stock levels. It is an important part of Target's computerized system to reduce costs by managing inventory more effectively.

the US and Canadian border crossings. Hence, Canadians can avoid paying tariffs by buying merchandise after they leave the US, but before they enter Canada.[14]

Perhaps the most intriguing international retail markets are to come in Eastern Europe, where demand for consumer goods is high but the political environment remains unstable.[15] McDonald's has opened restaurants in Moscow, Rome, and Prague, with dramatic success. PepsiCo is also testing the waters of the Eastern European markets with its Pizza Hut and KFC stores.

Technological advances

Retailers have embraced the *technological perspective,* and advances in retail technology have developed at a phenomenal pace. A familiar example is the scanner linked to computerized inventory systems that greatly improve a retailer's efficiency level. Scanners speed the checkout process, reduce computational errors, and instantaneously input the transaction into the inventory system. This allows retailers to precisely track sales on a per-item basis, minimize out-of-stock problems, and judge the effectiveness of various pricing and marketing communications tactics. Other technological advances that directly influence customers include items such as automated cash registers that can issue temporary charge cards, gift certificates, and customer information, and process customer payments;[16] electronic kiosks that allow consumers to take simulated test-drives of various automobiles in mall showrooms;[17] new Universal Product Code scanners that have over a 90 percent success rate in scanning items on the first pass, an improvement estimated to save retailers millions;[18] and cashless grocery shopping that allows consumers to pay by credit card or bank ATM card.[19]

EXECUTIVE ROUNDTABLE COMMENT | **Don North, president of Stuckey's Family Favorites, emphasizes the important role of technology:**

It is the retailer's responsibility to meet consumer needs in the most efficient and effective way possible. In today's market, consumers are in a hurry, and they are becoming intolerant of delays and mistakes. If scanners reduce the error rate and speed checkout in a given situation, the retailer had best use scanners—or fall victim to a competitor that does.

Consistent with an *execution perspective,* some technological advances are directed at influencing consumer buying decisions. VideOcart, Inc., for example, sells shopping carts equipped with video screens that provide information on

Retailers go interactive with video kiosks

Video kiosks are an alternative way for retailers to communicate with their customers. Moving beyond the traditional means of merchandising—hand it or stack it—kiosks offer consumers information about their choices, suggest alternatives, and collect consumer information.

Blockbuster Video is selling through video kiosks in a joint venture with IBM. As a joint partner, IBM is testing new consumer-related applications for the touch-screen technology it has been developing since 1980. The kiosks provide previews of nearly 300 films and critics' ratings on more than 1,000 titles.

Soon to be introduced are kiosks that ask consumers which titles they have seen and enjoyed. The kiosks will then suggest other titles the consumer may enjoy from Blockbuster's 8,000 titles per store. The suggestions are intended to spur rentals of older films and expand consumer interest beyond new releases. Blockbuster is extending its interactive marketing communications to television. Call-in participants in an interactive trivia game receive coupons and a chance to win a European vacation.

Sources: "Retailers Go Interactive: Blockbuster Kiosks Hype Films, Gather Data," *Advertising Age,* February 24, 1992, p. 29. Copyright Crain Communications, Inc. Reprinted with permission. All rights reserved. "Interactive Award Finalists," *Advertising Age,* March 21, 1994, p. IM–12.

sale items, recipes, store directories, and even local news and weather reports. The messages on the screen can be keyed to infrared signals strategically placed in the store. When the shopper passes the soft-drink aisle, for example, the screen flashes promotional messages for Coke and Pepsi.[20] For another technological advance directed to the customer, see **The Technological Edge: Retailers Go Interactive with Video Kiosks.**

Customer service in retailing

Customer service refers to the activities that increase the quality and value customers receive when they shop and purchase merchandise. During the 1970s, inflation forced retailers to cut services to keep operating costs under control. At the same time, deregulation in industries such as airlines and banks also produced reduced services as these industries engaged in price wars. During this period, many US retailers had little interest in customer service and the *quality/value perspective;* they concentrated mainly on short-term profitability. Today, retailers rush to give lip service to the importance of customer service, but many still fall woefully short of providing it. Today's consumers are tougher, more informed, and so sensitive to poor service they often walk away and never come back to a store rather than point out the service problem to the retailer. Experts estimate the average business does not hear from 96 percent of its unhappy customers. Worse yet, the average consumer with a service problem tells 9 or 10 other people.[21]

Different types of retailers offer a variety of customer services to correspond with the image they need to project. Exhibit 15.3 compares some department store services with those offered by the typical discount store.

Store loyalty is the major reward of customer service, a benefit that builds on itself, as customers well served are customers retained. Obtaining new customers can cost a retailer five times more than generating repeat business from an existing customer base.[22] Through outstanding customer service, Direct Tire of Watertown, Massachusetts, has built store loyalty, even while selling tires priced at $10 to $20 over the nearest competitor. Services include immaculate waiting rooms stocked with current issues of popular magazines, complementary fresh hot coffee, observation areas where customers can watch technicians work,

Exhibit 15.3	Customer services offered by retailers

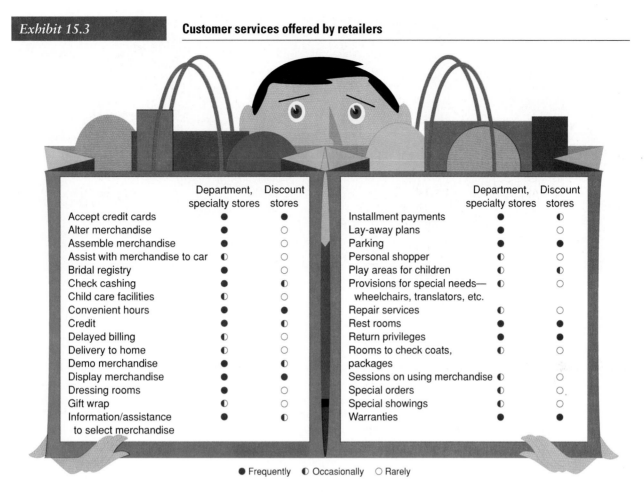

	Department, specialty stores	Discount stores		Department, specialty stores	Discount stores
Accept credit cards	●	●	Installment payments	●	◐
Alter merchandise	●	○	Lay-away plans	●	○
Assemble merchandise	●	○	Parking	●	●
Assist with merchandise to car	◐	○	Personal shopper	◐	○
Bridal registry	●	○	Play areas for children	◐	◐
Check cashing	●	◐	Provisions for special needs— wheelchairs, translators, etc.	◐	○
Child care facilities	◐	○	Repair services	◐	○
Convenient hours	●	●	Rest rooms	●	●
Credit	●	◐	Return privileges	●	●
Delayed billing	◐	○	Rooms to check coats, packages	◐	○
Delivery to home	◐	○	Sessions on using merchandise	◐	○
Demo merchandise	●	◐	Special orders	◐	○
Display merchandise	●	●	Special showings	◐	○
Dressing rooms	●	○	Warranties	●	●
Gift wrap	◐	○			
Information/assistance to select merchandise	●	◐			

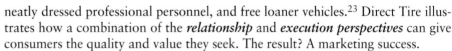

● Frequently ◐ Occasionally ○ Rarely

neatly dressed professional personnel, and free loaner vehicles.[23] Direct Tire illustrates how a combination of the *relationship* and *execution perspectives* can give consumers the quality and value they seek. The result? A marketing success.

Retailers can provide good service without necessarily providing expensive personal service. Automated teller machines, credit card–processing gas pumps, and point-of-sale audio-visual materials in home improvement stores are examples of how technology can assist in providing customer service.

Nonstore retailing

Traditional retailing is generally thought of as the selling of products and services in stores or some other physical structure. In contrast, **nonstore retailing** refers to sales outside a physical structure. Although stores account for 90 percent of all retail sales, the growth rate of nonstore retailing has far surpassed that of store-based retailing in the past few years.

Nonstore retailing, which includes catalog shopping, offers consumers the convenience of selecting and purchasing merchandise according to their own schedules. Merchandise is delivered directly to consumers or shipped to convenient vending locations, methods that particularly appeal to consumers with few store choices, busy people who care little for shopping, those who are bored or dissatisfied with store shopping, and consumers with limitations on movement, such as some nondrivers or disabled people. Disadvantages of nonstore retailing include limited assortments and no chance to try on merchandise, test it out, or have it altered before delivery.

The three most common forms of nonstore retailing are direct marketing, direct selling, and vending machine sales.[24] Direct marketing and direct selling are discussed in more detail in Chapter 21.

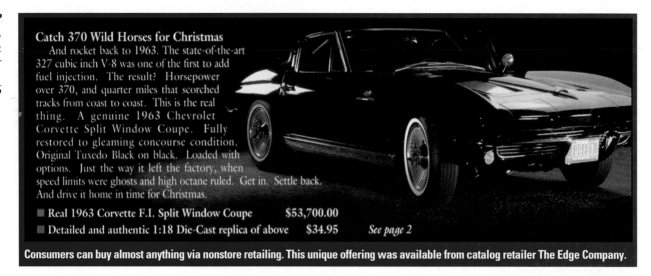

Catch 370 Wild Horses for Christmas
And rocket back to 1963. The state-of-the-art 327 cubic inch V-8 was one of the first to add fuel injection. The result? Horsepower over 370, and quarter miles that scorched tracks from coast to coast. This is the real thing. A genuine 1963 Chevrolet Corvette Split Window Coupe. Fully restored to gleaming concourse condition. Original Tuxedo Black on black. Loaded with options. Just the way it left the factory, when speed limits were ghosts and high octane ruled. Get in. Settle back. And drive it home in time for Christmas.

■ Real 1963 Corvette F.I. Split Window Coupe $53,700.00
■ Detailed and authentic 1:18 Die-Cast replica of above $34.95   *See page 2*

Consumers can buy almost anything via nonstore retailing. This unique offering was available from catalog retailer The Edge Company.

Direct marketing

Direct marketing can be defined as "the distribution of goods, services, information, or promotional benefits to targeted consumers through interactive communication while tracking response, sales, interests, or desires through a computer database."[25] The consumer is exposed to the merchandise through a non-personal medium (catalogs, TV shopping programs, interactive electronic networks), and then purchases the merchandise by mail or telephone. Direct marketing is growing rapidly. In the 1982–92 decade, the total percentage of Americans shopping direct increased 77 percent, while the population grew 16 percent. Over half of all US households (55 percent in 1992) have made a purchase by mail or phone. In 1992, consumers spent $51.5 billion on catalog merchandise and another $2 billion shopping by television.[26]

Approximately 13.5 billion catalogs are mailed each year, from which consumers can buy practically any type of merchandise. Sporting goods, clothing, computer hardware and software, books, recorded music, travel services, home

Spiegel is one of the most successful direct marketers in the world.

Avon, a leading direct seller with a *global perspective*, has sales in more than 100 countries and approximately 500,000 sales representatives in the United States.

furnishings, mutual funds, stocks and bonds, electronic equipment, tools—the list is practically endless. Direct marketing offers an example of the *execution perspective* as more than 93 percent of those who have tried it report that they were satisfied with the experience.[27]

Familiar catalog retailers include L. L. Bean, Spiegel, Fingerhut, Lands' End, and Lillian Vernon. More recently, TV home shopping has become a legitimate form of retailing (see the QVC/Home Shopping case at the end of the chapter), and major retailers Spiegel, Nordstrom, Bloomingdale's, and The Sharper Image are involved in TV home shopping programs. Videotext retailing involves an interactive electronic network that transmits data and graphics via telephone or cable lines to the consumer's computer terminal or television set. Prodigy and Compuserve are two popular videotext retailers.

Direct selling

In **direct selling,** salespeople reach consumers directly or by telephone primarily at home or at work. A small amount of direct selling is done in other locations, including exhibitions, theme parks, and fairs. Industry statistics reveal that 78 percent of all direct sales occur in the home and another 10 percent in the workplace. In 1992, direct selling generated $14.1 billion in sales. There are 5.5 million salespeople in direct selling, almost all of whom are independent contractors, not employees of the selling companies. Approximately 9 out of 10 direct salespeople work part-time.[28] Mary Kay, Avon, Cutco Cutlery, and Tupperware are familiar examples of companies that use direct selling.

Vending machine sales

Vending machines allow customers to purchase and receive merchandise from a machine. Sales from vending machines generate over $20 billion annually, with offerings of predominantly beverages, food, candy, and cigarettes. They are frequently located at work sites, hospitals, schools, tourist destinations, and travel facilities.

Exhibit 15.4

Understanding retail strategy: Selected controllable and uncontrollable factors

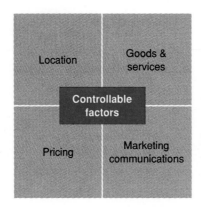

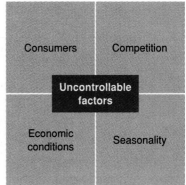

Developing retailing strategy

The scope of retail products and services and the demands of consumers combine to produce a constantly changing business environment. A successful retailer must effectively manipulate the factors it can control to survive in a largely uncontrollable environment. A few uncontrollable and controllable factors of interest to retailers are listed in Exhibit 15.4.

Uncontrollable factors

A number of constantly changing factors in the retail environment are beyond the retailer's control. To survive, the retailer must constantly monitor and adapt to changing, uncontrollable factors in the marketing environment such as legal restrictions, discussed later in the chapter, and advances in technology. The important uncontrollable factors we describe here are consumers, competition, economic conditions, and seasonality.

Consumers

Consumer demographics and lifestyles undergo constant changes, which retailers must recognize to satisfy the needs of their customers. For example, approximately half the US adult working population is female. This means the traditional female role of housekeeper and shopper has all but disappeared. Retailers, showing an *execution perspective,* are adapting to this change by offering longer store hours, time-saving appliances, and prepackaged, self-service items. Because many women have the buying power to make major independent purchases such as automobiles, retailers of big-ticket items now target this segment directly with marketing communications. Similarly, consumer product ads are directed to men and teenagers, who now do much of the routine grocery shopping.

Competition

Whether from new entries into the marketplace or from existing marketers, retail competition is fierce. One indicator of competition intensity, retail bankruptcies, hit an all-time high of 19,005 in 1992.[29] Robert Verdisco, president of the International Mass Retailing Association, notes, "The market is essentially fixed; under that circumstance, a retailer can increase business only by taking it from someone else."[30]

Exhibit 15.5

Poor economic conditions inflicted losses upon retailers (1988–1990)

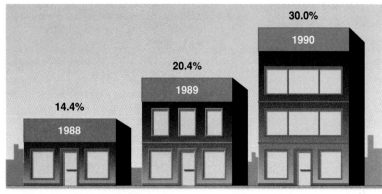

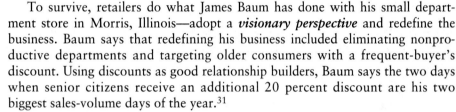

Percent of retailers reporting losses

To survive, retailers do what James Baum has done with his small department store in Morris, Illinois—adopt a *visionary perspective* and redefine the business. Baum says that redefining his business included eliminating nonproductive departments and targeting older consumers with a frequent-buyer's discount. Using discounts as good relationship builders, Baum says the two days when senior citizens receive an additional 20 percent discount are his two biggest sales-volume days of the year.[31]

In a broad sense, there are two major types of competition: intratype and intertype. **Intratype competition** describes competition among retailers that use the same type of business format. McDonald's, Wendy's, and Burger King are intratype competitors, for example; they are all fast-food restaurants. **Intertype competition** prevails among retailers using different types of business to sell the same products and services. McDonald's intertype competitors would include all other food retailers, ranging from vending machines to fine restaurants. Retail businesses that appreciate both types of competition tend to be better prepared to face challenges and avoid the pitfalls of marketing myopia, that is, too narrowly defining the scope of their business.

Economic conditions

Economic conditions are another factor beyond the retailer's control. During the early 1990s, for example, the economy dramatically affected interest rates, unemployment, taxes, and subsequently, retail sales (see Exhibit 15.5). Since the peak of retail employment in early 1990, the number of workers employed in the retail industry has fallen by more than 230,000.[32]

Large traditional retailers that offered top-rated products and services, such as Macy's and Federated department stores, have faced major financial woes, while discounters such as Wal-Mart and Kmart have thrived.[33] The positions occupied by traditional department stores and discount retailers provide an excellent example of how retailers can manipulate controllable factors to meet the challenges inherent in the uncontrollable environment. In this situation, the discounters manipulated prices downward on decent-quality merchandise, and consumers responded by spending a larger portion of their dollars with discounters. Consumers were seeking quality and value, and the discount retailers responded, illustrating the *execution perspective.*

Seasonality

Seasonality refers to demand fluctuations related to the time of the year, which may be moderated or exacerbated by unpredictable changes in weather and in consumer preferences. Retailers specializing in clothing, sporting equipment,

Exhibit 15.6	Selected criteria to consider when evaluating retail locations		
Strategic compatibility	**Accessibility**	**Legal considerations**	**Economic factors**
• Is site located near target markets? • Is type of shopping center or mall appropriate for the store? • What is the age & condition of the site? • Will adjacent stores complement/ compete with the store?	• What are the road patterns & conditions surrounding the site? • Do any natural or artificial barriers impede access to the site? • Does the site have good visibility from the street? • Is there a good balance between too much & too little traffic flow? • Is it easy to enter/exit the parking lot? • Is number/quality of parking spaces adequate? • Is the site accessible by mass transit? • Can vendor deliveries be easily made?	• Is the site zoning compatible with the store? • Does store's design meet building codes? • Are store's external signs compatible with zoning ordinances & building codes?	• What are the occupancy costs? • What will improvements & other one-time costs incurred during initial occupancy be? • Are amenities available at the site worth the cost?

amusement parks, fresh food, hotels, and car rentals are particularly affected by seasonality. A retailer may minimize the effects of seasonality by adjusting some controllable variables within its retail strategy mix. For example, some retailers initiate special promotions to encourage consumers to buy during the off-season. Other retailers, like sporting goods stores, alter their product mix by focusing on different products for different seasons.

Controllable factors

The four categories of controllable factors we discuss are location, the goods and services the retailer offers, the prices the retailer charges for products and services, and the marketing communications consumers receive.

Location

The old saying is—and experts confirm it—that the three most important factors in retailing are location, location, and location. To most retailers, location is the most crucial factor in the *execution perspective* and the least flexible element of retail strategy. A retailer can modify prices, products and services, and marketing communications relatively easily, but a poor location is difficult for even the best merchant to overcome. Moving is complicated by lease agreements, the transfer of inventory from one location to another, and perhaps even the sale of the building if the retailer owns it.

Evaluation of prospective locations requires analysis of strategic compatibility, accessibility, legal considerations, and economic factors. Key questions related to each of these criteria are presented in Exhibit 15.6.

In broad terms, retail sites are defined as isolated locations, unplanned business districts, or planned shopping centers. **Isolated locations** are freestanding locations, that is, there are no adjoining buildings. These are best suited for large retailers that can attract and hold a large customer base on their own and for convenience-related businesses such as gasoline stations and fast-food restaurants.

Unplanned business districts are made up of independently owned and managed retail operations. They generally evolve in a more spontaneous fashion than

Aldi, a German grocery chain, uses isolated locations in the United States. By avoiding major intersections and strip malls, Aldi keeps its operating costs below many of its competitors, thus focusing on the *productivity perspective.*

do planned business districts. Among the types of unplanned business districts are central business districts, secondary business districts, neighborhood business districts, and string locations. **Central business districts,** commonly known as downtown areas, represent the greatest concentration of office buildings and retail stores. **Secondary business districts** are defined by the intersection of two major thoroughfares. They make good locations because of this traffic flow.

Located in the midst of residential areas, **neighborhood business districts** consist of a small grouping of stores, with the largest generally being a supermarket or variety store. A **string location** is a grouping of stores that sell similar goods and services. Automobiles and mobile homes are often sold in string locations.

Planned shopping centers are centrally owned and managed, have ample parking availability, and offer a variety of stores. There are approximately 39,000 planned shopping centers in the US,[34] and their growth over the last 40 years has been dramatic. Smaller shopping centers have recently attracted an increasing number of shoppers, while the popularity of larger malls is declining.[35]

Goods and services

Another controllable factor in the retail strategy is the goods and services offered for sale. Retailers must decide on the number of product lines to carry, referred to as width or variety. They must also decide on the assortment of each product line, called length or depth. These decisions require several considerations. Major product considerations include compatibility (how well the product fits in with existing inventory), attributes (such as bulk, required service, selling levels), and profitability. Market considerations include stage in the product life cycle, market appropriateness (a product's appeal to the store's current target market), and competitive conditions. Finally, supply considerations such as product availability and supplier reliability need to be explored.

Retailers must be alert to the effects of changes in their product mix and open to a redefinition of competitors, reflecting both the *execution* and *visionary perspectives.* For example, the practice of adding unrelated product categories to existing product lines is referred to as **scrambled merchandising.** In the not-too-distant past, grocery stores predominantly sold food items. Today, consumers can buy motor oil or rent movies at grocery stores. Scrambled merchandising allows grocery stores to obtain higher profit margins than the traditional 1 to 2 percent made on food items. Consumers, in turn, enjoy the extra

Exhibit 15.7   Scrambled merchandising

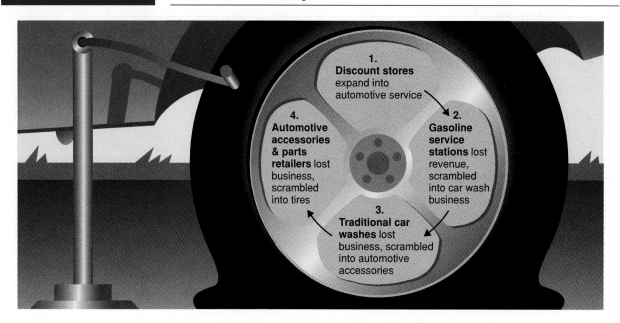

1.
Discount stores expand into automotive service

2.
Gasoline service stations lost revenue, scrambled into car wash business

3.
Traditional car washes lost business, scrambled into automotive accessories

4.
Automotive accessories & parts retailers lost business, scrambled into tires

convenience of one-stop shopping provided by a wide array of merchandise—in effect, they have received improved quality and value in their overall shopping experience.

EXECUTIVE ROUNDTABLE COMMENT | **Don North, president of Stuckey's Family Favorites, states:**

Time is something most consumers feel they don't have nearly enough of. If you can encourage them to pick up a few products while shopping in your store—whether these products are traditional or not for your type of store—you have taken another step toward being profitable in a tough market. Saving consumers time is one way of giving them more value.

Scrambled merchandising has had a chain reaction effect something like that shown in Exhibit 15.7. When discount stores aggressively expanded into automotive service, traditional gasoline service stations lost revenue and scrambled into the car wash business. Traditional car wash operations then expanded their sale of automotive accessories, causing lost volume for traditional automotive accessory and parts retailers. These retailers responded by scrambling into tires to supplement their lost sales on accessories.

Pricing

Retailers also control the final prices they charge consumers for their products and services. Retail prices are ultimately based on the store's target market, the desired store image, and the congruence between price and other elements of the retail mix (location, quality of products and services, marketing communications). Although price-conscious consumers may appear to dominate in many markets, successful retailers are found at all price ranges, from high to low.

Everyday-low-pricing (EDLP) strategies, pioneered by Wal-Mart in the 1980s, are now used by about 50 percent of all retailers. With EDLP, retailers demand low prices from their suppliers, minimize costly advertising and promotions, and keep their retail prices consistently low to lure consumers. Now, many

Giant Food Incorporated uses extensive advertising as part of its marketing communications program. It also gains favorable publicity from outdoor advertising, as seen at Baltimore's Oriole Park at Camden Yards.

retailers are adopting a *quality/value perspective* in "low-price leader" or "value pricing" programs. These programs feature low competitive prices across the board and a continual mix of special offers to keep consumers coming back.[36]

Marketing communications

Decisions about the mix of marketing communications are also controllable. These decisions specify how the retailer allocates resources among personal selling, advertising, public relations, direct marketing, and sales promotion. Retailers such as The Limited emphasize personal in-store selling and do very little advertising; convenience stores promote sales by placing signs in their windows; others promote "a sale a week."

Marketing communications influence **store image,** the picture shoppers conjure up of a store's identity. This image is a composite of shoppers' perceptions of the store's location, goods and services sold, and atmospherics. Essentially, store image is a reflection of consumers' feelings about a store. It affects consumer perceptions of the quality of products and services offered, prices, and the store's fashionability.

Types of strategy mixes

Retailers differentiate themselves from one another according to the **strategy mix** they pursue. The elements of the retail strategy mix are the controllable variables we have discussed—location, products and services, pricing, and marketing communications. Exhibit 15.8 describes a whole range of retailers and their strategy mixes. Although a multitude of combinations exist, specialty stores, department stores, and convenience stores are the more obvious examples of how retailers combine the strategy mix variables in different ways to achieve their desired positions in the marketplace.

Specialty stores

Specialty stores sell a narrow variety of products but offer a deep assortment of product choices. Typical examples of specialty stores are The Limited, Radio Shack, and The Sharper Image.

Because many specialty stores are not large enough to generate sufficient customer traffic on their own, most are commonly located in shopping clusters

Exhibit 15.8		Examples of retail strategy mixes			
Type of retailer	**Location**	**Merchandise**	**Prices**	**Atmosphere & services**	**Marketing communications**
Convenience store	Neighborhood	Medium width & low depth of assortment; average quality	Average to above average	Average	Moderate
Superstore	Community shopping center or isolated site	Full assortment of supermarket items, plus health & beauty aids & general merchandise	Competitive	Average	Heavy use of newspapers & flyers; self-service
Warehouse store	Secondary site, often in industrial area	Moderate width & low depth; emphasis on national brands purchased at discounts	Very low	Low	Little or none
Specialty store	Business district or shopping center	Very narrow width of assortment; extensive depth of assortment; average to good quality	Competitive to above average	Average to excellent	Heavy use of displays; extensive salesforce
Department store	Business district, shopping center, or isolated store	Extensive width & depth of assortment; average to good quality	Average to above average	Good to excellent	Heavy use of ads; catalogs; direct mail; personal selling
Full-line discount store	Business district, shopping center, or isolated store	Extensive width & depth of assortment; average to good quality	Competitive	Slightly below average to average	Heavy use of newspapers; price-oriented; moderate salesforce
Factory outlet	Out-of-the-way site or discount mall	Moderate width, but very poor depth of assortment; some irregular merchandise; low continuity	Very low	Very low	Little; self-service

(malls, shopping centers) where their product selections complement goods provided by neighboring retailers. The marketing communications mix of a specialty store generally includes personal selling along with advertising that emphasizes the uniqueness of offerings and the depth of assortment. Specialty stores are also known for their medium to high prices.

Department stores

Department stores are characterized by a wide variety of merchandise and extensive depth of assortment, and they offer customers one-stop convenience for multiple shopping needs. Operations are typically organized around sales departments such as apparel, home furnishings, cosmetics, and housewares. Employees also work within centralized functional departments such as buying, merchandising, and advertising. Some of the more well-known department stores are Bloomingdale's, Dillard's, and Macy's.

Department stores generally occupy **anchor positions** in shopping centers, shopping malls, or downtown areas; that is, they are strategically placed at different ends of the shopping cluster. Because department stores generate a lot of customer traffic, this placement creates a traffic flow throughout the entire shopping facility.

Customers sample the wares in a Bangkok department store owned by Isetan of Tokyo.

Marketing communications for department stores focus on product selection and quality; services offered such as alterations, gift wrapping, and credit; shopping atmosphere; and store image. Department stores are heavy users of newspaper advertising, catalogs, direct mail, and personal selling. As do specialty stores, department stores commonly charge at or above competitive prices.

Convenience stores

Convenience stores have developed their own unique marketing mix. They carry a modest variety and shallow assortment of products. Prices are high, which consumers tolerate because of the ease of shopping offered by such retailers. Convenience stores often occupy **interceptor locations** between residential areas and the closest supermarket. The store's marketing communications are predominantly limited to the store's sign and banners displayed in the front windows.

Two convenience stores, Circle K and 7-Eleven, have been in bankruptcy, and the entire industry faces a predicted decline in new-store growth over the next decade. The industry's problems can be traced to three main sources. First, the industry is overbuilt, with the proliferation of convenience stores constructed by major oil companies such as Exxon and BP. Second, as drugstores and supermarkets extend their hours of operation, convenience stores have increasing difficulty differentiating themselves on convenience. Moreover, increases in the minimum wage, store rents, and other general expenses have dramatically increased operating costs.

To survive, many convenience stores have repositioned themselves as quick-service eateries specializing in "one-handed" food—items you can eat with one hand while driving with the other, such as hot dogs, corn dogs, pizza, burritos, and egg rolls.[37]

Margin and turnover strategy mixes

Besides type of store, another distinction between retailers is gross margin and inventory turnover. **Gross margin** refers to sales revenue less the retailer's cost of goods sold. A retailer with higher margins makes more from each dollar of sales. **Inventory turnover** refers to how quickly merchandise is sold; it describes the number of times the retailer sells its average inventory during the year. Margin and turnover concepts are illustrated in Appendix A at the end of the text.

There are three strategic combinations of gross margin and inventory turnover among successful retailers. Jewelry stores exemplify a high margin/low turnover strategy. They realize high profits per sale but make fewer sales. Such retailers are also noted for their attention to personal service and attractive atmospheres that help support the store's merchandise.

Grocery stores use a low margin/high turnover strategy. They typically have a net profit margin of 1 to 2 percent but turn merchandise over very quickly. The third option is high margin/high turnover, demonstrated by convenience stores.

Ethical and legal issues in retailing

Retailers engage in highly visible activities, and their marketing communications are similarly visible and thus subject to a fair amount of scrutiny. Ethical or legal violations that retailers have been accused of include deceptive advertising, dishonest sales practices, charging unreasonably high prices to disadvantaged consumers, selling potentially harmful products without adequate control, and selling prohibited products to underage consumers.

Four additional factors pose special concerns for retailers: shoplifting, slotting allowances, the use of personal customer information, and ecological considerations.

Shoplifting

Retailers lose approximately $9 billion a year to shoplifting.[38] Nationwide, the incidence of shoplifting increased sharply in the 1980s, then declined slightly in the early 1990s.[39] Experts claim the primary contributors to shoplifting are fewer salesclerks per store and new floor layout arrangements that divide stores into separate boutiques. This type of layout creates barriers between departments, which makes it easier for shoplifters to conceal their activities.[40] Specialty clothing stores, drugstores, convenience stores, and department stores are hit hardest by shoplifting. Items most frequently stolen are fashion accessories, costume jewelry, fine jewelry, recorded music, health and beauty aids, sporting goods, radios, and television sets.[41]

Employees account for one-third of merchandise loss. To combat shoplifting, some retailers use ink tags attached to clothing. The tags spray indelible ink when improperly removed and permanently damage the merchandise. The logic behind this approach is that if potential shoplifters know the stolen merchandise will be rendered useless, they will have less incentive to steal it.[42]

A new means of controlling shoplifting that portrays a *technological perspective* is an electronically equipped surveillance dummy called Anne Droid. Outfitted with a closed-circuit camera in its eye, infrared illuminators for "seeing" in the dark, and a microphone in its ear, Anne Droid can spot shoplifters with practically no risk of being detected.[43] Some other methods for deterring shoplifting are detailed in Exhibit 15.9.

Slotting allowances

Another retailing issue that has legal or ethical implications is the use of slotting allowances. **Slotting allowances** are fees manufacturers pay to retailers or wholesalers to obtain shelf or warehouse space for their products. In other words, retailers and wholesalers receive money from manufacturers in exchange for allocation of shelf space.

Exhibit 15.9

Shoplifting deterrents

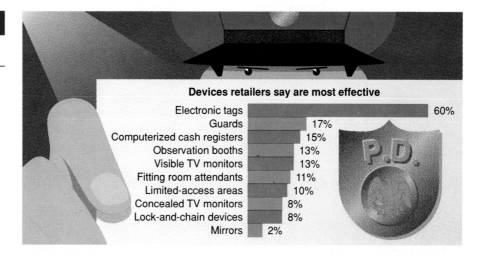

Devices retailers say are most effective

Device	Percentage
Electronic tags	60%
Guards	17%
Computerized cash registers	15%
Observation booths	13%
Visible TV monitors	13%
Fitting room attendants	11%
Limited-access areas	10%
Concealed TV monitors	8%
Lock-and-chain devices	8%
Mirrors	2%

Slotting allowances are controversial. Large manufacturers resist paying these questionable fees, while large wholesalers and retailers insist slotting fees be paid as a condition of doing business. In effect, slotting allowances place manufacturers in direct opposition to their customers—wholesalers and retailers.

Overall, slotting allowances are predominantly associated with negative consequences. They may increase conflict between channel members and reduce competitiveness at some levels. Large channel members can demand the slotting allowances that increase their profit margins, while the smaller members must fend for themselves.

Slotting allowances may also reduce customer service by forcing fewer brand choices, higher retail prices, and less prepurchase information. This could ultimately threaten the quality of product provided to the consumer. Additional research is needed to confirm these suspicions, but getting manufacturers, wholesalers, and retailers to discuss slotting allowances openly is not an easy task.[44]

Use of customer information

Advances in database technology provide retailers greater access to and storage of consumer information and purchase histories. For example, when a customer calls Spiegel to check a catalog order, the service rep has instant access, via an order number, to the customer's previous sales and service transactions. This information can be used to sell other products and service warranties and to process orders more efficiently.

Are retailers free to use such information for any purpose, or is the customer's right to privacy being violated? Although this question is the subject of much debate, public sentiment favors the protection of consumer privacy. Some of the major videotape rental firms no longer maintain records of customers' past rentals. Other companies that fear adverse publicity will quite likely take a right-to-privacy stance.

Ecological considerations

Retailers have begun to pay more attention to how their operations affect the environment. Wal-Mart, for example, won an award from the UN for designing a store in Lawrence, Kansas, that minimizes the impact on the environment.[45] The store uses recycled material in its parking lot, signage, carpet, and vestibule mats. Its air conditioning system uses a refrigerant that does not deplete the ozone layer, and solar energy lights the store's main sign. In addition, 1,200 square feet of the store's space is dedicated to environmental education, and the store is a site for community recycling.

Another indication that retailers are becoming more concerned with environmental issues is a move to ban smoking in shopping malls. Since the Environmental Protection Agency released a report on the dangers of secondhand smoke, shopping centers across the country have not waited for legal prompting—instead, they have taken the initiative to ban smoking. A spokesperson for the International Council of Retailers says that because so many malls have rushed to ban smoking, the organization cannot keep a current count of them. Not all shopping malls have joined the ban, however, fearing it would alienate consumers. But it appears that most customers favor the ban, so more malls are likely to follow suit.[46]

Summary

1. *Understand the economic importance of retailing and its role in the marketing channel.* The role of retailing in the marketing channel is to provide products and services to the ultimate, or final consumer. Retailing is an important economic activity in that (1) there are approximately 1.3 million retailers in the US; (2) nearly 19 million people, one-eighth of the US labor force, are employed in retail or retail-related activities; and (3) retailers generate approximately $1.8 trillion in sales. Retailers differ from other channel members in that they sell smaller quantities more frequently, offer assortments of products, and emphasize atmospherics in their selling.

2. *Cite evidence of the globalization of retailing.* Toys "Я" Us, McDonald's, Wal-Mart, Sears, and J. C. Penney are but a few companies expanding retail operations around the globe. Markets in countries with highly developed economies such as the US are somewhat saturated, thus retailers are increasingly eager to expand to less competitive markets.

3. *Discuss some of the advances in retailing technology.* Retailing has benefited from various technologies in recent years. VideOcarts, automated cash registers, electronic kiosks, Universal Product Code scanners, and cashless grocery shopping are some examples of technology put to good use in retailing. The explosive growth in nonstore retailing is fueled in part by new computer and communications technology.

4. *Explain the reasons behind the growth of nonstore retailing.* Busy people like to shop at their preferred times in the convenience of their own homes. Successful catalog retailing has encouraged consumers to try other forms of nonstore retailing such as TV and videotext shopping. The growth of nonstore retailing is probably also the result of consumer boredom and dissatisfaction with some traditional retail stores.

5. *Describe key factors in the retail marketing environment, and understand how they relate to retail strategy.* Controllable factors include location, products and services, pricing, and marketing communications. Uncontrollable factors are consumers, competition, economic conditions, and seasonality. To be successful, retailers must effectively manipulate the controllable factors to manage the environment created by always-changing uncontrollable factors.

6. *Cite important ethical and legal issues facing retailers.* Routine legal restrictions govern practically every aspect of retailing. Contemporary ethical and legal issues of special concern are shoplifting, the use of slotting allowances, the use of customer information, and ecological considerations. Employee, consumer, and supplier theft all figure into shoplifting. Slotting allowances are fees manufacturers pay to retailers or wholesalers to obtain shelf or warehouse space for their products. It's an ethically questionable practice and may be illegal. Other concerns are the retailer's use of customer information versus the individual's right to privacy, and the ecological impact of retail operations.

Key terms & concepts

Review & discussion questions

1. What evidence can you cite supporting the economic importance of retailing?

2. How do retailers differ from other members in the channel of distribution?

3. Review the opening example of Toys "Я" Us in Japan. Why has it been difficult for retailers to enter the Japanese market?

4. Review **The Technological Edge: Retailers Go Interactive with Video Kiosks.** Do you think consumers will quickly accept the use of such technology?

5. Review **The Entrepreneurial Spirit: sMall Shops Test Big Ideas.** What do you think would be the advantages and disadvantages of leasing such a shop?

6. What uncontrollable factors affect the retail environment? What can retailers do to minimize the impact of these factors on sales?

7. What types of locations are possible alternatives for retailers? Briefly define each type of location.

8. List and describe the three types of nonstore retailing. What are the advantages and disadvantages of nonstore retail operations?

9. Discuss the benefits of retail franchising from both the franchisor's and franchisee's point of view.

10. Discuss some of the key ethical and legal issues in retailing.

Application exercises

1. Retailers that sell secondhand merchandise, such as flea markets or Salvation Army stores, have been doing relatively well in recent years. Can you explain their success in terms of economic conditions and consumer preferences discussed in this chapter?

2. Tune in to a television shopping program once a week for a month, and analyze the products sold and the sales methods used. In particular, assess the following issues:

   - What is the primary pricing strategy?
   - What role do celebrities play in the programming?
   - Can you generalize about the size and colors offered in apparel sales?
   - Is it important to have merchandise with easy-to-demonstrate features?

3. For each of the following types of retail operations, suggest complementary products, either goods or services, that could logically be added to the merchandise mix:

   - A small coffee shop that features light desserts, pastries, espresso, cappuccino, and gourmet coffees.
   - A small independent bookstore located near a retirement community.
   - A large parking garage adjacent to a downtown office building.
   - A hairstyling salon.
   - A pet supplies store.

Case 15.1   QVC Network: TV home shopping takes off

In mid-1993, the business press was filled with the news of a pending merger between the QVC Network and the Home Shopping Network (HSN). Analysts agreed that nonstore retailing, especially home shopping, via television, was finally beginning to take off.

Several factors led to the increasing popularity of televised home shopping in the early 90s. Busy consumers had little time for long shopping trips, and many were dissatisfied with routine mall shopping. Crowds, traffic, and safety concerns were simply turning consumers off. Also, catalog shopping had become extremely popular, and many of these shoppers were ready and willing to try yet another new way to shop.

On the seller's side, business conditions practically forced manufacturers and retailers to try new distribution methods. In the sluggish economic climate of the early 90s, retail sales were weak, and price reductions were simply not bringing in enough customers. Retailers needed relief, and home shopping offered a low-cost distribution system. Using such a system, retailers had no need for hundreds, perhaps thousands, of stores, each with its own inventory.

Besides cutting back retailers' inventory expense, home shopping eliminates rent and combines the sales function with advertising on the air. These positive aspects enticed leading store and catalog retailers into home shopping—either with their own networks or via existing networks. But the most important factor is that it works. For example, Joan Rivers has sold over $60 million of jewelry on QVC, and designer Diane Von Furstenburg sold $1.2 million in dresses in a mere 90 minutes.

With the QVC/HSN merger, a single company now dominates televised home shopping. And since home shopping accounts for less than 2 percent of total retail sales, there is plenty of room for growth. The force behind the merger was Barry Diller, founder of the Fox Broadcasting Company. Diller plans to grow the merged company with specialized shopping programs to match consumer lifestyles and interests. He is also moving rapidly to expand outside the United States. Already, QVC broadcasts in Japan, Canada, parts of Europe, and Mexico. Another possibility is selling through computer networks such as Prodigy.

Questions:

1. From the consumer's point of view, what makes nonstore retailing an attractive alternative to shopping in stores?

2. What factors interest retailers in selling via televised home shopping networks?

3. What types of lifestyle-oriented shopping programs do you think would be successful on home shopping networks?

Sources: Scott Donaton, "Home Shopping Networks Bring Shoppers on Board," *Advertising Age,* April 19, 1993, p. S8; "Nordstrom Gears Up for Catalogue Operation and Interactive TV," *Marketing News,* June 21, 1993, p. 5; Kevin Maney, "Wall Street Tunes In to QVC Stock," *USA Today,* July 15, 1993, p. B3; and Laura Zinn, Gail de George, Rochelle Shoretz, Dori Jones Yang, and Stephanie Anderson Forest, "Retailing Will Never Be the Same," *Business Week,* July 26, 1993, pp. 54–60.

Case 15.2 — Pier 1: Riding the wave of global expansion

For over three decades, Texas-based Pier 1 focused on the US and Canada, where it has more than 600 stores. By selling unique home furnishings from around the globe at reasonable prices, Pier 1 has enjoyed healthy sales growth for almost three decades.

Pier 1 is well poised for global expansion. Chairman Clark A. Johnson believes that Southeast Asia, Mexico, and Central and South America are among the most promising areas, where Pier 1 could ride the wave of population growth to increased sales. By the year 2000, Pier 1 plans to open approximately 550 new stores, 300 outside the US and Canada.

In expanding beyond North America, Pier 1 faces a number of challenges. Management must decide whether to invest in direct ownership of stores in foreign countries or whether to enter into joint ventures with foreign partners. Or it can seek franchisees. According to Johnson, Pier 1 is leaning toward direct investment in English-speaking countries. The company might opt for joint ventures and franchising in non–English-speaking locations, preferring to use local businesspeople who know the local language and culture.

In many European countries, the cost of land for retail sites is extremely high, in turn affecting store size, warehousing and distribution costs, and many other general costs. According to a Pier 1 executive in the UK, Europe is similar to Manhattan when it comes to location: good locations are hard to find, and they are expensive.

As the Pier 1 retail empire grows, so must its support functions. Pier 1 plans to open a major buying and administrative office in Southeast Asia. Although the addition of office staff can be expensive, Pier 1 maintains a fairly low overhead in its stores, thanks to inexpensive merchandising practices.

Transplanting retail operations from one culture to another is difficult. For one thing, it is hard to determine which merchandise will most appeal to shoppers. Pier 1 offers an eclectic assortment, a sort of multicultural mix-and-match. Preliminary plans call for tailoring merchandise to the locale. For example, furniture in Japan will be sized to fit smaller Japanese homes and apartments. Chopsticks, popular in the US, will not be sold in Japan. Pier 1 expects arts and crafts from the US and posters of pop heroes to be big sellers in the Far East and Europe. In Puerto Rico, the same merchandise mix sold in Florida works quite well.

There are reasons to believe Pier 1 will be successful in its global expansion. The company has a reputation for making good use of input from customers in formulating marketing strategy and selecting merchandise. Its in-store displays are visually appealing, and management has done a great job in establishing a strong network of dependable vendors.

As Pier 1 faces the future, president Marvin Girouard urges his employees to seek merchandise where no other retailers look, learn local cultures, and take the time to establish trust with vendors and customers.

Global catalog retailing is another possibility, which makes sense, given high land costs and the increasing "time poverty" of dual income families in many major cities.

Questions:

1. How has Pier 1 been successful in the highly competitive home furnishings market?

2. With such a successful operation in North America, why would Pier 1 be interested in global expansion?

3. What are the key decision areas for Pier 1 as it implements a global expansion strategy?

Sources: Leonard R. Berry, "Qualities of Leadership," *Supermarket News,* May 1992, pp. 178–79; Stephanie Anderson Forest and Ruth Golby, "A Pier 1 in Every Port?" *Business Week,* May 31, 1993, p. 88; and Allyson Stewart, "US Puts Pier Pressure on Europe's Retailers," *Marketing News,* August 2, 1993, pp. 6–7.

Wholesaling and Logistics Management

After studying this chapter you should be able to:

1. Understand wholesaling and describe the three basic categories of wholesalers.

2. Identify and discuss the roles of different types of full-service and limited-function wholesalers.

3. Explain differences among the functions of agents, brokers, and commission merchants.

4. Understand the differences between manufacturers' sales branches and offices.

5. Appreciate how slow growth rates and globalization will affect wholesaling in the future.

6. Define logistics management and explain its key role in marketing.

7. Understand logistics activities, including warehousing, materials handling, inventory control, order processing, and transporting.

8. Discuss how some of the key ethical and legal issues affect logistics.

Little Debbie: Taking the cake in distribution

*L*ittle Debbie is the nation's best-selling snack-cake brand, far outdistancing Hostess, Tastykake, and Dolly Madison in market share. Its cakes and cookies, also sold under the Sunbelt label, routinely sell for 50 to 70 percent less than competitors' products. McKee Foods, the baking company that makes and sells Little Debbie, has a very simple marketing strategy—to undersell the competition. By offering low prices and streamlining its distribution system, McKee Foods has become one of the most profitable companies in the baking industry.

Little Debbie products contain natural preservatives that prolong shelf life to 30 days; Hostess Twinkies, by comparison, turn stale in 7 to 10 days. The longer shelf life eliminates the need for weekly delivery, thus cutting distribution costs. In addition, McKee ships to independent warehouses around the country, from which distributors deliver to the stores. Most of McKee's competitors sell and deliver directly to retail stores, incurring the added expense of a salesforce and the higher transportation costs of delivering to individual stores. To ensure dependable deliveries to the warehouses, McKee emphasizes the role of their fleet mechanics, a key to safe, reliable operation.

The future looks bright for McKee Foods. An already-strong demand is increasing, and McKee only produces to fill orders. Competitors will have a hard time matching McKee's low prices, as most are large corporations with high overhead costs. Even if competitors tried to lower costs to compete with McKee, it would take years to achieve the economies of scale McKee enjoys by virtue of its dominant market share. According to a Merril Lynch market analyst, the McKees have so dominated this end of the market that it would be difficult for the competition to step in.

By keeping a watchful eye on distribution expenses and product quality, McKee Foods has built a loyal following for Little Debbie throughout the marketing channel—from wholesaler to retailer to ultimate consumer.

Sources: William Stern, "Mom and Dad Knew Every Name," *Forbes,* December 7, 1992, pp. 172–74; and Carol Birkland, "Rodeo Roundup," *Fleet Equipment,* June 1992, pp. 30–31.

The Little Debbie example highlights the importance of the distribution function in the marketing of a product or service. First, note that the marketing channel strategy must be compatible with the product. Little Debbie has a longer shelf life than its competitors, which allows McKee Foods to use a less costly distribution method. This in turn allows McKee to pursue a marketing strategy based primarily on low prices to retailers.

Low prices are attractive when retailers are squeezed by most distributors to accept increased prices. Low prices also appeal to buyers, especially snack-cake buyers 15 years old and younger—fully 50 percent of Little Debbie's market. But beyond that, independent warehouses and distributors fulfill storage and delivery functions for Little Debbie, performing well against competitors' salesforces and direct delivery to the stores. In a highly competitive market, McKee Foods offers a fine example of the *execution* and *productivity perspectives.*

In this chapter we discuss two key areas related to the marketing channel and the other marketing mix elements: wholesaling and logistics management. Briefly, **wholesalers** are intermediaries in the marketing channel that sell to customers other than individual or household consumers. **Logistics management** is the planning, implementing, and movement of raw materials and products from point of origin to point of consumption.

Wholesalers are often involved in all five key functions of the marketing channel: marketing communications, inventory management, physical distribution, provision of market feedback, and assumption of financial risk. Logistics management also has some relevance to those functions, but it normally relates more specifically to inventory management and physical distribution activities.

Wholesaling

Wholesaling is an important aspect of the marketing channel strategy for many firms. It refers to the marketing activities associated with selling products to purchasers that resell the products, use them to make another product, or use them to conduct business activities. Wholesaling does not include transactions with household and individual consumers, nor does it include the small purchases businesses occasionally make from retail stores. Essentially, wholesalers sell to manufacturers and industrial customers, retailers, government agencies, other wholesalers, and institutional customers such as schools and hospitals.

Garbo Lobster is a US-Canadian wholesaler that sells live lobsters to restaurants and grocers worldwide.

Garbo Lobster
We put our name on it

Garbo Lobster Company, Inc.
Stonington, Connecticut 06378 USA
Phone: (203)535-1590 Fax: (203)535-2149

Garbo Lobster Limited
Deer Island, New Brunswick, CANADA

WORLDWIDE WHOLESALE EXPORTERS OF
LIVE LOBSTER

Visit our Booth No. 4402 at the
Boston Seafood Show

We mentioned in Chapter 14 that all intermediaries in a marketing channel, including wholesalers, must justify their existence by performing at least one function better than any other channel member. For wholesalers, this often means adding value to goods and services as they pass through the channel. For example, Lotus Development Corporation uses intermediaries called **value-added resellers (VARs)** to sell *Notes,* a database technology that allows workers in groups to share information.[1] The VARs add value to the Lotus software program in many ways, including educating potential users and designing specific applications tailored to differing user needs.

EXECUTIVE ROUNDTABLE COMMENT | **Bob Heimbrock, regional sales manager for Pomeroy Computer Resources, comments on the constant need for resellers to justify their position in the channel:**

With firms like IBM, Compaq, Apple, and AT&T telling the corporate customer that the value-added reseller channel is the best source for their products, companies like ours have experienced tremendous growth. It is too expensive for the manufacturers to sell to business end-users, and it is exactly what we are designed to do. At Pomeroy, our expertise in systems integration, networking, and computer applications allows us to be partners with our customers.

Types of wholesalers

According to the US Department of Commerce, the three basic categories of wholesalers are merchant wholesalers; agents, brokers, and commission merchants; and manufacturers' sales branches and offices. Exhibit 16.1 shows the three categories and the main types of wholesalers within each. Independent wholesalers that take title to the products they sell are called **merchant wholesalers.** Wholesalers in the second category, agents, brokers, and commission merchants, do not take title to the products bought or sold. They are sometimes referred to as *functional middlemen.* Those in the third category, manufacturers' sales branches and offices, are owned by producers or manufacturing firms.

Exhibit 16.1   **Categories and types of wholesalers**

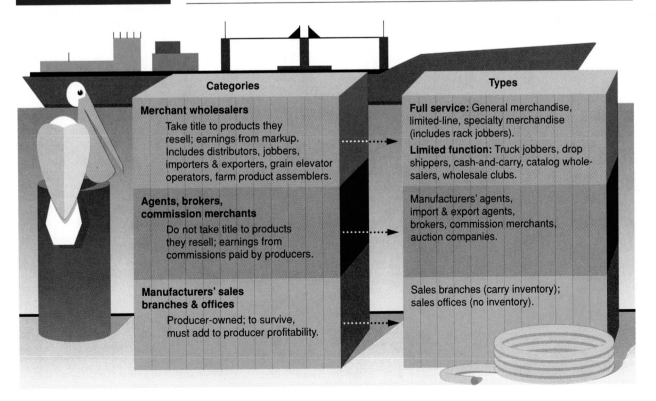

Categories

Merchant wholesalers
Take title to products they resell; earnings from markup. Includes distributors, jobbers, importers & exporters, grain elevator operators, farm product assemblers.

Agents, brokers, commission merchants
Do not take title to products they resell; earnings from commissions paid by producers.

Manufacturers' sales branches & offices
Producer-owned; to survive, must add to producer profitability.

Types

Full service: General merchandise, limited-line, specialty merchandise (includes rack jobbers).

Limited function: Truck jobbers, drop shippers, cash-and-carry, catalog wholesalers, wholesale clubs.

Manufacturers' agents, import & export agents, brokers, commission merchants, auction companies.

Sales branches (carry inventory); sales offices (no inventory).

Exhibit 16.2   **Functions performed by wholesalers**

Type of wholesaler	Marketing communications*	Inventory mgmt & storage	Physical distribution	Market feedback/ Advisory Board	Financial risk/ offer credit+
Full-service merchant wholesalers	Yes	Yes	Yes	Yes	Yes
Truck jobbers	Yes	Yes	Yes	Sometimes	Sometimes
Drop shippers	No	No	Yes	Yes	Yes
Cash & carry	No	Yes	No	Sometimes	No
Catalog wholesalers	Yes	Yes	Yes	Sometimes	Sometimes
Wholesale clubs	Sometimes	Yes	No	Sometimes	No
Mfrs' agents	Sometimes	Sometimes	Sometimes	Yes	No
Auction companies	Yes	Sometimes	No	No	No
Import & export agents	Sometimes	Sometimes	Sometimes	Yes	No
Brokers	No	No	No	Yes	No
Commission merchants	Yes	Yes	Sometimes	Yes	Sometimes
Mfrs' sales branches	Sometimes	Yes	Yes	Yes	Yes
Mfrs' sales offices	Sometimes	No	No	Yes	Yes

Note: Refer to Exhibit 14.1 for multiple examples of each functional area.

* By definition, all wholesalers are involved in at least one form of marketing communications (selling).

+ All wholesalers not classified as agents, brokers, or commission merchants incur financial risk when they assume ownership, or take title, to the products they subsequently resell. This exhibit refers to the financial risk taken by wholesalers that offer credit to their customers.

Merchant wholesalers

According to the *Census of the Wholesale Trade,* published by the Department of Commerce, there are almost 400,000 merchant wholesalers based in the US, accounting for 83 percent of the wholesale establishments in the country.[2] Merchant wholesalers, often called *distributors,* are categorized as either full-service wholesalers or limited-function wholesalers.

Full-service wholesalers.   **Full-service wholesalers** by definition perform a wide range of services for their customers and the parties from which they purchase. These wholesalers might perform all key activities in an entire marketing channel (as in Exhibit 16.2), while limited-function wholesalers are likely to specialize in only a few activities.

Full-service wholesalers include general merchandise, limited-line, and specialty-line wholesalers. For a better idea of services available from full-service wholesalers, see Exhibit 16.3 (pp. 392–93). **General merchandise wholesalers** carry a wide variety of products and provide extensive services for their customers. A typical example is Alabama Paper Company, which serves retail, industrial, and business customers throughout Alabama from its Birmingham warehouse. Its diverse product line, in excess of 5,000 items, includes consumer electronics, fishing and hunting merchandise, industrial adhesives and packaging materials, office supplies, and home improvement items. As a full-service wholesaler, Alabama Paper performs many marketing channel functions and provides services for its customers and their suppliers.

Limited-line wholesalers do not stock as many products as general merchandise wholesalers, but they offer more depth in their product offering. Merisel International, for example, is a limited-line wholesaler specializing in personal computer products. Demonstrating a *global perspective,* Merisel concentrates on selling Compaq personal computers and related supplies to retail stores around the world. Limited-line wholesalers often provide extensive services for their customers, as Merisel does.

Among merchant wholesalers, **specialty-line wholesalers** carry the most narrow product assortment—usually a single product line or part of one. To justify their existence, specialty-line wholesalers must be experts on the products they sell.

Rack jobbers, a category of specialty-line wholesalers, sell to retail stores. They set up and maintain attractive store displays and stock them with goods sold on consignment (the retailer pays for the goods only when sold). Rack jobbers are also called *service merchandisers,* a term that better captures the service-oriented aspects of their roles. Retailers depend on rack jobbers particularly in the provision of health and beauty aids, hosiery, and books and magazines. Some rack jobbers might be considered limited-function wholesalers if they carry very small inventories or fail to provide other services listed in Exhibit 16.2.

Limited-function wholesalers. Exhibit 16.1 shows five primary types of **limited-function wholesalers:** truck jobbers, drop shippers, cash-and-carry wholesalers, catalog wholesalers, and wholesale clubs. As Exhibit 16.2 shows, these wholesalers do not offer the comprehensive services of full-service wholesalers.

Producers of fast-moving or perishable goods that require frequent replenishment often use **truck jobbers.** These limited-service wholesalers deliver within a particular geographic area to ensure freshness of certain goods (bakery, meat, dairy). Marketers often choose truck jobbers, with their quick delivery and frequent store visits, to wholesale miscellaneous high-margin items such as candy, chewing gum, cigarettes, novelty items, and inexpensive toys sold in retail stores. Retailers hate to be out of these items, for consumers will usually buy them at the next most convenient store instead.

Drop shippers arrange for shipments directly from the factory to the customer. Although they do not physically handle the product, drop shippers do take title and all associated risks while the product is in transit. They also provide the necessary sales support. Drop shippers operate in a wide variety of industries, including industrial packaging, lumber, chemicals, and petroleum and heating products.

As the term implies, **cash-and-carry wholesalers** do not deliver the products they sell, nor do they extend credit. Small retailers and other businesses whose limited sales make them unprofitable customers for larger wholesalers are the primary customers for cash-and-carry wholesalers. For example, Oxford Seafood in Oxford, Mississippi, makes a daily trip to cash-and-carry seafood wholesalers in Louisiana, purchases crates of fresh seafood, and trucks them back to Oxford for sale later the same day.

Catalog wholesalers serve both major population centers and remote geographic locations and offer an alternative to cash-and-carry wholesalers. Most catalog wholesalers use delivery services such as UPS and require prepayment by check, money order, or credit card. Catalog wholesalers such as BrownCor International have established a large customer base by offering a wide range of competitively priced products, including office furniture, equipment and supplies, directional signs, packaging materials, and shelf and storage systems. These products can be conveniently ordered using toll-free telephone or fax systems.

Distributor services	To manufacturer	To retailer
Exhibit 16.3		**Services provided by full-service wholesalers/distributors**
Sensible buying	• Market feedback improves production planning, reducing costs of raw materials, components.	• Distributor buying clout passed on through low prices. • Dealing with only one or two wholesalers cuts purchasing costs, leads to one-stop shopping.
Distribution flow	• Reduces storage needs, moves products faster, cuts inventory costs. • Products stored closer to retailer for faster delivery; may cut need for costly distribution centers.	• Weekly deliveries reduce need for product storage, increase selling space. • Faster turnover increases profits.
Timely delivery	• Large orders, retail delivery fleets, & coordinated back-haul programs reduce transportation costs, keeping product prices competitive.	• Regular deliveries permit better planning, cut receiving costs. • Fast restocking of high-demand products for immediate display.
Traffic-building promotion	• Centralized co-op programs maximize ad dollar at local level. • Increases consumer awareness, establishes products, builds market share.	• Direct-mail circulars, ads, etc., build retail traffic, increase store capabilities, save administrative effort. • Co-op programs save time, money.
Marketing	• Reduces selling costs, frees executive time as distribs serve many retail accounts; products receive wider representation.	• Retail sales training, merchandising, display, layout improve with distrib aid. • Computer systems provide price stickers, program margin requirements, optimize profits. • Hundreds of mfrs' products in one retail location.

Note how the services of a wholesaler can benefit other channel members (in this case, manufacturers and retailers) in the implementation of key marketing perspectives. This exhibit illustrates the *relationship, quality/value, productivity, technological,* and *execution perspectives.*

continued

Another type of catalog wholesaler is the mail-order pharmacy, which sells prescription drugs to corporations seeking to cut their health care benefits costs. Industry leader Medco Containment Systems sells via catalog to companies like General Electric, Alcoa, and Mobil. Employees purchase the prescription drugs from the corporation rather than from a traditional pharmacist, and the corporation realizes as much as a 20 percent reduction in prescription bills.[3]

Wholesale clubs are a growing phenomenon. These enterprises, which also serve retail customers under the same roof, are especially popular with small-business customers, civic and social organizations, and church groups. Wholesale club members pay an annual fee that entitles them to make tax-free

W. W. Grainger, a nationwide distributor of equipment, components, and supplies to commercial, industrial, contractor, and institutional markets, provides an example of the *technological perspective* with its use of an electronic catalog to reach more than 4,000 customers.

Exhibit 16.3	Services provided by full-service wholesalers/distributors (concluded)	

Distributor manages assets	Manufacturer benefits	Retailer benefits
Product inventory	• Storage & delivery costs reduced to minimum. • Feedback on item movement improves production planning & use of assets.	• Turnover improved, promotional impact maximized, cash flow/return on investment increased. • In stock, good prices, superior service.
Physical plant	• Majority of plant used for production, not storage. • Need for regional redistribution facilities reduced or eliminated.	• More productive use of square footage ensured by lower inventory requirements, distrib printouts on product movement and margin management. • Market impact from merchandising assistance, in-store displays, signing, customer traffic flow.
Cash flow and credit	• Receivables minimized, credit risks reduced. • Administrative workload reduced.	• Cash flow accelerated through more frequent small purchases; less cash tied up in inventory. • Best credit terms, extended dating, less paperwork.
People	• Can concentrate on mfring & marketing; distribs take product to market. • Concentrating on distributor customers enhances strong relationships with fewer customers.	• Selling techniques, product knowledge enhanced through distrib training, sales aids. • One-on-one contact with distrib mgmt to seize market opportunities.

purchases at lower-than-retail prices. As leaders such as Costco, Pace Warehouse, and Sam's Club enjoy rapid expansion, wholesale clubs are making major inroads into markets once dominated by older forms of wholesaling, such as office supply and institutional food wholesalers. They are also taking business away from certain types of retailers, such as supermarkets and tire dealers. Wholesale clubs reflect the *quality/value, productivity, execution,* and *visionary perspectives.*

Sam's Club, a division of Wal-Mart, expanded rapidly by acquiring competitive wholesale clubs and opening new clubs in the US and Mexico. Its newest clubs are large enough to incorporate departments selling fresh produce, meat, and bakery items.

Phillips, auction house and appraisers since 1796, has offices and galleries worldwide, including New York, London, Brussels, and Stockholm.

Agents, brokers, and commission merchants

More than 40,000 agent, broker, and commission merchant organizations operate at the wholesale level, making up approximately 9 percent of all wholesale establishments. As Exhibit 16.1 indicates, these wholesalers do not take title to the products they resell. They perform a limited number of marketing channel activities, emphasizing sales or purchases (see Exhibit 16.2). Since these wholesalers perform so few marketing channel functions, they must be very knowledgeable and adopt the *relationship perspective* with their customers and suppliers to generate income through commissions.

Agents.   **Manufacturers' agents**, also called manufacturers' representatives or reps, constitute the largest group in this wholesale merchant category. There are more than 24,000 manufacturers' agents in the country, all of which sell related but noncompeting product lines for manufacturers. For example, Becker Marketing Services, Inc., an Atlanta-based manufacturers' agent, sells foodservice items such as disposable tablecloths, plastic plates, salt and pepper shakers, and napkins, all furnished by different manufacturers. Manufacturers' agents frequently work by contract with the companies they represent, and usually have exclusive rights to represent each manufacturer within a specified geographic area.

Another type of agent is the auction company, of which there are approximately 1,300 in the United States. Auction companies, also called **auction houses**, sell merchandise at a given time and place to the highest bidder. They typically promote the sale of the merchandise through advertising that specifies the time, date, and location of the auction, along with a description of the merchandise to be sold and the auction rules.

Auction houses are a popular way to sell livestock, tobacco, used automobiles, and art and antiques. Famous art auctioneers are Sotheby's, Phillips, and Christie's in New York, where works by noted artists sometimes fetch millions of dollars. Following the savings and loan scandal of the early 1990s, auction houses were used to liquidate approximately $35 million worth of real estate and loan portfolios seized from failed financial institutions. Auction houses also helped sell off $10 billion in "personal property" of the unscrupulous savings and loan executives and their associates—everything from office furniture to art collections to Arabian show horses.[4]

Two other types of agents, import and export, specialize in international trade. **Import agents**—approximately 700 in the US—find products in foreign countries to sell in their home countries. For example, cut flowers, available at lower cost outside the US, are flown into the country daily. On a typical day, import agents arrange for seven Boeing 747s to deliver inexpensive carnations and roses from Colombia to the United States.[5] In many countries, it is extremely difficult (or even illegal) to try to sell products from another country without going through an import agent or similar intermediary.[6]

On the other hand, **export agents** locate and develop markets abroad for products manufactured in their home countries. Basically, they function as manufacturers' agents in the home country and are paid a commission by the companies they represent. There are more than 500 export agents in the United States.

Many export agents embody the *entrepreneurial perspective* when they match suppliers in one country with customers in another. In some instances, these agents can be successful with limited capital resources. For example, Barry Grimes-Hardy, a seafood company manager in Silver Spring, Maryland, set up his own export company, Bridgeline, with no cash. When he received a $36,000 order for two trailer-sized refrigerated containers of fish to be exported to Mali, West Africa, he financed the deal through another exporter.[7]

Brokers. **Brokers** are intermediaries that bring buyers and sellers together. They are paid a commission by either the buyer or the seller, depending on which party they represent in a given transaction. Unlike manufacturers' agents, brokers do not enter into contracts for extended time periods with the parties they represent. Instead, they work on a transaction-by-transaction basis.

There are almost 9,000 wholesale broker firms in the US, many of them in food and agricultural businesses. The *execution perspective* is portrayed by FoodMatch, a broker that serves the $3 billion produce market within a 200-mile radius of Memphis, Tennessee.[8] Growers pay FoodMatch a 3 percent commission to find grocery store buyers. By using FoodMatch as a broker, the growers gain access to a large market, while the grocery chains can get fresher produce from distant markets.

Commission merchants. **Commission merchants** provide a wider range of services than agents or brokers, often engaging in inventory management, physical distribution, and promotional activities, and offering credit and market feedback to the companies they represent. More than 6,000 commission merchants operate in the US, primarily working to sell agricultural products for farmers.

Manufacturers' sales branches and offices

More than 35,000 manufacturer-owned wholesalers operate in the United States. Approximately two-thirds of these, or 22,000, are **manufacturers' sales branches,** which maintain inventory and perform a wide range of functions for the parent company. Manufacturers' sales branches handle delivery and act as an extension of the manufacturer to provide credit, market feedback, and promotional assistance.

Manufacturers' sales offices are the other significant type of producer-owned wholesaler, with more than 14,000 outlets in the United States. Sales offices do not maintain inventory, but they perform a limited range of functions, including assisting with sales and service, providing market feedback, and handling billing and collection of products sold.

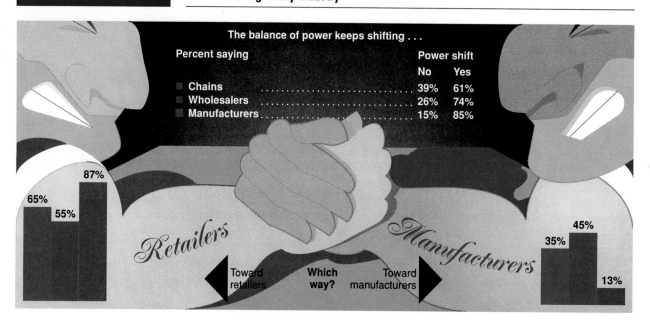

Exhibit 16.4   Power in the grocery industry

The balance of power keeps shifting . . .

Percent saying	Power shift	
	No	Yes
Chains	39%	61%
Wholesalers	26%	74%
Manufacturers	15%	85%

Developments in wholesaling

Three developments in wholesaling deserve special attention—the continuing struggle to grow, the globalization of wholesaling, and the increasing emphasis on developing relationships with others in the marketing channel.

Wholesalers face slow growth

According to the National Association of Wholesaler-Distributors (NAW), gross profits for wholesalers declined in the early 1990s after the industry experienced average growth rates in excess of 5 percent in the late 1980s.[9] In the food industry, where wholesalers are a major factor, growth in the early 1990s was hurt by the economic recession, a decrease in new-store construction, and competition from chains like Kroger and Safeway.[10] Chains, which usually prefer to buy directly from manufacturers, grabbed a larger part of the market in other areas like home improvement, with Home Depot the market leader.[11]

Ironically, while tough economic conditions can squeeze wholesalers as both large chains and small buyers seek lower prices, a booming economy can have a negative effect too. If retail sales grow rapidly, for example, the retailer may decide to cut out the wholesaler and buy directly from manufacturers. Fleming Companies, the largest food wholesaler in the world, once supplied Wal-Mart's Supercenter stores and Phillips grocery stores, but it lost a $375 million account when Wal-Mart completed its own grocery distribution center in Clarksville, Arkansas.[12]

Wholesalers' positions in markets served by retailers could grow even more precarious. Industry observers see power in the channel continuing to shift toward retailers. As shown in Exhibit 16.4, chains, wholesalers, and manufacturers generally agree that power is shifting in the grocery industry. Wholesalers are split on which way the power is shifting—55 percent say toward retailers, 45 percent say manufacturers. The point is that wholesalers are caught in a crossfire between retailers and manufacturers, with both sectors eager to improve their own profitability.

Grocery industry analysts say that wholesalers are more threatened by power shifts than are retailers and manufacturers.[13] For wholesalers, this

Exhibit 16.5

Cyclical wholesaling patterns by stages of economic development

Stages of economic development	Wholesaling patterns
Simple economy	Dominance of international wholesalers (channels controlled by all-purpose wholesale merchants)
Expanding economy	Emergence of interregional wholesalers (regional specialization)
Maturing economy	Growth of specialized wholesalers (product-line & functional specialization)
Advanced economy	Decline of conventional wholesalers and regrouping by wholesalers (channels controlled by large-scale retailers & manufacturers)
Global economy	Reemergence of international wholesalers

means a constant battle to improve service (*quality/value perspective*) and keep costs of operations and selling prices to a minimum (*productivity* and *execution perspectives*).

Globalization of wholesaling

In response to tougher conditions in domestic markets, many American wholesalers have adopted a *global perspective*. The **North American Free Trade Agreement (NAFTA)** makes it far easier to do business across three countries (Mexico, the US, Canada), encouraging wholesalers to expand their operations. The NAW predicts that by the year 2000 approximately 18 percent of US wholesalers' business, about double the 1992 share, will come from foreign markets.[14] According to observers of the wholesale sector, a decision to stick only with domestic markets may mean a decision not to grow.[15]

If US wholesalers become more prominent in international trade, they will follow a pattern of development shown in Exhibit 16.5. This pattern suggests that international wholesalers play an important role in servicing the needs of a country with a simple economy. As the country's economy reaches the advanced stage, however, the role of conventional wholesalers becomes less important. Finally, when the country becomes part of a global economy, international wholesalers reemerge as an important element in the economic system. The United States, along with its primary trading partners, is part of a growing global economy, a factor that may help wholesalers maintain or expand their base of business.

Wholesalers that expand via globalization should expect to face a new set of challenges—competition from established wholesalers, and new languages, legal systems, and cultural differences. Nonetheless, the effort to globalize can pay off. For an example of wholesaling success through globalization, see **The Entrepreneurial Spirit: Swedish Classics Goes International.**

Relationships in wholesaling

Mike Norberg, president of the Specialty Tool & Fastener Distribution Association (STAFDA), confirms the importance of a *relationship perspective:* "Partnering seems to be the buzzword these days. It is a major topic of discussion throughout our association." Frank Williams, former president of STAFDA, adds, "Partnership *is* the buzzword of the 90s—and it is appropriate."[16]

Swedish Classics goes international

*E*ntrepreneur Peter Nielsen of Oxford, Maryland, found that importing hard-to-get parts for vintage Volvos complemented his auto repair and restoration business, Swedish Classics. In an attempt to boost margins and cut costs, Nielsen went directly to manufacturers in England and Sweden. Later, he used the services of an import agent to handle all shipping arrangements.

With his foray into the global market, Nielsen became the exclusive US distributor for a highly profitable line of Volvo emblems. He also distributes thousands of Volvo parts. He advises would-be international distributors to look closely at their total product costs (including purchase cost from the factory, freight charges, custom duties, interest on bank letters of credit, and import-agent fees) before deciding to take the plunge. Other importers point out the importance of making a binding agreement with foreign suppliers to ensure product quality.

Source: "How to Navigate the Importing Seas," *Inc.,* September 1992, p. 28. Reprinted with permission, *Inc.* magazine, September 1992. Copyright 1992 by Goldhirsh Group, Inc., 38 Commercial Wharf, Boston, MA 02110.

The struggle of wholesalers to grow in a tough business environment has fostered interest in developing strong relationships—even partnerships—between wholesalers and customers and suppliers. One wholesaler who believes in the partnership approach is Jim Beckstein, CEO of Mill Supplies, Inc., in Fort Wayne, Indiana. Beckstein advises wholesalers to work closely with manufacturers: "Explain customer needs and problems to them. Encourage manufacturers to send their salespeople out into the field with you and your people. This gives suppliers' salespeople the opportunity to listen to the distributors' customers, understand their needs, and show them directly the benefits their products can provide."[17]

EXECUTIVE ROUNDTABLE COMMENT | **Bob Heimbrock, regional sales manager for Pomeroy Computer Resources, reinforces the importance of establishing strong customer relationships:**

Strong relationships are the key to success. Products can be acquired from hundreds of resellers. By providing the right services, such as training and equipment maintenance, we can increase customer comfort levels about us—that's what sets us apart.

Logistics management

Logistics management, as defined at the beginning of the chapter, deals with the movement of raw materials and products from point of origin to point of consumption. It also includes the management of information about materials and products as they move through marketing channels. In the late 1980s, for example, Federal Express pioneered satellite-based tracking systems that allow employees and customers to check on the status of shipments at any point in the logistics process.

The importance of logistics management has increased in today's environment, marked by the use of speed as a competitive edge (to deliver customers' orders, for example), development of exciting new computer technologies, and increased realization that overall operating costs are extremely sensitive to the

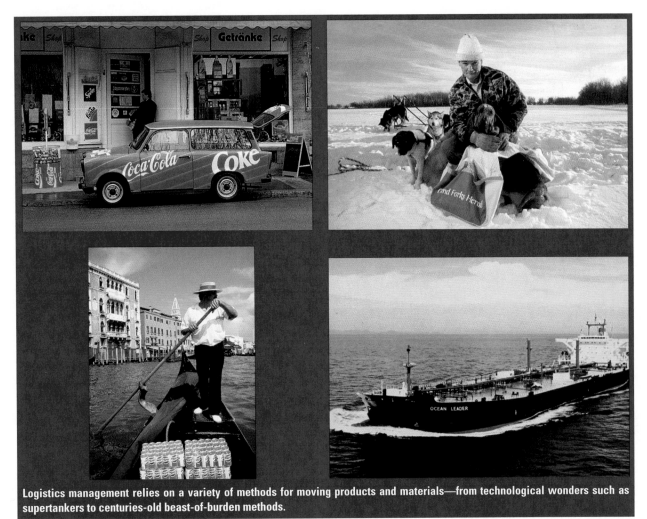

Logistics management relies on a variety of methods for moving products and materials—from technological wonders such as supertankers to centuries-old beast-of-burden methods.

various costs of handling and holding inventory. These factors point to the necessity of firms taking *productivity* and *technological perspectives* in their logistics operations. Recently, logistics management has become a differentiating factor in marketing strategy, reflecting the *execution perspective*.[18] As Gerry Clusic, logistics manager for Kellogg Company, puts it, "Logistics will become an increasingly important part of a business. It will be more integrated into the strategic planning process . . . I see companies using logistics as a competitive tool."[19]

Importance of logistics to marketing

The drive to enhance customer satisfaction while simultaneously improving productivity and profitability has put logistics in the spotlight in the marketing efforts of many successful firms. Helene Curtis, for example, revamped its logistics system, replacing six older warehouses with a streamlined distribution center. In the new center, computer-controlled forklifts place packages on laser-equipped conveyor belts that read bar codes and speed products on their way to customers. According to a Helene Curtis executive, "Ten years ago, sales reps would have to spend the first five minutes of their presentation time apologizing for what happened with the last shipment. Just giving them five more minutes to sell is a big competitive advantage."[20] Not only has Helene Curtis made its customers happier, but the firm has cut its distribution costs by 40 percent.[21]

Exhibit 16.6

Customer expectations of suppliers' logistics systems

- Ease of inquiry & order entry
- Reliable, timely delivery information
- Accurate, undamaged, complete order fulfillment
- On-time delivery
- Error-free paperwork, especially with invoicing
- Responsive postsale support
- Claims handled with ease

To keep customers satisfied, a logistics system should be easy to use and dependable and offer timely information. These attributes are detailed in Exhibit 16.6.

Key activities in logistics

Logistics includes five key functions: warehousing, materials handling, inventory control, order processing, and transporting raw materials and finished products from origin to destination. In the best logistics systems, these areas are carefully coordinated to gain customer satisfaction at an affordable cost.

Warehousing

Companies can choose private or public warehouses or distribution centers. *Private warehouses* are operated by the company using the warehouse. *Public warehouses* are for-hire facilities available to any business requiring storage or handling of goods. Public warehouses charge fees for storage and handling (receiving and moving goods out of storage).[22] Changes in marketing strategy can affect the choice between a private and a public warehouse. For example, 50-Off Stores serviced its stores from a private warehouse in San Antonio until it expanded into the midsouth region of the country. The 700-mile trip from San Antonio to the new stores was hard on its truckers, so 50-Off began using a public warehouse in Memphis to service its midsouth stores. This move, an example of the *productivity perspective,* allowed 50-Off Stores to concentrate on expansion and the efficient management of its stores.[23]

Distribution centers are private "superwarehouses" that serve a large geographic area. These automated warehouses do more than store products; they receive, process, and ship customer orders. Technological advances have allowed companies to save money and provide better service through distribution centers. Among the many companies using distribution centers are manufacturers such as Nike, Komatsu Dresser (heavy equipment), and Troll Associates (children's books), and retailers such as 50-Off Stores, Athlete's Foot, Williams-Sonoma, Wal-Mart, and McCrory Stores.

This picture may be changing, however. A 1992 survey revealed that although 86 percent of chain-store retailers had at least one distribution center, plans for near-term expansion were modest. Distribution centers may decline in importance in the retail sector, as retailers seek to order directly from vendors for delivery to individual stores.[24]

Materials handling

Materials-handling activities include receiving, identifying, sorting, and storing products, and retrieving the goods for shipment. The *technological perspective* is extremely important in this area of logistics. Bar coding is among the most noteworthy of the technological advances in materials handling, particularly in

McKesson Drug's distribution center in St. Louis, Missouri, features bar-code scanners for routing orders through an automated system that selects the items to be shipped, prints customer invoices, and sends products to the shipping docks. This is an example of the *technological* and *productivity perspectives* in action.

distribution centers. **Bar coding,** which allows a product to be identified by its computer-coded bar pattern, is used in a variety of logistics functions. According to Dave Skinner, distribution manager at Hamilton Beach-Proctor Silex, "There's a lot of emphasis on bar-code technology today; customers are requiring this as part of doing business. Anything we can do to move our product with a minimum amount of time is profitable for everybody."[25] The logistics manager for Tupperware's 300,000-square-foot distribution center in Tennessee adds, "You've come from pencil and paper and manual labor to fully automated warehousing operations with very little manpower and no paper."[26]

Inventory control

Another key area of logistics is inventory control, which attempts to ensure adequate inventory to meet customer needs without incurring additional costs for carrying excess stock. Two such inventory control systems that exemplify the *execution perspective* are in place in many industries: just-in-time and quick-response systems. By 1995, nearly 40 percent of shipments are expected to be made via these types of systems.[27]

Frito-Lay's manufacturing plant in Texas requires on-time, fresh potato shipments from North Dakota. Burlington Northern meets this customer requirement with a program called Precision Execution that matches customer needs with railcar delivery schedules—an example of the *execution perspective.*

Exhibit 16.7

Key activities in quick-response systems

- Retailers track sales & inventory for each item (stock-keeping unit).
- Automatic replenishment systems monitor stock to support smaller, more frequent shipments.
- Retailers assume responsibility for inventory carrying costs.
- Vendors commit to high level of service, stressing shipping accuracy and on-time delivery.
- Retailers share data with vendors to help plan production & commit to specific volume of purchases.
- Vendors mark shipping containers to speed delivery through distribution center to stores.

Just-in-time (JIT) inventory control systems apply primarily to the materials-handling side of logistics. These systems deliver raw materials, subassemblies, and component parts to manufacturers shortly before the scheduled manufacturing run that will consume the incoming shipment, thus the JIT label.

Chrysler uses a JIT system for scheduling incoming inventory to its assembly plants. The company has precisely synchronized inventory control with manufacturing, down to scheduling the delivery of auto parts as little as 30 minutes before they will be used in the assembly process.[28]

EXECUTIVE ROUNDTABLE COMMENT | **Don Johnson, traffic manager for Sharp Manufacturing Company of America in Memphis, Tennessee, comments on the JIT process:**

A JIT inventory process places a large amount of pressure on the transportation process to adjust to changes in a manufacturing process. This pressure is increased even more with a transportation system that may extend halfway around the world. The key to a successful JIT program is up-to-the-minute communications on all shipments, so that all processes are coordinated.

Quick-response (QR) inventory control systems are used by companies that provide retailers with finished goods. Quick-response systems are based on frequent but small orders, since inventory is restocked according to what has just been sold—yesterday, or even today in some systems. By melding strategy and technology, retailers such as Wal-Mart, Kmart, and Dillard's have matched up with vendors like Procter & Gamble, Gitano, and baby-clothes manufacturer Warren Featherstone to improve both responsiveness to the marketplace and productivity. Exhibit 16.7 describes the key steps required to implement a QR system.

Participants in quick-response systems must join together in a logistics partnership. A true partnership is necessary because buyers and sellers share sensitive information and must maintain constant communication. In fact, QR systems require so much information exchange that they take massive investments to implement. Bar coding and point-of-retail-sale scanning devices are needed. **Shipping container marking (SCM)** systems must be installed so tracking information can be fed into a computerized information system. This system is referred to as an **electronic data interchange (EDI)**.

EDIs are becoming increasingly popular for firms operating according to a *global perspective.* For example, Stride-Rite Corporation uses an EDI system to help manage the movement of its footwear from Asian manufacturers to US retailers. Every pair of shoes has a bar code that facilitates tracking, customs clearance, and unloading. Chrysler uses EDI to manage its annual export of 65,000 vehicles. The Chrysler program, known as HarperLink, provides worldwide inventory control, invoicing, and information about ports, carriers, and customs documentation.[29]

Exhibit 16.8

Potential benefits of quick-response inventory control

- Reduced negotiating costs for both buyer & seller
- Increased responsiveness to marketplace needs
- Stability of supply to buyer & demand to the seller
- Smoothing of production runs (fewer peaks & valleys)
- Decreased investment in inventory & storage space
- Fewer out-of-stock occurrences
- Higher levels of customer satisfaction

With a true partnership agreement, technology such as electronic data interchanges, and other resources such as personnel and training, QR systems offer the potential benefits shown in Exhibit 16.8.

Although JIT and QR systems offer impressive advantages, they can present drawbacks as well. Saturn, for example, had to stop the flow of its popular automobiles to 200 dealers around the country when a strike in a supplier's parts-manufacturing facility compromised the JIT inventory system.[30] Saturn resolved the problem within a matter of days, but it serves as a reminder that marketers are never completely insulated from inventory control problems, whatever the technological advances. Cautious marketers may shun quick-response systems in favor of carrying extra inventory, at a cost.

Order processing

Order-processing activities are critical to ensure that customers get what they order, when they want it, properly billed, and with appropriate service to support its use or installation. Accuracy and timeliness are key goals of order-entry processes. QR and JIT systems automatically handle order-processing activities. In other situations, order processing includes order entry, order handling, and scheduling for delivery. The term *order* here refers either to a customer's purchase order or to an order transmitted by a salesperson. Order handling entails procedures such as communicating the order to the shipping department or warehouse, clearing the order for shipping, or scheduling it for production. Eventually, the order is selected from stock, packaged, and scheduled for delivery. The order documentation becomes part of the customer's file of transactions with the seller. See Appendix A for mathematical calculations related to the determination of order quantities.

Transporting

The final logistics activity we consider in this chapter is transporting, which starts with selecting modes of transportation for delivery of products or materials. Transporting is an area of keen interest in implementing the *productivity perspective* for two primary reasons. First, transportation costs are the single largest component of logistics costs, averaging over 50 percent of the total.[31] Second, in a competitive environment with a premium on speedy action, transportation can help or hinder the accomplishment of marketing strategies and objectives.[32]

Shippers have five basic ways to move products and materials from one point to another—rail, truck, air, pipeline, and water transport—and each has its advantages and disadvantages. Logistics managers must assess each mode for costs, reliability, capacity, ability to deliver to customer receiving facilities, transit time, and special handling requirements such as refrigeration and temperature control, safety controls, and the capacity to deliver undamaged goods.

Well-executed order-entry activities can help get customers
what they want. This ad expresses some common customer
expectations.

Central Transport services the US, Canada, and Mexico; this ad
promises customer satisfaction.

Railroads.   Major US railroads haul more then 250,000 carloads of materials
and finished goods in an average week, with coal accounting for almost 40 percent of the total.[33] Rail transport is fairly reliable but subject to interruption due
to periodic labor disputes. These interruptions are usually short, and the federal
government has often intervened to prevent massive shutdowns of rail service.
Rail provides a cost-effective means of moving bulk goods such as coal, grain,
pulp and paper products, chemicals, and metal products over long distances.

In recent years railroad companies have upgraded the quality of their service
and become more competitive with trucking companies. A sign of such progress
is Procter & Gamble's willingness to use rail for a significant portion ($125 mil-
lion in 1991) of its deliveries to retailers. With reconditioned railcars, precision
scheduling, and high-tech tracking systems in place, rail companies convinced
P&G they can deliver almost as well as trucks, and at less cost.[34]

Trucks.   Trucks can deliver almost anywhere, particularly important for customers that lack a rail siding. Their fairly fast transit time makes trucks
extremely effective and efficient for delivery to destinations within 500 miles.
Although generally reliable, trucks can be negatively affected by inclement
weather. Trucking has also been hampered at times by labor strikes, more so
than have railroads.

The trucking industry has worked hard to improve operations, as results
show. A survey of shipping managers indicates that trucking, when compared to

Satellite systems in trucking

Satellites and land-based mobile communications systems offer truckers the information they need to remain competitive with other carriers. These systems allow trucking firms to track the location of their vehicles and communicate with their drivers on a real-time basis, that is, with no delay due to transmission of the message. With such a system in place, drivers can send data and voice messages directly to their companies without having to pull off the road to find a telephone. It allows drivers to take uninterrupted naps and react better to accidents or potentially unsafe conditions. Further, trucks can be redirected while en route, resulting in more fully loaded trips, which ultimately leads to better financial performance for the company and higher driver compensation.

These systems have limited value for scheduled service that routinely travels the same route. But for specialized carriers that promise quick pickup of customer orders, such as Roadway's Robert Express Unit, these systems are real business enhancers. Analysts expect more use of land-satellite communications systems, as IBM and J. B. Hunt, the fifth largest trucking company in the nation, are joining forces to market their version.

Sources: Lou Ann Bell, "Satellite Systems Boost Efficiency, Competitiveness of TL Carriers," *Traffic World,* March 30, 1992, p. 26; and "Computers for the Road," *Marketing News,* October 25, 1993, p. 1.

other modes of transportation, is making the most progress in controlling costs, delivering on time, responding to customers, upgrading equipment, and planning for the long term.[35]

From a marketing viewpoint, the top priority for most trucking firms is recruiting, training, and retaining drivers.[36] Considering the role logistics can play in increasing customer satisfaction and profitability, trucking firms should emphasize hiring dependable drivers who can enhance customer relationships. To improve driver efficiency, major truckers such as Roadway Express, J. B. Hunt, and M. S. Carriers use mobile communications and tracking systems. These systems are described in **The Technological Edge: Satellite Systems in Trucking.**

Air freight.   Air freight is tops in speed but highest in transportation cost. Sometimes air freight is an integral part of an *execution perspective,* as with catalog companies or firms marketing perishable items from faraway destinations

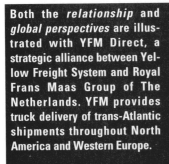

Both the *relationship* and *global perspectives* are illustrated with YFM Direct, a strategic alliance between Yellow Freight System and Royal Frans Maas Group of The Netherlands. YFM provides truck delivery of trans-Atlantic shipments throughout North America and Western Europe.

(such as Maine lobster delivered to seafood restaurants in California). In other situations, a firm may justify the cost of air freight to take advantage of a marketing opportunity. For example, Toys " Я " Us used air freight to rush a new Nintendo machine to its stores. According to a spokesperson, the company uses air cargo to transport "maybe one in 10,000" of its products to its stores.[37] The market for air freight shipments is growing at about 12 percent per year, a rate expected to hold up for several years.[38]

Pipelines.   Pipelines, such as the Alaska Pipeline, transport chemicals, gases, liquefied fossil fuels, and petroleum products. They offer fairly low-cost, reliable transportation to a limited number of destinations. Although the operation of a pipeline uses little energy, pipeline construction arouses environmental concerns about the land over which the line must travel.

Water.   Water transport is a good, low-cost alternative for large quantities of bulky products that must be shipped long distances. This includes bulk shipments of agricultural products, automobiles to and from foreign countries, and petroleum from distant oil-producing nations.

In the United States, water transport is available primarily in the eastern part of the country. The Mississippi River carries a large proportion of the country's water transport, and other rivers serve Cincinnati and Chicago. Rivers are also shipping routes for large amounts of cargo along the Gulf Coast between New Orleans and Houston, and between the Pacific Ocean and Portland, Oregon.

In the Great Lakes region, freighters carry huge shipments of raw materials such as iron ore to Detroit to service the automobile manufacturing industry. Other destinations served via the Great Lakes include Milwaukee, Buffalo, Chicago, and Toronto. The St. Lawrence Seaway, stretching from Lake Ontario to Montreal, can handle both barge traffic and oceangoing vessels. This project was jointly financed by the US and Canada, with Canada providing approximately three-fourths of the necessary funds.

Intermodal.   Although one mode of transportation may get the job done for a given shipper, marketers today show an increased interest in **intermodal shipping.** This involves the use of two or more modes of transportation. Loaded trailers, for example, may travel piggyback on railcars or in "stack trains." The Con-Way Intermodal program called Con-Quest combines the local pickup and delivery strategy of Con-Way trucks with the long-haul capabilities of five major railroads in a nationwide stack train service.[39]

Intermodal shipping is likely to increase as marketers implementing the *productivity perspective* find it an effective and economical way to move products and materials.

Shipping managers indicate that intermodal shipping is three times more likely to increase in the future than shipments by air, rail, or trucking.[40] A shortage of qualified truck drivers, the expense of moving large shipments by truck, and an emphasis on the *productivity perspective* have contributed to the growing use of intermodal shipping.[41] Rail can economically move goods for long hauls, with trucks completing the delivery in a timely manner.

Ethical and legal issues in logistics

The legal environment for logistics is shaped by thousands of local, state, national, and international laws, tax codes, and tariff regulations that govern the movement of materials and products. The Interstate Commerce Commission, Federal Maritime Commission, and Department of Transportation are the major US regulatory agencies.

One aspect of the legal environment that has affected logistics since the late 1970s is **deregulation,** which seeks to promote free competition among carriers. The pioneering laws affecting the transportation industry are the Airline Deregulation Act of 1978, the Staggers Rail Act of 1980, and the Motor Carrier Act of 1980.

A fierce debate raged prior to the passage of deregulation legislation. The proponents of deregulation predicted it would bring about a rather utopian marketplace, giving shipping customers more choices among competing shippers and, as a result, better service and lower shipping costs. Opponents predicted an economic disaster for both shippers and carriers, marked by mass exit of shippers from the marketplace and declining service levels to some communities.[42]

A decade and a half after deregulation, the effects are mixed. In the sluggish economic era of the 1980s and early 1990s, deregulation created a chaotic atmosphere and forced many companies into bankruptcy. For other companies, deregulation presented an opportunity to operate more efficiently. It allowed many to globalize their marketing efforts, improve customer service, and create business partnerships, all ingredients for success in the modern economy.

According to a survey of 453 shipping companies, deregulation has led to more companies adopting an *ethical perspective* in the trucking industry. Approximately 87 percent of the respondents believe that ethical standards of trucking company salespeople increased since the passage of the Motor Carrier Act.[43] A few comments from respondents indicate how ethical standards have evolved:

- The growth of coordinated shipping effort among previously decentralized corporate business units reduced local options to shift business for nonbusiness reasons, thus cutting incentives for unethical conduct.

- Most of the marginal operators that depended on questionable activities to gain business have been eliminated due to competition resulting from deregulation.

- Carriers are more image conscious and they realize there is more attention being paid to the carrier's service and performance than previously. "A slap on the back and a fifth under the table" no longer get the job done.

As suggested by the previous discussion, firms should view ethical considerations as an integral part of logistics management. Currently, shippers and carriers face safety issues such as the handling of hazardous materials and the safety of oversized "truck trains," trucking rigs pulling two 28-foot trailers. Such issues raise ethical questions. For example, the American Automobile Association (AAA) claims that numerous studies "show that combination vehicles (truck trains) are overinvolved in crashes and fatal accidents, and instill fear in other drivers because of their ominous size."[44] The trucking industry disagrees, claiming that truck trains are safe, are driven by the best drivers, and have a lower fatality rate than standard combination trucks. Further, the trucking industry accuses the railroad industry of orchestrating the public attack on truck trains.[45]

Some new laws will encourage the adoption of an *ecological perspective* by both shippers and transportation firms. In Maine, for example, a referendum renamed the transportation section of the state constitution the Sensible Transportation Policy Act. This law, similar to others cropping up around the country, requires that transportation decisions be made to "minimize the harmful effects of transportation on public health and on air and water quality, land use, and other natural resources."[46]

An example of the impact of environmental concerns on logistics is the "environmentally awarehouse," a concept put into practice in Elkhart, Indiana. This warehouse, specially designed for Miles Laboratories, uses nonpolluting electric forklift trucks and an advanced technology for preventing the leakage of dangerous chemicals in the event of a fire or spill.[47]

In addition, there are notable recycling programs in logistics, among them a plastics recycling program for Target Stores. Target collects the plastic film used to protect goods during shipping and delivers it to a recycler in Kentucky, which in turn sells it to a company that manufactures garbage bags. Target then purchases the bags from that manufacturer and sells them in its stores as an "environmentally correct" product.[48]

As logistics managers and wholesalers face the future, they must surely see the exciting prospect of playing an ever-increasing critical role in marketing. Change and adaptation will be necessary for survival of individual firms, and the management of information will play a key role for survivors. But wholesalers and logistics managers have tremendous technology at their disposal and can remain strong links in the chain that ultimately delivers customer satisfaction, profitability, and success.

Summary

1. *Understand wholesaling and describe the three basic categories of wholesalers.* An important part of marketing, wholesaling refers to the activities associated with selling products to purchasers that resell the products, use them to make another product, or use them to conduct business activities.

   The three basic categories of wholesalers are merchant wholesalers; agents, brokers, and commission merchants; and manufacturers' sales branches and offices. Some of these wholesalers provide a wide range of services, while others offer a narrow range of specialized services.

2. *Identify and discuss the roles of different types of full-service and limited-function wholesalers.* There are three main types of full-service wholesalers: general merchandise, limited-line, and specialty-line wholesalers. Of these, general merchandise wholesalers carry the broadest assortment of products and

provide extensive services to their customers. These services may involve promotional assistance, inventory management and storage, physical distribution, market feedback, assumption of financial risk, and offering of credit.

   The two others carry progressively smaller and more specialized assortments and provide different levels of service. Limited-function wholesalers include truck jobbers, drop shippers, cash-and-carry wholesalers, catalog wholesalers, and wholesale clubs. Of these, catalog wholesalers and wholesale clubs showed the most growth in recent years.

3. *Explain differences among the functions of agents, brokers, and commission merchants.* Agents, brokers, and commission merchants concentrate on making sales or purchases. They do not take title to the products they resell. These types of wholesalers must be quite knowledgeable in order to develop strong

relationships with their customers and suppliers. They are paid a commission, a percentage of the value of each completed sale or purchase.

4. *Understand the differences between manufacturers' sales branches and offices.* Manufacturers' sales branches maintain inventory, handle delivery, and act as an extension of the manufacturer for a wide variety of services. Manufacturers' sales offices offer a narrower range of services, primarily because they do not maintain inventory.

5. *Appreciate how slow growth rates and globalization will affect wholesaling in the future.* Slow growth rates in most developed economies are putting a significant amount of pressure on wholesalers, which often face declining profit margins. As large retail chains gain more power and increase direct purchases from manufacturers, wholesalers can expect tough operating conditions to continue.

To cope with slow growth, wholesalers often enter into relationships with manufacturers, customers, and in some cases, other wholesalers. Global markets offer more potential of growth for some wholesalers. As trade between nations becomes easier, wholesalers will have opportunities that have been difficult to realize in the past. Further, as developing economies grow, wholesalers that have the capability to conduct business outside the domestic marketplace can benefit by supplying them.

6. *Define logistics management and explain its key role in marketing.* Logistics management describes the planning, implementing, and controlling of the movement of raw materials and products from point of origin to point of consumption. In recent years, logistics management has grown more important in overall marketing strategies, because customer satisfaction is greatly affected by factors such as responsiveness to special shipping requirements and condition of delivered merchandise.

7. *Understand logistics activities, including warehousing, materials handling, inventory control, order processing, and transporting.* Some firms use independently owned public warehouses; others operate their own private warehouses or distribution centers. Materials-handling activities include receiving, identifying, sorting, storing, and retrieving goods for shipment. Inventory control is used to meet customer stock requirements without incurring excessive costs of carrying inventory. Just-in-time and quick-response systems are examples of inventory control programs used in a wide variety of industries.

Order processing, triggered by the customer's purchase order, includes order entry, order handling, and delivery scheduling. The final part of logistics is transporting, which requires decisions about how to ship the product. Shippers may choose among rail, truck, air, pipeline, and water transport, or some combination of these modes.

8. *Discuss how some of the key ethical and legal issues affect logistics.* The continued push for deregulation in freight delivery is having both positive and negative effects. Ultimately, the aim of deregulation is to create more competition among carriers, which should lead to lower costs for shippers and perhaps lower prices for consumers.

These benefits are not possible, however, without some negative consequences. For example, smaller trucking firms are disappearing, creating job losses and the possibility of poorer service to smaller communities. There is also great concern over the environmental impact of transportation on the quality of air, water, and land. In addition, groups are increasingly assessing how logistics facilities, such as warehouses, may affect the environment.

Key terms & concepts

wholesalers *388*
logistics management *388*
wholesaling *388*
value-added resellers (VARs) *389*
merchant wholesalers *389*
full-service wholesalers *390*
general merchandise wholesalers *390*
limited-line wholesalers *391*
specialty-line wholesalers *391*
rack jobbers *391*
limited-function wholesalers *391*
truck jobbers *391*

drop shippers *391*
cash-and-carry wholesalers *391*
catalog wholesalers *391*
wholesale clubs *392*
manufacturers' agents *394*
auction houses *394*
import agents *395*
export agents *395*
brokers *395*
commission merchants *395*
manufacturers' sales branches *395*
manufacturers' sales offices *395*

North American Free Trade Agreement (NAFTA) *397*
bar coding *401*
just-in-time (JIT) inventory control systems *402*
quick-response (QR) inventory control systems *402*
shipping container marking (SCM) *402*
electronic data interchange (EDI) *402*
intermodal shipping *406*
deregulation *407*

Review & discussion questions

1. What is wholesaling? What are the three basic categories of wholesalers?

2. Which category of wholesalers does not take title to products they resell? What types of wholesalers fall into this category?

3. How do manufacturers' agents differ from manufacturers' branch offices?

4. In the grocery industry, are wholesalers becoming more or less powerful in the marketing channel?

5. Review **The Entrepreneurial Spirit: Swedish Classics Goes International.** Is globalization a threat or an opportunity for the wholesaling sector?

6. Why has logistics management become more important in marketing during recent years?

7. What are the key activities in logistics management?

8. What are the benefits of a quick-response inventory control system?

9. What are the five basic ways to move products and materials from one point to another? What are the key factors to be considered when choosing among these modes of transport?

10. Review **The Technological Edge: Satellite Systems in Trucking.** What other examples of the use of technology to enhance wholesaling or logistics management can you cite from this chapter?

Application exercises

1. Assume you are the traffic manager for a large manufacturer of consumer goods. Your company is designing a quick-response delivery system for several large retail accounts. The system includes railcar delivery to distribution centers, direct-to-store truck delivery in a few isolated locations, and emergency service by air freight. What can you do to get feedback from your customers to aid in the design and implementation of the system?

2. During the midwestern flood of 1993, grain shippers that normally use barges for transport had to resort to other modes of transportation. Which other modes would be logical for shipping grain? How would massive flooding affect these modes?

3. An established rock group is thinking about firing its agent of five years. The agent gets 10 percent of all concert revenues and 1 percent of all other band-related profits, including those from merchandising agreements, commercial work, and paid TV appearances. The band members basically feel the agent is not really earning his seven-figure annual income. How would you advise the band? What factors should be considered before hiring another agent or, alternatively, eliminating the agent in favor of a less expensive salaried manager? [*Hint: this exercise pertains to the wholesaling portion of the chapter.*]

Case 16.1   *Fleming Companies: Building for the future*

The early 1990s were extremely difficult for US food wholesalers. Most had to cut prices to keep their grocery store customers from buying directly from manufacturers, already a common practice with large chains. As prices eroded, so did profits. Fleming Companies, the largest US food wholesaler, with more than $13 billion in sales, experienced hard times along with the rest of the industry. To chart the course for the future, Fleming management moved aggressively on two fronts: to increase the efficiency of its distribution system and to expand sales outside the United States.

Fleming is proud to be the nation's biggest food wholesaler, but it also wants to be known as the best. To John Gilbert, director of wholesale systems, this means lowering costs while providing faster service and greater productivity. To improve its distribution system, Fleming

plans to reduce the number of its warehouses from 35 to 25. Industry observers note the wisdom of this move, saying that a key to food wholesaling is driving as much volume as possible through each warehouse. The remaining centers are using state-of-the-art technology, an on-line computer system called *FOODS,* to manage inventory.

By the early 1990s, Fleming was convinced it had to move beyond its US market. The company's chairman noted, "There is a lack of real growth in the US food industry, so we can't get the sales increases we used to." A Fleming vice president added, "In foreign countries, some opportunities are greater than in the US, where most major cities are overstored."

To increase sales outside the US, Fleming looked to Mexico. Using forward integration as one strategy, Fleming became a partner in a 54-store supermarket chain.

Fortunately, the company avoided a major mistake by deciding not to name its stores "Super Mercado." Although the term means "supermarket," it has a bargain-basement connotation in Mexico. Instead, Fleming used the name "SuperMart" (in English), a more upscale alternative. The stores are similar to MegaMarket stores in the United States.

Fleming's move into Mexico was a calculated risk, but perhaps a necessary move. Its primary US customer base, independent grocers, was simply not growing. And, as the grocery chains strengthened their dominant position, the future for Fleming was none too bright. In Mexico, on the other hand, the economy is growing in double digits, inflation has slowed, and NAFTA has been passed.

Fleming plans to grow 25 percent each year in international sales. In addition to Mexico, the company is exporting to South and Central America, the Caribbean, Japan, and other Pacific Rim countries.

Questions:

1. Why did Fleming decide to move aggressively into markets outside the United States?

2. What obstacles might a US–based food wholesaler face in expanding into distant markets?

3. Discuss why a food wholesaler must have a sophisticated inventory management system to be competitive.

Sources: Laurel Campbell, "Middleman Fleming Fights to Stay on Top," *The Commercial Appeal,* May 10, 1992, pp. C1, C4; Robette Ledbetter, "At Fleming, Service Is Up and Film Is In," *Inform,* January 1992, pp. 34–35; Joseph Weber, "On a Fast Boat to Anywhere," *Business Week,* January 11, 1993, p. 94; and Steve Weinstein, "Spanning the Globe," *Progressive Grocer,* October 1992, pp. 65–70.

Case 16.2   *Mattel: Not toying with quick response*

Mattel, the California-based toy manufacturer, uses a quick-response inventory system to keep big retail customers in more than 100 countries satisfied. Acknowledging the importance of logistics management, Mattel vice president Fermin Cuza says, "Because of our growth, just-in-time inventory procedures, and today's advertising campaigns and commitment to customers, the availability of product on a timely basis is critical to the success of the company."

To ensure timely availability of its products, Mattel must coordinate production (none of it done in the US), shipping, storage, and delivery to retail stores. In addition, the company must deal with customs regulations all over the world. Before Mattel invested $100,000 in software to speed customs processing, shipments routinely took 3 to 5 days to clear customs. With its automated program, Mattel can give the required information to customs before the ship arrives, rather than waiting for hard-copy documents to arrive with the ship.

Mattel has also automated communications between its suppliers and its Hong Kong purchasing and logistics organization, the Mattel Trading Company. Rather than deal with individual suppliers, the California headquarters communicates with one source—the trading company. The trading company receives information from suppliers electronically, which it then transmits to California without reentering the data. For peak efficiency, however, Mattel can ship only on ocean carriers with automated capabilities. Since only about 10 percent of all ocean shippers are linked to their carriers electronically, Mattel is a pioneer in taking advantage of technology in worldwide shipping. Once goods are in the US, it is fairly simple to move them from one place to another. Retailers can set stringent standards for receipt of Mattel products and fully expect Mattel to meet the standards.

Now that Mattel has the Hong Kong–to–US quick-response system in place, it plans to expand the system to the other half of its market—the non-US portion. This will be quite a challenge, for implementing quick response in other countries is an entirely different situation. Technology is often not so advanced outside the United States. Bureaucracy can be the biggest problem, since most bureaucrats have no sense of urgency. For Mattel's global expansion of a QR system to become a reality, other customs authorities must automate their procedures, like US customs did. Mattel officials believe that other countries will follow the US example, and US officials have indicated a willingness to share the software for their automated commercial system at little or no cost to other countries.

Questions:

1. How can Mattel get a competitive edge by using computerized customs information as part of its quick-response system?

2. Mattel has spent untold amounts of time and money to implement its Hong Kong–to–US system. The $100,000 paid for customs processing software is but a fraction of the cost. Adopting new technology is expensive, and once one company has refined it, others will be able to get it at much lower cost. How can Mattel justify the time and money spent to lead the way?

3. What kind of information would ideally be contained in Mattel's quick-response system?

Sources: Robert J. Bowman, "The EDI Revolution: A Special World Trade Feature," *World Trade,* June 1993, pp. 38–48; Tony Seideman, "Mattel Doesn't Toy Around with Quick Response," *Consumer Goods Manufacturer,* June 1993, pp. 18–19; and Perry A. Trunick, Helen L. Richardson, and Thomas Andel, "Logistics Excellence Is Its Own Reward," *Transportation & Distribution,* September 1992, pp. 45–54.

PART

7

Integrated Marketing Communications

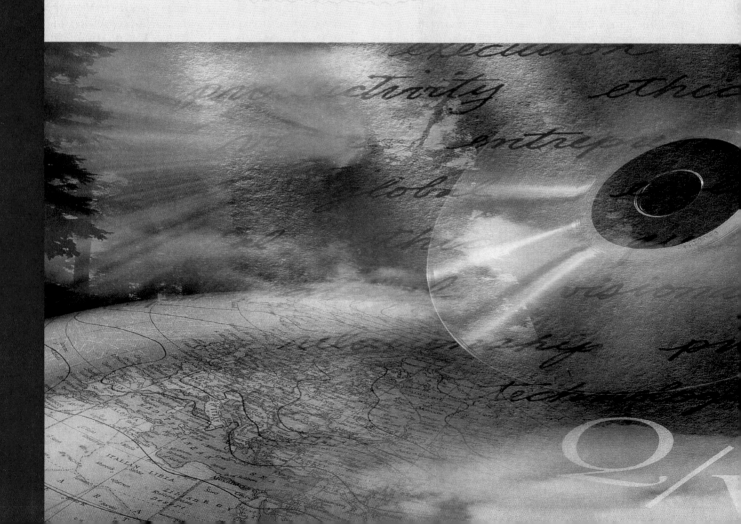

An integrated marketing communications program gives the marketer an extra edge in the race to reach customers.

V arious forms of marketing communications are discussed in the five chapters of Part 7. Chapter 17 provides an overview, explaining the marketing communications mix. Marketing communications objectives and planning considerations are also discussed, and the concept of integrated marketing communications is introduced. Chapter 18 discusses advertising, the best-known form of marketing communications. This chapter also covers public relations and publicity. Chapter 19 explains sales promotion. The chapter is divided into two sections, one dealing with consumer sales promotion, the other with trade sales promotion. Chapter 20 deals with personal selling and sales management. Finally, the increasingly important area of direct marketing communications is the topic for Chapter 21.

chapter 17

An Overview of Marketing Communications

After studying this chapter you should be able to:

1. Discuss the objectives of marketing communications.

2. Understand the marketing communications mix and its role.

3. Explain the key elements of the marketing communications process.

4. Discuss the seven steps in the marketing communications planning process.

5. Demonstrate awareness of some of the key ethical and legal issues related to marketing communications.

Barbara Mandrell and the No Nonsense Tour:
Integrating marketing communications

*K*ayser-Roth Hosiery, Inc., marketers of No Nonsense pantyhose, joined forces with country singer Barbara Mandrell in an integrated marketing communications campaign. Over an 18-month period, the company sponsored Mandrell's 80-city nationwide tour and contributed to one of her favorite causes, the Literacy Volunteers of America.

Kayser-Roth's acknowledged skill in coordinating the efforts of various activities was essential in the Mandrell/No Nonsense campaign. Personal selling played a key role, as No Nonsense salespeople worked with retail stores in all 80 tour cities to ensure that retail outlets were adequately stocked to meet demand. Salespeople also assisted in setting up in-store displays that featured Mandrell as the focal point. Advertising was intensive, with $10 million spent on television, radio, and newspaper ads.

Sales promotion directed to ultimate consumers included a coupon for a free pair of pantyhose packaged in Mandrell's CD/cassette and a free-trip sweepstakes. Sales promotion directed at retailers included concert tickets, free CDs and cassettes, and backstage visits with Mandrell.

The public relations effort was bolstered by the association with Literacy Volunteers of America. In addition, Mandrell's new CD/cassette was titled *No Nonsense.* The singer also touted her association with the company on numerous TV talk shows.

Even though concert tickets, cassettes, and CDs were bartered to help defray media and display costs, expenditures for the No Nonsense campaign totaled almost $12 million. It was money well spent. A 2 percent market share growth for No Nonsense more than covered the cost of the campaign.

Sources: "Barbara Mandrell's No Nonsense Tour," *Adweek's Marketing Week,* October 4, 1991, p. 28; and Frank A. Papa, "Linkage of Old and New," *Management Review,* January 1993, p. 63.

The campaign for No Nonsense pantyhose illustrates various facets of marketing communications and shows how a firm might integrate them into a comprehensive communications effort. **Marketing communications,** sometimes referred to as *promotion,* involve marketer-initiated techniques directed to target audiences in an attempt to influence attitudes and behaviors.

Marketers may use one or all of several marketing communications methods. There are five major categories: advertising, public relations, sales promotion, personal selling, and direct marketing communications. Together they constitute the **marketing communications mix,** often referred to as the *promotional mix.* As the No Nonsense campaign illustrates, several methods can be integrated to communicate more effectively with the target audience.

This chapter explores these five major categories, as well as the major objectives of marketing communications and the way the communications process works and is implemented. We discuss how the marketing environment, including ethical and legal concerns, can influence the marketing communications effort.

The role of marketing communications

The ultimate goal of marketing communications is to reach some audience to affect its behavior. There may be intermediate steps on the path to that goal, such as developing favorable consumer attitudes. Exhibit 17.1 lays out the three major objectives of marketing communications: to inform, to persuade, and to remind the marketer's audience.

Informing

Informing present or potential customers about a product is an important marketing communications function. Any time a new product is launched and promoted, marketing communications serve to inform audience members (the target market) about it. For example, two goals of the advertising for new movies by Warner Brothers, Paramount, and other major studios are to

Exhibit 17.1

The marketing communications mix

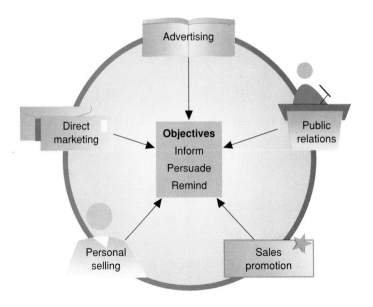

introduce offerings to potential moviegoers and announce when the movies will appear in local theaters.

Persuading

Marketing communications may concentrate on persuading customers to purchase a firm's market offering. For instance, Diet Pepsi set out to persuade Diet Coke drinkers to convert to Diet Pepsi with its "Convert a Million" campaign. One million cases of Diet Pepsi were home-delivered to Diet Coke drinkers in Pepsi's new "Uh-huh" package. Also included was a personalized letter signed by Ray Charles and a survey whose return automatically entered the consumer in a sweepstakes. The program also used television advertising, personal selling to retailers, and in-store promotions.[1]

Reminding

When consumers are aware of a firm's brand and have positive attitudes toward it, a reminding objective may be appropriate. Although consumers may be "sold" on the product, they are still vulnerable to competitors' appeals. Marketing

The thing about Chris is he doesn't like food that he has to chase around his plate. He's funny that way. Things to eat that are excessively small or cute bother him. Chris likes to sink his fork into his dinner without going for his reading glasses to see what he's getting.

Nobody likes food that's too weird or hard to get in your mouth.

Potatoes are steady. They're reliable. And they're good for you because they're a fresh vegetable. And they won't slide around just when you really need to eat them. Because when Chris comes home from a long hard day the last thing he wants is to have to wrestle his dinner off his own plate.

Potatoes

THEY'RE AT HOME ANYWHERE!

This "steaming" sign reminds millions of people every day of Eight O'Clock's status as America's top bean coffee.

communications can remind consumers of the product's benefits and reassure them they are making the right choice. Much of Coca-Cola's advertising, for instance, is aimed at keeping consumers aware of and sold on its product. Personal selling is another way to remind the buyer of the value of continuing the relationship and making repeat purchases. Among the best at using personal selling for reminder purposes are Alcoa, Eastman Kodak, Federal Express, Bethlehem Steel, Polaroid, Northwestern Mutual Life, Anheuser-Busch, and United Parcel Company.[2]

EXECUTIVE ROUNDTABLE COMMENT | Dorothy Brazil Clark, director of business development for Protein Technologies International, is aware of the need to maintain close relationships with customers, at a reasonable cost:

Viewing transactions as one-time occurrences is too costly. Acceptable returns on investment will best be achieved when the transactional benefits have been mutually identified and accepted by buyers and sellers. The emphasis on relationship marketing accelerates this process.

The marketing communications mix

To inform, persuade, and remind targeted consumers effectively, marketers rely on one or more of the five major elements of the marketing communications mix. We discuss these briefly here and in more detail in subsequent chapters.

Advertising

Advertising is nonpersonal, paid for by an identified sponsor, and disseminated through mass channels of communication to promote the adoption of goods, services, persons, or ideas. Marketers use media such as television, radio, outdoor, magazines, and newspapers to advertise. Its ability to reach a mass audience often makes advertising an efficient method for communicating with a large target market.

Traditionally, advertising has been the most recognized form of marketing communications largely because of its high visibility. We cannot escape the advertising that surrounds us in our daily lives. This high visibility is achieved through enormous expenditures. For example, the top 100 advertisers in the US

Elan Frozen Yogurt samples to success

*I*n 1986, Joanne and James Biltekoff founded Elan Frozen Yogurt Products. Short on the capital necessary for an extensive advertising program, they developed Elan into the leading premium brand in some regions primarily by distributing in-store samples.

The Biltekoffs found product sampling a cost-effective way to get consumers to try their yogurt. An in-store product demonstrator, at a cost of $100 a day, gives away free samples. To this is added the cost of the product consumed, the redemption cost of the distributed coupons, and the cost of training demonstrators. Demonstrators typically reach about 500 people a day, so the costs total about 30 cents per sample.

According to Joanne Biltekoff, sampling, if done correctly, is a great way to make your case. For Elan, this means getting the samples into the right mouths by distributing samples in the appropriate stores. It also means employing personable, well-trained employees to distribute the samples. The demonstrators wear uniforms and distribute samples from a stand that looks like an Elan yogurt carton, rather than from a makeshift setup.

Based in New York, Elan is now selling in 20 states. With an increase in capital, its marketing strategy has been updated to include television commercials and print ads. Product sampling, however, remains Elan's prominent communications method.

Source: "Product Sampling," *Inc.*, October 1991, p. 158. Reprinted with permission, *Inc.* Copyright 1991 by Goldhirsh Group, Inc., 38 Commercial Wharf, Boston, MA 02110.

alone spend over $33 billion per year to advertise.[3] Advertising expenditures, which had been declining since the mid-1980s, showed a five percent increase in 1993.[4]

Public relations

The **public relations** function identifies, establishes, and maintains mutually beneficial relationships between an organization and the various publics on which its success or failure depends.[5] Employees, customers, stockholders, community members, and the government are examples of various publics for many firms.

A key aspect of public relations is publicity. **Publicity** refers to non-paid-for communications about the company or product that appear in some media form, often the news media. Since the firm cannot completely control the message being disseminated, publicity may generate more believable messages than paid-for communications such as advertising. Many firms hire outside agencies to handle their public relations and publicity requirements.

Sales promotion

Sales promotion includes communications activities that provide extra value or incentives to ultimate consumers, wholesalers, retailers, or other organizational customers.[6] Sales promotion attempts to stimulate product interest, trial, or purchase. Coupons, samples, premiums, point-of-purchase displays, sweepstakes, contests, rebates, and trade show exhibits are all examples of sales promotion.

Consumer sales promotion is directed at ultimate users of the product or service; *trade sales promotion* is directed at retailers, wholesalers, or other business buyers. **The Entrepreneurial Spirit: Elan Frozen Yogurt Samples to Success** illustrates the use of product sampling, one method of sales promotion.

Exhibit 17.2   Spending for advertising versus consumer and trade sales promotion

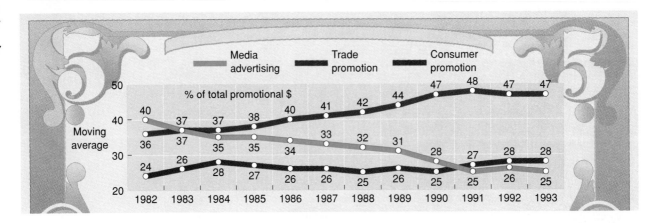

Marketers spend more money for consumer sales promotion than they do for advertising. Expenditures for trade sales promotion are significantly higher than for either advertising or consumer trade promotion (see Exhibit 17.2). This may be surprising to most people, for the behind-the-scenes promotion activities to business buyers are not easily observable outside an industry.

EXECUTIVE ROUNDTABLE COMMENT | **Dorothy Brazil Clark, director of business development for Protein Technologies International, points out the need to use multiple means of communicating with both resellers and consumers:**

With consumer goods, you cannot rely solely on advertising. There is nothing worse than having a consumer, properly informed and motivated to buy, go to a retailer in search of a hot new product and be turned off by lack of merchandise, poor merchandising, or not enough information at the point of sale. It is essential to promote the product throughout the channel to be sure it's available, attractively displayed, and sold at the right price when the consumer comes in to buy.

Marketers typically use sales promotion in conjunction with other marketing communications elements. For example, sales promotion programs such as sweepstakes or contests may use advertising to spread the word to mass consumer markets. Marketers also frequently link sales promotion with many forms of direct marketing, especially direct mail, or include it as part of a trade show (product giveaways, merchandise imprinted with ad messages or logos).

Unlike some other forms of marketing communications, sales promotion is usually intended to produce immediate results. This probably explains why marketers have increasingly turned to sales promotion to improve sales volume and market share in a wide variety of highly competitive markets.

Personal selling

Personal selling involves face-to-face interactions between the seller and the buyer to satisfy buyer needs to the mutual benefit of both parties. The personal nature of this method distinguishes it from nonpersonal forms of marketing communication. Personal selling allows immediate feedback, enabling a message to be tailored to fit the buyer's individual needs. Its dynamic nature and flexibility make personal selling an excellent communications medium for establishing and nurturing customer relationships.

Personal selling is an important element of marketing communications when the product is complex. The sale of medical equipment to hospitals and

This ad illustrates the combination of sales promotion and advertising. The sales promotion message (*lower right-hand corner*) is part of a magazine ad for a new product, Recharg A cell™ batteries, from two well-known companies, GE and Sanyo.

physicians would be practically impossible without well-informed salespeople who can provide the necessary details to prospective buyers.

Direct marketing communications

Direct marketing communications is a process of communicating directly with target customers to encourage response by telephone, mail, electronic means, or personal visit. Popular methods of direct marketing communications include direct mail, telemarketing, direct-response broadcast advertising, computer shopping services, cable television shopping networks, "infomercials," and in some instances, outdoor advertising.

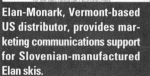

Elan-Monark, Vermont-based US distributor, provides marketing communications support for Slovenian-manufactured Elan skis.

Professional salespeople play an important role in the marketing communications effort for complex products. Shown is a marketing representative from Health Images, Inc., who educates physicians on the use of MRI (magnetic resonance imaging) equipment.

P
A
R
T

7

Direct marketing communications are used by all types of marketers, including retailers, wholesalers, manufacturers, and service providers. A fast-growing segment of the marketing communications field, direct marketing often uses precise means of identifying members of a target audience and compiling customer/prospect databases with addresses, telephone numbers, account numbers, or fax numbers to allow access to the buyers.

Integrated marketing communications

Today's highly competitive business environment puts considerable pressure on marketing communications to reach and spur busy, value-conscious consumers to buy. For marketers, this calls for an emphasis on the *productivity* and *execution perspectives.* As a result, marketers are increasingly turning to **integrated marketing communications (IMC),** which is the strategic integration of multiple means of communicating with target markets to form a comprehensive, consistent message. The Mandrell/No Nonsense campaign is an example of IMC. According to an expert in the field, "The strength of the IMC process is that each planning activity is considered individually for each specific group of consumers using a set of marketing communications tools that have been selected specifically for the task."[7]

The importance of integrated marketing communications has been documented in a survey of 100 marketing executives. They predict that integrated marketing communications will be the most important factor in shaping marketing strategy in the 1993–98 period, ahead of consumer lifestyle trends, economic trends, everyday-low-pricing strategies, new retail formats, and globalization.[8]

In one sense, marketing communications are integrated horizontally, or across various methods of communications. For example, the advertising message must be consistent with the personal selling message. The No Nonsense campaign also illustrates integration in a vertical sense, extending from the marketer down through the marketing channel. Recall, for example, that No Nonsense salespeople were dispatched to retailers to arrange for adequate inventory levels and to assist in setting up in-store displays.

Another aspect of integrated marketing communications is that it considers any contact with a brand, product, or company to be part of marketing

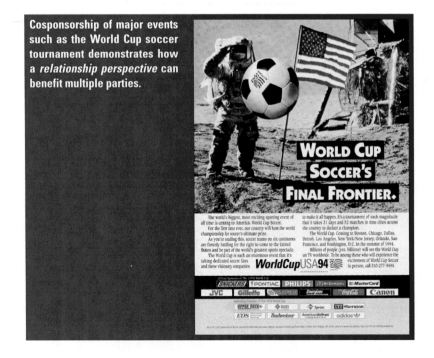

Cosponsorship of major events such as the World Cup soccer tournament demonstrates how a *relationship perspective* can benefit multiple parties.

communications. As a result of integrated marketing communications, consumers could see a product in a movie, a commercial message or brand name on a T-shirt, and a company name prominently displayed on a hot-air balloon.

Coca-Cola and Procter & Gamble are masters at integrating their marketing communications efforts. Both are well known for consumer advertising. Their sales promotion efforts, in the form of coupons, sweepstakes, and contests are also familiar to millions of consumers. The average consumer, however, does not see their highly trained salespeople who call on wholesalers and retailers. Both P&G and Coke have used direct marketing effectively. Like many others, Coca-Cola and Procter & Gamble also manage sophisticated public relations and publicity efforts to support their marketing communications campaigns.

Sponsorship programs may be an important part of an integrated marketing communications strategy. The Barbara Mandrell/No Nonsense campaign is an example—an investment in causes and events to support overall corporate objectives and marketing objectives.[9] Sponsors may back a single event, such as the Olympics or the World Series, or multiple events, as Buick does with golf tournaments on the PGA tour.

The marketing communications process

Communication is the process of establishing shared meaning, exchanging ideas, or passing information between a source and a receiver. Exhibit 17.3 shows how the marketing communications process works. Note that the intended target for any basic communication is the **receiver**. This could be a purchasing agent listening to a sales presentation, a consumer reading a magazine ad, or another of the various publics served by the marketer, such as stockholders or government officials.

Exhibit 17.3   **The marketing communications process**

| Source | → | Encoding | → | Message | → | Channel | → | Decoding | → | Receiver |

Feedback

NOISE

Response to message

| Company | → | Encoding | → | Marketing message | → | Media:
• Advertising
• Personal selling
• Public relations
• Sales promotion
• Direct marketing | → | Decoding | → | Company's publics:
• Prospects
• Customers
• Employees
• Stockholders
• Community
• Government |

Dallas Cowboys quarterback Troy Aikman is a credible presenter of marketing communications messages, especially in regional campaigns for Logo 7 sports apparel, Kroger supermarkets, and Nike.

Sources of marketing communications

The marketer is the **source**, or message sender of marketing communications. Two types of sources normally play a role in marketing communications, the message sponsor and the message presenter. The **message sponsor** is typically the organization attempting to market its goods, services, or ideas. The **message presenter**, perhaps a salesperson, actor, or television personality, actually delivers the message. For instance, Nike is a message sponsor, while Troy Aikman is one of Nike's message presenters.

Communications messages

The source sends a message through a channel to a receiver. The **marketing communications message** represents what the company is trying to convey about its products. A **message channel** is the means by which the message is conveyed. In advertising, message channels are often referred to as *media,* a reference to advertising vehicles such as newspapers, television, magazines, outdoor, and radio. Mail, telephones, audio and video cassettes, salespeople, and computer disks are also examples of message channels.

Encoding and decoding

The source does the **encoding** by choosing the words, pictures, and other symbols used to transmit the intended message. **Decoding** is the process by which the receiver deciphers the meaning of the words, pictures, and other symbols used in the message. When the message is not decoded as the source intended, a lack of communication results. For example, a consumer may find the copy in a magazine ad too technical and thus not understand the message.

Feedback

Feedback is the part of the receiver's response that is communicated to the sender. Depending on the nature of the communication, the sender can assess feedback to judge the effectiveness of the communication. Personal selling and many forms of sales promotion offer relatively quick feedback. Feedback is not so immediate for mass advertising and public relations, and only subsequent sales figures or marketing research will indicate the effectiveness of the message. New forms of interactive advertising media are now allowing for quicker feedback from the receiver, as evidenced in **The Technological Edge: Interactive Media Revolutionizes Marketing Communications.**

Noise

Noise is any distraction or distortion during the communication process that prevents the message from being effectively communicated. Competing messages and interruptions, such as a telephone call during a salesperson's sales presentation,

Interactive media revolutionizes marketing communications

*A*dvances in interactive communications media are changing the way companies communicate with consumers. The Federal Communications Commission has approved two-way interactive video and data services, a technology advocated by TV Answer, a communications company.

The system runs on a VCR-sized radio-controlled box that attaches to the TV set. Viewers can interact via remote control when a special icon appears on a commercial. For instance, viewers might request more information about a product. The technology also lets consumers do home banking and shopping. The system is installed in a consumer's home for approximately $500.

Another rapidly emerging interactive medium is the computer disk. For instance, General Motors Buick Motor Division mailed disks to 150,000 potential customers who returned a direct-mail piece or responded to advertising. Prospects can play a simulated round of golf and then look over the latest Buicks, showcased through text, animated graphics, pictures, and sound. The 150,000-disk mailing is claimed to have led to sales of more than 1,000 new Buicks. L. L. Bean, the mail-order giant, is among the major companies now experimenting with electronic catalogs.

Sources: Bradley Johnson, "News Briefs and Developments in Interactive Technology," *Advertising Age*, February 17, 1992, pp. S1, S6; and Evan I. Schwartz, "This Magazine Could Be on Your PC Screen," *Business Week*, June 28, 1993, p. 56.

constitute noise. Noise can even come from within the message itself, sometimes at quite an expense. For example, in a TV commercial for Chef Boyardee, the actors spoke in such thick Italian accents the message was unintelligible.[10]

Marketing communications planning

There are seven key tasks in **marketing communications planning**: marketing plan review; situation analysis; communications process analysis; budget development; program development; integration and implementation of the plan; and monitoring, evaluating, and controlling the marketing communications program. These are diagrammed in Exhibit 17.4.

Marketing plan review

Marketing communications planning draws heavily on the firm's overall marketing strategy and marketing objectives. A review of the marketing plan is thus a logical place to start the process of marketing communications planning. The marketing plan often contains detailed information that is useful for marketing communications planning.

Situation analysis

An analysis of the marketing communications situation considers how internal factors, such as the firm's capabilities and constraints, and other marketing mix variables will affect marketing communications. The situation analysis is also

---

Exhibit 17.4   **Key tasks in marketing communications planning**

Marketing plan review → Situation analysis → Communications process analysis → Budget development → Program development → Integration & implementation → Monitoring, evaluating, controlling

concerned with the marketing environment now and in the future. For example, competitive, economic, and social factors affect marketing communications. The political and legal environments, discussed later in this chapter, are also addressed in the situation analysis.

The competitive environment

Marketing communications are often used to foil the actions of competitors. For example, competitive strategy affected marketing communications at Georgia-Pacific Corporation. G-P was having difficulty selling one of its plywood products because the competition's lower-grade product was less expensive. To convince lumber yards and building materials retailers that its product was a superior alternative to others, Georgia-Pacific sent out marketing communications literature that included samples.[11]

The economic environment

Budgets for marketing communications often decline in hard economic times. Yet, some well-known firms have benefited from increasing their marketing communications expenditures under adverse economic conditions. Such continuous marketing communications help to maintain market leadership, and for these firms, it is part of an *execution perspective.* Campbell's, Coca-Cola, Ivory, Kellogg, Kodak, Lipton, and Wrigley have all maintained an unwavering commitment to promoting their brands in good and bad times, and each is a leader in its market category.[12]

Economic conditions may cause firms to reconsider which components of the marketing communications mix to emphasize. During the recessionary period of the early 1990s, for example, H. J. Heinz cut its advertising expenditures to put more money into sales promotion. Heinz management felt that no amount of advertising would sell as well as price-oriented sales promotion in a recessionary retail environment.[13]

The social environment

Communications messages often reflect social trends. An *ecological perspective,* for instance, has caused many marketers to communicate supposed environmental benefits of their products. Similarly, consumer interest in health and fitness

Marketers recognize that women are buying products traditionally bought by men, and vice versa. This ad uses a humorous approach to encourage male patronage of a florist shop.

has led marketers to promote the healthful aspects of many products. Social conditions can also affect a firm's marketing communications. For example, shortly after riots broke out in Los Angeles in 1992 following the Rodney King case, Nike ran a new commercial encouraging racial harmony while promoting its athletic shoes.[14]

Keeping current with behavioral changes in the target market is an important requirement of situation analysis. For example, the traditional target market for household products such as groceries, cleaning supplies, and health and beauty aids has changed dramatically. With 70 percent of women holding jobs outside the home, men have become extremely active in this market. Research by Campbell Soup Company reveals that 80 percent of all men do at least some grocery shopping every month. In response to changes in the target market, consumer goods giants like Procter & Gamble, Johnson & Johnson, and Kmart now run male-oriented ads in publications such as *Sports Illustrated, Rolling Stone,* and *Field & Stream.*[15]

EXECUTIVE ROUNDTABLE COMMENT | **Dorothy Brazil Clark, director of business development for Protein Technologies International, comments on the need to consider the target market when developing marketing communications strategies:**

International marketing efforts require bridging cultural gaps and establishing communications pathways. There are significant differences in the values and attitudes of our customers around the world, and we absolutely must do our best to understand and adapt to these differences. It takes time and money, but we really don't have a choice—treating everyone the same just won't work.

Marketing mix considerations

Compatibility of product, price, and channel characteristics with marketing communications is essential to the *execution perspective.* The physical characteristics of a product or product package (color, size, shape, texture, ingredients) and its brand name communicate a lot to consumers. For instance, the bright colors on the Cheer detergent package imply it is powerful enough to get clothes bright and clean without fading them. Brand names such as Arrid Extra Dry, Finesse, Ivory, Total, Huggies, Sheer Energy, and Angel Soft convey certain messages about the products.

The product's price also conveys a message. Consumers often use price as an indicator of product quality. The $215,000 price tag on a Ferrari 512TR coupe indicates more than the cost of the vehicle; it also conveys a message of quality and prestige. Although both Rolex and Timex watches keep good time, each conveys a different message with its pricing strategy, and each has built an image consistent with its price.

The chosen marketing channel also communicates to the consumer. For instance, Wal-Mart and Neiman-Marcus each conveys a different message. Walmart stands for everyday low prices—products that are very expensive and of the finest quality are typically not found there. Consumers generally assume items sold at Neiman-Marcus are of high quality because of the store's well-established image. The prices of products at Neiman-Marcus help convey that message.

Communications process analysis

In this step, marketers analyze the various elements of the basic communications model shown in Exhibit 17.4. Objectives for marketing communications are also set in this part of the planning process.

Exhibit 17.5   **Examples of marketing communications objectives**

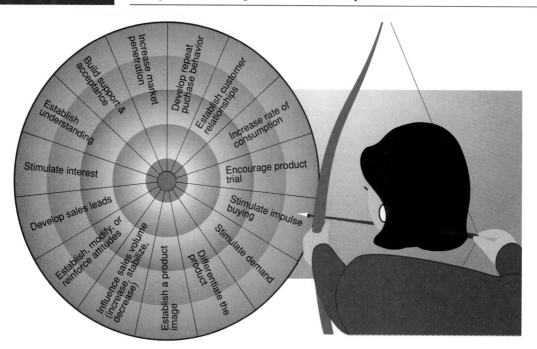

Applying the basic communications model

Marketers try to understand the decoding processes of potential receivers of marketing communications in order to create effective messages and select appropriate message channels. For example, will the consumer need detailed information from a well-trained salesperson to make a favorable decision? Or can simple point-of-sale displays achieve the desired results?

Setting marketing communications objectives

Exhibit 17.5 lists several general marketing communications objectives. Like all business objectives, a marketing communications objective should be stated as specifically as possible to help gauge the effectiveness of marketing communications efforts. It is also necessary to set objectives for each marketing communications effort, assuming separate programs are developed for individual products, product lines, geographic areas, customer groups, or different time periods. For example, greeting-card marketer Hallmark might run separate sales promotion programs to correspond with major occasions such as Christmas, Mother's Day, and Halloween.

Budget development

In developing a marketing communications budget, a firm must consider the *productivity perspective.* Determining the optimal amount to spend on marketing communications involves considerable subjective judgment. Further, it is hard to measure precise results achieved by marketing communication expenditures. For example, Apple Computer spends $45,000 per year on rent, food, and drink for a 16-seat skybox at Tampa Stadium. Selected customers are invited to attend Tampa Bay Buccaneers home football games with Apple representatives. Apple's regional manager says it is difficult to calculate the exact results of this activity, but believes it pays off by enhancing customer relationships.[16]

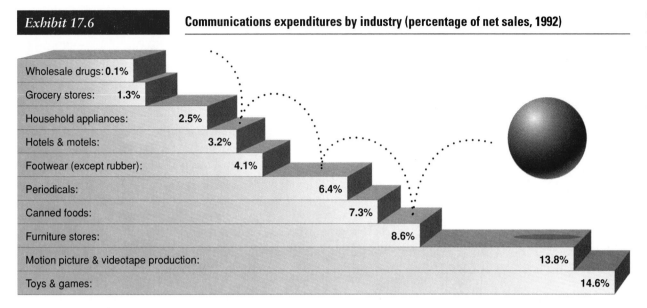

Exhibit 17.6   **Communications expenditures by industry (percentage of net sales, 1992)**

Wholesale drugs:	0.1%
Grocery stores:	1.3%
Household appliances:	2.5%
Hotels & motels:	3.2%
Footwear (except rubber):	4.1%
Periodicals:	6.4%
Canned foods:	7.3%
Furniture stores:	8.6%
Motion picture & videotape production:	13.8%
Toys & games:	14.6%

Influences on budgeting

The budget depends on the size of the company, its financial resources, the type of business, the market dispersion, the industry growth rate, and the firm's position in the marketplace. As shown in Exhibit 17.6, marketing communications expenditures also vary by industry.

High market-growth rates may indicate a large untapped market unaware of the product, and firms may then spend substantial amounts of money to reach these customers. Firms with larger market share may perceive high marketing expenditures as confirmation of dominance among competitors and as an effective way to discourage entry of new firms in the market, thus illustrating the *execution perspective.*[17]

Budgeting methods

Firms typically use any of four methods to determine the marketing communications budget: percentage of sales, competitive parity, all you can afford, and objective-task.

Percentage of sales.   Using the preceding year (or even a longer period) as a basis, a company can set its marketing communications budget as a percentage of sales. A drawback is that the assumed causal sequence of effects is reversed; that is, expenditures for marketing communications should partially determine sales levels, rather than past sales levels determining marketing communications expenditures.

Firms can also budget according to percentage of forecasted sales. When doing so, they often use industry standards such as those shown in Exhibit 17.6 as guidelines for determining a percentage. Percentage-of-sales approaches ensure some stability in planning, but they fail to consider competitive and economic pressures.

Competitive parity.   Some firms set marketing communications budgets to equal the percentage allocated by other companies in the industry. This approach at least acknowledges competitive actions. The disadvantage is it assumes that the competition is correct, that marketing communications dollars are spent with equal effectiveness across companies, and that other firms have similar objectives and resources. These assumptions may be dangerous oversimplifications of actual conditions.

All you can afford.   Sometimes firms spend what they can afford, or some amount left over after covering other costs. Such a budgeting technique fails to consider a firm's objectives and to commit expenditures necessary to achieve them. This is a questionable approach for the firm struggling to make a profit, because reduction of marketing communications expenditures may prevent any improvement and actually speed a downturn.

Objective-task.   More detailed than the other budgeting methods, this approach sets the budget at the level necessary to achieve stipulated marketing communications objectives. The objective-task method forces identification of tasks that must be achieved to meet established objectives and provides a way to evaluate results. It has the advantage of requiring management to spell out its assumptions about the relationships among dollars spent, exposure levels, product trial, and continuing consumer purchases.[18]

Marketing communications program development

Developing a marketing communications program involves developing general marketing communications strategies and allocating budgets to specific programs. A firm must decide the proper uses of explicit and implicit communications. And it must decide whether to adopt a push strategy, a pull strategy, or a combination strategy.

Explicit and implicit communications

Marketing communications may be either explicit or implicit. **Explicit communications** convey a distinct, clearly stated message through personal selling, advertising, public relations, sales promotion, direct marketing, or some combination of these methods. **Implicit communications** are what the message connotes about the product itself, its price, or the places it is sold. BMW, for instance, launched a marketing communications campaign to build a new image for its car. Ads suggested that BMWs are designed to improve a driver's ability the same way high-tech sports equipment enhances an athlete's performance.

This ad illustrates how both explicit and implicit marketing communications can be part of an *execution perspective.* Just like the watch, this rodeo cowboy can "take a licking and keep on ticking."

The ads explicitly focused on product features designed to improve drivers' skills, such as the suspension and steering systems, the exhaust sound, and wind noise.[19] As the BMW example illustrates, both implicit and explicit marketing communications can work together to convey a consistent message.

Push, pull, and combination strategies

A **push strategy** involves convincing intermediary channel members to "push" the product through the channel to the ultimate consumer. The company directs its marketing communications efforts toward promoting and selling the product to a reseller, which then does the same to another reseller or to the ultimate consumer. Personal selling is a primary tool in this method. Sales promotion and advertising directed at channel members may also be used. For example, manufacturers may provide sales incentives to retailers or place ads in retailer-oriented trade magazines.

A **pull strategy** attempts to get consumers to "pull" the product from the manufacturing company through the marketing channel. The company concentrates its marketing communications efforts on the consumer; that is, it hopes to stimulate interest and demand for the product at the end-user level. If consumers want and ask for the product, resellers are more likely to carry and distribute it. A firm with a new and unproven product might find a pull strategy useful if distributors are reluctant to carry the product. The firm then uses advertising and sales promotion tools such as coupons to get many consumers to go to the retail store and request the product, thus pulling it through the channel.

Many firms practice a **combination strategy**, aiming marketing communications at both resellers and ultimate consumers. A firm such as RJR Nabisco, for example, uses personal selling and trade promotions to sell its products to grocery retailers. At the same time, it makes extensive use of advertising and sales promotion directed at ultimate consumers. Strict reliance on either a push or a pull strategy does not take full advantage of the power of marketing communications. A firm with limited resources, however, may not be able to follow both strategies and may emphasize one over the other.

Integration and implementation

Implementation is setting the marketing communications plan into action. Depending on which tools the firm uses, it creates ads, purchases media time and space, and begins its sales promotion programs. If appropriate, the firm's personal selling, public relations, and direct marketing components also direct their efforts toward achieving the marketing communications objectives. As in the Barbara Mandrell/No Nonsense campaign, the key aspect of implementation is coordination.

Monitoring, evaluating, and controlling

Firms can use a variety of methods to monitor, evaluate, and control marketing communications. For example, a firm might monitor sales promotion by the number of coupons redeemed, or measure the effectiveness of a new personal selling strategy by looking at the number of new accounts opened by the salesforce. After an advertising campaign, a firm might run tests to see if consumers noticed the ad. The marketer could ask how many of those who noticed the ad linked the company name to it or actually read it. Researchers might also ask consumers about their attitude toward the company and the product both before and after a marketing communications program to see what effect, if any, the program had.

Marketers often rely on surveys and tests to evaluate marketing communications. Sometimes they look at sales results and attribute fluctuations in sales volume to the marketing communications, while largely ignoring the effects of other factors. Unfortunately, this narrow view prevails in many business settings.

Exhibit 17.7   **Ethical and legal concerns in marketing communications**

Marketing communications element	Ethical/Legal concerns
Advertising	• Using deceptive advertising • Reinforcing unfavorable ethnic/racial/sex stereotypes • Encouraging materialism & excessive consumption
Public relations	• Lack of sincerity (paying lip service to worthwhile causes) • Using economic power unfairly to gain favorable publicity • Orchestrating news events to give false appearance of widespread support for corporate position
Sales promotion	• Offering misleading consumer promotions • Paying slotting allowances to gain retail shelf space • Using unauthorized mailing lists to reach consumers
Personal selling	• Using high-pressure selling • Failing to disclose product limitations/safety concerns • Misrepresenting product benefits
Direct marketing communications	• Invading privacy by telemarketing • Using consumer database information without authorization of consumers • Creating economic waste with unwanted direct mail

Even though it may be difficult to measure the absolute effectiveness of most marketing communications, marketers have certainly not given up on the task. Quite the opposite is true, as the *productivity perspective* calls for marketers to increasingly justify money spent on communications.

Ethical and legal considerations

Exhibit 17.7 notes the ways the five areas of marketing communications may be subject to criticism from an ethical and legal viewpoint. Much to the dismay of upright professional marketers, ethical problems and legal violations in marketing communications continue. The good news is that an *ethical perspective* is also evident in marketing communications. In fact, marketing communications are frequently used to encourage responsible behavior such as contributing to charitable causes, practicing safe driving, and supporting community action programs. Marketing communications are also used to inform buyers about legal issues with reminders like "buckle up, it's the law," or "you must be 21 years old to purchase this product."

An example of marketing communications contributing to society is the "Friends of the Environment" campaign, which links package-goods manufacturers and groups such as the Nature Conservancy, International Wildlife Coalition, and Earth Island Institute. The program includes advertising, mass distribution of coupons (printed on recycled paper), and in-store displays in supermarkets. Consumers redeeming the coupons can designate the environmental

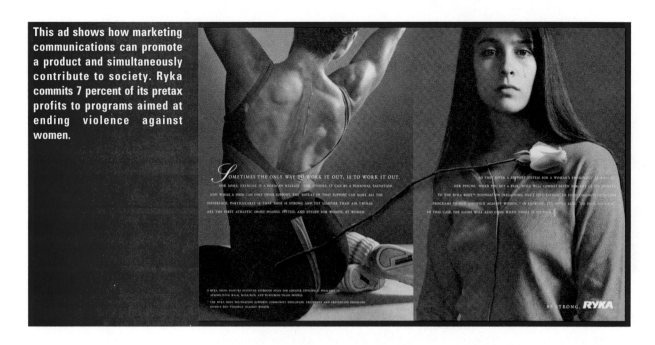

This ad shows how marketing communications can promote a product and simultaneously contribute to society. Ryka commits 7 percent of its pretax profits to programs aimed at ending violence against women.

projects they wish to support. Supporting companies then contribute 5 percent of the coupon's value toward the selected projects.[20] Such programs remind us that marketing communications are essential not only to profit-seeking marketers, but also to groups that support the improvement of our society. In some instance, the two constituencies overlap.

Legal—but ethical?

Some marketing communications may be technically legal but raise significant ethical questions. For example, the use of cartoon character "Old Joe" by R. J. Reynolds to promote Camel cigarettes poses ethical concerns. Reynolds claims to be aiming its Old Joe campaign at adults, but Camel's share of the market of young and underage smokers has risen dramatically since the campaign began. Although it is not illegal, the campaign certainly raises ethical concerns, and has prompted the US surgeon general to request that the FTC ban Old Joe ads.[21]

Similarly, alcohol ads using lifestyle themes to appeal to youth are ethically questionable. Beer manufacturers such as Anheuser-Busch and Miller Brewing Company, however, are trying to promote responsible drinking and curb teenage consumption. Anheuser-Busch has its "Know when to say when" campaign, while Miller features a "Think when you drink" theme.[22]

Deception in marketing communications

Exhibit 17.7 indicates that many problems relate to deception of consumers. Although this may happen in any area of the promotion mix, deceptive advertising is a prime concern. **Deceptive advertising,** communications intended to mislead consumers by making false claims or failing to disclose important information, is a major focus of the Federal Trade Commission (FTC), the government agency responsible for overseeing American business practices.[23]

An area particularly plagued by deceptive advertising is green marketing, or the promotion of a product as environmentally safe. Such claims, if false, subject a firm to Federal Trade Commission fines, damages, and injunctions.[24] Procter & Gamble, Kraft, General Foods, First Brands, Mary Kay Cosmetics, Jergens, and others have backed away from green claims because legislation in various states specifies different meanings for the terms, *recycled* and *recyclable*.[25] This inconsistency makes it extremely difficult for an advertiser to make green claims without a state-by-state review—a costly and time-consuming task.

This comparative ad points out that—unlike its competitors—Wesson Cooking Spray is alcohol free. The small type identifies the competing brands: Pam® and Mazola®.

Additional regulatory concerns

Additional FTC guidelines can affect marketing communications. The FTC requires that any claims made about product performance be capable of verification. Although the FTC provides for **comparative advertising** (which compares one or more products), it also requires that comparative claims be supported. If Pontiac wants to claim that its Bonneville costs thousands of dollars less than Lexus or BMW, it must make the basis for comparison clear to the consumer.

Product endorsers must be qualified to make judgments and must actually use the product being endorsed. Moreover, any demonstrations used in advertisements must be accurate representations and not misleading.[26]

Packaging and labeling practices of food and drug marketers are heavily scrutinized by consumers and regulatory agencies. At the national level, the Food and Drug Administration (FDA) keeps a watchful eye on health-related messages. Under pressure from the FDA, Kellogg changed the name of Heartwise cereal to Fiberwise, and Procter & Gamble stopped calling Citrus Hill "fresh" after the FDA took the juice off store shelves while investigating the freshness claim.[27] In 1991, the FDA's regulatory power was extended by legislation that requires manufacturers to disclose dietary and nutritional information on product labels about the amounts of fat, sugar, cholesterol, additives, and certain other elements in the product.

Effects of globalization

The increasing globalization of marketing often requires adjustment of the communications mix from country to country to avoid legal and ethical problems. For instance, although US tobacco advertisers are not allowed to advertise on television, they can advertise in magazines and outdoors and can sponsor sporting events. In Australia, however, the government is moving toward eliminating sponsorship of sports events and outdoor advertising by tobacco companies. Magazines may even be banned from the country if they run cigarette ads. The proposed ban would limit tobacco advertising in Australia to point of purchase.[28]

Summary

1. *Discuss the objectives of marketing communications.* The primary objective of marketing communications is to reach an audience to affect its behavior. In general, the three major objectives of marketing communications are to inform, to persuade, and to remind. The emphasis placed on one of the five primary communications

methods to achieve these objectives depends on the company's marketing and communications strategy.

2. *Understand the marketing communications mix and its role.* Marketing communications allow marketers to reach current and potential customers. Advertising, public relations, sales promotion, personal

selling, and direct marketing are the primary categories of marketing communications. Each of these tools has its unique advantages, providing a variety of techniques for reaching consumers.

It is important that marketing communications be consistent with a firm's overall corporate and marketing strategy. Marketing communications must be coordinated with product, price, and channel factors to reach the desired target audience effectively.

3. *Explain the key elements of the marketing communications process.* Communication occurs when there is shared meaning between source and receiver. Communication is considered effective to the extent that the source gets a desired response from the receiver.

From a marketing communications perspective, a firm as the source sends a marketing communications message through any of several message channels to its target audience, the receiver. The firm encodes the message by putting it into words, pictures, or symbols that best convey the message. Target audience members then decode the message by determining the

meaning of the words, pictures, and symbols. Sometimes the intended message is not received if there is noise in the communications process.

4. *Discuss the seven steps in the marketing communications planning process.* The key tasks of marketing communications planning include marketing plan review, situation analysis, communications process analysis, budget development, program development, integration and implementation of the plan, and monitoring, evaluating, and controlling the marketing communications process.

5. *Demonstrate awareness of some of the key ethical and legal issues related to marketing communications.* All areas of marketing communications have come under criticism for unethical and illegal activities. Some of the more frequently publicized problems include deceptive advertising, inability to substantiate comparative claims, unfair reinforcement of ethnic, racial, and sex stereotypes, and encouragement of materialistic values.

Key terms & concepts

marketing communications *416*
marketing communications
   mix *416*
advertising *418*
public relations *419*
publicity *419*
sales promotion *419*
personal selling *420*
direct marketing
   communications *421*
integrated marketing
   communications *422*
sponsorship *423*

communication *423*
receiver *423*
source *424*
message sponsor *424*
message presenter *424*
marketing communications
   message *424*
message channel *424*
encoding *424*
decoding *424*
feedback *424*
noise *424*

marketing communications
   planning *425*
percentage of sales budgeting *429*
competitive parity budgeting *429*
all you can afford budgeting *430*
objective-task budgeting *430*
explicit communications *430*
implicit communications *430*
push strategy *431*
pull strategy *431*
combination strategy *431*
deceptive advertising *433*
comparative advertising *434*

Review & discussion questions

1. Briefly define marketing communications and describe the elements of the marketing communications mix.

2. Refer to **The Entrepreneurial Spirit: Elan Frozen Yogurt Samples to Success.** Why do you think sampling is such an effective means of marketing communications for Elan frozen yogurt?

3. What is sponsorship? What are some of its advantages and disadvantages? Give an example of sponsorship, and comment on its effectiveness.

4. What is the goal of marketing communications? Name three major objectives of marketing communications. For each objective, give an example of how an actual firm uses marketing communications to reach it.

5. Give several examples of ethical or legal issues related to marketing communications.

6. What factors could cause a marketing communications message to be decoded differently from the way the source intended?

7. Review **The Technological Edge: Interactive Media Revolutionizes Marketing Communications.** Do you think interactive technology will increase the clarity of communications between marketers and consumers? Why or why not?

8. Briefly describe the steps in marketing communications planning.

9. How can other aspects of the marketing mix affect the marketing communications mix?

10. What influences the amount of money a company might spend on marketing communications?

Application exercises

1. Select a major marketer of consumer goods that has advertised on national television within the past month. Try to identify approaches other than television advertising that have been part of this company's recent marketing communications mix.

2. Identify several specific examples of marketing communications that you feel are either ethically or legally questionable. What elements in each communication cause the problem? How could each communication be improved to remove any doubt about its ethical or legal acceptability?

3. Choose a product you are familiar with, and illustrate how product, pricing, and marketing channel factors influence the marketing communications activities for the product.

Case 17.1   *The United Colors of Benetton: Social awareness and advertising*

Benetton, Italy's fastest-growing clothing empire, has long used arresting images in its advertising campaigns, some of which have attracted objections. Differing from most conventional views, Benetton's philosophy toward advertising is that it should create awareness of social problems around the world.

A recent worldwide $60 million print advertising campaign, "United Colors of Benetton," included images of a man dying from AIDS surrounded by his family; a horde of refugees struggling to climb aboard a huge ship; a soldier carrying a gun and holding what appears to be a human bone; an Indian couple waist-deep in flood waters; a burning car symbolizing terrorism; and the shrouded corpse of a Mafia hit victim.

Perhaps the most controversial ad from this campaign was the picture of the dying AIDS patient. The photo, originally shot for *Life* magazine, depicts AIDS patient David Kirby on his deathbed, surrounded by his family in a Columbus, Ohio, hospice. The Kirby family approved the ad, hoping that the love they expressed would help people see the disease differently. Instead, the ad prompted outrage that Benetton exploited AIDS to sell clothes. In fact, the Advertising Standards Authority in the UK banned the ad. Governmental regulatory agencies in France, Italy, and Great Britain have filed lawsuits against another Benetton ad campaign that showed photographs of body parts bearing a "HIV positive" tattoos.

Peter Fressola, Benetton's communications director, justifies the company's advertising strategy:

> We've become a shorthand for multiculturalism and a progressive world view . . . Exploitation isn't bad if there are no victims and some good is being served. Just as Jerry Lewis uses a poster child to raise money for muscular dystrophy, our powerful images compel people to think, call them to come together in a spirit of unity and equality. It's art in the service of commerce, positioning Benetton as a concerned, socially active

company in a modern global village . . . Consumers today are as concerned about a company's soul as about the price-value relationship of its products.

Consumer reactions to the ads vary. Some find them thought provoking, but others are upset and place angry calls to Benetton Services Corporation in New York. A 1992 *Advertising Age* survey found that 32 percent of Benetton's target market of 19- to 34-year-olds said the campaign is an effective marketing tool, and 41 percent believe the ads raise awareness of social issues.

Despite overall sales growth, Benetton has recently had difficult times in the US, where the company lost $10 million in 1991. Over time, American consumers have come to question Benetton's product quality and its notoriously high prices. Indeed, of its original 700 US stores, only 400 remained in 1992, with another 100 scheduled to close. Benetton failed to recognize Americans as price-conscious shoppers. It also faces tough US competition from The Gap and Limited Express.

Questions:

1. What is the goal of Benetton's advertising strategy? What does the company communicate about its products?

2. Should Benetton focus on the price-value relationship of its merchandise? In what way could Benetton address the fierce competition from other US clothing retailers?

3. Is Benetton acting in a socially responsible manner by running its controversial ads?

Sources: "AIDS Ad Angers," *The Commercial Appeal,* November 28, 1993, p. F5; "AIDS Agencies Sue Benetton," *Marketing News,* October 11, 1993, p. 1; Jacqueline Gold, "Lost in Translation," *Financial World,* July 7, 1992, pp. 22–24; Gary Levin, "Benetton Brouhaha," *Advertising Age,* February 17, 1992, p. 62; Dave Saunders, "The Benetton Ads: Exploration or Exploitation?" *Marketing Director International,* Spring 1993, pp. 33–35; Michael Schuman, "Unraveled," *Forbes,* May 24, 1993, p. 97; and Adrienne Ward, "Socially Aware or Wasted Money?" *Advertising Age,* February 24, 1992, p. 4.

Case 17.2   *Heinz's "Family Works!": An integrated marketing communications effort*

A recent trend in marketing has been the development of integrated marketing communications programs by which companies can deliver their messages more effectively to customers. Some of these integrated programs involve joint marketing communications efforts between two or more organizations. Such was the case when Heinz USA, maker of condiments and gravies, recently invested more than $10 million in its "Family Works!" program. This national program uses an integrated approach to communicate the issues facing the evolving American family and, in essence, to strengthen the reputation of the company's "homey" basic condiments.

The Milwaukee-based nonprofit organization Family Service America (FSA) cosponsored the program. FSA's basic agenda is to initiate public and private support for the American family in all its emerging forms. One objective of "Family Works!" was to provide modern solutions to the problems confronting American families today. The campaign kicked off in a TV special hosted by actress Ann Jillian. Although Heinz did not directly plug its products in the program content, it did so during commercial breaks and subsequent print and publicity campaigns. Heinz hoped to strengthen the reputation of its condiments and gravies by associating itself with FSA through the use of programming, cosponsored events, and retailer support.

Coordination of these events can be difficult, however, and must be achieved at all levels of the organization. For example, the Heinz campaign included a freestanding coupon insert in newspapers throughout the country. The inserts, in accordance with the objective of total integrated marketing, were customized for local markets and provided information on air times for the Ann Jillian show. Unfortunately, the insert in the New York–area papers inexplicably appeared a week *after* the show had aired. Other elements of the campaign included a series of 30-second TV commercials about family problems and solutions, various print ads, and the sponsorship of local events to encourage family participation.

The Heinz–FSA coordinated "Family Works!" program represents a comprehensive integrated marketing effort. The key words are *coordinated* and *effort*. According to Paul LaCamera, representative of Boston TV station WCVB and producer of some of the campaign's programs, "This takes a full commitment. When you've got a national sponsor, a local TV station, and local sponsors, you've really got to keep everyone on the same course to achieve the fullest potential. If you do, it can be a great success."

Questions:

1. Why would Heinz choose to cosponsor a campaign with a seemingly unrelated organization?

2. What are possible advantages and disadvantages that could result from an integrated marketing effort?

3. What criteria can Heinz use to measure the success of the campaign?

Sources: Laurie Petersen, "How Heinz's Family Works!" *Adweek's Marketing Week,* January 13, 1992, pp. 34, 36; "Customized Marketing's First Big Steps," *Adweek's Marketing Week,* March 18, 1991, p. 28; and Patricia Sellers, "H. J. Heinz: Has Cost Cutting Gone Too Far?" *Fortune,* November 2, 1992, pp. 81–82.

Advertising and Public Relations

After studying this chapter you should be able to:

1. Understand the characteristics, functions, and types of advertising.

2. Realize how people process advertising information, and how it affects buyer behavior.

3. Discuss approaches to developing advertising campaigns.

4. Describe different advertising objectives and the message strategies used to achieve them.

5. Understand the decisions involved in selecting media and scheduling advertising.

6. Explain how marketers assess advertising effectiveness.

7. Appreciate the roles of public relations and publicity in marketing.

Reno Air billboard campaign: Just the ticket for grabbing attention

Reno Air wanted to advertise its newest route connecting San Francisco and Lake Tahoe. As a new company, Reno Air could not afford television advertising, so it focused its efforts on newspapers and billboards. One billboard, selected by *Advertising Age* as the best out-of-home ad for 1992, was part of a $3 million ad campaign.

The billboard reflects many of the objectives of advertising. By being placed on the drive to Lake Tahoe from San Francisco, it exposed many potential customers to Reno's message. The placement of an authentic police car complete with a display figure of an officer eating a doughnut easily attracted attention. By slowing because of the police car, drivers and their passengers have additional time to understand and process the message: Reno's airfares cost less than a speeding ticket. The billboard is a prime example of a novel, attention-getting ad that presents a primary consumer benefit, low-cost air fares.

Reno combined the use of this billboard and two others on the same route with a series of newspaper ads. Both of these media are very effective at reaching localized audiences. The creativity embodied in Reno's novel marketing approach exemplifies the *entrepreneurial perspective.*

Sources: Riccardo A. Davis, "Out-of-Home—Reno Air Outdoor Board Just the Ticket for Attention Grabbing," *Advertising Age,* May 3, 1993, p. 515; and Greg Farrell,"The 1993 Obie Awards," *Adweek,* May 10, 1993, p. 3.

The Reno campaign is a good example of how marketers use different media and novel strategies to advertise products. Reno exposed the message to its most important target market, using two different media to present it. As a result of the campaign, Reno consistently fills most of its seats on flights to Lake Tahoe.

In this chapter, we explore issues associated with advertising—the most visible marketing activity. We discuss the related topic of public relations as well.

The nature of advertising

Advertising defined

Advertising is the activity consumers most associate with the term *marketing*. **Advertising** is defined as a marketing communications element that is persuasive, nonpersonal, paid for by an identified sponsor, and disseminated through mass channels of communication to promote the adoption of goods, services, persons, or ideas.[1]

Effective advertising can present information about new or existing products, demonstrate meaningful uses of the product, and establish or refresh the brand's image.[2] It can reach a diverse or wide audience with repeated communications and gives a company the opportunity to dramatize its products and services in a colorful way.

Advertising stimulates demand, helps build brand success, develops and shapes buyer behavior, and gives the seller a measure of certainty about the level of sales. In addition, it informs buyers about product characteristics and availability and makes markets more competitive.[3]

Advertising performs other functions as well. Some advertising supports personal selling efforts. For example, many companies advertise to increase consumer awareness of products, making later personal selling efforts easier. Such advertising, if executed effectively, generates sales leads and communicates product advantages to prospective buyers.

The advertising industry

Advertising is a huge industry, with annual global expenditures close to $300 billion worldwide. P&G, Philip Morris, GM, and Sears each spent more than $1 billion on media advertising in 1993.[4]

Exhibit 18.1 presents the amount advertisers spent in the US on each medium in 1992. Two of the fastest growing media are syndicated TV and cable

Exhibit 18.1   **Total national advertising spending by type of medium**

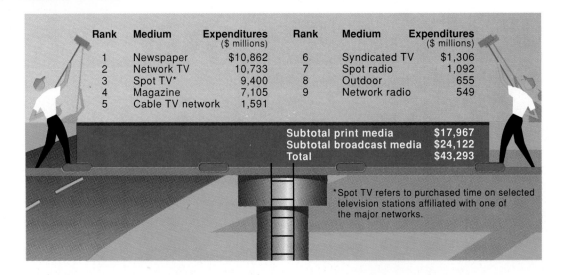

Rank	Medium	Expenditures ($ millions)	Rank	Medium	Expenditures ($ millions)
1	Newspaper	$10,862	6	Syndicated TV	$1,306
2	Network TV	10,733	7	Spot radio	1,092
3	Spot TV*	9,400	8	Outdoor	655
4	Magazine	7,105	9	Network radio	549
5	Cable TV network	1,591			

Subtotal print media	$17,967
Subtotal broadcast media	$24,122
Total	$43,293

*Spot TV refers to purchased time on selected television stations affiliated with one of the major networks.

TV networks; in fact, their growth has caused average nightly audience shares of the major networks (ABC, NBC, CBS) to drop to under 50 percent, hence network advertising revenues have dropped by more than 10 percent.[5]

Ad agencies

Many advertisers hire an **advertising agency** to create ad campaigns and to purchase media time and space. Exhibit 18.2 lists the world's top five advertising organizations as measured by gross income. All of them employ many people in organizations worldwide, and three have their central offices in London or Tokyo.

Ad agencies employ both creative people who develop unique advertising messages, and media specialists who provide media planning and scheduling. Creative strategies and a proven track record clearly are good reasons to hire an ad agency. To limit costs and save on commissions, however, some large companies like Benetton have in-house advertising functions to handle everything from creative design to media decisions. Other companies, like Procter & Gamble, now buy their own media space and time instead of relying entirely on ad agencies.

The choice of a competent ad agency is especially important for firms targeting new global markets. One US soap manufacturer, for example, simply dubbed its commercials showing people singing in the shower into Polish TV ads. Poles laughed heartily at the advertiser's naiveté: There are very few showers in Polish homes, and because hot water is so limited, no Pole would take a leisurely shower. Marketers can avoid such gaffes by establishing close partnerships with a capable advertising agency.[6]

Ad agencies derive much of their income from commissions. The major media usually give agencies a 15 percent discount on any time or space they purchase for their clients. For example, when an agency buys a full-page color ad from a magazine for a client for $25,000, the magazine charges $25,000 less 15 percent, or $21,250. The agency bills the advertiser the full $25,000 and keeps the difference.

An industry in transition

Today, marketers increasingly question each advertising expenditure. In fact, advertising's average share of marketing communication expenditures dropped from 43 percent in 1981 to 27 percent in 1992.[7] From the *productivity* and *execution perspectives,* targeting mass markets with advertising alone no longer makes sense for many companies. Simply buying air time during a specific TV program or buying a certain page in a specific magazine is not enough to reach

Exhibit 18.2	World's top five advertising organizations

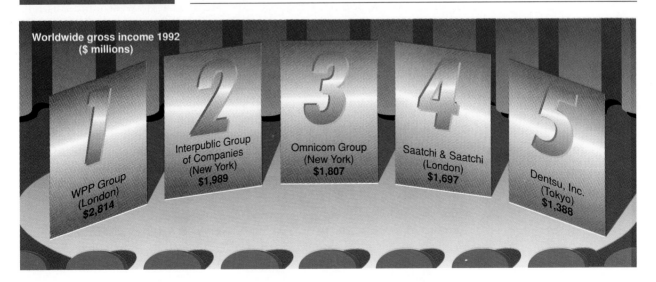

Worldwide gross income 1992 ($ millions)

1. WPP Group (London) $2,814
2. Interpublic Group of Companies (New York) $1,989
3. Omnicom Group (New York) $1,807
4. Saatchi & Saatchi (London) $1,697
5. Dentsu, Inc. (Tokyo) $1,388

Benetton's in-house advertising function handles its social awareness campaigns.

targeted audiences. Advertisers often must use multimedia campaigns, combining television, print ads, videos, billboards, trade shows, direct mail, and activities such as event sponsorship into an *integrated marketing communications program.*[8]

EXECUTIVE ROUNDTABLE COMMENT | Gerald Evans, vice president of field sales for Sara Lee Hosiery and former brand manager for Léggs, observes:

Many firms question the effectiveness of advertising. Today's consumer seems especially concerned about price due to economic trends and the rise of dominant, value-positioned retailers like Wal-Mart. Price appears to be the major variable in moving volume in every product category. Thus, at Sara Lee, we place more emphasis on sales promotion and less on advertising.

Globalization of marketing efforts is another example of changing times. Consistent with the **global perspective,** both product and advertising must meet local market needs and fit in with cultural practices. Religious-dominant areas such as Saudi Arabia and Iran, areas with multiple cultural influences such as Japan and Korea, and more homogeneous areas such as Sweden and Australia each require different advertising communications.[9] For example, Kraft advertised its processed cheese slices using a common theme (milk content) but different advertising styles and presentations to match the consumer preferences and uniqueness in Canada, the UK, Australia, and Spain.[10]

Japanese advertisers favor "soft selling" and often use indirect messages. The typical Western emphasis on product merit and use of spokespeople directly stating brand advantages are missing in much Japanese advertising.[11] And surprisingly, given the Japanese attraction to Western culture, the appearance of American images and settings has increased only modestly in Japanese advertising. Foreign advertisers in Japan should recognize these differences.

Technological changes keep the advertising industry in transition as well. The extension of cable TV, the widespread penetration of VCRs, and remote-control–capability all suggest some loss of effectiveness of TV commercials. Remote-control use, in particular, has given rise to **commercial zapping,** or changing the channels during commercials.[12] One study reveals that ads aired during competing sports events encountered audience losses up to 50 percent.

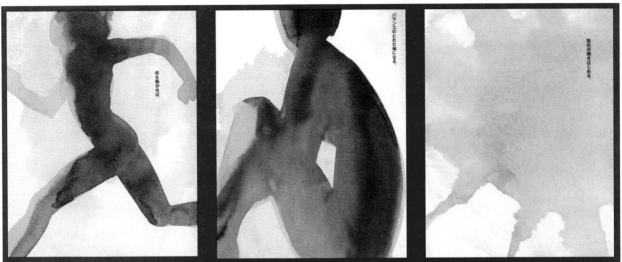

The copy accompanying these pages from a Nike insert specifically targeted to women in Japan reads, "As you work out . . . you can sleep tight . . . your body will be in better shape . . . your back straightens up . . . your heart becomes pure . . . and each and every day begins to shine . . . as you work out."

Zapping is heaviest during news and late-night programming.[13] In addition, younger viewers and members of higher-income households are more likely to get up and do something else during TV commercial breaks.[14]

What then does this transition mean for advertising? The future looks brightest for media that reach target audiences more efficiently than broadbased ones like network TV. The winners are expected to be radio stations, specialized cable networks, new kinds of in-store advertising, and weekly newspapers, all of which appeal to specific rather than to broad audiences.[15]

Classifications of advertising

Advertising can be classified by target audience, geographic area, medium, and purpose, as shown in Exhibit 18.3.[16] The special types discussed here are corporate image advertising, corporate advocacy advertising, public service advertising, classified advertising, direct-response advertising, business-to-business advertising, and cooperative advertising.

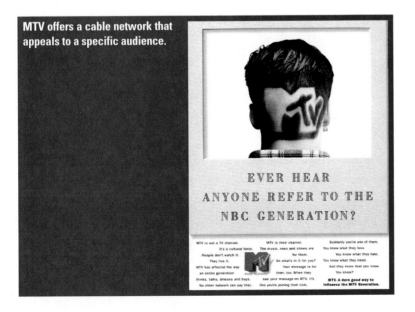

MTV offers a cable network that appeals to a specific audience.

EVER HEAR ANYONE REFER TO THE NBC GENERATION?

Exhibit 18.3 **Classifications of advertising**

By target audience	By geographic area	By medium	By purpose
Consumer advertising: aimed at people who buy the product for their own or someone else's personal use. **Business advertising:** aimed at people who buy or specify goods & services for use in business: • **Industrial:** aimed at people who buy or influence the purchase of industrial products. • **Trade:** aimed at wholesalers & retailers who buy for resale to their customers. • **Professional:** aimed at people licensed to practice under a code of ethics or set of professional standards. • **Agricultural (farm):** aimed at people in the farming or agricultural business.	**Local (retail) advertising:** advertising by businesses whose customers come from only one city or local trading area. **Regional advertising:** advertising for products sold in one area or region, but not the whole country. **National advertising:** advertising aimed at customers in several regions of the country. **International advertising:** advertising directed at foreign markets.	**Print advertising:** newspaper, magazine. **Broadcast (electronic) advertising:** radio, TV. **Out-of-home advertising:** outdoor, transit. **Direct-mail advertising:** advertising sent through the mail.	**Product advertising:** intended to promote goods & services. **Nonproduct (corporate or institutional advertising):** intended to promote firm's mission or philosophy rather than a product. **Commercial advertising:** intended to promote goods, services, or ideas with the expectancy of making a profit. **Noncommercial advertising:** sponsored by or for a charitable institution, civic group, or religious or political organization. **Action advertising:** intended to bring about immediate action on the part of the reader. **Awareness advertising:** attempts to build the image of a product or familiarity with the product's name and package.

Corporate image advertising, directed toward the general public or investors and stockholders, promotes an organization's image and role in the community as a corporate citizen, independent of any product or service. **Corporate advocacy advertising** announces a stand on some issue related to the firm's operation, often one threatening the company's well-being. For example, Exxon addressed environmental issues in advocacy advertising following its Alaska oil spill.

Public service advertising is donated by the advertising industry to promote activities for some social good. For example, the World Wildlife Fund presents environmental public service advertisements. Frequently, marketers donate advertising time to drug and alcohol abuse prevention efforts, such as the "Just Say No" program and Mothers Against Drunk Driving (MADD).

Direct-response advertising (discussed in more detail in Chapter 21) is intended to elicit immediate action, often a purchase. Direct-response ads on TV typically request immediate calls to telephone numbers shown on the TV screen. Direct-response ads also appear in magazines and direct mail. **Classified advertising,** mainly in newspapers, typically promotes transactions for a single item or service.

Firms use **business-to-business advertising** to promote their products or services directly to other firms. Most business advertising involves print ads in trade periodicals or direct-mail sent to targeted buyers. Some business marketers, such as Ricoh Copiers, IBM, and Federal Express, advertise on TV in time slots likely to reach sophisticated adult audiences.

Cooperative advertising entails manufacturers contributing to a local dealer or retailer's advertising expense. The amount is based on the quantity of product the retailer purchases. The local marketer typically runs manufacturer-developed advertising that includes the outlet's name and logo.

IT'S ONLY DEATH-DEFYING IF YOU LIVE THROUGH IT.

ADVANCED AEROBATIC FLIGHT TRAINING

屋外無人掃
屋內亦難逃劫數

🌸 清潔公眾地方 人人有責 ↑

Advanced Aerobic Flight Training advertises to consumers who will use its services.

A public service campaign directed at Hong Kong tenants who keep their apartments tidy but leave garbage in the halls: "Today, the corridor outside. Tomorrow . . ." and "Pitch in to clean up your block's shared areas."

Consumer ad processing

How then does advertising actually influence consumers? In this section, we explain how consumers process advertisements and how ads affect consumer attitudes and decisions.

In this business-to-business ad, Campbell's promotes its new advertising campaign to retailers. The breakthrough campaign includes new labels for its soup cans and a new theme: "Campbell's. Never underestimate the power of soup."

What's Red and White and Seen All Over?

Breakthrough Campbell's® Soup Ads Backed by Record Spending

You've never seen Campbell's Soup ads quite like these. And because we're determined to achieve big growth across our entire line, the whole country's about to see them all over the place. On TV and in print. Backed by a whopping 40% increase in media spending over last year.

So get ready. Major advertising support like this from the number one brand is going to mean real category expansion. Unprecedented excitement up and down the soup aisle. Increased store traffic. It's a sizzling new ad campaign with an important message for everybody: Campbell's. Never Underestimate The Power of Soup.

See your Campbell Representative for further details.

Campbell's
— Never Underestimate the Power of Soup —

Hierarchy of effects

Advertising's influence on consumers is often explained by using the hierarchy of effects, or information-processing, model. This sequence of effects—exposure, attention, comprehension, acceptance, retention—is shown in Exhibit 18.4. Of course, every consumer does not consciously, or even subconsciously, go through a sequence of steps for all ads. Yet each stage of this hierarchy represents a specific goal for advertisers to pursue.

A marketer achieves *message exposure* by placing ads in appropriate media, such as magazines, TV programs, or newspapers, which gives the consumer the opportunity to process the message.

Consumer *attention* is the next step. The ad must stimulate the consumer to direct mental effort toward it. The primary attention-getting properties of an ad are its physical characteristics. For print ads, these include size, number of colors, and brightness. Motion, attention-getting models, and novelty also help grab attention.[17]

Attention does not necessarily mean the consumer will process a message further. *Message comprehension,* the next stage, means the consumer understands the ad's meaning. Then, *message acceptance* must occur for the consumer to develop favorable attitudes about the advertised product or service and its subsequent purchase. *Message retention* occurs when the consumer stores ad information in long-term memory, which is critical for affecting later purchase decisions and behavior.

Influences on ad processing

Buyers' needs influence their processing of advertising messages. For example, a firm with a pressing need for waste removal would pay more attention to ads for this service than to esthetic ads from a plant service to beautify the corporate office.

In addition, the buyer's motivation, opportunity, and ability to process brand information come into play. *Motivation* is related to the concept of consumer involvement, or the personal relevance or importance of the marketing communications message. Motivation is the desire to process the information. When motivation is low, potential customers pay little attention and remember minimal information, if any. *Opportunity* is the extent to which distractions or limited exposure time affect the buyer's attention to brand information in an ad. *Ability* implies the buyer knows enough about the product category to understand the advertised message.[18]

Exhibit 18.4   **Advertising hierarchy of effects**

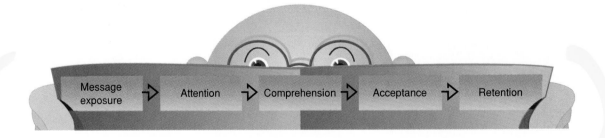

Developing an advertising campaign

An ad campaign requires an analysis of the marketing situation, the target market involved, and the firm's overall communication objectives. As Exhibit 18.5 shows, once the firm has selected its target market, it must determine advertising objectives, determine the advertising budget, design the creative strategy, select and schedule media, and evaluate advertising effectiveness.

Determining advertising objectives

Advertising objectives should be realistic, precise, and measurable, and consistent with the firm's overall marketing and communications objectives. One objective might be to increase brand awareness from 10 to 35 percent of all consumers within a particular market, say, cereal eaters between the ages of 18 and 55. Another might be to increase sales or market share, say, to achieve a sales growth of 2 percent in the next quarter. Setting objectives allows the firm to evaluate the effectiveness of its advertising expenditures, and focus on the *productivity* and *execution perspectives.*

Determining advertising budget

The size of the advertising budget depends on the size of the company, its financial resources, the industry growth rate, market dispersion, and the firm's position in the marketplace. Smaller firms usually spend less, while dominant firms may spend a disproportionately large amount to maintain market share and discourage competition. And, a growing industry may warrant higher advertising budgets to build awareness, sales, and market share.

As explained in Chapter 17, budgets are often based on percentage of sales, competitive parity, all the firm can afford, or allocation by objectives, the recommended approach.

Designing creative strategy

Creative strategy combines the "what is said" with the "how it is said." Typically, the advertiser specifies the general content or theme of the message, and the ad agency works with the company to develop the presentation.

Usually, the theme is the product's primary benefit or competitive advantage, presented in an attention-getting message the target audience can comprehend and remember. As competition for audience attention increases, highly creative and entertaining commercials become commonplace.[19]

Exhibit 18.5

Advertising development and evaluation

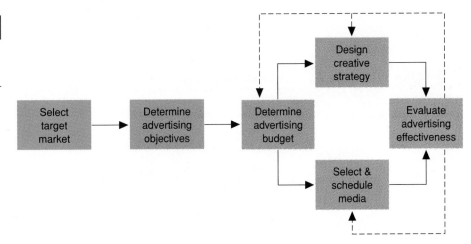

Don't touch that dial!

*O*n a shoestring, disc jockey Lee Baily and his wife Diane began producing "Radioscope" from their garage. The radio program, designed originally to appeal to young urban minorities, provides information about records and recording artists—it answers questions such as "Why did Jermaine Jackson switch labels?" and "What happened to the Stylistics?" The Bailys developed a sample program and mailed demonstration tapes to 50 radio stations. Ninety percent of the respondents reacted favorably to the promotion. Today, "Radioscope," "Hip Hop Countdown and Report," and "Inside Gospel" draw an estimated 15 million listeners in 47 countries.

The process was difficult, and the Bailys encountered significant obstacles. The company was undercapitalized and targeted to young urban blacks, a market some observers considered to be nonlucrative. The whole scheme, moreover, hinged on keeping three groups happy: listeners, radio stations, and advertisers.

Ultimately, the program's candor about the music industry and minority life attracted its first major advertiser. Chuck Morrison, Coca-Cola's vice president of sales and marketing for blacks and minorities, happened to be flipping the dial, heard a portion of the program, and promptly put a chunk of Coke's money behind it. As Lee Baily puts it, "Once we had Coke on board, things got easier—we moved out of the garage."

The Bailys' products are still no easy sell, however. "A lot of advertisers feel, if we do general advertising, we'll catch everyone. That's often not true," says Diane. The radio broadcasts do offer a unique means for advertisers to target an important market segment.

Source: Scott Wandus, "Lee and Diane Baily: Don't Touch That Dial," *Sales & Marketing Management,* January 1992, pp. 46–47.

Increasingly, advertisers recognize the influence of cultural diversity on advertising. As noted earlier, this is particularly true for international advertising, where standardization of advertising across national lines is on the decline. But national advertisers also target minority and other groups with specialized campaigns. **The Entrepreneurial Spirit: Don't Touch That Dial!** describes one such effort.

This Levi's Jeans for Women ad is part of a creative, attention-getting approach that differs from the traditional strategy of showing real models wearing the product.

Message strategy alternatives

Advertising messages can make objective or subjective claims. **Objective claims** describe product features or performance in measurable terms, such as "Chevy mid-sized vans are available with V-6 or V-8 engines." Objective claims often reflect a *quality/value perspective* by promoting the benefits received from the price paid. For example, Reebok advertises the custom fit from its pump technology. AT&T advertises service reliability for its monthly charges.

Subjective claims are not measurable, often stress image enhancement, and may include *puffery,* which is simply some level of acceptable exaggeration, such as Budweiser's "the King of beers" or Del Monte's "super natural" advertising phrases.[20]

Message strategies frequently attempt to convey a distinct product image or quality appeal. Timex ads, for example, consistently focus on product quality; Lexus ads appeal to buyers' self-images. Some messages appeal to the hedonistic, or pleasure-seeking, side of consumers.

Comparative advertising relates a sponsored brand to a competitive brand on at least one product attribute. Objective attribute comparisons seem to be most effective at enhancing consumer attitudes about the sponsoring brand. Well-known comparisons include MCI against AT&T; Subaru against Volvo; Toshiba computers against Compaq; Maxwell House coffee against Folgers; American Express credit cards against Visa; Pizza Hut versus Domino's; and Weight Watchers diet meals against Lean Cuisine.[21] In some countries, like Greece and Argentina, comparative advertising is restricted to brand X comparisons.

Typically, the advertiser claims superiority of its product on the most important features being compared. By not claiming superiority on a less important

Image-based appeals recognize the influence of others' reactions to the buyer's purchase. This Teva ad says: "There was an old lady who lived in a shoe. Do you want to live like an old lady?"

"The little box for head and tummy aches." Campaign for Alka-Seltzer in Belgium.

Norwegian Cruise Lines ad for trips to the Caribbean.

"If I were you, I'd order steak." Campaign for a steak restaurant in Amsterdam.

attribute, the advertiser implies admission of a slight shortcoming, which may actually enhance credibility of the other claims. An advertiser may also enhance a lesser-known product by comparing it to a well-known product.

Message strategies with *emotional appeals* attempt to evoke feelings, moods, and memories. Diet Pepsi and Dr Pepper commercials, for example, associate warm feelings with their brands. Marketers of insurance, tires, and automobiles may use *fear appeals* related to safety. The "baby in a tire" theme, produced by DDB Needham Advertising Agency of New York for Michelin Tires, recognizes the value of such advertising. And deodorant, shampoo, and toothpaste ads frequently play on the consumer's desire to be liked or to avoid disapproval.

Celebrity endorsements and *humor appeals* may be elements of creative message strategy. Well-known spokespersons, such as Elizabeth Taylor, Tim Allen, and Michael Jordan, can enhance the persuasive impact of a message. This strategy is not without some risk, however, as evidenced by problems encountered by former frequent endorsers Michael Jackson, Madonna, Burt Reynolds, and O. J. Simpson. Humor appeals can increase consumer attention and recall. Regardless of the punch celebrity endorsements or humor can have, however, the message still must reflect some competitive advantage, unique product benefit, and value.[22]

Celebrities are often selected because of their perceived expertise. The Nuprin–Jimmy Connors pairing promoting solutions for aches and pains from athletic competition is one example. In other instances, celebrity endorsements are intended to help consumers identify with the product. For example, ads that include professional athletes appeal to young people who dream of successful sports careers themselves.

A growing phenomenon is the **advertorial,** a special advertising section with some nonadvertising content included in magazines. Advertorials are typically sold as special deals to advertisers that would not normally advertise in the magazine. An example is the "Guide to Entertainment" presented in *The New Yorker,* paid for by Chrysler. Advertorials offer the advertiser a way to stand out in a cluttered media environment.[23] Television's counterpart, the infomercial, a 30-minute ad that resembles a talk show or news program, is described later in our chapter on direct marketing.

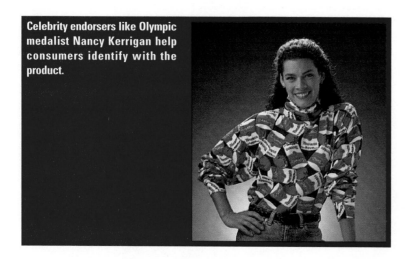

Celebrity endorsers like Olympic medalist Nancy Kerrigan help consumers identify with the product.

Selecting and scheduling media

Media planning involves decisions on *media class* (television, magazines) and on *media vehicles* (specific television programs, magazines). Marketers must then decide on *media schedules* (frequency, timing of ads).

Media classes

There are seven classes of advertising media: television, magazines, newspapers, radio, outdoor, transit, and direct mail. There are advantages and disadvantages of these, and the effectiveness of each approach depends on its unique capabilities.

Television, magazines, and radio are useful in building brand awareness. TV, in particular, can reach mass markets. And, with the advent of cable and specialized networks, TV can target specific markets at a relatively cheap cost per individual exposure. Television commercials, however, are expensive in total. Moreover, since TV ads typically last 15 to 30 seconds and are surrounded by other messages, consumers can easily tune them out.

Magazines can present complex and factual information. Messages can be read leisurely, have a long life, have pass-along exposure, and can be targeted to specific audiences. But magazine ads are subject to interference from competing ads and take a substantial time to develop and introduce.

Newspaper advertising is excellent for local retail sales promotions. It can be developed quickly and can effectively target particular locations. But newspapers contain many ads and do not typically generate much audience involvement. The production quality of newspaper advertising is fairly low, though newspaper inserts do enable higher quality. For retailers, however, newspaper advertising is an effective communications medium.

Radio advertising can be quite cost effective, the commercials can be targeted to specific audiences, and repetition of messages is possible. However, radio messages are subject to channel zapping and of course have no visual impact. Further, radio messages have a short life and typically generate only minimal involvement.

Outdoor advertising consists mainly of billboards constructed on leased property and rented to advertising companies. Billboards, like the Reno example at the start of the chapter, reach large numbers of consumers effectively and inexpensively. Billboard advertising is useful in supporting TV and radio campaigns and is particularly effective for building awareness of new brands. However, billboards present only limited message content, the span of exposure is brief, and messages must be viewed at a distance.

Billboards and transit ads are cost-effective ways to reach large numbers of customers.

Transit advertisements—signs and messages on or in public buses and trains—are billboards on wheels. Transit ads inside vehicles are low in cost and provide frequent and lengthy exposure to riders. But message space is limited and typically reaches a restricted audience. The vehicle environment may detract from the prestige of the advertiser or message, and crowded conditions during rush hours may limit the opportunity to process the messages.

Direct mail, among the fastest growing means of advertising today, has several significant advantages. It can reach narrow markets and enable the advertiser to elaborate on ad claims. Direct mail is also important in support of business-to-business marketing communications programs and is available to small and large companies. When coupled with 800 numbers or return envelopes, direct mail can generate direct-response sales. But the frequency of direct-mail advertising can limit its effectiveness. Many consumers perceive such ads as junk mail and don't pay much attention to them. The success of direct-mail campaigns depends on the quality of the mailing lists used to target customers. In addition, printing, mailing, and development costs can make direct-mail marketing expensive.

EXECUTIVE ROUNDTABLE COMMENT | Gerald Evans, vice president of field sales for Sara Lee and former brand manager for Léggs, notes that:

Print, cable, and syndicated television have emerged as lower-cost, more targeted media. However, for mass-marketed packaged goods brands, these media do not provide a sufficient impact on the target audience. They tend to complement a television plan rather than replace it. At Sara Lee, we are making more frequent use of cable and syndicated television for our advertising.

Media vehicles

Once the marketer has selected the media class, it must choose the specific advertising vehicles (specific magazines, radio, TV shows). The selection depends

Hindustan Lever sells soap in the villages with the help of video vans. This one visits Maharashtra.

on the cost effectiveness of a particular outlet for reaching desired market audiences. Factors include audience size and composition and the cost of running the ad. Firms such as Simmons Research Bureau can help here. For example, an advertiser can request data exposure or magazine readership for women with incomes over $30,000 who regularly purchase tennis equipment. Similar sources for TV and newspaper audiences are provided by Arbitron, A. C. Nielsen, and MediaMark.

A common method to evaluate vehicles within a specific medium is by **cost per thousand (CPM).** For magazines, the formula is:

$$\text{CPM} = [(\text{magazine page cost} \times 1{,}000)/\text{circulation}].$$

Assume *Sports Illustrated* charges $134,620 for a single-page, full-color ad and has a paid circulation of 3,573,915. The CPM for *SI* would be:

$$[(\$134{,}620 \times 1{,}000)/3{,}573{,}915] = \$37.67$$

Marketers can calculate this value for other magazines in that class and make comparisons for the decision. Rate and circulation statistics can be obtained from *Standard Rate & Data Services: Consumer Magazines.*

Media schedules

The most basic concepts in media scheduling are reach and frequency. **Reach** refers to the number of different people or households exposed to an ad or campaign over a specified time period (usually four weeks). **Frequency** refers to the number of times a person or household is exposed to a communication vehicle. Advertisers must address the basic question: Emphasize reach or frequency? When advertising is for a new brand, reach may be the paramount objective. Messages presenting detailed information or vying with heavily advertised competitors need greater frequency or repetition.

Advertisers are becoming increasingly concerned about reducing the waste of reaching consumers outside intended market segments. In response, media have taken steps to improve their efficiency. *Time, Reader's Digest, Newsweek,* and

Evaluating advertising effectiveness

other magazines, for example, have invested heavily in "selective binding" technology, which permits targeting of advertising to subscribers in specific ZIP code areas.

The evaluation of advertising typically includes pretesting or copytesting, posttesting, and sales effectiveness research. Firms pursuing the *productivity perspective* are making the evaluation of their advertising's effectiveness a much more important task.

Pretesting

In general, **pretesting** proposed print and broadcast ads is done by evaluating consumer reactions through direct questioning and focus groups. Marketers evaluate the ads for overall likability, consumer recall of information, message communication, and their effects on purchase intentions and brand attitudes.

Research Systems Corporation (RSC) evaluates advertising for marketers and ad agencies.[24] From 500 to 600 randomly chosen consumers view TV pilot programs and a number of commercials, including the ones being evaluated. Before the screening, participants are shown various consumer products and are asked to indicate which they would like to receive. After the screening, a second questionnaire is administered. A "persuasion score" is computed for each commercial, which indicates the differences in percentages of consumers selecting the advertised product before and after the screening. Respondents are also called 48 hours later to explore estimates of recall. These viewer reactions are used to predict sales effectiveness of the ads.

Posttesting

Marketers use **posttesting** through recall and attitude tests and inquiry evaluations to assess the effectiveness of an ad campaign. In **unaided recall tests** for print ads, respondents are questioned with no prompting about ads included in magazines. In **aided recall tests,** subjects are given lists of ads and asked which they remembered and read. An **inquiry evaluation** comes from the number of consumers responding to requests in an ad, such as using coupons or asking for samples or more product information.

Starch Message Report Services provides awareness and readership data about ads carried in consumer and business magazines. Burke Market Research administers a Day-after-Recall program (DAR) for TV commercials. DAR is the percentage of individuals in an audience who recall something specific about the ad being posttested. High levels of recall do not necessarily result in increased sales, however.

Sales effectiveness evaluations

Sales effectiveness evaluations are the most stringent tests of advertising efficiency. They assess whether the advertising resulted in increased sales. Given the many factors that affect sales and the number of competing messages, sales effectiveness evaluations are difficult, and marketers and ad agencies can differ on measures of results. Increasingly, however, evaluations of advertising effectiveness based on brand awareness will no longer be sufficient. Advertising evaluations instead will be based on its contributions to sales growth. **The Technological Edge: Muzak Goes Grocery Shopping** describes one advertising format that passed the sales effectiveness test.

Muzak goes grocery shopping

Muzak, the company that provides music in elevators and doctors' offices, is increasing its efforts toward in-store advertising. Muzak has over 200,000 telecommunication satellite receivers in businesses across the United States. Among these businesses are many of the large grocery chains, including A&P and Winn-Dixie. It is anticipated that by 1995, over 5,000 grocery stores will be linked in a single network available to national advertisers.

With growing concerns about the effectiveness of advertising dollars, companies are allocating more and more funds to in-store promotions. Also, consumers make up to two-thirds of their purchase decisions in the store. Hence, in-store advertising like that offered by Muzak, when combined with visual displays, are quite effective. These ads can be targeted to specific demographic areas. One recent test of the effectiveness of in-store advertising demonstrated consistent increases in sales for the advertised products.

Sources: Thomas Hoffman, "Muzak Offers New Tune for Data Flow," *Computerworld,* September 14, 1992, p. 72; Dori Jones Yang and Joan Warner, "Hear the Muzak, Buy the Ketchup," *Business Week,* June 28, 1993, pp. 70–72; and "Taco Bell Gets Data, Music—The Whole Enchilada," *Communications News,* June 1993, p. 30.

Recognizing the need to provide quality advertising that improves company performance, DDB Needham rebates a substantial portion of its fee if sales for an advertised product do not improve. If ad campaigns are successful, DDB Needham receives a bonus in addition to its fee.[25]

Ethical and legal issues in advertising

Advertising provides many useful functions for buyers, advertisers, and society. For buyers, benefits include comparative information about the availability and the characteristics of products and brands. For advertisers, advertising builds long-term brand recognition, introduces new products, and enhances corporate images. For society, advertising increases economic efficiency by enabling products to be sold in mass markets at lower unit costs and to be distributed over wide geographic areas.

Advertising does have its critics, however, and abuses do occur. In some instances, advertising malpractice receives considerable notoriety. Several years ago, Volvo Cars of North America altered cars in its "monster truck crushing" ads, for example. Other ethical issues related to advertising are more subtle. We discuss them below.

Is advertising manipulative?

Some critics charge that advertising stimulates needs and wants by creating unrealistic ideals about appearance and social identity. And indeed, students of marketing agree that advertising is intended to influence buyer behavior. But if it's so easy to manipulate people into buying, why do so many products fail? It would seem more likely that instead of being manipulated by advertising, the reverse is true, and buyers exercise control over the marketplace by the choices they make with their discretionary income.

Monster "Bearfoot" truck demolishes Volvos in a US Hot Rod Association restaging of the carmaker's controversial ad.

Is advertising deceptive or misleading?

The Federal Trade Commission (FTC), which monitors marketplace abuses, prohibits advertising messages that deceive consumers by presenting false claims, by omitting relevant information, or by giving misleading impressions that result in faulty decisions.

In some instances the FTC requires **corrective advertising** to remedy misleading impressions or information in an ad. The offending advertiser or marketer must develop and pay for advertising that counters the misperceptions. Corrective advertising is required most often when there have been outright misrepresentations of fact, rather than presentation of half-truths.

In one of the earliest cases, Warner-Lambert was required in 1975 to spend $10 million in advertising to correct misleading claims about the ability of Listerine mouthwash to combat colds.[26] Volvo was instructed to run corrective ads in local newspapers, *USA Today,* and *The Wall Street Journal* to explain its withdrawal of ads misrepresenting the effect of the monster truck crushing demonstration discussed above.[27] The FTC required Volkswagen (and Audi) to run a series of full-page national magazine ads to inform consumers about product performance problems. The magazine advertising was required to reach a nonduplicated audience of at least 75 million adults.

How does advertising affect children?

The youth market offers tremendous potential to business, and much advertising is directed toward children. Advertisers know young consumers influence parental decisions and exert significant buying power themselves. Concerns about advertising to children center largely on three important issues:

- Children's ability to understand advertising's intent to persuade.
- The nutritional value of food and candy products marketed to children.
- The influence of advertising on children's demands to parents for advertised products.

On the other hand, some opponents of limits on advertising to children argue that:

- Parents are better able than the FTC to help children interpret information and make decisions.

- Children know that fruits and vegetables are more nutritious than sugared foods.

- Banning TV advertising to children limits free speech.[28]

Is advertising intrusive?

Many people are irritated by unwelcome advertising messages that threaten their right to privacy. Most observers agree the marketplace is cluttered with advertising messages and that any one ad has limited ability to influence consumers. Yet recognition of this limitation only reinforces pressures to increase ad repetition.

Related questions have to do with methods of ad communications delivery. Is it ethical for infomercials to package commercial messages as regular programming? What about the practice of allowing TV advertisers into school classrooms?

Public relations

Public relations is an alternative to advertising, personal selling, and sales promotions for disseminating marketing communications. PR communications are not overtly sponsored and are a useful supplement to other forms of marketing communications. PR is an attempt to improve a company's relationship with its publics. Public relations may focus on customers, employees, stockholders, community members, news media, or the government. Most large corporations operate central PR departments to carry out coordinated public relations programs; and smaller companies with limited resources must also deal with PR issues. For example, AT&T and other companies support scientific studies to reduce fears about links between the use of cellular phones and cancer.[29] The Pharmaceutical Manufacturers' Association recently instituted an $8 million print campaign to inform the public that life-saving drugs represent only 5 percent of national health care costs.

As advertising becomes less effective, companies of all sizes try to build public awareness and loyalty by supporting customer interests. The general public increasingly demands that companies behave responsibly toward society as a whole and that they have obligations to more than their customers and stockholders. Profit maximization and social responsibility need not be incompatible, however. Today, companies show greater concern for employee welfare, minority advancement, community improvement, environmental protection, and other causes. A PR department plays a critical role in planning, coordinating, and promoting these visionary activities for an organization.[30] Some companies have effectively embodied public relations principles into their overall marketing communications program. For example, Members Only fashion company funded over $100 million worth of social consciousness–raising advertising about drug abuse and voter registration. More recent advertising promotes care for the homeless.

Public relations functions

Most frequently, PR functions support a firm's products and services. Often, however, public relations activity addresses corporate image and social responsibility. Exxon Corporation's varied program to maintain and improve

UAP, France's largest insur- ance company, sponsored ads promoting Jeu de Paume, a new modern art gallery in Paris that takes its name from an old French ball game. The ad's cap- tion reads, "The aim of the new Jeu de Paume is to catch art on the rebound."

LE NOUVEAU
JEU DE PAUME
CONSISTE
À ATTRAPER
L'ART
PENDANT QU'IL
REBONDIT.

L'UAP EST HEUREUSE DE SOUTENIR LES
ACTIONS DE LA GALERIE NATIONALE DU JEU DE PAUME.

its corporate image is a good example. Its PR activity ranges from an ongoing campaign about environmental damage from the Alaskan oil spill targeted toward the scientific community to charitable support of the Special Olympics.[31]

Public relations functions include: press relations; product promotions; internal and external corporate communications; lobbying to promote, defeat, or circumvent legislation and regulations; advising management about public issues and company positions and image; and overall, responding to a variety of occurrences in the marketplace.[32] Public relations can be proactive or reactive, as shown in Exhibit 18.6.

Publicity

Publicity, the generation of information by a company to the news media, has a narrower focus than public relations. The primary publicity techniques are news releases, press conferences, and feature articles, often presented in the business press.

One advantage of publicity is its relatively high credibility, because the messages are not paid for by a commercial sponsor. Information about a company presumably must be newsworthy to be published by an objective source. However, publicity messages may be revised by the media, then released at

| Exhibit 18.6 | Proactive and reactive marketing public relations |

Proactive marketing PR
• Product release announcements, statements by firm's spokespeople, event sponsorship, articles in business press.
• Corporate image enhancement & development of goodwill; corporate advocacy advertising supports certain position on given social issue.
• Cause-related marketing in which firm contributes specified amount to designated cause when customers buy firm's products.

Reactive marketing PR
• Firm's response to negative events & damaging publicity.
• Negative information comes from news media, consumer advocacy groups, government agencies; usually related to product defects or problematic company practices.
• Success depends on firm's ability to align its interests with the public's interests so both are served.

times most convenient to the broadcaster or publisher. Unfortunately, some publicity may be negative news stories beyond the firm's control, as when product tamperings occurred for Tylenol and Diet Pepsi. A firm's PR department must be prepared to react constructively and without delay when unfortunate events occur.

Vice President Gore leads a sophisticated public relations and publicity campaign to sell a government reorganization plan. The vice president made many public appearances, including one on "Late Show with David Letterman."

Summary

1. *Understand the characteristics, functions, and types of advertising.* Advertising, like other promotional elements, plays an important role in the total marketing communications program. Advertising is impersonal, paid for by an identified sponsor, and disseminated through mass channels of communication to promote the adoption of goods, services, persons, or ideas.

   Advertising can serve a number of functions, including heightening consumer awareness, disseminating information about a product's attributes or social value, shaping product images or emotional responses, persuading buyers to purchase, or reminding consumers about products, brands, or firms.

   Advertisements can be classified according to the target audience, geographic area, medium, and purpose. Corporate image advertising promotes an organization's image and role in the community as a corporate citizen. Other types are corporate advocacy, public service, classified, direct-response, business-to-business, and cooperative advertising.

2. *Realize how people process advertising information, and how it affects buyer behavior.* Advertisements rely on successive stages of processing by a targeted individual: exposure (presenting the information to a receiver); attention (the conscious direction of a receiver's mental effort toward the advertising stimulus); comprehension (the degree to which the receiver correctly understands the intended message); acceptance (the degree to which the receiver accepts or yields to the message); retention (the extent to which the receiver can recall or recognize the message at a later time).

   The relationships between these stages, and therefore the effectiveness of the advertising itself, may be affected by consumer needs as well as consumer motivations, opportunities, and abilities to process the information.

3. *Discuss approaches to developing advertising campaigns.* The steps in developing an ad campaign are (1) determining advertising objectives, (2) determining advertising budget, (3) designing appropriate creative strategies, (4) selecting and scheduling media, and (5) evaluating ad effectiveness.

4. *Describe different advertising objectives and the message strategies used to achieve them.* Advertising objectives should be consistent with the organization's overall marketing objectives and be realistic, precise, and measurable. Advertising objectives may be to inform, to persuade, or to remind.

   Many different message strategies can be used to achieve the advertising objective. One strategy is to compare the advertised brand to another. Celebrity endorsements, humor, and fear appeals are other tactics used to enhance the persuasive impact of advertisements.

5. *Understand the decisions involved in selecting media and scheduling advertising.* Decisions on media class involve choosing the most appropriate media channels, such as television, magazines, or radio. This choice depends on both the size and characteristics of the firm's target markets and the characteristics of the message itself.

   Decisions on media vehicles refer to the selection of the specific outlets within the chosen media class. These decisions usually depend on factors such as cost and the size and characteristics of the audience. Reach and frequency are important considerations in making these decisions.

6. *Explain how marketers assess advertising effectiveness.* Effectiveness evaluations involve some combination of pretesting, posttesting, sales response, and media research. Pretesting usually involves evaluating consumer reactions to proposed advertisements. Posttesting is used to measure the effectiveness of the chosen strategy during or after the ad campaign. Posttesting may include aided or unaided recall measurements, attitude evaluations, and sales impact effects.

7. *Appreciate the roles of public relations and publicity in marketing.* Public relations functions include the dissemination of press releases, product promotion efforts, and corporate communications, as well as lobbying and advising corporate executives about public issues affecting the firm. Publicity refers to the dissemination of nonpaid communication in news outlets and represents only a part of the larger activity of public relations.

   Marketing-oriented public relations can be proactive or reactive. Proactive marketing public relations refers to the initiation of positive public relations; it may take the form of corporate image advertising, advocacy advertising, or cause-related marketing. Reactive marketing public relations refers to defending an organization from negative and potentially damaging information, including negative events and adverse publicity.

Key terms & concepts

advertising *440*
advertising agency *441*
commercial zapping *442*
corporate image advertising *444*
corporate advocacy advertising *444*
public service advertising *444*
direct-response advertising *444*
classified advertising *444*
business-to-business advertising *444*

cooperative advertising *444*
objective claims *449*
subjective claims *449*
comparative advertising *449*
advertorial *450*
cost per thousand (CPM) *453*
reach *453*
frequency *453*
pretesting *454*

posttesting *454*
unaided recall tests *454*
aided recall tests *454*
inquiry evaluation *454*
sales effectiveness evaluations *454*
corrective advertising *456*
public relations *457* *actually expensive*
publicity *459*

Review & discussion questions

1. What different functions can advertising perform?

2. What are advertising agencies, and what services do they provide?

3. Explain why advertising expenditures have declined during recent years.

4. Define the following: business-to-business advertising; corporate image advertising; corporate advocacy advertising; direct-response advertising; and corrective advertising.

5. What steps are involved in a consumer's processing of advertisements? Why is understanding this sequence of these stages important to advertisers?

6. What can advertisers do to increase exposure, attention, and retention? How does audience involvement influence these processes? Refer to **The Technological**

Edge: Muzak Goes Grocery Shopping. How is the Muzak approach consistent with these concepts?

7. Identify the steps involved in the development of an advertising campaign.

8. What are media class decisions, and how do they differ from media vehicle decisions? Refer to **The Entrepreneurial Spirit: Don't Touch That Dial!** What audience characteristics would an advertiser evaluate in considering the Bailys' programs as message outlets?

9. Contrast pretesting with posttesting in the evaluation of advertising effectiveness. Explain the problem with using sales results as a measure of advertising effectiveness.

10. Explain the differences between advertising and public relations.

Application exercises

1. Collect two examples each of: (*a*) corporate image advertising; (*b*) corporate advocacy advertising; (*c*) public service advertising; (*d*) comparative advertising; (*e*) classified advertising; (*f*) direct-response advertising; and (*g*) business-to-business advertising.

2. Collect one example each of magazine, radio, television, and outdoor advertising. Describe how each works to get consumers' attention and ensure retention.

3. The current average issue circulation for *People* magazine is 3,224,770. The cost for a one page ad in a regular issue is $82,390. Estimate the CPM for that magazine. Compare it with similar data for *Time*: page cost, $113,700; circulation, 2,962,168. What might you advise a potential advertiser of personal computers? of cosmetics?

Case 18.1   *Diet Pepsi: Can "uh-huh" sell soft drinks?*

In the early 1990s, almost any US consumer could name Ray Charles' favorite soft drink: Diet Pepsi. In the successful ad campaign, Charles, after tasting a Diet Coke, then a Diet Pepsi, proclaims Diet Pepsi "the right one."

Most Pepsi commercials before 1991 featured some sort of taste test between the two best-selling colas. Although Diet Pepsi consistently outscored Diet Coke in consumer preferences during these tests, it still lagged behind its chief competitor in sales. Then came the 1991 Super Bowl. Pepsi chose this annual advertising spectacular to unveil its new campaign featuring Ray Charles and the Raylettes. What began that January evening led to the most popular commercial in each quarter of 1991, according to Video Storyboard Tests' rankings—an unprecedented feat.

The morning after the Super Bowl, the ad's slogan, "You got the right one baby, uh-huh," began to catch on. Pepsi quickly tried to capitalize on the phenomenon, spending $70 million in 1991 and $50 million in 1992 on variations of this campaign to get consumers to say "uh-huh" to Diet Pepsi. The ad's strong popularity prompted a series of commercials featuring Ray Charles, the Raylettes, and their hit slogan.

The popular campaign helped Diet Pepsi cut into Diet Coke's lead in consumer awareness tests. Previously, when asked to pick only one of the two brands, consumers consistently named Diet Coke over Diet Pepsi 70 percent of the time. After the ads aired, Diet Pepsi began slightly outperforming Diet Coke. Consumers also consistently identified Diet Pepsi as the brand advertised in these commercials, which doesn't happen with many advertisements.

For all its apparent success, however, some observers question whether the extensive campaign made a significant enough impact on sales to warrant its expense. Most analysts would agree that, although Coke sells more product, Pepsi consistently produces better ads and out markets its competitors. Even Diet Coke's own advertising theme, "There's just one," created very little stir compared to Diet Pepsi's ads. But the gap between the two colas has remained virtually unchanged despite the "uh-huh" cam-

paign. Industry research showed a majority of consumers could remember seeing the ad, but fewer than 1 percent actually switched to Diet Pepsi.

Undaunted by the campaign's apparent failure to increase sales, Pepsi plans to stay with it for some time. The company has even decided to air the commercials in Japan, where the brand is still somewhat new.

Assuredly, Pepsi understands that the most popular advertising may not always be the most effective. Because measures of this campaign suggest mixed results, the company should at least proceed with caution. Some experts call this campaign a gem of advertising; others are not so sure.

Questions:

1. Would you classify the Diet Pepsi advertising campaign as successful or unsuccessful? Why?

2. Do you believe that the campaign justifies the millions of dollars Diet Pepsi is spending on it? Should the company continue to do so? Why or why not?

3. Explain how the advertisements can be so popular yet sales percentages have not improved.

4. Why is it important for Diet Pepsi's advertising to foster a desired image with consumers? What impact, if any, do you believe this campaign has had on Diet Pepsi's image?

5. Are consumers' attitudes toward advertisements important for marketers such as Diet Pepsi?

Sources: Laura Bird, "Marketing and Media—Advertising: Study Suggests That Ad Dazzle Rarely Turns into More Dollars," *The Wall Street Journal*, May 19, 1992, p. B8; Yumiko Ono, "Marketing—Focus on Japan," *The Wall Street Journal*, April 21, 1992, p. B1; Joshua Levine, "Affirmative Grunts," *Forbes*, March 2, 1992, pp. 90–91; James Warren, "Uh-Uh!: Ray Charles Ads Haven't Helped Diet Pepsi Close Gap with Diet Coke," *Chicago Tribune*, February 20, 1992, p. 5-2; Greg W. Prince, "You Got 1991. You Got a Bigger CCE, More Beer, and Less Malt Liquor. You Got Anything Else?: Uh-Huh!" *Beverage World*, December 1991, pp. 28–33; Michael J. McCarthy, "Advertising: Diet Coke Frets Its Jingle Isn't Right One, Baby," *The Wall Street Journal*, August 28, 1991, p. B1; and Patricia Winters, "Diet Colas Drop Comparative Tactic," *Advertising Age*, January 21, 1991, pp. 24, 28.

Case 18.2   *Toyota: Advertising drives to success in Europe*

More and more international companies are moving away from international advertising, that is, presenting the same advertising campaign in every country in which the company conducts business. A standardized strategy often fails to provide the most effective advertising for a given geographical area, because each area has its own distinctive political, legal, and cultural characteristics. The use of advertising suited to the particular characteristics of a country may be more effective.

Toyota has always taken an unstandardized approach, tailoring its advertising on a country-by-country basis. It lets the local marketers handle all the aspects of advertising for their particular area on the theory that they know the market best. Toyota simply supplies the local advertisers with the necessary raw materials (information pertinent for promoting Toyota vehicles) to develop effective advertisements for their area. This system has been effective for Toyota, which enjoys a significant market share in countries in North America, Asia, and Europe.

Eased trade conditions within the European Community could allow Toyota to reevaluate just how integrated (if at all) it wants to make its advertising within the EC. Today Toyota uses an integrative European approach to its advertising for only one brand, the Lexus luxury automobile, which has met with some success. The company might also find it profitable to reduce the number of advertising agencies it works with in Europe. Becoming more standardized in its advertising could offer Toyota certain economies of scale.

Of course, the issue of cultural differences would remain. Consumers in France still differ from those in Italy or the United Kingdom. But the EC is bound to increase European consumers' familiarity with the culture of the other European countries, particularly when it comes to business and consumer considerations. Although each country will maintain its own identity and cultural values, their marketplace identities are at least converging somewhat.

In 1990, Toyota established Toyota Motor Marketing Europe in Brussels. With production facilities throughout Europe, the time could be right for Toyota to consider standardizing its approach to European marketing.

Questions:

1. Enumerate and explain the advantages and disadvantages to Toyota of using an integrative, standardized approach versus maintaining its current approach to advertising in Europe.

2. What would you recommend Toyota do regarding its advertising in Europe? Why?

3. Explain the impact that differing cultural values, legal considerations, and economic considerations have on international advertising.

4. Explain why Toyota should or should not promote the Lexus differently from its other automobile brands.

Sources: A. Faye Borthick and Harold P. Roth, "Will Europeans Buy Your Company's Products?" *Business Credit,* November–December 1992, pp. 23–24; David Kilburn, "Oh, What a Feeling: Toyota Marketing Drives Quality Image Abroad," *Advertising Age,* October 7, 1991, p. 38; and Nicholas di Talamo, "Europe's Gates Are Now Open," *Direct Marketing,* September 1991, pp. 46–48.

Consumer and Trade Sales Promotion

After studying this chapter you should be able to:

1. Explain the role and significance of sales promotion in the marketing communications mix.

2. Understand why sales promotion use and expenditures have increased in recent years.

3. Discuss the objectives and techniques of consumer sales promotion.

4. Discuss the objectives and techniques of trade sales promotion.

5. Explain the limitations of sales promotion.

6. Realize how deceptive and fraudulent sales promotion victimizes both consumers and marketers.

Kimberly-Clark and Colgate-Palmolive
American Heart: Increasing sales through sales promotion

What connects Timex Corporation to the makers of Kleenex and Colgate toothpaste? They combined efforts in a successful consumer and retailer sales promotion. The program won a MOTI (for *Moti*vation), an annual award given at a national trade show sponsored by the Illinois-based firm Hall-Erickson.

The program, called "Kimberly-Clark and Colgate-Palmolive American Heart," offered a Timex Aerobix watch to consumers redeeming eight proofs of purchase from Kimberly-Clark brands and six from Colgate-Palmolive brands, while it made a $3 donation to the American Heart Association. To increase product visibility and sales, the program also provided retailer incentives. For placing a 25-case display, retailers received an Aerobix watch; for a 50-case display, a more upscale Triathlon watch; and for a 100-case display, a Titanium watch. Kimberly-Clark also offered watches to key retail personnel at cost. The five-week promotion was augmented with advertising inserts in large-circulation newspapers and point-of-purchase displays with tear-off pads and American Heart Association exercise booklets.

The incentives motivated both retailers and consumers. Retail display increased 22 percent during the promotion. Kimberly-Clark distributed 15,000 watches to dealers; Colgate-Palmolive 7,000. Consumers ordered more than 100,000 watches, resulting in a $300,000 donation to the American Heart Association.

The sales promotion effort achieved its key objective: to increase sales. Kimberly-Clark increased sales approximately 24 percent, and Colgate-Palmolive, about 22 percent. According to Ed Dowdle, manager of premium sales for Timex, "The dramatic increase in sales for the kind of staple, everyday products Colgate-Palmolive and Kimberly-Clark sell *must* be attributed, in some part, to new customers."

Sources: Nora Ganim and Debra Fitzgibbons, "Strategic Marketing for Charitable Organizations," *Health Marketing Quarterly,* Summer–Fall 1992, pp. 103–14; and Melissa Campanelli, "Motivating, Moti Style," *Sales & Marketing Management,* June 1991, pp. 125–26.

465

As this experience illustrates, sales promotion can be a strong contributor to the *execution perspective*—it is designed to boost sales. **Sales promotion** consists of media and nonmedia marketing communications employed for a predetermined, limited time to stimulate trial, increase consumer demand, or improve product availability.[1] Common sales promotion tools are coupons, samples, displays, contests, and sweepstakes. Sales promotion may be directed at ultimate consumers, retailers, or wholesalers.

The opening example also illustrates the *relationship perspective* in action with two major types of sales promotion, **consumer sales promotion** (directed at consumers) and **trade sales promotion** (directed at resellers). The three-firm/one-organization collaboration suggests that successful sales promotion may be integrated with other forms of marketing communications. In the case of the Kimberly-Clark and Colgate-Palmolive American Heart program, advertising accompanied the sales promotion.

This chapter examines the growing role of sales promotion in marketing communications. The objectives, techniques, and limitations of consumer and trade sales promotion are explored. The chapter also looks at ethical and legal issues related to sales promotion.

The role of sales promotion

A unique characteristic of sales promotion is that it offers an incentive for action. A consumer might receive a rebate for making a purchase, for instance, or a retailer may be offered an allowance for purchasing a specific quantity of a product within a specified time period. In contrast to many forms of advertising, sales promotion is oriented toward achieving short-term results. As the opening example illustrates, sales promotion activities rarely stand alone; they are typically combined with other forms of marketing communications to create an integrated program.

Sales promotion is aimed at both resellers and ultimate consumers. This AT&T offer is aimed at business customers; and the company also directs sales promotions at ultimate consumers.

Effective sales promotion, like all forms of marketing communications, should result from adequate planning as discussed in Chapter 17. Since sales promotion seeks results in the near future, it is possible to set specific, measurable objectives and to accurately monitor results. Since sales promotion often works in conjunction with other communications, coordination of messages and timing is crucial for success. Exhibit 19.1 presents the primary considerations in sales promotion planning.

The significance of sales promotion

The role of advertising declined during the latter half of the 1980s and the early 1990s. During this same era, the importance of sales promotion grew. The marketing environment of recent years and the outlook in coming years suggest a healthy future for sales promotion.

Sales promotion expenditures

The combined expenditures on consumer and trade sales promotion are almost triple the expenditures on advertising. Observers see no end to increased spending on sales promotion. Expenditures in the US are expected to grow at a compound annual rate of 7.6 percent through 1996, reaching $159.9 billion.[2]

Reasons for the growth of sales promotion

What has motivated the growth of sales promotion in recent years? Changes in the marketing environment—consumer attitudes, demographic shifts, and lifestyle changes—are favorable for sales promotion, as are emerging technology and changes in retailing.[3] Also, marketers are under pressure to perform well in the short term and are increasingly accountable for achieving measurable results.

Consumer factors

With the US population growing at less than 1 percent annually, most mature products see only modest growth in per capita consumption. The natural result

---

Exhibit 19.1   **The 10 commandments of creative sales promotion**

1. **Set specific objectives.** Undisciplined, undirected creative work is a waste of time and resources.
2. **Know how basic promotion techniques work.** A sweepstakes shouldn't be used to encourage multiple purchases or a refund to get new customers. A price-off deal can't reverse a brand's downward sales trend.
3. **Use simple, attention-getting copy.** Most promotions are built around a simple idea: "save 75 cents." Emphasize the idea & don't try to be cute.
4. **Use contemporary, easy-to-track graphics.** Don't expect to fit 500 words & 20 illustrations into a quarter-page, freestanding insert.
5. **Clearly communicate the concept.** Words & graphics must work together to get the message across.
6. **Reinforce the brand's advertising message.** Tie promotions to the brand's ad campaign.
7. **Support the brand's positioning & image.** This is especially important for image-sensitive brands & categories—like family-oriented Kraft.
8. **Coordinate promotional efforts with other marketing plans.** Be sure to coordinate schedules & plans. A consumer promotion should occur simultaneously with a trade promotion; a free-sample promotion should be timed in conjunction with the introduction of a new line.
9. **Know the media you work through.** Determine which media will work best. Should samples be distributed in store, door to door, or through direct mail? Does the promotion need newspaper or magazine support?
10. **Know when to break the other nine commandments.** A confident, creative person knows when breaking these rules is the smartest way to go.

is increased competition for market share, thus placing a premium on the *execution perspective.* Sales promotion techniques, particularly price breaks, are therefore key.

Today's busy consumer cares less about shopping. If two spouses work outside the home, shopping time is limited. This makes consumers inevitably more responsive to sales promotion deals that encourage multiple purchases and to in-store displays.

Another factor in favor of sales promotion is simply that consumers like it. One study claims that 56 percent of all households—up from 47 percent in 1988—favor grocery brands promoted by coupons, premiums, refunds, and other incentives.[4]

Impact of technology

There is ample evidence of technology as a stimulus for the growth of sales promotion. Computerized scanning devices have changed retailing. Scanners let retailers know what is and what is not selling every day. They also provide quick input on which brands are most profitable. In the case of trade sales, portable computers in the hands of field salespeople let vendors track product movement practically instantaneously. As a result, both retailers and manufacturers can follow a *productivity perspective* by measuring the effectiveness of various sales promotion programs very quickly. Manufacturers can thus adjust or eliminate unproductive programs, freeing up investment for more productive ones. H. J. Heinz, Philip Morris, and McNeil Consumer Products Company are some of the well-known users of scanner-tracked promotional programs.[5]

Increased retail power

Huge retailers such as Wal-Mart and Kmart wield tremendous clout by virtue of their immense purchasing power. Sales promotions directed at both retailers and consumers make the manufacturer's product more appealing, an example of the *execution perspective* at work.

As retailers gain more power, they have tried to increase sales of their own private-label products. Although retailers can tout their private labels while limiting in-store promotions for national brands, they cannot do much about sales promotion efforts such as couponing. No doubt the struggle of national brand marketers against private labels has contributed to the growth of sales promotion.[6]

The private-label trend is also occurring in European markets, where a lingering recession has compelled consumers to see more value for their money. Private-label products, which account for approximately 30 percent of supermarket sales in Britain, are increasing in France, Switzerland, and Italy. To combat private-label sales, multinationals with a *global perspective,* such as Unilever and Nestlé, are promoting both their traditional brands and "Eurobrands," products designed for the entire European market.[7]

Consumer sales promotion

Consumer sales promotion, with techniques such as coupons and rebates, helps pull the product through the channel of distribution. Both small and large companies can effectively use it with either new or existing products. Sometimes sales promotion may increase interest in mature or mundane products by imparting a sense of urgency to buy before the promotion ends.

Exhibit 19.2

Objectives of consumer sales promotion

- Stimulate trial
- Increase consumer inventory & consumption
- Encourage repurchase
- Neutralize competitors
- Increase sales of complementary products
- Stimulate impulse purchasing
- Allow flexible pricing

Objectives of consumer promotions

Sales promotion may accomplish a variety of objectives, all related to affecting present or prospective consumers' behavior. As Exhibit 19.2 shows, objectives may be to stimulate trial; increase consumer inventory and consumption; encourage repurchase; neutralize competitive promotions; increase the sales of complementary products; stimulate impulse purchasing; and allow for flexible pricing.

Stimulate trial

Marketers commonly use sales promotion to stimulate product trial—to get consumers to try a product. This is particularly so for newly introduced or improved products. The decision to buy a new product entails risk, which may prompt buyer resistance. Sales promotion techniques that reduce consumer cost, such as coupons, rebates, or samples, help alleviate this risk. When Hershey wanted to encourage trial of its Hershey's Dark candy bar, for example, it offered buyers coupons redeemable for a free candy bar. In the minds of most people, no cost means no risk.

Increase consumer inventory and consumption

Sales promotion sometimes encourages consumers to increase their inventory or consumption of a product by enticing them to buy more than they would in the

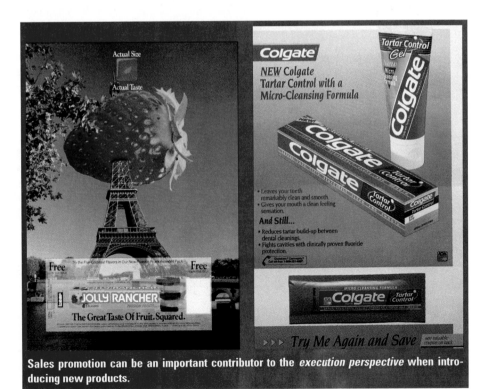

Sales promotion can be an important contributor to the *execution perspective* when introducing new products.

absence of a special incentive. The idea is that people tend to consume greater quantities of a product if it is on hand. For instance, a buy-one-get-one-free special on potato chips may stimulate the consumer to buy more than normal. Because chips can get stale if not eaten within a certain time, and since they are around the house, people are likely to eat more than they normally would. Also, the more inventory of a given brand that consumers have, the less interest they have in stocking up on a competitor's brand.

Encourage repurchase

Sales promotion offers a variety of ways to help establish repeat-purchase patterns, on which the product's survival ultimately depends. Hotels are heavily involved in repeat-purchase promotions. An example of the *global perspective,* Holiday Inns Worldwide Priority Club encourages travelers to accumulate points redeemable anywhere in the world. Some of the more popular destinations for award winners are the Bavarian Alps, complete with tour of castles, and the sunny beaches of Cancun, Mexico.[8] Other examples of repeat-purchase promotions are special price incentives magazines use to gain subscription renewals and on-the-package coupons for future discounts that companies such as Domino's and Pizza Hut feature.

Neutralize competitive promotions

Sometimes marketers use sales promotions to combat competitive promotions. Consider the perennial battle between Coca-Cola and Pepsi-Cola, for example. Both firms constantly use promotions to attract consumers. As a result, the two firms often compete on price. Promotions to neutralize other retailers are also commonplace in the fast-food industry.

EXECUTIVE ROUNDTABLE COMMENT | **Shaun Singleton Masters, director of merchandising, artwear division of Signal Apparel in Chattanooga, TN, comments on the versatility of sales promotion:**

Marketing is filled with uncertainty, but we do know one thing—it's a lot more profitable to work with an established customer base than it is to recreate your market from scratch every day. Sure, Signal uses sales promotion to bring us new business, but mostly we use it to develop tailored programs for our current customers and let them know we value their business.

Increase sales of complementary products

Using sales promotion to attract buyers to one complementary product can increase sales of the other. A rebate Gillette offered for its Sensor razor, for example, allowed the consumer to get the product for practically nothing. Gillette hoped to cash in on sales of its Sensor razor blades, a complementary product the consumer must buy on a recurring basis. The promotion worked as planned, and Sensor is now a leading brand.

Stimulate impulse purchasing

Many people do not take the time to develop a shopping list. This tends to increase impulse purchasing. As the term implies, an impulse purchase is unplanned. It satisfies a strong desire to acquire a product quickly, without a lot of forethought. Retailers use special feature displays to generate impulse purchases.

Exhibit 19.3

Consumer sales promotion techniques

- Price deals
- Coupons
- Rebates
- Cross-promotions
- Contests, sweepstakes, games
- Premiums
- Sampling
- Advertising specialties

Allow price flexibility

Sales promotion facilitates tailored price changes, which allow the marketer to pursue opportunities as they arise. Suppose a manufacturer has set relatively high list prices, intending to appeal to the least price-sensitive segment of the market. Later the manufacturer can appeal to price-sensitive segments of the market through sales promotions. Automobile manufacturers follow this strategy despite the advent of no-haggle pricing.

Consumer sales promotion techniques

Most people recognize the familiar consumer sales promotion techniques and have probably participated in some. Exhibit 19.3 lists some popular ones.

Price deals

A **price deal** is a temporary reduction in the price of a product. Marketers may use price deals to introduce a new or improved brand, to convince current users to purchase more, or to encourage new users to try an established brand. There are two primary types of price deals: cents-off deals and price-pack deals. **Cents-off deals** offer a brand at less than the regular price. Sometimes the manufacturer's package itself specifies a price reduction in dollars or cents or by a certain percentage, say 25 percent off. Such deals are often promoted in the store in some manner and may also be advertised.

Price-pack deals offer consumers something extra through the packaging itself. Perhaps they can buy a package of Martha White brownie mix 20 percent bigger than usual or a box of Double-Chex with 40 percent more cereal for the price of the normal size.

Marketers with a *productivity perspective* would be smart not to overuse price deals, however. If a brand is frequently offered on a price deal, consumers come to expect it. They hold off purchasing the product until it comes on deal again. Frequent deals on the same product eventually erode its normal retail selling price and may diminish its brand value.

Coupons

A **coupon** is typically a printed certificate giving the bearer a stated price reduction or special value on a specific product, generally for a specific period of time. Coupons allow the manufacturer to reduce the product's price at any time. They are particularly useful in encouraging new-product trials.

Couponing is on the rise. In the US packaged goods industry, more dollars are spent on it than any other consumer sales promotion tool.[9] It has also become a global marketing activity, growing in importance in Canada, Italy, and the United Kingdom.[10]

Sales promotion does not require a huge budget. Small service businesses with the *entrepreneurial perspective,* such as Fuller's Car Washes, can use couponing and other consumer promotions to build sales volume and repeat purchases.

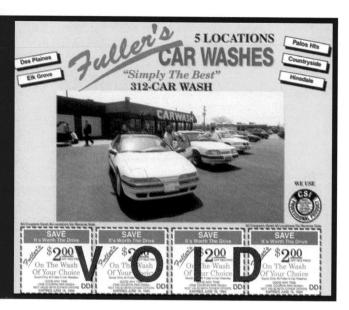

Research has identified certain characteristics associated with coupon users. Coupon-using households are more educated, have higher incomes, live in urban areas, and are less loyal to brands or particular stores. Furthermore, households tend to be consistent in their use of coupons across product classes.[11] A study by NCH Promotion Services indicates that half of coupon users decide which ones to use prior to leaving home for shopping.[12]

The outlook for couponing is favorable, as marketers expect large numbers of consumers to continue to respond to price appeals. Also, the cost of handling coupons has fallen three-quarters of a cent per coupon since 1983 because of lower processing fees, reduced interest rates, and an increase in the number of coupons redeemed.[13] This ultimately allows marketers that use couponing to stretch marketing communications dollars farther.

Coupons may be distributed in several ways. The most popular method is through the **freestanding insert (FSI),** a preprinted coupon (sometimes contained in an ad) placed into a separate publication, such as a newspaper. In 1992, the FSI was the primary method of coupon delivery, accounting for 80.2 percent of the 310 billion coupons distributed. Coupons printed in newspapers declined from 5.3 percent the previous year to 4.1 percent, while magazine coupon inserts increased to 2.8 from 2.3 percent. The percentage of coupons distributed by direct mail also grew, up from 4.0 to 4.4 percent in 1992. In-store couponing, on the rise in previous years, remained constant at 5 percent of all coupons.[14]

One technique to distribute in-store coupons, **on-shelf couponing,** uses a dispenser mounted near the manufacturer's particular product. Retailers also use in-store **checkout dispensers.** Catalina Marketing, the leading dispenser company, operates checkout dispensers in approximately 8,000 supermarkets in the

Coupons have traditionally been distributed through mail and printed media such as newspapers and magazines. ACTMEDIA offers retailers an instant coupon machine for dispensing coupons in stores.

The checkout kings hit the target

Catalina Corporation's checkout coupons system uses scanner data to distribute more than 3 million coupons daily. The system is in operation in more than 8,000 grocery stores, allowing manufacturers to reach more than 50 million households per week. Catalina's system instantly matches data about a consumer's specific purchase to an equally specific promotion for another product or service. Initially, the system dispensed coupons for products similar to those purchased by the consumer. Now, one of the fastest-growing segments of Catalina's business is for beyond-the-store promotions. For example, Sears Portrait Studios uses the system to issue coupons to shoppers who buy baby products in the supermarket.

Catalina has expanded into Europe and is moving into frequent-shopper programs. It also provides promotional support by training retailers to get more information from the system. Although this method is more expensive per thousand than other ways of dispensing coupons, it incurs less waste. On the whole, many manufacturers believe it is a cost-efficient way to promote sales.

Sources: Kate Fitzgerald, "Paper Coupons Losing Lure in High-Tech Store," *Advertising Age,* March 21, 1994, p. S-14; Ronald Grover, Laura Zinn, and Irene Recio, "Big Brother Is Grocery Shopping with You," *Business Week,* March 29, 1993, p. 60; and Laurie Peterson, "The Checkout Kings," *Adweek's Marketing Week,* October 21, 1991, pp. 22–23.

United States. Although coupons dispensed through Catalina are more expensive to the manufacturer than those in newspapers (7 cents versus a penny), consumers redeem in-store coupons at a much higher rate. Some companies, such as Clorox and PepsiCo, use Catalina's dispensing service until they get enough new customers to warrant the expense, then stop using the service.[15] Catalina is described in **The Technological Edge: The Checkout Kings Hit the Target.**

Rebates

A **rebate** is a cash reimbursement to a buyer for purchasing a product. The consumer typically must mail a rebate form, the purchase receipt, and some proof of purchase (often the universal product code) to the manufacturer within a certain time. Although consumers often purchase as a direct result of a rebate offer, many forget to send for the reimbursement or run out of time. Incentives such as coupons are easier to use, and rebates may not offer consumers the instant gratification that makes other incentives attractive.[16]

Rebates serve several functions. They act as an economic appeal to attract customers, particularly price-conscious buyers.[17] They have a deadline, thus consumers are encouraged to act by a certain time. They also offer a good way to reduce the perceived risk in trying a new brand, as a lower price represents less risk to most consumers.

Rebates also encourage increased consumption. The Quaker Oats Company, for instance, may offer a rebate on the purchase of two or more packages of instant oatmeal when the typical purchase is for only one package. Offering a rebate also allows the manufacturer to maintain a brand's original price while enjoying the benefits of a temporary price reduction.

Cross-promotions

A **cross-promotion,** sometimes called a *tie-in,* is the collaboration of two or more firms in a sales promotion. The program of the American Heart Association, Timex, Kimberly-Clark, and Colgate-Palmolive described in the chapter

In this instance, Motorcraft offers staggered rebates on both auto parts and batteries—an extra incentive to use its products.

opener is an example. Cross-promotions enhance the communications effort of all the participating firms. For example, Frito-Lay's Ruffles brand potato chips collaborated with MCI in a cross-promotion. With a purchase of potato chips, consumers received free long-distance minutes on MCI. Frito-Lay benefited, as consumers were attracted to buy the chips, while MCI gained an opportunity to promote its long-distance calling card.

Cross-promotions offer several advantages. Relationships forged between strong brands reinforce the image of each. The image of a new product, or one with low market share, may be enhanced through association with a leading brand. Also, the resources pooled in a cross-promotion enable larger incentives to be offered and generate more fanfare in introducing the promotion to consumers.[18]

Contests, sweepstakes, and games

A **contest** offers prizes based on the skill of contestants. The participant must use a skill or some ability to address a specified problem to qualify for a prize. In an attempt to boost ratings and awareness of regularly scheduled non-news programs, CNN sponsored a contest entitled, "Showbiz Box Office Busters," in which viewers had to guess which upcoming movie releases would gross the most money. Prizes included a Hollywood tour and a spending spree on Rodeo Drive in Beverly Hills. Entry forms appeared next to ads in *Entertainment Weekly* and *People* magazines.[19]

A **sweepstakes** offers prizes based on a chance drawing of participants' names. Sweepstakes have strong appeal because they are easier to enter and take less time than contests and games. Wendy's "Summer of 99" sweepstakes, highlighting its 99-cent Super Value Menu, offered customers a chance to win their choice of 99 prizes. They entered the drawing of their choice, each for a specific prize, by filling out forms available in the stores. By law, purchase cannot be a requirement to enter a sweepstakes.

Games are similar to sweepstakes, but they cover a longer period. They encourage consumers to continue playing in order to win. Another CNN promotion involved a watch-and-win game centered on "Sports Tonight," a half-hour

This cross-promotion offers free ski lessons to those who travel via American Airlines to designated resort locations in Wyoming and Colorado.

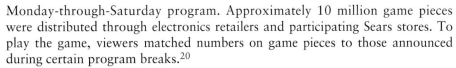

Monday-through-Saturday program. Approximately 10 million game pieces were distributed through electronics retailers and participating Sears stores. To play the game, viewers matched numbers on game pieces to those announced during certain program breaks.[20]

Contests, sweepstakes, and games can create interest and motivate consumption by encouraging consumer involvement. Contest, sweepstakes, and games are often used in integrated marketing communications programs along with in-store displays (part of trade promotion) and advertising.

Premiums

An item given free or at a bargain price to encourage the consumer to buy is called a **premium.** NBC, for example, gave subscribers to their pay-for-view coverage of the Olympics their choice of a "free" warm-up jacket or a Universal remote-control unit for cable systems. Premiums are intended to improve the product's image, gain goodwill, broaden the customer base, and produce quick sales. Premiums that require saving in-pack coupons or proofs of purchase to be redeemed can create consumer loyalty. For instance, Totino's pizza offered NFL jackets and sweaters to customers mailing in a certain number of proofs of purchase.

The use of premiums is well established and popular in a variety of industries, yet not growing in importance. For example, roughly two-thirds of the manufacturers in the packaged goods industry use premiums, a ratio that has remained fairly constant over the past few years.[21]

Sampling

A **sample** is a small size of a product made available to prospective purchasers, usually free of charge. Marketers use samples to demonstrate a product's value or use and encourage future purchase. Sampling reduces the consumer's perception of risk by allowing product trial before purchase of a full-size version.

Marketers find sampling particularly useful for new brands with features that are difficult to describe adequately through advertising. Samples also draw heightened attention to a brand. For instance, Stouffer's Lean Cuisine French Bread Pizza samples offered to customers in a grocery store draw attention to and create interest in the brand.

Although usually mailed to prospective customers, samples may be distributed door to door, at trade shows, or in store. They sometimes accompany the purchase of a related product, such as a free sample of laundry detergent with the purchase of a washing machine.

Emerging methods of sampling include distribution in theaters and newspapers. To get its new Wild Bunch fruit-flavored colas distributed in Kroger supermarkets in Atlanta, Pepsi gave away free samples to some 10,000 moviegoers and told them where they could buy more—at their neighborhood Kroger store.[22]

NewsPac, a flat 7-by-11-inch envelope that looks like an ad but comes stuffed with a sample packet, allows marketers to distribute samples via newspaper. A major drawback to this method is that samples can be no more than one-fourth of an inch thick.[23] Samples may also be distributed person to person, as is the case with Chesebrough-Pond's new "younger skin" products. Although the products are available only through retail stores, a direct-sales company hands out samples and literature to encourage sales.[24]

Sampling can be expensive, and according to the *productivity perspective,* marketers must determine the most cost-effective manner of distribution. This depends on the target audience and the size of the sample. Although larger samples cost more, the sample should be big enough for consumers to make an adequate evaluation. For an example of a successful sampling plan, see **The Entrepreneurial Spirit: Stonyfield Farms Successfully Scoops Its Customers.**

Advertising specialties

An **advertising specialty** is an item of useful or interesting merchandise given away free of charge and typically carrying an imprinted name or message. These items are typically low in cost, although some can be expensive. Examples of advertising specialties include pens or pencils, calendars, yardsticks, coffee mugs, notebooks, key chains, T-shirts, and letter openers.

Specialty advertising has several common uses. It can reinforce other advertising media to strengthen a message. It can also produce or foster high levels of

Stonyfield Farms successfully scoops its customers

Stonyfield Farms, a $14 million New Hampshire yogurt maker, was founded to expand markets for New England dairy farmers. Creative, low-cost marketing, including the use of sampling, has made the company successful. According to Stonyfield president, Gary Hirshberg, "We don't advertise, and we can't afford supermarket slotting fees, so getting people to taste our product is our entire focus."

One successful sampling program ran in conjunction with Rebecca's Cafe, a Boston chain of upscale fast-food restaurants. The promotion offered diners a free scoop of Stonyfield's frozen yogurt on any dessert they ordered. Rebecca's sold about 15 percent more desserts during the 30-day program, and in a slow month for yogurt, Stonyfield exposed 1,250 customers to its product.

The costs of the promotion, in addition to product costs, were for inexpensive point-of-purchase display placards, which Stonyfield and Rebecca's split. For small and large businesses, sampling can be an extremely effective means of promoting the product.

Sources: "Sampling with a Twist," *Inc.*, August 1992, p. 80; and Jacqueline Davidson, "Responsibility Reaps Rewards," *Small Business Reports,* February 1993, pp. 56–64.

brand recognition when the item has a relatively long life. A unique specialty advertising item can attract interest among target audience members and perhaps stimulate action. In addition, a useful specialty item can create a positive attitude toward the provider. Poor-quality merchandise, however, may detract from the marketer's image.

Trade sales promotion

Trade sales promotion at the wholesale and retail level helps push products through the marketing channel. Unlike consumer sales promotion, trade promotion is not easily observed by ultimate consumers. Although consumer sales promotions are very visible, in fact they are dwarfed by the magnitude of trade sales promotion. Marketers spend approximately twice as much money on trade promotion.

Objectives of trade promotions

Sales promotions aimed at the trade have many and varied objectives. As listed in Exhibit 19.4, common trade promotion objectives are to gain or maintain distribution; influence resellers to promote a product; influence resellers to offer a price discount; increase reseller inventory; defend a brand against competitors; and avoid reduction of normal prices.[25] Trade promotions may be conducted by manufacturers, service providers, or wholesalers, all directing their efforts toward other channel members, most notably retailers.

Gain or maintain distribution

Sales promotion influences resellers to carry a product. Manufacturers selling directly to retailers may strike special introductory deals to get established with the retailer. Later, sales promotion may help maintain distribution in the face of competition or a flat sales period. Such is the case in the soft-drink market, where Coke and Pepsi use sales promotion on a regular basis. Other incentives, such as providing free in-store displays, may encourage retailers to purchase by reducing their perceived risk. A trade show is another example of sales promotion that may provide a way to introduce the product to potential distributors and gain their business.

Influence resellers to promote the product

Getting a product into the reseller's inventory is not always enough to realize sales objectives. In other words, it's not enough to get the product "on the shelf"; it may take sales promotion to move it "off the shelf." Ways manufacturers can influence retailers to promote a product include offering incentives to the retail salesforce, splitting advertising costs with the retailer, furnishing free display

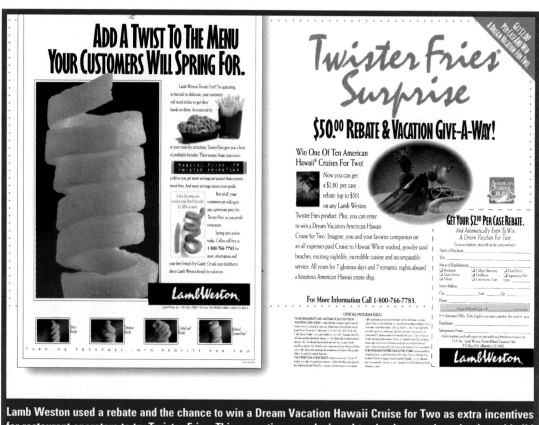

Lamb Weston used a rebate and the chance to win a Dream Vacation Hawaii Cruise for Two as extra incentives for restaurant operators to try Twister Fries. This promotion was designed to simultaneously maintain and build distribution through Lamb Weston distributors.

This ad from a grocery industry magazine gives retailers four reasons to fill their shelves with Vlasic® Early California® ripe olives.

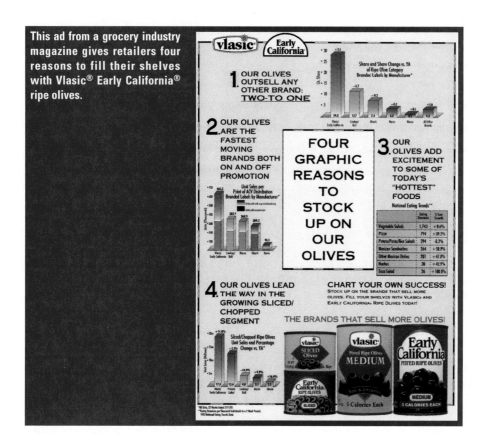

materials, or various other techniques. Quaker State, for example, could encourage service station attendants to promote the sale of motor oil by paying them 25 cents per can sold during a contest period. At the end of the contest, the attendant with the most sales would receive two free tickets to a NASCAR race. The basic idea is for additional sales volume to offset expenses involved in running the promotion or for sales to clear the dealers' inventory to make way for more profitable sales in the future.

Influence resellers to offer a price discount

Sometimes the manufacturer gives wholesalers and retailers allowances or discounts so that its product will be offered at a reduced price. The manufacturer hopes the lower price will lead to increased sales. This often occurs with end-of-season merchandise. For example, fishing equipment manufacturer Zebco might offer sporting goods stores a clearance price on factory-premarked rods and reels and a special display barrel with promotional signs indicating "Rod & Reel Riot! $12.99 While They Last!"

Increase reseller inventory

Suppliers do not want channel members to run out of stock. A product being out of stock results in more than lost sales; it creates dissatisfaction among customers seeking to make a purchase. Sometimes a manufacturer may want to shift products to wholesalers or retailers because of the costs involved in holding inventory. The other channel members, of course, are well aware of the cost and risks of holding excess inventory, and the supplier may grant them special deals in exchange for doing so. Such an approach is commonplace in the greeting card industry, where suppliers offer retailers special pricing and deferred payment to book orders well in advance.

EXECUTIVE ROUNDTABLE COMMENT | **Dave Moore, vice president of sales for Ruddell & Associates, Inc., a manufacturers' representatives firm in San Francisco, comments on the cost of holding inventory:**

Neither the manufacturer nor the retailer wants an oversupply of plastic pumpkins waiting for next Halloween. So the manufacturer offers a "buy now, pay later" program to reduce the retailer's financial risk and encourage a good stock position. Retailers hate to be out of a hot item, but they don't want to pay for it any sooner than they have to.

Defend against competitors

Just as at the consumer level, sales promotion can stave off competitors at the trade level. An incentive may prompt channel members to choose one firm's brand over a competing one.

Avoid price reductions

Rather than reduce the price of a product permanently, marketers may use some form of trade promotion to offer channel members a temporary price reduction. If there is a momentary oversupply of product on the market, for example, a manufacturer might elect to maintain sales volume by offering a "1 free with 10" program of short duration. In effect, the customer gets a discount in the form of free goods, but the manufacturer avoids a permanent price reduction.

Trade sales promotion techniques

Trade sales promotion techniques can be applied independently or in combinations. And, as illustrated in the chapter-opening cross-promotion, firms often link trade sales promotion with consumer sales promotion and other elements of the communications mix, reflecting the *execution perspective*. Some frequently used trade sales promotion techniques are shown in Exhibit 19.5.

Trade allowances

Trade allowances are short-term special allowances, discounts, or deals granted to resellers as an incentive to stock, feature, or in some way participate in the cooperative promotion of a product. There are several kinds of allowances, including slotting allowances, which we discussed in Chapter 15. Another type, the *buying allowance,* is payment of a specified amount of money to a reseller for purchasing a certain amount of a product during a particular period. The payment may be by check or as a credit against an invoice. A manufacturer usually offers a buying allowance to increase the size of the reseller's order.

A *display allowance* is money or a product provided to a retailer for featuring the manufacturer's brand in an agreed-upon in-store display. An *advertising*

Exhibit 19.5

Trade sales promotion techniques

- Trade allowances
- Dealer loaders
- Trade contests
- Point-of-purchase displays
- Trade shows
- Training programs
- Push money

allowance is money paid a reseller for including the manufacturer's product, along with other products, in the reseller's advertising efforts. Somewhat similar to this, *cooperative advertising* occurs when the manufacturer helps finance the reseller's advertising efforts featuring only the manufacturer's product. For example, Pioneer may help a local electronics store pay for a newspaper ad featuring Pioneer products.

Dealer loaders

A **dealer loader** is a premium given to a reseller to encourage development of a special display or product offering. Loader techniques help ensure proper stock and display of the item, of particular interest to many manufacturers at certain seasons or holidays.

There are two common types of loaders. A *buying loader* is a gift, such as a free trip, for buying, displaying, and selling a certain amount of a product within a specified time. A *display loader* allows the reseller to keep some or all of the display when the promotion ends. A tennis racket manufacturer, for example, might allow qualifying retailers to keep an expensive, custom-produced lighted display featuring action photos of top players to help promote sales.

Trade contests

A **trade contest** typically associates prizes with sales of the sponsor's product. As do consumer contests, trade contests generate interest, which makes them useful for motivating resellers. Effective trade contests are held periodically, rather than all the time—otherwise, they lose some of their motivating potential. Effective contests can boost short-term sales and improve relations between manufacturer and reseller.

Point-of-purchase displays

Point-of-purchase displays are generally used at the retail level to call customer attention to a featured product. Typically provided free or at low cost by the manufacturer to the reseller, point-of-purchase displays attract consumers while they shop, encouraging purchase of the particular product. With much of retailing self-service today, point-of-purchase displays support the retail sales effort by highlighting the product and offering information. Given that consumers make many purchase decisions in the store rather than before entering it, these displays can be important selling tools.

A disadvantage of displays is that manufacturers must assemble and place them. Retailers are busy, and they are deluged with point-of-purchase materials, many of which never make it to the sales floor. Displays often become unused throwaways, an unnecessary waste in marketing communications and a concern for supporters of an *ecological perspective.*

EXECUTIVE ROUNDTABLE COMMENT | **Shaun Singleton Masters, director of merchandising, artwear division of Signal Apparel in Chattanooga, TN, comments on display design:**

Point-of-purchase displays have to really grab people and pull them in for a closer look. Designing these displays is like walking a tightrope—you want to be creative, but you have to consider the store layout, image, and size constraints. If you get a bit too cute, or not cute enough depending on the retailer, the display will just gather dust somewhere off the sales floor.

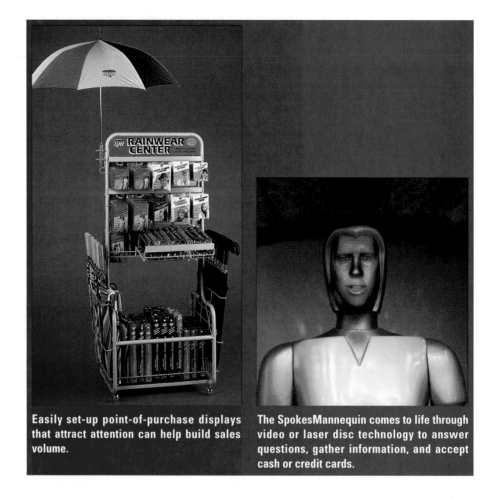

Easily set-up point-of-purchase displays that attract attention can help build sales volume.

The SpokesMannequin comes to life through video or laser disc technology to answer questions, gather information, and accept cash or credit cards.

Displays come in many varieties, including special racks, display cartons, banners, signs, price cards, video monitors, and mechanical dispensers. A relatively new and novel display is the SpokesMannequin, an advanced version of holographic "talking heads" images of the 1980s. Through video or laser disc technology, the device conveys the likeness, voice, and performance of a human being in the form of a dummy. Its creators claim the SpokesMannequin can answer questions, gather information, and accept cash or credit cards.[26]

Trade shows

A **trade show** is a periodic, semipublic event sponsored by trade, professional, and industrial associations at which suppliers rent booths to display products and provide information to potential buyers. Trade shows are big business, attracting more than 70 million visitors in the US per year.[27] They are also extremely important in many overseas markets, including Europe, the Middle East, Africa, Asia, and Latin America. In many of these markets, trade shows are a more influential part of the marketing process than in the United States.[28]

Marketers can use trade shows to accomplish any number of objectives, including demonstrating products, acquiring new-prospect leads, making sales, providing information, comparing competing brands, introducing new products, enhancing the corporate image, and strengthening relationships with existing customers.

Some shows are simply too large for customers to effectively visit each exhibit. Many companies use preshow mailings or phone calls to boost exhibit traffic.[29] Companion promotional products are also effective for generating traffic and creating a memorable exhibit. For example, Corhart Refractories Corporation mailed headphones for an AM/FM radio to registered attendees prior to a trade

A large selection of Mercedes-Benz products was one of the chief attractions of the first Hanover (Germany) Commercial Vehicle Show.

Armstrong Tile holds training sessions for retailers on its products and how to sell them.

show and invited them to visit Corhart's booth to pick up the radio.[30] Passing out T-shirts or other specialty advertising items carrying the company's name and logo or constructing an unusual and eye-catching display can also generate booth traffic.

It is important for companies to have well-trained salespeople available at a trade show. In addition, follow-up after the show is critical for successful implementation of the *relationship perspective.* Major trade shows are held in large cities; thus lodging and associated expenses for company personnel can be expensive.

Training programs

Some manufacturers sponsor or pay for training programs for customer employees. Armstrong Tile, for example, a manufacturer of floor tile, provides sales training to teach some of its key dealer personnel how to sell or use its products.

Marketers may also provide training on a number of other topics, including retail and wholesale management procedures, safety issues, or current technical developments in an industrial field. Training programs are expensive, and results are often hard to measure. To be effective, training should be continual, or at least periodically reinforced, thus adding to the expense. Training can add a lot to the *relationship perspective,* but its costs and hard-to-measure results are indeed subjects of interest to those interested in the *productivity perspective.*

Push money

Push money, also called **spiffs,** is what a manufacturer pays to retail salespeople to encourage them to promote its products over competitive brands. Push money may also be used to encourage the retail sale of specific products in the manufacturer's line. This extra incentive helps to get the manufacturer's brand special representation or favored treatment. The disadvantage is that the retail salesperson's extra enthusiasm for the manufacturer's product may wane once the spiff is eliminated, especially if another manufacturer offers a new spiff.

Limitations of sales promotion

Although sales promotion can accomplish a variety of objectives, there are certain things it cannot do. By understanding the limitations of sales promotion, marketers can better decide how it facilitates the *relationship, productivity,* and *execution perspectives.* Sales promotion can help boost sales, but it cannot reverse a genuine declining sales trend. If sales are slipping, the marketer should evaluate, and perhaps change the product's marketing strategy. Attempting to use sales promotion as a quick fix may temporarily postpone worsening of the problem, but it cannot eliminate it.

In a similar vein, marketers cannot reasonably expect sales promotion to convert rejection of an inferior product into acceptance. Consumers judge a product on whether it satisfies their needs. Products that do not meet consumer needs naturally fade from the market over the course of time.

Beyond its inability to improve a brand's image, sales promotion may even weaken the brand image. As a sales promotion develops a life of its own, perceived product differentiation may be blurred; consumers come to see the deal as more important than any other real or perceived brand difference.[31] In essence, buyers reach a point at which they fail to see any differences among brands, and the marketer has unwittingly created short-run price-oriented behavior. In the soft-drink market, for instance, many consumers see Coca-Cola and Pepsi-Cola as interchangeable, and decide which of the two they will purchase primarily on the basis of price (which is the better deal?).

Sales promotion, far more than other marketing activity, has also been blamed for encouraging competitive retaliation.[32] Promotions can be developed quickly, and one company can respond to a competitor's sales promotion with its own. Quick response may stave off the potential of sales lost to the competitor's promotion. Although a promotion battle benefits the consumer, two firms that compete head-to-head often both lose profits. Other forms of marketing communications are less likely to evoke such quick retaliatory efforts.

Sales promotion can result in manufacturers gaining short-term volume but sacrificing profit. Special incentives and deals promote **forward buying,** both among distributors and consumers. That is, people buy more than they need at the deal price. They purchase enough to carry them to the next deal, when once again they can stock up at low prices.[33] Thus, the manufacturer may sell more at the expense of less profit.

To overcome this problem, manufacturers are increasingly using **pay-for-performance trade promotions,** through which retailers are rewarded for making sales to consumers rather than making purchases from manufacturers. Scanner data can be used to measure results, and the incentive to overload warehouses to take advantage of lower prices during deal periods is reduced.[34]

Ethical and legal issues in sales promotion

The *ethical perspective* is found in the American Marketing Association Code of Ethics, which stipulates the "avoidance of sales promotion that uses deception or manipulation." Sales promotion provides an environment ripe for exploitation, and many of the ethical and legal problems in marketing communications are related to questionable promotions. Deception and fraud are the primary issues. Global marketing poses added ethical concerns because of requirements specific to different cultures.

Deception

According to pollster Lou Harris, more than 92 percent of American adults have received a letter or postcard "guaranteeing" they have won a prize they can claim by dialing an 800 or 900 number. More than 50 million people have responded to such notifications, and virtually all of them lost money doing so.[35]

This survey is but one of many indicators that deceptive sales promotions are all too common. According to the National Consumers League, guaranteed-prize scams presented as legitimate sales promotions cost consumers approximately $40 million per year.[36]

Another popular consumer sales promotion tool, the sweepstakes, is often used deceptively. As a result, a variety of regulatory agencies, including the US Postal Service and the Federal Trade Commission, actively police sweepstakes. In addition, all 50 states have various combinations of gambling, lottery, and consumer protection laws that regulate sweepstakes. At least nine states regulate the use of simulated checks, and separate restrictions exist for sweepstakes promoting tobacco, liquor, milk, and time-share lodging.[37]

Caution is the best policy when designing a sweepstakes program. In fact, the same could be said for any sales promotion to ensure that manufacturers, wholesalers, and retailers steer clear of unethical or illegal activity. Basically, marketers must tell consumers the truth and clearly spell out the action necessary to enter the sweepstakes. In addition, marketers must take responsibility for the fair and equitable treatment of buyers and nonbuyers during a promotion, taking care not to make it significantly more difficult for nonbuyers to enter. Finally, a legitimate sweepstakes program entails honest distribution of prizes, which may require the services of a sweepstakes management company to avoid insider rigging.

Fraud

Diverting also can involve fraud and kickbacks. For example, the FBI investigated a New Jersey firm that set up bogus export companies to buy large quantities of deeply discounted Hershey's cocoa for sale in West Africa. The cocoa was then diverted to stores in the US, and the firm paid a $100,000 fine after pleading guilty to mail fraud.[38]

Another significant problem involves coupon and rebate fraud, with manufacturers the intended victims. Exhibit 19.6 points out some of the ways cheaters can profit from coupons and mail-in offers. The Coupon Information Center estimates that companies pay coupon refunds totaling more than $800

| Exhibit 19.6 | Examples of coupon and rebate fraud |

The Fake Storefront

A scam artist rents space cheap, sets up a store, then starts sending in coupons to manufacturers for payment. Pretty soon the store's shelves are bare, but the "owner" is still sending in coupons obtained illegally.

Stuffing the Ballot Box

A retailer legitimately obtains cash from clearinghouses & manufacturers for coupons handed in by shoppers, but boosts the take illegally by sending in extra coupons purchased at steep discounts from various sources, such as unscrupulous printers.

Playing the Middleman

An ambitious operator makes money supplying other operators—collecting coupons by the pound & selling them to retailers, buying & selling proofs of purchase, or counterfeiting coupons & proofs of purchase.

The Redemption Scam

Manufacturers offer big cash rebates on large items to shoppers who mail in forms, together with proofs of purchase—receipts, labels, or box tops. A con artist uses the rebate forms & proofs of purchase, real or counterfeit, to illicitly collect refunds without buying products.

million a year to undeserving retailers and consumers. Approximately $500 million goes to retailers that submit coupons to manufacturers fraudulently.[39]

Manufacturers have resorted to high-tech methods to combat coupon fraud. To circumvent coupon counterfeiting, special inks produce the word *void* on coupons exposed to the light used in copier machines. New checkout scanner technology now polices misredemption at the store level. Even low-tech methods, such as shortening the redemption period, are used. Gillette, for instance, shortened the redemption lifetime of its coupons from as long as a year to just a month or two.[40]

As with couponing, fraud is a factor in rebates. The Coupon Information Center estimates manufacturers pay approximately $320 million annually to con artists illegally sending in rebate forms.[41] Either the rebate forms or the accompanying proofs of purchase required for redemption may be counterfeit.

The most widespread effect of fraud and deceptive sales promotions is that in the long run consumers pay more for products than they would otherwise. Consumers also pay through taxes for the considerable government regulation needed to combat fraud and deception.

Diverting

Consumers are not the only victims of unethical and illegal sales promotion. Manufacturers can also be the targets of fraud. A controversial, yet commonplace, activity is **diverting** (also called *arbitraging*), or secretly purchasing a product where it is less expensive, usually as a result of a trade promotion, and reselling in areas where prices are higher.

Diverters use up-to-the-minute computerized information to find out where the deals are, purchase merchandise for shipment to a buyer authorized by the manufacturer to receive the deal, then divert all or part of the shipment to an unauthorized location while the goods are in transit. Diverters include both intermediaries and chain stores. Intermediaries are fairly tight-lipped about diverting, although some even maintain secret operations in the offices of legitimate wholesalers and supermarket chains.

Diverting can distort supply and demand and cause marketing strategies to backfire on manufacturers. Industry analysts believe diverting is inevitable so long as manufacturers offer the same products at different prices in different geographic markets. Some manufacturers, most notably Procter & Gamble, have instituted a one-price nationwide policy to reduce diverting.[42]

Global concerns

The *global perspective* requires marketers to make an extra effort to become familiar with local laws and customs. In Spain, for example, it is legal to require the purchase of the product for entry in sales promotion contests, while such a requirement is illegal in most other European countries. Further, according to an expert on sales promotion in Spain, the Spanish people are generally keen on gambling and participate heavily in promotional games of chance. Logically, sales promotion in Spain is extremely popular, more so than in other European countries with stricter regulations. As a result, it is impossible to design a sales promotion campaign for the entire European market—marketers must adapt programs to the appropriate legal framework.

In Canada, a variety of laws affect sales promotion. For example, if entry into a contest requires that the consumer send in a UPC label, entrants are also allowed to submit a handwritten facsimile of the label. In Quebec, language laws require that most marketing communications be in French. Also, most contests must be structured to require that entrants answer a skill-testing question to be eligible for a prize.

These examples from Spain and Canada are reminders that marketing activities should be conducted to meet varying applicable local requirements, often a composite of national, state (or province), and local laws. As most sales promotion tools involve mass distribution of written documents, extreme caution should be used to ensure compliance with relevant laws.

Summary

1. *Explain the role and significance of sales promotion in the marketing communications mix.* Sales promotion is one way firms may communicate with intended target audiences. Sales promotion uses media and nonmedia marketing communications for a predetermined, limited time at either consumer, retailer, or wholesaler level to stimulate trial, increase consumer demand, or improve product availability. Sales promotion is unique in that it offers an extra incentive for action. Its importance is evidenced by the considerable amount of money firms invest in it.

2. *Understand why sales promotion use and expenditures have increased in recent years.* Expenditures in sales promotion have been fueled by changes in consumer demographics, lifestyles and attitudes, technological advances, a shift of power to retailers, a focus of firms on the short term, and an increasing emphasis on accountability for results.

   Many shoppers today are busy and price-conscious, making sales promotion attractive. Scanning technology allows both retailers and manufacturers an opportunity to gauge the effectiveness of promotions quickly and accurately, thus reinforcing the use of sales promotion. Retailers have gained considerable power in the marketing channel in recent years, and manufacturers are virtually required to engage in sales promotion to increase or maintain distribution. Since sales promotion is generally short term, it fits with the time horizon most favored today in business. Finally, the results of sales promotion are easier to assess than the results of advertising, prompting its use in an era of accountability.

3. *Discuss the objectives and techniques of consumer sales promotion.* Consumer sales promotion attempts to stimulate trial, increase consumer inventory and consumption, encourage repurchase, neutralize competitive promotions, increase the sales of complementary products, stimulate impulse purchasing, and allow for flexible pricing policies. Consumer sales promotion techniques include price deals, coupons, rebates, cross-promotions, contests, sweepstakes, games, premiums, sampling, and advertising specialties.

4. *Discuss the objectives and techniques of trade sales promotion.* Trade sales promotion can help gain or maintain distribution, influence retailers to promote a product or to offer a price discount, increase reseller inventory, defend against competitors, and avoid price reductions. Popular trade sales promotion techniques involve trade allowances, dealer loaders, trade contests, point-of-purchase displays, trade shows, training programs, and push money.

5. *Explain the limitations of sales promotion.* Sales promotion cannot permanently reverse a genuine decline in sales, nor can it work to capture enduring acceptance of an inferior product. Overused sales promotion may actually weaken a brand image, rather than strengthen it. Because it is short term and often highly visible, sales promotion can spur retaliation from competitors, which tends to diminish its effectiveness. In addition, consumers and resellers may engage in forward buying to take advantage of sales promotions, possibly causing the manufacturer to gain volume at the expense of declining profitability.

6. *Realize how deceptive and fraudulent sales promotion victimizes both consumers and marketers.* Consumers lose money on deceptive sales promotions such as bogus guaranteed-winner sweepstakes. Manufacturers pay consumers and resellers more than $800 million a year for fraudulently submitted rebates and coupons. The average consumer eventually pays a higher price for products to cover the cost of fraud in sales promotion. In addition, taxpayers have a heavier burden due to the increased costs of regulation at the federal, state, and local levels.

Key terms & concepts

sales promotion 466
consumer sales promotion 466
trade sales promotion 466
price deal 471
cents-off deals 471
price-pack deals 471
coupon 471
freestanding insert (FSI) 472
on-shelf couponing 472
checkout dispensers 472

rebate 473
cross-promotion 473
contest 474
sweepstakes 474
games 474
premium 475
sample 475
advertising specialty 476
trade allowances 480
dealer loader 481

trade contest 481
point-of-purchase displays 481
trade show 482
push money 483
spiffs 483
forward buying 484
pay-for-performance trade
  promotions 484
diverting 486

Review & discussion questions

1. What factors have contributed to the growth in sales promotion?

2. What are the objectives of consumer sales promotion?

3. Define and briefly discuss these consumer sales promotion techniques: price deals, coupons, rebates, cross-promotions, contests, sweepstakes, games, premiums, sampling, and advertising specialties.

4. How do the objectives of trade sales promotion differ from those of consumer sales promotion?

5. Define and briefly discuss these trade sales promotion techniques: trade allowances, dealer loaders, trade contests, point-of-purchase displays, trade shows, training programs, and push money.

6. How would these parties be affected if consumer and trade sales promotions on grocery products were banned by law? (*a*) consumers; (*b*) retailers; (*c*) manufacturers with their own brands.

7. Discuss the issue of deception in sales promotion, and give examples of deceptive sales promotion.

8. Discuss the problem of coupon and rebate fraud, and identify several ways unscrupulous operators could exploit manufacturers through fraud.

9. Refer to **The Technological Edge: The Checkout Kings Hit the Target.** How does scanner technology allow marketers to do a better job with consumer promotions?

10. Refer to **The Entrepreneurial Spirit: Stonyfield Farms Successfully Scoops Its Customers.** Why is sampling an effective promotion technique for small companies?

Application exercises

1. Consult the Sunday edition of a local newspaper. Identify examples of as many consumer trade promotion techniques as possible. You may find examples of price deals, coupons, rebates, cross-promotions, contests, sweepstakes, games, premiums, and even sampling. Select one example from each category of consumer sales promotion techniques that you have identified, and try to determine the main objective of the promotion: stimulating trial, increasing consumer inventory and consumption, encouraging repurchase, neutralizing competitive promotions, or increasing the sale of complementary products.

2. Look again at the Sunday newspaper. Collect a minimum of 10 coupons or other sales promotion materials intended to stimulate trial of a new product. You may need to review the paper for a couple of weeks to collect 10 examples. Now, visit local retailers to determine whether the new products are in stock. If the product is in stock, note any other point-of-purchase materials that encourage a purchase. If the product is not in stock, see if you can find out why.

3. Assume you are the owner of a small independent bookstore in a large metropolitan area. You face heavy competition from large national chains such as B. Dalton, Walden Books, and Bookstar. Your clientele is more upscale, educated, and intellectual than that of your competition. You are attempting to develop a sales promotion program to encourage your clientele to become loyal customers. Explain how you would choose one or more consumer sales promotion techniques to accomplish this objective.

Case 19.1   *Ocean Spray Cranberries: Juicy promotion*

High-profile consumer sales promotions are often accompanied by behind-the-scenes trade promotions to get the extra effort needed in a competitive marketplace. Retail store shelves are crowded, and consumers are bombarded with product choices, ads, and all sorts of promotional fanfare.

In the crowded beverage market, Ocean Spray Cranberries, Inc., teamed up with Sony in a splashy summer 1994 promotion called "Beach Blanket Bingo." The program was designed to boost short-term sales and reinforce Ocean Spray's category-leading status in the minds of consumers and retailers as the top seller of multiserve, canned and bottled juice drinks. Also, Ocean Spray hoped to update its image by association with state-of-the-art Sony stereo products.

The primary promotional vehicle was bottle labels, stylized with the Beach Blanket Bingo logo, which ap-
peared on both new and established products. Consumers could win in three ways. First, the back of each label included a mail-in offer for deeply discounted Sony music CDs and cassettes. Second, if the label was an instant winner, consumers could win Ocean Spray and Sony products as prizes. Third, consumers could collect imprinted labels to eventually spell BINGO and win a Sony stereo rack system. The three-pronged approach encouraged multiple purchases, either to spell out BINGO, take advantage of the mail-in music offer, or to be an instant winner.

The program combined the consumer awards with a trade program for retailers. According to Carol Trifone, Ocean Spray's marketing promotions manager, the company wanted a promotion that could work nationally in the mass market but could be specifically tailored for key accounts in the retail division. To support retailers' key role in the promotion, Ocean Spray emphasized catchy in-store displays to build consumer awareness and participation. The 18,000 participating retailers across the US also chose "from a menu of options ranging from in-store sweepstakes for free groceries to multiple-purchase rebates or near-pack prizes (single-song CDs for each purchase of an Ocean Spray product)," says Trifone.

Coordination with retailers was a critical element of this program. Ocean Spray's regional managers and Connecticut-based Reach Marketing personnel educated retailers about their options. Inventory planning was important to ensure adequate stock on store shelves from late April through August. The promotion required additional coordination to allow consumers to claim prizes through October.

Although specific sales results were not yet available by mid-summer 1994, Gianna Hausman of Reach Marketing declared the program an apparent success. Hausman said the retailers especially liked having a choice of promotion options, which allowed tailoring to local market conditions and consumer preferences.

Questions:

1. Why do you think Ocean Spray offered retailers a choice of in-store promotions (sweepstakes or specially priced single-play Sony CDs with purchase of Ocean Spray products) or rebates for multiple purchases?

2. What specific consumer behavior was Ocean Spray seeking by offering consumers three ways to win? Is this behavior a reasonable expectation of sales promotion?

3. One stated goal of Beach Blanket Bingo was to update Ocean Spray's image by association with modern Sony products. How realistic is it to think that sales promotion can improve brand image?

Sources: "Promoting a Leading Image," *Sales & Marketing Management,* May 1994, p. 26; conversation with Gianna Hausman of Reach Marketing, July 6, 1994.

Case 19.2   *PepsiCo: Fiasco in the Philippines*

The prelude to what will go down in history as one of sales promotion's biggest blunders began routinely enough. Pepsi-Cola Products of Philippines, with the assistance of the owner of 19 percent of its stock, New York–based PepsiCo Inc., ran television ads proclaiming "Today, you could become a millionaire!" In this poor country, the advertising generated a great deal of interest in Pepsi bottle-cap collecting, as the campaign promised to pay one million pesos (about $40,000 US) to anyone holding a bottle cap marked with the winning number.

When Pepsi announced that anyone holding a cap marked with the number 349 would be a million-peso winner, the campaign quickly moved from routine sales promotion to front-page news. Through an inexplicable computer error, approximately 800,000 caps had been printed with the winning number, rather than the single winning cap.

To borrow a line from rock star Warren Zevon, Pepsi executives probably felt like singing in unison: "Send lawyers, guns, and money . . . ," as the public's outrage led to confrontation and acts of violence. Pepsi officials in the Philippines now travel with bodyguards, and heavily armed security personnel ride shotgun on delivery trucks. Even so, 32 delivery trucks were stoned, torched, or overturned.

Consumers have also turned to the courts for relief. More than 22,000 people have filed 689 civil suits seeking damages from Pepsi, and there are an additional 5,200 criminal complaints for fraud and deception. It will take years to settle all the suits, not to mention a huge amount of money.

After spending millions trying to calm angry claimants, Pepsi still faces the contempt of consumers who feel cheated by what they see as an unfair scheme. Thus far, almost a half-million consumers have produced a "winning" cap, and it is impossible to predict how many more will file suit. Pepsi's original budget for the promotion was $2 million; the company has already paid an additional $10 million for more prizes, along with a $6,000 fine to the country's consumer protection agency—the maximum fine the law permits.

Pepsi officials vow they will not pay any additional money to those claiming to be winners. They equate the current consumer protest in the Philippines to extortion and terrorism, saying the company will no longer be "held hostage."

This problem may not go away without additional negative consequences. In a nation known for volatile politics and public demonstrations, nothing has united Philippine consumers like their displeasure with Pepsi. The protest movement includes communist rebels and army generals, upscale Manila consumers and barefoot rural peasants—citizens from all walks of life are joining in the fight against Pepsi. Even though the sales volume of Pepsi brands jumped by 40 percent during the promotion, the company's officials undoubtedly wish the program had never been executed.

Questions:

1. Could Pepsi have prevented this fiasco? What specific suggestions can you make that would prevent such mistakes?

2. Do you think consumers in the US would react the same way to this sort of mistake? Why?

3. Is it reasonable to think that Pepsi owes every holder of a "winning" bottle cap the announced prize of a million pesos?

Sources: Bob Drogin, "Pepsi Marketing Goof Has Filipinos Enraged," *The Courier-Journal,* July 27, 1993, pp. A1, 5; and "Uh, Huh! PepsiCo Claims They Got the Wrong One," *The Wall Street Journal,* June 1, 1992, p. A5.

Personal Selling and Sales Management

After studying this chapter you should be able to:

1. Understand the role and importance of personal selling in the promotion mix.

2. See how the key steps in personal selling depend on a relationship perspective.

3. Identify the similarities and differences in the job responsibilities of salespeople and sales managers.

4. Describe the key activities in sales management.

5. Appreciate important ethical issues faced by salespeople and sales managers.

ALICO: *Ensuring successful selling from Japan to Pakistan*

American Life Insurance Company (ALICO) has grown from its Shanghai origins in 1919 to become one of the world's largest insurers. With a sales organization of 15,000 agents and brokers operating in 50 countries, ALICO must adapt its sales management practices to diverse operating environments.

The company's former president notes that the traditional methods of choosing sales agents "must be tweaked and tailored to fit local customs and cultures. This is done to seize a competitive advantage and penetrate the markets." In Japan, ALICO abandoned the Japanese custom of employing a part-time salesforce to sell life insurance. Instead, it chose to sell through property-casualty agents and developed a Western-style, full-time, career-oriented salesforce.

Life insurance sales had never been seen as a profession in Japan, so this took considerable time and effort. By offering intensive training and strong market support to its agents, ALICO has become the market leader among non-Japanese life insurance companies operating in the country.

In the Persian Gulf region, ALICO often recruits third-country nationals who lack experience in life insurance sales. These agents are highly effective in selling to other third-country nationals and foreign workers—the largest labor force in the region.

ALICO's sales training emphasizes the identification of client needs and the effectiveness of laptop computers for making sales presentations. Some of the more popular training programs were developed in the UK and then modified to fit cultural, language, and currency differences in other countries.

ALICO's plan includes sales incentive contests, service awards, and agent participation in educational conferences. Agents compete for Caribbean cruises, trips to the Olympic Games, and a coveted place in a headquarters showcase called the Gallery of Stars.

According to the company's former president, "The key to building a profitable field force away from home is to remember that results are in direct proportion to the effort of the development."

Sources: Richard R. Collins, "Taking Your Act on the Road," *LIMRA's Marketfacts*, September–October 1991, pp. 86–88; and William Glasgall, "Mr. Risk," *Business Week*, December 7, 1992, pp. 104–9.

The ALICO example illustrates several points of interest for this chapter. For example, success in personal selling and sales management depends on selecting and hiring the right people for the tasks—and an *entrepreneurial perspective* is often a key. In Japan, ALICO rejected the traditional practice of recruiting part-time salespeople and ultimately built a highly successful full-time salesforce. A successful sales organization, however, cannot rely entirely on the talents of salespeople to reach its goals. ALICO management supports its salespeople through training, compensation, and recognition programs.

The development of a sound sales strategy is essential for success also, as illustrated by ALICO's practice of reaching the Persian Gulf labor market through third-country sales agents. Further, ALICO's practice of focusing on client needs is another key to its success.

In this chapter, we explore another element of the marketing communications mix, **personal selling**—the face-to-face interaction between a seller and a buyer for the purpose of satisfying buyer needs to the benefit of both.

This chapter describes the roles of professional salespeople and illustrates various types of sales jobs. We look at the key personal selling activities, especially the way salespeople work with customers to establish mutually beneficial business relationships.

The remainder of the chapter deals with sales management. In simple terms, **sales management** provides leadership and supervision of an organization's personal selling function. Besides managing sales personnel, sales managers develop and implement sales strategy. As in other areas of marketing, personal selling and sales management roles are being redefined to meet the challenges of today's competitive, customer-driven marketplace.

We also discuss ethical issues in personal selling and sales management. Salespeople are among the most visible representatives of an organization's marketing effort, and they operate under considerable pressure to generate sales revenue. Because of these factors, it is extremely important for salespeople and sales managers to be aware of their ethical and legal responsibilities.

The multiple roles of salespeople

Salespeople fulfill multiple roles that contribute to the overall success of a business. We look at these roles in two ways: as contributions to the marketing effort, and as functional roles, or the different types of personal selling jobs.

Contributions of personal selling to marketing

Personal selling contributes to a firm's marketing efforts by producing sales revenue, meeting buyer expectations, and providing marketplace information. The key to successful marketing lies in understanding customer requirements, and then matching a firm's offerings to those requirements. Because salespeople are often the most direct link between a firm and its customers, they can heavily influence whether or not the firm succeeds.

Producing sales revenue

Salespeople make perhaps their most important contribution to the marketing function as revenue producers. Businesses scrambling for survival in a highly competitive world have become more profit-oriented in recent years. To produce an adequate bottom-line profit, it is imperative to achieve a suitable top-line, or sales revenue, figure. And salespeople are on the front line, supported of

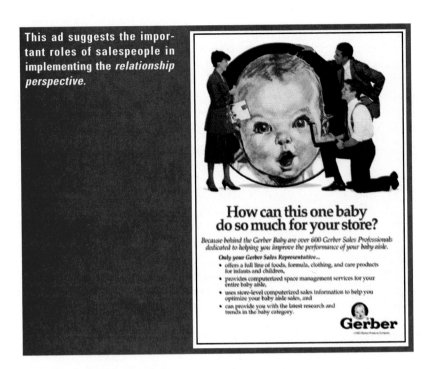

How can this one baby do so much for your store?

Because behind the Gerber Baby are over 600 Gerber Sales Professionals dedicated to helping you improve the performance of your baby aisle.

Only your Gerber Sales Representative...
- offers a full line of foods, formula, clothing, and care products for infants and children,
- provides computerized space management services for your entire baby aisle,
- uses store-level computerized sales information to help you optimize your baby aisle sales, and
- can provide you with the latest research and trends in the baby category.

Gerber

course by marketing research, product development, distribution, and other areas of the business. Sales personnel, along with management, are the prime bearers of the burden of contributing to profit by producing revenue.

Meeting buyer expectations

To succeed in a competitive marketplace, salespeople must—at a minimum—meet buyer expectations. Salespeople are at the heart of the *relationship perspective.* There is no question that the recent tough economic environment has given buyers more clout in dealing with salespeople. According to the National Association of Purchasing Managers, buyers are less likely to tolerate salespeople who waste their time with poorly prepared sales presentations or who will not address their concerns.[1] Dennis Ferguson, a buyer for California-based Rayley's supermarkets, advises salespeople: "I'm busier than ever. Don't tell me what I already know. Tell me why and how your product . . . will disappear off the shelf."[2]

Exhibit 20.1 presents a number of dos and don'ts for salespeople. As suggested by the exhibit, many buyers today take a no-nonsense attitude when dealing with salespeople. They expect straightforward, honest communication. In short, they expect salespeople to live up to high professional standards.

Providing marketplace information

Because personal selling involves face-to-face interaction with the buyer, salespeople can get immediate feedback from customers. Just as marketplace feedback can help in a firm's development of future products and promotional programs, direct customer feedback adds value to the personal selling function. Feedback to the company can include information on competition and analysis of existing and potential customers and markets, which is useful in sales forecasting.

Exhibit 20.1   **What buyers expect from salespeople**

DOs	DON'Ts
• Know your product & its competition better than the buyer. • Be a tough, but open, negotiator. • Have the backing of your company to make strategic partnerships. • Understand the customer's future plans & offer ideas about how your company can help further them. • Be willing to change your processes & products. • Offer something unique—a technological change, a new way of delivering, or a large price concession. • Get to know all the people interested in the product, from purchasing managers to engineers. • Keep on top of potential product problems. • Be able to explain how your company plans to improve the quality & reliability of its products.	• Use industry buzzwords without knowing what you're talking about. • Portray your company as quality-conscious if it's not. • Focus exclusively on short-term sales goals. • Talk about strategic alliances without having the support of your company. • Say, "We want your business, and we'll make it up later." • Try to persuade purchasers to buy something that doesn't meet their needs. • Simply talk pricing. • Give a canned presentation. • Come without ideas. • Knock the competition. • Fly by the seat of your pants. • Offer product today that you're not likely to have tomorrow. • Roll over dead in negotiations.

New technologies continue to improve the efficiency and effectiveness of sales rep feedback to the company. For example, a study of 185 companies with over 10,000 salespeople reports that approximately one-third of the companies used electronic mail (an integrated computer-telephone system) to allow better communications with the salesforce.[3]

The benefits of electronic mail and other feedback-enhancing technologies are expressed by Ray Garacino, an executive with Robert Mondavi, a California winery:

The fact that our reps can call in any time eliminates problems with time zone differences. For example, we needed information from one of our reps in Japan. It was 9 AM Pacific time and 2 AM in Japan. But with voice mail we were able to leave a message regarding the information we wanted and to retrieve his response from the system the following day. It actually expands the hours of the workday.[4]

Job roles of salespeople

Although all personal selling involves face-to-face interactions with customers, there are distinct differences in the nature of these interactions. Salespeople's contributions to the overall company effort may be made in a variety of job roles. Exhibit 20.2 classifies personal selling jobs into two major categories: business-to-business and direct-to-consumer.

Business-to-business sales

Business-to-business selling involves the sale of products and services that are resold by the customer; used as part of the customer's manufacturing process; or used to facilitate the operation of the customer's business. Business selling involves three major types of salespeople: sales support, new business, and existing business.

Sales support salespeople are not directly involved in concluding customer purchases. Rather, they support the personal selling function by promoting a product or providing technical support. Sales support salespeople work in

Professional selling often involves the use of the latest portable communications equipment, an example of the *technological perspective.*

coordination with other salespeople who actually solicit customer purchases, and their activities can be modified to meet the needs of individual customers.

One primary type of sales support job is that of the *missionary.* Missionary salespeople, like religious missionaries, work at the grassroots level to spread the "gospel," that is, help promote their company's products. In this instance, the grassroots level means with product users or with a channel intermediary such as a retail store. Missionaries are a particularly important element of the *execution perspective* in the grocery and pharmaceutical markets. Broker organizations often use sales support personnel to visit individual grocery stores, assisting in merchandising and providing point-of-purchase sales information, thereby providing support to build sales volume for the broker's products.

In the pharmaceutical industry, highly specialized missionaries, or *detailers,* work for most major drug firms. Detailers call on medical professionals and provide them with technical information and product samples to encourage doctors to write prescriptions for the company's drugs.

Exhibit 20.2	Types of personal selling jobs

Business-to-business	
Sales support:	Promote the product or provide technical service. Includes missionaries & detailers.
New business:	Focus on sales growth by selling new products or new customers. Some salespeople are trade show specialists & some work in the field (out of the office).
Existing business:	Maintain & enhance relationships with an established customer base. Includes salespeople who follow an established route, writing up routine orders.
Direct-to-consumer	
	Represent the seller in transactions with ultimate consumers. Includes retail salespeople & representatives of direct selling firms & most real estate & financial services.

This Colgate sales support rep in Brazil explains antiplaque benefits to a dentist, depicting *global, relationship,* and *execution perspectives.*

An illustration of the *technological perspective,* this sales rep works with hospitals to ensure a smooth transition to US Surgical's suture product line.

Technical support salespeople are an element of the sales support function. They have expertise in areas such as design and installation of complex equipment and may provide specialized training to customer employees. Technical support salespeople are especially effective in sales teams formed to address customer needs. For example, the shipping and weighing division of Pitney Bowes sells sophisticated computerized systems that weigh, rate, and track packages for customers like Federal Express and UPS. The Pitney Bowes sales team includes a sales rep and two sales support personnel—a shipping expert and a sales engineer.[5]

Members of the salesforce who concentrate on selling new products or selling to new customers are called **new-business salespeople.** These people are extremely important to companies focusing on sales growth. Suppose a newly established franchising firm depends on the sale of new franchises to achieve its growth objectives. Salespeople representing the franchising company may then travel the country in search of new franchisees.

Many salespeople are assigned to work with established customers to produce a steady stream of sales revenue. **Existing-business salespeople,** sometimes called *order takers,* include wholesaler reps who follow an established route, writing up fairly routine orders from their customers.

Business-to-business salespeople often represent some combination of the sales support, new-business, and existing-business roles. For example, salespeople from General Mills serve all three functions. They seek new business when new grocery retailers enter the market or when General Mills introduces a new product; they work with existing grocery chains and co-ops to maximize sales of existing and new products; and they provide sales support as they visit individual grocery stores to maximize the General Mills presence at the point of sale.

Direct-to-consumer sales

Direct-to-consumer salespeople sell to individuals who personally use the products and services. This category includes over 4.5 million retail salespeople and

Exhibit 20.3 | **The sales process: A relationship approach**

Salesperson attributes
• Customer-oriented
• Honest
• Dependable
• Competent
• Likable

Selling strategy
• Sales territory
• Each customer
• Each sales call

Initiating customer relationships
• Prospecting
• Precall planning
• Approaching the customer

Developing customer relationships
• Sales presentation delivery
• Gaining customer commitment

Enhancing customer relationships

over a million others who sell residential real estate and financial securities to ultimate consumers. Several additional million direct-to-consumer salespeople represent firms such as Mary Kay, Tupperware, Nu-Skin, Lands' End, and other direct selling companies.

The sales process: A relationship approach

Whatever their role, salespeople try to maximize their effectiveness in the **sales process**, which involves initiating, developing, and enhancing long-term, mutually satisfying relationships with customers. This view of selling—called **relationship selling**—is a departure from the old approach that focused more on a salesperson's ability to make a compelling, and often manipulative, sales presentation than on customer needs. Exhibit 20.3 describes its components.

EXECUTIVE ROUNDTABLE COMMENT | Dave Moore, vice president of sales for Ruddell and Associates, Inc., a manufacturers' representatives firm in San Francisco, comments on relationship selling:

Going to the marketplace without a customer-oriented attitude is like playing in the NFL without a helmet—mortal injury is a distinct possibility. My customers are feeling the heat to improve their profitability, and they have a simple way of looking at salespeople—"help me make money and improve my business or I really don't have time for you. Have a nice day."

Exhibiting trust-building attributes

To succeed in relationship selling, salespeople must have certain attributes. Although specific attributes vary depending on the sales context, the ability to build trust is basic. Research has shown that five attributes help to build relationships with customers. Salespeople must be customer-oriented, honest, dependable, competent, and likable.[6] Teresa McBride, head of a consulting firm that is the nation's fastest-growing Hispanic-owned business, says the smartest sales policy is one based on honesty. By following a trust-based sales strategy, the 31-year-old McBride doubled sales revenue to Fortune 500 clients in a single year.[7]

Sales rep Merideth Melin-Lock of the *Duluth News-Tribune* developed a selling strategy of offering her assistance in creating high-quality color ads for local auto dealers such as Mark Johnson, owner of Sonju Motors. The strategy resulted in increased advertising for the newspaper, an example of the *execution perspective*.

Developing a selling strategy

It is not enough for salespeople to exhibit the right attributes. Consistent with an *execution perspective,* they must also develop a selling strategy, an overall plan for a course of action. As part of integrated marketing communications programs, selling strategies should be developed at three levels: sales territory, customer, and individual sales call.

A sales territory, usually defined geographically, consists of specific customers assigned to a specific salesperson. Salespeople should have an overall territory strategy focusing on specific customer needs they can satisfy. The territory strategy of an advertising sales rep for *Sports Illustrated,* for example, might be to provide high-quality, cost-effective print advertising to those who wish to reach an active, upscale audience.

Selling strategy should next be developed for each customer within a given sales territory. The *Sports Illustrated* salesperson might focus on the manufacturer of Prince tennis racquets and develop an advertising plan to coincide with tennis Grand Slam events: the Australian Open, the French Open, Wimbledon, and the US Open. The salesperson might develop entirely different sales strategies for other tennis racquet manufacturers, depending on the needs of the customer.

Finally, each sales call, or every meeting with the customer, should be guided by a strategy compatible with customer needs. By developing a specific plan of action for each sales call, the salesperson capitalizes on a major advantage of personal selling as a marketing communications tool. The *Sports Illustrated* salesperson, for example, would probably have to meet with Prince executives individually and in groups, along with ad agency personnel several times to gain a commitment for the Grand Slam advertising program.

Initiating customer relationships

Exhibit 20.3 breaks initiating customer relationships into three primary activities: prospecting, precall planning, and approaching the customer. These activities, like the other parts of the sales process, are highly interrelated. They are not necessarily separately distinguishable actions.

Prospecting

Prospecting is defined as the seller's search for and identification of qualified buyers. Potential prospects come from a variety of sources, including existing

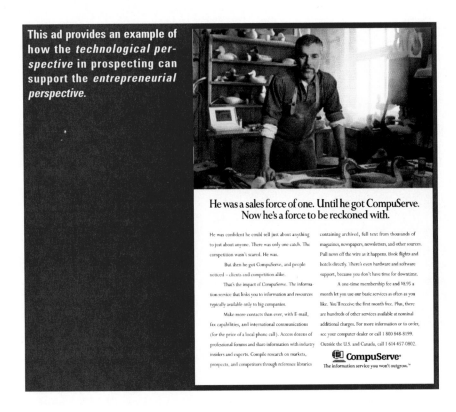

This ad provides an example of how the *technological perspective* in prospecting can support the *entrepreneurial perspective.*

customers, personal contacts, directories, computerized databases, trade publications, and trade shows. Prospects may respond to advertising by placing a telephone call or writing for more information. Such responses, called *inquiries,* are often assigned to salespeople for follow-up.

A qualified buyer must be reasonably accessible to the seller, able to afford the purchase, and at least willing to consider making it. To define qualified prospects, salespeople or companies may establish additional criteria involving elements such as geographical proximity, marketplace function (sales only to wholesalers, for example), or minimum sales-volume levels.

Precall planning

In **precall planning,** the salesperson focuses on learning more about the customer's situation, a crucial task for implementing the *relationship perspective.* Salespeople might visit the prospect's place of business to learn more about their needs. Bell-South, a major telecommunications company headquartered in Atlanta, instructs its salespeople to follow up a "qualifying" call with an information-gathering meeting with the prospect. After the proper information is gathered, the BellSouth account rep plans a sales presentation to be delivered at a later date.

A sales rep must consider a multitude of factors in planning a specific sales presentation. A good idea is to formulate a measurable *sales call objective* to guide the planning process. This should specify the desired customer action resulting from the call; for instance, "the customer will place an order of 400 units for immediate shipment."

Planning involves selecting a format for the sales presentation. In most cases, a two-way dialog between the buyer and the seller may be facilitated by an *organized sales presentation,* a mental or written outline developed by the salesperson. The outline should be flexible enough to allow **adaptive selling;** that is, the salesperson must be able to adjust her or his behavior to respond appropriately to the situation and to address the issues that are most important to the customer.[8]

Interactive electronic media

*I*nteractive electronic media (IEM) make it possible to produce diskette-based sales aids for personal and laptop computers. These computerized tools can greatly improve sales presentation effectiveness. Dun's Marketing Services, a subsidiary of Dun & Bradstreet, turned to an IEM system when seeking a dramatic way to illustrate how customers could use its BusinessLine mailing lists for a variety of marketing functions, including market analysis and promotional planning.

The firm developed an electronic brochure that uses animation to illustrate BusinessLine use. The customer and the salesperson have access to a topic "hotkey" on the computer, which allows questions to be answered immediately. A busy customer learns about topics of interest, rather than all the details about BusinessLine's many applications.

The graphics and animation capabilities of Dun's IEM system, according to product manager Patricia Saydah, allow the "entire sales team to deliver a sales presentation on this technically complex product and prequalify prospects for a live demonstration."

Source: David Furham, "Interactive Electronic Media," *Sales & Marketing Management*, January 1991, pp. 44–47.

A format at the other extreme from adaptive selling is a *canned sales presentation*. In effect, this is a fully scripted presentation that the sales rep memorizes; it could even be an automated presentation using audiovisual media. Although generally ineffective in business-to-business personal selling, canned presentations have worked well in consumer settings such as the sale of encyclopedias to families. Although they may be complete and logical, the relative inflexibility of canned presentations limits their usefulness.

Word processing supported by graphics facilitates another presentation format, the *written sales proposal*. Long used in major sales, written sales proposals can now easily be tailored to individual customers with diverse needs. Sales proposals are usually accompanied by face-to-face meetings between the buying and selling parties to define product specifications and negotiate details.

During precall planning, salespeople also decide how to use sales tools such as brochures, audiovisual support material, and computer technology. As an example, Dun's Marketing Services, a subsidiary of Dun & Bradstreet, greatly improved the effectiveness of its sales presentations by using a computer to demonstrate how its BusinessLine product works. This application is explained in **The Technological Edge: Interactive Electronic Media.**

Precall planning requires a salesperson to think about communicating to customers how various product or service features translate into explicit benefits. A **feature** is merely a statement of fact about some aspect of a product or service. A **benefit** describes what the feature can do for the customer. For example, one feature of a Mitsubishi portable fax machine is a built-in speakerphone. The benefit of the speakerphone is that it allows hands-free conversation. Effective salespeople communicate more about benefits than features, focusing on benefits of particular interest to each customer.

Approaching the customer

The final phase of initiating the relationship is approaching the customer. This involves arranging the sales call, usually by making an appointment, and extends into the first sales call when introductions are made and the salesperson attempts to develop the basis for further sales activity. Common courtesy and

The Pacific Rim on a shoestring

*F*or small companies, the task of selling overseas can be somewhat daunting. Problems with language and cultural differences, customs restrictions, and unexpected tariffs are just a few of the difficulties associated with selling in foreign markets. Indiana-based Electronic Liquid Fillers (ELF), a $12 million packaging equipment company, views a foreign country as "just another state."

ELF sales manager Jeff Ake made a seven-week trip to Pacific Rim countries, such as Taiwan, the Philippines, and New Zealand, where he contacted 90 potential buyers and sellers for his products. The trip was well worth his costs, which ran $19,000.

Ake used a fax machine to contact 400 prospects before planning his trip. Approximately 100 prospects responded, and Ake sent each a letter seeking an appointment and requesting information about their business. That allowed Ake to plan his sales calls and set priorities for scheduling purposes. As he traveled in various countries, his Indiana office worked as an advance team, faxing the prospects to reconfirm and set up appointments. Ake gained over $2 million in new sales, clearly showing that global selling is not limited to large companies.

Source: "Selling Overseas: The Pacific Rim on a Shoestring," *Inc.*, June 1991, pp. 122–23. Reprinted with permission, *Inc.* magazine. Copyright 1991 by Goldhirsh Group, Inc., 38 Commercial Wharf, Boston, MA 02110.

business etiquette can help make a good initial impression. Improper behavior, on the other hand, can diminish the salesperson's opportunity to proceed in the sales process. Examples of behaviors to avoid are shown in Exhibit 20.4. Avoidance of these behaviors is part of the *ethical* and *relationship perspectives.*

The initiation of relationships with buyers in foreign countries is important in many firms, both large and small, to achieve sales growth. An example of a small US company's success in developing customer relationships in the Pacific Rim is summarized in **The Entrepreneurial Spirit: The Pacific Rim on a Shoestring.**

Developing customer relationships

After successfully approaching the customer, the salesperson can begin to develop the customer relationship. To do this, he or she must deliver an effective sales presentation or, more likely, multiple sales presentations. The relationship is established when the customer makes a commitment to take an action such as making a purchase.

Exhibit 20.4   **Approaching the customer: Violations of ethics and etiquette**

A survey of 250 secretaries, administrative assistants, & other "gatekeepers" responsible for scheduling appointments for visiting salespeople revealed these violations of sales etiquette and sales ethics.

• Arriving unannounced to make a sales call.
• Pretending to know the decision maker.
• Treating secretaries disrespectfully.
• Being reluctant to state the purpose of the proposed visit.
• Arriving late for appointments.
• Being overly persistent in attempts to get an appointment.
• Wasting time with unnecessary conversation.
• Failing to cancel appointments that cannot be met.

Exhibit 20.5   **Questioning and listening in sales**

- Remember that you cannot possibly suggest solutions for your clients if you have not listened to what they have said.
- When you are a good listener, you run less chance of dominating the conversation and losing the client's attention.
- You will always learn something valuable from listening. In building customer relationships, this learning process never stops.
- Listening provides feedback on how your sales presentation is going. React to what the prospect is telling you. Clarify the prospect's message when necessary.
- Plan and organize your presentation so you know which questions to ask. Make your questions clear and concise to avoid confusing the client.
- During the presentation, take notes to ensure appropriate follow-up activities, or to plan for the next call.

Sales presentation delivery

To make a successful sales presentation, the salesperson must achieve **source credibility**—that is, the customer must perceive its needs being satisfied by the combination of the salesperson, the product or service, and the salesperson's company. The salesperson's personal characteristics such as dress, appearance, and manner may be important in achieving source credibility.

Certain sales techniques can also help achieve source credibility. Prospect-oriented questioning and active listening, as illustrated in Exhibit 20.5, is important.[9] The salesperson should be careful not to overstate any claims about the product or service and should be prepared to substantiate any that are made. Using third-party evidence such as letters from satisfied customers, called *testimonials,* can enhance source credibility. Finally, pointing out guarantees and warranties that reduce the buyer's risk can assist in establishing source credibility.

During the sales presentation, the sales rep should expect to resolve buyer concerns before the customer makes a commitment to buy. Buyer concerns, called *objections,* come in many forms ("Your price is too high"; "I don't like the color"; "I am happy with my current supplier") and must be dealt with successfully to make a sale. Objections are a form of *sales resistance,* which also includes unspoken customer concerns. To the extent possible, the salesperson should anticipate these concerns and formulate appropriate customer-oriented responses prior to the sales presentation. Salespeople must understand that questions and concerns are part of the buyer's attempt to make a sound purchase decision; addressing these concerns is an integral element in the sales process.

Many buyer concerns arise when a sales rep has not taken enough time to qualify a buyer and thus calls on a marginal prospect—perhaps one who cannot afford the product or will derive only limited benefits from a purchase. Under any set of circumstances, salespeople should treat buyer questions with patience and respect. Exhibit 20.6 details some ideas on how to deal with customers' unreasonable concerns and objections.

Gaining customer commitment

In most cases, a buyer can choose from among a number of potential sellers—hence, sales reps are responsible for gaining customer commitment. This remains true even when the seller is the only available alternative, for a customer may elect to make no purchase at all.

Exhibit 20.6   **Dealing with unreasonable customer concerns and objections**

When a customer lodges a completely unjustified objection, one that is knowingly untrue or unreasonable, salespeople can follow these guidelines for responding.

- Allow customers to retain their dignity. State your position politely.

- Do not argue with a customer. Winning an argument can have detrimental effects on the relationship.

- Appeal to the customer's sense of fair play. Tell the customer you want to do what is right, and try to reach agreement on a course of action to be taken.

- Stand firm, so long as your position is based on facts.

- Do not use company policy as a reason for your position. This tends to invite criticism of the policy.

- If absolutely necessary, be prepared to say no to an unreasonable demand. Agreeing to an unreasonable demand can open the door for more of the same, which will ultimately endanger or ruin the relationship.

A successful relationship between a buyer and a seller requires a firm commitment from both parties. Essentially, customer commitment involves an economic transaction between the buyer and the seller (customer buys when salesperson "closes" a sale), or an agreement between the two parties that moves them toward such a transaction. Some customer commitments take the form of a purchase order. Other examples are agreeing to continue sales negotiations, signing a long-term distribution contract, or accepting the seller's suggestion to maintain specified inventory levels to meet local demand.

To gain a commitment, a professional salesperson is willing to spend the time necessary to give the customer all the pertinent information. Further, professional salespeople understand that when buyers do not want to make a commitment, it is because they see a commitment as simply not in their best interest at that time.

Relationship-oriented salespeople must walk a fine line between being persuasive and being overly persistent or pushy in an attempt to gain commitment. Buyers do not like being pressured into making decisions they feel are premature, and salespeople must realize that decisions made under pressure are likely to create postpurchase doubts. This can jeopardize the relationship and even lead to its termination.

EXECUTIVE ROUNDTABLE COMMENT | **Claudia Bowers, executive vice president of TRC Industries, Inc., reflects on how risk affects commitment:**

In love, war, and business, nobody wants to be a loser. When customers are not quite ready to commit to your proposition, it's because they perceive more risk than benefit. They see some chance of being a loser. If that's the case, can you blame them for not committing their dollars—or maybe their job security—to you? Good buyers are risk-averse, and it's your job to show them how your proposition offers benefits well beyond any risk factors.

Enhancing customer relationships

The final phase of the sales process shown in Exhibit 20.3 is enhancing customer relationships. The purpose of this step is to ensure that customer expectations are met or exceeded, so that an ongoing mutually satisfying relationship between the buyer and seller may continue. This stage involves postsale follow-up activities such as entering and expediting customer orders, providing training for the customer's employees, assisting in merchandising and installation activities, and solving customer problems.

Salespeople can enhance the relationship by continuing to provide timely information, alerting the customer to forthcoming product improvements, monitoring customer satisfaction and making improvements as necessary, showing

During a sales training session, Astra/Merck Group Pharmaceutical Specialists discuss how they can most effectively respond to customer needs in the changing health care environment.

the customer additional ways to use the product, and acting as a consultant to the prospect's business. It is not unusual for salespeople to become confidants of customers, offering opinions when asked on a wide range of topics, some of which are unrelated to the sales offering.

Salespeople should seek feedback from customers, rather than wait for problems to surface. Questions such as "How are we doing as your supplier?" are important, as well as follow-up action to continually build value for the customer. As part of the *quality/value perspective,* salespeople must never take existing customers' business for granted. The added value to customers can be reinforced through periodic business reviews, where salespeople and perhaps their management meet with customers to analyze sales and profit performance and identify areas for future emphasis.

Sales management activities

Sales managers must move their salesforces toward the ideal. Typically, successful sales managers were outstanding salespeople before being promoted. They usually continue some form of personal selling after becoming managers, perhaps selling to their own set of customers, accompanying salespeople on sales calls, or serving as a member of a selling team. Exhibit 20.7 presents management activities, including defining the strategic role of the sales function, designing the sales organization, developing and directing the salesforce, and determining effectiveness and performance.

These activities require more of sales managers than is expected of salespeople. While salespeople concentrate mainly on relationships with customers, sales managers must work well with customers, salespeople, and many other people in the company to do a good job.

Defining the strategic role of the sales function

To be successful, the sales function must develop an appropriate relationship strategy and a proper sales channel strategy. These must be consistent with overall corporate, marketing, and business-unit strategies to enact the *execution perspective.* Further, the strategic role of the sales function is not constant; it changes with the marketplace.

Exhibit 20.7	Key sales management activities

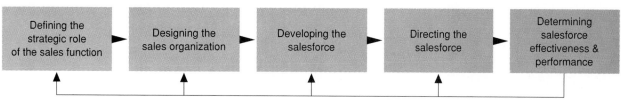

Defining the strategic role of the sales function ▶ Designing the sales organization ▶ Developing the salesforce ▶ Directing the salesforce ▶ Determining salesforce effectiveness & performance

Developing a relationship strategy

We have said that relationship selling is a good description for today's sales process. A **relationship strategy** provides a framework for managing dealings with customers. Exhibit 20.8 specifies three types of strategies for relationship selling: counselor, supplier, or systems designer. All three are examples of the *relationship perspective*.

The **counselor strategy** requires the sales team to have sufficient knowledge to act as an advisor to the customer. Merrill Lynch uses this counselor strategy with its "wrap account" program. A wrap account matches an investor with an individual money manager, and a broker acts as an intermediary between the investor and the money manager. By teaming a broker with a money manager, Merrill Lynch is trying to provide superior service and high-quality information to the client.[10]

The **supplier strategy** may be appropriate when customers know what they want to buy but value some sales assistance. The supplier strategy requires that the salesperson make regularly scheduled sales calls to inform the customer about new products and promotional programs, coordinate order entry, and solve any problems that may arise. Major companies such as PepsiCo, Procter & Gamble, and Beecham Products use supplier strategies in selling to chain stores such as Kroger, Wal-Mart, and Walgreen's.

Exhibit 20.8	Relationship selling strategies

Type of relationship	Customer	Sales team
Counselor	• Knows general objective or desired condition but doesn't know how to implement a solution. • Places high value on personalized attention & easy access to the salesperson.	• Understands the customer's desired goals & objectives. • Has extensive expertise in various solutions to customer's problems & objectives. • Keeps solutions matched to changing needs & goals of customers in a dynamic environment.
Supplier	• Knows the objective he/she wants to attain. • Knows what type of product/service will be needed to achieve objective. • Needs assistance in procuring specific product or service.	• Secures specific brands of goods & services the customer has indicated are needed. • Solves any logistical problems that occur such as shipping, billing, or replacing damaged goods. • Keeps buyer informed of new offerings & their availability.
Systems designer	• Does not see ways to perform an activity or function in a more efficient way. • Expects total solution to a problem once it has been established that a better approach exists.	• Conceptualizes a better system for performing a function the customer is now performing. • Implements the new system in the customer's environment. • Upgrades the system to optimize its efficiency, when necessary.

Emery Worldwide, a Consolidated Freightways company, uses a systems-designer strategy to adapt to each customer's shipping needs, an example of the *relationship perspective.*

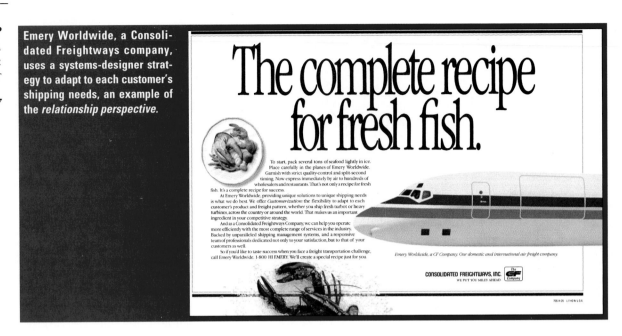

Sales managers using a **systems-designer strategy** expect their salespeople to determine solutions to the customer's problems or to visualize opportunities to enhance the customer's business through new or modified business systems. This strategy requires knowledgeable salespeople who can conceptualize, implement, and upgrade customer systems. AT&T, for example, uses this selling strategy to reach the market for its office systems products.

Developing a customer contact strategy

The **customer contact strategy** (sometimes called *sales channel strategy*), addresses how the company initiates and maintains contact with customers. It may involve the use of a company field salesforce, telemarketing, independent sales reps, distributors, or trade shows.[11] Customer contact strategy should ensure that customers receive the necessary attention from the salesforce. Consistent with the *productivity perspective,* the contact strategy must be both effective (get the job done) and efficient (at a reasonable cost).

Since NAFTA took effect in early 1994, many US, Mexican, and Canadian companies have implemented new sales channel strategies to reach North American markets more efficiently and effectively. Many smaller companies, for example, followed the lead of Xerox and Microsoft. These two giants decided to sell through extensive distributor networks in Mexico, rather than hiring company salesforces.[12]

A customer contact alternative receiving more attention in today's era of relationship selling is **team selling.** With this option, a company assigns accounts to sales teams of specialists according to the customer's purchase-information needs. Team selling is not new to industry leaders such as IBM, Baxter Healthcare, Stanley Tool, Dial Corporation, or Digital Equipment Corporation. And Procter & Gamble assigns customer-account teams to specific wholesalers and retailers, a method first implemented with Wal-Mart.[13]

Some companies use team selling to give special sales attention to key customers, or *major accounts*. Companies design such programs for high-potential customers in recognition of the importance of the account. They often offer customized products and services, purchase rebate incentives, and streamlined communications procedures.

The *relationship perspective* is typified in team selling. Zurich-American uses a team approach to sell liability insurance to health care providers.

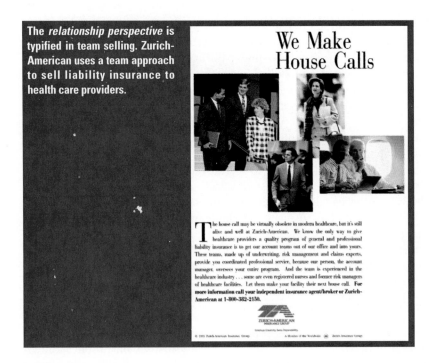

We Make House Calls

The house call may be virtually obsolete in modern healthcare, but it's still alive and well at Zurich-American. We know the only way to give healthcare providers a quality program of general and professional liability insurance is to get our account teams out of our office and into yours. These teams, made up of underwriting, risk management and claims experts, provide you coordinated professional service, because one person, the account manager, oversees your entire program. And the team is experienced in the healthcare industry . . . some are even registered nurses and former risk managers of healthcare facilities. Let them make your facility their next house call. **For more information call your independent insurance agent/broker or Zurich-American at 1-800-382-2150.**

Designing the sales organization

To implement a successful selling strategy, the company must design an appropriate sales organization and adjust it according to subsequent strategic changes. Some key questions to address in designing the sales organization include:

- Should the salesforce be generalists (salespeople who sell the entire product line) or specialists?

- If specialists are used, should they be product specialists, market or customer specialists, or functional (new-business or existing-business) specialists?

- Should tight control be maintained with a centralized salesforce, or should sales activities and decision making be moved closer to the customer with a decentralized salesforce?

- How much total selling effort is needed to provide adequate sales coverage? How large should the salesforce be?

- How should specific customers and geographic areas be assigned to salespeople to form sales territories?

- How should *salesforce turnover* (the proportion of salespeople who leave their jobs) be factored into sales organization design decisions?

All these decisions are complex, and they may be addressed with any number of analytical tools. Computer algorithms and sophisticated decision models can give some quantitative input. Dictaphone, for example, used a computerized mapping program to realign sales territories when its poorly designed territories caused high salesforce turnover. An example of the *technological* and *productivity perspectives* in action, the reconfiguration reduced salesforce turnover and improved morale and productivity.[14]

Developing the salesforce

There are three main activities in developing the salesforce: recruiting, selecting, and training salespeople.

Recruiting and selecting salespeople

Recruiting is the process of finding prospective job candidates; *selecting* involves choosing the candidates to be hired. Recruiting and selecting salespeople are challenging tasks. According to one survey, over 30 percent of 645 firms reported "some difficulty" or "great difficulty" in recruiting salespeople in the early 1990s. More of these firms expect similar difficulty by 1996. There simply are not enough well-educated and skilled workers. For example, for its salesforce, pharmaceutical firm G. D. Searle recruits registered nurses and pharmacists, of which there are severe shortages in the United States.[15] Approximately 60 percent of all sales reps in the pharmaceutical industry are pharmacy school graduates, but the difficulty of recruiting pharmacists may cause some firms to seek candidates with nonpharmaceutical backgrounds.[16]

Another problem is lack of time to recruit qualified salespeople. In one survey, sales executives said that because of a lack of time, they sometimes rely on "warm body" recruiting—hiring under pressure to fill a vacancy.[17]

Observers predict that to meet the challenges in recruiting and selecting salespeople, companies will hire more part-time and older salespeople and increase efforts to diversify their salesforces ethnically and culturally. The number of women entering sales is also expected to continue to grow.

Training the salesforce

There are two categories of sales training: initial and continual. Newly hired salespeople receive *initial training,* which typically focuses on product knowledge and sales techniques. *Continual training* for all salespeople is becoming more standard as firms attempt to stay current and competitive in an ever-changing environment.

EXECUTIVE ROUNDTABLE COMMENT | **Claudia Bowers, executive vice president of TRC Industries, Inc., believes that continual improvement is absolutely essential for professional selling:**

The sales world is changing so fast that it can almost be scary. But it can be a lot of fun, too, if you can keep up with the changes and every so often, get ahead of the wave. You really don't have much of a choice—to be successful in sales, you had best be completely committed to a lifetime of learning and continual improvement—there's just not a lot of demand for obsolete salespeople.

Sales training is a key for companies interested in continual improvement, an element of the *quality/value perspective.* At Union Pacific, for example, salespeople go through 21 courses over a five-year period to learn to deliver total quality management, including the improvement of customer relationships. The first year focuses on product knowledge and selling skills. The second year concentrates on working effectively in teams. In the third year, salespeople learn how to be team leaders. Then training moves to advanced stages of total quality management. According to Fred Henderson, vice president of sales and marketing, "We had to create a company strategy that was focused on the true requirements of the customer and the marketplace, and then build a training strategy to take it there."[18]

Directing the salesforce

Directing salespeople to meet goals and objectives consumes much of the typical sales manager's time. These activities include motivation, supervision, and leadership of the salesforce.

Motivation

Salesforce motivation involves maximizing the effort salespeople direct toward specific objectives and helping them persist in the face of adversity. Most sales companies offer a variety of financial and nonfinancial rewards in their salesforce motivation programs.

C
H
A
P
T
E
R

2
0

Money remains the most sought-after reward among salespeople, with the opportunity for promotion into management also highly desired.[19] Most companies pay salespeople a combination of salary and incentives. Incentive pay could include commissions, bonuses, or both. About three-fourths of US firms use a combination pay plan; less than 15 percent pay a straight salary; and some 10 percent pay by straight commission.[20]

Incentive pay can have dramatic effects on salesforce motivation. Creative Works, a Northbrook, Illinois, school supply company, established an additional 2 percent bonus on top of the existing 5 percent commission for the addition of new customers. The company also introduced a one dollar per case bonus on the opening order of any new products sold to new or existing accounts. In one year, sales jumped from $700,000 to $3 million and the customer base grew from 80 to 200.[21]

Most companies also use sales contests and formal recognition programs to motivate their salesforces. Such programs may offer exotic travel, merchandise, or high-visibility award ceremonies in addition to money as an incentive.

Supervision and leadership

Supervision of a salesforce deals with direction of day-to-day operations. Computerized **sales automation systems** are one way to assist sales managers in routine supervisory chores such as processing salespeople's call reports, itineraries, and expense reports.

Leadership activities, on the other hand, use more subtle communication to influence salespeople to achieve the company's overall objectives. One leadership function is *coaching,* or providing guidance and feedback on a regular basis to direct salespeople's activities. Another important leadership activity is conducting sales meetings that unite a salesforce in an effort to meet common goals.

The supervision and leadership of salespeople is very much a human endeavor, despite the help of technology. Sales managers routinely deal with human relations problems such as drug and alcohol abuse, sexual harassment,

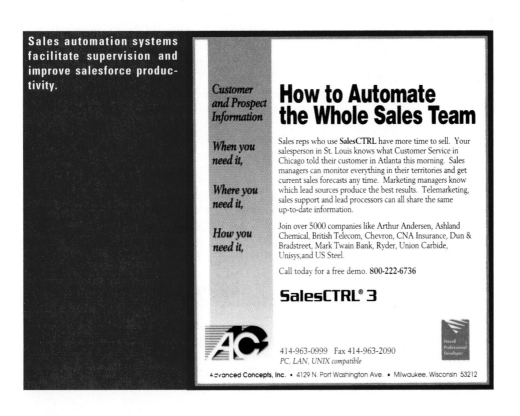

Determining performance and effectiveness

employee job stress, expense account fraud, and any number of other people problems. Salespeople are no different from any other group of employees when it comes to problem areas.

Sales managers must establish standards by which performance and effectiveness are measured, evaluate performance and effectiveness against these standards, and then take appropriate follow-up action. *Salesperson performance* refers to how well individual salespeople meet job expectations. An evaluation of *salesforce effectiveness* is in fact an assessment of the entire sales organization. Factors within and outside the sales organization, such as product quality or competitors, can also influence salesforce effectiveness.

Setting salesforce standards

Standards by which performance and effectiveness are assessed usually relate to quantitative outcomes, or *quotas,* such as total sales volume, gross margin, market share, number of new accounts added, and accounts retained. These quotas typically are based on a forecast developed at least in part by the sales manager.

To carry out the **productivity perspective,** sales managers must also get the job done within a specified budget. Given the high costs of personal selling, achieving objectives within budget constraints is a constant challenge. For example, the median cost per sales call exceeds $200, despite increased efforts to trim sales costs. Travel-related costs, such as lodging and meals, continue to climb, along with salespeople's pay levels.[22]

It is becoming increasingly difficult to raise selling price only because of increasing sales costs. Thus, to maintain favorable sales-expense-to-sales-revenue ratios, most salespeople are asked to sell more each year—whether economic conditions are favorable or not.

Evaluating salesperson performance

To evaluate individual salesperson performance, sales managers may take a behavior-based perspective, an outcome-based perspective, or a combination of the two. A *behavior-based perspective* defines the sales behaviors expected, such as how many sales calls to make or which sales presentation tactics to use. The salesperson is then evaluated on how well he or she executes the behaviors. An *outcome-based perspective* focuses on the results of sales behavior, such as total sales volume. As relationship selling spreads, the behavior-based perspective to evaluate salesperson performance is gaining more acceptance than the outcome-based approach.

Analyzing sales organization effectiveness

Managers may analyze sales, costs, profitability, and productivity to evaluate the effectiveness of the sales organization. They compare figures of one year to those of the previous year to gauge progress. Managers also compare their own salesforce effectiveness to that of competitors, if possible. For example, in the packaged-grocery business, market share data by brand are readily available, and comparisons to key competitors are commonplace.

A simple example of salesforce productivity analysis is shown in Exhibit 20.9. Note that District 2 is tied for the lead with District 4 in total sales volume. Also, the sales per salesperson and expenses per salesperson figures in District 2 compare favorably with the other districts. Yet the number of sales calls made per salesperson is low. This may explain why expenses are low, but it may also suggest that salespeople in District 2 may not be providing adequate contact with their customers.

Exhibit 20.9

Example of a salesforce effectiveness evaluation

	District 1	District 2	District 3	District 4
Sales	$10,000,000	$12,000,000	$10,000,000	$12,000,000
Selling expenses	$ 1,000,000	$ 1,200,000	$ 1,500,000	$ 1,500,000
Sales calls	5,000	4,500	4,500	6,000
Proposals	100	105	120	120
Number of salespeople	10	15	10	15
Sales per salesperson	$ 1,000,000	$ 800,000	$ 1,000,000	$ 800,000
Expenses per salesperson	$ 100,000	$ 80,000	$ 150,000	$ 100,000
Calls per salesperson	500	300	450	400

Numbers, then, do not tell the whole story; but analysis of the numbers can suggest areas worth further investigation by the sales manager. By combining quantitative analysis with personal observation, information from customers, and review with salespeople, sales managers can evaluate the effectiveness of their salesforces.

Ethical and legal issues in personal selling

Because personal selling activities are highly visible, ethical and legal issues are extremely important for salespeople and sales managers. In building trust-based customer relationships, ethical behavior is even more critical. Major professional groups such as Sales and Marketing Executives International, the American Marketing Association, and the Direct Selling Association have adopted strict codes of ethics for salespeople, as have many companies. An example is shown in Exhibit 20.10.

Sales managers must take responsibility for the proper behavior of their salespeople, and they must also lead by example. They must know the laws related to buyer-seller interactions, the gathering of competitive information, and the management of personnel.

Exhibit 20.10

Code of ethics for professional salespeople

As a Certified Professional Salesperson, I pledge to the following people & organizations:

1 The Customer. In all customer relationships, I pledge to:

Maintain honesty & integrity in my relationships with customers & prospective customers.

Accurately represent my product or service in order to place the customer or prospective customer in a position to make a decision consistent with the principle of mutuality of benefit & profit to the buyer & seller.

Keep abreast of all pertinent information that would assist my customers in achieving their goals as they relate to my product(s) or service(s).

2 The Company. In relationships with my employer, co-workers & other parties whom I represent, I will:

Use their resources that are at my disposal for legitimate business purposes only.

Respect & protect proprietary & confidential information entrusted to me by my company.

3 The Competition. Regarding those with whom I compete in the marketplace, I promise:

To obtain competitive information only through legal & ethical methods.

To portray my competitors & their products & services only in a manner that is honest, truthful & that reflects accurate information that can or has been substantiated.

Exhibit 20.11   **Unethical sales behaviors**

Research indicates sales behaviors that are unethical in the eyes of customers:

- Exaggerates the features & benefits of his/her products/services.
- Lies about availability to make a sale.
- Lies about the competition to make a sale.
- Sells products/services people don't need.
- Is interested only in own interests, not the clients'.
- Gives answers when doesn't really know the answers.
- Lies about competitors.
- Falsifies product testimonials.

- Passes the blame for something he/she did onto someone else.
- Poses as a market researcher when conducting telephone sales.
- Misrepresents guarantees/warranties.
- Makes oral promises that are not legally binding,
- Does not offer information about an upcoming sale that will include merchandise the customer is planning to buy.
- Accepts favors from customers so the seller will feel obliged to bend the rules/ policies of the seller's company.
- Sells dangerous or hazardous products.

To be on the safe side, salespeople should be honest in their dealings with customers and be informed of relevant laws governing their business situation. All salespeople are subject to some form of contract law, which regulates transactions. Purchase orders are binding contracts, as are oral commitments made by a salesperson. An extensive review of 50 years of legal cases reveals that salespeople can, by inappropriate oral statements, create undesirable legal obligations for their firms. Problems include creation of unintended warranties, understatement of warning messages, disparagement of competitors' offerings without substantiation, misrepresentation of company offerings, and illegal interference with business relationships.[23]

Exhibit 20.11 reveals some specific sales behaviors deemed unethical by buyers. Salespeople interested in developing lasting relationships with their customers should refrain from these behaviors, for research suggests that buyers will go out of their way to avoid doing business with salespeople they see as unethical.[24]

There are also numerous ethical and legal issues relevant to relationships between sales managers and salespeople. For example, the Civil Rights Act of 1964 prohibits discrimination based on age, race, color, religion, sex, or national origin. The act has implications for recruiting and selecting salespeople and evaluating and rewarding their performance. The Americans with Disabilities Act of 1992 also affects recruiting and other sales management functions, as do guidelines for minimizing sexual harassment issued by the Equal Employment Opportunity Commission.

This is only a brief discussion of the ethical and legal consequences of marketers' actions. Given the pressure on the sales function to generate revenue, it is particularly important for sales managers to know and adhere to the laws of the marketplace and the workplace. They should be models, provide adequate training, and monitor, reinforce, and direct sales personnel. In developing trust-based relationships with customers, marketers should follow these guidelines not just because of laws or because it's the right thing to do—it is also a sound business practice.

C
H
A
P
T
E
R

2
0

Summary

1. *Understand the role and importance of personal selling in the promotion mix.* Personal selling is a valuable part of the promotion mix and the overall marketing effort of many companies. Salespeople fulfill the extremely important role of generating revenue. In today's competitive environment, paying close attention to customer needs and expectations is necessary, and personal selling can help in this endeavor. Salespeople provide crucial marketplace information to their companies, which may further improve the marketing effort.

2. *See how the key steps in personal selling depend on a relationship perspective.* The sales process involves three steps: initiating, developing, and enhancing customer relationships. To initiate customer relationships, salespeople must first locate qualified potential customers through prospecting. They must then plan the initial sales call and the way to approach the customer.

In developing customer relationships, salespeople must be able to deliver effective sales presentations. During a sales call, it is extremely important that the salesperson use questioning and listening skills to attend to all of the customer's requirements and to gain a commitment from the customer.

To enhance relationships with customers, salespeople must be customer-oriented and continue to meet or exceed customer expectations. Relationship selling also requires that salespeople formulate and implement different strategies for different customers and that they minimize wasted time in each sales call.

To be successful in relationship selling, salespeople gain the trust of their customers. To build trust, salespeople should be customer-oriented, honest, dependable, competent, and likable.

3. *Identify the similarities and differences in the job responsibilities of salespeople and sales managers.*

Along with their other job duties, sales managers are usually involved in personal selling to some degree. Using an athletic team analogy, the salespeople are the players, and the sales manager is the coach. The sales manager must do everything necessary to field a competitive sales team year after year, including developing the team strategy. Salespeople concentrate on taking care of their customers; sales managers must work not only with customers, but also with others in the company to ensure success.

4. *Describe the key activities in sales management.* The key job activities of sales managers are defining the strategic role of personal selling, designing the sales organization, developing the salesforce, directing the salesforce, and determining performance and effectiveness. Sales managers must recruit and select salespeople and provide them with sufficient resources to be effective. Most sales managers play an active role in training their salespeople. They must also help motivate salespeople to reach their full potential and evaluate their performance. Sales managers must accomplish all these activities in a rapidly changing environment, which means they may need to adapt sales strategies to remain competitive.

5. *Appreciate important ethical issues faced by salespeople and sales managers.* Salespeople can develop trust with their customers by avoiding a range of unethical sales behaviors. Examples are lying, selling customers products they do not need, withholding information, and selling dangerous products.

Sales managers lead by example. They must not abuse the power of their positions in dealing with their employees. Sales managers must also be prepared to deal with human relations issues such as drug abuse, sexual harassment, and employee job stress. Ignoring such issues would be less than ethical.

Key terms & concepts

personal selling 492
sales management 492
sales support salespeople 494
technical support salespeople 496
new-business salespeople 496
existing-business salespeople 496
direct-to-consumer salespeople 496
sales process 497

relationship selling 497
prospecting 498
precall planning 499
adaptive selling 499
feature 500
benefit 500
source credibility 502

relationship strategy 505
counselor strategy 505
supplier strategy 505
systems-designer strategy 506
customer contact strategy 506
team selling 506
sales automation systems 509

Review & discussion questions

1. Discuss the three major roles salespeople play in the overall marketing effort.

2. How are the roles of sales support salespeople different from those of new-business salespeople?

3. Give several examples of different types of direct-to-consumer salespeople.

4. To practice relationship selling, salespeople must be able to cultivate the trust of their customers. What

attributes should salespeople have to cultivate the trust of their customers?

5. The first step in the sales process is to initiate customer relationships. Discuss the three primary activities during this initial step.

6. Review **The Technological Edge: Interactive Electronic Media.** Do you think the use of IEM technology helps the salesperson develop trust-based relationships with customers? Explain.

7. How important is ethical behavior by salespeople in dealing with customers? Think about trust-building salesperson attributes, and consult Exhibits 20.3 and 20.10 before completing your answer.

8. Consult **The Entrepreneurial Spirit: The Pacific Rim on a Shoestring.** How can small firms compete with larger competitors through personal selling? How would personal selling be implemented differently in a small firm as contrasted with a large Fortune 500 firm?

9. Describe the key responsibilities of sales managers in each of the five activity areas shown in Exhibit 20.7.

10. How are the recruitment and selection of salespeople related to designing the salesforce?

Application exercises

1. Review the unethical sales behaviors in Exhibit 20.11. Can you recall from your own experiences as a consumer examples of any of those behaviors? In those instances, did you eventually come to trust the salesperson? Did you make purchases? What kind of sales behavior could you suggest for salespeople who wish to earn the trust of their customers?

2. When a commitment is not readily forthcoming from a prospect, some salespeople might use a "buy now" method to get the sale, which gives the buyer a good reason to make an immediate purchase. For example, the salesperson might suggest that the buyer can avoid a planned price increase by placing an immediate order. If no such price increase is actually planned, has the salesperson acted unethically? What if the buyer has been promising to place an order for months, but never has, and now seems to be stalling?

3. Visit a retail store with the aim of getting some details about a product you plan to buy at some future date. Evaluate the listening skills of the salesperson you encounter. Is the salesperson a good listener or not? How was the salesperson's credibility affected by his or her listening skills?

Case 20.1   *Saturn: Taking a STEP to equip its salesforce*

In the late 1980s, the American automobile industry was struggling. Consumers were unhappy with product quality, pricing, advertising, and inane industry sales practices. Foreign automakers were continuing to build market share at the expense of domestic manufacturers. In this environment, General Motors departed from tradition and offered a "different kind of car from a different kind of company." The Saturn success story had begun.

By 1993, Saturn had become a force to be reckoned with. Sales were soaring, and GM was eager to transplant Saturn's winning ways to other divisions. Industry analysts cited several reasons for Saturn's rise to prominence: no-haggle pricing, customer-oriented selling, elimination of confusing rebates, and basically, a good car for a reasonable price.

Many competitors followed Saturn's lead with a one-price, no-haggle selling strategy. American automobile manufacturers also improved product quality, and many dealers adopted one-price policies similar to Saturn's. In the face of intensified competition, Saturn's salesforce has helped to sustain the company's edge in the marketplace. A key element in equipping the salesforce is the Saturn Training and Education Partnership, or STEP, a comprehensive program designed to develop job skills.

The STEP program reinforces five key values Saturn wants to instill in all facets of its operations: customer enthusiasm, excellence, teamwork, trust and respect, and constant improvement.

To reinforce these values in sales training, Saturn established the objectives for STEP long before its first dealership opened. Sales managers refined the program with salespeople from dealers who were interested in becoming Saturn dealers, and then with salespeople who had been hired to staff the still-unopened Saturn outlets.

The STEP program requires salespeople to abandon the conventional way of selling cars, which often involves high-pressure manipulative sales techniques. Instead, Saturn's sales philosophy casts the salesperson in a consultative role to build customer enthusiasm, with six key elements: listening to the customer; creating an environment of mutual trust; exceeding customer expectations; creating a "win-win" culture; following up to ensure that customer expectations are met; and constantly improving customer perceptions of quality.

The sales training consists of self-study modules and seminars. The self-study portion, which takes about 11 hours to complete, features learning activities based on short reading assignments and video vignettes. The short assignments can easily be completed one at a time, allowing training to be interspersed with other job activities.

Saturn measures the effectiveness of its training in three ways. For each module, trainees provide a written evaluation of materials, methods, and trainers. Each module is followed by a written test. Sixty days later, trainees are evaluated in a performance check that requires demonstration of the skills developed in training. All indicators point to a successful sales training program.

Questions:

1. Did Saturn face any risks in implementing its STEP program?

2. Would previous sales experience be an asset to a Saturn job candidate? If so, what kind of experience?

3. How would Saturn's recruiting, selection, motivation, and evaluation of sales performance likely differ from that of a high-volume, conventional automobile dealer's sales operation?

Sources: "STEP . . . Training to Integrate the Saturn Difference," *Marketing Journal,* Winter 1993, pp. 1–2; Dorothy Cottrell, Larry Davis, Pat Detrick, and Marty Raymond, "Sales Training and the Saturn Difference," *Training and Development,* December 1992, pp. 38–43; and Andrea Sawyers, "No-Haggle Pricing Hits Full Throttle," *Advertising Age,* March 22, 1992, p. S10.

Case 20.2   *Purolator: An overnight success*

Purolator Courier Limited is the top overnight delivery service company in Canada, with a 45 percent market share. However, things were not always so rosy for the firm; it barely escaped bankruptcy in 1986. The bankruptcy scare was precipitated by Purolator's investment in an inoperable parcel tracking system based in a huge New Jersey warehouse and an ambitious but costly purchase of a new fleet of cargo jets. How did Purolator turn the corner and rise to prominence in Canada? By focusing on the customer and rebuilding its sales organization.

Purolator used two key concepts as cornerstones of its sales strategy. First, the firm concentrates on building partnerships with its customers. Second, it uses a team selling approach to build the partnerships.

One goal of the partnership is to help Purolator's customers provide better service to their customers. The other objective is to define the unique needs of each customer and adapt to those needs. Barbara Leclair, manager of government services, fully understands the importance of defining the needs of each account: "Government accounts don't fit the mode most salespeople are used to. They require a great deal of flexibility from the sales team because each agency has numerous decision makers and operates with a unique set of rules and needs."

To build partnerships, Purolator salespeople follow a carefully planned process. A sales team approaches each prospect to establish contact at multiple levels. For larger national accounts, a minimum of 10 senior-management contacts are required. For example, Purolator's senior vice president of marketing contacts the customer's senior purchasing officer, and similar contacts are made at other levels of the prospect's organization.

Knowing the prospect's organization at different levels allows Purolator to maximize value—defined by the company as the optimum combination of low price and great service. In a highly competitive, price-sensitive market, service has to be good, if not great, to avoid a large number of low-priced competitors.

Purolator also uses technology to deliver better service. The firm offers a fully staffed management information systems group to help customers integrate their systems with the Purolator system. For example, software giant Microsoft became a customer after the Purolator sales team displayed the effectiveness of automatic order entry and shipping over Microsoft's manual order system. By linking the electronic data processing systems of the two companies, Purolator built a partnership.

To implement the team selling approach, Purolator revamped its training and motivation programs. Clear performance expectations are documented in a 12-page manual for salespeople. The manual details specific tasks to be completed during each phase of the sales process, frequently in the company of sales managers, who spend three days a week in the field with salespeople.

Incentives such as vacation trips to resorts are offered to executives, salespeople, sales support staff, and secretaries. This supports the concept of "everybody sells" at Purolator and adds an element of fun and anticipation to the work environment.

In a tough market, Purolator's success story could be tomorrow's tale of woe. If, however, the company continues to take its cues from customers and do its part to build mutually beneficial partnerships, its competitors will have a tough selling job ahead.

Questions:

1. Purolator's team selling has worked well, although such an approach is not appropriate for all situations. Identify some disadvantages of team selling, and specify some situations where it would not be appropriate.

2. Which parts of the sales process are most important if a seller sees itself entering into partnerships with customers?

3. How has Purolator supported its salespeople and reinforced performance expectations?

Sources: Andrea Biesada, "Penny-Wise . . . Pound-Foolish?" *Financial World,* December 1990, pp. 24–27; Malcolm K. Fleschner, II, "Overnight Success," *Personal Selling Power,* October 1992, pp. 54–58; and Andrew Tausz, "Shakeout in Canada's Domestic Marketplace," *Distribution,* April 1991, pp. 42–46.

Direct Marketing Communications

After studying this chapter you should be able to:

1. Understand the objectives of direct marketing communications and describe its distinguishing characteristics.

2. Discuss the factors driving the growth in direct marketing communications.

3. Understand traditional direct marketing communications techniques such as direct mail, direct selling, broadcast and print media, and telemarketing.

4. Recall examples of the use of technology such as electronic media in direct marketing communications.

5. Understand some of the ethical and legal issues facing marketers that use direct marketing communications.

Direct marketing communications: Circling the Pacific Rim

Progressive companies in industries such as automobiles, financial services, cosmetics, computers, publishing, and medical equipment use direct marketing communications to build sales volume around the globe. Their ranks include well-known marketers like American Express, Estée Lauder, L.L. Bean, Nestlé, Citibank, BMW, and Chrysler. One of the hottest areas for direct marketers in recent years has been the Pacific Rim, including a dozen countries from Asia to New Zealand.

Stories of direct marketing communications success in the Pacific Rim abound. American Express, for example, built a cardholder-based mailing list of more than 400,000 people in Asia that annually brings in millions of dollars of extra revenue. Chrysler used direct marketing communications to sell millions of dollars worth of outdated assembly equipment for small motors. L.L. Bean is successfully using a direct-mail catalog campaign to complement its opening of retail stores in Japan.

Leading advertising agencies, including Ogilvy & Mather and J. Walter Thompson, have established direct marketing communications departments specializing in helping clients market throughout the Pacific Rim. These agencies advise clients to concentrate on markets with a large, literate, middle class. Direct marketers are best able to approach markets where credit cards are in use and postal and telecommunications systems are operational. According to J. Walter Thompson, all these characteristics exist in Japan, Singapore, Hong Kong, and Korea. Taiwan, Thailand, and Malaysia have some of the desirable characteristics, while India, Indonesia, and China lag far behind.

Generally, reliable mailing lists are hard to find in Asia, and they are fairly expensive. Postal rates can also be high, as is the case in Hong Kong and Singapore. But labor rates are low in these countries, which leads to lower production costs for mail pieces and may even encourage delivery by courier. Some direct marketers have direct-mail pieces produced in countries with low labor rates and then mail from Malaysia, where postal rates are low.

Some notable failures at direct marketing in Asia (Sears, Reader's Digest, The Sharper Image) remind us that communications must adapt to local cultures and operating conditions to be successful. For example, in most Asian countries, direct-mail offers cannot use a hard-sell approach or impose a time limit. A J. Walter Thompson executive says, "You will insult Asians if they feel pressured to buy a product. It's interesting, because they'll never tell you they're offended, but they'll also never do business with you again."

Sources: Drayton Bird, "Running with the Dragons," *Direct*, June 1993, pp. 46–47; and Aimee Stern, "Spanning the Bridge to the Pacific," *Direct*, April 1992, pp. 31–33.

In Chapter 17, we saw that traditional marketing communications methods, such as mass advertising through broadcast and print media, are giving way to more narrowly targeted means for reaching consumers. Most marketers use more than one way to communicate with their target markets. These multiple means of reaching target markets are sometimes developed into integrated marketing communications (IMC) programs. At the heart of many of these programs lies direct marketing communications. This chapter discusses the role and characteristics of direct marketing communications and examines the reasons for its growth. Direct marketing communications (DMC) methods are discussed, including a variety of interactive media such as mail, video, telephone, salesperson, and computer. The chapter concludes with a discussion of ethical and legal issues in direct marketing communications.

Role of *direct marketing communications*

Direct marketing communications have two primary objectives, both of which fit the *relationship perspective*. The first is to establish relationships by soliciting a direct and immediate response from prospects or customers. Customer response could be a purchase, a request for additional information from the marketer, or a reply that furnishes data related to the customer's desires and interests. The second, and increasingly important, objective of DMC is to maintain and enhance customer relationships—whether those relationships have been established by direct marketing communications or by some other means.

Direct marketing communications techniques are used to reach both individual consumers and businesses. In one survey, for example, 35 percent of the respondents use direct marketing to reach business consumers; 28 percent use it to tap into consumer markets. Thirty-eight percent of the respondents use direct marketing to reach both business customers and ultimate consumers.[1]

Direct marketing can be an important ingredient in the *execution perspective,* especially as part of integrated communications strategies. Avon is one example of a consumer-goods company that uses direct marketing communications as part of a sophisticated IMC program. Avon delivers a series of coordinated messages through a combination of media—telemarketing, response-specific direct mail, more than 400,000 direct salespeople, media advertising, and cable

Avon, shown here in Guangzhou, China, takes a *global perspective,* using direct selling, direct-mail advertising, and telemarketing in its worldwide integrated marketing communications effort.

television. In combination, these marketing communications tools allow Avon to communicate directly with the 3 million consumers in its database. Avon expects to communicate directly with 10 million consumers by 1995.[2]

In the business-to-business area, Kodak uses direct marketing in its imaging division (copiers and desktop publishing). The Kodak strategy blends direct marketing with sales promotion (trade shows) and personal selling to reach business and government buyers at various levels.[3]

Characteristics of direct marketing communications

Several characteristics distinguish direct marketing from other marketing communications methods. First, direct marketing targets a carefully selected audience, as opposed to a mass audience. Second, it typically involves two-way communication; direct responses from customers make it interactive. Finally, direct-response results are quite measurable—marketers can determine what works and what does not.

Customer databases

A key element of direct marketing communications is the use of a list or database of current or potential customers. **Lists** of names and addresses may also provide telephone numbers and data on demographics, lifestyles, brand and media preferences, and consumption patterns.[4] Lists can be developed from customer-transaction records, newspapers, trade show registration, or other sources that identify specific groups of customers or prospects. Rather than compiling its own lists, a company can rent, reproduce, or use a list on a one-time basis.[5]

Lists, often in the form of sophisticated computerized databases, allow direct marketers to focus on a precisely defined target market, as opposed to using mass-market appeals. **Database marketing** has become commonplace (see Exhibit 21.1). According to one survey, 61 percent of the leading advertising agencies said that more than half their clients maintain a customer database for direct marketing purposes.[6] These databases can be quite large. Cahners Direct Marketing Services, for example, manages and sells access to a list of more than 6 million names of corporate decision makers, and consumer databases are often much larger.[7]

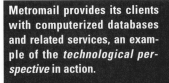

Metromail provides its clients with computerized databases and related services, an example of the *technological perspective* in action.

Exhibit 21.1

Customer database aids communications planning, integration, and execution

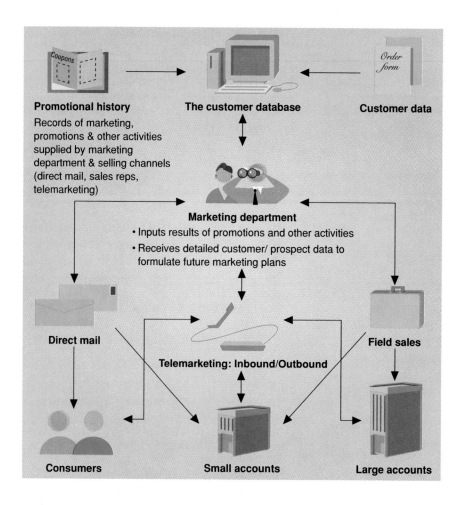

Companies use database information to deliver marketing communications tailored to the unique needs of a target audience. Kimberly-Clark and Procter & Gamble, for example, build databases by collecting names of new mothers from hospitals, doctors, and other sources. Both companies use this information to send coupons for disposable diapers and other baby products to new mothers soon after they come home from the hospital. As the child grows older, the manufacturers send coupons for larger diapers.[8]

SKI Ltd., operators of resorts in Vermont and California, compiled a computerized database of over 2.5 million skiers worldwide. Illustrating the *productivity* and *execution perspectives,* the company "wields this information like a scalpel, dissecting its customer base" for special communications. One particularly successful program targeted 90,000 weekend-only skiers who lived at least three hours away by car. The company offered them discounted midweek lift tickets. As a result, midweek skiing now accounts for half the resort's revenue.[9]

Immediate-response orientation

Direct marketing communications often have deadlines for action and offer special incentives for taking immediate action. An example would be a direct mail piece from a bank saying, "Call now for super-low 7 percent mortgages. Free property survey. Offer expires June 1st." Other marketing communications methods are not typically oriented toward gaining an immediate response from prospects and customers. Publicity, for example, and many forms of advertising are aimed more at achieving results over a period of time. Personal selling seeks a response, but salespeople typically cultivate customers for some time.

Measurable action objectives

Although all marketing communications should try to achieve measurable results, their objectives are generally not as action-specific as those of direct marketing. For instance, an advertising campaign for a new brand may have the goal of achieving brand awareness among 65 percent of its target audience. In DMC, however, marketers usually set much more specific action objectives, such as a purchase or a request for information. Achievement of such objectives can then be measured by calculating the number of purchases or requests for information that result from the campaign.

Action objectives allow the marketer to test several different forms of a direct marketing communication. The marketer can then adjust the message and the medium to achieve optimum results, consistent with the *productivity perspective*. For example, Citicorp tested three direct marketing combinations to see which could do the best job of gaining new accounts while cutting marketing costs. Test one used direct mail and a toll-free number, resulting in a 7 percent increase in the number of customers while cutting costs by 63 percent. When telemarketing was added in test two, 13 percent more customers were gained, and costs were cut 72 percent. Finally, print advertising was added to the mix in the third test, and Citicorp gained 15 percent more customers while reducing costs 71 percent.[10] This fusion of DMC and print advertising yielded the most favorable test results, offering another illustration of integrated marketing communications.

EXECUTIVE ROUNDTABLE COMMENT | **Chuck Sawyer, account executive with Metromail, an R. R. Donnelly & Sons Company in Chicago, feels that direct marketing communications contribute to productivity and execution:**

If you work for a pet food manufacturer and you are marketing dog food, you have a market where only 26 percent of US households own a dog. If you could use a medium that allowed you to focus more of your advertising and promotional budget on households that actually own a dog, why would you ever spend money promoting dog food to the other 74 percent? Direct marketing communications give you more focus and less waste.

Growth of direct marketing communications

Direct marketing communications have become a larger part of the total marketing communications picture in recent years. While mass-media advertising expenditures dwindle, spending on DMC continues to rise. Leading the way is spending on direct-mail advertising, exceeding $26 billion annually in the United States.[11] Approximately 64 billion pieces of direct mail are delivered yearly, up 37 percent in the last decade.[12] This results in the average US household receiving approximately 1.7 direct-mail pieces per day.[13] More recently, however, the flood of direct mail seems to be subsiding. Expenditures for third-class postage, the most popular method for sending direct mail, have been fairly stable in recent years; but expected increases in those rates will probably hold down direct-mail growth.[14]

Other DMC methods are relatively new but have grown rapidly. Telemarketing, infomercials, interactive shopping networks, and marketing via fax became factors in the 1990s. When these new methods are added to the mature yet still-growing direct mail and direct selling industries, it is clear that direct marketing communications are indeed growing. In the remainder of this section, we examine the global growth of DMC and some of the catalysts for it.

Global direct marketing communications

Direct marketing communications are becoming more important in global marketing efforts. A survey reveals that approximately 29 percent of direct marketers for consumer products marketed outside the US in 1992; another 28 percent intend to do so. Business-to-business direct marketers are farther ahead, with 36 percent already in international markets and another 31 percent intending to enter. Manufacturers and publishers are the most active industries in global direct marketing.[15] As in the US, computer companies are also actively involved in direct marketing communications in Europe. For example, Olivetti, an Italian firm, is using DMC programs in the UK, France, Germany, Spain, Denmark, and Belgium.[16]

Growth catalysts

The forces that have contributed to the decline of mass advertising are also propelling the growth of direct marketing communications. The increase in customized products, fragmented markets, and product price sensitivity; shrinking audiences for network television and newspapers; and emphasis on immediate sales all contribute to the decline of mass advertising and the expansion of direct marketing communications. Marketers are now forced to identify their target markets more specifically in order to reach them more effectively.[17]

Other forces also contribute to the growth of direct marketing communications. Changes in lifestyles create a need for convenient, time-saving, and dependable ways to shop. Two-worker families have more discretionary income but less time. These conditions make shopping at home, at one's leisure, very appealing. The *quality/value perspective* applies, as the ease of communication between buyer and seller, combined with the increased use of credit cards and acceptable products, makes direct purchasing an attractive alternative for many consumers.

A major reason for the growth in direct marketing communications has been advancing technology, which allows more precise construction and manipulation of customer databases. **Predictive modeling** on a database allows the marketer

Precision targeting with neural networks

Spiegel Inc. uses neural networks to fine-tune its direct-mail campaign. The campaign involves mailing 200 million catalogs and brochures to customers each year. To concentrate on its most profitable customers, the company wanted to separate one-time catalog purchasers from those most likely to purchase again.

To accomplish this task, Spiegel hired NeuralWare, Inc., a neural network software company. The company combined lifestyle and demographic data such as age, income, family makeup, and home ownership for each addressee in Spiegel's database with a huge list of people who had made just one catalog purchase. It found, for instance, that a young suburban couple, housebound with a first baby, is five times more likely to buy regularly from a catalog than a similar couple without kids.

Using thousands of trends like these, NeuralWare programmers developed a method to dispense with mailing to 60 percent of the customers not likely to purchase again; it continues to mail to 90 percent of those who would. Spiegel expects savings of at least $1 million annually as a result of its ability to target customers better.

Sources: Len Egol, "Neural Networks Add 'Brainpower' to Data," *Direct*, February 1992, p. 17; and "Smart Programs Go to Work," *Business Week*, March 2, 1992, pp. 97–102.

to reach a desired target more effectively, thus avoiding waste and enhancing profits. Sophisticated computerized statistical techniques known as *neural networks* can calculate weights for customer characteristics such as age, income, education, or time on the job. Using artificial intelligence, neural networks "learn" which targets are more likely to respond by examining data examples and calculating the relationships between predictor characteristics and known results. For an application of this technology, see **The Technological Edge: Precision Targeting with Neural Networks.**

Direct marketing communications techniques

Direct marketing communications include a variety of techniques. Two of the most popular are direct mail and direct selling. Direct marketing communications also include some forms of broadcast advertising, such as infomercials and direct-response television and radio advertising. Direct-response advertising appears in newspapers and magazines as well. Other techniques include telemarketing and supplementary electronic media.

Direct mail

Direct mail includes any form of advertising addressed to prospects through public or private delivery services. It can range in complexity from a simple flyer to a package including a letter, multipage brochure, video, and response card. The direct-mail response rate per thousand people reached is generally higher than for any other advertising medium,[18] which may explain why both small companies and industry giants such as IBM, General Motors, Lockheed, and American Express use direct mail as part of the *execution perspective.* Advantages and disadvantages of direct mail are summarized in Exhibit 21.2.

Direct mail has considerable flexibility in its self-contained message and the form used to convey it. A message could be written on a postcard or conveyed

| Exhibit 21.2 | Advantages and disadvantages of direct mail |

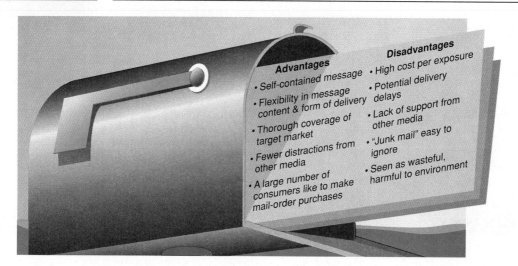

by videocassette. Moreover, direct mail can appeal to a narrow audience and be designed to suit a prospect's specific needs. Midwest Corvette Specialties, for example, can reach Corvette owners through its parts magazine. Working from a list of Corvette owners, the company avoids advertising to consumers who have no interest in its products.

The marketer can achieve nearly 100 percent coverage of the intended target market with direct mail, with fewer distractions than in some other media. For example, television or radio commercials are broadcast along with other ads and the regular programming. And magazine ads are juxtaposed with articles and other ads. A direct-mail piece, however, is typically viewed with less competition.

Perhaps the biggest advantage of direct mail is its potential effectiveness. One survey found that 48 percent of respondents had bought something by mail order in the past six months. This trend has prompted upscale businesses traditionally not known for using direct mail to do so. For example, Merrill Chase Galleries distributes a quarterly newsletter to 30,000 selected customers.[19]

Direct mail does have its flaws, however. It has one of the highest costs per thousand of any form of advertising; and it suffers potential delivery delays. It may take up to six weeks for bulk mail to reach its destination. In addition, consumers can easily ignore it, tossing the "junk mail" without ever being exposed to its message.[20] And finally, consumers increasingly view direct mail as wasteful and harmful to the environment.[21]

E X E C U T I V E R O U N D T A B L E C O M M E N T | **Chuck Sawyer, account executive with Metro-mail, comments on effective direct mail:**

From a consumer's point of view, "junk mail" is simply a communication that is not relevant. If you own a boat and are an avid sailor, a mail piece about the newest offerings for sail material and rigging would interest you. But your neighbor who has no interest in sailing would consider it "junk mail." The challenge to marketers is to target the market effectively and then match a relevant message to that target. This leads to greater effectiveness, but also greater efficiencies since waste is reduced.

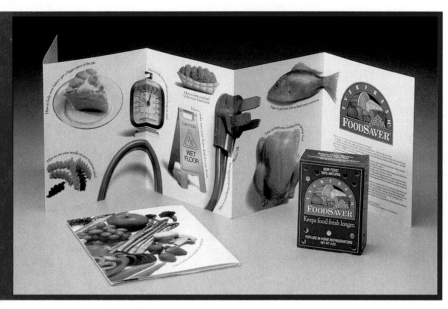

Direct mail can be as simple as a one-piece flyer or a multi-piece mailer. Landmark Products, distributor of products to the food-service industry, won the 1993 Echo Gold Mailbox award for the most innovative use of direct mail.

Types of direct mail

Direct mail comes in many formats, as shown in Exhibit 21.3. The most common form of direct mail is the *sales letter,* which typically includes the recipient's name and may be mailed with brochures, price lists, and reply cards and envelopes. *Postcards* generally offer discounts, announce sales, or generate customer traffic. Quantum Laboratories, a clinical lab in Washington, sent postcards to 750 physicians' office managers culled from a list of 3,500. The mailing generated $300,000 of new business; and Quantum's continued use of direct mail helped boost overall sales by more than 50 percent.[22]

Some companies produce publications referred to as *house organs* for mailing to particular audiences. These may be newsletters, consumer magazines, stockholder reports, or dealer publications. American Express distributes its *Your Business* quarterly, free of charge, to more than 1 million customers carrying the American Express Small Business Corporate Card. The publication gives card owners useful information not found elsewhere in hopes they will keep and use the travel service's charge card.

Exhibit 21.3

Types of direct mail

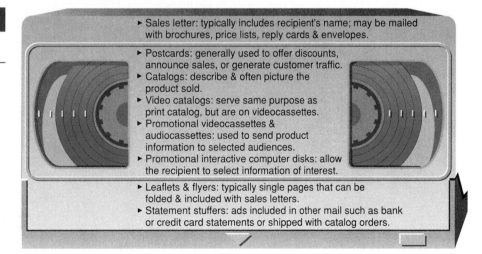

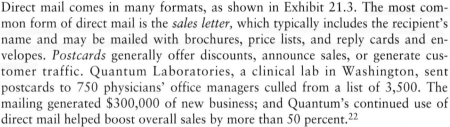

► Sales letter: typically includes recipient's name; may be mailed with brochures, price lists, reply cards & envelopes.

► Postcards: generally used to offer discounts, announce sales, or generate customer traffic.
► Catalogs: describe & often picture the product sold.
► Video catalogs: serve same purpose as print catalog, but are on videocassettes.
► Promotional videocassettes & audiocassettes: used to send product information to selected audiences.
► Promotional interactive computer disks: allow the recipient to select information of interest.

► Leaflets & flyers: typically single pages that can be folded & included with sales letters.
► Statement stuffers: ads included in other mail such as bank or credit card statements or shipped with catalog orders.

Office Depot's house organ *Business News* is a full-color, 40-page magazine of how-to's and free advice sent to 1.3 million businesspeople.

More than 100 million shoppers spend an estimated $60 billion on merchandise from more than 13,000 *catalogs* per year.[23] Lands' End, Eddie Bauer, Patagonia, and J. C. Penney produce well-known catalogs. An innovative twist on catalogs is the *video catalog,* put into videocassette format. Hartmarx, for example, sent a video catalog to 150,000 of its best customers.[24]

Promotional videocassettes and *audio cassettes* filled with product information are becoming popular direct-mail pieces. Chrysler Corporation mailed a videocassette promoting changes in its 1991 minivan to 400,000 current minivan owners.[25] Newstrack, an executive tape service, uses a sales letter and audiocassette to sell its news service. *Promotional interactive computer disks* are another medium. MCI successfully promoted its long-distance services by mailing computer disks to top executives. Compaq, the computer manufacturer, received four times greater response using promotional computer disks than with any previous direct-mail campaign.[26]

Leaflets or *flyers* are typically single pages printed on one or both sides of standard-sized paper (8½ by 11 inches) and folded. *Statement stuffers* are ads included in other mail such as bank or credit card statements.

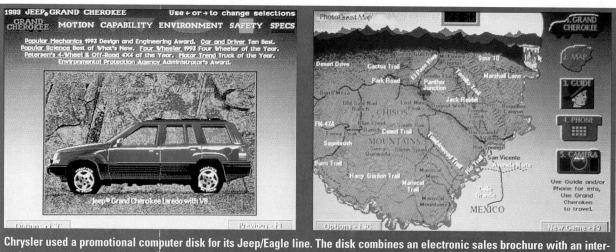

Chrysler used a promotional computer disk for its Jeep/Eagle line. The disk combines an electronic sales brochure with an interactive survival game set in the rugged terrain of Big Bend National Park in Texas.

Exhibit 21.4	Business-to-business mailings: Executive opinions

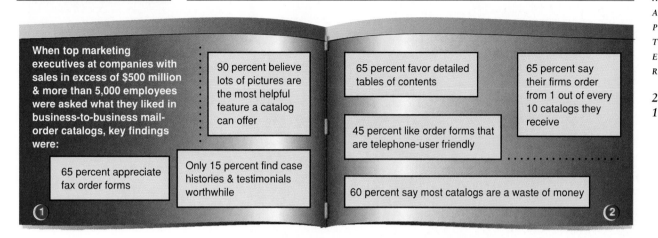

When top marketing executives at companies with sales in excess of $500 million & more than 5,000 employees were asked what they liked in business-to-business mail-order catalogs, key findings were:

90 percent believe lots of pictures are the most helpful feature a catalog can offer

65 percent favor detailed tables of contents

65 percent say their firms order from 1 out of every 10 catalogs they receive

45 percent like order forms that are telephone-user friendly

65 percent appreciate fax order forms

Only 15 percent find case histories & testimonials worthwhile

60 percent say most catalogs are a waste of money

Business-to-business direct mail

All the forms of direct mail discussed above are frequently used in business-to-business marketing. With the increasing costs of sales calls, marketers use direct mail to generate sales leads, solicit sales, and provide after-sale support and service information. Motorola, for instance, designed a 3-D direct-mail campaign featuring an Indy 500 theme to recruit resellers of its computer products.[27] For an indication of what makes a successful business-to-business direct-mail piece, see Exhibit 21.4.

Mail-order pharmacies use business-to-business direct-mail to gain sales in the $4 billion prescription drug market. Medco Containment Systems, the industry leader with about 2,500 clients, competes effectively against Baxter International, as well as mail-order divisions of Walgreens and the Thrift Drug chain. Direct-mail companies have sold corporate giants like General Electric, Alcoa, and Mobil on the notion of cutting their health care costs by up to 20 percent through mail-order purchase.[28]

Implications for direct-mail users

There are several noteworthy marketing implications for users of direct mail. Direct mail requires a thorough knowledge of postal laws, FTC regulations, and state statutes. It also requires an ongoing research effort to meet the needs and expectations of the target market. The traditional catalog shopper, for example, is described as a female, married, college-educated, homeowner in a dual-income household earning $30,000 to $99,000 annually.[29] Yet a multitude of female direct-mail target markets do not fit this stereotype, and must be approached with a strong marketing research effort. Without research, careful targeting is impossible.

Direct mail also requires that the user pay close attention to other elements of the marketing mix, especially in the physical distribution and logistics areas. For example, direct-mail users must know the status of inventory at all times, and order forms should be designed to allow easy access to key information at various points in the order entry-to-shipping cycle.

Direct selling

Direct selling is the selling of goods or services to consumers through personal demonstration and explanation. Intermediaries are eliminated from the process. Companies such as Amway, Tupperware, Avon, and Mary Kay all use direct selling as a primary means of reaching consumers.

An Avon representative in the United Kingdom. Direct selling eliminates intermediaries and allows the salesperson to demonstrate products and answer customer questions personally.

There are an estimated 12 million direct salespeople worldwide, with approximately 5 million in the US and more than 1.5 million in Japan. Almost half the estimated $40 billion in worldwide sales through direct selling is produced in Japan, while approximately one-fourth of the total comes from the United States. An indication of the size of the industry is that Amway, a direct seller, has joined IBM, Coca-Cola, Mobil, Du Pont, and Exxon as one of the 10 largest companies in Japan.[30]

Direct selling takes three primary forms: person-to-person selling in homes or workplaces; selling in temporary locations such as booths at shopping malls; and selling at planned "parties" where a host presents products for sale to guests. The primary advantage of direct selling is that salespeople can demonstrate a product and answer consumer questions. From a practical viewpoint, some products almost demand a demonstration to convince consumers. Electrolux, for example, sells vacuum cleaners door to door, and demonstrations are an integral part of the sales presentation. Exemplifying the *execution perspective,* Electrolux's sales volume is over $300 million in North America.[31]

One disadvantage of direct selling is the less-than-favorable image of some direct sellers who use misleading tactics in their sales presentations and in recruiting salespeople. Legitimate direct sellers must devote extra effort to gain customer trust and recruit a sufficient number of salespeople. We discuss this further in the section on ethical and legal issues.

Broadcast media

Although used mostly for mass advertising, television and radio are also used for direct marketing communications. Infomercials and direct-response advertising on TV and radio are popular DMC formats.

Infomercials

Infomercials are extended (usually 30-minute) commercials cast in a television show format. Mixing information and entertainment, they strive to look more like a regular TV program than a commercial. Infomercials generated revenues of over $4.5 billion in 1993.[32] As they gain favor among mainstream advertisers such as Volvo, Club Med, Panasonic, Braun, MCA Records, American Airlines, and General Motors, continued growth seems quite likely.[33]

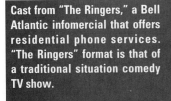

Cast from "The Ringers," a Bell Atlantic infomercial that offers residential phone services. "The Ringers" format is that of a traditional situation comedy TV show.

The infomercial format provides an opportunity to stand out in a cluttered environment. A 30-second commercial is more likely to get lost in the shuffle than a 30-minute one. Second, its length makes it possible to explain an advertised product more fully. For instance, the Juiceman, Jay Kordich, increased sales of food and juice processors by over 500 percent to more than $30 million a year through explanatory infomercials.[34]

By featuring a direct-response telephone number, an infomercial guarantees a quick means for measuring results, a desirable characteristic for the *productivity perspective.* Moreover, information obtained from those ordering can be used to develop a database. Finally, it can be cost-effective. Airtime for twenty-five 30-minute infomercials runs about the same price as one 30-second nationally televised commercial, which ranges from $250,000 to $500,000.[35]

Infomercials also have certain disadvantages. For one thing, airing is confined largely to cable TV and late-night programming on major networks, perhaps making it difficult to reach the target market with the desired message. Only 11 percent of the respondents to a national survey said they had watched infomercials, which may help account for infomercials' 85 percent industrywide failure rate.[36] One notable failure was "Nightcap," which featured Robin Leach ("Lifestyles of the Rich and Famous") and actress Rae Dawn Chong selling exercise gear and karaoke players. The program was canceled after a lackluster four-week run.[37]

Although potentially cost-effective, average production costs for infomercials are high—between $250,000 and $400,000.[38] Thus, production costs added to air-time costs make infomercials more expensive than most direct marketing communications methods.

Finally, infomercials have a poor image. Many suffer from exaggerated claims, low-quality production standards, and unprofessional presentation.[39] Moreover, there is some concern that they are deceptive by appearing in the guise of programs. Problems such as these may be overcome as the format develops and attracts more credible sponsors.

One source of growth for infomercials is in politics. Independent candidate Ross Perot used them in his bid for the US presidency in 1992, for instance. This marketing communications strategy won him Adman of the Year honors from *Advertising Age.*[40] Perot's infomercial-dominated effort gained 19 percent of the popular vote, a fact not likely to go unnoticed by other campaigners. Interestingly, Perot was denied infomercial time by the three major networks in his ill-fated attempt to block the passage of NAFTA in 1993.

Selling teddy bears via radio

*T*he Vermont Teddy Bear Company was having difficulty selling its teddy bears. Although its bears were on the shelves of major toy retailers, they were not selling in the face of stiff competition from better-known toy companies.

This prompted the company to skip retail distributors and go directly to consumers with inexpensive radio commercials. Using simple, folksy spots read by local announcers and an easy-access, toll-free order number, Vermont Teddy Bear avoided direct in-store competition from other manufacturers. The company's telephone orders increased by 300 percent in only one year after the first radio commercial aired. Eighty percent of the company's customers are adults, and many are men.

The company now buys time on 40 stations in six cities. Sales revenues climbed to $5.2 million from $1.7 million and are projected to top $12.5 million in 1992. Its founder, John Sortino, attributes the growth to its new distribution and marketing campaign, which now also includes a direct-mail program. The success of the Vermont Teddy Bear Company attests to the power of direct-response radio advertising.

Sources: Jenny C. McCune, "Switch on the Radio," *Success,* April 1992, p. 23; Ray Jutkins, "Mail Order Bears," *Target Marketing,* October 1992, pp. 22–24; and Emily DeNitto, "Bullish on Teddy Bears," *Advertising Age,* December 13, 1993, p. 44.

Direct-response television advertising

Direct-response television advertising includes an 800 or 900 telephone number and an address for placing orders in a typical 30-, 60-, or 90-second commercial. Unlike typical mass advertising, direct-response ads attempt to get an immediate answer from the consumer. The campaign for the near-legendary Ginsu knife is an example, but many mainstream companies use this format. MCI, for instance, ran commercials with an 800 number to elicit response for its "Friends and Family" calling plan.

Although sometimes aired on network television, direct-response commercials are more widely broadcast on cable TV. Expected to have almost 70 million subscribers in the US by 1995, cable TV allows effective targeting of audiences through **narrowcasting,** or special-interest programming.[41] Bass Pro Shops, a Springfield, Missouri, catalog retailer, for example, uses direct-response advertising on popular cable-TV fishing programs. As with infomercials, this form of DMC enables database building and immediate assessment of results.

Direct-response radio advertising

Direct-response radio advertising also offers the ability for immediate feedback through a telephone number or address provided with the commercial. In addition, it can be directed toward a very targeted audience and is relatively inexpensive compared to other forms of direct marketing communications. Radio, however, is not a particularly dynamic medium. Radio audiences tend to be too preoccupied with other things to focus on an address or a telephone number. Certainly a listener hearing a radio commercial while driving cannot easily record an address. Yet radio can be effective, as shown in **The Entrepreneurial Spirit: Selling Teddy Bears via Radio.**

Nordic Track uses telefocus telemarketing to market its line of aerobic exercise equipment. Inbound telemarketing handles prospective customers' requests for a video and brochure. Outbound telemarketing follows up with prospects after they have received the video and brochure.

Print media

Although not so tightly targeted as other direct marketing communications media, newspapers and magazines can also provide an opportunity for direct response. Consumers can respond to ads carrying an address, order form, coupon, or telephone number. The response can be either to purchase or to request additional information. One way to use direct-response print advertising is with a freestanding insert (FSI), discussed in Chapter 19.

Magazines may include other forms of direct marketing communications. Some marketers insert reply cards into magazines. **Reader-response cards** are sometimes used in conjunction with ads to allow consumers to request additional information. Readers wanting more information on a product would circle a number on the card corresponding to the product's ad in the magazine and send the card to the magazine's publisher. One of the newest magazine inserts is the floppy disk. *Forbes* magazine, for example, included a disk that contained information from such advertisers as American Express, Chevrolet, Embassy Suites, and Merrill Lynch, among others.

Telemarketing

Telemarketing is an interactive direct marketing communications approach that uses the telephone to initiate, develop, and enhance relationships with customers. On a cost-per-contact basis, telemarketing is less expensive than personal selling, but much more expensive than mass advertising and direct mail. However, its high return often justifies the added expense.

Outbound telemarketing occurs when the marketer actively solicits customers or prospects. Inbound telemarketing occurs when a customer calls the marketer to obtain information or place an order. Either case offers the advantage of two-way conversation, allowing the respondent to ask questions and give answers and the marketer to tailor a message to the individual needs of the prospect.

Promotional campaigns often include telemarketing as one of the elements. **Telefocus telemarketing** is an integrated technique that combines telemarketing efforts with a direct-mail campaign using video brochures. This technique has been used to market such high-ticket items as home exercise equipment, European vacations, and cars, by companies such as Nordic Track, Soloflex, Air France, and General Motors.[42]

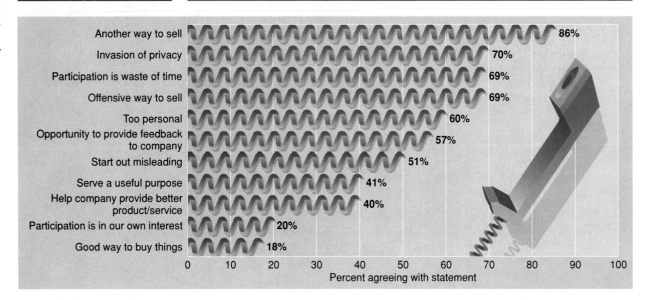

Exhibit 21.5   **Consumer opinions of telemarketing**

Statement	Percent agreeing
Another way to sell	86%
Invasion of privacy	70%
Participation is waste of time	69%
Offensive way to sell	69%
Too personal	60%
Opportunity to provide feedback to company	57%
Start out misleading	51%
Serve a useful purpose	41%
Help company provide better product/service	40%
Participation is in our own interest	20%
Good way to buy things	18%

Percent agreeing with statement

Very popular in business-to-business marketing, telemarketing can be effective in expanding international marketing operations. Gateway, the direct supplier of computers, established a telemarketing center in Dublin, Ireland, as a first step toward entry into European markets.

Technology has made telemarketing very productive. **Predictive dialing systems** save telemarketers as much as 20 minutes an hour by passing over answering machines, busy signals, and no answers. Predictive dialers automatically dial a designated amount of numbers per minute. Completed calls are immediately passed on to a live telemarketer, who simultaneously receives customer information on a computer terminal.

Unfortunately, telemarketing does not have a good image. Consumers view telemarketers as uninvited nuisances. According to one survey, as shown in Exhibit 21.5, two out of three Americans feel that telemarketing is an invasion of privacy, an offensive way to sell, and a waste of the consumer's time.[43] Telemarketers, then, should provide short, compelling messages, as most people will not spend more than a few minutes on the phone for an uninvited sales call.

Electronic media

Several other electronic forms of direct marketing communications are available besides broadcast media. Although not used as often as other methods, interactive computer services and kiosks and fax machines are growing in popularity.

Interactive computer services

Interactive computer services allow consumers and marketers to communicate with each other through telephone lines and a personal computer. For instance, IBM and Sears provide Prodigy, a computer-based shopping and information service available to PC owners in major markets across the country. Marketers using the service, such as BMW, Panasonic, United Airlines, and Columbia House, can reach more than 2 million Prodigy subscribers. Subscribers are issued an ID code that indicates particular demographics. The system uses this information to deliver specific information and shopping programs tailored to subscriber needs. More than 700 news, banking, travel, and other services are offered through Prodigy.[44]

Interactive computer services are also available for business-to-business marketers. Digital Equipment Corporation's Electronic Connection, for example, links customers by modem. Using a PC, customers can query DEC's inventory database, find out if an item is available, check the contract price, and place an order. All this can be done without talking to a sales rep.[45]

EXECUTIVE ROUNDTABLE COMMENT | **Chuck Sawyer, account executive with Metromail, points out the potential for improving marketing communications as interactive computer networks continue to evolve:**

The "information super highway" will deliver over 500 channels to the home television set. Through their computers, consumers will be able to select topics of interest and have information stored for retrieval at their convenience. This will allow consumers to process information more efficiently, thus becoming better-informed buyers.

Interactive computer kiosks

A fairly new electronic marketing medium is the **interactive computer kiosk,** usually located in retail stores. These kiosks typically use touch-screen technology that allows the consumer to access specific information of interest. Some interactive computer kiosks include catalogs (video or paper) featuring items not stocked in the retail store, with a direct toll-free number for placing orders. Interactive computer kiosks may transmit in-store information to boost sales and increase customer service. Kmart, for instance, is testing a kiosk at which shoppers touch a screen to access store maps and receive information on products and weekly promotions.[46]

Catalog retailers are also using computer kiosks to gain additional exposure and sales from mall shoppers. In Chicago and in metropolitan areas of Delaware, 30 kiosks sell merchandise from catalogers Hammacher Schlemmer, Lands' End, J. C. Penney, and the Wine Enthusiast. Each cataloger sells 50 to 100 items, with quarterly updates to allow changes in merchandise, presentation, or pricing.[47]

Fax machines

Fax machines allow customers to transmit written documents via telephone. However, their use as a direct marketing communications tool has been restricted primarily to business-to-business customers. Direct marketers routinely use fax machines to receive customer orders. New technology called **fax-on-demand systems** allows instant response to 800-number requests for information using a fax.[48] In these systems, a fax machine receives the request for information and immediately faxes the information back to the requester.

One problem with using fax machines in business-to-business marketing communications is that most businesses do not want to tie up their incoming fax lines with unsolicited information. It is now a fairly common practice to send unsolicited marketing communications after normal business hours, a practice made easy by delayed-dialing capabilities of most fax machines. Some states, including Texas, Oregon, and Florida, prohibit the transmission of unsolicited fax communications.[49]

Many business-to-business marketers, including accounting firms and equipment manufacturers, depend on disseminating information as a means of attracting clients. Some of these marketers find an advantage in transmitting information in written, rather than audio or video form. Many prospective customers would rather read a customized report than listen to one, since it is easier to access important parts of the written report. Prices, product availability, shipping schedules, and other marketing mix variables can change frequently, and the fax is extremely accommodating when such changes occur. Many fax documents are never in hard copy form, but exist in computer files that can be changed with the flick of a key stroke just before dissemination.

Fax machines are also becoming increasingly popular as an interactive medium. For example, a jeweler in Topeka can call RapNet, a diamond exchange, and use touch-tone technology to get fax price quotes from as far away as Antwerp.[50]

Ethical and legal issues in direct marketing communications

In this section, we discuss four key areas of ethical and legal concern in direct marketing communications: invasion of privacy, deceptive practices, pyramid schemes, and waste of natural resources.

Invasion of privacy

As consumer databases become more sophisticated, there is growing concern among some buyers about invasion of privacy. Most people do not object to a company storing information on its own customers for information-management purposes.[51] They may be less likely to approve of that company renting its list to another firm, however, even though list rental is legal.

US marketers are leery of legislative attempts to regulate potential threats to consumer privacy. Consumers in other countries are accustomed to strict privacy statutes. German firms, for example, cannot make outbound prospecting calls; laws restrict them to calling only on their own customers or people requesting such contact. French companies cannot sell or exchange customer information with each other.[52]

To ward off potential legislative action, some direct marketing companies are taking actions to avoid invading consumers' privacy. Fewer firms make their in-house lists available for rental to other companies. McDonald's, Fisher-Price, and Citicorp, for example, no longer rent their customer lists.[53] Many firms allow consumers to choose whether or not they are included on lists made available to other firms. Others ask consumers how often they would like to receive mail solicitations.[54]

Sensitivity to consumers' privacy, however, does not appear to be the primary reason for restricting list use. Industry observers say that despite exhortations from the Direct Marketing Association and continued legislative threats, few companies cite the invasion of privacy issue as the key reason to keep a list off the market.[55] Most list owners that decide not to rent do so to keep their competitors from getting their customer information.

To match marketers' efforts to self-regulate, the Direct Marketing Association launched a $2.5 million campaign to combat privacy legislation. The association claims it is attempting to counteract an "explosion" of bills aimed at expansion of credit information and telemarketing technology.[56] For a closer examination of telemarketing legislation, see Exhibit 21.6.

Deceptive practices

Attempts at telemarketing legislation have increased at least in part to address numerous telemarketing abuses. Consumers exhibit high levels of trust in sellers when they order and pay for a product sight unseen. Direct-response marketers rely on this trust. Yet, as some examples illustrate, certain direct-marketing activities have damaged that trust.[57]

After 25 years, marketers have finally convinced consumers that 800-number telephone calls are toll free. But some marketers ask 800-number callers to punch codes into their telephones that, unbeknownst to them, convert the call to a billable 900 number. Another abuse comes from sweepstakes marketers who promote 900-number calls for prizes worth much less than the cost of the call.

Automatic number identification and **caller ID intrusion** systems pose additional ethical and legal problems. These systems let incoming telephone numbers of respondents to an ad or a promotion be identified at the onset of the call

| Exhibit 21.6 | Examples of telemarketing legislation |

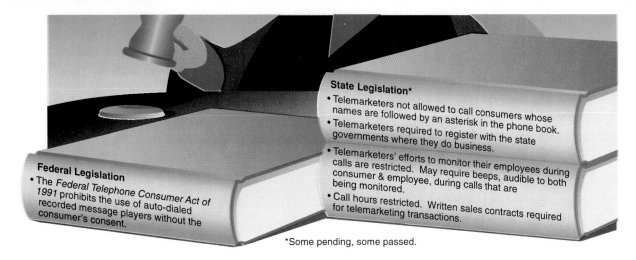

State Legislation*
• Telemarketers not allowed to call consumers whose names are followed by an asterisk in the phone book.
• Telemarketers required to register with the state governments where they do business.
• Telemarketers' efforts to monitor their employees during calls are restricted. May require beeps, audible to both consumer & employee, during calls that are being monitored.
• Call hours restricted. Written sales contracts required for telemarketing transactions.

Federal Legislation
• The *Federal Telephone Consumer Act of 1991* prohibits the use of auto-dialed recorded message players without the consumer's consent.

*Some pending, some passed.

without the caller's consent or knowledge. Not only is this a possible invasion of privacy, but it also presents an opportunity to capture and sell unlisted numbers.

The question of basic fairness often arises in direct marketing communications. Consumers may wonder if they have a legitimate chance to win sweepstakes and contests, two sales promotion activities that often use direct marketing communications. Publishers Clearing House (PCH) faced a class-action suit over the administration of one of its sweepstakes programs. A sanitation worker in New York discovered 2,000 discarded unopened sweepstakes entries, mostly from nonmagazine buyers. This added fuel to the common perception that the odds of winning a sweepstakes are much higher for a buyer than a nonbuyer. In settling the suit, PCH agreed to enter the names of over 40 million consumers who had not previously ordered magazines from PCH in upcoming sweepstakes.[58]

Pyramid schemes

In **multilevel marketing,** sometimes called **network marketing,** the salesperson-distributor recruits other salespeople into the sales organization. The original salesperson-distributor earns commissions on his or her own sales to consumers, plus a percentage of sales made by the recruited salespeople.

Legitimate multilevel marketing organizations should not be confused with **pyramid schemes,** "illegal scams in which large numbers of people at the bottom of the pyramid pay money to a few people at the top."[59] According to the Direct Selling Education Foundation, some pyramid schemes copy legitimate multilevel marketing firms by taking on a line of products presumably for sale to consumers. In reality, however, no substantial effort is made to sell to consumers. Instead, money is made from new recruits, who are pressured into buying large amounts of practically worthless products. Since pyramid operators can be quite crafty in their deception, potential investors in multilevel marketing should follow the precautions shown in Exhibit 21.7.

Waste of natural resources

The *ecological perspective* calls for a consideration of the environmental consequences of marketing decisions, thus increasing attention on use of natural resources. In the direct-mail industry, consumer complaints and regulatory interest concerning junk mail have motivated discussion about excessive contributions to landfills, impact on timber production and harvesting, and the economic waste associated with rising paper costs.[60]

The US Postal Service estimates that more than 5.6 billion pieces, or 9 percent of all third-class mail, are simply undeliverable.[61] It is also commonly known

Exhibit 21.7   **Evaluating multilevel marketing opportunities**

Srikumar Rao of the University of Long Island recommends these steps in evaluating a multilevel marketing opportunity:

1. *Evaluate the product.* Is it competitive, a reasonable value for the money?

2. *Check the financial status of the company.* Commercial credit companies like Dun & Bradstreet can provide information, and suppliers can be queried.

3. *Check the legal record.* Equifax can provide a pending-legislation report. Check with the Better Business Bureau and the Department of Consumer and Regulatory Affairs. Also check with the Direct Selling Association in Washington, DC.

4. *Avoid frontloading,* a requirement to buy large amounts of inventory each month to qualify for commissions. Good companies forbid frontloading.

5. *Check the ethics.* Ethical companies forbid exaggerated product and potential-income claims.

that consumers do not want to receive all their unsolicited mail. Two alternatives are easily available to marketers who wish to cut down on waste by minimizing undeliverable and unwanted direct-mail pieces. First, the marketer can increase the accuracy of a mailing list by running it through the US Postal Service's national file on changes of address. By using this service, which has change-of-address information on 100 million people, mailers could cut down on undeliverable pieces and perhaps qualify for lower postage rates in the process.[62]

In addition, direct marketers could better inform consumers of their right to remove their names from mailing lists. The Direct Marketing Association coordinates a "preference" program that allows consumers to stop mail and telephone solicitation if they so choose. There may be some way marketers can make consumers more aware of this program, which would eventually lead to less unwanted mail and more efficient direct marketing communications.

Cutting out waste in DMC requires that consumers join with concerned companies to bring about the desired changes. This is true of most ethical and legal problems facing marketing. For example, when asked about invasion of privacy, the president of the National Consumers League said, "Are consumers being exploited? Most certainly. Is it an invasion of privacy? Probably not. Most consumers are willing to disclose the information." Whether we are talking about invasion of privacy, deceptive practices, illegal pyramid schemes, waste of natural resources, or any other significant ethical or legal issue in marketing, the consumer must take an active role in effecting favorable change.

Summary

1. *Understand the objectives of direct marketing communications and describe its distinguishing characteristics.* Direct marketing communications are directed at target audiences using one or more media. One objective of direct marketing communications is to elicit a response by telephone, mail, or personal visit from a prospect or customer. Another objective, to maintain and enhance customer relationships, is growing in importance.

Direct marketing is distinguished from other marketing communications methods in several ways. First, it uses customer databases, or lists, to target an audience

precisely. Next, it is oriented more toward an immediate response than most other forms of marketing communications. Finally, its objectives are specific consumer actions, so results are highly measurable.

2. *Discuss the factors driving the growth in direct marketing communications.* Increasingly fragmented markets make the narrowly focused methods of direct marketing quite attractive. Changes in lifestyles have created a need for convenient, time-saving, and dependable ways to shop. Perhaps one of the biggest motivators of growth in direct marketing communications

has been the emergence of database marketing, which gives marketers a more in-depth understanding of productive target customers.

3. **Understand traditional direct marketing communications techniques such as direct mail, direct selling, broadcast and print media, and telemarketing.** Direct mail is the most popular method, and it comes in a variety of forms, from postcards to video catalogs. Direct selling is a huge part of direct marketing communications, with more than 10 million salespeople worldwide.

   Print and broadcast media are used for direct-response advertising, and the infomercial has become a significant means of communicating directly with the target market. Inbound and outbound telemarketing have become extremely popular, even though outbound telemarketing is a nuisance to many consumers. Each of these methods has unique capabilities and limitations, one reason marketers typically use multiple methods to reach a given audience.

4. **Recall examples of the use of technology such as electronic media in direct marketing communications.** Interactive computer services, interactive computer kiosks, and fax machines are three examples of relatively new technology now widely used in direct marketing communications. These tools offer immediate information to consumers and business-to-business buyers, and sometimes allow the customer to do business with the seller after normal business hours.

5. **Understand some of the ethical and legal issues facing marketers that use direct marketing communications.** As database lists become more sophisticated, there is increased concern about invasion of privacy. Abuse of consumers' privacy is likely to lead to legislation to curb it. Telemarketing has come under the heaviest attacks, as unethical marketers use deceptive methods in dealing with consumers. Actions can and should be taken to avoid unwarranted or abusive intrusion. Some firms posing as legitimate multilevel marketers use illegal pyramid schemes. Junk mail has been accused of wasting natural resources. Concerned marketers, consumers, and associations such as the Direct Marketing Association and the Direct Selling Association must work together to curb these problems. Otherwise, it is certain that some consumers will be victimized and that legislation will be enacted to address the issues.

Key terms & concepts

direct marketing
   communications   *518*
lists   *519*
database marketing   *519*
predictive modeling   *522*
direct mail   *523*   rent
direct selling   *527*
infomercials   *528*
direct-response television
   advertising   *530*

narrowcasting   *530*
direct-response radio
   advertising   *530*
reader-response cards   *531*
telemarketing   *531*
telefocus telemarketing   *531*
predictive dialing systems   *532*
interactive computer services   *532*

interactive computer kiosk   *533*
fax-on-demand systems   *533*
automatic number
   identification   *534*
caller ID intrusion   *534*
multilevel marketing   *535*
network marketing   *535*
pyramid schemes   *535*

Review & discussion questions

1. Define direct marketing communications and describe their distinguishing characteristics.

2. What is database marketing? How has it contributed to the growth of direct marketing communications?

3. Review **The Technological Edge: Precision Targeting with Neural Networks.** How can neural networks benefit marketers involved in direct marketing communications?

4. Describe advantages and disadvantages of direct mail.

5. What is an infomercial? What types of products do you think would benefit most from using this type of advertising and why?

6. Refer to **The Entrepreneurial Spirit: Selling Teddy Bears via Radio.** If this company was so successful using direct-response radio advertising, why don't more companies use this method?

7. What is an interactive computer service? How does it differ from an interactive computer kiosk?

8. Database marketing has come under attack from those who believe it is an invasion of privacy. Should marketers be concerned about this? What can be done to deal with consumers' concerns? Please explain.

9. What are the differences between legitimate multilevel marketing firms and illegal pyramid schemes?

10. What can direct marketers do to cut down on the waste generated by their communications methods?

Application exercises

1. Working in groups of three to five students, analyze two current infomercials to see if they meet the standards of conduct as set forth by the National Infomercial Marketing Association:

    a. A "paid advertisement" disclosure must appear at the beginning and end of each infomercial and at each ordering opportunity.

    b. The name of the sponsor must be disclosed.

    c. There can be no misrepresentations as to format, no false claims or deception through omission, and no indecent or offensive material.

    To what extent do the members of the group agree on the last point? Summarize your opinions for class discussion.

2. Assume you are the chair of an alumni fund-raising committee for your college or university. The committee is charged with the task of contacting approximately 30,000 alumni to solicit donations for a new library. The goal is to raise $1 million from the alumni within the next 18 months. The first order of business is to determine what form of communication is to be used in the campaign. The alumni are scattered across the US, and approximately 10 percent live in a variety of foreign countries. Which means of reaching these alumni would you recommend the committee consider? Briefly explain your reasoning.

    a. Direct mail
    b. Telemarketing
    c. Personal selling
    d. Direct-response television advertising
    e. Direct-response radio advertising
    f. Fax solicitation

3. Which types of direct marketing communications would you choose for each task?

    a. Informing your customers of an upcoming sale in your retail store.

    b. Introducing yourself and your company to new prospects in your sales territory.

    c. Inviting current customers to visit your booth at a trade show next month.

    d. Demonstrating a new software program offered by your company.

    e. Familiarizing European construction managers with your latest piece of earth-moving equipment.

    f. Bringing your 1,200 dealers up to date on a variety of happenings in your company.

Case 21.1   *Club Med: From self-indulgence to self-improvement*

By the mid-1980s, Club Med was old news to jet-setters. Business was steady but not growing. With its annual number of visitors at a plateau, the company began trying to move beyond its singles-only, self-indulgent image to a family orientation, featuring self-improvement as the key attraction. Suddenly, hedonism was out, spiritual uplift was in.

To promote its new theme "Take Home a Club Med Vacation," the company hired a new ad agency and expanded its direct marketing communications efforts. The key to its new tactics was Club Med's detailed, internally generated database of 2.5 million names. About 40 percent are singles; 60 percent are couples and families. The database provides information about preferred activities, family size, and residential location that can be used to plan and execute direct marketing communications.

Club Med uses a variety of formats to reach its audience: infomercials, direct mail, direct-response TV and radio commercials, and telemarketing. According to Club Med president Michael Kubin, targeting the customer is crucial, since most vacationers look for locations that fit their specific interests. Database information makes it possible to sort previous customers by activity and geographic preferences, two common segmentation bases used for new communications. For example, a customer might get a direct-mail piece that says, "You enjoyed horseback riding and hiking in the Rockies, now try the West Coast . . ."

Club Med also uses direct mail to reach a highly adventurous, athletic, affluent target market (mostly couples) for the Club Med I sailing ship. Kubin maintains that direct marketing communications is the only practical means of reaching this market and that mass communications would be extremely wasteful.

Technology has aided the Club Med direct marketing communications effort. Its computerized database allows the company to seek new business without alienating the travel agencies on which it relies for most of its business. More than 150,000 potential vacationers were identified from a list of those who had called in for a premium, promotional video, or brochure, but had never booked a room. These prospects were pursued via telemarketing, perhaps the most promising of Club Med's direct marketing methods.

Technology has expanded the productive working hours for telemarketing sales reps (TSRs). Automatic-dialing voice-recognition systems detect a human voice on the other end of the telephone line even before the party can say "hello." The call is then automatically switched to an available TSR, who can initiate the conversation without the customer being aware that the call was placed automatically. These systems make it feasible to place calls during the day, a low-return activity for TSRs placing their own calls.

Club Med is happy with its DMC program and is applying it to new areas. For example, a membership benefits program is under way. Members will receive discounts on products and services such as exercise equipment and car rentals. Expansion also calls for direct communications to targeted consumers not on the internally generated Club Med list.

Questions:

1. Club Med is moving away from mass advertising toward direct marketing communications. Why do you think this is the case?

2. The president of Club Med says that targeting the customer is the key to direct marketing communications. In addition to vacation activity and geographic preferences, how could Club Med segment its target market?

3. Could Club Med's direct marketing communications program be implemented without computerized database and telemarketing systems? Does Club Med's use of a database and other technological devices pose any ethical problems?

Sources: Risa Bauman, "Club Med Steers '90s Course," *Direct,* October 1991, p. 19; Martin Everett, "Extra! Extra! Gannett Helps Club Med Mine Its Database," *Sales & Marketing Management,* October 1992, pp. 120–22; and Joshua Levine, "You've Got to Be Perfect, but Not Plastic Perfect," *Forbes,* September 30, 1991, pp. 152–54.

Case 21.2   *Coldwater Creek: Cataloging customers*

Dennis and Ann Pence left New York City and their big-company management positions behind when they moved to Sandpoint, Idaho, to launch Coldwater Creek Inc., a catalog retailing business, featuring American Indian jewelry, crafts, and apparel. Sandpoint, a town of 6,000, is 50 miles south of the Canadian border, just west of the Continental Divide.

The Coldwater formula for success is driven by a focus on the customer. The typical customer, according to Dennis, is "a 40-year-old woman whose Volvo is stuck in traffic on the San Diego freeway. She wants to spend the weekend in Yosemite, but doesn't have time." When Pence worked as national marketing manager for Sony, he learned the valuable lesson of determining who the customers are, defining their needs, and working hard to meet those needs. According to Pence, the motto at Sony was "Ready, aim, aim, aim, aim, fire!"

This motto served the Pences well and is certainly appropriate for direct marketing communications. The Pences figured that if they could execute every step in the buyer's buying process better than anyone else, making purchasing a pleasant experience, satisfied customers would fuel future growth. They figured right, and in only a few years Coldwater Creek grew into one of the nation's most successful catalog operations.

To provide outstanding service and pleasant buying experiences, Coldwater Creek relies on technology, strong relationships with vendors, and direct marketing communications, all of which combine to produce a powerful marketing machine. Orders are received 365 days a year, 24 hours a day, by inbound telemarketing, fax, and mail. Incoming calls are answered in an average of three seconds, and only 0.2 to 0.3 percent of callers hang up before a Coldwater representative picks up, compared to the industry average of 3 to 5 percent.

Orders are processed immediately. Approximately 90 percent are shipped the same day, and almost 100 percent within 24 hours. For an additional $5 charge, customers can specify special Wild Goose Express priority delivery.

To ensure that orders are shipped correctly, Coldwater formed a team of 16 employees to study shipping procedures. They identified 16 sources of possible mistakes and created systems to prevent them. Coldwater reports an error rate of about two errors per 1,000 orders—five times better than the industry average. When a return of merchandise is necessary (less than 3.5 percent of all orders), Coldwater Creek reimburses the original shipping and handling charges, something rarely offered in the catalog business.

At the heart of Coldwater's operation is a million-dollar Hewlett-Packard computer system that keeps up with the details of the business, allowing personnel to focus on customer interactions. The computer system also forecasts sales far enough in advance to allow vendors to schedule production and shipping to keep Coldwater in stock, enhancing supplier relationships.

Dennis says, "It's a lot of computer for a company of our size, but . . . it provides us with a competitive advantage." He also notes that they spent a lot on computer equipment just to seem smaller and nontechnical to customers. Calls from customers are not answered by an automated operator, nor are customers put on hold.

Coldwater Creek is also sensitive to the ethical and ecological issues. It uses order blanks printed on recycled paper. In addition, the company clearly informs customers that since its mailing list is available to other marketers, they can choose to remove their names from it.

Questions:

1. An entrepreneurial perspective emphasizes creativity, innovation, and risk taking in all marketing activities. How have the Pences displayed these characteristics?

2. Coldwater's order forms are printed on recycled paper, but its catalogs are printed on top-quality paper. The use of recycled paper is often identified with ecologically enlightened marketing. Is Coldwater justified in its use of top-quality paper for its catalog?

3. Technology can overcome many time and distance problems faced by most store retailers. How does this statement relate to Coldwater Creek?

Sources: Matthew Schifrin, "Know Thy Customer," *Forbes,* May 10, 1993, pp. 122–23; John Case, "How to Launch an Inc. 500 Company," *Inc.,* October 1992, pp. 91–99; Harry Chevan, "With Product Suppliers, Be Specific," *Catalog Age,* February 1993, p. 12; and *Coldwater Creek: A Northcountry Catalog,* Winter 1993.

IN THE IDITAROD, THE IDEA THAT THERE ARE ONLY SNOWMEN IS ABOMINABLE.

The Ten Key Marketing Perspectives

1 G — GLOBAL
A global perspective
A global view of the marketplace to include searching for marketing opportunities around the world, competing against international competitors & working with multicultural suppliers, employees, channel participants & customers.

2 R — RELATIONSHIP
A relationship perspective
An emphasis on long-term, mutually beneficial relationships to include customer relationships, organizational partnerships & teamwork within a company.

3 E — ETHICAL
An ethical perspective
Viewing ethical and social responsibility issues as important considerations in all marketing decisions & activities.

4 QV — QUALITY/VALUE
A quality/value perspective
Generating customer satisfaction by providing the quality desired by customers & continuously improving quality to increase the value customers receive.

5 P — PRODUCTIVITY
A productivity perspective
Constant attention to improving the productivity of marketing resources by doing the same things better or by doing different things.

6 T — TECHNOLOGICAL
A technological perspective
Looking for ways to use the latest technological advances to improve marketing practice & as a source for new products.

7 E — ECOLOGICAL
An ecological perspective
A consideration of the environmental consequences of marketing decisions & capitalizing on environmental marketing opportunities.

8 E — ENTREPRENEURIAL
An entrepreneurial perspective
An emphasis on creativity, innovation & risk taking in all marketing activities.

9 E — EXECUTION
An execution perspective
A focus on the effective implementation of sound marketing strategies.

10 V — VISIONARY
A visionary perspective
A broad, long-term view of what a company is trying to accomplish & a willingness to continually make the changes needed to achieve desired goals.

The Timberland Company

A worldwide winner

Founded in 1955, family-run Timberland of Hampton, New Hampshire, has become highly successful in marketing its line of rugged footwear, outdoor apparel, and accessories in 51 countries. Timberland's sales volume reached almost $250 million in 1992, and in 1993 reached $418.9 million. These results are especially impressive given the rather stagnant global economy.

Both everyday customers and athletic competitors in the spotlight give Timberland products high marks for quality. The crew members of America's Cup competitors *Il Moro di Venezia* and *New Zealand Challenge* sported Timberland's One Design boat shoes. Participants in the famous Iditarod® Trail Sled Dog Race are outfitted from head to toe in Timberland products. Through its growing base of satisfied customers and high-profile marketing communications efforts, Timberland has earned the status of a premium brand.

Timberland's success defies the conventional wisdom that American manufacturers cannot compete with lower-cost foreign competition. While some American manufacturers are seeking protection from Congress against Asian imports, Timberland is rapidly expanding its exports, including impressive growth in Hong Kong, Taiwan, and Japan.

According to chairman Sidney W. Swartz, Timberland is responsible for five major constituencies: stockholders, employees, business partners, the community, and consumers. Speaking of consumers, Swartz says they "deserve great quality and value with service beyond expectation." He adds, "Our standards are high because our customers count on us in a sometimes harsh world."

In a business environment that pressures most marketers into seeking short-term results, Timberland has achieved success with visionary management that focuses on long-term results. The Timberland mission statement validates its commitment to its constituencies and issues a call to responsible action in the social and natural environments.

The Timberland Mission

*H*uman history is the experience of individuals confronting the world around them. Timberland participates in this process, not just through our products or through our brand, but through our belief that each individual can, and must, make a difference in the way we experience life on this planet. As a team of diverse people motivated and strengthened by this belief, we can and will deliver world-class products and service to our customers and create value for our shareholders around the world.

The Timberland boot stands for much more than the finest waterproof leather. It represents our call to action. Pull on your boots and make a difference. With your boots and your beliefs, you will be able to interact responsibly and comfortably within the natural and social environments that all human beings share. When confronting the world around you, nothing can stop you.

Sources: *The Timberland Company 1992 Annual Report;* "Timberland: Walking Tall," *The Economist,* August 4, 1990, pp. 56–57; William J. Cook, "Four Better Mousetraps," *U.S. News and World Report,* August 24, 1992, pp. 52–55; Securities and Exchange Commission, *The Timberland Company, Form 10-K,* for year ended December 31, 1992; "The Timberland Company: Selling Customer Service," *Customer Service Manager's Letter,* April 10, 1992, pp. 3–6; "Timberland Co.: Outdoor-Wear Maker Seeks Growth outside US," *Barron's,* June 24, 1991, p. 47; Mark Maremont, "Timberland Comes Out of the Woods," *Business Week,* September 13, 1993, p. 78; and company sources, June 1994.

---

*T*imberland has done an outstanding job of implementing the ten key marketing perspectives that were integrated in the discussion throughout this text. Timberland takes a **global perspective,** with sales in 51 countries. Its chairman expresses Timberland's commitment to a **quality/value perspective.** The **entrepreneurial perspective** is evident in the family-run company's evolution from manufacturing a single product to producing and marketing a complete line of footwear, outdoor apparel, and accessories for men and women.

The other seven key marketing perspectives are the **relationship, ethical, productivity, technological, ecological, execution,** and **visionary perspectives.** The text presents numerous examples of these perspectives. In this Epilog, we illustrate the way one firm, the Timberland Company, implements all ten of these perspectives to achieve a position of market leadership.

Timberland's family-run top management: Chairman Sidney Swartz (*left*) and President Jeffrey Swartz (*right*).

The Timberland Company succeeds by implementing the ten key marketing perspectives.

Global perspective

To implement a global perspective, marketers search for opportunities and face competitors from around the world. They work with multicultural suppliers, employees, channel participants, and customers. Traditionally, close to half of Timberland's total sales volume, for example, comes from outside the United States. Timberland sells globally through distributors, commission agents, and subsidiaries in England, France, Germany, Spain, Australia, and New Zealand. These subsidiaries offer sales, administrative, and warehousing support for the independent retailers that carry the Timberland line. The company also operates its own specialty stores in Germany (Munich, Düsseldorf), France (Paris, Lyon), England (London), Austria (Vienna), and New Zealand (Aukland).[1]

Many of Timberland's chief competitors are located primarily in the United States. Internationally, Timberland faces competition from numerous manufacturers of footwear, some of which attempt to copy the company's styles. In apparel and accessories markets, Timberland encounters a variety of competitors, including direct merchants and wholesalers.

Timberland showcases its products in more than 400 Concept Shops in upscale stores and over 5,000 retail locations worldwide.

In building its international business, Timberland learned valuable lessons from some of its customers. Some of these lessons helped build sales in other countries and, concurrently, provided insights that have applied in the United States. For example, some customers encouraged Timberland to use selective distribution for its products and pointed out the value of public relations in building brand image.

In expanding its international sales base, Timberland learned that while a single marketing strategy could work in the United States, it is risky to try a single strategy for all of Europe. What works in England does not necessarily appeal to German consumers, who are said to have reacted to Timberland ads with comments like "How can people show a dirty shoe on a clean piece of carpet?" Timberland learned the importance of building relationships with international customers according to their own cultures, customs, and business protocol. This in turn has led to more effective marketing programs in the United States.

Timberland is using the lessons learned in European expansion

Asia offers new markets for Timberland, as this Thai ad shows.

to grow in Asia, primarily in Hong Kong and Japan. There is no question that a global perspective contributes significantly to Timberland's success and bright future as a world-class marketer.

Relationship perspective

A relationship perspective requires emphasis on long-term, mutually beneficial relationships with customers and other organizations, as well as teamwork within the company. A focus on long-term success, as noted in Timberland's 1991 annual report, "is at the core of all our strategies for marketing the Timberland brand." According to the 1992 annual report, strong relationships with customers, employees, and members of the world community are ultimately the foundation on which a successful business is built.

Timberland's implementation of a relationship perspective dominates its approach to customer service. The director of corporate customer operations at Timberland says, "The role of the customer service representative is evolving into a frontline representation of the company to the customer." At Timberland, customer service reps do much more than fill orders and handle complaints. They are the primary contact for customers, fulfilling a liaison role between the customer and the company. In this capacity they provide information and advice on a wide range of topics, including new marketing programs and delivery schedules. In this respect, they "are" the company.[2]

Corporate headquarters in Hampton, NH, where customer service reps are Timberland's front-line representatives to customers.

While customer service reps concentrate on dealing with customers, customer service managers represent the total service quality concept to senior managers and managers of other departments. This helps everyone at Timberland understand customers and their needs better, leading to continual improvement of already outstanding service.

At Timberland, service is important enough to managers that they personally staff the telephones in customer service twice a year. This program, called "Rubber Meets the Road," sells the concept of customer service to middle and senior managers. This certainly aids in the implementation of a relationship perspective, not only with customers but also with employees.

Timberland's relationship perspective extends to its suppliers and resellers. In the 1992 annual report, chairman Swartz tells stockholders: "We will continue to push hard to expand distribution with our partners and to work even more closely with our strategic retail allies. Through great suppliers and committed retailers, we will continue to satisfy Timberland customers."

Ethical perspective

Companies that embrace an ethical perspective view ethical and social responsibility issues as important considerations in all marketing decisions and activities. Timberland started with an honest idea—the waterproof boot—and takes pride in the integrity of its products. The company's ethical perspective is reflected further in its willingness to tackle tough social issues. A Timberland program called "Give Racism the Boot" was launched in Germany, France, the US, and the UK to speak out against hatred and intolerance globally. Proceeds from the sales of posters, T-shirts, and buttons in the US support a host of community service programs, including the City Year urban peace corps, a Boston-based community service program that is expanding nationally. Timberland recently invested $1 million in City Year, consequently becoming its primary corporate sponsor.

Other socially conscious policies of Timberland include offering each employee 16 hours of paid leave to perform community service; ceasing manufacturing in China since 1993, due to its unacceptable human rights conditions; and designating a Vice President of Community Enterprises to act as a link between Timberland and the community.[3]

Quality/value perspective

The quality/value perspective generates customer satisfaction by providing the quality customers desire and constantly improving it to increase the value they receive. Timberland's commitment to total quality management translates to high-quality products, a distinct competitive advantage for the company. In Asia, where the company faces intense price competition from local manufacturers, it remains able to sell at premium price levels.[4]   Timberland products feature top-notch exclusive waterproof leathers, waterproof Gore-Tex fabric, rustproof fittings, and other quality performance features.

Another aspect of the quality/value perspective at Timberland is value pricing. Following price cuts on its Weatherback line of casual, waterproof shoes, 1993 sales increased 300 percent over the previous year, as reported in *USA Today.*[5]

E
P
I
L
O
G

5
4
5

Productivity perspective

This perspective involves paying constant attention to improving the productivity of marketing resources by doing the same things better or by doing new things. To remain a formidable global competitor and sustain high growth and profitability rates, Timberland assiduously seeks productivity improvements in many areas. Through better coordination of product management, manufacturing, and shipping, both inventories and accounts receivables have dropped as a percentage of sales. The number of products in the Timberland line was cut almost in half, allowing more efficient inventory management and prompt delivery to customers.[6]

A key to increasing efficiency is a multidisciplinary approach to Timberland processes. For example, teams of people from finance, marketing, sales, and manufacturing work together on product development. This has allowed quicker response to changing consumer needs, tastes, and desires—without sacrificing product quality.

The implementation of a productivity perspective requires constant assessment to gauge progress. In customer service at Timberland, one measure of productivity is the number of telephone calls required per transaction—the productivity goal is one call. A customer service manager at Timberland says, "You might find you need additional productivity tools—such as a new computer—or you may find that you need to change a process or procedure or a particular policy."[7]

Scanners automatically track inventory and create shipping bills, making it as efficient to handle small orders as big ones.

Technological perspective

By looking for ways to use the latest technological advances to improve marketing practice and as a source of new products, Timberland exemplifies the technological perspective. Technology has played an important role since introduction of the first Timberland boot in 1973. Boots are submerged in water to find out where they leak, and the application of exclusive technology has allowed the development of waterproof, yet breathable, footwear. The leather is waterproofed through a proprietary process with leather manufacturers, and coating the stitches with latex plugs the

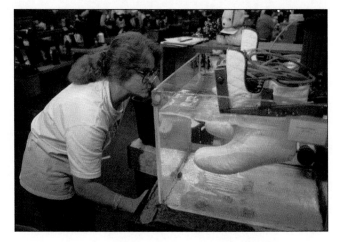

leaks caused by sewing needles. Special nylon thread is used to avoid the wicking effects of other types of thread. Soles are now formed by injecting polyurethane into a mold so that a bond to the leather upper is achieved with no stitches, holes, or—most important—leaks.

The waterproof footwear technology has served Timberland well as it has continued to evolve for over two decades. The company uses the latest technology not only in its new products; it also puts

technology to work to improve marketing operations. It has revamped manufacturing to allow just-in-time deliveries.[8]

CEO Jeffrey Swartz notes the importance of quick-response shipping to retail accounts, even in foreign markets: "If consumers can't get what they want when they want it, then the retailer's going to make sure they can find something else. If Timberland can provide its foreign retailers with that kind of quick response, and combine it with our product and image, then you'd have a preemptive position."

Ecological perspective

An ecological perspective takes into consideration the environmental consequences of marketing decisions and capitalizes on environmental opportunities. Timberland has supported educational programs and lobbying efforts for the environment. In 1993, the company became a signatory to the CERES Principles, a set of 10 environmental objectives of ethics that guide environmental conduct. The CERES Principles were introduced in 1989 by the Coalition for Environmentally Responsible Economics with the belief that meeting business objectives and protecting the environment need not be mutually exclusive.[9]

Timberland developed its own magazine called *Elements: The Journal of Outdoor Experience*, which gives the company an opportunity to softsell its products. The articles, on topics such as spring storms and polar exploration, celebrate the outdoor experience and position Timberland as an authentic resource for environmentally concerned consumers.[10]

Entrepreneurial perspective

An entrepreneurial perspective emphasizes creativity, innovation, and risk taking in all marketing activities. A letter to shareholders states that Timberland strives "to combine the entrepreneurial energy and vitality which has traditionally defined our Company, with the disciplines and controls required to build and market our brand in more than 50 countries worldwide."[11]

Throughout our discussion, we have cited examples of Timberland's creativity and innovation in product design and development. As for risk taking, Timberland encounters risk on a daily basis. First, a company in the footwear and apparel business is subject to quick-changing customer tastes. At present, Timberland's sales are fueled by consumers' affection for a rugged, outdoor look and the popularity of outdoor activities in the 90s. Customers have been spotted in sundresses and Timberland boots, but no one knows how long the rugged look will be the hot fashion. Fashion businesses are always at risk, and Timberland must continue to take chances to be successful. To some extent, Timberland has reduced the fashion-market risk by stressing the quality, ruggedness, timeless style, and core values of its product rather than making fashion statements with its advertising.

Risk also comes with international operations. Timberland supplements its US manufacturing facilities with a plant in the Dominican Republic, which the company points out "is subject to the usual risks of doing business abroad. These risks include political or labor disturbances, expropriation, acts of war, and other similar risks."[12]

Execution perspective

The execution perspective puts a premium on the effective implementation of sound marketing strategies. A quick review of Timberland's market performance leaves little doubt that this company knows how to execute. Industry analysts rave: "They're turning in terrific numbers . . . It's a great company with a great product and a terrific brand name . . . Business has been just phenomenal. Timberland continues to gain market share in the rapidly exploding market for casual shoes and boots."[13]

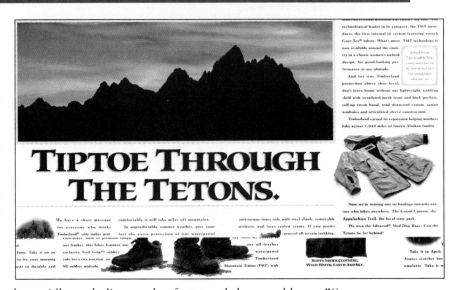

Timberland's ability to execute sound marketing strategies shows in its advertising program. Four years after introduction, Timberland's print advertising has become one of the most awarded campaigns in history. With its agency, Mullen Advertising, the firm's "Tiptoe Through the Tetons" and "In the Iditarod, the Idea That There Are Only Snowmen Is Abominable" ads earned nominations for the prestigious 1993 MPA Kelly Award, widely regarded as the top award for print advertising.[14]

Timberland's advertising is helping generate record sales. But the implementation of other strategies is also contributing to growth. Expansion in foreign markets and in the US is part of Timberland's strategy. Always well known in the Northeast, Timberland is gaining distribution elsewhere, especially in specialty stores in the South and Midwest. Value pricing is another well-executed Timberland strategy.[15] As with all successful marketers, the integration and coordination of all marketing activities is a key to execution.

Visionary perspective

To implement a visionary perspective, management must have a broad, long-term view of what the company is trying to accomplish and be willing to make the changes needed to achieve desired goals. Timberland has developed dramatically over the last few years to become a major player in a worldwide market. The company constantly adapts to make the changes necessary to maintain its current position as a market leader. These changes have included the implementation of advertising and public relations, revamping of manufacturing and delivery systems, expansion into new geographic

As this ad says, unlike some companies that slavishly follow the winds of change, Timberland takes its inspiration—its vision—from the elements themselves. "Timberland: boots, shoes, clothing, wind, water, earth, and sky."

markets, introduction of new products, and the improvement of internal processes to realize gains in productivity.

The willingness to continue to change is clear in an excerpt from the company's 1992 10-K:

The Company intends to continue its growth through a combination of internal development and the establishment of business relationships with other manufacturers, suppliers, distributors, and retailers capable of adhering to the strict performance specifications and rigid quality control procedures of Timberland. The Company may, from time to time, consider the possibility of acquiring other companies which produce or distribute quality footwear, apparel, accessories or related products which complement the Company's existing product lines. However, the Company currently has no plans for such acquisitions.[16]

Perhaps the most telling part of this statement is the final sentence. A truly visionary company does not necessarily have current plans for something it may do in the future, but it keeps the door open. To do otherwise would restrict future opportunities.

Finally...

This sketch of the Timberland Company offers a solid example of how a highly successful firm implements the ten key marketing perspectives featured throughout this text. Timberland is joined by successful companies in every industry that are setting the standards for today's best marketers.

We hope you will continue to learn from the Timberlands of the world and from other progressive marketing organizations such as those represented in our **Executive Roundtable**, so that the practice of marketing continues to evolve and improve during your careers. Whatever your major field of study or the career path you follow, we believe an understanding of marketing and its key perspectives will be crucial to your success. Best wishes and good luck!

A

Applications of Mathematical and Financial Tools to Marketing Decisions

Marketing decisions are often enhanced by the use of mathematical and financial analyses. These computations are helpful in setting prices, evaluating financial aspects of the firm, evaluating suppliers, determining inventory order quantities, and estimating segment potentials. Analysis of the firm's income statement is crucial for control and performance evaluation. This appendix describes and presents example calculations for some of the most frequently used mathematical and financial tools.

Exhibit A.1

Simplified weighted decision matrix

Evaluation criteria	Importance weight	Supplier A Score	Supplier A Total	Supplier B Score	Supplier B Total
Quality performance	16%	9.6	154	9.3	149
Delivery performance	22	8.1	178	7.6	167
Technical capability	8	10.0	80	8.0	64
Quoted price	44	7.5	330	9.3	409
Service factors	10	6.4	64	8.8	88
Overall total	100%	—	806	—	877

Supplier selection

Business buyers frequently use weighted indexes to evaluate suppliers. As explained in Chapter 6, buyers base decisions on selection of suppliers or vendors on the criteria they consider most important. Exhibit A.1 shows a simplified weighted index approach for evaluating two suppliers, A and B. This example is from the experiences of General Electric and its purchases of electrical wiring devices.[1]

In this example, five criteria are used to evaluate two suppliers: quality performance, delivery performance, technical capability, quoted price, and service factors. Price and delivery performance are weighted most heavily. These weights reflect a consensus of managerial judgment and past experiences with purchases of this type of product. Each supplier is evaluated on a 1 to 10 scale for each attribute, with 10 being the best possible rating. The scores are multiplied by an importance weight for each criterion. The "total" columns are summed to produce a score for each supplier. In this case, supplier B, with an overall total score of 877, is selected as the preferred vendor.

Estimating segment potentials

The "Survey of Buying Power" published annually by *Sales & Marketing Management* magazine, enables the computation of the *buying power index (BPI)* for individual geographic market segments. Frequently used to evaluate market segment potentials, the BPI is a measure of a particular market's ability to buy. The index converts three basic elements—population, effective buying income (EBI), and retail sales—into a measure of a market's ability to purchase, expressed as a percentage of the total US potential.[2] The three elements are weighted as follows: 0.2, population; 0.3, US retail sales potential; and 0.5, EBI, or disposable personal income, that is, income available after taxes. The latter weight reflects the importance of income to buying potential. The BPI for a market can be computed as:

$$BPI = (0.5)(EBI) + (0.3) \text{ (Retail sales \%)} + (0.2) \text{ (Population \%)}$$

The computations in Exhibit A.2 provide an example. Specifically, a skiing equipment company in West Virginia is considering expanding its sales operations into one of two neighboring states, Pennsylvania or Kentucky. The company offers premier equipment that it sells at premium prices. Their equipment is targeted toward young adults, aged 25 to 45 years old, with an EBI of at least $35,000.

Exhibit A.2

Evaluating geographic target segments

	Pennsylvania	Kentucky	United States
Households aged 25–45	1,805,780	590,118	41,231,931
Households EBI > $35,000	2,046,065	483,254	42,555,244
General merchandise stores' sales ($000)	$9,230,884	$3,448,368	$182,310,557

To construct a customized BPI for evaluating each state, the company made the following calculations:

Step 1. The ratio of each state's markets to those of the entire US are:

Pennsylvania

% of households aged 25–45:
1,805,780/41,231,931 = .043

% of households EBI > $35,000:
2,046,065/42,555,244 = .048

% of general merchandise stores' sales:
$9,230,884/$182,310,557 = .051

Kentucky

% of households aged 25–45:
590,118/41,231,931 = .014

% of households EBI > $35,000:
483,254/42,555,244 = .011

% of general merchandise stores' sales:
$3,448,368/$182,310,557 = .019

Step 2. The company assigns importance weights as follows:

Households aged 25–45	(20%) or .20
Households EBI > $35,000	(50%) or .50
General merchandise stores' sales	(30%) or .30

Note: These weights sum to 1.0.

Step 3. The BPI is the weighted sum of the three components:
Pennsylvania
(.20 x .043) + (.50 x .048) + (.30 x .051) = .0479
Kentucky
(.20 x .014) + (.50 x .011) + (.30 x .019) = .0140

The figures in Exhibit A.2 suggest that Pennsylvania offers the greatest potential as a market. However, other factors such as the cost of living, competition, and the legal environment may differ between these two states as well. Consequently, BPI comparisons should be used in conjunction with other information.

Price determination

In this section of the appendix, we discuss the break-even formula, elasticities of demand, and methods for computing retail markups. First, we present break-even formulas for quantity (units) and revenue (dollars). Second, we look at examples of other forms of elasticity and discuss profit maximization. Third, we explain markups and markdowns.

Break-even analysis

The traditional break-even formula is based on the premise that the break-even point in units occurs when total revenues equal total costs. The break-even quantity in units is defined as:

$$Q(BE) = \frac{\text{Fixed costs}}{\text{Price} - \text{Variable cost per unit}}$$

The break-even point in dollars is computed as:

$$Q(BE\$) = \frac{\text{Fixed costs}}{1 - (\text{Variable cost/Price})}$$

Exhibit A.3

Break-even points from different prices and quantity demanded

Price	Quantity demanded (000s)	Total revenue ($000)	Total fixed costs ($000)	Total variable costs ($000)	Total costs ($000)	Break-even quantity (000s)	Profit ($000)
$10	5.0	$50.0	$15.0	$35.0	$50.0	5.00	$0.0
11	4.8	52.8	15.0	33.6	48.6	3.75	4.2
12	4.7	56.4	15.0	32.9	47.9	3.00	8.5
13	4.6	59.8	15.0	32.2	47.2	2.50	12.6
14	4.0	56.0	15.0	28.0	43.0	2.14	13.0
15	3.4	51.0	15.0	23.8	38.8	1.87	12.2

The *BEP* in units is derived as follows. Remember that the *BEP* occurs where total costs equal total revenues:

$$TR = TC$$

$$P \times Q = FC + VC \times Q \text{ (because } TR = P \times Q)$$

$$\text{and } TC = FC + VC \times Q$$

$$P \times Q - VC \times Q = FC \text{ (transposing the } VC \text{ term)}$$

$$Q (P - VC) = FC \text{ (factoring out } Q)$$

Therefore, the *BEP* in units is $Q (BEP) = FC/(P - VC)$.

This analysis can be extended by considering the effects of different prices and quantity demanded. For example, the data presented in Exhibit A.3 show how the break-even quantity can vary as prices rise and demand declines. Notice the inverse relationship between price and demand. In this example, total fixed cost is $15,000 and variable cost per unit is $7.

This "sensitivity analysis" allows managers to consider alternative assumptions and conditions. It greatly enhances the managerial usefulness and realism of the break-even approach.

Elasticity

Price elasticity represents the change in quantity demanded from a change in price. Elasticities greater than one indicate elastic demand; that is, a 1 percent change in price causes a greater percentage change in demand. Inelastic demand occurs when a 1 percent price change results in less than a 1 percent change in demand. A commonly used computational approach for estimating elasticity is to compute the arc elasticity, where the price elasticity of demand is measured over a range using the average price and quantity as the base.

Arc elasticity of demand is computed as follows:

$$E_d = \frac{(Q_2 - Q_1)/[(Q_1 + Q_2)/2]}{(P_2 - P_1)/[(P_1 + P_2)/2]}$$

For example, at the price of $6 per ticket, the average moviegoer demands two tickets per month. At a price of $4 per ticket, the average moviegoer purchases six tickets per month.[3] The price elasticity for this example is:

$$E_d = \frac{(6 - 2)/[(6 + 2)/2]}{(4 - 6)/[(4 + 6)/2]} = -2.5$$

Therefore, the price elasticity of demand over this price range is elastic. Remember that price elasticities are normally negative and typically the negative sign, while shown here, is omitted.

Cross-price elasticity reflects quantity changes in one good or service caused by changing prices of other goods or services. This concept is useful for examining relationships among complementary goods (printers, personal computers) and substitutes (competitive brands, items in a product line, and pure substitutes such as videotape rental charges and movie prices). Conceptually, cross elasticity can be expressed as:

$$E_c = \frac{\text{Change in quantity demanded for product A}}{\text{Change in price for product B}}$$

If E_c is positive, products A and B are substitutes. If E_c is negative, the two products are complementary.

Assume the price of a Kodak 35-millimeter camera is $145 and a comparable Minolta is $149. Further, assume the quantities demanded for the Kodak and Minolta cameras at these prices are 50,000 and 100,000 units, respectively. When Kodak lowers its price to $142, the demand increases to 60,000. The Minolta demand, however, declines to 95,000 units.[4] The cross-price elasticity for the Minolta camera is:

$$E_c = \frac{-5,000/100,000}{-\$3/\$145} = 2.42$$

In this example, the two cameras are substitutes; hence, decreasing the price of one brand decreases the demand for the other.

Profit maximization

The traditional economic perspective on price setting is based on the premise that profits are maximized when marginal revenue equals marginal cost. Marginal revenue is the amount obtained from selling one additional unit of a product—this is usually the price paid for the unit. Marginal cost is the cost of producing and selling one additional unit of a product.

The cost and revenue data presented in Exhibit A.4 can be used to analyze these relationships for a hypothetical manufacturer of personalized T-shirts. The

Exhibit A.4
Sales and cost information for personalized T-shirts

(1) Quantity Q	(2) Price p	(3) Total revenue $TR = Q \times p$	(4) Marginal revenue MR	(5) Total cost TC	(6) Average total cost $ATC = \frac{TC}{Q}$	(7) Marginal cost MC	(8) Profit $\pi = TR - TC$
0	$10	$ 0		$ 2.00	—		$–2.00
1	9	9	$9	9.00	$9.00	$ 7.00	0.00
2	8	16	7	14.00	7.00	5.00	2.00
3	7	21	5	15.00	5.00	1.00	6.00
4	6	24	3	18.00	4.50	3.00	6.00
5	5	25	1	22.50	4.50	4.50	2.50
6	4	24	–1	30.00	5.00	7.50	–6.00
7	3	21	–3	49.00	7.00	19.00	–28.00

corresponding cost and revenue curves are depicted in Exhibit A.5. Note that in columns 4, marginal revenue, and 7, marginal cost, the manufacturer continues to expand output as long as marginal revenue exceeds marginal cost. Any expansion in output beyond this point would increase costs more than it would revenue. Therefore, the optimal output is four units priced at $6. Profits are maximized at that level:

$$\text{Profits} = TR - TC = \$24 - \$18 = \$6$$

Exhibit A.5 plots these findings. It shows that profits are maximized when price equals $6 and quantity equals 4. Notice that marginal costs initially decline as output increases. The shaded profit area is computed by multiplying unit profit times quantity of output:

$$\begin{aligned}\text{Profits} &= (AR - ATC) \times Q \\ &= (\$6 - \$4.50) \times 4 \\ &= \$6\end{aligned}$$

In this case, unit profit is the difference between average revenue and average total cost.

Markups and markdowns

Retail markups can be computed on either cost or the selling price. Markup as a percentage of cost is calculated as:

$$\text{Markup} = \frac{\text{Selling price} - \text{Cost}}{\text{Cost}}$$

Assume, for example, that a new Wilson tennis racket costs a retailer $90 and the markup is $50. Therefore, the selling price is $140. The markups on cost and price are:

Markup on cost = $50/$90 = 56%
Markup on price = $50/$140 = 36%

Exhibit A.5

Intersection of marginal cost and marginal revenue curves

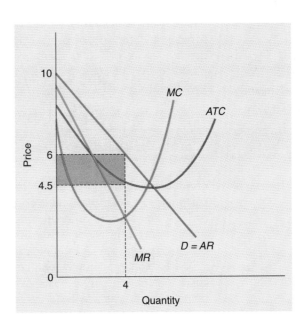

Frequently, retailers desire to convert markup percentages on cost to markup percentages on price and vice versa. The computational procedures for making these conversions are:

$$\text{Markup on cost} = \frac{\text{Markup on selling price}}{100\% - \text{Markup on selling price}}$$

$$\text{Markup on price} = \frac{\text{Markup on cost}}{100\% + \text{Markup on cost}}$$

Price reductions are common practice in retailing. In these instances, the retailer may wish to know what the percentage markdown is:

$$\text{Markdown on initial selling price} = \frac{\text{Initial selling price} - \text{Reduced sale price}}{\text{Initial selling price}}$$

$$\text{Markdown on reduced sale price} = \frac{\text{Initial selling price} - \text{Reduced sale price}}{\text{Reduced sale price}}$$

Return on inventory investment

Retailers evaluate merchandising performance of departments using the *gross margin return on inventory investments (GMROI)*. The GMROI combines the effects of both profits and turnover. Since both are considered, the GMROI enables comparison between retail store areas that differ in turnover and gross margin. It is computed as:[5]

$$GMROI = \frac{\text{Gross margin}}{\text{Net sales}} \times \frac{\text{Net sales}}{\text{Average inventory}} = \frac{\text{Gross margin}}{\text{Average inventory}}$$

Average inventory is usually expressed in terms of costs.

Inventory turnover, which is also used to evaluate how well investments in inventory are used, is the number of times inventory turns over or is sold, typically in a year. Inventory turnover is computed as:

$$\text{Inventory turnover} = \frac{\text{Costs of goods sold}}{\text{Average inventory cost}}$$

where average inventory equals (Beginning inventory + Ending inventory)/2. If for example, the cost of goods sold during a year was $600,000 and the average inventory was $200,000, then inventory turnover was 3. This value can be compared to that of competitive firms to evaluate inventory investment and firm performance.

Balancing physical distribution costs

One of the objectives of a distribution system is to provide adequate levels of customer service at reasonable costs. Companies would like to carry high inventories so they can fill orders promptly and maintain high service levels. As inventories increase, however, costs to the firm rise as well. These relationships are depicted graphically in Exhibit A.6.

As Exhibit A.6 shows, total costs represent the sum of two offsetting sets of costs. Order-processing costs, which decline as average inventory increases, include setup costs, manufacturing costs, and administrative costs. Inventory-carrying costs increase as average inventory increases. Carrying costs include

Exhibit A.6

Determining optimal order quantity

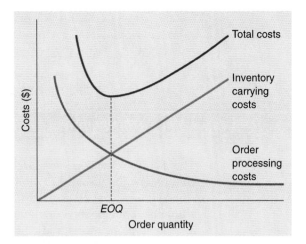

storage, insurance, investment, and obsolescence costs. The *economic order quantity (EOQ)* model offers one approach for determining inventory order quantities that balance these costs. Specifically, the EOQ model can be derived from the total cost relationships presented in Exhibit A.6 as follows:

$$\text{Total costs} = \text{Carrying costs} + \text{Ordering costs}$$

$$= \frac{QCI}{2} + \frac{RS}{Q}$$

where

Q = order quantity,
C = unit cost,
I = opportunity cost (%),
R = annual demand, and
S = ordering, setup cost.

Note that $(Q/2)$ is the average inventory and (R/S) is the number of orders required per year. The objective is to select the quantity that minimizes the total cost curve (see Exhibit A.6). Therefore, using basic calculus, the above equation can be differentiated with respect to Q:

$$TC'\ (Q) = \frac{CI}{2} + (-1)\frac{RS}{Q^2} = 0$$

By setting the above to zero and solving for Q, the EOQ model is derived:

$$EOQ = \sqrt{\frac{2RS}{CI}}$$

The model assumes that the pattern of demand is constant, that the lead time from order to delivery is constant, that all the order is received in a batch, and that stockouts do not occur. This approach can easily be modified to include the maintenance of safety stocks to further enhance service levels.

As an example, assume a manager wishes to determine the economic order quantity for a product that costs $3 and has annual sales of 600 units. The ordering cost is $80, and the opportunity cost of capital is 20 percent.

$$EOQ = \sqrt{\frac{2(600)(\$80)}{(\$3)(.2)}} = 400 \text{ units}$$

Total inventory costs for this product then would be:

$$TC = \frac{400}{2}(3)(.2) + \frac{600}{400}(80) = 120 + 120 = \$240$$

Income statement and performance ratios

The income statement summarizes the firm's revenues and expenses over an accounting period, usually 12 months beginning either July 1 or January 1. The income statement shown in Exhibit A.7 is for a manufacturer and marketer of aluminum components for compact disc manufacturers. (Income statements can also be developed for specific brands or projects.) Total and net sales are shown at the top of the statement. Net sales ($780,212) are determined by subtracting returns, allowances, and discounts from total sales. Gross profit is the amount remaining after costs of goods sold are subtracted from net sales. Operating income ($106,558) is the amount of funds available after operating expenses have been subtracted from gross profits. Net income is the final amount left after nonoperating items (interest expenses) and corporate income taxes have been paid.

Exhibit A.7

Income statement for year ended December 31, 1993

Sales revenue		$839,490
Less: Returns & allowances	$ 43,345	
Discounts	15,933	
Total		59,278
Net sales		780,212
Less: Cost of goods sold		416,296
Gross profits on sales (gross margin)		363,916
Operating expenses		
Salaries	$136,000	
Rent	19,000	
Miscellaneous office	2,046	
Marketing	52,812	
Depreciation	30,000	
Insurance	2,320	
Utilities	4,750	
Payroll taxes	9,230	
Bad debts	1,200	
Total operating expenses		257,358
Operating income		106,558
Nonoperating items		
Interest expense	$ 9,600	
Purchase discounts lost	534	
Total nonoperating items		10,134
Net income before corporate income taxes		96,424
Less: Corporate income taxes		48,212
NET INCOME		$ 48,212
Net income per weighted share of common stock outstanding		5.3487

This statement is useful in evaluating the performance of the firm. From the income statement, a number of frequently used ratios can be determined. Performance ratios based on the income statement include gross margin ratio, net income ratio, cost-of-goods-sold ratio, operating expense ratio, sales efficiency ratio, and return on investment (ROI).

$$\text{Gross margin ratio} = \frac{\text{Gross margin}}{\text{Net sales}} = \frac{\$363,916}{\$780,212} = 47\%$$

This ratio represents the percentage of sales revenue available to cover operating expenses and profit objectives.

$$\text{Net income ratio} = \frac{\text{Net income}}{\text{Net sales}} = \frac{\$48,212}{\$780,212} = 6\%$$

The net income ratio reflects the percentage of each sales dollar that is profit before corporate income taxes.

$$\text{Costs-of-goods-sold ratio} = \frac{\text{COGS}}{\text{Net sales}} = \frac{\$416,296}{\$780,212} = 53\%$$

This ratio reflects the percentage of sales used to manufacture goods sold. If it is high, costs are either excessive or prices may be too low.

$$\text{Operating expense ratio} = \frac{\text{Total expenses}}{\text{Net sales}} = \frac{\$257,358}{\$780,212} = 33\%$$

This ratio reflects the company's operating efficiency and represents the percentage of each dollar needed to cover expenses.

$$\text{Sales efficiency ratio} = \frac{\text{Net sales}}{\text{Gross sales}} = \frac{\$780,212}{\$839,490} = 93\%$$

This ratio reflects adjustments to gross sales from returns, allowances, and discounts.

$$\text{Return on investment (ROI)} = \frac{\text{Net profit before taxes}}{\text{Total investment}}$$

Information regarding total investment from the firm's balance sheet is required to compute ROI. ROI figures can be compared with industry averages and opportunity costs of investing elsewhere to evaluate the firm's performance.

appendix  B

A Product
Marketing Plan

A general strategic planning process is presented in Chapter 4. The basic stages include: examine the current situation, identify potential threats and opportunities, set objectives, and develop strategies. This appendix illustrates the types of information typically appearing in each section of a product marketing plan.

The example

In early 1994, Eastman Kodak is the market leader for 35mm film in the US. The company is making strategic changes to improve performance. Kodak would likely develop a 35mm film product marketing plan to articulate the marketing strategy and execution plan for 1994. The example below is hypothetical, but is illustrative of what Kodak would probably include in such a product marketing plan. Some of the information about Kodak and the 35mm film market has been taken from published sources; some has been fabricated to emphasize specific points.

1994 Product Marketing Plan for 35mm Film

Current situation

This section of the product marketing plan presents a snapshot of Kodak's current situation. It describes the general marketing strategy, provides some assessment of recent performance, and evaluates the competitive landscape. Typical information in this section includes:

- Kodak has two 35mm brands: Kodak Royal Gold (premium quality and price) and Kodak Gold (medium quality and price).
- Kodak is perceived to offer the highest-quality film by many consumers.
- Kodak's share of the 35mm film market dropped from 90 percent to 68 percent during the past 10 years.
- The size of the 35mm film market was 750 million rolls in 1993.
- Major competitors and market shares are Fuji Photo Film USA (25 percent), and Konica and private-label brands (7 percent).

Threats and opportunities

This section of the product marketing plan presents the major opportunities and threats facing Kodak during the next year. This information is obtained by identifying important trends in the marketing environment and assessing the potential impact of these trends on Kodak's marketing situation (see Chapter 3). The threats and opportunities are typically presented in order of importance. Examples for this section include the following items.

Threats

- Economic uncertainties are making many consumers more price conscious when purchasing products such as 35mm film.
- Fuji Photo Film USA is expected to try to increase market share through very aggressive marketing.
- Private-label sales of 35mm film are expected to increase.

- New electronic imaging technologies might replace the use of film by some consumers.
- Consumers' continuing desire for convenience is increasing the use of disposable cameras.

Opportunities

- Total sales of 35mm film are projected to increase by 5 percent in 1994.
- A growing number of consumers desire the highest quality pictures.
- Even price-conscious consumers are concerned about picture quality.

Set objectives

This section of the product marketing plan presents the objectives for the year. These objectives are expectations about what can be accomplished given the threats and opportunities facing Kodak. Example objectives include:

- Increase market share by 2 percent to 70 percent.
- Increase profits by 5 percent.

Marketing strategies

This section of the product marketing plan presents the marketing strategies Kodak will use to achieve the objectives within the marketing environment it faces in 1994. An *execution action plan* is also included to indicate what needs to be done, by whom, and when. Examples of marketing strategy information and an execution action plan include the following actions.

Marketing strategy

- Expand target market to include price-conscious consumers.
- Introduce low-price brand called Kodak Funtime.
- Achieve widespread distribution of Kodak Funtime.
- Price Kodak Gold 20 cents more than Kodak Funtime.
- Price Kodak Royal Gold 9 cents more than Kodak Gold.
- Increase advertising support for Kodak Super Gold with an emphasis on quality and value to differentiate the brand from brand and private-label competitors.
- Maintain advertising support for Kodak Gold.
- Promote Kodak Funtime at the point-of-purchase, but do not support with media advertising.

Execution action plan

- March 31: Advertising purchases network time and media space for Kodak Super Gold and Kodak Gold fall ads.

- April 30: Advertising gets Kodak Funtime point-of-purchase materials to salesforce.

- June 30: Salesforce gets retail distribution of Kodak Funtime with point-of-purchase materials set up.

- July 31: Advertising, product managers, and sales managers approve fall ads for Kodak Super Gold and Kodak Gold.

Conclusion

This sample product marketing plan illustrates several important points. Kodak's performance in the 35mm film market has been slowly eroding due to a changing market and increased competition. An assessment of the marketing environment indicates serious threats that are likely to reduce performance further, if current strategies are continued. There are, however, some opportunities in overall market growth and for reaching specific consumers. In addition, Kodak has a strong market position, high-quality image, and extensive distribution of its 35mm film.

Kodak wants to increase both market share and profits during 1994. The marketing strategies to achieve the desired objectives address the threats, build on Kodak's strengths, and take advantage of market opportunities. The new film, Kodak Funtime, appeals to price-conscious consumers and attacks low-priced competitors, especially private labels. The sales from this product should increase market share and, because of low marketing expenditures, contribute to a profit increase. Increased advertising for high-profit Kodak Royal Gold should increase both market share and profits. Some of the specific activities needed to implement the marketing strategies are indicated in the execution action plan.

Sources: Specific industry and company information taken from Riccardo A. Davis, "Kodak Unveils Ad Effort Framed around New 35mm Film Strategy," *Advertising Age,* May 23, 1994, p. 8; Riccardo A. Davis, "Kodak's Future Picture May Include Private Label," *Advertising Age,* June 20, 1994, p. 8; and Mark Maremont, "The New Flash at Kodak," *Business Week,* May 16, 1994, p. 32.

Glossary of Marketing Terms

ability the consumer's knowledge about the product category sufficient to understand the advertised message, *p. 446*

acceptable price range the range of prices buyers are willing to pay for a product; prices above the range may be judged unfair, while prices below the range may generate concerns about quality, *p. 320*

accessibility the degree to which a firm can reach intended target segments efficiently with its products and communications, *p. 184*

adaptive selling a salesperson's adjustment of his or her behavior between and during sales calls to respond appropriately to the situation and address issues important to the customer, *p. 499*

administered marketing channel system system designed to control a line or classification of merchandise; channel members agree on a comprehensive plan but no channel member owns another member, *p. 343*

adoption process the steps consumers follow in deciding whether to use a new product, *p. 246*

advertising the element of the marketing communications mix that is nonpersonal, paid for by an identified sponsor, and disseminated through mass channels of communication to promote the adoption of goods, services, persons, or ideas, *p. 418*

advertising agency a company that develops advertising messages and provides media planning and scheduling for marketers, *p. 441*

advertising allowance money paid a reseller for including the manufacturer's product, along with other products, in the reseller's advertising efforts, *p. 480*

advertising specialty an item of useful or interesting merchandise given away free and typically carrying an imprinted name or message; for example, a pen, calendar, or coffee mug, *p. 475*

advertorial a special advertising section with some editorial (nonadvertising) content included in magazines, *p. 450*

aided recall tests posttesting in which consumers are given lists of ads and asked which they remembered and read, *p. 454*

AIO statements survey responses concerning activities, interests, and opinions (AIO), used in psychographic research, *p. 189*

all you can afford budgeting a method for determining the marketing communications budget that involves spending whatever's left over after other costs without considering the firm's objectives, *p. 430*

Americans with Disabilities Act (ADA) a US law passed in 1990 to prohibit discrimination against consumers with disabilities, *p. 512*

anchor position retail stores, often department stores, that are strategically placed in malls, shopping centers, or downtown shopping areas to attract customers and stimulate traffic flow throughout the shopping area, *p. 378*

arbitraging see **diverting**, *p. 486*

arc elasticity of demand the price elasticity of demand measured over a range using the average price and quantity as the base, *p. 553*

atmospherics a retailer's combination of architecture, layout, color scheme, sound and temperature monitoring, special events, prices, displays, and other factors that attract and stimulate customers, *p. 362*

attention the consumer's mental notice directed at a marketing communication (such as an ad), often stimulated by its physical characteristics; the second step in the information-processing model, *p. 446*

attitudes learned predispositions to respond favorably or unfavorably to a product or brand; based on beliefs about its attributes (price, service level, quality), *p. 111*

auction house a company that sells merchandise at a given time and place to the highest bidder, *p. 394*

automatic number identification a system that identifies incoming phone numbers of respondents to an ad or promotion at the beginning of the call without the callers' knowledge, *p. 534*

backward integration a corporate marketing channel system in which the channel member owns one or more of its suppliers upstream (as opposed to forward integration, where it owns buyers downstream), *p. 342*

bait and switch advertising a product at an attractively low price to get customers into the store but not making it available, so customers must trade up to a more expensive version, *p. 326*

balanced matrix organization an approach to new-product development in which a project manager oversees the project and shares responsibility and authority with functional managers, *p. 249*

bar coding a computer-coded bar pattern that identifies a product; see also **Universal Product Code**, *p. 401*

bases of segmentation the distinguishing characteristics of market segments (such as demographics, benefits sought) within a firm's overall product or service market, *p. 186*

basic price mix the basic components that define the size and means of payment exchanged for goods and services; less comprehensive than the price promotion mix, *p. 283*

battle of the brands intense competition between manufacturer and distributor brands, *p. 224*

behavior-based perspective a way of evaluating salesperson performance that defines the sales behaviors expected, such as how many calls to make or which presentation tactics to use; see also **outcome-based perspective**, *p. 510*

benefit what a product feature can do for a particular customer; for example, a speakerphone built into a fax machine is a feature, but the fact that it allows hands-free conversation is a benefit, *p. 500*

benefit segmentation segmenting the market by the attributes or benefits consumers need or desires, such as quality, service, or unique features, *p. 191*

best-value strategy purchasing the lowest-cost brand available with the desired level of quality, *p. 297*

bids in government markets, written proposals from qualified suppliers in response to published governmental requirements or specifications, *p. 144*

brand a name, term, sign, symbol, design, or combination that a firm uses to identify its products and differentiate them from competitors, *p. 221*

brand awareness when target consumers know about a brand and it comes to mind when thinking about the product category; for example, Kleenex comes to mind when thinking about tissues, *p. 223*

brand competitors direct competitors that offer the same types of products (for example, Domino's Pizza and Pizza Hut), *p. 72*

brand equity the value a brand has in the marketplace due to reputation and goodwill, *p. 223*

brand image consumers' impression about a brand, *p. 223*

branding identifying a firm's products to distinguish them from competitors' similar products, *p. 221*

brand loyalty when consumers purchase a specific brand all or most of the time, *p. 223*

brand mark the element of a brand that cannot be vocalized (for example, the MGM lion or the Texaco star), *p. 221*

brand name the element of a brand that can be vocalized (for example, IBM, Tide, Coke), *p. 221*

break-even analysis calculation of the number of units that must be sold at a certain price for the firm to cover costs (break even); revenues earned past the break-even point contribute to profits, *p. 321*

broker an intermediary that brings buyers and sellers together and is paid a commission by whichever party it represents in a given transaction, *p. 395*

budgeting allocating to various aspects of marketing communications monetary sums based on factors such as the size of the company, its financial resources, the type of business, the market dispersion, the industry growth rate, and the firm's position in the marketplace, *p. 428*

bundling marketing two or more products in a single package at one price (for example, computer systems or ski weekends), *p. 318*

business analysis the stage of new-product development where initial marketing plans are prepared, including a tentative marketing strategy and estimates of sales, costs, and profitability, *p. 243*

business firms   manufacturers of tangible goods and firms that provide services such as health care, entertainment, and transportation, *p. 134*

business level   the smaller units within a complex organization that are managed as self-contained businesses, *p. 81*

business products   goods and services purchased by a firm for its own use (as opposed to consumer products), *p. 213*

business strategic plan   a plan for how each business unit in the corporate family intends to compete in the marketplace, given the vision, objectives, and growth strategies of the corporate strategic plan, *p. 82*

business-to-business advertising   promoting products or services directly to other firms, often through print ads in trade periodicals or direct-mail promotions to targeted potential buyers, *p. 444*

business-to-business buying behavior   the decision making and other activities of organizations as buyers, *p. 132*

buying allowance   payment of a specified amount of money to a reseller for purchasing a certain amount of a product during a particular period, *p. 480*

buying center   business purchasing decision makers made up of people throughout all levels of the organization, not just the purchasing department; the buying center makeup may vary as purchasing decisions change, *p. 143*

buying loader   a dealer premium in the form of a gift, such as a free trip, for buying, displaying, and selling a certain amount of a product within a specified time, *p. 481*

buying power index (BPI)   a measure of a particular market's relative ability to buy, based on population, effective buying income, and retail sales and expressed as a percentage of the total US potential, *p. 551*

caller ID intrusion system   see **automatic number identification**, *p. 534*

canned sales presentation   a fully scripted presentation that the sales rep memorizes, or even an audiovisual presentation, that is not adaptable to individual customers, *p. 500*

cannibalization   when a new product takes sales away from existing products, which leads merely to a shift in the company's sales instead of a gain, *p. 267*

capital products   expensive items that are used in business operations but do not become part of any finished product; examples include physical facilities (office buildings) and accessory equipment (copiers and forklifts), *p. 216*

cash-and-carry wholesaler   a limited-function wholesaler that does not extend credit for or deliver the products it sells; its primary customers are small retailers, *p. 391*

catalog wholesaler   a limited-function wholesaler that offers a wide range of competitively priced products that customers order by phone or fax, *p. 391*

category   an assortment of items seen by the customer as reasonable substitutes for each other, *p. 361*

category killers   discount retailers that offer a complete assortment and can thus dominate a product category, giving them the clout to negotiate excellent prices from suppliers and be assured of dependable sources of supply, *p. 361*

causal research   experiments in which researchers manipulate independent variables and observe the dependent variable(s) of interest to identify cause and effect relationships, *p. 160*

celebrity endorsement   the use of a famous spokesperson, say a sports or movie star, to promote a product, *p. 450*

central business district   a downtown area, representing a city's greatest concentration of office buildings and retail stores, *p. 375*

cents-off deal   an offering of a brand at less than the regular price, *p. 471*

channel conflict   conflict between members of a marketing channel, which may stem from poor communication, a power struggle, or incompatible objectives, *p. 352*

channel cooperation   a cooperative spirit among members of a marketing channel that helps reduce and resolve conflicts, *p. 352*

channel leader   a marketing channel member with enough power to control others in the channel, *p. 352*

channel objectives   specific, measurable goals of a marketing channel that are consistent with the firm's marketing objectives and are often stated in terms of sales volume, profitability, market share, cost, number of wholesale or retail outlets, or geographic expansion, *p. 345*

channel of distribution   see **marketing channel**, *p. 334*

channel power   ways marketing channel members can gain control to enhance their position, including reward power, legitimate power, expert power, and referent power, *p. 351*

channel strategy   an expression of a general action plan and guidelines for allocating resources to achieve the objective of a marketing channel, *p. 345*

childhood consumer socialization   the process by which young people acquire skills, knowledge, and attitudes to help them function as consumers in the marketplace, *p. 114*

Child Protection Act   a US law passed in 1990 to regulate advertising on children's TV programs, *p. 68*

Child Safety Act   a US law passed in 1966 that prohibits the marketing of dangerous products to children, *p. 68*

classified advertising   advertising that typically promotes transactions for a single item or service and usually appears in newspapers, *p. 444*

Clayton Act   a US law passed in 1914 that prohibits anti-competitive activities, *p. 294*

cluster sampling   a probability sampling technique in which units are organized into similar clusters, such as neighborhoods; clusters are then selected randomly and each house in the selected clusters is included in the sample, *p. 169*

coaching   the leadership function of providing guidance and feedback on a regular basis to direct salespeople's activities, *p. 509*

coercive power   power a member of a marketing channel uses to pressure another member to do something; for example, a manufacturer threatens to cut off a distributor's credit unless the distributor pays its bills more promptly, *p. 352*

cognitive dissonance   a consumer's postpurchase doubt about the appropriateness of a purchase decision; caused by an imbalance of information because each alternative has attractive features; most likely to occur when the purchase is important and visible, the perceived risk is high, and the decision involves a long-term commitment, *p. 123*

collaborative venture   an arrangement in which two or more firms share in the rights to market specified products; may take the form of a strategic partnership, strategic alliance, joint venture, or licensing agreement, *p. 237*

combination strategy   aiming marketing communications at both resellers and ultimate consumers in a push-pull approach, *p. 431*

commercialization   the stage of new-product development after the product tests successfully and the firm introduces it on a full-scale basis, *p. 246*

commercial zapping   changing the channels during TV commercials, *p. 442*

commission merchant   a wholesaler that provides a wider range of services than agents or brokers, often engaging in inventory management, physical distribution, and promotional activities and offering credit and market feedback to the companies it represents, *p. 395*

communication   the process of establishing shared meaning, exchanging ideas, or passing information between a source and a receiver, *p. 423*

comparative advertising   advertising that compares a sponsored brand to a competitive brand on at least one product attribute (such as MCI versus AT&T services), *p. 434*

competitive advantage   trying to get consumers to purchase one's products instead of competitors' products, through either lower prices or differentiation, *p. 91*

competitive environment   all the organizations that attempt to serve the same customers, including both brand competitors and product competitors, *p. 72*

competitive parity   a budgeting method for marketing communications based on the percentage allocated by other companies in the industry, *p. 429*

competitive pricing   pricing strategies based on a firm's position in relation to its competition; includes penetration pricing, limit pricing, and price signaling, *p. 317*

composite of salesforce estimates   a means of forecasting sales in which sales reps give forecasts for their territories, which can then be combined, *p. 198*

concentrated strategy   a strategy in which a firm seeks a large share of one or a few profitable segments of the total market, often concentrating on serving the selected segments innovatively and creatively, *p. 194*

concept development   the process of shaping and refining the idea for a new product into a complete description, *p. 242*

concept testing   having the concept for a new product evaluated by potential customers, *p. 243*

consolidated metropolitan statistical area (CMSA)   the largest designation of geographic areas based on census data; the 20 largest market areas in the US that contain at least two PMSAs, *p. 188*

consumer behavior   the mental and emotional processes and the physical activities people engage in when they se-lect, purchase, use, and dispose of products or services to satisfy particular needs and desires, *p. 106*

Consumer Credit Protection Act   a US law passed in 1968 that requires full disclosure of financial charges for loans, *p. 68*

consumer decision process   a four-step process: (1) recognizing a need or problem, (2) searching for information, (3) evaluating alternative products or brands, and (4) purchasing a product, *p. 108*

consumerism   a social movement in which consumers demand better consumer information, quality, service, dependability, and fair prices, *p. 63*

consumer learning   a process that changes consumers' knowledge or behavior patterns through marketing communications or experience, *p. 112*

consumer products   goods and services purchased by consumers for their own personal use (as opposed to business products), *p. 213*

Consumer Product Safety Commission (CPSC)   an agency of the US government that protects consumers from unsafe products, *p. 70*

consumer protection laws   laws that state what firms must do to give consumers the information they need to make sound purchasing decisions or to make sure the products they buy are safe, *p. 68*

consumer rights   four inherent rights of consumers: (1) to safety, (2) to be informed, (3) to choose, and (4) to be heard, *p. 125*

consumer sales promotion   sales promotion directed at ultimate users of the product or service (as opposed to trade sales promotion), *p. 419*

contest   a sales promotion that offers prizes based on the skill of contestants, *p. 474*

continual training   ongoing sales training that helps firms stay current and competitive in an ever-changing environment, *p. 508*

convenience products   consumer may prefer a specific brand but do not want to spend much time shopping for it; will buy another brand if preferred one is not available; normally low-priced, often-purchased goods, *p. 214*

convenience store   retail store that carries a modest variety and shallow assortment of products and has high prices but offers a convenient location and hours, *p. 379*

cooperative advertising   advertising for a local dealer or retailer whose expense is contributed to by the manufacturer, *p. 444*

corporate advocacy advertising   advertising that announces a stand on some issue related to the firm's operation, often one threatening the company's well-being, *p. 444*

corporate image advertising   advertising directed toward the general public or investors and stockholders promoting an organization's image and role in the community as a corporate citizen, independent of any product or service, *p. 444*

corporate level   the highest level in any organization, at which managers address issues concerning the overall organization and their decisions and actions affect all other organizational levels, *p. 81*

corporate strategic plan a plan that determines what a company is and wants to become and that guides strategic planning at all organizational levels; it involves developing a corporate vision, formulating corporate objectives, allocating resources, determining how to achieve desired growth, and establishing business units, *p. 82*

corporate vision the basic values of an organization, specifying what it stands for, where it wants to go, and how it plans to get there, and addressing the organization's markets, principal products or services, geographic domain, core technologies, objectives, basic philosophy, self-concept, and desired public image, *p. 85*

corrective advertising advertising the FTC mandates to remedy misleading impressions and information in an ad, *p. 456*

cost per thousand (CPM) a factor in evaluating the cost effectiveness of a particular outlet for reaching desired market audiences, *p. 453*

counselor strategy a selling approach in which the sales team is knowledgeable enough to act as an advisor to the customer to provide superior service and high-quality information, *p. 505*

countersegmentation combining market segments to appeal to a broad range of consumers and assuming an increasing consumer willingness to accept fewer product and service variations for lower prices; *p. 195*

countertrade trade between developed and less developed countries that involves barter and exchanges instead of just currency, *p. 282*

coupon a printed certificate giving the bearer a stated price reduction or special value on a specific product, generally for a specific time period; especially useful in encouraging new-product trials; may be distributed in an ad, in a freestanding insert, or on the store shelf, *p. 474*

creative strategy combining what is said in an ad with how it is said; typically the marketer specifies the general theme of the message and the ad agency develops the presentation, *p. 447*

cross elasticity of demand the relation of the percentage change in quantity demanded for one product to percentage price changes for other products; a price increase for one brand of cola will increase demand for a substitute brand, but a price increase for computers will decrease demand for printers, a complementary product, *p. 308*

cross-functional teamwork having employees from different functional areas of a firm work together to satisfy customer needs, *p. 97*

cross-promotion the collaboration of two or more firms in a sales promotion; also called a **tie-in**, *p. 473*

cross-sectional study a survey of customers administered at a given time to assess, for example, perceived satisfaction with service, *p. 160*

cultural environment factors and trends related to how people live and behave, including the values, ideas, attitudes, beliefs, and activities of specific population subgroups; a component of the social environment, *p. 61*

culture the values, ideas, attitudes, and symbols people adopt to communicate, interpret, and interact as members of a society; a society's way of life, learned and transmitted from one generation to the next, that includes both abstract and material elements. Culture determines the most basic values that influence consumer behavior patterns and can be used to distinguish subcultures that represent substantial market segments and opportunities, *p. 112*

customary pricing pricing strategies that modify the quality, features, or service of a product without adjusting the price; customary price beliefs reflect consumers' strongly held expectations about what the price of a product should be, *p. 319*

customer contact strategy sometimes called **sales channel strategy**; addresses how the company initiates and maintains contacts with customers, *p. 506*

customer service the assistance a firm provides to help a customer with the purchase or use of a product or service; providing exceptional customer service can give a firm a marketing advantage, *p. 228*

customized marketing strategy implementing a different marketing mix for each target market country in international marketing, *p. 96*

database marketing the collection and use of individual customer-specific information stored on a computer to make marketing more efficient, *p. 174*

dealer loader a premium given to a reseller to encourage development of a special display or product offering, *p. 481*

deceptive advertising communications intended to mislead consumers by making false claims or failing to disclose important information, *p. 433*

decline stage the fourth and final stage of the product life cycle, when falling sales and profits persist, *p. 261*

decoding the process in communications by which the receiver deciphers the meaning of the words, pictures, and other symbols used in the message, *p. 424*

demand curve relationship that shows how many units a market will purchase at a given price in a given time period; generally, customers buy more units as prices drop and fewer units as prices rise, *p. 307*

demographic environment the size, distribution, and growth rate of groups of people with different traits that relate to buying behavior; a component of the social environment, *p. 56*

department store a retail store characterized by a wide variety of merchandise and extensive depth of assortment; typically organized around sales departments like apparel, cosmetics, and housewares, *p. 378*

derived demand demand for business-to-business products that is dependent upon demand for other products in consumer markets, as when increased consumer demand for new automobiles causes a demand for products used to make them also go up, *p. 132*

descriptive research research directed by one or more formal research questions or hypotheses, usually involving a survey or questionnaire, *p. 160*

differential pricing selling the same product to different buyers at a variety of prices; such price discrimination works because there are differences in reactions to price among consumers or consumer segments, *p. 315*

differential responsiveness the degree to which market segments exhibit varying responses to different marketing mix combinations, *p. 185*

differentiated strategy using different marketing strategies for different segments; either marketing a unique product and communications campaign to each segment, or marketing a common product to different segments with various communication strategies, *p. 194*

differentiation offering consumers products or services that are better than the competition; one way to gain a competitive advantage, *p. 182*

diffusion process the adoption of an innovative product form over time, *p. 260*

direct investment investing in production, sales, distribution, and/or other operations in a foreign country; requires a large investment of resources but gives the marketer much control over operations, *p. 96*

direct mail any form of advertising addressed to prospects through public or private delivery services, including everything from a simple flyer to a package that contains a letter, multipage brochure, video, and response card, *p. 523*

direct marketing distributing goods, services, information, or promotional benefits to carefully targeted consumers through interactive (two-way) communication while tracking response, sales, interests, or desires through a computer database, *p. 370*

direct marketing channel a way to move the product from producer to user without intermediaries, *p. 338*

direct marketing communications (DMC) a process of communications directly with target customers to encourage response by telephone, mail, electronic means, or personal visit; examples of DMC methods include direct mail, telemarketing, computer shopping services, TV shopping networks, and infomercials, *p. 421*

direct-response advertising advertising intended to elicit immediate purchase; for example, TV commercials that show a toll-free phone number, *p. 444*

direct-response radio advertising radio ads that provide a phone number or address to elicit immediate feedback from the consumer, *p. 530*

direct-response TV advertising TV ads that include an 800 or 900 phone number and an address for placing orders in an attempt to get an immediate answer from the consumer, *p. 530*

direct selling a method in which salespeople reach consumers directly or by telephone primarily at home or at work and sell through personal demonstration and explanation, *p. 371*

direct-to-consumer salespeople sales reps who sell to individuals who personally use the products and services; they include retail salespeople, real estate agents, and financial securities agents, *p. 496*

discounts reductions from the market price; for example, cash discounts for prompt payment or quantity discounts for large orders. See also **trade sales promotion allowances**, *p. 321*

display allowance money or a product provided to a retailer for featuring the manufacturer's brand in an agreed-on in-store display, *p. 480*

display loader a dealer premium that lets the reseller keep some or all of the display when the promotion ends, *p. 481*

distribution center an automated "superwarehouse" that serves a large geographic area and receives, processes, and ships customer orders in addition to storing products, *p. 400*

distributor brand a brand sponsored by a distributor such as a wholesaler or retailer; the distributor is responsible for the product's quality and marketing. Also called a **store brand, private brand,** or **private label**, *p. 224*

diversification strategy expanding into new products and new markets; the riskiest growth strategy, since the company cannot build directly on its strengths in its current markets or products, *p. 88*

diverting secretly purchasing a product where it is less expensive, usually due to a trade promotion, and reselling it where prices are higher, *p. 486*

downward stretch strategy adding products to the lower end of a product line; for example, IBM entered the market with high-priced microcomputers and later added lower-priced ones, *p. 267*

drop shipper a limited-function wholesaler that arranges for shipments directly from the factory to the customer; it does not physically handle the product but does take title and all associated risks while the product is in transit, as well as providing sales support, *p. 391*

dumping selling a product in a foreign country at a price lower than in the home country and lower than its marginal cost of production, *p. 294*

durability the stability of market segments and whether distinctions between them will diminish or disappear as the product category or the markets mature, *p. 184*

early adopters the second group to adopt a new product (after innovators); they represent about 13.5 percent of a market, *p. 260*

early majority the third group to adopt a new product (after innovators and early adopters); they represent about 34 percent of a market, *p. 260*

ecological perspective considering the environmental consequences of marketing decisions and capitalizing on environmental marketing opportunities, *p. 43*

economic environment factors and trends that are related to the production of goods and services and population incomes and that affect the purchasing power of markets, *p. 64*

economic order quantity (EOQ) a way to determine inventory order quantities that balances carrying costs and ordering costs, *p. 557*

effective buying income (EBI) disposable personal income (income available after taxes), *p. 551*

elastic demand demand for a product that changes substantially in response to small changes in price; when demand is elastic, a small decrease in price may substantially increase total revenues, *p. 307*

electronic data interchange (EDI) a computerized system that allows exchange of information between parties; part of a quick-response inventory control system, *p. 402*

embargo prohibition against trade with a particular country, imposed by the UN or individual governments, *p. 67*

emotional appeals ad message strategies that attempt to evoke feelings, moods, and memories to sell a product, *p. 450*

encoding the process in communications by which the source chooses the words, pictures, and other symbols used to transmit the intended message, *p. 424*

entrepreneurial perspective an emphasis on innovation, risk taking, and proactiveness in all marketing activities, *p. 44*

entry strategy the approach used to begin marketing products internationally; options run the gamut from exporting to joint ventures to direct investment, *p. 95*

Environmental Protection Agency (EPA) agency of the US government whose goal is to protect the environment, *p. 70*

environmental scanning identifying relevant factors and trends and assessing their potential impact on the organization's markets and marketing activities, *p. 56*

ethical perspective addressing the morality of marketing decisions and practicing social responsibility, *p. 34*

ethnic patterns the norms and values of specific groups or subcultures, which may be formed around nationality, religion, race, or geographic factors, *p. 113*

ethnographic research technique in which market researchers record how consumers actually use products, brands, and services from day to day by entering their homes, observing consumption behavior, and recording pantry and garbage content, *p. 168*

European Union (EU) the world's largest consumer market, consisting of 16 European nations: France, Germany, Italy, the Netherlands, Belgium, Luxembourg, Britain, Ireland, Denmark, Greece, Spain, Portugal, Sweden, Finland, Norway, and Austria, *p. 295*

everyday-low-price (EDLP) policy suppliers reduce discounts and promotions to retailers; and retailers demand low prices from suppliers and minimize advertising and sales promotions to keep prices consistently low, *p. 376*

exchange the transfer of something tangible or intangible, actual or symbolic, between two or more social actors, *p. 12*

exchange rate the price of one country's currency in terms of another country's currency, *p. 284*

exclusive dealing agreement a marketing channel arrangement between producer and reseller that restricts the reseller from carrying a competing product line, *p. 354*

exclusive distribution using only one outlet in a geographic marketplace, *p. 346*

exclusive territories a marketing channel arrangement between a producer and a reseller that prohibits other resellers from selling a particular brand in a given geographic area, *p. 354*

execution perspective a focus on the effective implementation of sound marketing strategies, *p. 46*

existing-business salespeople sales reps who work with established customers, writing up fairly routine orders, to provide a steady stream of sales revenue, *p. 496*

expert opinion a qualitative approach to forecasting sales in which analysts ask executives within the company or other experts to provide forecasts based on their own judgments, *p. 198*

expert power power a member of a marketing channel gains by accumulating expertise and knowledge; for example, large retailers have gained much expert power using point-of-sale scanners to gauge product movements, price sensitivities, and trade promotion effectiveness, *p. 351*

explicit communications a distinct, clearly stated message conveyed through personal selling, advertising, public relations, sales promotion, direct marketing, or some combination of these methods, *p. 430*

exploratory research research carried out to gain greater understanding or develop preliminary background and suggest hypotheses for a detailed follow-up study; may involve literature reviews, case analyses, interviews, and focus groups, *p. 160*

export agent a wholesaler that locates and develops markets abroad for products manufactured in its home country, operating on commission, *p. 395*

exporting selling products to buyers in international markets, either directly or through intermediaries, *p. 95*

extensive problem solving using considerable mental effort and a substantial search for information, usually in response to a high-involvement decision, *p. 111*

external reference prices prices charged by other retailers or comparison prices a retailer provides to enhance perceptions of the advertised price, *p. 297*

external secondary data secondary data that are collected from outside the firm and may be proprietary (provided by commercial marketing research firms) or nonproprietary (available from public sources), *p. 162*

external sourcing acquiring specific brands from another firm or purchasing the entire firm to obtain ownership of its products, *p. 237*

fad a subcategory of fashion that has a very short product life, *p. 262*

Fair Credit Report Act a US law passed in 1970 to regulate the reporting and use of credit information, *p. 68*

Fair Debt Collections Practice Act a US law passed in 1970 to regulate methods for collecting on debts, *p. 68*

Fair Packaging & Labeling Act a US law passed in 1965 to regulate the packaging and labeling of products, *p. 68*

family brand name strategy branding all items in a product line or even the entire product mix with a family name or the company name, *p. 271*

family life cycle the sequence of steps a family goes through, from young single adults to the married couple whose children have left home; household consumption patterns vary greatly across the family life cycle, *p. 115*

fashion a component of style whose products reflect what is currently popular, *p. 262*

fax-on-demand systems direct marketing technology that lets consumers request information by fax (via an 800 number) and lets the marketer reply instantly, also by fax, *p. 533*

fear appeal a type of emotional appeal used in an ad message strategy; for example, Michelin's "baby in a tire" theme, *p. 450*

feature a statement of fact about some aspect of a product or service (as opposed to a benefit, which is what the feature can do for the customer), *p. 500*

Federal Communications Commission (FCC) agency of the US government that regulates the interstate communications industry, *p. 70*

Federal Trade Commission (FTC) agency of the US government that regulates business practices; established by the Federal Trade Commission Act of 1914, *p. 69*

feedback the part of the receiver's response that is communicated to the sender, *p. 336*

fieldwork the process of contacting respondents, conducting interviews, and completing surveys in market research, *p. 170*

five Cs of pricing five critical influences on pricing decisions—costs, customers, channels of distribution, competition, and compatibility, *p. 289*

fixed costs costs that cannot be changed in the short run and do not vary with the quantity produced; they include plant investments, interest, and the costs of production facilities. See also **variable costs**, *p. 308*

flyer a single-page piece of direct mail printed on one or both sides of 8½-by-11 inch paper and folded, *p. 526*

FOB origin pricing a form of geographic pricing in which buyers are charged the unit cost of goods plus shipping costs, which vary with location; in FOB (free on board), the goods are placed on a carrier and shipped to the customer, who pays the transportation charges, *p. 322*

focus group an explorary research method in which a moderator leads 8 to 12 people in a focused, in-depth discussion on a specific topic; used most for examining new-product concepts and advertising themes, investigating the criteria underlying purchase decisions, and generating information for developing consumer questionnaires, *p. 164*

Food and Drug Administration (FDA) an agency of the US government that regulates the food, drug, and cosmetics industries; established by the Food, Drug & Cosmetic Act of 1938, *p. 70*

forward buying when distributors or consumers stock up on enough of a product at a deal price to carry them over to the next sale, *p. 484*

forward integration a corporate marketing channel system in which a channel member owns one or more of its buyers downstream (as opposed to backward integration, where it owns suppliers upstream), *p. 341*

franchisee party that is granted rights (by the franchisor) to distribute and sell specified goods and services, *p. 343*

franchise system a contractual marketing channel system where the franchisor grants a franchisee the right to distribute and sell specified goods and services and the franchisee agrees to operate according to marketing guidelines set forth by the franchisor under a recognized trademark or trade name, *p. 343*

franchisor parent company that grants rights to a franchisee to distribute and sell its goods and services, *p. 343*

freestanding insert (FSI) a preprinted ad, usually containing a coupon, placed in a separate publication, such as a newspaper, *p. 472*

freight absorption pricing a form of geographical pricing in which the seller absorbs freight costs, *p. 322*

frequency the number of times a person or household is exposed to a communication vehicle such as an ad, *p. 453*

full-service wholesaler a wholesaler that performs a wide range of services for its customers and the parties from which it purchases, *p. 390*

functional level the various functional areas within a business unit, where most of the unit's work is performed (for example, marketing and accounting are functional areas), *p. 81*

functional middleman a wholesaler that does not take title to the products it sells, *p. 389*

game a sales promotion that offers prizes like sweepstakes but covers a longer time period, *p. 474*

gatekeepers decision makers who control the flow of information and communication among buying-center participants, *p. 143*

General Agreement on Tariffs and Trade (GATT) an agreement under which countries meet periodically to negotiate matters related to trade and tariffs; in 1993, GATT was signed by 108 countries representing 80 percent of all global trade, *p. 67*

general merchandise wholesaler a wholesaler that carries a wide variety of products and provides extensive services for its customers, *p. 390*

generics products that are not branded; they are labeled only by their generic name (tomato soup) and usually cost less and may be of lower quality than their branded competitors, *p. 223*

geodemographics the combination of geographic information and demographic characteristics; used in segmenting and targeting specific segments, *p. 189*

global conversation concept that the world is tied together in a single electronic market moving at the speed of light (a term coined by former Citicorp chairman Walter Wriston), *p. 28*

global perspective a view of the marketplace that includes searching for marketing opportunities around the world, competing internationally, and working with multicultural suppliers, employees, channel participants, and customers, *p. 29*

goods physical products such as cars, golf clubs, soft drinks, or other concrete entities (in contrast to services, which are nonphysical products), *p. 211*

government market federal, state and local government organizations that purchase goods and services for use in many activities, *p. 134*

green marketing implementing an ecological perspective in marketing or promoting a product as environmentally safe, *p. 44*

gross domestic product (GDP)   the total size of a country's economy measured in the amount of goods and services produced, *p. 64*

gross margin   sales revenue minus the retailer's cost of goods sold, *p. 379*

gross margin return on inventory investments (GMROI)   a calculation of ROI that combines the effects of profits and turnover, *p. 559*

growth stage   the second stage in the product life cycle, when sales and profits increase rapidly, *p. 261*

hard-core browns   consumers who are antienvironmentalist in their purchasing behavior (about 15–30 percent of the US population), *p. 44*

hierarchy of effects model   see **information-processing model**, *p. 446*

high-involvement decisions   purchasing decisions that involve high levels of importance or personal relevance, thorough information processing, and substantial differences between alternatives, *p. 110*

house organs   newsletters, consumer magazines, stockholder reports, or dealer publications mailed to particular audiences, *p. 525*

idea generation   the initial stage of the new-product development process, requiring creativity and innovation to generate ideas for potential new products, *p. 240*

idea screening   evaluating the pool of new-product ideas to reduce it to a smaller, more attractive set, based on consistency with the company vision and strategic objectives, potential market acceptance, fit with the firm's capabilities, and possible long-term contribution to profit, *p. 242*

implicit communications   what the marketing message connotes about the product, its price, or the places it is sold, *p. 430*

import agent   a wholesaler that finds products in foreign countries to sell in its home country; in many countries, it is illegal to sell imported products without going through an import agent or similar intermediary, *p. 395*

incentive pay   commissions, bonuses, or both; about 75 percent of US firms use a combination pay plan, less than 15 percent pay a straight salary, and 10 percent pay straight commission, *p. 509*

income statement   summary of a firm's revenues and expenses over an accounting period, usually 12 months, *p. 558*

independent retailers   retailers that own and operate only one retail outlet; they account for more than three-fourths of all US retail establishments, *p. 363*

indirect marketing channel   a way to move the product from producer to user with the help of intermediaries that perform functions related to buying or selling the product, *p. 338*

individual brand name strategy   establishing specific and different brand names for each individual product in a product line, *p. 271*

individual product   any brand or variant of a brand in a company's product line, *p. 259*

inelastic demand   the demand that exists when price changes do not result in significant changes in the quantity of a product demanded, *p. 307*

infomercial   a program-length TV ad that resembles a talk show or news program, *p. 528*

informational influence   an interpersonal process, based on consumers' desire to make informed choices and reduce uncertainty, in which they seek information and advice from people they trust, *p. 117*

information-processing model   the sequence of advertising's effects: (1) exposure, (2) attention, (3) comprehension, (4) acceptance, and (5) retention; also called the **hierarchy of effects model**, *p. 446*

initial training   sales training that focuses on product knowledge and sales techniques, *p. 508*

innovators   consumers who are most willing to try new products (about the first 2.5 percent of product adopters), *p. 247*

inquiry evaluation   posttesting of an ad based on the number of consumers responding to requests in it, such as using coupons or asking for samples or more product information, *p. 454*

institutional environment   all the organizations involved in marketing products and services, including marketing research firms, ad agencies, wholesalers, retailers, suppliers, and customers, *p. 73*

institutional market   includes organizations such as profit or nonprofit hospitals, educational and religious institutions, and trade associations, *p. 134*

integrated marketing communications   the strategic integration of multiple means of communicating with target markets to form a comprehensive, consistent message; communications are integrated horizontally (across various methods of communications) and vertically (from the marketer down through the marketing channel), *p. 422*

intensive distribution   distributing a product or service through every available outlet, *p. 346*

interactive computer kiosk   an electronic marketing medium, usually located in retail stores, that uses touch-screen technology to let the consumer access information of interest, *p. 533*

interactive computer services   systems that allow consumers and marketers to communicate with each other through phone lines and a personal computer, *p. 532*

interceptor location   a location between a residential area and the closest supermarket, where a convenience store does business, *p. 379*

intermarket segments   well-defined, similar clusters of customers across national boundaries that let firms standardize marketing programs and offerings for each segment globally, *p. 181*

intermediaries   middlemen directly involved in the purchase or sale of products as they flow from originator to user; they include retailers and wholesalers, *p. 334*

intermodal shipping   using two or more modes of transportation to ship products; for example, loaded trailers may travel piggyback on railcars, *p. 406*

internal development a way to generate new products in which a firm creates the products itself, possibly subcontracting product design, engineering, or test marketing or working in partnership with another firm, *p. 237*

internal reference prices comparison price standards that consumers remember and use to judge the fairness of prices; they include the expected price, the price last paid, the average retail price, and the price the consumer would like to pay now, *p. 298*

internal secondary data secondary data collected within a firm, including accounting records, salesforce reports and customer feedback, *p. 162*

Interstate Commerce Commission (ICC) agency of the US government that regulates interstate transportation, *p. 70*

intertype competition competition among retailers that use different business formats to sell the same products; for example, McDonald's intertype competitors include all food retailers, from vending machines to fine restaurants, *p. 373*

intratype competition competition among retailers that use the same business format, *p. 373*

introduction stage the first stage in the product life cycle, when a new product is launched into the marketplace; it continues the commercialization stage of the new-product development process, *p. 260*

inventory turnover the number of times a retailer sells its average inventory during the year, or how quickly merchandise is sold, *p. 379*

involvement the level of importance, interest, or personal relevance generated by a product or a decision, which varies by the decision at hand and by the person's needs or motives, *p. 110*

ISO 9000 the International Standards Organization's 25-page set of quality standards; certification shows that a company meets world standards, *p. 70*

isolated locations freestanding retail sites where there are no adjoining buildings; best suited for large retailers that can attract a customer base on their own or for convenience businesses, *p. 374*

joint venture an arrangement between two or more organizations to market products internationally, through licensing agreements, contract manufacturing deals, or equity investments in strategic partnerships, *p. 96*

just-in-time (JIT) inventory control system a system that delivers raw materials, subassemblies, and component parts to manufacturers shortly before the scheduled manufacturing run that will consume the incoming shipment, *p. 402*

label a printed description of a product on a package, *p. 226*

laggards the final group to adopt a new product; they represent about 16 percent of a market, *p. 260*

Lanham Trademark Act a US law passed in 1946 that protects trademarks and brand names, *p. 68*

late majority the fourth group to adopt a new product; they represent about 34 percent of a market, *p. 260*

leaflet see **flyer**, *p. 526*

leased departments sections in a retail store that the owner rents to another party; typically department stores rent their jewelry, shoe, hairstyling, and cosmetic departments, *p. 365*

legitimate power power a member of a marketing channel gains through ownership or contractual agreements, *p. 351*

licensing the right to use a trademark in exchange for paying royalties on the sale of the licensed product, *p. 226*

lifestyle a person's pattern of living, as expressed in activities, interests, and opinions; lifestyle traits are more concrete than personality traits and more directly linked to the acquisition, use, and disposition of goods and services. See also **psychographics**, *p. 189*

limited-function wholesaler a truck jobber, drop shipper, cash-and-carry wholesaler, catalog wholesaler, or wholesale club, that does not offer the comprehensive service of a full-service wholesaler, *p. 391*

limit pricing a competitive pricing strategy that involves setting prices low to discourage new competition, *p. 317*

limited-line wholesaler a full-service wholesaler that does not stock as many products as a general merchandise wholesaler but has more depth in its product offering, *p. 391*

limited problem solving a situation between routinized response behavior and extensive problem solving; the consumer understands the relevant product attributes but may need some new information to, say, evaluate a new brand in a familiar product class, *p. 111*

line-filling strategy adding products in various places within a product line to fill gaps that may not be at either the high or the low end, *p. 267*

lists databases of current or potential customers that include their names, addresses, telephone numbers, and perhaps data on demographics, lifestyles, brand and media preferences, and consumption patterns, *p. 519*

logistics management planning, implementing, and moving raw materials and products from point of origin to point of consumption, *p. 388*

longitudinal research research conducted over time, typically on a panel of consumers or stores, *p. 160*

low-involvement decisions purchase decisions that involve fairly little personal interest, relevance, or importance and simple decision processes, *p. 110*

Magnusson-Moss Act a US law passed in 1975 to regulate warranties, *p. 68*

mail surveys marketing research method that involves sending questionnaires via mail, often to large, geographically diverse groups of people, *p. 166*

major accounts key, high-potential customers, *p. 506*

majority fallacy pursuing large "majority" market segments because they offer potential gains while overlooking the fact that they also may attract overwhelming competition, *p. 196*

mall intercept interviews   market research method in which consumers are interviewed one-on-one while shopping, *p. 167*

manufacturer brand   a brand sponsored by the product's manufacturer, who is responsible for its quality and marketing. Also called a national brand or regional brand, *p. 224*

manufacturers' agent   a merchant wholesaler that sells related but noncompeting product lines for various manufacturers; also called **manufacturers' rep**, *p. 394*

manufacturer's sales branch   a manufacturer-owned wholesaler that maintains inventory and performs a wide range of functions for the parent company, *p. 395*

manufacturer's sales office   a producer-owned wholesaler that differs from the manufacturer's sales branch in that it does not maintain inventory or perform as many functions for the parent company, *p. 395*

marginal costs   costs that are incurred in producing one additional unit of output; they typically decline early due to economies of scale but increase as the firm approaches capacity, *p. 309*

marginal revenue   the additional revenue a firm will receive if one more unit of product is sold (MR is usually the price of the product), *p. 309*

market   a group of people or organizations with needs to satisfy or problems to solve, the money to satisfy needs or solve problems, and the authority to make expenditure decisions, *p. 54*

market coverage   the number of outlets used to market a product; may involve intensive, selective, or exclusive distribution, *p. 346*

market expansion strategy   a corporate growth strategy of marketing existing products to new markets (different market segments in the same geographic area or the same target market in different geographic areas), *p. 88*

market forecast   the amount of sales predicted based on the marketing effort (expenditures) put forth by all the companies competing to sell a particular product or service in a specific period, *p. 196*

marketing   the process of planning and executing the conception, pricing, promotion, and distribution of ideas, goods, and services to create exchanges that satisfy individual and organizational goals, *p. 6*

marketing as a societal process   a process and the institutions that facilitate the flow of goods from producers to consumers in a society, *p. 10*

marketing channel   a combination of organizations and individuals (channel members) who perform the activities required to link producers to users to products to accomplish marketing objectives; also called channel of distribution, *p. 334*

marketing communications   marketer-initiated techniques directed to target audiences in an attempt to influence attitudes and behaviors; its three main objectives are to inform, persuade, and remind consumers; also called **promotion**, *p. 335*

marketing communications activities   activities that include advertising and public relations, sales promotion, personal selling, and direct marketing, *p. 335*

marketing communications message   what the company is trying to convey about its products, *p. 424*

marketing communications mix   the combination of advertising, public relations, sales promotion, personal selling, and direct marketing; also called the **promotional mix**, *p. 416*

marketing communications planning   a seven-step process: (1) marketing plan review, (2) situation analysis, (3) communications process analysis, (4) budget development, (5) program development, (6) integration and implementation of the plan, and (7) monitoring, evaluating, and controlling the marketing communications program, *p. 425*

marketing concept   the interrelated principles that (1) an organization's basic purpose is to satisfy customer needs, (2) satisfying customer needs requires integrated, coordinated efforts throughout the organization, and (3) organizations should focus on long-term success, *p. 9*

marketing decision support system (MDSS)   a comprehensive entity that encompasses all data, activities, and computerized elements used to process information relevant to marketing decisions; designed to enhance managerial decision making and firm performance by providing timely, relevant internal and external information, *p. 173*

marketing environment   the uncontrollable environment within which marketers must operate, encompassing social, economic, competitive, technological, legal/political, and institutional environments; all factors outside an organization that can affect its marketing activities, *p. 54*

marketing management   specific strategic decisions for individual products and the day-to-day activities needed to execute these strategies successfully, *p. 85*

marketing mix   the overall marketing effort to appeal to the target market, consisting of decisions in four basic areas: product, pricing, communications, and distribution, *p. 14*

marketing philosophy   an organization's emphasis on satisfying customers' needs; a focus on the marketing concept, *p. 9*

marketing research   activities linking marketer, customer, and public through information used to identify marketing opportunities; generate, refine, and evaluate marketing actions; monitor marketing performance; and improve understanding of marketing as a process. Marketing research specifies the information required to address these issues, designs the methods for collecting information, manages and implements the data collection process, analyzes the results, and communicates the findings and implications, *p. 156*

marketing research designs   general strategies or plans of action for addressing research problems, data collection, and analysis, *p. 159*

marketing research process   a six-step sequence: (1) problem definition, (2) determination of research design, (3) determination of data collection methods, (4) development of data collection forms, (5) sample design, and (6) analysis and interpretation, *p. 158*

marketing strategic plan   a functional plan for how marketing managers will execute the business strategic plan, addressing the general target market and marketing mix, *p. 83*

marketing strategies   selecting a target market and developing a marketing mix to satisfy that market's needs, *p. 14*

market mavens people who share with other consumers their knowledge about kinds of products, places to shop, and other facets of the market, *p. 118*

market penetration strategy achieving corporate growth objectives with existing products within existing markets, by persuading current customers to purchase more of the product or capturing new customers, *p. 88*

market potential the maximum amount of industry sales possible for a product or service for a specific period, *p. 196*

market scope how broadly a business views its target market, *p. 90*

market segmentation dividing the market for a product into subsets of customers who behave in the same way, have similar needs, or have similar characteristics that relate to purchase behavior, *p. 180*

market share a firm's percentage of the total market or total industry sales of a product, *p. 286*

market tests marketing a new product in test locations using the planned promotion, pricing, and distribution strategies, *p. 198*

markup pricing pricing where markup is the difference between the cost of an item and the retail price, expressed as a percentage, *p. 310*

maturity stage the third stage of the product life cycle, when competition intensifies and sales growth slows, *p. 261*

maybe-greens consumers who express environmental attitudes but do not always purchase in an ecologically sound way (about 55–80 percent of the US population), *p. 43*

measurability the degree to which the size and purchasing power of market segments can be assessed, *p. 184*

media class one of seven classes of advertising media: TV, magazines, newspapers, radio, outdoor, transit, and direct mail, *p. 451*

media schedule the frequency and timing of ads and commercials. See also **reach** and **frequency**, *p. 453*

media vehicle a specific TV program, magazine, or the like in any of the seven media classes, *p. 452*

megatrends broad trends that will have effects on many organizations and will affect markets and marketing activities (for example, the move from an industrial to an information society and from a national to a global economy), *p. 74*

merchant wholesaler an independent distributor that takes title to the products it sells; may be either a full-service or a limited-function wholesaler, *p. 389*

message acceptance the point where the consumer develops favorable attitudes about the advertised product and subsequent purchase; step 4 in the information-processing model, *p. 446*

message channel the means by which a company conveys its message about its products; for example, advertising vehicles like newspapers, TV, and billboards, *p. 424*

message comprehension the point where the consumer understands an ad's meaning; step 3 in the information-processing model, *p. 446*

message exposure that a marketer achieves by placing ads in appropriate media, giving consumers the opportunity to process the message; step 1 in the information-processing or hierarchy of effects model, *p. 446*

message presenter a person, perhaps a salesperson, actor, or TV personality who actually delivers the message, *p. 424*

message retention the point where a consumer stores ad information in long-term memory, which is critical for affecting later purchase decisions and behavior; step 5 in the information-processing model, *p. 446*

message sponsor the organization that is attempting to market its goods, services, or ideas, *p. 424*

metropolitan statistical area (MSA) a geographic area identified by census data to contain a city with a population of at least 50,000 or be an urbanized area with 50,000 people that is part of a county of at least 100,000 residents, *p. 188*

micromarketing using computer analysis of census and demographic data to identify clusters of households that share similar consumption patterns (for example, the PRIZM market segmentation system), *p. 201*

middlemen see **intermediaries**, *p. 334*

missionary salespeople sales support personnel who work at the grassroots level to promote their company's products; especially important in the grocery and pharmaceutical markets, *p. 495*

mission statement an element in the strategic planning process that expresses the company's basic values and specifies the boundaries within which business units, marketing, and other functions must operate, *p. 86*

modified rebuy decisions business purchasing decisions that call for the evaluation of new alternatives; could involve considering new suppliers for current purchase needs or new products offered by current suppliers; an example is the purchase of complex component parts from a new supplier, *p. 141*

motivation the desire to process ad information; a state or condition within a person that prompts goal-directed behavior; it generally occurs when some need or problem is recognized and it can affect information search, information processing, and purchase behavior, *p. 119*

multilevel marketing marketing in which the salesperson-distributor recruits other salespeople into the organization, earning commissions on his or her own sales to consumers plus a percentage of sales made by the recruited reps, *p. 535*

multiple-channels marketing strategy distributing a product through more than one channel to reach customers (for example, Prell shampoo is widely available at discount, drug, and grocery stores), *p. 340*

narrowcasting special-interest programming on cable TV, *p. 530*

national brand see **manufacturer brand**, *p. 224*

negative disconfirmation an experience where a purchase does not turn out as well as the consumer expected, *p. 122*

negotiated pricing pricing in which negotiation between vendor and supplier replaces multiple bids; common for large investments. See also **sealed-bid pricing**, *p. 323*

neighborhood business district a small grouping of stores, the largest usually a supermarket or variety store, located in the midst of a residential area, *p. 375*

network marketing see **multilevel marketing**, *p. 535*

network organizations firms involved in many different types of organizational partnerships, including strategic alliances, joint ventures, and vendor partnering, *p. 33*

neural networks sophisticated statistical techniques that can use a database to calculate weights for such traits as age, income, education, or time on the job, *p. 523*

new-business salespeople members of the salesforce who concentrate on selling new products or selling to new customers, *p. 496*

new-task decisions business purchasing decisions that occur when the buying problem is new and a great deal of information must be gathered; relatively infrequent decisions for a company, and the cost of making a wrong decision is high, *p. 140*

noise any distraction or distortion during the communication process that prevents the message from being communicated effectively, *p. 424*

nonprice competition competition between brands for sales based on factors other than price, such as quality, service, or specific product features, *p. 288*

nonprobability sampling market research in which selection of the sample is based on the researcher's or field worker's judgment, *p. 169*

nonproprietary secondary data secondary data that are available from libraries, computer databases, and other public sources, *p. 162*

nonstore retailing the selling of products and services outside a physical structure through, for example, direct marketing, direct selling, or vending machine sales, *p. 369*

norms the expectations, real or imagined, of other individuals or groups of people, *p. 117*

North American Free Trade Agreement (NAFTA) a treaty that eliminates many trade barriers among the United States, Mexico, and Canada, *p. 397*

objections buyer concerns about a product, *p. 502*

objective claims advertising messages that describe product features or performance in measurable terms, often reflecting a quality/value perspective, *p. 449*

objective price see **price**, *p. 282*

objective-task budgeting a budgeting method for marketing communications based on achieving stipulated objectives, identifying tasks to meet those objectives, and evaluating results, *p. 430*

observation research market research technique where a researcher or a video camera monitors customer behavior, or anonymous shoppers evaluate the quality of services offered, *p. 168*

odd-even pricing setting prices at just below an even amount (for example, contact lenses for $199.95 instead of $200), *p. 319*

on-shelf couponing distributing coupons via a dispenser mounted near the manufacturer's product on a store shelf, *p. 472*

operational products products that are used in a firm's activities but do not become part of any finished product; examples include light bulbs, cleaning materials, and services (such as accounting or advertising), *p. 217*

opinion leaders people who influence consumer behavior through word-of-mouth communications based on their interest or expertise in particular products, *p. 117*

opportunities areas where a company's performance might be improved; typically ranked by managers so the most important can be addressed first in the next strategic planning stage, *p. 54*

opportunity the extent to which distractions or limited exposure time affect the buyer's attention to brand information in an ad, *p. 446*

order in order processing, either a customer's purchase order or an order transmitted by a sales rep, *p. 403*

order takers see **existing-business salespeople**, *p. 496*

Organization of Petroleum Exporting Countries (OPEC) a loose federation of many of the oil-producing countries, designed to influence market prices and short-term profits for crude oil, *p. 295*

organized sales presentation a mental or written outline developed by the salesperson that is flexible enough to allow adaptive selling, *p. 499*

outcome-based perspective a way of evaluating salesperson performance that focuses on the results of sales behavior, such as total sales volume; see also **behavior-based perspective**, *p. 510*

outsourcing a firm's decision to purchase products and services from other companies rather than to make the products or perform the services internally; examples include components for computers, shipping, telecommunications, payroll administration, *p. 135*

package the container or wrapper for a product, including the label, *p. 226*

pay-for-performance trade promotion a sales promotion in which retailers are rewarded for making sales to consumers rather than purchases from manufacturers, *p. 484*

penetration pricing setting a low initial price to encourage initial product trial, stimulate sales growth and lower unit production costs, increase total revenues, and enhance profits, *p. 286*

perceived monetary price the consumer's subjective perception of whether the price of a product is high or low, fair or unfair (in contrast to objective price), *p. 296*

perceived value the buyer's overall assessment of a product's utility based on what is received and what is given; the quality per dollar, *p. 296*

percentage of sales budgeting a budgeting method for marketing communications based on the preceding year's or forecasted coming year's sales, *p. 429*

perceptual maps spatial representations of consumer perceptions of products or brands, used to evaluate brand positions in a market, *p. 201*

periodic discounting offering occasional discounts to take advantage of consumer segments' differing price sensitivity; includes price skimming, *p. 316*

personal interviews one-on-one interactions between a consumer, customer, or respondent and a market researcher to gather data, *p. 167*

personality a person's consistent response to his or her environment, linked to susceptibility to persuasion and social influence and thereby to purchase behavior, *p. 119*

personal selling the element of the marketing communications mix that involves face-to-face interactions between seller and buyer to satisfy buyer needs for their mutual benefit, *p. 420*

planned shopping center a retail center that is centrally owned and managed, has ample parking, and offers a variety of stores, *p. 375*

plus-one dialing method of telephone interview where a phone number is randomly selected from the local directory and a digit or digits added to it; allows inclusion of unlisted numbers in the sample, *p. 165*

point-of-purchase display a sales promotion, often provided free by the manufacturer to the retailer, to call customer attention to a featured product, *p. 481*

political/legal environment factors and trends related to governmental activities and specific laws and regulations that affect marketing practice, *p. 66*

positioning developing an overall image for a product or brand by designing a marketing program, including the product mix, that a market segment will perceive as desirable, *p. 200*

positive disconfirmation an experience where a purchase turns out better than a consumer expected, *p. 122*

postcards as direct-mail pieces, they generally offer discounts, announce sales, or generate customer traffic, *p. 525*

posttesting recall and attitude tests and inquiry evaluations marketers use to assess the effectiveness of an ad campaign, *p. 454*

precall planning focusing on learning more about the customer's situation before making a sales call, *p. 499*

predatory dumping dumping intended to drive rivals out of business, *p. 294*

predatory pricing charging very low prices to drive competition from the market and then raising prices once a monopoly has been established, *p. 326*

predictive dialing systems automated dialing machines that make telemarketing more productive by passing over answering machines, busy signals, and no answers and passing live calls on to a live telemarketer, *p. 532*

predictive modeling manipulating a customer database to reach a desired target more effectively, using neural networks and other technologies, *p. 522*

prelaunch activities marketing research studies conducted before commercialization of a new product, *p. 250*

premium an item given free or at a bargain price to encourage the consumer to buy, *p. 475*

premium pricing setting higher prices on one or more product versions; a popular strategy for beer, clothing, appliances, and cars, *p. 319*

prestige pricing keeping prices high to maintain an image of product quality and appeal to buyers who associate premium prices with high quality, *p. 288*

pretesting evaluating consumer reactions to proposed ads through focus groups and direct questioning, based on overall likability, consumer recall of information, message communication, and effects on purchase intentions and brand attitudes, *p. 454*

price the amount of money a buyer pays a seller in exchange for products and services, *p. 282*

price-aversion strategy buying the lowest-priced brand (in contrast to the best-value strategy, which takes quality into account), *p. 297*

price competition competition between brands for sales based on price alone; most common for similar brands and for customers with limited budgets and weak brand loyalties; see also **nonprice competition**, *p. 287*

price deal a temporary reduction in the price of a product, in the form of a cents-off or price-pack deal, used to introduce a new brand, convince current users to purchase more, or encourage new users to try an established brand, *p. 471*

price discrimination selling the same product to different customers at different prices; restricted in the United States by the Robinson-Patman Act; see also **differential pricing**, *p. 315*

price elasticity the responsiveness of customer demand to changes in a product's price, *p. 283*

price-pack deal a product that offers consumers something extra through the packaging itself; for example, a box of cereal with 20 percent more cereal for the regular price, *p. 471*

price promotion mix the basic price plus such supplemental components as sale prices, temporary discounts, coupons, and favorable payment and credit terms; encourages purchase behavior by strengthening the basic price during relatively short periods of time, *p. 283*

price/quality relationship the extent to which a consumer associates a higher product price with higher quality, *p. 297*

price-seeking strategy purchasing the highest-priced brand to maximize expected quality, *p. 297*

price-sensitivity measurement (PSM) a pricing approach that incorporates input from potential buyers, who read a product description and then plot on a scale the prices they would pay, yielding price estimates high enough to reflect the product's perceived value but low enough to avoid sticker shock, *p. 314*

price signaling a competitive pricing strategy that puts high prices on low-quality products, *p. 297*

price skimming setting prices high initially to appeal to consumers who are not price sensitive, then lowering prices sequentially to appeal to the next market segments, *p. 287*

price threshold the point at which buyers notice a price increase or decrease; the threshold level depends on a product's average price (for example, a 10-cent reduction on a 50-cent product is more meaningful than on a $10 product), *p. 320*

primary data data collected for a particular research problem, for example, survey information; typically more current and relevant than secondary data but more expensive to gather, *p. 162*

primary demand   general demand for a new product form, which marketing tries to generate at the introduction stage of the product life cycle, *p. 262*

primary metropolitan statistical area (PMSA)   a major urban area, often located within a CMSA, that has at least one million inhabitants, *p. 188*

private brand   see **distributor brand**, *p. 224*

private response   a complaint in which a dissatisfied consumer bad-mouths a product to friends or family, *p. 123*

private warehouse   a warehouse operated by the company that uses it, *p. 400*

PRIZM   potential rating index by ZIP markets, which divides every neighborhood in the United States into one of 40 distinct cluster types that reveal consumer data; PRIZM+4 uses ZIP+4 codes for even greater detail covering individual demographics, individual credit records, model-specific auto registration, and purchase behavior data from private sources, *p. 189*

probability sampling   market research in which each person in the population has a known, nonzero chance of being selected by some objective procedure; such unbiased selection increases the sample's representativeness, *p. 169*

problem definition   the first step in the marketing research process; identifying the difference between the way things should be and the way they are or the issues that need to be investigated, *p. 159*

product   an idea, a physical entity (a good), a service, or any combination that is an element of exchange to satisfy individual or business objectives, *p. 210*

product competitors   companies that offer different kinds of products to satisfy the same basic need (for example, Domino's Pizza and Kentucky Fried Chicken both attempt to satisfy a consumer need for fast food but offer somewhat different products and services), *p. 72*

product design   the styling, aesthetics, and function of a product, which affect how it works, how it feels, and how easy it is to assemble, fix, and recycle, *p. 220*

product differentiation   circumstance in which a firm's offerings differ or are perceived to differ from those of competing firms on any attribute, including price, *p. 182*

product expansion strategy   marketing new products to the same customer base, *p. 88*

production philosophy   an organization's emphasis on the production function, valuing activities related to improving production efficiency or producing sophisticated products and services, *p. 9*

production products   raw materials and components that become part of some finished product (for example, steel and paper), *p. 216*

productivity perspective   getting the most output for each marketing dollar spent, by doing the same things better and/or doing different things, *p. 40*

product life cycle (PLC)   the advancement of a product through the stages of introduction, growth, maturity, and decline, *p. 258*

product line   a group of individual products that are closely related in some way, *p. 257*

product line contraction   deleting individual products from a product line, *p. 268*

product line length   the number of products in any one product line, *p. 258*

product-line pricing   offering multiple versions of the same product, with those priced at the low end used to build traffic and those at the high end creating a quality image for the entire product line, *p. 317*

product marketing plans   plans within each business unit that focus on specific target markets and marketing mixes for each product and includes both strategic decisions (what to do) and execution decisions (how to do it), *p. 83*

product mix   the total assortment of products and services marketed by a firm, *p. 257*

product mix consistency   the relatedness of the different product lines in a product mix; for example, all of Schwab's product lines are investment related, but J&J sells everything from contact lenses to baby powder, *p. 258*

product mix width   the number of product lines in a company's product mix, *p. 257*

projective techniques   market research methods, such as word association or sentence completion, that let researchers elicit feelings that normally go unexpressed, *p. 167*

project matrix organization   an approach to new-product development in which a project manager has primary responsibility and authority, and functional managers assign personnel as needed, *p. 250*

project team organization   an approach to new-product development in which a project manager heads a core group of people selected from various functional areas; managers from the different functional areas are not formally involved, *p. 250*

promotional interactive computer disks   a relatively new format for direct-mail campaigns in which the information is presented on disk and the consumer can respond, *p. 526*

proprietary secondary data   data provided by commercial marketing research firms that sell their services to other firms; examples are diary panels and scanner data, *p. 162*

prospecting   the seller's search for and identification of qualified buyers, defined as buyers who are reasonably accessible to the seller, able to afford the purchase, and willing to consider making it, *p. 498*

prototype development   converting the concept for a new product into an actual product, using the information obtained from concept tests to design a tangible product that can be tested further, *p. 244*

psychographics   a concept for dividing a market into lifestyle segments on the basis of consumer interests, values, opinions, personality traits, attitudes, and demographics to develop marketing communications and product strategies, *p. 189*

psychological pricing   the recognition that buyers' perceptions and beliefs affect their evaluations of prices, *p. 319*

publicity   information about the company or product that appears, unpaid for, in the news media; primary publicity techniques are news releases, press conferences, and feature articles, often presented in the business press, *p. 458*

public relations the element of the marketing communications mix that identifies, establishes, and maintains mutually beneficial relations between an organization and the various publics on which its success or failure depends, for example, customers, employees, stockholders, community members, and the government, *p. 419*

public relations functions press relations; product promotions; internal and external corporate communications; lobbying to promote, defeat, or circumvent legislation and regulations; advising management about public issues and company positions and image; and overall responding to various occurrences in the marketplace, either reactively or proactively, *p. 458*

public service advertising (PSAs) advertising donated by the ad industry to promote activities for some social good, *p. 444*

public warehouse a for-hire facility available to any business that requires storage or handling of goods, *p. 400*

puffery advertising that contains claims including acceptable exaggeration, *p. 448*

pull strategy concentrating marketing communications on consumers to stimulate demand in an attempt to get consumers to "pull" a product from the manufacturing company through the marketing channel, *p. 431*

push money what a manufacturer pays retail salespeople to encourage them to promote its products over competitive brands or to sell specific products in the manufacturer's line, *p. 483*

push strategy directing marketing communications toward intermediary channel members to "push" a product through the channel to the ultimate consumer, *p. 431*

pyramid scheme an illegal scam in which large numbers of people at the bottom of the pyramid pay money to a few people at the top, *p. 535*

quality the totality of features and characteristics of a product or service that bear on its ability to satisfy stated or implied needs, *p. 36*

quality/function deployment (QFD) a procedure in the new-product development process that links specific consumer requirements with specific product characteristics, *p. 245*

quality/value perspective continually improving the quality of products and services and offering this quality to customers at lower prices, *p. 35*

quick-response (QR) inventory control system a system for providing retailers with finished goods in which inventory is restocked according to what has just been sold, based on small but frequent orders, *p. 402*

quotas the quantitative outcomes (such as total sales volume, gross margin, market share, number of new accounts added, and accounts retained) used to assess sales reps' performance and effectiveness, *p. 510*

rack jobber a specialty-line wholesaler that sells to retail stores, setting up and maintaining attractive store displays and stocking them with goods sold on consignment, *p. 391*

random-digit dialing a method of telephone interviewing where, for example, four random digits are added to three-digit telephone exchanges to reach consumers, *p. 165*

reach the number of different people or households exposed to an ad or campaign over a specified time period (usually four weeks), *p. 453*

reader-response cards card inserts in magazines, used in conjunction with ads, that make it easy for readers to send for more information on a product, *p. 531*

rebate cash reimbursement for purchasing a product, in which the buyer must mail a rebate form, the receipt, and proof of purchase to the manufacturer within a certain time, *p. 473*

receiver the intended target for any basic communication; for example, a purchasing agent listening to a sales presentation or a consumer reading a magazine ad, *p. 423*

reciprocity occurs when firm A purchases from supplier B, who in turn buys A's own products and services; practice may be illegal if it restricts competition, *p. 147*

reference groups interpersonal influences beyond the family, including friends and co-workers, *p. 117*

referent power power a member of a marketing channel gains through another member's desire to be associated with it, *p. 352*

regional brand see **manufacturer brand**, *p. 224*

related diversification branching out into new products and markets that have something in common with existing operations (for example, a video rental store diversifying into music retailing), *p. 88*

relationship marketing developing, maintaining, and enhancing long-term profitable relationships with customers, *p. 31*

relationship perspective building partnerships with firms outside the organization and encouraging teamwork among different functions within the organization to develop long-term customer relationships, *p. 31*

relationship selling see **relationship marketing**, *p. 497*

relationship strategy a framework for working with customers based on relationship selling, it includes the counselor strategy, the supplier strategy, and the systems-designer strategy, *p. 505*

repositioning developing new marketing programs to shift consumer beliefs and opinions about an existing brand; see also **positioning**, *p. 200*

reseller market firms that purchase goods and in turn sell them to others at a gain; includes wholesalers and retailers, *p. 134*

reservation price the highest price a person is willing to pay for a product; one form of a consumer's internal reference price, *p. 298*

retail chain a retailer that owns and operates multiple retail outlets; chains represent 20 percent of all retailers and account for 50 percent of all retail sales, *p. 364*

retail cooperative a group of stores that remain independently owned but adopt a common name and storefront and band together to increase their buying power, *p. 365*

retailer-owned cooperative group a contractual marketing channel system in which the retailers own the wholesaler, *p. 343*

retail franchising   a form of chain ownership in which a franchisee pays the franchisor (parent company) fees or royalties and agrees to run the franchise by prescribed norms in exchange for use of the franchisor's name, *p. 363*

retailing   all of the activities involved in selling products and services to the final consumer; retailers include independents, chains, franchises, leased departments, cooperatives, and various forms of nonstore retailers, *p. 360*

retail sales   sales to final consumers, as opposed to wholesale sales; a firm's retail sales must be at least half of its total revenues for it to be classified a retailer, *p. 360*

retail strategy mix   the controllable variables of location, products and services, pricing, and marketing communications, *p. 377*

return on investment (ROI)   ratio of income before taxes to total operating assets associated with a product, such as plant and equipment and inventory, *p. 287*

reward power   power a member of a marketing channel gains when it can offer another member widespread distribution, special credit terms, or some other reward, *p. 351*

Robinson-Patman Act   a US law passed in 1936 to prohibit price discrimination, *p. 293*

rollout studies   marketing research studies performed on a new product after it has been introduced, *p. 250*

routinized response behavior   a quick, habitual decision with limited search for information in response to some need, *p. 110*

sales automation systems   computerized systems sales managers use for routine supervisory chores such as processing sales reps' call reports, itineraries, and expense reports, *p. 509*

sales effectiveness evaluations   the most stringent tests of advertising efficiency, they assess whether the advertising resulted in increased sales, *p. 510*

salesforce turnover   the proportion of salespeople who leave their jobs, *p. 507*

salesforce effectiveness   how well the entire sales organization is performing, including an evaluation of individual salespeople's performance, *p. 454*

sales letter   the most common form of direct mail, it includes the recipient's name and may be mailed with brochures, price lists, and reply cards and envelopes, *p. 525*

sales management   managers who oversee the personal selling function, managing sales personnel and developing and implementing sales strategy, *p. 492*

salesperson performance   how well individual salespeople meet job expectations, evaluated from a behavior-based perspective, an outcome-based perspective, or a combination of the two, *p. 510*

sales potential   the maximum amount of sales a specific firm can obtain for a specified time period, *p. 196*

sales process   the process of initiating, developing, and enhancing long-term, mutually satisfying relationships with customers, *p. 497*

sales promotion   the element of the marketing communications mix that provides extra value or incentives to consumers, wholesalers, retailers, or other organizational customers to stimulate product interest, trial, or purchase; media and nonmedia marketing communications employed for a predetermined, limited time to stimulate trial, increase consumer demand, or improve product availability, *p. 419*

sales resistance   customer concerns about a product, both spoken (objections) and unspoken, *p. 502*

sales support salespeople   employees who support the personal selling function by promoting a product or providing technical support, working in coordination with the salespeople who actually solicit customer purchases, *p. 494*

sales territory   usually defined geographically, a territory consists of specific customers assigned to a specific salesperson, *p. 498*

sample   a small size of a product made available to prospective purchasers, usually free, to demonstrate a product's value or use and encourage future purchase, *p. 169*

sample size   the size of a sample in market research, based on the anticipated response rate, variability in the data, cost, and time considerations and desired level of precision, *p. 170*

sampling frame   the outline or working description of the population used in sample selection for market research, *p. 170*

sanctions   restrictions imposed by the UN or individual governments to limit trade with specific countries, *p. 67*

scanner data   a type of proprietary data derived from UPC bar codes, *p. 162*

scrambled merchandising   adding unrelated product categories to existing product lines, *p. 375*

sealed-bid pricing   pricing in which sellers submit sealed bids for providing their products or services and the buyer chooses among them. See also **negotiated pricing**, *p. 322*

search costs   the cost to buyers in time and effort to obtain information about which firms sell what products and at what prices, *p. 315*

seasonality   product demand fluctuations related to the time of year, which may be affected by unpredictable changes in weather and in consumer preferences, *p. 373*

secondary business district   a concentration of retail stores defined by the intersection of two major thoroughfares, *p. 375*

secondary data   proprietary and nonproprietary data already collected for some other purpose and available from various sources (such as library research); typically cheaper than collecting primary data but may be less current or relevant, *p. 162*

secondary demand   demand for a specific brand of new product form, which marketing tries to generate after competing brands are introduced, *p. 262*

second-market discounting   a form of differential pricing in which different prices are charged in different market segments (for example, foreign markets), *p. 315*

selecting   choosing the candidates to be hired for a sales job, *p. 507*

self-concept   a person's overall perception and feelings about himself or herself; consumers buy products that are consistent with or enhance their self-concept, *p. 119*

selling philosophy an organization's emphasis on the selling function to the exclusion of other marketing activities, *p. 9*

selling strategy an overall plan for a salesperson's course of action, developed at three levels: sales territory, customer, and individual sales call, *p. 498*

service merchandiser see **rack jobber**, *p. 391*

service retailers all retailers that sell services, from rental businesses to movie theaters, hotels, and car repair shops, *p. 360*

services nonphysical products such as a haircut, a football game, or a doctor's diagnosis (in contrast to goods, which are physical products), *p. 211*

Sherman Act a US law passed in 1890 to prohibit monopolistic practices, *p. 293*

shipping container marking (SCM) system feeds information into a computerized tracking system to facilitate shipping of products, *p. 402*

shopping products items consumers do not know exactly what they want and are willing to spend time shopping for; usually expensive items such as cars, TVs, *p. 215*

simple random sampling a probability sampling approach in which each unit has an equal chance of being selected, *p. 169*

simulated test marketing evaluating a new product prototype in situations set up to be similar to those where consumers would actually purchase or use the product (for example, intercepting shoppers at a high-traffic location in a mall), *p. 245*

single-channel marketing strategy using only one means to reach customers (for example, Nexxus shampoo is distributed exclusively through hair care professionals), *p. 340*

single-source data data produced by proprietary systems that combine information on product purchase behavior with TV viewing behavior, *p. 163*

slotting allowances fees manufacturers pay to retailers or wholesalers to obtain shelf or warehouse space for their products, *p. 380*

social classes divisions within a society that contain people with similar values, needs, lifestyles, and behavior; social class is influenced most strongly by education level and occupation and influences the purchases consumers make and the activities they pursue, *p. 114*

social environment all factors and trends related to groups of people, including their number, characteristics, behavior, and growth projections, *p. 56*

socialization absorbing a culture, a process that continues throughout life and produces many specific preferences of products and services, shopping patterns, and interactions with others, *p. 112*

social responsibility minimizing social costs, such as environmental damage, and maximizing the positive impact of marketing decisions on society, *p. 35*

source the message sender; in marketing communications, the marketer, *p. 424*

source credibility the state in which a customer perceives that its needs are satisfied by the combination of the sales rep, the product or service, and the rep's company, *p. 502*

sources companies or individuals who sell products and services directly to buying organizations; also called **suppliers** or **vendors**, *p. 132*

specialty-line wholesaler a wholesaler that sells only a single product line or part of a line but is expert on those products, *p. 391*

specialty products items for which consumers want a specific brand and are willing to hunt for it; they won't switch brands (as with convenience products) or shop to evaluate alternatives (as for shopping products), *p. 216*

specialty store a retail store that sells a narrow variety of products but offers a deep assortment of product choices; usually located in a shopping cluster where its product selection complements that of neighboring retailers, *p. 377*

spiff see **push money**, *p. 483*

sponsorship programs investments in causes and events to support overall corporate and marketing objectives, *p. 423*

Standard Industrial Classification (SIC) system a federal government numerical scheme for categorizing businesses from general industry groupings to specific product categories, *p. 133*

standardized marketing strategy implementing the same product, price, distribution, and communications programs in all international markets, *p. 96*

standard test marketing testing a new product prototype and its marketing strategy in actual market situations, *p. 246*

statement stuffers promotional pieces that are included in other mail, such as bank or credit card statements, *p. 526*

statistical demand analysis forecasting sales from equations in which price, promotion, distribution, competitive, and economic factors are independent variables, *p. 198*

store brand see **distributor brand**, *p. 224*

store image the picture shoppers have of a store's identity, composed of their perceptions of its location, goods and services sold, and atmospherics, *p. 377*

straight rebuy decisions most common type of business purchasing decision in which products and services are simply repurchased; delivery, performance, and price are critical considerations, *p. 141*

strategic business unit (SBU) a unit of a company that focuses on a single product or brand, a line of products, or a mix of related products that meet a common market need and whose management oversees the basic business functions, *p. 89*

strategic marketing marketing activities that encompass three functions: (1) helping to orient everyone in the organization toward markets and customers, (2) helping to gather and analyze information needed to examine the current situation, identify trends in the marketing environment, and assess their potential impact, and (3) helping to develop corporate, business, and marketing strategic plans, *p. 84*

stratified sampling a probability sampling technique in which the population is divided into mutually exclusive groups, such as consumers with different income levels, and random samples are taken from each group, *p. 169*

string location a grouping of stores that sell similar goods and services (for example, cars or mobile homes), *p. 375*

style a unique form of expression that is defined by a product's characteristics and has a fluctuating life cycle, *p. 262*

subjective claims advertising claims that are not measurable and often stress image enhancement, *p. 449*

substantialness the degree to which identified target segments are large enough and have sufficient sales and profit potential to warrant separate marketing programs, *p. 184*

suppliers see **sources**, *p. 132*

supplier strategy a selling strategy in which the sales reps make regularly scheduled sales calls to inform customers about new products and promotional programs, coordinate order entry, and solve any problems that arise, *p. 505*

survey of buyers' intentions sales forecast based on surveys of what either consumers or organizational buyers say they will do; such surveys are most reliable when the buyers have well-formed intentions and are willing to disclose them accurately, *p. 198*

sweepstakes a sales promotion that offers prizes based on a chance drawing of participants' names, *p. 474*

systems-designer strategy a selling strategy in which sales reps are knowledgeable enough to determine solutions to the customer's problems or visualize opportunities to enhance the customer's business through new or modified business systems, *p. 506*

targeting selecting which segments in a market are appropriate to focus on and designing the means to reach them, *p. 182*

target market a defined group of consumers or organizations with whom a firm wants to create marketing exchanges, *p. 14*

target-return pricing a cost-oriented approach that sets prices to achieve a desired rate of return, with cost and profit estimates based on some expected volume or sales level, *p. 313*

team selling a sales approach in which a company assigns accounts to sales teams of specialists according to the customers' purchase-information needs, *p. 506*

technical support salespeople the people in sales support who have expertise in areas such as design and installation of complex equipment and may provide specialized training to customer employees, *p. 496*

technological environment factors and trends related to innovations that affect the development of new products or the marketing process, *p. 71*

technological perspective using new and emerging technologies as sources for new products and services and to improve marketing practice, *p. 40*

telefocus telemarketing an integrated promotional technique that combines telemarketing efforts with a direct-mail campaign using video brochures, *p. 531*

telemarketing an interactive direct marketing communications approach that uses the phone to initiate, develop, and enhance relationships with customers, *p. 531*

testimonials third-party evidence, such as letters from satisfied customers, that enhance source credibility, *p. 502*

test marketing testing the prototype of a new product and its marketing strategy in simulated or actual market situations, *p. 245*

third-party response a complaint about a product in which the consumer takes legal action or files a complaint with a consumer affairs agency instead of dealing just with the company, *p. 123*

threats trends in the marketing environment that might adversely affect a company's situation; typically ranked by managers so the most important threats can be addressed first in the next strategic planning stage, *p. 54*

tie-in see **cross-promotion**, *p. 473*

total costs the sum of variable costs and fixed costs, *p. 309*

total quality management (TQM) programs that emphasize long-term relationships with selected suppliers instead of short-term transactions with many suppliers, *p. 28*

total revenue total sales, or unit price multiplied by the quantity of the product sold; (before-tax) profits equal total revenue minus total costs, *p. 309*

trade allowance the amount a manufacturer contributes to a local dealer or retailer's advertising expense, *p. 480*

trade contest a sales promotion at the reseller level that associates prizes with sales of the sponsor's product, *p. 481*

trademark a brand or part of a brand that is registered with the US Patent and Trademark Office, giving the owner exclusive rights to use the brand, *p. 222*

trade sales promotion sales promotion directed at retailers, wholesalers, or other business buyers to help push products through the marketing channel, *p. 419*

trade sales promotion allowances concessions a manufacturer allocates to wholesalers or retailers to promote its products (for example, supermarkets' cooperative advertising), *p. 322*

trade show a periodic, semipublic event sponsored by a trade, professional, or industrial association at which suppliers rent booths to display products and provide information to potential buyers, *p. 482*

traditional retailing the selling of products and services in stores or some other physical structure; it accounts for 90 percent of all retail sales, *p. 369*

transaction marketing producing sales in the short run at any cost, *p. 31*

transaction value the perceived merits of the deal itself; retailers provide comparison pricing in an effort to boost products' transaction value by raising shoppers' internal price standard, *p. 299*

trend analysis a quantitative forecasting approach that examines historical sales data for predictable patterns (also known as time-series analysis), *p. 198*

truck jobber a limited-function wholesaler that delivers within a small geographic area to ensure freshness of goods (for example, bakery, meat, dairy), *p. 391*

two-way stretch strategy adding products at both the low and the high end of a product line, *p. 267*

tying contract a marketing channel arrangement in which a manufacturer requires a reseller to buy products in addition to the one it really wants, *p. 354*

unaided recall tests posttesting in which consumers are questioned with no prompting about ads, *p. 454*

undifferentiated strategy marketing a single product using a single promotional mix for the entire market; most often used early in the life of a product category, *p. 194*

uniform delivered price a form of geographical pricing in which each customer, no matter where located, is charged the same average freight amount, *p. 322*

unit pricing price information presented on a per-unit weight or volume basis so shoppers can compare prices across brands and across package sizes within brands, *p. 326*

Universal Product Code (UPC) bar code that is scanned at grocery checkouts and can provide secondary data for marketing research, *p. 162*

unplanned business district shopping area that evolved spontaneously and is made up of independently owned and managed retail operations; types include central business districts, secondary business districts, neighborhood business districts, and string locations, *p. 374*

unrelated diversification branching out into products or services that have nothing in common with existing operations, *p. 88*

upward stretch strategy adding products at the higher end of a product line; for example, Japanese carmakers entered the US market at the low end and gradually added higher-priced cars, *p. 267*

US-Canada Trade Act a law passed in 1988 to allow free trade between the United States and Canada, *p. 68*

utilitarian influence compliance with the expectations of others to achieve rewards or avoid punishments (for example, peer disapproval), *p. 117*

value-added resellers (VARs) intermediaries that add value to goods and services as they pass through the marketing channel, *p. 389*

value-expressive influence a desire to enhance self-concept through identification with others (for example, by purchasing a product endorsed by a celebrity), *p. 117*

value-in-use pricing basing pricing on customer estimates of the costs if the service could not be obtained (downtime costs if a computer could not be repaired), *p. 291*

values shared beliefs or cultural norms about what is important or right, which directly influence how consumers view and use products, brands, and services, *p. 112*

Values and Lifestyles Program (VALS2) a lifestyle program from SRI International that segments consumers into eight

groups: actualizers, fulfillers, believers, achievers, strivers, experiencers, makers, and strugglers, *p. 190*

variable costs costs that change with the level of output, such as wages and raw materials; see also **fixed costs**, *p. 309*

vendors see **sources**, *p. 132*

vertical marketing systems centrally coordinated, highly integrated operations in which the product flows down the channel from producer to ultimate consumer; the basic vertical types are corporate, contractual, and administered channel systems, *p. 341*

VideOcarts shopping carts equipped with video screens that provide promotional messages, information on sale items, recipes, store directories, and even local news and weather, *p. 367*

video catalog a direct-mail catalog in videocassette form, *p. 526*

visionary greens consumers whose buying behavior is very ecologically oriented (about 5 to 15 percent of the US population), *p. 43*

visionary perspective a well-articulated picture of how everything fits together to make an organization what it wants to become (very important for entrepreneurial marketers), *p. 47*

voice response a complaint about a product in which the customer seeks satisfaction directly from the seller, *p. 123*

wholesale club a club whose members pay an annual fee that entitles them to make tax-free purchases at lower-than-retail prices, *p. 392*

wholesaler-sponsored voluntary group a contractual marketing channel system consisting of independent retailers that operate under the name of a sponsoring wholesaler, *p. 342*

wholesale sales sales to other businesses that resell the product or service or use it in running their own businesses (as opposed to retail sales), *p. 360*

written sales proposal a detailed written presentation of a product's capabilities, benefits, and costs, often tailored to the individual customer, *p. 500*

zone pricing a form of geographical pricing in which customers within one area (say, the Northeast) are charged one freight price and more distant zones are charged higher freight amounts, *p. 322*

Endnotes

Chapter 1

[1]Reprinted from Peter D. Bennett, ed., *Dictionary of Marketing Terms* (Chicago: American Marketing Association, 1988), p. 54.

[2]Reported in "Business Bulletin," *The Wall Street Journal*, June 3, 1993, p. A1.

[3]Adapted from Nancy J. Perry, "Even Bankers Can Learn to Sell," *Fortune*, July 2, 1993, pp. 96–97.

[4]Reported in Susan B. Garland, Richard S. Dunham, and Laura Zinn, "Polling for Policy," *Business Week*, February 22, 1993, pp. 34–35.

[5]Reported in Howard Schlossberg, "Competition Sparks Gas Company to Become Customer Friendly," *Marketing News*, April 12, 1993, p. 8.

[6]"New Church Uses Marketing to Appeal to Baby Boomers," *Marketing News*, April 12, 1993, p. 11.

[7]Personal conversations with David Fleming, senior vice president, Jewish Hospital, during January and February 1994.

[8]This section is adapted from Martin Everett, "On the Run with Roger Dow," *Sales & Marketing Management*, September 1993, pp. 76–83.

[9]For different perspectives concerning the marketing concept see Franklin S. Houston, "The Marketing Concept: What It Is and What It Is Not," *Journal of Marketing*, April 1986, pp. 81–87; Frederick E. Webster, Jr., "The Rediscovery of the Marketing Concept," *Business Horizons*, May–June 1988, pp. 29–39; Lynn W. McGee and Rosann L. Spiro, "The Marketing Concept in Perspective," *Business Horizons*, May–June 1988, pp. 40–45; and Ajay K. Kohli and Bernard J. Jaworski, "Market Orientation: The Construct, Research Propositions, and Managerial Implications," *Journal of Marketing*, April 1990, pp. 1–18.

[10]The first three quotations are taken from "Today's Leaders Look to Tomorrow," *Fortune*, March 26, 1990, pp. 30, 37, 42.

[11]Taken from Kenichi Ohmae, *The Borderless World* (New York: HarperBusiness, 1990), p. 103.

[12]See John C. Narver and Stanley F. Slater, "The Effect of a Market Orientation on Business Profitability," *Journal of Marketing*, October 1990, pp. 20–35; and Bernard J. Jaworski and Ajay K. Kohli, "Market Orientation: Antecedents and Consequences," *Journal of Marketing*, July 1993, pp. 53–70.

[13]William Symonds and Bart Ziegler, "NT Phones Home," *Business Week*, July 12, 1993, p. 38.

[14]Reported in Joseph Kahn, " 'Dynasty' in Shanghai Is Aiming for Profit," *The Wall Street Journal*, December 2, 1993, p. A13.

[15]Reported in Avraham Shama, "Management under Fire: The Transformation of Managers in the Soviet Union and Eastern Europe," *The Executive*, February 1993, pp. 22–35.

[16]See Franklin S. Houston and Jule B. Gassenheimer, "Marketing and Exchange," *Journal of Marketing,* October 1987, pp. 3–18, for a more complete discussion of exchange and marketing.

[17]Richard P. Bagozzi, "Toward a Formal Theory of Marketing Exchange," in *Conceptual and Theoretical Developments in Marketing,* eds. O. C. Ferrell, Stephen W. Brown, and Charles W. Lamb, Jr. (Chicago: American Marketing Association, 1979), p. 434.

[18]Reported in Robert Davis, "Sales Pitch for Gun Buybacks," *USA Today,* March 24, 1994, p. 3A.

[19]Reported in Jack Honomichi, "Spending for Research in US Shows 3.4% Real Growth," *Marketing News,* June 8, 1992, p. H2.

[20]This section draws heavily from the historical analysis and marketing evolution conceptualization presented in Ronald A. Fullerton, "How Modern Is Modern Marketing? Marketing's Evolution and the Myth of the 'Production Era,' " *Journal of Marketing,* January 1988, pp. 108–25.

[21]Arch W. Shaw, *An Approach to Business Problems* (Cambridge: Harvard University Press, 1916), p. 104.

Chapter 2

[1]Thomas A. Stewart, "Welcome to the Revolution," *Fortune,* December 13, 1993, pp. 66–78; and Frederick E. Webster, Sr., "Defining the New Marketing Concept," *Marketing Management* 2, no. 4, pp. 23–31.

[2]Reported in Alan M. Webber, "What's So New about the Economy?" *Harvard Business Review,* January–February 1993, p. 25.

[3]Reported in Michael R. Czinkota and Ilkka A. Ronkainen, "Global Marketing 2000: A Marketing Survival Guide," *Marketing Management,* Winter 1992, pp. 37–45.

[4]Reported in "Today's Leaders Look to Tomorrow," *Fortune,* March 26, 1990, p. 60.

[5]Walecia Konrad and Andrea Rothman, "Cola Wars: All Noisy on the Western Front," *Business Week,* January 27, 1992, pp. 94–95.

[6]Julie Tilsner, "Duracell Looks Abroad for More Juice," *Business Week,* December 21, 1992, pp. 52–56.

[7]"America's Little Fellows Surge Ahead," *The Economist,* July 3, 1993, pp. 59–60.

[8]Reported in "Today's Leaders Look to Tomorrow," *Fortune,* March 26, 1990, pp. 30–31.

[9]Neal Weinstock, "The Switch Is On in Japan," *World Trade,* June 1993, pp. 55–58.

[10]Brian Dumaine, "P&G Rewrites the Marketing Rules," *Fortune,* November 6, 1989, pp. 34–48.

[11]Reported in *Fortune,* March 26, 1990, p. 32.

[12]Frederick E. Webster, Jr., "The Changing Role of Marketing in the Corporation," *Journal of Marketing,* October 1992, pp. 1–17.

[13]Kirkpatrick, 1992, p. 54.

[14]Reported in Mary Walton, *The Deming Management Method* (New York: Dodd, Mead, 1986), pp. 139–44.

[15]Taken from Gene R. Laczniak and Patrick E. Murphy, "Incorporating Marketing Ethics into the Organization," in *Marketing Ethics: Guidelines for Managers,* eds. Gene R. Laczniak and Patrick E. Murphy (Lexington, MA: Lexington Books, 1985), pp. 97–105.

[16]Cyndee Miller, "Rediscovering the Inner City," *Marketing News,* January 17, 1994, pp. 1–2.

[17]Herman Bryant Maynard, Jr., and Susan E. Mehreus, *The Fourth Wave: Business in the 21st Century* (San Francisco: Berret-Koehler, 1993).

[18]Reported in "Business Ethics Get Renewed Push," *The Wall Street Journal,* February 6, 1990, p. A1.

[19]Reported in Ross Johnson and William O. Winchell, *Marketing and Quality* (Milwaukee: American Society for Quality Control, 1989), pp. 1–2.

[20]Jerry G. Bowles, "The Race to Quality Improvement," *Fortune,* September 25, 1989.

[21]Reported in Stephen Phillips, Amy Dunkin, James Treece, and Keith Hammonds, "King Customer," *Business Week,* March 12, 1990, pp. 88–94.

[22]Reported in "Jack Welch's Lessons for Success," *Fortune,* January 25, 1993, p. 86.

[23]These examples are presented in Christopher Power, Walecia Konrad, Alice Z. Cuneo, and James B. Treece, "Value Marketing," *Business Week,* November 11, 1991, pp. 132–40.

[24]Michael Treacy and Fred Wiersema, "Customer Intimacy and Other Value Disciplines," *Harvard Business Review,* January–February 1993, pp. 84–93.

[25]Larry Armstrong, "Altima's Secret: The Right Kind of Sticker Shock," *Business Week,* January 18, 1993, p. 37.

[26]These figures are reported in Richard Gibson, "Marketers' Mantra: Reap More with Less," *The Wall Street Journal,* March 22, 1991, pp. B1–B2.

[27]Ibid., p. B2.

[28]Ibid., p. B1.

[29]Ibid.

[30]"But Will They Get Their Own Water Coolers?" *Business Week,* July 19, 1993, p. 32.

[31]Reported in John Carey, "The Myth That America Can't Compete," *Business Week,* June 15, 1990, pp. 44–48.

[32]The scenario and quotation are taken from Tom Eisenhart, "Automation Inevitable for 90s Marketers," *Business Marketing,* January 1990, pp. 44–49.

[33]Ibid., p. 49.

[34]Jeffrey Rothfeder, Jim Bartimo, Lois Therrien, and Richard Brandt, "How Software Is Making Food Sales a Piece of Cake," *Business Week,* July 2, 1990, pp. 54–55.

[35]Howard Gleckman, John Carey, Russell Mitchell, Tim Smart, and Chris Roush, "The Technology Payoff," *Business Week,* June 14, 1993, pp. 57–68.

[36]Reported in "Survey: Consumers More Aware, Still Want More Info," *Marketing News,* December 9, 1991, p. 6; "Teens Say They Look for Environmentally Friendly Products," *Marketing News,* December 9, 1991, p. 6; and Rose Gutfeld, "Eight of 10 Americans Are Environmentalists, at Least They Say So," *The Wall Street Journal,* August 2, 1991, pp. A1–A8.

[37]These examples are taken from David Kirkpatrick, "Environmentalism: The New Crusade," *Fortune,* February 12, 1990, pp. 44–54.

[38]Michael H. Morris and Gordon W. Paul, "The Relationship between Entrepreneurship and Marketing in Established Firms," *Journal of Business Venturing,* 1987, pp. 247–59.

[39]Jacqueline Graves, "Most Innovative Companies," *Fortune,* December 13, 1993, p. 11.

[40]Joyce E. Davis, "A Master Class in Radical Change," *Fortune,* December 13, 1993, p. 84.

[41]Taken from Phillips et al., "King Customer," pp. 88–94.

[42]William Holstein, Stanley Reed, Jonathan Kapstein, Todd Vogel, and Joseph Weber, "The Stateless Corporation," *Business Week,* May 14, 1990, pp. 98–105.

43John Helyar, Meg Cox, and Elizabeth Jensen, "How Fox Stole the Football Away from CBS," *The Wall Street Journal,* December 20, 1993, pp. B1, B6.

Chapter 3

1These statistics are reported in Nafis Sadik, "World Population Continues to Rise," *The 1992 Information Please Almanac* (Boston: Houghton Mifflin, 1991), p. 131.

2Reported in John W. Wright, *The Universal Almanac 1993* (Kansas City, MO: Andrews and McMeel, 1992), p. 326.

3 Ibid., p. 279.

4Dom Del Prete, "Wall Street Bullish on Mature Adults," *Marketing News,* December 6, 1993, pp. 1–2.

5Cyndee Miller, "Xers Know They're a Target Market, and They Hate That," *Marketing News,* December 6, 1993, pp. 2,15.

6"They Understand Your Kids," *Fortune,* Autumn–Winter 1993, pp. 29–30.

7Reported in Diane Crispell, Thomas Exter, and Judith Waldrop, "Snapshots of the Nation," *The Wall Street Journal,* March 9, 1991, pp. R12–R13.

8Reported in Laura Zinn, Heather Keets, and James B. Treece, "Home Alone—with $660 Billion," *Business Week,* July 29, 1990, pp. 76–77.

9Robin Tierney, "Pop Culture," *World Trade,* October 1993. p. 20.

10Reported in Michael J. Mandel, Christopher Farrell, Dori Jones Yang, Gloria Lau, Christina Del Valle, and S. Lynne Walker, "The Immigrants: How They're Helping to Revitalize the US Economy," *Business Week,* July 13, 1992, pp. 114–22.

11Cyndee Miller, "Cosmetics Firms Finally Discover the Ethnic Market," *Marketing News,* April 30, 1993, p. 2.

12Andrew E. Serwer, "42,496 Secrets Are Bared," *Fortune,* January 24, 1994, pp. 13–14.

13Elizabeth Lesly, "Does Snapple Have the Juice to Go National?" *Business Week,* January 18, 1993, pp. 52–53.

14"Fingerhut Considers Launching a TV Shopping Channel," *Marketing News,* January 3, 1994, p. 13.

15"On-Line in Japan," *Marketing News,* January 3, 1994, p. 28.

16Marvin Cetron and Owen Davies, *Crystal Globe* (New York: St. Martin's Press, 1991), pp. 353–54.

17Howard Schlossberg, "Report Says Environmental Claims Level Off," *Marketing News,* May 24, 1993, p. 12.

18Mark Landler and Geoffrey Smith, "The MTV Tycoon," *Business Week,* September 21, 1992, pp. 56–62.

19John Ward Anderson, "Thundering Herd," *The Courier-Journal* (Louisville, KY), January 2, 1994, p. A8.

20Reported in Valerie Rietman, "US Firms Turn to the Developing World," *The Wall Street Journal,* August 4, 1993, p. A2.

21"Poland Sees Sustained Growth," *The Wall Street Journal,* August 26, 1993, p. A7.

22"E Pluribus Unum," *The Economist,* January 8, 1994, pp. 49–50.

23Jay M. Tannon, "NAFTA Is Good News for US Trade," *Business First,* November 29, 1993, p. 7.

24Louis S. Richman, "What's Next after GATT's Victory," *Fortune,* January 10, 1994, pp. 66–70; and "From Uruguay to Marrakesh," *The Economist,* April 16, 1994, pp. 73–74.

25Cyndee Miller, "Opening the Vietnam Market," *Marketing News,* April 12, 1993, pp. 1–2; David Rogers, "In the New Vietnam, Baby Boomers Strive for Fun and Money," *The Wall Street Journal,* January 7, 1994, pp. A1–A5; Urban C. Lehner, "US

Firms Head for Vietnam, but Find Asian, European Firms Already There," *The Wall Street Journal,* February 10, 1994, p. A14; and James Walsh, "Peace Finally at Hand," *Time,* February 14, 1994, pp. 34–36.

26Bob Ortega, "Wal-Mart Loses Predatory-Pricing Case in Arkansas Court but Plans to Appeal," *The Wall Street Journal,* October 15, 1993, p. B9.

27Robert S. Greenberger, "Syria Enjoys Economic Boom, Boosted by Freedom Allowed under Law No. 10," *The Wall Street Journal,* January 4, 1994, p. A5.

28Maxine S. Lans, "New Laws on Green Marketing Are Popping Up All the Time," *Marketing News,* February 15, 1993, pp. 22, 24.

29Elyse Tanouye, "Warner-Lambert Drug Is Approved for Epilepsy Cases," *The Wall Street Journal,* January 4, 1994, p. B12.

30Bob Davis and Bruce Ingersol, "Clinton's Team Moves to Extend Regulation in Variety of Industries," *The Wall Street Journal,* April 13, 1993, pp. A1, A8.

31Jonathan B. Levine, "Want EC Business? You Have Two Choices," *Business Week,* October 19, 1992, pp. 58–59.

32Neil Gross, "Come One, Come All to the Cellular Sweepstakes," *Business Week,* April 25, 1994, p. 50.

33"Business and Finance," *The Economist,* April 16, 1994, p. 7.

34More specific statistics on R&D expenditures and patents are available in Peter Coy, Jonathan B. Levine, Joseph Weber, Richard Brandt, and Neil Gross, "In the Labs, the Fight to Spend Less, Get More," *Business Week,* June 28, 1993, pp. 102–4; and Peter Coy, John Carey, and Neil Gross, "The Global Patent Race Picks Up Speed," *Business Week,* August 9, 1993, pp. 57–62.

35Trends reported in Marvin Cetron and Owen Davies, *Crystal Globe* (New York: St. Martin's Press, 1991), pp. 329–34.

36Ibid., p. 358.

Chapter 4

1Reported in Tom Peters, *Liberation Management* (New York: Alfred A. Knopf, 1992), p. 45.

2Michael H. Morris and Leyland F. Pitts, "The Contemporary Use of Strategy, Strategic Planning, and Planning Tools by Marketers: A Cross-National Comparison," *European Journal of Marketing,* 1993, pp. 36–57.

3Reported in Ronald Grover and Eric Schine, "Can Hilton Draw a Full House?" *Business Week,* June 8, 1992, pp. 88–89.

4Adapted from William Keenan, Jr., "America's Best Sales Forces: Six at the Summit," *Sales & Marketing Management,* June 1990, pp. 66–72; Brian Dumaine, "PG Rewrites the Marketing Rules," *Fortune,* November 6, 1989, pp. 34–48; and Alecia Swasy, "In a Fast-Paced World, Procter & Gamble Sets Its Store in Old Values," *The Wall Street Journal,* September 21, 1989, pp. A1–A2.

5Frederick E. Webster, Jr., "The Changing Role of Marketing in the Corporation," *Journal of Marketing,* October 1992, pp. 1–17.

6Adapted from John A. Pearce II and Fred David, "Corporate Mission Statements: The Bottom Line," *Academy of Management Executive,* May 1987, p. 109.

7"Consumer Service: Blockbuster Entertainment," *Sales & Marketing Management,* August 1993, p. 41.

8Reported in Teri Lammers, "The Effective and Indispensable Mission Statement," *Inc.,* August 1992, pp. 75–77.

9These examples are reported in Gilbert Fuchsberg, " 'Visioning' Missions Becomes Its Own Mission," *The Wall Street Journal,* January 7, 1994, pp. B1, B4.

[10]"Tootsie Roll Industries," *Fortune*, January 10, 1994, p. 109.

[11]David W. Cravens, *Strategic Marketing* (Homewood, IL: Richard D. Irwin, 1994), pp. 46–47.

[12]Gary McWilliams, "DEC's Comeback Is Still a Work in Progress," *Business Week*, January 18, 1993, p. 75.

[13]Julia Flynn, David Greising, Kevin Kelly, and Leah Nathans Spiro, "Smaller but Wiser," *Business Week*, October 12, 1992, pp. 28–29.

[14]Reported in Andrea Rothman, Gail DeGeorge, and Eric Sheine, "The Season of Upstart Startups," *Business Week*, August 31, 1992, pp. 68–69.

[15]"General Excellence: Southwest Airlines," *Sales & Marketing Management*, August 1993, p. 38.

[16]Kevin Kelly, Wendy Zellner, and Aaron Bernstein, "Suddenly Big Airlines Are Saying: 'Small Is Beautiful,' " *Business Week*, January 17, 1994, p. 37.

[17]Joseph B. White, "GM Saturn Unit Trumpets Profit Turned in 1993," *The Wall Street Journal*, January 6, 1994, p. A4.

[18]Edmund Faltermayer, "Competitiveness: How US Companies Stack Up Now," *Fortune*, April 18, 1994, pp. 52–64.

[19]Gary McWilliams, "Wang's Great Leap Out of Limbo," *Business Week*, March 7, 1994, pp. 68–69.

[20]"Cadbury Buys Spanish Concern," *The Wall Street Journal*, April 22, 1994, p. A6.

[21]These examples reported in Kathy Rebello and Neil Gross, "A Juicy New Apple?" *Business Week*, March 7, 1994, pp. 88–90; "Ciba-Geigy Plans China Venture," *The Wall Street Journal*, April 22, 1994, p. A6; and Brian Coleman and Bridget O'Brian, "Delta Airlines, Virgin Atlantic Forge Alliance," *The Wall Street Journal*, April 13, 1994, p. A4.

[22]"Nissan Motor Inc.," *The Wall Street Journal*, April 14, 1994, p. B4.

[23]David M. Szymanski, Sundar G. Bharadwaj, and P. Rajan Varadarajan, "Standardization versus Adaptation of International Marketing Strategy: An Empirical Investigation," *Journal of Marketing*, October 1993, pp. 1–17; Subhash C. Jain, "Standardization of International Marketing Strategy: Some Research Hypotheses," *Journal of Marketing*, January 1989, pp. 70–79; and John A. Quelch and Edward J. Hoff, "Customizing Global Marketing," *Harvard Business Review*, May–June 1986, pp. 59–68.

[24]Quelch and Hoff, "Customizing," p. 59.

[25]James E. Ellis, "Why Overseas? 'Cause That's Where the Sales Are," *Business Week*, January 10, 1994, p. 63.

[26]Richard A. Melcher and Stewart Toy, "On Guard, Europe," *Business Week*, December 14, 1992, pp. 54–55.

[27]Ellis, "Why Overseas?" p. 63.

[28]Sally Solo, "How to Listen to Consumers," *Fortune*, January 11, 1993, pp. 77–78.

[29]Edward F. McQuarrie and Shelby McIntyre, "The Customer Visit: An Emerging Practice in Business-to-Business Marketing," *Marketing Science Institute*, May 1992, p. 10.

[30]Ginger Trumfio, "Kodak Adjusts Its Focus," *Sales & Marketing Management*, January 1994, p. 20.

Chapter 5

[1]*Economic Report of the President* (Washington, DC: US Government Printing Office, February 1994).

[2]Frank Rose, "If It Feels Good, It Must Be Bad," *Fortune*, October 21, 1991, p. 100.

[3]*What the Customer Wants: The Wall Street Journal's Guide to Marketing in the 1990s* (New York: Dow Jones, 1990), p. vi.

[4]Bernard J. Jaworski and Ajay K. Kohli, "Market Orientation: Antecedents and Consequences," *Journal of Marketing*, July 1993, p. 53.

[5]Peter R. Dickson, "Toward a General Theory of Competitive Rationality," *Journal of Marketing*, January 1992, p. 70.

[6]James F. Engel, Roger D. Blackwell, and Paul W. Miniard, *Consumer Behavior*, 7th ed. (Ft. Worth, TX: Dryden Press, 1993), pp. 276–77.

[7]Thomas S. Robertson, "Low-Commitment Consumer Behavior," *Journal of Advertising Research*, April 1976, pp. 19–24.

[8]Jeffrey J. Stoltman, James W. Gentry, Kenneth A. Anglin, and Alvin C. Burns, "Situational Influences on the Consumer Decision Sequence," *Journal of Business Research*, November 1990, p. 196.

[9]Lynn R. Kahle, Sharon E. Beatty, and Pamela Homer, "Alternative Measurement Approaches to Consumer Values: The List of Values (LOV) and Values and Life Style (VALS)," *Journal of Consumer Research*, December 1986, p. 406.

[10]Engel et al., *Consumer Behavior*, p. 87.

[11]Joel Garreau, *The Nine Nations of North America* (Boston: Houghton Mifflin, 1981).

[12]Richard P. Coleman, "The Continuing Significance of Social Class to Marketing," *Journal of Consumer Research*, December 1983, pp. 265–80.

[13]Jerry C. Olson, *Consumer Behavior and Marketing Strategy*, 3rd ed. (Homewood, IL: Richard D. Irwin, 1993), p. 490.

[14]Greg J. Duncan, Timothy M. Smeeding, and Willard Rogers, "The Incredible Shrinking Middle Class," *American Demographics*, May 1992, p. 38.

[15]John C. Mowen, *Consumer Behavior*, 2nd ed. (New York: Macmillan, 1990), p. 527; and Scott Ward, "Consumer Socialization," *Journal of Consumer Research*, September 1974, pp. 1–14.

[16]"Getting 'Em while They're Young," *Marketing*, September 9, 1991, p. 94; and James U. McNeal, "The Littlest Shoppers," *American Demographics*, February 1992, pp. 48–53.

[17]Robert Bontilier, "Pulling the Family's Strings," *American Demographics*, August 1993, p. 46.

[18]William D. Danko and Charles M. Schaninger, "An Empirical Evaluation of the Gilly-Enis Updated Household Life Cycle Model," *Journal of Business Research*, August 1990, p. 39; Mary C. Gilly and Ben M. Enis, "Recycling the Family Life Cycle: A Proposal for Redefinition," in *Advances in Consumer Research*, vol. 9, ed. Andrew Mitchell (Ann Arbor, MI: Association for Consumer Research, 1982), pp. 271–76; Patrick Murphy and William Staples, "A Modernized Family Life Cycle," *Journal of Consumer Research*, June 1979, pp. 12–22; and Charles M. Schaninger and William D. Danko, "A Conceptual and Empirical Comparison of Alternative Household Life Cycle Models," *Journal of Consumer Research*, March 1993, pp. 580–94.

[19]"The Changing American Household," *American Demographics Desk Reference Series*, July 1992, p. 2; and "The Future of Households," *American Demographics*, December 1993, pp. 27–40.

[20]Lawrence F. Feick and Linda L. Price, "The Market Maven: A Diffuser of Marketplace Information," *Journal of Marketing*, January 1987, pp. 83–97.

[21]Aimee L. Stern, "MCI's Campaign of Converts," *The New York Times*, January 1, 1993, p. 5.

[22]Terry L. Childers and Akshay Rao, "The Influence of Familial and Peer-Based Reference Groups on Consumer Decisions," *Journal of Consumer Research*, September 1992, p. 204; and William

O. Bearden and Michael J. Etzel, "Reference Group Influence on Product and Brand Purchase Decisions," *Journal of Consumer Research,* September 1982, p. 184.

[23]M. Joseph Sirgy, "Self-Concept in Consumer Behavior: A Critical Review," *Journal of Consumer Research,* December 1982, pp. 287–88.

[24]Beth A. Walker and Jerry L. Olson, "Means-End Chains: Connecting Products with Self," *Journal of Business Research,* March 1991, p. 111.

[25]Harold H. Kassarjian and Mary Jane Sheffet, "Personality and Consumer Behavior: An Update," in *Perspectives in Consumer Behavior,* 4th ed., eds. H. H. Kassarjian and T. S. Robertson (Englewood Cliffs, NJ: Prentice Hall, 1990), pp. 281–363.

[26]John L. Lastovicka, "On the Validation of Lifestyle Traits: A Review and Illustration," *Journal of Marketing Research,* February 1982, p. 126.

[27]William L. Wilkie, *Consumer Behavior* (New York: John Wiley & Sons, 1986), p. 307.

[28]Abraham H. Maslow, *Motivation and Personality,* 2nd ed. (New York: Harper and Row, 1970).

[29]Russell W. Belk, "An Exploratory Assessment of Situational Effects in Buyer Behavior," *Journal of Marketing Research,* May 1974, p. 156.

[30]Gordon C. Brunner, "Music, Mood, and Marketing," *Journal of Marketing,* October 1990, pp. 94–104; and Ronald E. Milliman, "Using Background Music to Affect the Behavior of Supermarket Shoppers," *Journal of Marketing,* Summer 1982, pp. 86–91.

[31]Brian Wansink and Michael L. Ray, *How Expansion Advertising Affects Brand Usage Frequency: A Programmatic Evaluation,* MSI Report Summary, Report No. 93–126 (Cambridge, MA: Marketing Science Institute, 1993), p. 1.

[32]Stephen J. Hoch and John Deighton, "Managing What Consumers Learn from Experience," *Journal of Marketing,* April 1989, pp. 1–20.

[33]Walter R. Nord and J. Paul Peter, "A Behavior Modification Perspective on Marketing," *Journal of Marketing,* Spring 1980, p. 41; and Michael L. Rothschild and William C. Gaidis, "Behavioral Learning Theory: Its Relevance to Marketing and Promotions," *Journal of Marketing,* Spring 1981, pp. 70–78.

[34]Richard L. Oliver, "A Cognitive Model of the Antecedents and Consequences of Satisfaction Decisions," *Journal of Marketing Research,* November 1980, pp. 460–61.

[35]Richard L. Oliver, "Cognitive, Affective, and Attribute Bases of the Satisfaction Response," *Journal of Consumer Research,* December 1993, p. 419.

[36]Marsha L. Richins and Peter H. Bloch, "Post-Purchase Product Satisfaction: Incorporating the Effects of Involvement and Time," *Journal of Business Research,* September 1991, pp. 145–58.

[37]Jagdip Singh, "Consumer Complaint Intentions and Behavior: Definitional and Taxonomical Issues," *Journal of Marketing,* January 1988, pp. 93–107.

[38]For a detailed discussion of managerial reactions to complaint behavior, see Alan J. Resnik and Robert R. Harmon, "Consumer Complaints and Managerial Response: A Holistic Approach," *Journal of Marketing,* Winter 1983, pp. 86–97; see also Howard Schlossberg, "Customer Satisfaction: Not a Fad, but a Way of Life," *Marketing News,* June 10, 1991, p. 18; and Judith Waldrop, "Educating the Customer," *American Demographics,* September 1991, p. 45.

[39]Waldrop, "Educating the Customer," p. 45.

[40]Stephanie Anderson Forest, "Customers 'Must Be Pleased, Not Just Satisfied,' " *Business Week,* August 3, 1992, p. 52.

[41]Waldrop, "Educating the Customer," p. 44.

[42]For additional explanation regarding the role of cognitive dissonance in marketing and consumer behavior, see William H. Cummings and M. Venkatesan, "Cognitive Dissonance and Consumer Behavior: A Review of the Evidence," *Journal of Marketing Research,* August 1976, pp. 303–8; and Pradeep K. Korgaonkar and George P. Moschis, "An Experimental Study of Cognitive Dissonance, Product Involvement, Expectations, Performance, and Consumer Judgments of Product Performance," *Journal of Advertising* 11, no. 3 (1982), pp. 32–44.

[43]Mowen, *Consumer Behavior,* p. 764.

[44]Carolyn Gatten, "Social Issues Guide Consumer Buying," *Marketing News,* December 9, 1991, p. 80.

[45]Mowen, *Consumer Behavior,* p. 766.

Chapter 6

[1]Harper W. Boyd, Jr., and Orville C. Walker, Jr., *Marketing Management: A Strategic Approach* (Homewood, IL: Richard D. Irwin, 1990), p. 147.

[2]Ibid, p. 163.

[3]Ernest Raia, "Top 100, 1993," *Purchasing,* November 11, 1993, pp. 69–85.

[4]Eugene W. Muller and Carla S. Lallatin, "At Work with State and Local Government and Institutional Purchasers," *NAPM Insights,* November 1993, pp. 49–51.

[5]Eric J. Adams, "Well Connected," *World Trade,* November 1993, p. 46.

[6]B. G. Yovovich, "Outsourcing Trend Reshapes Marketing," *Business Marketing,* May 1994, p. 36.

[7]"Outsourcing Trend," *Personal Selling Power,* April 1994, p. 34.

[8]Bob Donath, "Important Commandment: Know Thy Customer," *Marketing News,* May 23, 1994, p. 16.

[9]"Rubbermaid, Inc.," *The Wall Street Journal,* April 27, 1994, p. B4.

[10]Personal conversation with Jesse Schook, June 21, 1994.

[11]Ibid.

[12]Jill Miller, "The Customer, the Purchaser, and the Supplier," *NAPM Insights,* May 1994, pp. 30–32.

[13]Philip Kotler, "Philip Kotler Explores the New Marketing Paradigm," *Marketing Science Institute Review,* Spring 1991, p. 9.

[14]Kathy Stuesser and Landon J. Napoleon, "A High-Tech Quest to Reduce Landfill," *NAPM Insights,* February 1994, pp. 61–63.

[15]Harold Leibovitz, "Cost-Effective Systems for Recycling Plastics," *NAPM Insights,* March 1994, pp. 42–44.

[16]"Case Study 1: J. C. Penney," *Stores,* February 1991, pp. A16–A17.

[17]Landon J. Napoleon, "Increasing the Value," *NAPM Insights,* May 1994, pp. 37–40.

[18]Personal conversations with Wayne Whitworth, June 21, 1994.

[19]Ibid.

[20]Marilyn Lester, "What's in a Name," *NAPM Insights,* October 1993, pp. 41–43.

[21]Susan Zimmerman, "Competition Changes the Buying Landscape," *Purchasing,* February 6, 1992, pp. 50–53.

[22]For a revised and expanded version of this typology, see Michele D. Bunn, "Taxonomy of Buying Decision Approaches," *Journal of Marketing,* January 1993, pp. 38–56. See also Patrick J. Robinson, Charles W. Faris, and Yoram Wind, *Industrial Buying and Creative Marketing* (Boston: Allyn and Bacon, 1967).

[23]Barry Rehfeld, "How Large Companies Buy," *Personal Selling Power,* September 1993, p. 31.

[24]Elizabeth Wilson, Gary L. Lilien, and David T. Wilson, "Developing and Testing a Contingency Paradigm of Group Choice in Organizational Buying," *Journal of Marketing Research,* November 1991, pp. 452–53.

[25]Erin Anderson, Wujin Chu, and Barton Weitz, "Industrial Purchasing: An Empirical Exploration of the Buyclass Framework," *Journal of Marketing,* July 1987, p. 72.

[26]Laura M. Birou and Stanley E. Fawcett, "International Purchasing: Benefits, Requirements, and Challenges," *International Journal of Purchasing and Materials Management,* Spring 1993, p. 34.

[27]Jagdish N. Sheth, "A Model of Industrial Buyer Behavior," *Journal of Marketing,* October 1973, p. 52.

[28]William H. Ducker, "Research Is Also Vital for Business Marketers," *Marketing News,* September 13, 1993, p. 17.

[29]Joseph R. Carter and Ram Narasimhan, "Purchasing in the International Marketplace: Implications for Operations," *Journal of Purchasing and Materials Management,* Summer 1990, p. 10.

[30]John R. Ronchetto, Jr., Michael D. Hutt, and Peter H. Reingen, "Embedded Influence Patterns in Organizational Buying Systems," *Journal of Marketing,* October 1989, p. 51.

[31]Hokey Min and William P. Galle, "International Purchasing Strategies of Multinational US Firms," *International Journal of Purchasing and Materials Management,* Summer 1991, p. 11.

[32]*Economic Report of the President* (Washington, DC: US Government Printing Office, 1993).

[33]*Commerce Business Daily,* May 18, 1992, p. 1.

[34]Boyd and Walker, *Marketing Management,* p. 166.

[35]Mary Beth Marklein, "Selling to Uncle Sam," *Nation's Business,* March 1991, p. 29; and Vanessa Gallman, "Winning the Government Procurement Game," *Black Enterprise,* February 1991, p. 154.

[36]*1991 Statistical Abstract of the United States* (Washington, DC: US Department of Commerce, Bureau of the Census, 1991); and Michael Levy and Barton Weitz, *Retail Management* (Homewood, IL: Richard D. Irwin, 1992), p. 21.

[37]Christopher Rauen, "Buying Groups Deliver Discounts," *Nation's Business,* May 1992, p. 41.

[38]Lawrence B. Chonko and Shelby D. Hunt, "Ethics and Marketing Management: An Empirical Investigation," *Journal of Business Research,* August 1985, pp. 339–59.

[39]Gregory T. Gundlach and Patrick E. Murphy, "Ethical and Legal Foundations of Relational Marketing Exchanges," *Journal of Marketing,* October 1993, pp. 35–46; and N. Craig Smith and John A. Quelch, *Ethics in Marketing* (Homewood, IL: Richard D. Irwin, 1983), pp. 40–43.

[40]Kevin Kelly and Kathleen Kerwin, "There's Another Side to the Lopez Saga," *Business Week,* August 23, 1993, p. 26; and John Templeman, Stuart Toy, and Paula Dwyer, "How Many Parts Makers Can Stomach the Lopez Diet?" *Business Week,* June 28, 1993, pp. 45–46.

[41]Min and Galle, "International Purchasing Strategies," p. 16.

Chapter 7

[1]Vincent P. Barabba, "The Market Research Encyclopedia," *Harvard Business Review,* January–February 1990, p. 105.

[2]"AMA Board Approves New Marketing Definition," *Marketing News,* March 1, 1985, pp. 1, 14.

[3]John Tarsa, "Ocean Spray Marketing Research: Delivering Insights in a Customer-Supplier Relationship," *Marketing Research: A Magazine of Management and Application,* September 1991, p. 8.

[4]Adapted from Gilbert A. Churchill, Jr., *Marketing Research: Methodological Foundations,* 5th Ed. (Chicago: The Dryden Press, 1991), p. 9.

[5]Earl Babbie, *The Practice of Social Research,* 5th ed. (Belmont, CA: Wadsworth, 1989), p. 80.

[6]See William R. Dillon, Thomas J. Madden, and Neil A. Firtle, *Marketing Research in a Marketing Environment,* 2nd ed. (Homewood, IL: Richard D. Irwin, 1990), p. 29; and Churchill, *Marketing Research,* pp. 130–43.

[7]See, for example, Johan K. Johansson and Ikujiro Nonaka, "Market Research the Japanese Way," *Harvard Business Review,* May–June 1987, pp. 16–18, 22; and Tim Powell, "Despite Myths, Secondary Research Is Valuable Tool," *Marketing News,* September 2, 1991, p. 28.

[8]Ed Campbell, "CD-Roms Bring Census Data In-House," *Marketing News,* January 1992, p. 15.

[9]For several recent descriptions, Joseph M. Winski, "Gentle Rain Turns to Torrent," *Advertising Age,* June 3, 1991, p. 34; Blair Peters, "The 'Brave New World' of Single Source Information," *Marketing Research: A Magazine of Management and Applications,* December 1990, pp. 13–21; and "Nielsen, NPD Start Single Source Service," *Marketing News,* August 28, 1987, p. 1.

[10]Thomas G. Exter, "The Next Step Is Called GIS," *American Demographics,* May 1992, p. 2.

[11]Jack Szergold, "Getting the GIS of Things," *Management Review,* July 1993, p. 6.

[12]David Churbuck, "Geographics," *Forbes,* January 6, 1992, pp. 262–67; and Eric Schine, "Computer Maps Pop Up All over the Map," *Business Week,* July 26, 1993, p. 75.

[13]See Bobby J. Calder, "Focus Groups and the Nature of Qualitative Marketing Research," *Journal of Marketing Research,* August 1977, pp. 353–64; and Edward F. Fern, "The Use of Focus Groups for Idea Generation: The Effects of Group Size, Acquaintanceship, and Moderator on Response Quantity and Quality," *Journal of Marketing Research,* February 1982, pp. 1–13.

[14]Jonathan Jameson, "Marketing: Back to the Basics," *Restaurant Business,* September 1, 1991, p. 82; and Cyndee Miller, "Right Package Sets Mood for Image-Driven Brands," *Marketing News,* August 5, 1991, p. 2.

[15]Howard Gershowitz, "Entering the 1990s—The State of Data Collection —Telephone Data Collection," *Applied Marketing Research,* Spring 1990, pp. 16–19.

[16]Jack Honomichl, "Legislation Threatens Research by Phone," *Marketing News,* June 24, 1991, p. 4.

[17]Stephen W. McDaniel, Perry Verille, and Charles S. Madden, "The Threats to Marketing Research: An Empirical Reappraisal," *Journal of Marketing Research,* February 1985, pp. 74–80; and Gershowitz, "Entering the 1990s."

[18]Michael P. Cronin, "On-the-Cheap Market Research," *Inc.,* June 1992, p. 108.

[19]Pamela Rogers, "One-on-Ones Don't Get the Credit They Deserve," *Marketing News,* January 2, 1991, p. 9.

[20]Susan Kraft, "Who Slams the Door on Research?" *American Demographics,* September 1991, p. 9.

[21]Alan J. Bush and Joseph F. Hair, Jr., "Mall Intercept versus Telephone Interviewing Environment," *Journal of Marketing Research,* May 1985, pp. 158–68.

[22]Howard Schlossberg, "Shoppers Virtually Stroll through Store Aisles to Examine Packages," *Marketing News,* June 6, 1993, p. 2.

[23]Sharon Hollander, "Projective Techniques Uncover Real Consumer Attitudes," *Marketing News,* January 4, 1988, p. 34.

[24]See Stephen Groves and Raymond P. Fisk, "Observational Data Collection Methods for Services Marketing: An Overview," *Journal of the Academy of Marketing Science,* Summer 1992, pp. 217–24.

[25]Rebecca Piirto, "Socks, Ties, and Videotape," *American Demographics,* September 1991, p. 6.

[26]Daphre Chandler, "8 Common Pitfalls of International Research," in *The Resurgence of Research in Decision-Making: 1992 CASRO Annual Journal* (Port Jefferson, NY: The Council of American Survey Research Organizations, 1992), pp. 81–85.

[27]Elizabeth Loken, "Probing Japanese Buyers' Minds," *Business Marketing,* 1987, pp. 85–86.

[28]Howard N. Gundee, "Council Joins Industrial Effort to Support Research," *Marketing News,* January 4, 1993, p. 22.

[29]McDaniel, Verille, and Madden, "Threats to Marketing Research."

[30]Wade Lettwich, "How Researchers Can Win Friends and Influence Politicians," *American Demographics,* August 1993, p. 9.

[31]"The Persistence of Surveying," *Marketing News,* September 28, 1992, p. 4.

[32]Ishmael P. Akaah and Edward A. Riordan, "Judgments of Marketing Professionals about Ethical Issues in Marketing Research: A Replication and Extension," *Journal of Marketing Research,* February 1989, p. 113.

[33]Patrick E. Murphy and Gene R. Laczniak, "Emerging Ethical Issues Facing Marketing Researchers," *Marketing Research,* June 1992, pp. 6–7.

[34]Tom Eisenhart, "After 10 Years of Marketing Decision Support Systems, Where's the Payoff?" *Business Marketing,* June 1990, pp. 46–48, 50.

[35]Alan J. Greco and Jack T. Hogue, "Developing Marketing Decision Support Systems," *Journal of Business and Industrial Marketing,* Summer–Fall 1990, p. 28; and Alan J. Greco and Jack T. Hogue, "Developing Marketing Decision Support Systems in Consumer Goods Firms," *Journal of Consumer Marketing,* Winter 1990, pp. 56–64.

[36]Rajerdra S. Sisodia, "Marketing Information and Decision Support Systems for Services," *Journal of Services Marketing,* Winter 1992, p. 53.

[37]Lisa Beneson, "Bull's Eye Marketing," *Success,* February 1993, pp. 43–44.

[38]Rochelle Kass, "Know Your Customers," *Bank Systems and Technology,* November 1992, p. 35.

Chapter 8

[1]William L. Wilkie, *Consumer Behavior* (New York: John Wiley and Sons, 1986), p. 288.

[2]For an in-depth review, see Gary L. Lilien and Philip Kotler, *Marketing Decision Making: A Model Building Approach* (New York: Harper and Row, 1983); and Peter R. Dickson and James L. Ginter, "Market Segmentation, Product Differentiation, and Marketing," *Journal of Marketing,* April 1987, pp. 1–10.

[3]Harper W. Boyd, Jr., and Orville C. Walker, Jr., *Marketing Management: A Strategic Approach* (Homewood, IL: Richard D. Irwin, 1990), p. 186.

[4]Cyndee Miller, "Researcher Says US Is More of a Bowl than a Pot," *Marketing News,* May 10, 1993, p. 6; and Cynthia Webster, "The Effects of Hispanic Subcultural Identification on Information Search Behavior," *Journal of Advertising Research,* September/October 1992, pp. 54–62.

[5]Daniel F. Hansler and Donald R. Riggin, "Geodemographics: Targeting the Market," *Fund Raising Management,* December 1989, pp. 35–43.

[6]Saeed Samiee, "A Conceptual Framework for International Marketing," in *International Business: Inquiry: An Emerging Vision,* eds. B. Toyne and Douglas Nigh (Columbia, SC: USC Press, 1994) see also Theodore Leavitt, "The Globalization of Markets," *Harvard Business Review,* May–June 1983, pp. 99–102; and Saeed Samiee and Kendall Roth, "The Influence of Global Marketing Standardization on Performance," *Journal of Marketing,* April 1992, pp. 1–17.

[7]Ugar Yavas, Bronislaw J. Verhage, and Robert T. Green, "Global Consumer Segmentation versus Local Market Orientation: Empirical Findings," *Marketing International Review,* 1992, pp. 266–68.

[8]Peter D. Bennett, ed., *Dictionary of Marketing Terms* (Chicago: American Marketing Association, 1988), p. 199.

[9]Marian B. Wood and Evelyn Ehrlich, "Segmentation: Five Steps to More Effective Business-to-Business Marketing," *Sales & Marketing Management,* April 1991, p. 60.

[10]Gary L. Berman, "The Hispanic Market: Getting Down to Cases," *Sales & Marketing Management,* October 1991, p. 66.

[11]Shirley Young, Leland Ott, and Barbara Feign, "Some Practical Considerations in Market Segmentation," *Journal of Marketing Research,* August 1978, pp. 405–12.

[12]Ronald Grover, "Old Rockers Never Die—They Just Switch to CDs," *Business Week,* August 17, 1992, p. 54.

[13]Maria Mallory, "Working Up to a Major Market," *Business Week,* March 23, 1992, p. 70.

[14]Roger J. Calantone and Alan G. Sawyer, "The Stability of Benefit Segments," *Journal of Marketing Research,* August 1978, pp. 395–404.

[15]Howard Schlossberg, "Success with Seniors Depends on Dialogue and Long-Range Plans," *Marketing News,* January 4, 1993, p. 2.

[16]Henry Assael, "Segmenting Markets by Response Elasticity," *Journal of Advertising Research,* April 1976, pp. 27–35.

[17]Hartmarx, *Annual Report* (Chicago: Hartmarx Corporation, 1992).

[18]"The American Dream Is Alive and Well—In Mexico," *Business Week,* September 30, 1991, p. 102.

[19]Philip Kotler, *Marketing Management: Analysis, Planning, Implementation, and Control,* 8th ed. (Englewood Cliffs, NJ: Prentice Hall, 1994), p. 265.

[20]See Yoram Wind and Richard Cardoza, "Industrial Market Segmentation," *Industrial Marketing Management,* March 1974, pp. 153–66, for a similar outline of business-to-business segmentation bases.

[21]Jon Berry, "An Empire of Niches," *Superbrands,* 1991, p. 22.

[22]Kathleen Kerwin and Larry Armstrong, "Why Motown Is Going the Extra Mile in California," *Business Week,* October 12, 1992, p. 70.

[23]"A User's Guide to the Survey of Media Markets," *Sales & Marketing Management,* October 26, 1992, p. 8.

[24]Daniel F. Hansler and Don L. Riggen, "Geodemographics: Targeting the Market," *Fund Raising Management,* December 1989, p. 35.

[25]Nick Fuller, "Finding Cable's Target," *Marketing,* February 18, 1992, p. 27.

[26]See also: William D. Wells and Douglas J. Tigert, "Activities, Interests, and Opinions," *Journal of Advertising Research,* August 1971, pp. 27–35; and William D. Wells, "Psychographics: A Critical Review," *Journal of Marketing Research,* May 1975, pp. 196–213. See also Allen M. Clark, "'Trends' That Will Impact New Products," *Journal of Consumer Marketing,* Winter 1991, pp. 29–34; P. Valette-Florence and A. Jolibert, "Social Values, A.I.O., and Consumption Patterns: Exploratory Findings," *Journal of Business Research,* March 1990, pp. 109–22; and Steven Hoch, "Who Do We Know: Predicting the Interests and Opinions of the American Consumer," *Journal of Consumer Research,* December 1988, pp. 315–24.

[27]Wells and Tigert, "Activities, Interests, and Opinions," p. 30.

[28]Brian Davis and Warren A. French, "Exploring Advertising Usage Segments among the Aged," *Journal of Advertising Research,* February–March 1989, pp. 22–29.

[29] Michael Gates, "VALS Changes with the Times," *Incentive,* June 1989, p. 27.

[30]Martha Farnsworth Riche, "Psychographics for the 1990s," *American Demographics,* July 1989, p. 30.

[31]Russell I. Haley, "Benefit Segmentation: A Decision-Oriented Tool," *Journal of Marketing,* July 1968, pp. 30–35.

[32]Ibid.; and Paul E. Green, Abba M. Krieger, and Catherine M. Schagger, "Quick and Simple Benefit Segmentation," *Journal of Advertising Research,* June–July 1985, pp. 9–17.

[33]Kristaan Helson, Kamel Jedidi, and Wayne S. DeSarbo, "A New Approach to Country Segmentation Utilizing Multinational Diffusion Patterns," *Journal of Marketing,* October 1993, p. 61.

[34]David A. Chambers, "Data Technology Boosts Popularity of Lifestage Marketing," *Marketing News,* October 28, 1991, p. 16.

[35]Robert H. Waterman, Jr., "Successful Small- and Medium-Sized Firms Stress Creativity, Employ Niche Strategy," *Marketing News,* March 15, 1984, p. 24.

[36]Harper W. Boyd and Orville C. Walker, Jr., *Marketing Management: A Strategic Approach* (Homewood, IL: Richard D. Irwin, 1990), p. 294.

[37]Raymond Serafin and Cleveland Horton, "Buick Ads Target ZIP codes," *Advertising Age,* April 1, 1991, pp. 1, 36.

[38]Martin R. Lautman, "The ABCs of Positioning," *Marketing Research: A Magazine of Management and Applications,* Winter 1993, p. 12.

[39]Mita Sujan and James R. Bettman, "The Effects of Brand Positioning Strategies on Consumers' Brand and Category Perceptions: Some Insights from Schema Research," *Journal of Marketing Research,* November 1989, p. 454.

[40]Paula Munier Lee, "The Micromarketing Revolution," *Small Business Reports,* February 1990, pp. 73–82.

[41]Howard Schlossberg, "Packaged Goods Experts: Micromarketing the Only Way to Go," *Marketing News,* July 6, 1992, p. 8.

[42]N. Craig Smith and John A. Quelch, *Ethics in Marketing* (Homewood, IL: Richard D. Irwin, 1993), pp. 188–95.

Chapter 9

[1]Adapted from Peter D. Bennett, ed., *Dictionary of Marketing Terms* (Chicago: American Marketing Association, 1988), p. 153.

[2]"Business-to-Business Product: Hewlett-Packard," *Sales & Marketing Management,* August 1993, p. 42.

[3]Based on communication from Wayne Whitworth, purchasing manager at Brown-Forman, April 16, 1993.

[4]Tom Peters, *Liberation Management* (New York: Alfred A. Knopf, 1992), p. 295.

[5]Wendy Zellner, "Penney's Rediscovers Its Calling," *Business Week,* April 5, 1993, pp. 51–52.

[6]"Pen Wars," *Forbes,* January 6, 1992, pp. 88–89.

[7]Based on communication from David J. Faulds, June 1994. The data supporting this section are available in David J. Faulds, *Consumer Product and Manufacturer Ratings,* vols. 1 and 2 (Detroit: Gale Research Inc., 1993).

[8]Brian Dumaine, "Design That Sells and Sells and . . . ," *Fortune,* March 11, 1991, pp. 86–94.

[9]Ron Stodghill II, "Joe Montgomery's Wild Ride," *Business Week,* April 19, 1993, pp. 50–51.

[10]Kathleen Deveny, "Today's Toothbrushes: 'Improved' and Pricey," *The Wall Street Journal,* November 10, 1992, pp. B1, B10.

[11]C. Merle Crawford, *New Products Management* (Homewood, IL: Richard D, Irwin, 1991), p. 361.

[12]This discussion is adapted from Kevin Lane Keller, "Conceptualizing, Measuring, and Managing Customer-Based Brand Equity," *Journal of Marketing,* January 1993, pp. 1–22.

[13]Patricia Krantz, "In Moscow, the Attack of the Killer Brands," *Business Week,* January 10, 1994, p. 40.

[14]These examples are reported in Lois Therrien, Maria Mallory, and Zachary Schiller, "Brands on the Run," *Business Week,* April 19, 1993, pp. 26–29.

[15]"Shoot Out at the Check-Out," *The Economist,* June 5, 1993, pp. 69–72.

[16]Bob Ortega, "Wal-Mart Develops New Private Label for Packaged Food," *The Wall Street Journal,* April 7, 1993, p. B7.

[17]Diana T. Kurylko, "Product Namer Attempts to Capture a Car's Feeling," *Business First,* April 5, 1993, pp. 30–31.

[18]Valerie Reitman, "P&G Uses Skills It Has Learned at Home to Introduce Its Brands to the Russians," *The Wall Street Journal,* April 14, 1993, pp. B1, B3.

[19]"Licensed Product Value Falls," *Marketing News,* March 1, 1993, p. 1.

[20]John Chamberlain, "Look for the Label on U of L Products," *Inside U of L,* April 16, 1993, p. 3.

[21]"Big Blue," *The Economist,* July 10, 1993, p. 22.

[22]Richard Gibson, "Label Law Stirs Up Food Companies," *The Wall Street Journal,* June 2, 1993, pp. B1, B6; and Nancy Hellenich, "New Food Labels Help to Balance Your Dietary Budget," *USA Today,* May 2, 1994, p. 40.

[23]Kathleen Deveny, "Toothpaste Makers Tout New Packaging," *The Wall Street Journal,* October 10, 1992, pp. B1, B10.

[24]Michael Connor, "Services Research Should Focus on Service Management," *Marketing News,* September 13, 1993, pp. 36, 41.

[25]James B. Miller, "Bailing Out Customers," *Sales & Marketing Management,* January 1994, p. 29.

[26]John R. Graham, "Customer Service Redefined: It's What You Know, Not What You Sell," *Marketing News,* January 3, 1994, p. 25.

[27]Martin Everett, "Relate Is Good, Elate Is Better," *Sales & Marketing Management,* January 1994, pp. 31–32.

Chapter 10

[1]Reported in Christopher Power, Kathleen Kerwin, Ronald Glover, Keith Alexander, and Robert D. Hof, "Flops," *Business Week,* August 16, 1993, p. 82.

[2]Alan Farnham, "America's Most Admired Company," *Fortune,* February 7, 1994, pp. 50–54.

[3]Power et al., "Flops," p. 77.

[4]Rahul Jacob, "Beyond Quality and Value," *Fortune,* Autumn–Winter 1993, pp. 8–11.

[5]Cyndee Miller, "Little Relief Seen for New Product Failure," *Marketing News,* June 21, 1993, pp. 1, 10.

[6]Brenton R. Schlender, "How Sony Keeps the Magic Going," *Fortune,* February 24, 1993, pp. 76–84.

[7]James P. Miller, "Hallmark Cards to Acquire RHI for $365 Million," *The Wall Street Journal,* April 27, 1994, p. B10.

[8]Suein Hwang, "Colgate-Palmolive Profit Rose 11% in Third Quarter," *The Wall Street Journal,* October 22, 1993, p. B5.

[9]John Naisbitt, *Global Paradox* (New York: William Morrow and Company, 1994), p. 70.

[10]Michael J. McCarthy, "PepsiCo to Test Two New Lines of Fruit Drinks," *The Wall Street Journal,* April 22, 1993, pp. B1, B8.

[11]Thomas D. Kuczmarski, *Managing New Products: Competing through Excellence* (Englewood Cliffs, NJ: Prentice-Hall, 1988), pp. 37–39.

[12]Power et al., p. 77.

[13]Robert L. Simison and Neal Templin, "Ford Is Turning Heads with $6 Billion Cost to Design 'World Car,'" *The Wall Street Journal,* March 23, 1993, pp. A1, A6.

[14]Dori Jones Young, "When the Going Gets Tough, Boeing Gets Touchy-Feely," *Business Week,* January 17, 1994, pp. 65–67.

[15]Power et al., "Flops," p. 77.

[16]"Mercury's Mystique Tries No-Tuneup Tack," *The Courier-Journal,* February 3, 1994, p. D1.

[17]Kevin Kelly, "The New Soul of John Deere," *Business Week,* January 31, 1994, pp. 64–66.

[18]Linda Rochford and Thomas R. Wotruba, "New Product Development under Changing Economic Conditions," *Journal of Business and Industrial Marketing,* 8, no. 3, 1993, pp. 4–12.

[19]Alan Farnham, "America's Most Admired Company," *Fortune,* February 7, 1994, pp. 50–54.

[20]Kathleen Devery, "Failure of Its Oven Lovin' Cookie Dough Shows Pillsbury Pitfalls of New Products," *The Wall Street Journal,* July 17, 1993, pp. B1, B8.

[21]Power et al., "Flops," p. 80.

[22]Christopher Power, "Will It Sell in Podunk? Hard to Say," *Business Week,* August 10, 1992, p. 46.

[23]William R. Dillon, Thomas J. Madden, and Neil H. Firtle, *Essentials of Marketing Research* (Homewood, IL: Richard D. Irwin, 1993), p. 732.

[24]Warren B. Brown and Necmi Karagozoglu, "Leading the Way to Faster New Product Development," *The Executive,* February 1993, pp. 36–47.

[25]Kyle Pope, "Compaq Is Set to Introduce 'Subnotebook,'" *The Wall Street Journal,* February 2, 1994, p. 85.

[26]This section draws heavily from Robert G. Cooper and Elko J. Kleinschmidt, "Stage Gate Systems for New Product Success," *Marketing Management,* 1, no. 4, pp. 20–26.

[27]Susan Caminiti, "A Star Is Born," *Fortune,* Autumn–Winter 1993, pp. 44–47.

Chapter 11

[1]Peter Bennett, *Dictionary of Marketing Terms* (Chicago: American Marketing Association, 1988), p. 156.

[2]Ibid.

[3]Emerson Andrew Torgan, "Not Ready for Prime Time: PDAs," *Home Office Computing,* January 1994, pp. 70–74; and Jim Carlton, "Apple Unveils New Version of Newton in Bid to Recover from Marketing Flop," *The Wall Street Journal,* March 4, 1994, p. B10.

[4]Marcy Magiera and Melanie Wells, "New Age Road Leads Coke to Fruitopia," *Advertising Age,* March 7, 1994, pp. 4, 47.

[5]Christy Fisher, "Line Extension No Recipe for Success in Candy," *Advertising Age,* January 31, 1994, pp. 3, 38.

[6]Riccardo A. Davis, "Kodak's Future Picture May Include Private Label," *Advertising Age,* June 20, 1994, p. 8.

[7]Gabriella Stern, "Makers of Frozen Diet Entrees Start Some Diets of Their Own," *The Wall Street Journal,* January 4, 1994, pp. B1, B7.

[8]Elizabeth A. Lesly, "Borden Faces Facts: It's Time to Shed the Flab," *Business Week,* November 9, 1992, p. 44.

[9]Geoffrey Smith and Nathans Spiro, "Fidelity Jumps Feet First into the Fray," *Business Week,* May 25, 1992, pp. 104–6.

[10]"Circuit City Stores Plans to Try Its Hand at Peddling a New Product—Used Cars," *The Wall Street Journal,* April 7, 1993, p. B6.

[11]Greg Bowens, "Wiping the Mess from Gerber's Chin," *Business Week,* February 1, 1993, p. 32.

[12]Ronald Grover, "Coors Is Thinking Suds 'R' Us," *Business Week,* June 8, 1992, p. 34.

[13]Kyle Pope, "Texas Instruments Sees Path on Information Highway," *The Wall Street Journal,* March 9, 1994, p. B4.

[14]Allen D. Shocker, Rajendra K. Srivastava, and Robert W. Ruekert, "Challenges and Opportunities Facing Brand Management: An Introduction to the Special Issue," *Journal of Marketing Research,* May 1994, pp. 149–58.

[15]Srinivas K. Reddy, Susan L. Holak, and Subodh Bhat, "To Extend or Not to Extend: Success Determinants of Line Extensions," *Journal of Marketing Research,* May 1994, pp. 243–62.

[16]Gene R. Laczniak and Patrick E. Murphy, *Ethical Marketing Decisions: The Higher Road* (Boston, MA: Allyn and Bacon, 1993), p. 81.

[17]Fred W. Morgan, "Incorporating a Consumer Product Safety Perspective into the Product Development Process," in N. Craig Smith and John A. Quelch, eds., *Ethics in Marketing,* (Homewood, IL: Richard D. Irwin, 1993), pp. 351–59.

[18]Reported in Douglas Lavin, "Chrysler Corp. Discloses a Third Recall of Its Neon Model for Brake Problem," *The Wall Street Journal,* April 8, 1994, p. A3; and "Some Crayon Brands are Recalled by US, Citing Lead Levels," *The Wall Street Journal,* April 7, 1994, p. A8.

[19]Mary Agnes Carey, "Popcorn at Movies Gets Thumbs Down for Being Full of Fat," *The Wall Street Journal,* April 26, 1994, p. A5.

[20]Laczniak and Murphy, *Ethical Marketing Decisions,* p. 89.

[21]Marcus W. Brauchli, "Chinese Flagrantly Copy Trademarks of Foreigners," *The Wall Street Journal,* June 20, 1994, pp. B1, B5.

[22]Laczniak and Murphy, *Ethical Marketing Decisions,* p. 103.

Chapter 12

[1]Stuart Sinclair, "A Guide to Global Pricing," *Journal of Business Strategy,* May–June 1993, p. 16.

[2]Walter van Waterschoot and Christophe Van den Butle, "The 4P Classification of the Marketing Mix Revisited," *Journal of Marketing,* October 1992, p. 90.

[3]Michael V. Marn and Robert Rosiello, "Managing Price, Gaining Profit," *Harvard Business Review,* September–October 1992, p. 86.

[4]Ibid., p. 84.

[5]Hermann Simon, "Pricing Opportunities and How to Exploit Them," *Sloan Management Review,* Winter 1992, p. 56; and Gerard J. Tellis, "The Price Elasticity of Selective Demand: A Meta-Analysis of Econometric Models of Sales," *Journal of Marketing Research,* November 1988, p. 331–41.

[6]See Kent. B. Monroe, *Pricing: Making Profitable Decisions* (New York: McGraw-Hill, 1990), pp. 8–10; and Paul W. Farris and John A. Quelch, "In Defense of Price Promotion," *Sloan Management Review,* Fall 1987, p. 63.

[7]Sinclair, "A Guide to Global Pricing," p. 16.

[8]William Spindle, "Can't Get Enough of That Super Yen," *Business Week,* October 4, 1993, p. 50.

[9]Michael D. Mondello, "Naming Your Price," *Inc.,* July 1992, p. 80.

[10]Thomas T. Nagle, *The Strategy and Tactics of Pricing: A Guide to Profitable Decision Making* (Englewood Cliffs, NJ: Prentice Hall, 1989), p. 8.

[11]"Cruise Lines Deep in Discounts," *Advertising Age,* February 3, 1992, p. 16.

[12]Zachary Schiller, "Procter & Gamble Hits Back," *Business Week,* July 19, 1993, p. 20.

[13]Peter R. Dickson, *Marketing Management* (Fort Worth, TX: The Dryden Press, 1994), p. 476.

[14]Robert Jacobson and David A. Aaker, "Is Market Share All That It's Cracked Up to Be?" *Journal of Marketing,* Fall 1985, pp. 11–22.

[15]Greg Bowers, "Wiping the Mess from Gerber's Chin," *Business Week,* February 1, 1993, p. 32.

[16]Monroe, *Pricing,* p. 8.

[17]Marn and Rosiello, "Managing Price, Gaining Profit," pp. 84–85.

[18]Nagle, *Strategy and Tactics of Pricing,* pp. 114–15.

[19]Simon, "Pricing Opportunities," p. 64.

[20]"Sheraton's New Pricing Makes Rivals Cry Foul," *Advertising Age,* May 11, 1992, p. 6.

[21]Mondello, "Naming Your Price," p. 80.

[22]Doug Carroll, "Price Wars Make Airlines Shrink," *USA Today,* November 24, 1993, p. 18B.

[23]Allan J. McGrath, "Ten Timeless Truths about Pricing," *Journal of Business and Industrial Marketing,* Summer–Fall 1991, p. 17.

[24]Raymond Serafin, "US Cars Build Share with Value Pricing," *Advertising Age,* July 12, 1993, p. 4; and Wendy Zeller, "Penney's Rediscovers Its Calling," *Business Week,* April 5, 1993, p. 51.

[25]Donald F. Blumberg, "What Is Your Service Really Worth?" *Success,* July–August 1992, p. 13.

[26]Monroe, *Pricing,* p. 204.

[27]Susan M. Broniarczyk and Joseph W. Alba, "The Importance of the Brand in Brand Extension," *Journal of Marketing Research,* May 1994, pp. 214–25. For recent reviews, see David A. Aaker and Kevin Lane Keller, "Consumer Evaluations of Brand Extensions," *Journal of Marketing,* January 1990, pp. 27–41; and C. Whan Park, Sandra Milberg, and Robert Lawson, "Evaluation of Brand Extensions: The Role of Product Feature Similarity and Brand Concept Consistency," *Journal of Consumer Research,* September 1991, pp. 185–93.

[28]Kent B. Monroe and Susan M. Petroshius, "Buyers' Perceptions of Price: An Update of the Evidence," in *Perspectives in Consumer Behavior,* 3rd ed., ed. H. H. Kassarjian and T. S. Robertson (Glenview, IL: Scott, Foresman, 1991), p. 44.

[29]Valarie Zeithaml, "Consumer Perceptions of Price, Quality, and Value: A Means-End Model and Synthesis of Evidence," *Journal of Marketing,* July 1988, p. 10; and Peter R. Dickson and Alan G. Sawyer, "The Price Knowledge and Search of Supermarket Shoppers," *Journal of Marketing,* July 1990, pp. 42–53.

[30]Zeithaml, "Consumer Perceptions," p. 14.

[31]Kent B. Monroe and R. Krishnan, "The Effect of Price on Subjective Product Evaluations," *Perceived Quality: How Consumers View Stores and Merchandise,* ed. Jacob Jacoby and Jerry Olson (Lexington, MA: Lexington Books, 1985), pp. 209–32.

[32]Gary Levin, "Price Rises as Factor for Consumers," *Advertising Age,* November 8, 1993, p. 37.

[33]Robert A. Peterson and William R. Wilson, "Perceived Risk and Price-Reliance Schema and Price-Perceived-Quality Mediators," in *Perceived Quality: How Consumers View Stores and Merchandise,* ed. Jacob Jacoby and Jerry Olson (Lexington, MA: Lexington Books, 1985), pp. 247–68. Studies of firm behavior reveal that pursuit of product-quality strategies can improve profitability and that price and quality are related at the firm level. See Robert Jacobson and David A. Aaker, "The Strategic Role of Product Quality," *Journal of Marketing,* October 1987, pp. 31–44.

[34]Donald R. Lichtenstein and Scot Burton, "The Relationship between Perceived and Objective Price Quality," *Journal of Marketing Research,* November 1989, pp. 429–43.

[35]Gerard J. Tellis and Gary J. Gaeth, "Best Value, Price-Seeking, and Price Aversion: The Impact of Information and Learning on Consumer Choices," *Journal of Marketing,* April 1990, pp. 34–45.

[36]Robert Jacobson and Carl Obermiller, "The Formation of Expected Future Price: A Reference Price for Forward-Looking Consumers," *Journal of Consumer Research,* March 1990, p. 421.

[37]Noreen M. Klein and Janet E. Oglethorpe, "Cognitive Reference Points in Consumer Decision-Making," in *Advances in Consumer Research,* vol. 14, ed. M. Wallendorf and J. Anderson (Provo, UT: Association for Consumer Research, 1987), pp. 183–97.

[38]Joel E. Urbany and Peter R. Dickson, *Consumer Knowledge of Consumer Prices: An Exploratory Study and Framework,* Report No. 90-112 (Cambridge, MA: Marketing Science Institute, 1990), p. 18.

[39]Dickson and Sawyer, "Price Knowledge and Search," p. 42–53.

[40]Aradha Krishna, "Effect of Dealing Patterns on Consumer Perceptions of Deal Frequency and Willingness to Pay," *Journal of Marketing Research,* November 1991, pp. 441–51.

[41]Abhijit Biswas and Edward A. Blair, "Contextual Effects of Reference Prices in Retail Advertisements," *Journal of Marketing,* July 1991, p. 4.

[42]Richard Thaler, "Mental Accounting and Consumer Choice," *Marketing Science,* Summer 1985, pp. 199–214.

Chapter 13

[1]Harper W. Boyd, Jr., and Orville C. Walker, Jr., *Marketing Management: A Strategic Approach* (Homewood, IL: Richard D. Irwin, 1990), p. 461.

[2]Michael Parkin, *Microeconomics,* 2nd ed. (Reading, MA: Addison-Wesley, 1992), p. 109.

[3]Philip Kotler, *Marketing Management: Analysis, Planning, Implementation, and Control,* 8th ed. (Englewood Cliffs, NJ: Prentice Hall, 1994), p. 495.

[4]Rockney G. Walters, "Assessing the Impact of Retail Price Promotions on Product Substitution, Complementary Purchase, and Interstore Sales Displacement," *Journal of Marketing*, April 1991, p. 17.

[5]Paul A. Samuelson and William D. Nordhaus, *Economics*, 14th ed. (New York: McGraw-Hill, 1992), p. 210.

[6]Ford S. Worthy, "Japan's Smart Secret Weapon," *Fortune*, August 12, 1991, pp. 72–73.

[7]John B. Elmer, " '3-D' Pricing Helps to Overcome Marketing Myopia," *Marketing News*, August 5, 1991, p. 6; and Peter H. van Westenoorp, "Price Sensitivity Meter (PSM)—A New Approach to Study Consumer Perception of Prices," *NSS, N. V. Nederlanouse Stichting voor Statistiek (NSS)*, 1975, pp. 140–67.

[8]The organization and content of this section are based on the typology and discussion of Gerard J. Tellis, "Beyond the Many Faces of Price: An Integration of Pricing Strategies," *Journal of Marketing*, October 1986, pp. 146–60.

[9]Kent B. Monroe, *Pricing: Making Profitable Decisions*, 2nd ed. (New York: McGraw-Hill, 1990), p. 490.

[10]Kotler, *Marketing Management*, p. 512.

[11]Gerard J. Tellis and Gary J. Gaeth, "Best Value, Price-Seeking, and Price Aversion: The Impact of Information and Learning on Consumer Choices," *Journal of Marketing*, April 1990, p. 36.

[12]Tellis, "Beyond the Many Faces of Price," p. 153.

[13]Monroe, *Pricing*, p. 304.

[14]Joseph P. Guiltinan, "The Price Bundling of Services: A Normative Framework," *Journal of Marketing*, April 1987, p. 74.

[15]Gary J. Gaeth, Irwin P. Levin, Goutam Ghakraborty, and Aron Levin, "Consumer Evaluation of Multi-Product Bundles: An Information Integration Analysis," *Marketing Letters*, December 1990, p. 47; and Francis J. Mulhern and Robert P. Leone, "Implicit Price Bundling of Retail Products: A Multiproduct Approach to Maximizing Store Profitability," *Journal of Marketing*, October 1991, pp. 63–76.

[16]Tim Clark, "Four H-P Success Story Strategies," *Business Marketing*, July 1993, pp. 18, 20.

[17]Kotler, *Marketing Management*, p. 514.

[18]Michael Mandel, Neil Gross, and Lois Therrien, "Stuck! How Companies Cope when They Can't Raise Prices," *Business Week*, November 15, 1993, p. 146.

[19]For research regarding acceptable price limits, see Peter R. Dickson and Alan G. Sawyer, "The Price Knowledge and Search of Supermarket Shoppers," *Journal of Marketing*, July 1990, pp. 42–53; Rustan Kosenko and Don Rahtz, "Buyer Market Price Knowledge on Acceptable Price Range and Price Limits," in *Advances in Consumer Research*, vol. 15, ed. Michael J. Houston (Provo, UT: Association for Consumer Research, 1987), pp. 328–33; and Patricia Sorce and Stanley M. Widrick, "Individual Differences in Latitude of Acceptable Prices," in *Advances in Consumer Research*, vol. 18, ed. Rebecca H. Holman and Michael R. Soloman (Provo, UT: Association for Consumer Research, 1991), pp. 802–5.

[20]Kate Fitzgerald, "Target Accuses Wal-Mart in Ads," *Advertising Age*, March 29, 1993, pp. 1, 50.

[21]Alan Radding, "Big Blue Takes Aim at Toshiba, Compaq," *Advertising Age*, March 25, 1991, pp. 1, 48; Kathy Rebello and Stephanie Anderson, "They're Slashing as Fast as They Can," *Business Week*, February 17, 1992, p. 40; and Hal Lancaster and Michael Allen, "Compaq Computer Finds Itself Where It Once Put IBM," *The Wall Street Journal*, January 13, 1992, p. B4.

[22]Kathleen Madigan, Joseph Weber, and Geoffrey Smith, "The Latest Mad Plunge of the Price Slashers," *Business Week*, May 11, 1992, p. 36.

[23]Hugh M. Cannon and Fred W. Morgan, "A Strategic Pricing Framework," *Journal of Business and Industrial Marketing*, Summer–Fall 1991, p. 62.

[24]Monroe, *Pricing*, p. 427.

[25]Michael L. Mellot, "Systematic Approach to Pricing Increases Profits," *Marketing News*, May 24, 1993, p. 3.

[26]Jim Hansen, "Fees for Loans: Just Part of the Marketing Equation," *Credit Union Executive*, November–December 1992, pp. 42–45; Clifford L. Ratza, "A Client-Driven Model for Service Pricing," *Journal of Professional Services Marketing*, 8 (2), 1993, pp. 55–64; and Madhav N. Segal, "An Empirical Investigation of the Pricing of Professional Services," *Journal of Professional Services Marketing*, 1991, pp. 169–81.

[27]Kristen Young, "When Morris Took Flight, Fares Fell," *USA Today*, August 30, 1993, pp. 1B–2B.

[28]Guiltinan, "The Price Bundling of Services," p. 74.

[29]Zachary Schiller, Susan Garland, and Julia Flynn Siler, "The Humana Flap Could Make All Hospitals Feel Sick," *Business Week*, November 4, 1991, p. 34.

[30]Gwendolyn K. Ortmeyer, "Ethical Issues in Pricing," in *Ethics in Marketing*, ed. N. Craig Smith and John A. Quelch (Homewood, IL: Richard D. Irwin, 1993), p. 401; and Andrea Rothman, "The Airlines Get Out the Good China," *Business Week*, February 3, 1992, p. 66.

[31]Marc Rice, "Profiteering Claimed as Wood Prices Rise," *The Commercial Appeal*, August 28, 1992, pp. B4–B5; and "Home Depot Offers Storm Victims Break," *The Commercial Appeal*, August 29, 1992, p. B4.

[32]*Code of Federal Regulations*, 16, 233.0 FTC, Office of the Federal Register National Archives and Records Administration, Washington, DC, pp. 26–30.

[33]"News Release," Colorado Department of Law, Attorney General, June 21, 1989, pp. 2–3.

[34]Nagle, *Strategy and Tactics of Pricing*, p. 324.

[35]Ortmeyer, "Ethical Issues in Pricing," pp. 396–97.

Chapter 14

[1]Adapted from Peter D. Bennett, ed., *Dictionary of Marketing Terms* (Chicago: American Marketing Association, 1988), p. 29.

[2]Zachary Schiller, Wendy Zellner, Ron Stodghill II, and Mark Maremont, "Clout!" *Business Week*, December 21, 1992, pp. 66–73.

[3]"Making Customer Roundtables Work," *Inc.*, February 1992, pp. 99–100.

[4]Karen Blementhal, "Zale Faces Bankruptcy Court, Battle," *The Wall Street Journal*, January 31, 1992, p. B4.

[5]"Zale Upswing," *USA Today*, August 2, 1993, p. B1.

[6]Toddi Gutner, "Food Distributors," *Forbes*, January 6, 1992, p. 148.

[7]Peter Burrows, "Beyond Rock Bottom," *Business Week*, March 19, 1994, pp. 80–82; Stephanie Anderson Forest, Catherine Arnst, Kathy Rebello, and Peter Burrows, "The Education of Michael Dell," *Business Week*, March 22, 1993, pp. 82–88; Julie Pitta, "Why Dell Is a Survivor," *Forbes*, October 12, 1992, pp. 82–91; Patrick Oster and Igor Reichlin, "Dell: Mail Order Was Supposed to Fail," *Business Week*, January 20, 1992, p. 89; and "The Best Entrepreneurs," *Business Week*, January 13, 1992, p. 131.

[8]From an advertisement in *Fortune*, September 23, 1991, p. 8.

[9]Carolyn T. Greer, "Insurance," *Forbes,* January 6, 1992, p. 163.

[10]Michael David Harkavy and The Philip Lief Group, *The 100 Best Companies to Sell For* (New York: John Wiley & Sons, 1989), pp. 197–99.

[11]Bennett, *Dictionary of Marketing Terms,* p. 211.

[12]Phyllis Berman and Jean Sherman Chatzky, "Closer to the Consumer," *Forbes,* January 20, 1992, pp. 56–57.

[13]Allan J. Magrath, "Collaborative Marketing Comes of Age—Again," *Sales & Marketing Management,* September 1991, pp. 61–64.

[14]William Heuslin, "Famous Shmaymous," *Forbes,* December 20, 1993, pp. 146–48; and Martin Everett, "Profiles in Marketing: Keith Lively," *Sales & Marketing Management,* July 1993, p. 12.

[15]Martin Everett, "Mike Williams: Corn in the USA," *Sales & Marketing Management,* February 1992, pp. 26–27.

[16]Daniel M. Gold, "The Retailers Respond," *Adweek's Marketing Week,* February 10, 1992, pp. 36–37.

[17]Amy Barrett, "Detergents, Aisle 2, Pizza Hut, Aisle 5," *Business Week,* June 7, 1993, pp. 82–83.

[18]Laura Brennan, "For US Vendors in Europe, Planning Is Everything," *PC Week Business,* January 14, 1991, p. 122.

[19]Magrath, "Collaborative Marketing," pp. 61–64.

[20]Michael J. Swenson, Marjorie F. Utsey, and Patricia F. Kennedy, "Interactive Effects of Marketing Mix Variables: Issues, Findings, and Outlook," in *Review of Marketing 1990,* ed. Valarie A. Zeithaml (Chicago: American Marketing Association, 1990), pp. 393–94.

[21]Julia Flynn Siler and Stephanie Anderson Forest, "OshKosh B'Gosh May Be Risking Its Upscale Image," *Business Week,* July 15, 1991, p. 140.

[22]Graham Button, "Room at the Top," *Forbes,* January 20, 1992, p. 106.

[23]James E. Ellis, "Sony's 'Gallery' Has Retailers Hearing Footsteps," *Business Week,* December 23, 1991, p. 29.

[24]Matthew Grimm, "Reebok's Direct Sales Spark a Revolt," *Adweek's Marketing Week,* December 2, 1991, p. 7.

[25]Cara Applebaum, "Fighting over Future of Water," *Adweek's Marketing Week,* January 27, 1992, pp. 4–5.

[26]Jean Sherman Chatzky, "Changing the World," *Forbes,* March 2, 1992, pp. 83–84.

[27]"Wal-Mart Typifies Co-Operation between Supplier, Retailer," *The Commercial Appeal,* July 14, 1991, p. C1.

[28]Laurel Touby, "Blimpie Is Trying to Be a Hero to Franchisees Again," *Business Week,* March 22, 1993, p. 70.

[29]Zachary Schiller, "Not Everyone Loves a Supermarket Deal," *Business Week,* February 17, 1992, pp. 64–68.

[30]The types of power discussed in this section can be traced back to John French, Jr., and Bertram Raven, "The Bases of Social Power," in *Studies in Social Power,* ed. D. Cartwright (Ann Arbor, MI: University of Michigan Press, 1959), pp. 150–67.

[31]David Woodruff, "Winning the War of Battle Creek," *Business Week,* May 13, 1991, p. 80.

[32]John R. Wilke, "Digital to Cut Personal Computer Prices, Begin Marketing, Mail-Order Campaign," *The Wall Street Journal,* January 13, 1992, p. B3.

[33]Lois Therrien and Barbara Buell, "Whatever Happened to the Corner Computer Store?" *Business Week,* May 20, 1991, pp. 131–37.

Chapter 15

[1]Gary Kirkland, "Franchise Has Appeal, but Not Guarantees," *The Star-News,* June 28, 1992, p. E1.

[2]Michael Levy and Barton Weitz, *Retail Management* (Homewood, IL: Richard D. Irwin, 1992), p. 21.

[3]Ibid.

[4]Ibid., p. 7.

[5]Cyndee Miller, "Glitzy Interiors Transform Stores into 'Destinations,' Boost Sales," *Marketing News,* August 30, 1993, p. 1.

[6]"USA Snapshots," *USA Today,* August 11, 1993, p. B1.

[7]Barry Berman and Joel R. Evans, *Retail Management: A Strategic Approach* (New York: Macmillan, 1992), p. 67.

[8]Kirkland, "Franchise Has Appeal."

[9]Carol Steinberg, "International Franchising: American Franchises to Go," *World Trade,* November 1992, pp. 118–22; and Carol Steinberg, "A Guide to US Franchise Strategies," *World Trade,* May 1994, pp. 64A–66J.

[10]Ibid.

[11]Linda L. Hyde, Carl E. Steidtmann, and Daniel J. Sweeney, *Retailing 2000—The New Dimensions* (Columbus, OH: Management Horizons, 1990), p. 11.

[12]"Biggest Mac's," *The Commercial Appeal,* June 28, 1992, p. E9.

[13]William C. Symonds, Geri Smith, and Stephen Baker, "Border Crossings," *Business Week,* November 22, 1993, pp. 40–42; and William C. Symonds, "Invasion of the Retail Snatchers," *Business Week,* May 9, 1994, pp. 72–73.

[14]William C. Symonds, Marti Benedetti, and Dori Jones, "Invasion of the Booty Snatchers," *Business Week,* June 24, 1991, pp. 66–69; and James Lyons, "Border Merchants," *Forbes,* August 19, 1991, pp. 56–57.

[15]James E. Ellis, "Why Overseas? 'Cause That's Where the Sales Are," *Business Week,* January 10, 1994, pp. 62–63.

[16]Herbert McCann, "Terminals to Cost 7,000 Sears Jobs," *The Commercial Appeal,* January 8, 1992, p. B4; and Julie Voorman, "Stores Test Automated Checkouts," *The Commercial Appeal,* December 26, 1992, p. B3.

[17]"Whittle Weighing Mall 'Test Drives,' " *The Commercial Appeal,* September 10, 1991, p. B4.

[18]Howard Schlossberg, "Scanning Improvements Introduced," *Marketing News,* February 17, 1992, pp. 1–2.

[19]"Cashless Grocery Shopping Coming to New England," *Marketing News,* August 5, 1991, p. 7.

[20]Richard Shulman, "New Systems, Old Practices Create a POS 'Generation Gap,' " *Supermarket Business,* November 1993, pp. 17–18.

[21]Karl Albrecht and Ron Zemke, *Service America!* (Homewood, IL: Richard D. Irwin, 1985), p. 6.

[22]Laura Lisawood, "Once You've Got 'Em, Never Let 'Em Go," *Sales & Marketing Management,* November 1987, pp. 73–77.

[23]Rahul Jacob, "How to Retread Customers," *Fortune,* Autumn–Winter 1993, pp. 23–24.

[24]The material on nonstore retailing is based on Levy and Weitz, *Retail Management.*

[25]Stan Rapp, "Getting the Words Right," *Direct,* July 1993, p. 98.

[26]Statistics from "News and Information," a press release from the Direct Marketing Association, New York, December 17, 1993.

[27]Ibid.

[28]Statistics from "Fact Sheet: Summary, 1993 Direct Selling Growth & Outlook Survey," furnished by the Direct Selling Association, Washington, DC, December 17, 1993.

[29]Meg Whittemore, "Survival Tactics for Retailers," *Nation's Business*, June 1993, pp. 20–25.

[30]Ibid.

[31]Ibid.

[32]Laura Zinn, "The New Stars of Retailing," *Business Week*, December 16, 1991, pp. 120–21.

[33]Jeffrey Trachtenberg, "Macy Will Close 57 Special Shops," *The Wall Street Journal*, March 6, 1992, pp. A3, A6; and Laurel Campbell, *The Commercial Appeal*, January 5, 1992, pp. C1, C4.

[34]Gretchen Morgenson, "The Fall of the Mall," *Forbes*, May 24, 1993, pp. 106–12.

[35]Julie Stacey, "Big Malls Slump," *USA Today*, May 28, 1993, p. B1; and Howard L. Green, "New Consumer Realities for Retailers," *Marketing News*, April 25, 1994, pp. 4–5.

[36]Kate Fitzgerald, "In Retailing, Price Stranglehold Lessens," *Advertising Age*, November 1, 1993, p. S6.

[37]Linda Romine, "Multitude of Challenges Face Owners of Convenience Stores," *Memphis Business Journal*, September 16, 1992, pp. 29–32; and "Down but Not Out," *Forbes*, January 18, 1993, p. 14.

[38]Barbara Bradley, "Shoplifters Steal Season's Cheer," *The Commercial Appeal*, November 26, 1993, pp. C2, C9.

[39]Ibid.

[40]Karen Pulfer Focht, "Increases in Shoplifting Defy Modern Deterrents," *The Commercial Appeal*, December 15, 1991, pp. C1, C2.

[41]Ibid.

[42]Ibid.

[43]Leslie Cauley, "Mannequins Play Cop," *USA Today*, December 21, 1992, p. B2.

[44]Judy A. Siguaw and K. Douglas Hoffman, "The Role of Slotting Allowances in Retail Channel Relationships," *Enhancing Knowledge Development in Marketing*, Robert P. Leane and V. Kumar, eds. (Chicago: 1992 American Marketing Association Summer Educators' Conference), pp. 494–95.

[45]"Wal-Mart Wins Environmental Impact Award for New Store," *The Commercial Appeal*, July 6, 1993, p. B4.

[46]Ellen Neuborne, "More Malls Are Snuffing Out Smoking," *USA Today*, August 5, 1993, p. B1; and "Complaints Are Few as Malls in Ark. Begin Smoking Ban," *The Commercial Appeal*, May 16, 1994, p. B2.

Chapter 16

[1]Joe Mullich, "Lotus Enlists VARs to Promote Notes," *Business Marketing*, July 1993, pp. 12–13.

[2]*1987 Census of the Wholesale Trade*, publication no. WC87-S-4 (Washington, DC: US Department of Commerce, Bureau of the Census), pp. 4-3 through 4-74.

[3]"Mail-Order Pharmacies Mushroom," *Marketing News*, January 18, 1993, p. 3.

[4]George Chelekis, "Has Uncle Sam Got a Deal for You," *Nation's Business*, June 1993, p. 32.

[5]Joshua Levine, "Halloween Boo-quets, Anyone?" *Forbes*, October 26, 1992, pp. 206–8.

[6]Thomas N. Ingram, Thomas R. Day, and George H. Lucas, Jr., "Dealing with Intermediaries: Guidelines for Sales Managers," *Journal of Global Marketing*, Fall 1992, pp. 65–80.

[7]Bruce G. Posner, "Money for 'Pre-Export,' " *Inc.*, August 1993, p. 31.

[8]Charles Conner, "Area Growers, Buyers Form Co-op," *The Commercial Appeal*, January 11, 1992, p. B3.

[9]Joseph Weber, "On a Fast Boat to Anywhere," *Business Week*, January 11, 1993, p. 94.

[10]Laurel Campbell, "Middleman Fleming Fights to Stay on Top," *The Commercial Appeal*, May 10, 1992, p. C1; and Toddi Gutner, "Food Distributors," *Forbes*, January 3, 1994, pp. 148–50.

[11]Cyndee Miller, "Big Chains Battle for Market Share in Home Improvement," *Marketing News*, September 28, 1992, pp. 1, 10.

[12]Campbell, "Middleman Fleming."

[13]"The Rumors of Peace Remain Unfounded," *Progressive Grocer*, April 1992, pp. 24–26.

[14]Weber, "On a Fast Boat."

[15]Neal Weinstock, "Hot Exports!" *World Trade*, April 1994, pp. 30–38.

[16]"Partnering for Profit," *Sales Manager's Bulletin*, August 30, 1992, p. 5.

[17]Ibid., p. 1.

[18]Joseph B. Fuller, James O'Connor, and Richard Rawlinson, "Tailored Logistics: The Next Advantage," *Harvard Business Review*, May–June 1993, pp. 87–98.

[19]Gregory Powell, "Logistics Takes Distribution beyond Moving Merchandise," *Memphis Business Journal*, July 15–19, 1991, p. 29.

[20]Rita Koselka, "Distribution Revolution," *Forbes*, May 25, 1992, p. 60.

[21]Ibid., p. 54.

[22]Peter D. Bennett, ed., *Dictionary of Marketing Terms* (Chicago: American Marketing Association, 1998), p. 213.

[23]Angeline Maxie, "Mid South Warehouse to Handle Freight for Retail Clothing Chain," *The Commercial Appeal*, July 20, 1992, p. B3.

[24]"Retail Distribution and Logistics: Distribution Centers," *Chain Store Age Executive*, April 1992, pp. A10, A11.

[25]David Yawn, "High-Tech Gadgetry Tracks Goods in Today's Warehouses," *Memphis Business Journal*, June 29–July 3, 1992, p. 33.

[26]Ibid., p. 44.

[27]Thomas A. Foster, "Logistics Costs Drop to Record Low Levels," *Distribution*, July 1993, pp. 6–10.

[28]John D. Schultz, "Chrysler Expands Just-in-Time with Six 'Lead Logistics' Companies," *Traffic World*, January 13, 1992, pp. 10–12.

[29]Robert J. Bowman, "The EDI Revolution: A Special World Trade Feature," *World Trade*, June 1993, pp. 38–48.

[30]Kevin McKenzie, "Just-in-Time Philosophy Shuts Saturn," *The Commercial Appeal*, August 29, 1992, p. B4.

[31]William A. Cunningham, "Transportation User Fees: The Government's New Source of Revenue," *Business Perspectives*, Spring 1992, pp. 8–12.

[32]"1992: A Pivotal Year?" *Chain Store Age Executive*, April 1992, pp. A6, A7.

[33]"Weekly Loadings of American Railroads," *The Commercial Appeal*, January 11, 1993, p. B5.

[34]Joseph Weber, "Big Rail Is Finally Rounding the Bend," *Business Week,* November 11, 1991, pp. 128–29.

[35]Kevin McKenzie, "Survey Indicates Anxieties about Transportation System," *The Commercial Appeal,* September 6, 1993, p. B4.

[36]Roger Gilroy, "Wooing and Winning Drivers No. 1 Priority for Truckload Carriers," *Traffic World,* March 30, 1992, pp. 21–23; Kevin McKenzie, "Truckers Lamenting State of the Wheel," *The Commercial Appeal,* January 17, 1994, p. B4; and R. Lee Sullivan, "It's First-Class Here, Man," *Forbes,* March 14, 1994, pp. 102–04.

[37]Rahul Jacob, "Christmas Could Come Early for Toys 'Я' Us," *Fortune,* September 23, 1991, p. 28.

[38]"Company Spotlight: Airborne Express," *West of Wall Street,* June 28, 1991, p. 7.

[39]Kevin McKenzie, "Con-Way Provides Link to Railroads," *The Commercial Appeal,* May 3, 1993, p. B5.

[40]Robert J. Bowman, "Trying Harder," *World Trade,* April 1994, pp. 80–87.

[41]Nicky Robertshaw, "Competition, Shortage of Drivers Fuel Growth of Intermodal," *Memphis Business Journal,* June 7–11, 1993, pp. 33–42.

[42]The text discussion of the effects of deregulation draws on James P. Rakowski, R. Neil Southern, and Judith L. Jarrell, "The Changing Structure of the US Trucking Industry: Implications for Logistics Managers," *Journal of Business Logistics,* January 1993, pp. 111–29.

[43]Kenneth C. Schneider and James C. Johnson, "Professionalism and Ethical Standards in a Deregulated Environment: A Case Study of the Trucking Industry," *Journal of Personal Selling and Sales Management,* Winter 1992, pp. 33–43.

[44]Robert R. Sharp, "Truck Trains Derailed," *AAA Going Places,* August 1991, p. 6.

[45]"Open Forum: Tandem Trucking," *AAA Going Places,* October 1991, p. 12.

[46]Lou Ann Bell, "New Laws Reflect 'Green' Trend," *Traffic World,* January 6, 1992, p. 11.

[47]E. J. Muller, "The Greening of Logistics," *Distribution,* January 1991, pp. 26–34.

[48]Ibid.

Chapter 17

[1]Risa Bauman, "They've Got the 'Right One' Now," *Direct,* May 1992, p. 22.

[2]William Keenan, Jr., "America's Best Sales Forces," *Sales & Marketing Management,* September 1992, p. 48.

[3]"100 Leading Advertisers," *Advertising Age,* January 3, 1994, p. 14.

[4]Robert J. Coen, "Ad Gain of 5.2% in '93 Marks Downturn's End," *Advertising Age,* May 2, 1994, p. 4.

[5]Scott M. Cutlip, Allen H. Center, and Glen M. Broom, *Effective Public Relations,* 6th ed. (Englewood Cliffs, NJ: Prentice Hall, 1985), p. 4.

[6]George E. Belch and Michael A. Belch, *Introduction to Advertising and Promotion: An Integrated Marketing Communications Perspective,* 2nd ed. (Homewood, IL: Richard D. Irwin, 1993), p. 16.

[7]Don E. Schultz, "Objectives Drive Tactics in IMC Approach," *Marketing News,* May 9, 1994, pp. 14, 18.

[8]Scott Hume, "Integrated Marketing: Who's in Charge Here?" *Advertising Age,* March 22, 1993, p. 3.

[9]T. Bettina Cornwell, "Sponsorship-Linked Marketing," working paper, The University of Memphis, 1994.

[10]Bob Garfield, "Chef Boyardee Garbles Return to Italian Roots," *Advertising Age,* April 13, 1992, p. 60.

[11]"Using Mailings as an Incentive Springboard," *Business Marketing,* February 1992, pp. T7–T9.

[12]"In a Recession, the Best Defense Is a Good Offense," *Adweek's Marketing Week,* November 11, 1991, p. 12.

[13]Judann Dagnoli, "Sorry, Charlie, Heinz Puts Promos First," *Advertising Age,* March 30, 1992, pp. 3, 62.

[14]Bob Garfield, "Nike Scores Points with Spike's Unity Plea," *Advertising Age,* June 8, 1992, p. 50.

[15]Laura Zinn, "Real Men Buy Paper Towels, Too," *Business Week,* November 9, 1992, pp. 75–76.

[16]David Jacobson, "Apple Dealers Strike Paydirt," *Business Marketing,* January 1991, pp. 24–25.

[17]Siva K. Balasubramanian and V. Kumar, "Analyzing Variations in Advertising and Promotional Expenditures: Key Correlates in Consumer, Industrial, and Service Markets," *Journal of Marketing,* April 1990, p. 65.

[18]Adapted from Philip Kotler, *Marketing Management: Analysis, Planning, and Control,* 8th ed. (Englewood Cliffs, NJ: Prentice Hall, 1994), pp. 612–13.

[19]Raymond Serafin, "BMW Launches New Image Ads," *Advertising Age,* March 2, 1992, pp. 3, 34.

[20]Kate Fitzgerald, "Couponing for a Cause," *Advertising Age,* July 19, 1993, p. 21.

[21]Ira Teinowitz and Steven W. Colford, "Old Joe a Winner Even with Ad Ban," *Advertising Age,* August 16, 1993, p. 1; and Nicole Caroll, "Surgeon General's Warning: Tobacco Firms Target Kids," *USA Today,* February 25–27, p. 1A.

[22]Julia Flynn Siler, "It Isn't Miller Time Yet, and This Bud's Not for You," *Business Week,* June 24, 1991, p. 52.

[23]William Wells, John Burnett, and Sandra Moriarty, *Advertising Principles and Practice* (Englewood Cliffs, NJ: Prentice Hall, 1992), pp. 52–58.

[24]Kathyleen O'Brien, "Green Marketing: It Can Be Harmful to Your Health," *Industry Week,* April 20, 1992, pp. 55–60.

[25]Jennifer Lawrence, "Marketers Drop 'Recycled,' " *Advertising Age,* March 9, 1992, pp. 1, 48.

[26]Fara Warner, "What Happened to the Truth?" *Adweek's Marketing Week,* October 28, 1991, pp. 4–5.

[27]Ibid.

[28]Geoffrey Lee Martin, "Tobacco Sponsors Fear Aussie TKO," *Advertising Age,* April 27, 1992, p. 18.

Chapter 18

[1]Charles H. Patti and Charles F. Frazer, *Advertising: A Decision-Making Approach* (Chicago: The Dryden Press, 1988), p. 4.

[2]Laurie Petersen, "A Short-Sighted View of Advertising," *Adweek's Marketing Week,* November 11, 1991, p. 9.

[3]John Kenneth Galbraith, "Economics and Advertising: Exercise in Denial," *Advertising Age,* November 9, 1988, p. 81.

[4]"100 Leading National Advertisers," *Advertising Age,* January 3, 1994, p. 14.

[5]Dean M. Krugman and Roland T. Rust, "The Impact of Cable and VCR Penetration on Network Viewing: Assessing the Decade," *Journal of Advertising Research,* January–February 1993, pp. 67–73; and Joe Mandese, "Nets Get Less for More," *Advertising Age,* March 2, 1992, p. 1.

[6]Mel Mandell, "Getting the Word Out," *World Trade,* November 1993, p. 30.

[7]Howard E. Potter, "Ziff Chairman: Faith in Advertising Declines," *Marketing News,* April 27, 1992, p. 16; and Glen Heitsmith, "Still Climbing," *Promo,* July 1993, p. 131.

[8]Allan J. Magrath, "The Death of Advertising Has Been Greatly Exaggerated," *Sales & Marketing Management,* February 1992, p. 23.

[9]Sergey Frank, "Avoiding the Pitfalls of Business Abroad," *Sales & Marketing Management,* March 1992, p. 57.

[10]James M. Kolts, "Adaptive Marketing," *Journal of Consumer Marketing,* Summer 1990, pp. 39–40.

[11]C. Anthony Di Benedetto, Marik Tamate, and Rajan Chandran, "Developing Creative Advertising Strategy for the Japanese Marketplace," *Journal of Advertising Research,* January/February 1992, pp. 39–48.

[12]Fred S. Zufryden, James H. Pendrick, and Avu Sankaralingam, "Zapping and Its Impact on Brand Purchase Behavior," *Journal of Advertising Research,* January–February 1993, p. 58.

[13]Joanne Lipman, "TV Ad Deals to Set Big Price Increases," *The Wall Street Journal,* June 25, 1992, p. B8.

[14]Judith Waldrap, "And Now a Break from Our Sponsor," *American Demographics,* August 1993, pp. 16–18.

[15]Dana Wechsler Linden and Vicki Contavespi, "Media Wars," *Forbes,* August 19, 1991, p. 38.

[16]William F. Arens and Courtland L. Bovée, *Contemporary Advertising,* 5th ed. (Burr Ridge, IL: Richard D. Irwin, 1994), p. 8.

[17]Scott B. MacKenzie, "The Role of Attention in Mediating the Effect of Advertising on Attribute Importance," *Journal of Consumer Research,* September 1986, pp. 174–95.

[18]Deborah J. MacInnis, Christine Moorman, and Bernard J. Jaworski, "Enhancing and Measuring Consumers' Motivation, Opportunity, and Ability to Process Brand Information from Ads," *Journal of Marketing,* October 1991, pp. 32–53.

[19]Joann Lublin, "As VCRs Advance, Agencies Fear TV Viewers Will Zap More Ads," *The Wall Street Journal,* January 4, 1991, p. B3.

[20]Gary T. Ford, Darlene B. Smith, and John L. Swasy, "Consumer Skepticism of Advertising Claims: Testing Hypotheses from Economics of Information," *Journal of Consumer Research,* March 1990, pp. 433–41.

[21]Thomas E. Barry, "Comparative Advertising: What Have We Learned in Two Decades," *Journal of Advertising Research,* March–April 1993, p. 20.

[22]Scott Hume, "Best Ads Don't Rely on Celebrities," *Advertising Age,* May 25, 1992, p. 20; and Kevin Goldman, "Candice Bergen Leads the List of Top Celebrity Endorsers," *The Wall Street Journal,* September 17, 1993, pp. B1, B6.

[23]Scott Donaten, "Advertorials Are like a Drug," *Advertising Age,* March 9, 1992, p. S16.

[24]Cyndee Miller, "Study Says 'Likability' Surfaces as Measure of TV Ad Success," *Marketing News,* January 7, 1991, p. 14.

[25]Faye Rice, "A Cure for What Ails Advertising?" *Fortune,* December 16, 1991, p. 121.

[26]William L. Wilkie, Dennis L. McNeill, and Michael B. Mazis, "Marketing's 'Scarlet Letter': The Theory and Practice of Corrective Advertising," *Journal of Marketing,* Spring 1984, pp. 11–31.

[27]Raymond Serafin and Gary Levin, "Ad Industry Suffers Crushing Blow," *Advertising Age,* November 12, 1990, pp. 1, 76, 77.

[28]David A. Aaker, Rajeev Batra, and John G. Myers, *Advertising Management,* 4th ed. (Englewood Cliffs, NJ: Prentice-Hall, 1992), p. 557.

[29]Donald P. Robin and R. Eric Reidenbach, "Social Responsibility, Ethics, and Marketing Strategy: Closing the Gap between Concept and Application," *Journal of Marketing,* January 1987, pp. 44–58.

[30]Patricia Winters, "Drugmakers Portrayed as Villains, Worry about Image," *Advertising Age,* February 22, 1993, p. 1; Kate Fitzgerald, "Health Concerns Don't Slow Down Cellular Phones," *Advertising Age,* February 8, 1993, p. 4; Annetta Miller, "Do Boycotts Work?" *Newsweek,* July 6, 1992, p. 56; and Howard Schlossberg, "Members Only to Introduce Homeless in Cause Marketing," *Marketing News,* July 20, 1992, p. 6.

[31]Caleb Solomon, "Exxon Attacks Scientific Views of Valdez Oil Spill," *The Wall Street Journal,* April 15, 1993, p. B1.

[32]Philip Kotler, *Marketing Management: Analysis, Planning, Implementation, and Control,* 8th ed. (Englewood Cliffs, NJ: Prentice Hall, 1994), pp. 676–77.

Chapter 19

[1]Adapted from Peter D. Bennett, ed., *Dictionary of Marketing Terms* (Chicago: American Marketing Association, 1988), p. 179.

[2]Joe Mandese and Scott Donaton, "Media, Promotion Gap to Narrow," *Advertising Age,* June 29, 1992, p. 6.

[3]Robert D. Buzzell, John A. Quelch, and Walter J. Salmon, "The Costly Bargain of Trade Promotion," *Harvard Business Review,* March–April 1990, pp. 141–49.

[4]"Consumers Remain High on Promotions," *Marketing Times,* March–April 1993, p. 11.

[5]Julie Liesse, "Pay for Performance Picking Up Speed," *Advertising Age,* August 9, 1993, p. 19.

[6]Richard Gibson, "Store-Brand Pricing Has to Be Just Right," *The Wall Street Journal,* March 23, 1992, p. B1.

[7]Patrick Oster, Gabrielle Saveri, and John Templeman, "The Eurosion of Brand Loyalty," *Business Week,* July 19, 1993, p. 22; and Laurel Wentz, "Private Labels on the March in Europe, Too," *Advertising Age,* May 9, 1994, p. 53.

[8]Ibid.

[9]"Where's the Money?" *Direct,* July 1993, p. 56.

[10]"Pump Up the Volume," *Direct,* September 1992, p. 5.

[11]Kapil Bawa and Robert W. Shoemaker, "The Coupon-Prone Consumer: Some Findings Based on Purchase Behavior across Product Classes," *Journal of Marketing,* October 1987, pp. 99–110.

[12]"Coupon Users Need Incentive," *Promotional Sense,* June 1992, p. 1.

[13]Scott Hume, "Study Shows Decline in Handling Fees for Coupons," *Advertising Age,* May 25, 1992, p. 20.

[14]Scott Hume, "Couponing Sets Record, but Pace Slows," *Advertising Age,* February 1, 1993, p. 25.

[15]Ronald Grover, Laura Zinn, and Irene Recio, "Big Brother Is Grocery Shopping with You," *Business Week,* March 29, 1993, p. 60.

[16]Howard Schlossberg, "Coupons Likely to Remain Popular," *Marketing News,* March 29, 1993, pp. 1, 7.

[17]Ibid.

[18]"Cross-Promotional Power," *Success,* March 1993, p. 68.

[19]Alison Fahey, "CNN Tries Promo Hook," *Advertising Age,* March 16, 1992, p. 6.

[20]Ibid.

[21]"Where's the Money?"

[22]Laurie Petersen, "Showtime for Product Samples," *Adweek's Marketing Week,* November 11, 1991, p. 28.

[23]James Cox, "Newspaper Ads to Pack Punch You Can Mix," *USA Today,* August 15, 1991, p. B1.

[24]Pat Sloan, "Just Call It 'Pond's Direct,' " *Advertising Age,* August 16, 1993, p. 3.

[25]Adapted from Robert C. Blattberg and Scott A. Neslin, *Sales Promotion, Concepts, Methods, and Strategies* (Englewood Cliffs, NJ: Prentice Hall, 1990), p. 314.

[26]"What's New on the Floor?" *Adweek's Marketing Week,* November 11, 1991, p. 30.

[27]*A Guide to the US Exposition Industry* (Denver: Trade Show Bureau, 1994), p. 15.

[28]Jaideep Motwani, Gillian Rice, and Essam Mahmoud, "Promoting Exports through International Trade Shows: A Dual Perspective," *Review of Business,* Spring 1992, pp. 38–42.

[29]Eric J. Adams, "Trade Show Sizzle," *World Trade,* February 1994, pp. 144–47.

[30]"Promotional Products Build Traffic, Research Shows," *Promotional Sense,* June 1992, pp. 1–2.

[31]John Philip Jones, "The Double Jeopardy of Sales Promotions," *Harvard Business Review,* September–October 1990, pp. 145–52; and Cyndee Miller, "Moves by P&G, Heinz Rekindle Fears That Brands Are in Danger," *Marketing News,* June 8, 1992, pp. 1, 15.

[32]Jones, "Double Jeopardy."

[33]Ibid.

[34]Ira Teinowitz, "Grocery Trade Deals Set to Enter New Era," *Advertising Age,* May 17, 1993, p. 3.

[35]"Beware of Callers Bearing Gifts," *Parade Magazine,* November 22, 1992, pp. 12–13.

[36]Ibid.

[37]John Awerdick, "On Sweepstakes," *Direct,* September 1992, pp. 22–23.

[38]Matthew Schrifin, "Arbitraging Dog Food," *Forbes,* May 10, 1993, pp. 80–81.

[39]Christopher Power, "Coupon Scams Are Clipping Companies," *Business Week,* June 15, 1992, pp. 110–11.

[40]Ibid.

[41]Ibid.

[42]Melissa Campanelli, "What's in Store for EDLP?" *Sales & Marketing Management,* August 1993, pp. 56–59.

Chapter 20

[1]Derrick C. Schnebelt, "Turning the Tables," *Sales & Marketing Management,* January 1993, pp. 22–23.

[2]David Topus, "Keep It Short . . . and Smart," *Selling,* August 1993, p. 30.

[3]Thayer C. Taylor, "Laptop Fever Grips Marketers," *Sales & Marketing Management,* July 1991, pp. 68–69.

[4]Kerry Rottenburger, "The Next Voice You Hear . . . ," *Sales & Marketing Management,* July 1991, p. 52.

[5]Tom Murray, "Team Selling: What's the Incentive?" *Sales & Marketing Management,* June 1991, pp. 89–92.

[6]Jon M. Hawes, Kenneth E. Mast, and John E. Swan, "Trust Earning Perceptions of Sellers and Buyers," *Journal of Personal Selling and Sales Management,* Spring 1989, pp. 1–8.

[7]Ingrid Abramowitz, "The Trust Factor," *Success,* March 1993, p. 18.

[8]Rosann L. Spiro and Barton A. Weitz, "Adaptive Selling: Conceptualization, Measurement, and Nomological Validity," *Journal of Marketing Research,* February 1990, pp. 61–69.

[9]"Pipe Down," *Sales & Marketing Management,* January 1994, p. 22.

[10]"Brokers Get Friendlier—For a Price," *Fortune,* March 11, 1991, pp. 24–25.

[11]David W. Cravens, Thomas N. Ingram, and Raymond W. LaForge, "Evaluating Multiple Sales Channel Strategies," *Journal of Business and Industrial Marketing,* Summer–Fall 1991, pp. 37–48.

[12]Geoffrey Brewer, "New World Orders," *Sales & Marketing Management,* January 1994, pp. 59–63.

[13]Jennifer Lawrence, "P&G Redirects Sales Force," *Advertising Age,* June 28, 1993, p. 52.

[14]Bob Attanasio, "How PC-Based Sales Quotas Boost Productivity and Morale," *Sales & Marketing Management,* September 1991, pp. 148–50.

[15]"Taking Aim at Tomorrow's Challenges," *Sales & Marketing Management,* September 1991, pp. 66–67.

[16]Francy Blackwood, "A Prescription for Change," *Selling,* August 1993, pp. 22–25.

[17]William Keenan, Jr., "Time Is Everything," *Sales & Marketing Management,* August 1993, pp. 60–62.

[18]"Sales Training Points the Way toward Successful Total Quality Management," *Sales and Marketing* (newsletter of the American Society of Training and Development), Winter 1993, pp. 1, 6.

[19]Lawrence B. Chonko, John F. Tanner, Jr., William A. Weeks, and Melissa R. Schmitt, "Reward Preferences of Salespeople," Research Report No. 91–3 (Waco, TX: Center for Professional Selling, Baylor University, 1991).

[20]"Compensation and Expenses," *Sales & Marketing Management,* June 28, 1993, p. 65.

[21]"Bonuses for Breaking New Ground," *Inc.,* March 1993, p. 27.

[22]"Compensation and Expenses," p. 65.

[23]Karl A. Boedecker, Fred W. Morgan, and Jeffrey J. Stoltman, "Legal Dimensions of Salespersons' Statements: A Review and Managerial Suggestions," *Journal of Marketing,* January 1991, pp. 70–80.

[24]I. Frederick Trawick, John E. Swan, Gail McGee, and David R. Rink, "Influence of Buyer Ethics and Salesperson Behavior on Intention to Choose a Supplier," *Journal of the Academy of Marketing Science,* Winter 1991, pp. 17–23.

Chapter 21

[1]"The *Direct* '92 Forecast," *Direct,* December 1991, pp. 23–29.

[2]"Avon Rings Millions of New Bells," *Sales & Marketing Management,* October 1992, p. 35.

[3]James G. Kimball, "Kodak Unit Developing Strategy with Direct Marketing," *Business Marketing,* June 1993, p. 10.

4Greg Johnson, "Knowledge-Based Marketing Adds Value to Mailing Lists," *Marketing News,* January 20, 1992, pp. 15, 18; and Karen Burka, "The Database Race," *Direct,* June 1992, pp. 13–14.

5Definitions in this section are based on a glossary developed by the Direct Marketing Association, as reproduced in Tracy Emerick, "Infobase Management: Creating the Right Chemistry," *Sales & Marketing Management,* October 1992, p. 103.

6Gary Levin, "Database Draws Fevered Interest," *Advertising Age,* June 8, 1992, p. 31.

7Joe Mullich, "Integrated Push Requires Muscle," *Business Marketing,* August 1993, p. 57.

8Walecia Konrad, "Smoking Out the Elusive Smoker," *Business Week,* March 16, 1992, pp. 62–63.

9David H. Freedman, "An Unusual Way to Run a Ski Business," *Forbes ASAP,* December 7, 1992, pp. 27–32.

10Ernan Roman, "Timing Is Everything," *Direct,* October 1991, pp. 33–35.

11Martin Everett, "This One's Just for You," *Sales & Marketing Management,* June 1992, pp. 119–26.

12James R. Rosenfield, "Getting It Right: The Next Step," *Direct,* April 1992, pp. 34–39.

13Carrie Goerne, "Direct Mail Spending Rises, but Success May Be Overblown," *Marketing News,* March 2, 1992, p. 6.

14Len Egol, "Expect Higher Postage," *Direct,* September 1993, pp. 1, 30.

15"What's in Store?" *Direct,* December 1992, pp. 26–35.

16"Olivetti Tries Direct Marketing," *Business Marketing,* June 1993, p. 16.

17Don E. Schultz, "Technology Putting an End to Mass Marketing," *Business Marketing,* June 1993, p. 56; and Scott Shepard, "Grocers Shifting Media-Buying Power to Direct Mail," *Memphis Business Journal,* August 30–September 3, 1993, p. 10.

18Courtland L. Bovee and William F. Arens, *Contemporary Advertising,* 3rd ed. (Homewood, IL: Richard D. Irwin, 1990), p. 492. The discussion on advantages of direct mail draws on this source.

19Carrie Goerne, "The Art of Direct Mail: Galleries Use It to Improve Relationships with Customers," *Marketing News,* April 27, 1992, p. 6.

20Goerne, "Direct Mail Spending Rises."

21Rosenfield, "Getting It Right."

22Teri Lammers, "The Elements of the Perfect Pitch," *Inc.,* March 1992, pp. 53–55.

23"Good Times Keep On Rolling," *Direct,* August 1993, p. 5; Ellen Neuborne, "Shoppers Seem to Prefer Mail over Mall," *USA Today,* August 12, 1993, p. 4B; and "USA Snapshots: Mass Mailings," *USA Today,* August 19, 1993, p. 1A.

24Laurie Peterson, "The 14-Minute Holiday Workout," *Adweek's Marketing Week,* October 14, 1991, p. 9.

25Everett, "This One's Just for You."

26Chris Lyons, "Disk-Based, Interactive Marketing Yields Greater Response Rates," *Business Perspectives,* Spring 1993, pp. 10–11.

27"Fast Times at Motorola Inc.," *Business Marketing,* February 1992, pp. 30–32.

28Michael Clements, "Medco Makes Over Mail-Order," *USA Today,* August 10, 1993, p. 5B; and Mariann Caprino, "Mail-Order Pharmacies Compete in Growing Market," *The Commercial Appeal,* November 25, 1992, pp. B3, B7.

29Paul Hughes, "Winning Ways," *Entrepreneur,* February 1994, pp. 80–88; and Erika Kotite, "Mail Order Technology," *Entrepreneur,* February 1994, pp. 91–93.

30Elaine Underwood, "Building the Recovery, Door-to-Door," *Adweek's Marketing Week,* January 27, 1992, p. 16; and "Distributing International Passports to Success," *Business Korea,* April 1991, pp. 79–80.

31Underwood, "Building the Recovery."

32"Superselling," *Success,* September 1993, p. 12.

33Gary Strauss, "Show-and-Tell Format Called 'New, Fresh,'" *USA Today,* February 23, 1993, pp. 1A–2A; and Mark Landler, "The Infomercial Inches toward Respectability," *Business Week,* May 4, 1992, p. 175.

34Gary Slutsker, "The Power of Juicing," *Forbes,* March 2, 1992, pp. 82–83.

35"Making an Infomercial," *Direct,* supplement, February 1992, pp. 15–16.

36"Infomercial Network Launched," *Marketing News,* September 30, 1991, p. 21.

37Strauss, "Show-and-Tell Format."

38Kathy Haley, "Infomercials Lure More Top Marketers," *Advertising Age,* May 9, 1994, p. IN-2.

39"Making an Infomercial."

40"Moneyline," *USA Today,* December 21, 1992, p. 1B.

41Dana Wechsler Linden and Vicki Contavespi, "Media Wars," *Forbes,* August 19, 1991, pp. 38–40.

42Richard L. Bencin, "Telefocus: Telemarketing Gets Synergized," *Sales & Marketing Management,* February 1992, pp. 49–53.

43Karen Burka, "Does Outbound Still Work?" *Direct,* October 1992, pp. 34–36.

44John P. Cortez, "Flowers Flourish through Interactive Media," *Advertising Age,* July 12, 1993, p. 12; and Len Egol, "Prodigy Goes After a Broader Base," *Direct,* August 1993, p. 19.

45Len Egol, "Tomorrow Is Here," *Direct,* June 1992, p. 22.

46John P. Cortez, "Kmart Tunes Up In-Store Radio," *Advertising Age,* March 16, 1992, pp. 3, 50.

47Risa Bauman, "CD Catalog Kiosks Tested in Two Areas," *Direct,* June 1993, p. 55.

48Karen Burka, "Just the Fax, Ma'am," *Direct,* February 1992, p. 32.

49John H. Awerdick, "Wrong Numbers," *Direct,* October 1992, pp. 39–41.

50Don Peppers and Martha Rogers, *The One to One Future* (New York: Doubleday, 1993), pp. 233–48.

51"Recession Not Hurting Database Growth: Exec," *Advertising Age,* January 13, 1992, pp. 25, 30.

52Gray Ligon, "Distribution Challenges of International Direct Marketing," working paper (Greenville, NC: East Carolina University, 1992).

53Karen Burka, "Owners Say No to List Revenue," *Direct,* December 1992, p. 38.

54"Take Your Blinders Off," *Direct,* June 1992, pp. 1, 12.

55Burka, "Owners Say No."

56Bruce Murray, "Trust Me . . . Not," *Direct,* June 1992, pp. 57–58.

57Ibid.

58Karen Burka, "Should PCH Have Done More?" *Direct,* December 1992, pp. 8, 10; and Burka, "PCH Settles Lawsuit," *Direct,* January 1993, p. 55.

[59]*Pyramid Schemes: Not What They Seem* (Washington, DC: Direct Selling Education Foundation, 1991).

[60]Howard Schlossberg, " 'Project Clean Mail' Would Fine-Tune Marketing," *Marketing News,* September 14, 1992, pp. 18–19.

[61]"Marketing Mix," *Promotional Sense,* June 1992, p. 3.

[62]Ibid.

Epilog

[1]Material in this section is drawn from Ed Fishbein, "One Giant Step for Timberland," *World Trade,* December 1992, pp. 32–35; *Form 10-K, The Timberland Company,* for the fiscal year ended December 31, 1992 (Washington, DC: Securities and Exchange Commission); "Timberland Co.: Outdoor-Wear Maker Seeks Growth outside US," *Barron's,* June 24, 1991, p. 47; and company sources, June 1994.

[2]"CS Close-Up: The Timberland Company," *Customer Service Manager's Letter,* April 10, 1992, pp. 3–6.

[3]*The Timberland Company, 1992 Annual Report;* and company sources, June 1994.

[4]"Timberland: Walking Tall," *The Economist,* August 4, 1990, p. 57.

[5]Donna Rosato, "Timberland Boots Take Giant Step," *USA Today,* October 28, 1993, p. 1B.

[6]Mark Maremont, "Timberland Comes Out of the Woods," *Business Week,* September 13, 1993, p. 78.

[7]"CS Close-Up," p. 4.

[8]Fishbein, "One Giant Step," p. 35.

[9]Company sources, June 1994.

[10]Ibid.

[11]*The Timberland Company, 1991 Annual Report.*

[12]*The Timberland Company, Form 10-K,* for the fiscal year ended December 31, 1992.

[13]David Craig and Donna Rosato, "Best Buy, Timberland Hot Third-Quarter Stocks," *USA Today,* September 30, 1993, p. 4B; and Rosato, "Timberland Boots Take Giant Step."

[14]"MPA Kelly Award," advertising supplement to *Advertising Age,* May 1993.

[15]Rosato, "Timberland Boots Take Giant Step."

[16]*The Timberland Company, Form 10-K,* for the fiscal year ended December 31, 1992, p. 4.

Appendix A

[1]Daniel L. Smytha and Michael W. Clemens, "Total Cost Supplier Selection Model: A Case Study," *International Journal of Purchasing and Materials Management,* Winter 1993, p. 43.

[2]William R. Dillon, Thomas J. Madden, and Neil H. Firtle, *Essentials of Marketing Research* (Homewood, IL: Richard D. Irwin, 1993), p. 87.

[3]William Boyes and Michael Melvin, *Microeconomics* (Boston: Houghton Mifflin, 1991), p. 178.

[4]Kent B. Monroe, *Pricing: Making Profitable Decisions,* 2nd ed. (New York: McGraw-Hill, 1990), p. 35.

[5]Michael Levy and Barton A, Weitz, *Retail Management* (Homewood, IL: Richard D. Irwin, 1992), p. 391.

Credits and Acknowledgments

Part 1
Photos/Ads   p. 3, Dynamic environment: © Imtek Imagineering/Masterfile.

Chapter 1
Exhibits   1.6, Rolph Anderson, *Professional Personal Selling* (Englewood Cliffs, NJ: Prentice Hall, 1991), p. 105. Reprinted by permission.
Photos/Ads   p. 5, Domino's European ad: Courtesy Domino's Pizza International.   p. 7, Mr. Rex billboard: Courtesy Pagano Schenck & Kay Agency.   p. 10, Johnson Controls ad: Courtesy Johnson Controls, Inc.   p. 11, New Federal States of Germany ad: © Economic Ministry of The Federal Republic of Germany.   p. 11, Colgate-Palmolive in Poland and Colgate-Palmolive in Maylaysia: Both photos courtesy Colgate-Palmolive Company.   p. 12, Welsh Jewelry & Loan billboards: Courtesy Adams Outdoor Advertising, Atlanta.   p. 18, Global Market Research ad: Courtesy BRX/Global, Inc.   p. 20, Historical consumer ads: Stock Montage, Inc.   p. 23, Citibank ad: Courtesy Citibank.

Chapter 2
Exhibits   2.4, Reprinted by permission of the American Marketing Association.   2.5, Jan W. Bol, Charles T. Crespy, James M. Stearns, and John R. Walton, *The Integration of Ethics into the Marketing Curriculum: An Educator's Guide* (Needham Heights, MA: Ginn Press, 1991), p. 27.   2.6, Adapted from Thomas R. Wotruba, "A Framework for Teaching Ethical Decision Making in Marketing," *Marketing Education Review,* Summer 1993, p. 5.   2.7, "Products That Will Change Your Life and in the Years After," *Business Tokyo,* June 1990, pp. 30–31.   2.8, Peter R. Dickson, *Marketing Management* (Fort Worth, TX: The Dryden Press, 1994), p. 8. Used with permission of the publisher.
Photos/Ads   p. 27, IBM photo: © Larry Ford.   p. 30, AIG ad: Courtesy American International Group, Inc.   p. 33, Mitel ad: Courtesy Hewson Bridge and Smith Ltd.   p. 34, J&J credo: Courtesy Johnson & Johnson.   p. 38, Ford Escort ad: Courtesy Ford Motor Company.   p. 39, Mita ad: Courtesy Mita Copystar America, Inc.; agency: Lord Dentsu & Partners.   p. 43, Zenith technology: Courtesy Zenith Electronics Corporation/Charlie Westerman.   p. 43, Lever ad: Courtesy of Lever Brothers Company.   p. 44, Timex Indiglo watch ad: Courtesy Timex Corporation.   p. 47, DHL ad: Courtesy DHL Worldwide.   p. 48, MagneTek: Photo courtesy of MagneTek, Inc.; Photographer: Randy Galling.

Chapter 3

Exhibits 3.3, Excerpt from *1994 Information Please Almanac* (Boston: Houghton Mifflin, 1994), pp. 132–33. Used with permission of the publisher. All rights reserved. 3.4, Excerpt from *1994 Information Please Almanac* (Boston: Houghton Mifflin, 1994), pp. 130–31. Used with permission of the publisher. All rights reserved. 3.5, Data from United Nations Population Division. 3.6, Data from John W. Wright, ed., *The United Almanac 1993* (New York: Andrews and McMeel, 1992), p. 285. Used with permission of publisher. All rights reserved. 3.7, Adapted with permission from "The World Economy in Charts," by Penn World Table and WEFA, in *Fortune*, July 26, 1993, p. 96. © 1993 Time Inc. All rights reserved. 3.10, John Naisbitt and Patricia Aberdein, *Megatrends 2000: Ten New Directions for the 1990s* (New York: William Morris, 1990), pp. 12–13.

Photos/Ads p. 53, LeSabre ad: Courtesy McCann-Erickson Detroit. p. 58, G. T. Global ad: Courtesy G. T. Global Financial Services, Inc. p. 60, Silver Spikers volleyball players: Reprinted with permission Eastman Kodak Company, and Hong Kong bank ad: Courtesy Hong Kong & Shanghai Banking Corporation Limited. p. 61, *Minnesota Bride* magazine: Courtesy Tiger Oak Publications, Inc. and *La Novia B. Linda* magazine: Division of Fantastica Bride Flora Ltd. p. 62, American Express ad: Courtesy American Express; agency: Wunderman Cato Johnson. p. 63, German Ford "I was a car" ad: Courtesy Young & Rubicam, Frankfurt. p. 65, Frito-Lay in India: Courtesy Pepsi-Cola International. p. 67, European traffic jam: Raphael Gaillarde/Gamma Liaison. p. 70, Wrigley gum ad: Courtesy Wm. Wrigley Jr. Company. p. 71, Airbus Industrie ad: Courtesy of Airbus Industrie. p. 73, Reynolds Plastic Wrap ad: Courtesy Reynolds Metals Company.

Chapter 4

Photos/Ads p. 79, Megastores: Courtesy Blockbuster Entertainment Corporation. p. 81, University of Chicago Business School: Courtesy Graduate School of Business/University of Chicago. p. 86, Owens-Corning vision statement: Courtesy Owens-Corning Fiberglass Corporation. p. 89, Fuji ad: Courtesy Fuji Photo Film Co., Ltd. p. 90, Clorox products: Courtesy The Clorox Company. p. 91, Rainbow Ecological Fibers ad: Courtesy Ecological Fibers, Inc. p. 93, Southwest Airlines ad: Courtesy Southwest Airlines. p. 95, Sharp scanner ad: Courtesy Sharp Electronics Corporation. p. 96, Saturn Suzanne Stehlik ad: Courtesy Saturn Corporation. p. 97, Coke in Cameroon, Africa: © Joe Stewardson. p. 98, Hallmark team: © James Schnepf.

Part 2

Photos/Ads p. 103, Pricing: © Howard Sochurek/The Stock Market.

Chapter 5

Exhibits 5.1, "Shoppers Squeeze Nickels—and Consumer Goods Makers," *Business Week*, September 30, 1991, p. 26; "Consumers Grow Greener," *Adweek's Marketing Week*, September 16, 1991, p. 8; Judith Waldrop, "Educating the Customer," *American Demographics*, September 1991, p. 44; Ken Dychtwald and Greg Gable, "Portrait of a Changing Consumer," *Business Horizons*, January–February 1990, p. 69; Carrie Goerne, "Scanning Service Targets In-Home Users," *Marketing News*, March 2, 1992, p. 5;

and Howard Schlossberg, "Conspicuous Consumption Is a Thing of the Past for Relaxed Consumers," *Marketing News*, January 1, 1993, p. 7. 5.2, Adapted from James F. Engel, Roger D. Blackwell, and Paul W. Miniard, *Consumer Behavior*, 6th ed (Ft. Worth, TX: The Dryden Press, 1993). 5.3, J. Paul Peter and Jerry C. Olson, *Understanding Consumer Behavior* (Burr Ridge, IL: Richard D. Irwin, 1994), p. 309. 5.4, Adapted from Kenneth Lubich, "Class in America," *Fortune*, February 7, 1994, p. 116. © 1994 Time Inc. All rights reserved. 5.5, Adapted from Robert Boutilier, "Pulling the Family Strings," *American Demographics*, August 1993, p. 46. © American Demographics, Inc., Ithaca, NY. 5.6, "The Changing American Household," *American Demographics Desk Reference*, July 1992, p. 2. © American Demographics, Inc., Ithaca, NY. 5.7, Terry L. Childers and Akshay Rao, "The Influence of Familial and Peer-Based Reference Groups on Consumer Decisions," *Journal of Consumer Research*, September 1992, p. 204; and William O. Bearden and Michael J. Etzel, "Reference Group Influence on Product and Brand Purchase Decisions," *Journal of Consumer Research*, September 1982, p. 185. 5.8, Adapted from Richard L. Oliver, "Cognitive, Affective, and Attribute Bases of the Satisfaction Response," *Journal of Consumer Research*, December 1993, p. 419. © 1993 by the University of Chicago.

Photos/Ads p. 105, Japanese Hush Puppies ad: Courtesy Wolverine World Wide, Inc. p. 107, Häagen-Dazs ad: Courtesy The Häagen-Dazs Company, Inc. p. 110, Saturn Barry & Cynthia ad: Courtesy Saturn Corporation. p. 110, New York Lottery ad: Courtesy DDB Needham Worldwide Inc. p. 113, Porsche ad: Courtesy Leagas Delaney, London; art director: Steve Dunn; copywriter: Tim Delaney; photographer: Uwe Duttmann. p. 117, Sunlight ad: Courtesy Lever Brothers Canada; agency: MacLaren-Lintas/Toronto; creative director: Bill Durnan; art director: Elspeth Lynn; copywriter: Craig Cooper. p. 117, Steel jeans ad: Courtesy Steel Sportswear; agency: No Comment Advertising Agency. p. 120, Honda airbag ad: Courtesy American Honda Motor Co., Inc. p. 124, Audi ad: Courtesy DDB Needham/Paris. p. 125, Whittaker House ad: Courtesy Whittaker House.

Chapter 6

Exhibits 6.2, "Data Supplement: US Totals for 4-Digit SIC Industries," *Sales & Marketing Management*, July 1991, p. 63. 6.3, Barry Rehfeld, "How Large Companies Buy," *Personal Selling Power*, September 1993, p.28. 6.4, Erin Anderson, Wujin Shu, and Barton Weitz, "Industrial Purchasing: An Empirical Exploration of the Buyclass Framework," *Journal of Marketing*, July 1987, p. 72. © 1987 by the American Marketing Association. Reprinted with permission.

Photos/Ads p. 131, Whirlpool business-to-business ad: Courtesy Whirlpool Corporation. p. 135, United Technologies photo: Courtesy United Technologies Automotive; photo by Frank White. p. 136, Castle Metals ad: Courtesy A. M. Castle & Co. p. 137, A&P coffee buyers: Courtesy The Great Atlantic & Pacific Tea Company. p. 138, Du Pont TV storyboard: Materials supplied by Du Pont. p. 141, Ernst & Young ad: Courtesy Ernst & Young; Photography by Ron Brello Jr. p. 142, Brown and Caldwell ad: Courtesy Brown and Caldwell. p. 144, Konica copiers ad: Courtesy Konica Business Machines U.S.A., Inc. p. 144, Harsco photos: Courtesy Harsco Corporation. p. 145, Libbey glassware ad: Courtesy Libbey Glass Inc. p. 146, Vascular imaging system: Courtesy Siemens AG p. 148, International business photo: SuperStock, Inc.

Part 3
Photos/Ads p. 153, Research and segmentation: © Bob Forrest.

Chapter 7

Exhibits 7.1, Adapted from Gilbert A. Churchill, Jr., *Marketing Research: Methodological Foundations*, 5th ed. (Chicago: The Dryden Press, 1991), p. 9. 7.2, Based on Churchill, *Marketing Research*, p. 69.

Photos/Ads p. 155, Fischer-Price ad: Courtesy Fischer-Price, Inc. p. 156, Swiss Miss Gels: Courtesy Hunt-Wesson, Inc. p. 158, Ford ad: Courtesy Ford Motor Company. p. 159, South Seas Plantation ad: Courtesy South Seas Plantation. p. 161, Maritz Marketing Research ad: Courtesy Maritz Marketing Research, Inc. p. 162, CF Motor Freight ad: Courtesy Consolidated Freightways. p. 163, Geodemographic map: Courtesy Strategic Mapping Inc. p. 167, Consumer survey: Courtesy Bristol-Myers Squibb. p. 170, *Advertising Age* cartoon: © Bill Whitehead. p. 171, Lea & Perrins ad: Courtesy Saatchi & Saatchi/Singapore. p. 175, Good Times magazine: Courtesy Kay Bee Toys & Hobby.

Chapter 8

Exhibits 8.4, "A User's Guide to the Survey of Media Markets," *Sales & Marketing Management*, October 26, 1992, p. 8. 8.5, SRI International. 8.7, David A. Chambers, "Data Technology Boosts Popularity of Lifestage Marketing," *Marketing News*, October 28, 1991, p. 16. © 1991 by the American Marketing Association. Reprinted by permission. 8.8, Philip Kotler, *Marketing Management: Analysis, Planning, Implementation, and Control*, 8th ed. (Englewood Cliffs, NJ: Prentice Hall, 1994), p. 286. © 1994. Adapted by permission. 8.9, Thomas N. Ingram and Raymond W. LaForge, *Sales Management: Analysis and Decision Making* (Chicago: The Dryden Press, 1992), p. 584. 8.10, Joseph P. Guiltinan and Gordon W. Paul, *Marketing Management: Strategies and Programs* (New York: McGraw-Hill, 1991), p. 110. © 1991 by McGraw-Hill, Inc. Reprinted by permission of the publisher. 8.11, *Automotive News*, May 11, 1992, pp. 1, 42; and William R. Dillon, Thomas J. Madden, and Neil N. Firtle, *Essentials of Marketing Research* (Homewood, IL: Richard D. Irwin, 1993), p. 353.

Photos/Ads p. 179, Loose Levi's ad: Courtesy Levi Strauss & Co. p. 180, Oxydol tough stain ad: © The Procter & Gamble Company. Used with permission. p. 182, Patek Phillippe watch ad: Courtesy Bozell SA Advertising. p. 183, AT&T USA Direct ad: Courtesy Young & Rubicam New York. p. 184, Essence pantyhose ad: Courtesy Acme-McCrary Corporation; agency: Trone Advertising Inc. p. 185, Hart Schaffner & Marx and Hickey Freeman ads: Courtesy Hartmarx Corporation. p. 190, Charles David boot ad: Courtesy Lambesis Advertising Agency. p. 192, Andersen Consulting ad: Courtesy Andersen Consulting. p. 195, Hi Pro ad: Reprinted with permission of Ralston Purina Co. p. 200, Nick Jr. ad: NICKELODEON. Used by permission. © 1994 MTV Networks. All Rights Reserved. NICKELODEON is a cable channel owned and operated by Viacom International Inc. p. 200, Schwinn Bicycle ad: Courtesy Schwinn Bicycle.

Part 4
Photos/Ads p. 207, Products and services: © Roy Wiemann.

Chapter 9

Exhibits 9.7, David J. Faulds, *Consumer Product and Manufacturer Ratings: 1961–1990* (Detroit: Gale Research, 1993). 9.8, Reprinted by permission of Interbrand.

Photos/Ads p. 209, Phone services: Myron J. Dorf/The Stock Market. p. 210, Du Pont ad: Materials supplied by Du Pont. p. 213, Singapore Airlines ad: Courtesy Singapore Airlines. Ltd. p. 215, Caramello ad: Courtesy Hershey Foods Corporation; Samsonite ad: Courtesy Samsonite Corporation; Bentley ad: Reprinted by permission of Rolls-Royce Motor Cars Inc. p. 216, Rockwell International ad: Courtesy Rockwell International. p. 219, Parker Pen ad: Courtesy Parker Pen. p. 220, Cannondale ad: Courtesy Cannondale Bicycle Corporation; agency: Pagano Schenck & Kay/Providence, RI; creative director: Woody Kay; art director: Terry Rietta; copywriter: Steve Bautista; photographer: George Simhoni; scenic artist: Kelvin Britton. p. 222, General Mills brands ad: Used with permission of General Mills, Inc. p. 225, Spartan brand products ad: Courtesy Spartan Stores, Inc. p. 228, Marriott ad: Courtesy Marriott Corporation.

Chapter 10

Exhibits 10.1, Adapted from C. Merle Crawford, *New Products Management*, 4th ed. (Burr Ridge, IL: Richard D. Irwin, 1994), p. 11. 10.4, James J. McKeown, "New Products from New Technologies," *Journal of Business and Industrial Marketing*, Winter–Spring 1990, p. 70. 10.8, Adapted from Robert G. Cooper and Elko J. Kleinschmidt, "Stage Gate Systems for New Product Success," *Marketing Management*, 1, no. 4, pp. 20–29. Reprinted by permission of the American Marketing Association. 10.9, William R. Dillon, Thomas J. Madden, and Neil H. Firtle, *Essentials of Marketing Research* (Homewood, IL: Richard D. Irwin, 1993), p. 50.

Photos/Ads p. 233, China Coast restaurant: Courtesy General Mills. p. 234, Little Tikes ad: Courtesy The Little Tikes Company. p. 236, Kelly-Springfield tire ad: Courtesy Kelly-Springfield Tire Company. p. 237, Ceremony luncheon for the formation of WorldPartners Company: Courtesy AT&T. p. 240, Ford product development team: Courtesy Ford Motor Company. p. 244, Du Pont prototype models: Materials supplied by Du Pont. p. 246, Campbell's Hong Kong test kitchen: Greg Girard/Contact Press Images. The Nestea Cool Out Caravan: "Nestea" is a registered trademark licensed to Coca-Cola Nestle Refreshments Company, USA. Used with permission. p. 247, Sony MiniDisc ad: Courtesy of Sony Electronics Inc. p. 248, CNN On-Line ad: Courtesy Journal Graphics, Inc. p. 250, Thermos Lifestyle team members: © 1994 James Schnepf.

Chapter 11

Exhibits 11.1, *The Charles Schwab Corporation 1992 Annual Report*. 11.4, Adapted from Eric N. Berkowitz, Roger A. Kevin, Steven W. Hartley, and William Rudelius, *Marketing*, 4th ed. (Burr Ridge, IL: Richard D. Irwin, 1994), p. 327.

Photos/Ads p. 255, *Beauty and the Beast* video cover: © The Walt Disney Company. p. 256, Philip Morris product lines: Reprinted by permission of Philip Morris Inc. p. 263, Pioneer ad: Advertisement for corporate image elevation and LaserActive product launch promotion. Provided by Pioneer Electronic Corporation. p. 254, Gillette Sensor montage: Courtesy The Gillette Company. p. 265, 1942 Cheerioats ad and Cheerios cereals: Used with permission of General Mills, Inc. p. 267, UPS ad: Courtesy United Parcel Service of America, Inc. p. 268, Zenith products: Courtesy Zenith Electronics Corporation; and Mercedes Benz commercial services: Courtey Mercedes Benz. p. 269, NEC ad: Courtesy NEC USA, Inc. p. 270, Arthur Andersen ad: Courtesy Arthur Andersen. p. 272, Reynolds Wrap: Courtesy Reynolds Metals Co. p. 274, US Customs photo: Bettmann.

Part 5

Photos/Ads   p. 279, Pricing: © Larry Hamill.

Chapter 12

Exhibits   12.2, Adapted from John A. Farris and John A. Quelch, "In Defense of Price Promotion," *Sloan Management Review*, Fall 1989, p. 64; and Rockney G. Walters, "Assessing the Impact of Retail Price Promotions on Product Substitution, Complementary Purchase, and Interstore Displacement," *Journal of Marketing*, April 1991, p. 17.   12.3, Adapted from Kent B. Monroe, *Pricing: Making Profitable Decisions*, 2nd ed. (New York: McGraw-Hill, 1990), p. 13. © 1990 by McGraw-Hill, Inc. Reprinted by permission of the publisher.   12.4, Hermann Simon, "Pricing Opportunities and How to Exploit Them," *Sloan Management Review*, Winter 1992, p. 59.   12.6, Copyright 1991, *USA Today*. Adapted with permission.   12.8, Adapted from Kent B. Monroe, *Pricing: Making Profitable Decisions*, 2nd ed. (New York: McGraw-Hill, 1990), p. 46; and William B. Dodds, Kent B. Monroe, and Druv Grewal, "Effects of Price, Brand, and Store Information on Buyers' Product Evaluations," *Journal of Marketing Research*, August 1991, p. 308.   12.9, Adapted from Joel E. Urbany and Peter R. Dickson, "Consumer Knowledge of Normal Prices: An Exploratory Study and Framework," report no. 90-112 (Cambridge, MA: Marketing Science Institute, 1990), p. 18.   12.10, Adapted from Abhijit Biswas and Edward A. Blair, "Contextual Effects of Reference Prices in Retail Advertisement," *Journal of Marketing*, July 1991, p. 4. © 1991 by the American Marketing Association. Reprinted with permission.

Photos/Ads   p. 281, Snapple ad: Courtesy Snapple Beverage Corporation; agency: Kirshenbaum & Bond.   p. 282, List price ad: Courtesy Cambro Manufacturing Co.   p. 286, Just Tires store: Courtesy The Goodyear Tire & Rubber Company.   p. 288, Compaq computer ad: Courtesy Compaq Computer Corporation.   p. 291, Safari ad: Courtesy Ralph Lauren Fragrances.   p. 292, Lee jeans ad: Courtesy Lee Apparel Co., Inc.   p. 296, Motel 6 ad: Courtesy The Richards Group.   p. 298, Daffy's ad: Courtesy Devito/Verdi.   p. 299, Jennifer Convertibles ad: Courtesy Jennifer Convertibles.

Chapter 13

Exhibits   13.1, Adapted from Harper W. Boyd, Jr., and Orville C. Walker, Jr., *Marketing Management: A Strategic Approach* (Homewood, IL: Richard D. Irwin, 1990), p. 461.   13.5, Adapted from Ford S. Worthy, "Japan's Smart Secret Weapon," *Fortune*, August 12, 1991, p. 73. © 1991 Time Inc. All rights reserved.

Photos/Ads   p. 305, Swatch ad: agency: Barbella Gagliardi Saffirio, Milan; creative director: Pasquale Barbella; art director: Agostino Toscana; copywriter: Roberta Sollazzi; photographer: Antonio Capa.   p. 308, Pampers Uni in Brazil: © Paulo Fridman/Sygma.   p. 310, Jergens ad: Courtesy The Andrews Jergens Company.   p. 316, RPS Air ad: Courtesy Roadway Services Company; and McDonald's ad: Courtesy McDonald's Corporation.   p. 317, Pharmacist Formula ad: Courtesy Leiner Health Products.   p. 318, Pulsar ad: Courtesy Pulsar Time.   p. 318, Dunkin' Donuts ad: Courtesy Dunkin Donuts.   p. 319, Wrigley's gum in China photo: © Mary Beth Camp/Matrix.   p. 321, Salute to Savings ad: Used with permission of General Mills, Inc.   p. 324, National Discount ad: Courtesy National Discount Brokers.   p. 326, Unit pricing photo: Michael J. Hruby.

Part 6

Photos/Ads   p. 331, Channels: © 1993 Steve Gottlieb.

Chapter 14

Exhibits   14.6, First appeared in *Success*, November 1991. Written by Richard Poe. Reprinted with permission of *Success* magazine. Copyright © 1991 by Hal Holdings Corporation.

Photos/Ads   p. 333, Lee Riders ad: Courtesy Lee Apparel Co., Inc.   p. 337, Spiegel catalog: Courtesy Spiegel, Inc.   p. 339, Rocky Mountain Log Homes ad: Courtesy Spiker Communications.   p. 342, Episode store: Courtesy Episode.   p. 345, Kroger ad: Courtesy Kroger Co. Advertising Department.   p. 347, Nestlé and General Mills ad: Used with permission of General Mills, Inc. and Cereal Partners Worldwide.   p. 348, Oshkosh B'Gosh ad: Courtesy Oshkosh B'Gosh, Inc.   p. 351, Ferrara Pan trade ad: Courtesy Ferrara Pan Candy Co.   p. 354, IBM Direct ad: Courtesy of International Business Machines Corporation.

Chapter 15

Exhibits   15.1, Data from *Fortune*, May 30, 1994, p. 214.   15.2, First appeared in *Success*, November 1992. Written by Michael Warshaw. Reprinted with permission of *Success* magazine. Copyright © 1992 by Hal Holdings Corporation.   15.3, Michael Levy and Barton A. Weitz, *Retail Management* (Homewood, IL: Richard D. Irwin, 1992), p. 602. © 1992 Richard D. Irwin. Reprinted with permission of publisher.   15.5, *USA Today*, September 20, 1991, p. B1. Copyright 1991, *USA Today*. Reprinted with permission.   15.6, Adapted from Michael Levy and Barton A. Weitz, *Retailing Management* (Homewood, IL: Richard D. Irwin, 1992), p. 337. © 1992 Richard D. Irwin. Reprinted with permission of publisher.   15.8, Adapted from Barry Berman and Joel R. Evans, *Retail Management: A Strategic Approach*, 5th ed. (New York: Macmillan, 1992), pp. 98–99. Copyright © 1992 by Macmillan College Publishing Company, Inc. Reprinted with permission of publisher.   15.9, Arthur Young-NMRI 6th Annual Study of Security and Shrinkage. From Dale R. Lewison, *Retailing*, 4th ed. (New York: Macmillan, 1991), p. 310.

Photos/Ads   p. 359, Toys "Я" Us in Japan: Courtesy Toys "Я" Us, Inc.   p. 362, World Foot Locker store: Courtesy Kinney Shoe Corporation.   p. 362, Knott's Camp Snoopy: Courtesy Mall of America; © 1993 Bob Perzel.   p. 364, Mail Boxes Etc. ad: Courtesy Mail Boxes Etc.   p. 365, True Value co-op ad: Courtesy Cotter & Co.   p. 366, BP Willkommen outlet in Dresden, Germany: photograph by British Petroleum.   p. 367, Target bar code scanner: © Steve Niedorf.   p. 370, *Edge* catalog: Courtesy The Edge Company.   p. 370, Spiegel order takers: Courtesy Spiegel, Inc.   p. 371, Avon ad: Courtesy Avon Products, Inc.   p. 375, Exterior and interior of Aldi prototype store: (*left*) © Michael J. Hruby; (*right*) Courtesy Aldi Inc.   p. 377, Giant Food ad in Baltimore Orioles ballpark: © Chuck Solomon/Sports Illustrated.   p. 379, Bangkok department store: Peter Charlesworth/JB Pictures.

Chapter 16

Exhibits   16.3, Adapted with permission of the International Hardware Distributors Association.   16.4, "The Rumors of Peace Remain Unfounded," April 1992 Annual Report of the Grocery Industry, *Progressive Grocer* magazine, © 1992 by Progressive Grocer.   16.5, Mushtaq Luqmani, Donna Goehle, Zahir A. Quraeshi, and Ugur Yavas, "Tracing the Development of Wholesaling Thought and Practice," *Journal of Marketing Channels*, April 1991, p. 95. Reprinted by permission of The Haworth Press, Inc.   16.6, Compiled from Patrick M. Byrne, "Eight Forces for Global Change," *Travel and Distribution*, April 1992, pp. 53–54; and "Preston Trucking Company, Inc.: Customer Service Is a Process," *Customer Service Manager's Letter*, September 10, 1992, p. 6.   16.7, Adapted from "Quick Response: What It Is; What It's Not," *Chain Store Age Executive*, March 1991, pp. B4, B5.

Photos/Ads   p. 387, Girl with Little Debbie Banana Twins: © Michael J. Hruby.   p. 388, Garbo Lobster ad: Courtesy Garbo Lobster Limited.   p. 392, Electronic catalog: Courtesy W. W. Grainger, Inc.   p. 393, Sam's Club interior: Courtesy of Sam's Club.   p. 394, Phillips Auctioneers & Valuers catalog items: Courtesy Phillips Auctioning & Appraising Since 1796.   p. 399, Coke station wagon: © Andreas Bottcher; dog sled: Courtesy of Knight-Ridder, Inc.; Pepsi gondola delivery: Courtesy Pepsi International; Amoco supertanker: Courtesy Amoco Corporation.   p. 401, McKesson distribution center: Jim Visser for *McKesson Today*.   p. 401, Frito Lay potatoes: Courtesy Burlington Northern Railroad; © Tom Graves.   p. 404, Federal Express ad: Courtesy BBDO/New York; and Central Transport ad: Courtesy McKinlay Transport Ltd.   p. 405, Yellow Freight Systems YFM Direct: Courtesy Yellow Freight Systems, Inc.   p. 406, Intermodal shipping photos: Courtesy Consolidated Freightways, Inc.

Part 7

Photos/Ads   p. 413, Integrated communications: © Telegraph Colour Library/FPG.

Chapter 17

Exhibits   17.2, Donnelley Marketing Annual Surveys of Promotional Practices for 1983–93.   17.6, "Advertising and Promotional Expenditures as a Percentage of Net Sales," *Sales & Marketing Management*, June 28, 1993, p. 73.

Photos/Ads   p. 415, Barbara Mandrell's No Nonsense tour: Courtesy Mandrell, Inc.; photo by Jon Cortez.   p. 417, Longhorn Steaks billboard: Courtesy Scharbo & Co.   p. 417, The Potato Board ad: Courtesy Ketchum Advertising.   p. 418, A&P Eight O'Clock coffee billboard: Courtesy The Great Atlantic & Pacific Tea Company, Inc.   p. 421, Sanyo/GE battery ad: Courtesy Sanyo Energy (U.S.A.) Corporation.   p. 421, Elan ski ad: Courtesy Elan; agency: Richardson, Myers & Donofrio/Baltimore.   p. 421, MRI equipment: © Flip Chalfant.   p. 422, World Cup Soccer sponsorship ad: Courtesy ISL Marketing AG; agency: Dentsu Corporation.   p. 424, Troy Aikman: Wide World Photos.   p. 426, Bailey's Nursery ad: Courtesy Bailey's Nursery; art director: Tim Ward; creative director/copywriter/photographer: Michael LaMonica.   p. 430, Timex cowboy ad: Courtesy Timex Corporation.   p. 433, Ryka ad: Courtesy Doyle Advertising and Design Group.   p. 434, Wesson comparative ad: Courtesy Hunt-Wesson, Inc.

Chapter 18

Exhibits   18.1, "National Ad Spending by Media," *Advertising Age*, May 3, 1993, p. 38. Reprinted with permission. Copyright Crain Communications, Inc. All rights reserved.   18.2, "World's Top 50 Advertising Organizations," *Advertising Age*, January 3, 1994, p. 27. Reprinted with permission. Copyright Crain Communications, Inc. All rights reserved.   18.3, Adapted with permission from William F. Arens and Courtland L. Bovée, *Contemporary Advertising,* 5th ed. (Burr Ridge, IL: Richard D. Irwin, 1994), p. 8. © 1994 Richard D. Irwin, Inc.   18.6, William M. Curry, "PR Isn't Marketing: Using Its Tools as a Sales Aid Masks Danger," *Advertising Age*, December 16, 1991, p. 18; and Donald P. Robin and R. Eric Reidenbach, "Social Responsibility, Ethics, and Marketing Strategy: Closing the Gap between Concept and Application," *Journal of Marketing*, January 1987, pp. 44–58.

Photos/Ads   p. 439, Reno Air billboard: Courtesy Goldberg Moser O'Neill, San Francisco.   p. 442, Benetton ad: Courtesy Benetton Services Corporation.   p. 443, Japanese Nike brochure: Courtesy Wieden & Kennedy/Portland.   p. 443, MTV ad: MTV: MUSIC TELEVISION. Used by permission. © 1994 MTV Networks. All rights reserved. MTV: MUSIC TELEVISION is a cable channel owned and operated by Viacom International Inc.   p. 445, Advanced Aerobic Flight Training ad: Courtesy Hunt Murray/Minneapolis; and Roaches: Courtesy Lintas Hong Kong Ltd.   p. 446, Campbell Soup trade ad: Courtesy Campbell Soup Company.   p. 448, Levi's for Women ad: Courtesy Levi Strauss & Co.   p. 449, TEVA ad: © 1993 TEVA. The Sport Sandal.   p. 450, Alka-Seltzer in Brussels ad: Courtesy McCann-Erickson/Brussels; Norwegian Cruise ad: Courtesy Goodby, Berlin, & Silverstein, San Francisco; Gauchos steak restaurant: Courtesy Campaign Company, Amsterdam; art director: Bela Stamenkovits; copywriter: Rob Floor; photographer: Nandor Stamen Kovits.   p. 451, Nancy Kerrigan for Campbell's: Courtesy Campbell Soup Company.   p. 452, MADD billboard: Courtesy MADD/Minnesota State Organization; created by Clarity Coverdale & Rueff; and Medieval Times transit ad: Courtesy Medieval Times Dinner Theater.   p. 453, Lever in Hindustan photo: Raulai/Magnum Photos.   p. 456, "Bearfoot" monster truck: UPI/Bettmann.   p. 457, French museum ad: Courtesy BDDP, Paris.   p. 459, Vice President Gore and Dave Letterman: Courtesy CBS Inc.; © Alan Singer.

Chapter 19

Exhibits   19.1, Adapted with permission from William F. Arens and Courtland L. Bovee, *Contemporary Advertising,* 5th ed. (Burr Ridge, IL: Richard D. Irwin, 1994), p. 505. © 1994 Richard D. Irwin, Inc.   19.6, Christopher Power, "Coupon Scams Are Clipping Companies," *Business Week*, June 15, 1992, pp. 110–11. Reprinted by special permission, copyright © 1992 by McGraw-Hill, Inc.

Photos/Ads   p. 465, American Heart Association collaborative consumer and retailer promotion: Courtesy National Premium Sales Executives Inc.; TIMES, AEROBIX, and TRIATHLON are registered trademarks of Timex Corporation.   p. 466, AT&T ad: Courtesy AT&T.   p. 469, Jolly Rancher ad: Courtesy Leaf, Inc.; agency: Ayer Chicago; John Lamb/Tony Stone Images; and Colgate Tartar Control free sample: Courtesy Colgate-Palmolive Company.   p. 472, Fuller's coupon ad: Courtesy Fuller's Car Washes.   p. 473, Instant coupon machine: Courtesy ACT-MEDIA.   p. 474, Motorcraft rebate ad: Courtesy Motorcraft.   p. 475, American Airlines ad: Courtesy Timberland McClain.   p. 476, Free samples in store: Courtesy The Great Atlantic & Pacific Tea Company.   p. 478, Lamb Weston ad: Courtesy Lamb Weston, Inc.; agency: Strahan Advertising, Inc.   p. 479, Vlasic trade ad: Advertisement used by permission from Vlasic Foods, Inc.; Early California is a registered trademark of Vlasic Foods, Inc.   p. 482, Point-of-purchase display: Courtesy J. Jay Products Co., Inc.; and SpokesMannequin: Courtesy PeopleVision.   p. 483, Hanover, Germany, commerical vehicle show: Courtesy Mercedes-Benz; and Armstrong training session: Courtesy Armstrong World Industries, Inc.

Chapter 20

Exhibits   20.1, Linda Corman, "The World's Toughest Customers," *Selling*, September 1993, p. 53.   20.3, Adapted from Thomas N. Ingram and Raymond W. LaForge, *Sales Management: Analysis and Decision Making,* 2nd ed. (Fort Worth, TX: The Dryden Press/Harcourt Brace Jovanovich, 1992), p. 52. Copyright © 1992 by The Dryden Press, reproduced by permission of the publisher. 20.4, Thomas N. Ingram, Michael D. Hartline, and Charles A. Schwepker, "Gatekeeper Perceptions: Implications for Improving Sales Ethics and Professionalism," *Proceedings of the Academy of Marketing Science,* 1992, pp. 328–32. 20.5, Phillip Schembra, "Often Overlooked Listening Habits," *The Selling Advantage,* January 1991, p. 3; and Phillip Schembra, "A Checklist on Asking Questions," *The Selling Advantage,* July 1991, p. 3. 20.6, Adapted from: *Making . . . Serving . . . Keeping Customers,* (Chicago: The Dartnell Corporation, 1990). 20.7, Adapted from Thomas N. Ingram and Raymond W. LaForge, *Sales Management and Decision Making,* 2nd ed. (Fort Worth, TX: The Dryden Press/Harcourt Brace Jovanovich, 1992), p. 2. Copyright © 1992 by The Dryden Press, reproduced by permission of the publisher. 20.8, Adapted from John I. Coppett and William A. Staples, *Professional Selling: A Relationship Management Process,* 2nd ed. (Cincinnati: South-Western, 1994), p. 65. Used with the permission of South-Western Publishing Co. All rights reserved. 20.9, Adapted from Thomas N. Ingram and Raymond W. LaForge, *Sales Management: Analysis and Decision Making,* 2nd ed. (Fort Worth, TX: The Dryden Press/Harcourt Brace Jovanovich, 1992), p. 533. Copyright © 1992 by The Dryden Press, reproduced by permission of the publisher. 20.10, Excerpted from Sales and Marketing Executives International Certified Professional Salesperson Code of Ethics (Cleveland: Sales and Marketing Executives International, 1994). 20.11, Rosemary R. Lagace, Thomas N. Ingram, and Michael Borom, "An Exploratory Study of Salesperson Unethical Behavior: Scale Development and Validation," forthcoming in the *Proceedings,* American Marketing Association Summer Educators' Conference, 1994.

Photos/Ads p. 491, ALICO photo: Courtesy American International Group, Inc. p. 492, Gerber ad: Courtesy Gerber Products Company. p. 495, RAM Mobile Data ad: Courtesy RAM Mobile Data. p. 496, Colgate sales rep in Brazil: Courtesy Colgate-Palmolive Company. p. 496, United States Surgical Corporation rep: Courtesy United States Surgical Corporation; photo by John Madere. p. 498, Selling strategy: Courtesy of Knight-Ridder, Inc. p. 499, CompuServe ad: Courtesy CompuServe, Inc. p. 504, Merck sales reps: Courtesy of Merck & Co., Inc.; photographer: Maureen Murphy. p. 506, Consolidated Freightways ad: Courtesy Consolidated Freightways, Inc. p. 507, Zurich-American ad: Courtesy Zurich-American Insurance Group. p. 509, Sales CTRL 3 ad: Courtesy Advanced Concepts, Inc.

Chapter 21

Exhibits 21.1, First appeared in *Success,* February 1993. Written by Jodi Hewgill. Adapted with permission of *Success* magazine. Copyright © 1993 by Hal Holdings Corporation. 21.4, "Survey: Marketers Like Faxes and Pictures," *Direct,* June 1992, p. 16. Reprinted with permission of *Direct* magazine, a Cowles Business Media publication. 21.5, Walker Group, an Indianapolis-based Business Information Holding company, whose subsidiaries offer Marketing Research, Customer Satisfaction, Direct Marketing, and Clinical Research. 21.6, Karen Burka, "The Telephone in Your

Future," *Direct,* February 1992, p. 32; and John Awerdick, "Wrong Numbers," *Direct,* October 1993, pp. 39–41. 21.7, First appeared in *Success,* March 1992. Reprinted with permission of *Success* magazine. Copyright © 1992 by Hal Holdings Corporation.

Photos/Ads p. 517, L.L. Bean catalog: Courtesy L.L. Bean, Inc. p. 518, Avon in China photo: Courtesy Avon Products, Inc. p. 519, Metromail ad: Courtesy R. R. Donnelley & Sons Company. p. 522, Johnson & Hayward ad: Courtesy Johnson & Hayward, Inc. p. 525, Everfresh FoodSaver direct marketing package: Courtesy Landmark Products Corporation; agency: Liggett-Stashower Direct. p. 526, Office Depot's *Business News* cover: Courtesy Office Depot Inc. p. 526, Jeep/Eagle disk and game: Courtesy Jeep Eagle; agency: Bozell/North. p. 528, Avon representative in the UK: Courtesy Avon Products, Inc.; The Direct Selling Education Foundation. p. 529, "The Ringers" infomercial: Courtesy Bell Atlantic. p. 531, Nordic Track ad: Courtesy Nordic Track, Inc.

Epilog

Photos/Ads p. 540, "Abominable" ad: Courtesy The Timberland Company; agency: The Mullen Agency; main photo: Kim Heacox; product shots: John Holt Studios/Boston. p. 541, Iditarod race: Jeff Schultz/Alaska Stock Images. p. 542, Sidney and Jeff Swartz: © Richard E. Schultz, 1993. p. 543, "British queen" ad: Courtesy Leagas Delaney, London; art director: Christine Jones; copywriter: Giles Montgomery; photographer: John Claridge. p. 543, Timberland specialty concept store: (*left*) © Michael J. Hruby; (*right*) Courtesy HSSI. p. 544, Timberland ad in Thailand: Courtesy The Timberland Company; agency: The Mullen Agency; main photo: Clint Clemmons; product shots: John Holt Studios/Boston. p. 544, Timberland headquarters photo: Andrew Edgar. p. 545, "Give racism the boot" ad: Courtesy The Timberland Company; agency: The Mullen Agency. p. 545, "Lot goes into boot" ad: Courtesy The Timberland Company. p. 546, Warehouse photo: © 1993 Richard E. Schultz. p. 546, Manufacturing photos: © Jeffrey Macmillan. p. 547, "Waterproof" ad: Courtesy The Timberland Company; agency: The Mullen Agency. p. 547, *Elements* magazine: Courtesy The Timberland Company. p. 548, Product shot: Courtesy The Timberland Company. p. 548, "Tiptoe through the Tetons" ad: Courtesy The Timberland Company; agency: The Mullen Agency; main photo: David Muench; tulip inset photo: Westlight. p. 549, "Elements of design" ad: Courtesy The Timberland Company; agency: The Mullen Agency.

Appendix A

Exhibits A.2, "1993 Survey of Media Markets" and "Survey of Buying Power," *Sales & Marketing Management,* October 25, 1993, pp. 11–17. A.4, Marilyn Hart McCarty, *Introductory Economics* (Glenview, IL: Scott, Foresman, 1988), p. 639. Reprinted by permission of HarperCollins College Publishers.

Name Index

Company and Brand Index

Procter & Gamble, 6, 36, 37, 83, 121, 221, 224,
    226, 228, 235, 235, 245, 265, 285, 349,
    402, 404, 423, 427, 433, 434, 440, 486,
    505, 506, 520, 603
    brand awareness, 223
    brand names, 271
    detergent market segments, 180
    differentiated strategy, 195–96
    marketing channel, 351
    marketing perspectives, 50
    retailers, 32
Prodigy, 92, 532
Produce Specialties, 18
Proof Positive, 209
Protein Technologies International, 418, 420, 427
Prudential, 212
Publishers Clearing House, 535
Pulsar Time, 604
Pulsar watches, 318
Purina Hi Pro, 195
Purolator, team selling, 515

Q

Qingdao Ciba Agro Ltd., 96
Qingdao Pesticides Factory, 96
Quaker Oats Bran, 266
Quaker Oats Company, 473
Quaker State, 478–79
Quality Inns, 222
Quantum Laboratories, 525
Quantum tools, 251
Quick Response Partnerships, 138
QVC, 63
QVC Network home shopping, 108, 371, 384

R

R. J. Reynolds, 433
R. R. Donnelly and Sons Company, 521, 606
Radioscope, 448
Radio Shack, 317, 334, 366, 376
Rainbow Ecological Fibers, 602
Raley's, 338, 341, 493
Ralph Lauren, 291
Ralph Lauren Fragrances, 604
Ralston Purina, 121, 195
RAM Mobile Data, 495
Ramsey Popcorn, 61–62
R & E Electronics, 309
Range Rover, 114
RapNet, 534
Raytheon, 150
RCA, 15, 337
RCA television, 29
RCA Videodisc, 234
RC Cola, 24
Reader's Digest, 201, 452, 517
Rebecca's Cafe, 477
Red Lobster, 233
Reebok, 72, 77, 337, 348, 424, 449
Reebok Pump, 220
Reese's, 267
Relaxed Rider, 333
RE/MAX, 365
Reno Air, 605
    billboard advertising, 439–40
Research Systems Corporation, 454
    ARS Persuasion system, 163
Revenue Rev-Up, 6
Revlon, 62
Reynolds Metal Company, 604
Reynolds Plastic Wrap, 73, 602
Reynolds Wrap, 272, 604
Rezide CD-ROM, 62
RHI Entertainment, 237
Richards Group, 604
Ricoh Copiers, 444
Riders brand jeans, 333

RJR Nabisco, 223, 231; *see also* Nabisco
Roadway Robert Express Unit, 405
Roadway Services Company, 604
Robert Mondavi winery, 494
Rockwell International, 216, 603
Rocky Mountain Log Homes, 339, 605
Roger Williams Park Zoo, 125
Rolex, 222, 341, 344, 352, 427
Rolling Stone, 427
Rolls-Royce Motor Cars, Inc., 603
Royal Appliance, 335
Royal Caribbean Cruise Line, 285
Royal Crown Cola, 24
Royal Frans Maas Group, 405
RPS Air, 316, 604
Rubbermaid, 136, 234, 241
Rubik's Cube, 155
Ruddell and Associates, 338, 341, 346, 480, 497
Ryka, 433, 605

S

S. C. Fang Brothers, 342
S. C. Johnson, 237
Saatchi and Saatchi, 18, 441, 603
Safari, 291
Safeway Stores, 341, 361, 396
Sam's Club, 360, 393, 605
Sam's Wholesale Club, 360
Samsonite bags, 215
Samsonite Corporation, 603
Sansabelt slacks, 185
Sanyo Energy Corporation, 67, 605
Sara Lee, 296
Sara Lee Hosiery, 442, 449, 452
Saturn auto plant, 94–95
Saturn car, 96, 110
Saturn Corporation, 602, 603; *see also* General
    Motors
    market, 201
    salesforce, 514–15
Scharbo Company, 504
Schick razors, 347
Schwinn Bicycle Company, 603
Schwinn bicycles, 200
SDR, Inc., 157, 158
Sears, 33, 348, 366, 440, 517
    brand names, 271
    past diversification, 89
    Prodigy, 92
Sears Merchandise Group, 89, 361
Sears Portrait Studios, 473
Sega Enterprises, competition with Nintendo, 329
Sega of America, 61
Seiko, 347
Selective Consolidated Dealers Co-op, 146
Send-a-Song Corporation, idea development, 253
Sentry Hardware, 365
7-Eleven stores, 379
Shanghai Television, 10–11
Sharp, 95, 262, 311
Sharp Electronics Corporation, 602
Sharper Image, 371, 376, 517
Sharp Manufacturing Company of America,
    402, 462
Sharp's nonalcoholic beer, 205
Sheer Energy, 427
Shell Oil, 25
Sheraton, price structure, 288
ShopKo, 333
Showbiz Box Office Busters, 474
Siemens, 33, 357, 603
Siemens Medical Systems, 147
Signal Apparel, 481
Silver Fox, competitive pricing, 302
Silver Spikers, 607
Silver Tab jeans, 179
Simmons Research Bureau, 452
Simpson, Bart, 231
Singapore Airlines, 213, 603
Singapore Telecom, 237

Sioux Valley Hospital, 56, 218, 268
SKI Ltd., 520
Smith Barney Shearson, Inc., 32, 73
    Financial Management Account, 265
SmithKline Beecham, 221
Snapple Beverage Corporation, 63, 604
    pricing strategy, 281–82
Snelling and Snelling, 343
Snickers candy, 223
Soloflex, 531
Sonju otors, 498
Sony brand, 224, 226
Sony Corporation, 6, 15, 72, 337, 352, 488, 604
    new products, 236
    predatory pricing, 294
    product design, 221
Sony Design Center, 221
Sony Gallery of Consumer Electronics, 348
Sony Mini disc, 247
Sotheby's, 394
Source Perrier, 349
South Central Bell, 228
Southern California Gas, 7
Southern Pacific Transportation, 139
South Seas Plantation, 159, 603
Southwest Airlines, 93–94, 290, 602
Southwestern Bell Corporation, 189
Spartan brand, 225
Spartan Stores, 604
Specialized Bicycle Components, 336
Special K cereal, 121
Special Olympics, 459
Specialty Tool and Fastener Distribution
    Association, 397
Spiegel, Inc., 63, 337–38, 370-71, 604
    neural networks, 523
SpokesMannequin, 482
Sports Illustrated, 427, 452, 498
Springfield Farms, 476–77
SRI International, 191
Stanley Tools, 340, 506
Starbucks Coffee Company, pricing strategy, 295
Starch Messsage Report Services, 454
StarSight Telecast, 268
Starter Corporation, licensing, 226
State Farm, 212
Steel jeans, 117
Steel Sportswear, 603
Stouffers, 157, 183, 476
Strategic Mapping, Inc., 603
Stride-Rite Corporation, 402
Strombecker Tootsie brand Bubble Sword, 155
Stuckey's Family Favorites, 364, 365, 376
Styrofoam, 227
Subaru, 449
Subway Sandwiches, 365
Success magazine, 20
Sucrets Lozenges, 340
Summer Olympic Games, 227
Summer Strawberry, 277
Sun Airways, 92
Sunlight, 603
Swatch, 604
Swatch watches, pricing, 305–6
Swedish Classics, 398
Swiss Miss Gels, 603

T

T. Rowe Price, 59
Taco Bell, 164, 296, 346
Talbot's, 366
Tampa Bay Buccaneers, 428
Tandy Corporation, 262, 334
Target Stores, 255, 321, 408, 605
    bar code scanning, 367
Tastykake, 387
Team Taurus, 33
Tektronix, 32
TEVA, 449, 606
Texaco, 25, 221

Subject Index